From
CHICAGO
to L.A.

To Lucy Hubbard Haugh and James Calvin Haugh,
     friends and supporters of the Southern California Studies Center

Michael J. Dear
Editor

With J. Dallas Dishman

From CHICAGO *to* L.A.

Making Sense of Urban Theory

Sage Publications
International Educational and Professional Publisher
Thousand Oaks ▪ London ▪ New Delhi

For information:

Sage Publications, Inc.
2455 Teller Road
Thousand Oaks, California 91320
E-mail: order@sagepub.com

Sage Publications Ltd.
6 Bonhill Street
London EC2A 4PU
United Kingdom

Sage Publications India Pvt. Ltd.
M-32 Market
Greater Kailash I
New Delhi 110 048 India

Printed in the United States of America

Library of Congress Cataloging-in-Publication Data

Main entry under title:

From Chicago to L.A.: Making sense of urban theory / by Michael J. Dear.
    p. cm.
Includes bibliographical references and index.
  ISBN 0-7619-2094-3 (cloth) — ISBN 0-7619-2095-1 (pbk.)
  1. Urbanization—California—Los Angeles Metropolitan Area.
  2. Los Angeles Metropolitan Area (Calif.)—Social conditions.
  3. Urbanization—United States. 4. Sociology, Urban—United States. I. Title.
HT384.U52 L673 2001
307.76′0973—dc21   2001000421

02   03   10   9   8   7   6   5   4   3   2   1

Acquiring Editor:	Catherine Rossbach/Marquita Flemming
Editorial Assistant:	MaryAnn Vail
Production Editor:	Diana E. Axelsen
Editorial Assistant:	Candice Crosetti
Copy Editor:	Alison Binder
Typesetter/Designer:	Marion Warren
Indexer:	Mary Mortensen
Cover Designer:	Michelle Lee

Contents

Preface

MICHAEL J. DEAR

More than seventy five years ago, the University of Chicago Press published a book of articles titled *The City: Suggestions for Investigation of Human Behavior in the Urban Environment.* Six of its ten chapters are by Robert E. Park, chair of the university's sociology department. There are also two chapters by Ernest W. Burgess, and one each from Roderick D. McKenzie and Louis Wirth. In essence, the book announced the arrival of the "Chicago School" of urban sociology, defining an agenda for urban studies that persists to this day.

The present volume begins the task of defining an alternative agenda for urban studies, based on the precepts of what some refer to as the "Los Angeles School." Quite evidently, adherents of the L.A. School take many cues from the Los Angeles metropolitan region or, more generally, from Southern California—a five-county region encompassing Los Angeles, Orange, Riverside, San Bernardino, and Ventura counties. This exceptionally complex, fast-growing megalopolis is already home to more than 16 million people. It is likely soon to overtake New York as the nation's premier urban region. Yet for most of its history, it has been regarded as an exception to the rules governing the growth of American cities, an aberrant outlier on the continent's western edge.

All this is changing. For the past two decades, Southern California has attracted increasing attention from multidisciplinary scholars and other social commentators. Los Angeles has become, for many, not the exception but rather a prototype of the city of the future. As the volume of academic and popular writings has accumulated, the prospect of an L.A. School of urbanism has also ascended. The purpose of this book is to critically examine the foundations and potential of a putative L.A. School.

The present volume is the final part of a trilogy (all published by Sage) that has attempted to shift the axis in urban thought away from the Chicago School and toward an L.A. School. The first in this series, *Rethinking Los Angeles* (1996), defined many of the changing conditions that created the imperative for an L.A. School. The second volume, *Urban Latino Cultures: La vida latina en L.A.* (1999), focused on the rising Latino majority as the principal demographic and cultural dynamic in the new city. This third volume, *From Chicago to L.A.*, critically examines some of the major precepts of the L.A. School. All three volumes could usefully be read alongside my monograph *The Postmodern Urban Condition,* which provides a more personal interpretation of current urban tendencies in Southern California.[1]

The particular conditions that have led now to the emergence of what some refer to as a Los Angeles School may be almost coincidental: (a) An especially powerful intersection of empirical and theoretical research projects has coalesced in this particular place at this particular time; (b) these trends are occurring in what has historically been the most understudied major city in the United States; (c) these projects have attracted the attention of an assemblage of increasingly self-conscious scholars and practitioners; and (d) the world is facing the prospect of a Pacific century, in which Southern California is likely to become a global capital. The vitality and potential of the L.A. School derive from the intersection of these events and the promise that they hold for a renaissance of urban theory. The validity of the school will be determined elsewhere, in careful comparative analyses that I hope this book will now encourage other urbanists to undertake.

> *While the city of Chicago is used as the laboratory for this investigation, it is assumed that the processes of urban life in one community are in certain ways typical of city life throughout the United States.*[2]

For most of the twentieth century, the precepts of the Chicago School guided urban analysts throughout the world. Shrugging off challenges from competing visions, the school has maintained a remarkable longevity that is tribute to its model's beguiling simplicity, to the tenacity of its adherents who subsequently constructed a formidable literature, and to the model's "working" in application to so many cities for such a long time. Now the hegemony of the Chicago School is being challenged by what some researchers are referring to as the Los Angeles School. This book examines the case for shifting the focus of urban studies from Chicago to Los Angeles.

Los Angeles is the least studied major city in the United States. To outsiders, Southern California has long been viewed as an exception to the rules governing American urban development. But to insiders, Los Angeles has simply confirmed what contemporaries have known throughout this century: that the city posited a different set of rules for understanding urban growth. This alternative urban metric is now overdue; as Joel Garreau observed in his 1991 study of edge cities, "Every American city that is growing, is growing in the fashion of Los Angeles."[3]

This book is one of a growing number of recent monographs that take Los Angeles seriously. Its purpose is fourfold:

- ▶ To uncover the underlying assumptions of the Chicago School of urbanism
- ▶ To jettison an obsolete lexicon of concepts that have hitherto blocked our understanding of Southern Californian cities

▶ To uncover and interpret the imaginative structures that people have been using to understand and explain Los Angeles

▶ To examine the utility of something we call the Los Angeles School of urbanism

In pursuit of these objectives, we have assembled a diverse group of experienced scholars from a variety of disciplines. Although each starts from a common point of departure in contemporary Los Angeles, we do not all seek, nor does anyone expect to achieve, an easy consensus about the merits of the putative L.A. School. Instead, we view the book as a *process* of intellectual inquiry, necessarily engaging in multiple modes of inquiry and a plurality of epistemologies that extend far beyond the confines of any single discipline.

The basic primer of the Chicago School, *The City*, was originally published in 1925. Still in print, the book retains a tremendous vitality far beyond its interest as a historical document. Needless to say, simply refuting *The City* would be a rather pointless task because so much has changed since 1925. Instead, we prefer to regard the book as emblematic of an analytical paradigm that remained coherent for most of the twentieth century. Its assumptions include the following:

▶ An individual-centered understanding of the urban condition; urban process in *The City* is typically grounded in the individual subjectivities of urbanites, their personal choices ultimately explaining the overall urban condition, including spatial structure, crime, poverty, and racism

▶ A "modernist" view of the city as a unified whole, that is, a coherent regional system in which the center organizes its hinterland

▶ A linear evolutionist paradigm, in which processes lead from tradition to modernity, from primitive to advanced, from community to society, and so on

There may be other important assumptions of the Chicago School, as represented in *The City*, that are not listed here. Finding them and identifying what is right or wrong about them are two of the tasks at hand, rather than excoriating the book's contributors for not accurately foreseeing some distant future.

Just as the Chicago School emerged at a time when that city was reaching new national prominence, Los Angeles is now making its impression on the minds of urbanists across the world. Few of them argue that the city is unique, or necessarily a harbinger of the future, although both viewpoints are at some level demonstrably true. At a minimum, however, they all assert that Southern California is an unusual amalgam—a polyglot, polycultural pastiche that is deeply involved in rewriting the American social contract. Moreover, their theoretical inquiries do not end with Southern California but are also focused on more general questions concerning urban sociospatial processes.

In *From Chicago to L.A.,* we use the ten original chapters of *The City* as points of departure for our own inquiries. Each contributor adopts some reference point from

The City (typically part of a chapter or topical focus) and develops his or her own meditation on the state of contemporary urban theory. The basic harmony of our book derives from its focus on a single place, although many of our contributors extend their geographic range beyond the city of Los Angeles to the Southern California region as a whole. Many chapters also consider evidence of wider national and international trends. Another concern common to each chapter is defining the emerging urban agenda (in both theory and practice) that will guide analysts and policymakers into the future.

This book is also, along the way, an assessment of the utility of the concept of a Los Angeles School. Perhaps this is not the moment to be suggesting an alternative urban paradigm that could become just one more metanarrative as hegemonic as the construct it purports to displace. (Indeed, the most appropriate response to the Chicago School may be some anonymous "antischool.") Yet the variety, volume, and pace of contemporary change almost *require* the development of alternative analytical frameworks; one can no longer make an unchallenged appeal to a single model for the myriad global and local trends that surround us. These proliferating social logics insist on multiple theoretical frameworks that overlap and coexist in their explanations of the burgeoning world order. The consequent epistemological difficulties are manifest in the problem of *naming* the present condition—witness the use of such terms as *postmodernity, hypermodernity,* and *supermodernity.*

Part I of the book begins by sketching a broad picture of Los Angeles and the rise of what has come to be called the L.A. School (Chapter 1). The special sociodemographic characteristics of Los Angeles are highlighted by comparing the region with Chicago, New York City, and Washington, D.C. (Chapter 2). Finally, an alternative model of urban structure is proposed, based on Los Angeles (Chapter 3).

The economy of cities is one important facet of urban process that was downplayed in the Chicago School's presentation in *The City.* To correct this imbalance, and to expand our description of the region, Part II of this book examines Los Angeles as a city of industry. Chapters 4 and 5 develop important themes in L.A.'s economic history, and Chapter 6 brings the historical record up to the present, focusing on trends in regional economic restructuring.

The theme of community lay at the heart of the Chicago researchers' agendas. In Part III, important aspects of contemporary community are explored. These include the significant role of immigration in the emerging character of Southern California (Chapter 7) and the growth of homelessness as a consequence of the region's burgeoning socioeconomic polarization (Chapter 8). Less anticipated in *The City,* perhaps understandably so, is the increasing presence of gangs (Chapter 9), religious communities (Chapter 10), and virtual communities in Los Angeles (Chapter 11). Taken together, these five chapters presage new ways of examining the social contract of America's urban democracies.

Finally, in Part IV, contributors begin the task of retheorizing the twenty-first-century city. Chapter 12 considers the place of the new media in representations of Southern California, and other contributors reconsider the utility of the original ecological metaphor of community adopted by the Chicago School (Chapter 13).

Any urban theory for a new century cannot avoid confronting environmental issues (Chapter 14), as well as the challenges of postmodern thought in ways of understanding the city (Chapter 15).

Each of the chapters in this book begins with a short editorial introduction followed by a brief excerpt from *The City,* to provide an orientation to each topical focus and a point of departure for the contributor's discussion. Page numbers in these introductions and excerpts refer to the 1984 Midway reprint of the original text.

ACKNOWLEDGMENTS

I am deeply grateful to contributors from many academic disciplines who made this volume possible and to the University of Chicago Press for generously allowing me to reproduce selections from *The City.*

At Sage Publications, I once again thank Catherine Rossbach, whose sustained support and encouragement brought this project to fruition. She also made valuable suggestions that have greatly improved the text. Thanks also go to Marquita Flemming, a model of an agreeable and efficient editor, who took over from Catherine when she moved to another position at Sage. Diana Axelsen has been my production editor on all three of the books in this trilogy. This team knows how to make a book look good, how to solve seemingly insuperable production problems expeditiously, and how to have fun while making books.

Special thanks go to the volume's contributors, and to J. Dallas Dishman for helping me assemble the manuscript, making invaluable design and layout suggestions and contributing one of his own chapters to this collection. Mike Murashige did a wonderful job in editing the entire volume. I would like to express my gratitude to Richard Parks and Clare Walker for their assistance in the assembling of this manuscript. Kathy War, at the University of Nevada, Las Vegas Special Collections, provided expert and efficient assistance from afar.

This project was supported by the Southern California Studies Center of the University of Southern California, through the office of its provost, Lloyd Armstrong Jr. USC's president, Steven Sample, and former dean of the College of Letters, Arts, and Sciences, Morty Schapiro, have also been strong supporters of the center. Additional funding was provided by The James Irvine Foundation.

NOTES

1. Michael J. Dear, *The Postmodern Urban Condition* (Malden, Mass.: Blackwell, 2000).

2. Robert E. Park, Ernest W. Burgess, and Roderick D. McKenzie, *The City: Suggestions for Investigation of Human Behavior in the Urban Environment* (Chicago: University of Chicago Press, 1925, 1967; Midway reprint, 1984), 143-144.

3. Joel Garreau, *Edge City: Life on the New Frontier* (New York: Doubleday, 1991), 3.

"Well, it winds from Chicago to LA;
More than two thousand miles all the way.
Get your kicks on Route 66."

PART 1

Los Angeles and the "L.A. School"

The Resistible Rise
of the L.A. School

EDITOR'S
COMMENTS

In the final chapter of *The City,* Louis Wirth provides a magisterial review of the field of urban sociology, titled (with deceptive simplicity and astonishing self-effacement) "A Bibliography of the Urban Community." But what Wirth does in this chapter, in a remarkably prescient way, is to summarize the fundamental premise of Chicago School urbanism and also to isolate two equally fundamental features of the urban condition at the beginning of the twenty-first century.

Specifically, Wirth establishes that the city lies at the center of, and provides the organizational logic for, a complex regional hinterland based on trade. But he also notes that the development of "satellite cities" is characteristic of the "latest phases" of city growth and that the location of such satellites can exert a "determining influence" on the direction of growth (185). He observes that modern communications have transformed the world into a "single mechanism," where the global and the local intersect decisively and continuously (186).

And there, in a sense, you have it all. In a few short paragraphs, Wirth anticipates the pivotal moments that separate Chicago-style urbanism from L.A.-style urbanism. He anticipated the shift from what I shall term a *modernist* to a *postmodern* city. In so doing, he foreshadows the necessity of the transition from the Chicago to the L.A. School. It is no longer the center that organizes the hinterland but the hinterland that determines what remains of the center; the imperative toward decentralization (including suburbanization) has become the principal dynamic in contemporary cities, and the twenty-first century's emerging world cities (including Los Angeles) are ground zero, pivotal loci in a globalizing political economy.

From a few, relatively humble first steps, we gaze out already over the abyss—the yawning gap of an intellectual fault line separating Chicago from Los Angeles. In Chapters 1 and 3, Dear and Flusty spell out the history and precepts of the L.A. School, while Dowell Myers describes fundamental ways in which L.A. differs from Chicago, New York City, and Washington, D.C. (Chapter 2).

QUOTES FROM
THE CITY

Far from being an arbitrary clustering of people and buildings, the city is the nucleus of a wider zone of activity from which it draws its resources and over which it exerts its influence. The city and its hinterland represent two phases of the same mechanism which may be analyzed from various points of view.

Just as Galpin, in his *Social Anatomy of Rural Community,* was able to determine the limits of the community by means of the area over which its trade routes extend, so the city may be delimited by the extent of its trading area. From the simpler area around it the city gathers the raw materials, part of which are essential to sustain the life of its inhabitants, and another part of which are transformed by the technique of the city population into finished products which flow out again to the surrounding territory, sometimes over a relatively larger expanse than the region of their origin. From another point of view the city sends out its tentacles to the remotest corners of the world to gather those sources of supply which are not available in the immediate vicinity, only to retail them to its own population and the rural region about it. Again, the city might be regarded as the distributor of wealth, an important economic role which has become institutionalized in a complex financial system. . . . (182-183)

One of the latest phases of city growth is the development of satellite cities. These are generally industrial units growing up outside of the boundaries of the administrative city, which, however, are dependent upon the city proper for their existence. Often they become incorporated into the city proper after the city has inundated them, and thus lose their identity. The location of such satellites may exert a determining influence upon the direction of the city's growth. These satellites become culturally a part of the city long before they are actually incorporated into it. . . . (185)

With the advent of modern methods of communication the whole world has been transformed into a single mechanism of which a country or a city is merely an integral part. The specialization of function, which has been a concomitant of city growth, has created a state of interdependence of world-wide proportions. Fluctuations in the price of wheat on the Chicago Grain Exchange reverberate to the remotest part of the globe, and a new invention anywhere will soon have to be reckoned with at points far from its origin. The city has become a highly sensitive unit in this complex mechanism, and in turn acts as a transmitter of such stimulation as it receives to a local area. This is as true of economic and political as it is of social and intellectual life. (186)

CHAPTER 1

The Resistible Rise of the L.A. School

The state of theory, now and from now on, isn't it California? And even Southern California?

—Jacques Derrida[1]

MICHAEL J. DEAR
STEVEN FLUSTY

What *does* Los Angeles mean? How should we read the texts of the urban as manifested by the chapters in this book? Does it make sense to speak of a Los Angeles School of urbanism, and, if so, with what consequences, apart from irritating those who live beyond the borders of that elusive place called Southern California? Constructing the historical meaning of such a place from the present is at the heart of our concern in this chapter. We argue for an L.A. School of urbanism, believing that a convincing, although in no way conclusive, case for its existence can be made. We are equally interested in the conditions that promote or inhibit the creation of such a school and in the consequences of assuming the school's existence. In essence, this chapter aims to map the intellectual landscape of contemporary urban theory, while leaving it for others to decide how they will navigate beyond it.

THE LOS ANGELES SCHOOLS

It may come as a surprise that a region notorious for a certain contempt for its own history should possess a rich intellectual, cultural, and artistic heritage. Mike Davis's history of Los Angeles encapsulates some of these traditions in a series of wicked metaphors—referring, as he does, to booster, debunker, noir, exile, sorcerer, communard, and mercenary traditions embedded in the city's past. More specifically, Todd Boyd (*Am I Black Enough for You?*) has identified a distinctive L.A. cultural studies; Richard Cándida Smith, a (Southern) Californian artistic canon (*Utopia and Dissent*); and David Fine, an L.A. literature (*Los Angeles in Fiction*). Victor

AUTHORS' NOTE: In preparing this chapter, we have been greatly helped by conversations with Dana Cuff, Kevin Daly, Phil Ethington, Jane Jacobs, and Jennifer Wolch. An earlier version of this chapter was presented in the Getty Research Center's seminar on the construction of historical meaning; we are grateful to Michael Roth for the invitation to present at the Getty and for the comments received at the seminar. USC colleagues who attended the on-campus series that led to this book also provided much valuable guidance. The opinions expressed in this chapter are, needless to say, solely those of the authors.

Burgin, Robbert Flick, Catherine Opie, Allan Sekula, and Camilo José Vergara are in the midst of creating a photographic record of L.A. landscapes, and there are also important public art and muralist traditions heavily influenced by Latino artists including Judy Baca and the ADOBE LA group. Finally, we cannot fail to mention the Hollywood school of filmmaking.

Closest to our concerns is the contemporary L.A. school of architecture, which has enjoyed a rigorous documentation because of the efforts of that most intrepid chronicler, Charles Jencks.[2] We hasten to add that there are many L.A. schools of architecture, both past and present, including Richard Neutra, Rudolph Schindler, Gregory Ain, and others in the 1930s,[3] as well as members of the current L.A. Forum on Architecture and Urban Design. According to Jencks, the current L.A. school of architecture includes such luminaries as Frank Gehry and Charles Moore and was founded amid acrimony in 1981:

> The L.A. School was, and remains, a group of individualized mavericks, more at home together in an exhibition than in each other's homes. There is also a particular self-image involved with this Non-School which exacerbates the situation. All of its members see themselves as outsiders, on the margins challenging the establishment with an informal and demanding architecture; one that must be carefully read.[4]

Jencks concurs with architectural critic Leon Whiteson that L.A.'s cultural environment is one that places the margin at its core: "The ultimate irony is that in the L.A. architectural culture, where heterogeneity is valued over conformity, and creativity over propriety, the periphery is often the center."[5] Jencks's interpretation is of particular interest here because of its implicit characterization of a school as a group of marginalized individuals incapable of surrendering to a broader collective agenda. This is hardly the distinguishing feature we had in mind for this inquiry into an L.A. School of urbanism. Our search was originally for some notion of an identifiable cohort knowingly engaged in a collaborative enterprise. Jencks's vision radically undermines this expectation as, in retrospect, have our personal experiences of the L.A. School of urbanism.

A large part of the difficulty involved in identifying a school is etymological. The *Shorter Oxford English Dictionary* provides fourteen principal categories, including a "group of gamblers or of people drinking together" and a "gang of thieves or beggars working together" (both nineteenth-century uses). Yet also from the mid-nineteenth century is something closer to the spirit of our discussion: "a group of people who share some principle, method, style, etc. Also, a particular doctrine or practice as followed by such a body of people."[6] The dictionary goes on to give as an example the "Marxist school of political thought."

In a broad examination of a "second" Chicago School, Jennifer Pratt uses the term *school* in reference to

> a collection of individuals working in the same environment who at the time and through their own retrospective construction of their identity and the impartations of

intellectual historians are defined as representing a distinct approach to a scholarly endeavor.[7]

Such a description suggests four elements of a working definition of the term *school*. The adherents of a school should be

1. engaged on a common project (however defined);

2. geographically proximate (however delimited);

3. self-consciously collaborative (to whatever extent);

4. externally recognized (at whatever threshold).

The parentheses associated with each of the four characteristics underscore the contingent nature of each trait. Conditions 1 through 3 may be regarded as the minimum, or least restrictive, components of this definition. Second-order criteria for defining a school could include the following:

5. that there exists broad agreement on the program of research;

6. that adherents voluntarily self-identify with the school and/or its research program;

7. that there exist organizational foci for the school's endeavors (such as a learned journal, meetings, or book series).

Most of these traits should be relatively easy to recognize, although no candidate for the school appellation might possibly satisfy all the criteria.

Verifying the existence of a school must always remain unfinished business, not least because we, who would identify such a phenomenon, are ourselves stuck in those particular circumstances of history and place to which our bodies have been consigned. But of greater practical concern is the fourth identifying characteristic, that is, the external recognition needed to warrant the title of *school*. Outside recognition traditionally arrives only after most (if not all) of its participants have died, simply because there are so many incentives to deny the existence of a school. Accolades from outsiders are routinely refused because of professional rivalries, or routinely attacked as crass careerism. Outsiders also appeal to alternative standards of evidence in rejecting a challenge, most commonly seen in appeals to the "hardness" of existing paradigms (as in "hard science"). Gertrude Himmelfarb, for example, refers to real history as "hard work" (something distinct from its postmodern analogue).[8] Yet another variant of denial of school status is the unthinking, perverse pleasure taken by many in puncturing a novice's enthusiasm, using claims such as, "There's nothing new in that. It's all been said and done before." With such curt put-downs, existing orders and authority remain undisturbed, and old hegemonies once again settle about us like an iron cage.

The refusal to even contemplate the existence of a distinctive (intellectually focused, place-based) school of thought is both intellectually and politically conservative. It stifles the development of a synoptic gaze, in both epistemological and material terms, and it inhibits the growth of intellectual and political alliances. In short, the unexamined dismissal of a school's claims is a denial of new ways of seeing and acting. Therefore, we do not intend to wait for outsiders' recognition or permission; it is a far, far better thing to declare a school's existence, raise the flag, and let the battle commence on one's own terms.

THE CHRYSALIS UNFOLDS ...

Most births are inherently messy, and the arrival of an L.A. School of urbanism is no exception. The genetic imprint of the school lies in some unrecoverable past, although we can identify the traces of inveterate city improver Charles Mulford Robinson somewhere in the process. In his 1907 plan to render Los Angeles as "City Beautiful," Robinson conceded that "the problem offered by Los Angeles is a little out of the ordinary."[9] A peculiarly Angeleno urban vision was more convincingly established in 1946, with the publication of Carey McWilliams's *Southern California: An Island on the Land.* This work remains the premier codification of the narratives of Angeleno (sur)reality, has served to establish L.A.'s status as "the great exception," and has since colored both popular and scholarly perceptions of the city. McWilliams emphasized L.A.'s uniqueness with the assertion that the area "reverses almost any proposition about the settlement of western America."[10] He describes Southern California as an engineered utopia attracting pioneers from faraway places such as Mexico, China, Germany, Poland, France, and Great Britain. Among the most exotic immigrants, however, were families from the American Midwestern states who were crushed beneath the heel of an open shop industrial system and generated a hothouse of segregated communities. In McWilliams's account, local communities were rife with bizarre philosophies, carnivalesque politics, and a confused cultural mélange of immigrant influences imperfectly adapted to local conditions. The whole enterprise was pervaded by apocalyptic undercurrents suitable to a fictive paradise situated within a hostile and simultaneously fragile desert environment.

McWilliams's exceptionalism was confirmed and consolidated by Robert Fogelson's *The Fragmented Metropolis,* which in 1967, the year of its publication, was the only account of the region's urban evolution between 1850 and 1930. Fogelson summarized the exceptionalist credo in this way: "The essence of Los Angeles was revealed more clearly in its deviations from [rather] than its similarities to the great American metropolis of the nineteenth and early twentieth centuries."[11] But perhaps the canonical moment in the prehistory of the L.A. School came with the publication in 1971 of Reyner Banham's *Los Angeles: The Architecture of Four Ecologies.* Responding to the notion that Southern California was devoid of cultural or artistic merit, Banham was the first to assert that Los Angeles should not be "rejected as inscrutable and hurled as unknown into the ocean."[12] Rather, he argued, the city should be taken seriously and read and understood only on its own terms instead of those used to make sense of other American cities. But although Los

Angeles was an object worthy of serious study, according to Banham, its structure remained exceptional: "Full command of Angeleno dynamics qualifies one only to read Los Angeles. . . . The splendors and miseries of Los Angeles, the graces of grotesqueries, appear to me as unrepeatable as they are unprecedented."[13] More than any other single volume to that date, Banham's celebration of L.A. landscapes legitimized the study of Los Angeles and temporarily neutralized the propensity of East Coast media and scholars to chart the eccentricities of their West Coast counterparts with mock amazement.

Not until the 1980s did a group of loosely associated scholars, professionals, and advocates based in Southern California become convinced that what was happening in the region was somehow symptomatic of a broader sociogeographic transformation taking place within the United States as a whole. Their common, but then unarticulated, project was based on certain shared theoretical assumptions, as well as on the view that Los Angeles was emblematic of a more general urban dynamic. One of the earliest expressions of an emergent L.A. School came with the appearance in 1986 of a special issue of the journal *Society and Space,* devoted entirely to understanding Los Angeles. In their prefatory remarks to that issue, Allen Scott and Edward Soja referred to Los Angeles as the "capital of the twentieth century,"[14] deliberately invoking Walter Benjamin's designation of Paris as capital of the nineteenth. They predicted that the volume of scholarly work on Los Angeles would quickly overtake that on Chicago, the dominant model of the American industrial metropolis.

Ed Soja's celebrated tour of Los Angeles (which first appeared in this journal issue and was later incorporated into his 1989 *Postmodern Geographies*) most effectively achieved the conversion of Los Angeles from the exception to the rule—the prototype of late twentieth-century postmodern geographies:

> What better place can there be to illustrate and synthesize the dynamics of capitalist spatialization? In so many ways, Los Angeles is the place where "it all comes together." . . . One might call the sprawling urban region . . . a prototopos, a paradigmatic place; or . . . a mesocosm, an ordered world in which the micro and the macro, the idiographic and the nomothetic, the concrete and the abstract, can be seen simultaneously in an articulated and interactive combination.[15]

Soja went on to assert that Los Angeles "insistently presents itself as one of the most informative palimpsests and paradigms of twentieth-century urban development and popular consciousness," comparable with Borges's Aleph: "the only place on earth where all places are seen from every angle, each standing clear, without any confusion or blending."[16]

As ever, Charles Jencks quickly picked up on this trend, taking care to distinguish its practitioners from the L.A. school of architecture:

> The L.A. School of geographers and planners had quite a separate and independent formulation in the 1980s, which stemmed from the analysis of the city as a new post-

modern urban type. Its themes vary from L.A. as the post-Fordist, post-modern city of many fragments in search of a unity, to the nightmare city of social inequities.[17]

This same group of geographers and planners (accompanied by a few dissidents from other disciplines) gathered at Lake Arrowhead in the San Bernardino Mountains on October 11-12, 1987, to discuss the wisdom of engaging in an L.A. School. The participants included, if memory serves, Dana Cuff, Mike Davis, Michael Dear, Margaret FitzSimmons, Rebecca Morales, Allen Scott, Ed Soja, Michael Storper, and Jennifer Wolch. Mike Davis later provided the first description of the putative school:

> I am incautious enough to describe the "Los Angeles School." In a categorical sense, the twenty or so researchers I include within this signatory are a new wave of Marxist geographers—or, as one of my friends put it, "political economists with their space suits on"—although a few of us are also errant urban sociologists, or, in my case, a fallen labor historian. The "School," of course, is based in Los Angeles, at UCLA and USC, but it includes members in Riverside, San Bernardino, Santa Barbara, and even Frankfurt, West Germany.[18]

The meeting was, we can attest, as perceptive as it was inconclusive, as exhilarating as hilarious. Davis described one evening as a

> somewhat dispiriting retreat . . . spent wrestling with ambiguity: "Are we the LA School as the Chicago School was the Chicago School, or as the Frankfurt School was the Frankfurt School?" Will the reconstruction of urban political economy allow us to better understand the concrete reality of LA, or is it the other way around? Fortunately, after a night of heavy drinking, we agreed to postpone a decision on this question. . . . So in our own way we are as "laid back" and decentralized as the city we are trying to explain.[19]

Yet despite these ambiguities and tensions (with their curious echoes in the L.A. school of architecture recorded by Jencks), Davis is clear about the school's common theme:

> One of the nebulous unities in our different research—indeed the very ether that the L.A. School mistakes for oxygen—is the idea of "*restructuring.*" We all agree that we are studying "restructuring" and that it occurs at all kinds of discrete levels, from the restructuring of residential neighborhoods to the restructuring of global markets or whole regimes of accumulation.[20]

Davis also recorded some substantive contributions made by the school's early cadre of perpetrators:

> To date [1989], the LA School has contributed original results in four areas. First, particularly in the work of Edward Soja and Harvey Molotch, it has given "placeness," as a social construction, a new salience in explaining the political economy of cities. Secondly, via the case studies by Michael Storper, Suzanne Christopherson, and Allen

Scott, it has deepened our understanding of the economies of high-tech agglomeration, producing some provocative recent theses about the rise of a new regime of "flexible accumulation." Thirdly, through both the writing and activism of Margaret FitzSimmons and Robert Gottlieb, it has contributed a new vision of the environmental movement, with emphasis on the urban quality of life. And, fourthly, through the collaboration of Michael Dear and Jennifer Wolch, it is giving us a more realistic understanding of the homeless and indigent, and their connection to the decline of unskilled inner city labor markets.[21]

Davis was, to the best of our knowledge, the first to mention a specific L.A. School of urbanism, and he repeated the claim in his popular contemporary history of Los Angeles, *City of Quartz* (1990). But truth be told, following those fateful and strange days of quasi-unity at Lake Arrowhead, the L.A. School had already begun to atomize, even as the floodgates opened and tentative claims for a prototypical Los Angeles trickled forth.

Journalist Joel Garreau understood more clearly than most urban scholars where the country was heading. The opening sentences in his 1991 book, *Edge City,* proclaimed: "Every American city that is growing, is growing in the fashion of Los Angeles."[22] By 1993, the trickle of Southern California studies had grown to a continuous flow. In his careful, path-breaking study of high technology in Southern California, Allen Scott noted,

> Throughout the era of Fordist mass production, [Los Angeles] was seen as an exception, as an anomalous complex of regional and urban activity in comparison with what were then considered to be the paradigmatic cases of successful industrial development. . . . [Yet] with the steady ascent of flexible production organization, Southern California is often taken to be something like a new paradigm of local economic development, and its institutional bases, its evolutionary trajectory, and its internal locational dynamics . . . as providing important general insights and clues.[23]

Charles Jencks added his own spin on the social forces underlying L.A.'s architecture when he argued that

> Los Angeles, like all cities, is unique, but in one way it may typify the world city of the future: there are only minorities. No single ethnic group, nor way of life, nor industrial sector dominates the scene. Pluralism has gone further here than in any other city in the world and for this reason it may well characterize the global megalopolis of the future.[24]

The foundations of a putative school were completed in 1993 with Marco Cenzatti's first explicit examination of the thing called an L.A. School of urbanism. Responding to Davis, he underscored that the school's practitioners combined precepts of both the Chicago and Frankfurt Schools:

> Thus Los Angeles comes . . . into the picture not just as a blueprint or a finished paradigm of the new dynamics, but as a laboratory which is itself an integral component of the production of new modes of analysis of the urban.[25]

Since then, the rate of scholarly investigations into Los Angeles has accelerated, just as Scott and Soja predicted it would. For instance, in a 1993 study of homelessness in Los Angeles, Wolch and Dear situated the analysis within the broader matrix of L.A.'s urbanism.[26] The pivotal year in the maturation of the L.A. School, however, may yet prove to be 1996, which saw the publication of three edited volumes on the region: *Rethinking Los Angeles* (Dear, Schockman, and Hise); *The City: Los Angeles and Urban Theory at the End of the Twentieth Century* (Scott and Soja); and *Ethnic Los Angeles* (Waldinger and Bozorgmehr). The forty or more chapters in these volumes represent a quantum leap in the collective understanding of the region and the implications of these new insights for national and international urbanisms. By 1996, there was also a growing number of predominantly university-based centers that legitimized scholarly and public policy analyses of the region, among them USC's Southern California Studies Center, UCLA's Lewis Center for Regional Policy Studies, and Loyola Marymount University's Center for the Study of Los Angeles. Other institutions consolidated parallel interests in regional governmental and nongovernmental agencies, including the Getty Research Institute and RAND.

. . . AND THE L.A. SCHOOL EMERGES

In these postmodern times, the gesture to an L.A. School might appear to be a deeply contradictory intellectual strategy. A school has semantic overtones of codification and "mastery"; it has structure and authority. Modernists and postmodernists alike might be inclined to shudder at the irony implied by these associations. Yet ultimately, we are comfortable in proclaiming the existence of a Los Angeles School of urbanism, although such a proclamation seems an after-the-fact conclusion for two reasons.

The first is one of *demonstrable traces.* The Los Angeles School exists as a body of literature. It exhibits an evolution through history, beginning with the analysis of Los Angeles as an aberrant curiosity distinct from other forms of urbanism. The tone of that history gradually shifts to the point that, at present, the city is now commonly represented as indicative of new forms of urbanism augmenting (and even supplanting) the older, established forms against which Los Angeles was once judged deviant. Further, the current body of literature on Los Angeles, and the swollen population of urbanists situated in the region, attest to the city's critical mass in contemporary urban theorizing. Second, we assert the existence of an L.A. School by reason of its existence as a *discursive strategy.* In acknowledging an L.A. School, we demarcate a space both for the exploration of new realities and for resistance to old hegemonies. The body of writing about Los Angeles provides alternative models to past orthodoxies on the "essential" nature of the city and is proving to be far more successful than its detractors at explaining the form and function of urbanism in a time of globalization.

In issuing a proclamation, however, we acknowledge the danger that a Los Angeles School could become another panoptic fortress from whence a new totalizing urban model is manufactured and marketed, running roughshod over divergent ways of seeing like the hegemonies it has so recently supplanted. This danger of creating a new overbearing urban paradigm stands at every step of our project: in defining the very boundaries of an L.A. School, in establishing a unitary model of Los Angeles, and in imposing the template and experiences of Los Angeles on the rest of the world. Let's consider each of these threats in turn.

Who is, and who is not, a member of the L.A. School? The fragmented and globally oriented nature of the Los Angeles School counters the threats of a new hegemony. The avowal of an L.A. School can become a decolonizing, postcolonial impulse, even as it warns us of new colonialisms marching down the historical path. In declaring our enterprise, therefore, we hope to promote inclusiveness. Those who worry about the hegemonic intent of an L.A. School may rest assured that the L.A. School is pathologically antileadership. Few of the contributors to this volume (or those discussed in their chapters) will readily identify themselves as members of an L.A. School, and some adamantly reject such a notion. But all are unable (so we believe) to deny their implication in the genealogy uncovered in this investigation. The programmatic intent of the L.A. School remains fractured, incoherent, and idiosyncratic even to its constituent scholars, who most often perceive themselves as occupying a place on the periphery rather than at the center. The L.A. School invites as members all those who take Los Angeles as a worthy object of study and a source of insight into the nature of contemporary urbanism. Such a school evades dogma by including divergent empirical and theoretical approaches rooted in philosophies both modern and postmodern, ranging from Marxist to Libertarian. Admittedly, such a school will be a fragmentary and loosely connected entity, always on the verge of disintegration—but then again, so is Los Angeles itself.

Is there a single Los Angeles to speak of? A unified, consensual description of Los Angeles necessitates excluding a plethora of valuable readings on the region. For instance, numerous discursive battles have been fought since the events of April 1992 in Los Angeles to decide what term best describes them or, more cynically, which term most effectively recasts them as a weapon adaptable to a particular rhetorical arsenal. Those who read the events as a spontaneous, visceral, opportunistic (and ill-justified?) reaction to the acquittal of the officers in the Rodney King case employ the term *riot.* For those who read the events within the context of economic evisceration and social polarization, the term *uprising* is preferred. Those who see in them a more conscious political intentionality apply the term *rebellion.* For its part, civic authority skirts these issues by relying on the supposedly depoliticized term *civil unrest.* But those concerned with the perspective of Korean participants, literally caught in the middle of the turmoil itself as well as the subsequent rhetoric war, deploy the Korean tradition of naming an occurrence by its principal date and so make use of the term, *Sa-I-Gu.* Which name is definitive? The polyvocality of the Los Angeles School permits us to replace the question, "Which is it?" with "Which is it, at which stage of events, at which location in the region, and from whose perspective?" Such an approach may well entail a loss of clarity and certitude, but in exchange it offers a richness of description and interpretation that would otherwise be forfeited in the name of achieving an "official" narrative.

Finally, is *Los Angeles the world?* Being Angelenos ourselves (more or less), we are sometimes tempted to answer this question in the affirmative. But contributors to the L.A. School are well aware that time and space regularly throw speed bumps in our path. On the one hand, the processes at work in Los Angeles may be simultaneously at work in other cities around the world. Yet from a temporal perspective, much work of the L.A. School explicitly recognizes the inherently peculiar and slippery nature of history, which influences us even as it allows us to differentiate the present character and function of one world city from another. There are industries and settlements in Los Angeles distinct from those in Paris, which, in turn, are a major contrast to those in Lagos and elsewhere. These differences cannot simply be conjured out of existence in the name of some vague Angeleno standard.

Spatially, L.A.'s urban landscapes are not necessarily original to Los Angeles. The luxury compound atop a matrix of impoverished misery, the self-contained secure community, and the fortified home can be found first in places such as Manila and São Paolo. Indeed, Anthony King has suggested that all things ascribed to postmodern urbanism can be seen decades earlier in the principal cities of the colonial world.[27] Thus, the L.A. School justifies a presentation of Los Angeles not as *the* model of contemporary urbanism, nor as the privileged locale from whence a cabal of theoreticians issue pronouncements about the way things really are, but as one of a number of space-time geographical prisms through which current processes of urban (re)formation may be advantageously viewed.

The literature of the L.A. School has largely (although not exclusively) shown itself to be less about looking to Los Angeles for models of the urban and more about looking for contemporary expressions of the urban in Los Angeles. Thus, the school and its concepts of contemporary Angeleno urbanism do not represent an emerging vision of contemporary urbanism in total so much as they are one component in a new interurban geography working from Los Angeles but requesting the participation of (and placing equal importance on) the continuing experiences and voices of Tijuana, Miami, São Paolo, Marseilles, and the like.

Even as we write, the claims of an L.A. School are being challenged by a nascent "Orange County School." In a chapter contained in *Postsuburban California*, Gottdeiner and Kephart claim that in Orange County,

> We have focused on what we consider to be a new form of settlement space—the fully urbanized, multinucleated, and independent county. . . . As a new form of settlement space, they are the first such occurrence in five thousand years of urban history.[28]

Although those who are familiar with the more southerly regions of Southern California may regard this as a somewhat exaggerated if not entirely melodramatic gesture, such counterclaims are an important piece of the comparative urban discourse that we hope this book will help generate. To repeat, we are certainly not trying to create an L.A. School in the counterproductive sense of an exclusionary, hegemonic, institutionalized mode of thought. Instead, in this book, we have simply begun to map the intellectual terrain surrounding a perspective on twenty-first-century cities. An important component in that landscape is Southern California. It may or may not be prototypical. It certainly is not unique. But it is redefining the way we understand cities, and we ignore its lessons at our peril.

NOTES

1. Jacques Derrida, 1990, quoted in Carrol, p. 63.
2. Jencks, 1993, p. 34.
3. See Gebhard and von Breton, 1989.
4. Jencks, 1993, p. 34.
5. Jencks, 1993, p. 34.
6. *Shorter Oxford English Dictionary,* 1999, p. 2714.
7. Quoted in Fine, 1995, p. 2.
8. Himmelfarb, 1992.
9. Robinson, 1907, p. 4.
10. McWilliams, 1973, p. 295.
11. Fogelson, 1993, p. 134.
12. Banham, 1971, p. 23.
13. Banham, 1971, p. 24.
14. Scott and Soja, 1996.
15. Soja, 1989, p. 191.
16. Soja, 1989, p. 248.
17. Jencks, 1993, p. 132.
18. Davis, 1989, p. 9.
19. Davis, 1989, pp. 9-10.
20. Davis, 1989, p. 10.
21. Davis, 1989, p. 10.
22. Garreau, 1991, p. 3.
23. Scott, 1993, p. 33.
24. Jencks, 1993, p. 7.
25. Cenzatti, 1993, p. 8.
26. Wolch and Dear, 1993.
27. King, 1992.
28. Gottdeiner and Kephart in Kling, Olin, and Poster, 1991, p. 51.

REFERENCES

Banham, Reyner. 1971. *Los Angeles: The architecture of four ecologies.* Harmondsworth, England: Penguin.

Boyd, Todd. 1997. *Am I black enough for you? Popular culture from the 'hood and beyond.* Bloomington: Indiana University Press.

Cenzatti, Marco. 1993. *Los Angeles and the L.A. school: Postmodernism and urban studies.* Los Angeles: Los Angeles Forum for Architecture and Urban Design.

Davis, Mike. 1989. Homeowners and homeboys: Urban restructuring in LA. *Enclitic* 11 (summer): 9-16.

Davis, Mike. 1990. *City of quartz: Excavating the future in Los Angeles.* New York: Verso.

Dear, Michael J., H. Eric Schockman, and Greg Hise, eds. 1996. *Rethinking Los Angeles.* Thousand Oaks, Calif.: Sage.

Derrida, Jacques, 1990. Quoted in Carrol, David, ed., *The states of "theory."* New York: Columbia University Press.

Fine, David, ed. 1995. *Los Angeles in fiction: A collection of essays.* Albuquerque: University of New Mexico Press.

Fine, Gary Alan, ed. 1995. *A second Chicago School? The development of a postwar American sociology.* Chicago: University of Chicago Press.

Fogelson, Robert. 1993. *The fragmented metropolis.* Berkeley: University of California Press.

Garreau, Joel. 1991. *Edge city: Life on the new frontier.* New York: Doubleday.

Gebhard, David, and Harriette von Breton. 1989. *Los Angeles in the thirties, 1931-1941.* Los Angeles: Hennessey & Ingalls.

Himmelfarb, Gertrude. 1992. Telling it as you like it: Post-modernist history and the flight from fact. *Times Literary Supplement,* October 16, p. 12.

Jencks, Charles. 1993. *Heteropolis: Los Angeles, the riots and the strange beauty of hetero-architecture.* New York: St. Martin's Press.

King, Anthony. 1992. The times and spaces of modernity. Paper presented at the conference on "A New Urban and Regional Hierarchy: Impacts of Modernization, Restructuring, and the End of Bipolarity," International Sociological Association, Research Committee 21, University of California, Los Angeles.

Kling, Rob, Spencer Olin, and Mark Poster, eds. 1991. *Postsuburban California: The transformation of Orange County since World War II.* Berkeley: University of California Press.

McWilliams, Carey. 1973. *Southern California: An island on the land.* Santa Barbara, Calif.: Peregrine Smith.

Robinson, Charles Mulford. 1907. *The city beautiful.* Report to the mayor, city council and members of the municipal art commission.

Scott, Allen J. 1993. *Technopolis: High-technology industry and regional development in Southern California.* Berkeley: University of California Press.

Scott, Allen J., and Edward W. Soja, eds. 1996. *The city: Los Angeles and urban theory at the end of the twentieth century.* Berkeley: University of California Press.

Shorter Oxford English dictionary. 1999. Oxford, England: Oxford University Press.

Smith, Richard Cándida. 1995. *Utopia and dissent: Art, poetry, and politics in California.* Berkeley: University of California Press.

Soja, Edward W. 1989. *Postmodern geographies: The reassertion of space in critical social theory.* New York: Verso.

Waldinger, Roger, and Mehdi Bozorgmehr, eds. 1996. *Ethnic Los Angeles.* New York: Russell Sage Foundation.

Wolch, Jennifer, and Michael J. Dear. 1993. *Malign neglect: Homelessness in an American city.* San Francisco: Jossey-Bass.

Demographic Dynamism in Los Angeles, Chicago, New York, and Washington, DC

The heart of the city is its peoples. Practitioners in the Chicago School placed the city and its inhabitants at the core of their inquiries, including consideration of human nature, the urban economy, and (above all) the evolution of communities and geographically defined neighborhoods. Their writings emphasized the organic nature of the growth of relatively homogeneous agglomerations of peoples on the basis of class, culture, race/ethnicity, and so on. At the same time, they also recognized the essential interrelatedness of all places in the city.

In this chapter, Dowell Myers opens our investigations by examining the "demographic dynamism" of contemporary cities. By comparing Los Angeles with three other U.S. metropolitan regions (Chicago, New York, and Washington, DC), Myers not only provides the essential demographic history that undergirds all the other inquiries in this book but also teases out the special (even unique) qualities of the demographic process in Southern California.

QUOTES FROM
THE CITY

The city . . . is something more than congeries of individual men and of social conveniences—streets, buildings, electric lights, tramways, and telephones, etc.; something more, also, than a mere constellation of institutions and administrative devices—courts, hospitals, schools, police, and civil functionaries of various sorts. The city is, rather, a state of mind, a body of customs and traditions, and of the organized attitudes and sentiments that inhere in these customs and are transmitted with this tradition. The city is not, in other words, merely a physical mechanism and an artificial construction. It is involved in the vital processes of the people who compose it; it is a product of nature, and particularly of human nature. . . . (1)

The city has been studied, in recent times, from the point of view of its geography, and still more recently from the point of view of its ecology. There are forces at work within the limits of the urban community—within the limits of any natural area of human habitation, in fact—which tend to bring about an orderly and typical grouping of its population and institutions. The science which seeks to isolate these factors and to describe the typical constellations of persons and institutions which the co-operation of these forces produce, is what we call human, as distinguished from plant and animal, ecology. . . . (1-2)

The city is not, however, merely a geographical and ecological unit; it is at the same time an economic unit. The economic organization of the city is based on the division of labor. The multiplication of occupations and professions within the limits of the urban population is one of the most striking and least understood aspects of modern city life. From this point of view, we may, if we choose, think of the city, that is to say, the place and the people, with all the machinery and administrative devices that go with them, as organically related; a kind of psychophysical mechanism in and through which private and political interests find not merely a collective but a corporate expression. . . . (2)

Physical geography, natural advantages and disadvantages, including means of transportation, determine in advance the general outlines of the urban plan. As the city increases in population, the subtler influences of sympathy, rivalry, and economic necessity tend to control the distribution of population. There spring up fashionable residence quarters from which the poorer classes are excluded because of the increased value of the land. Then there grow up slums which are inhabited by great numbers of the poorer classes who are unable to defend themselves from association with the derelict and vicious.

In the course of time every section and quarter of the city takes on something of the character and qualities of its inhabitants. Each separate part of the city is inevitably stained with the peculiar sentiments of its population. The effect of this is to convert what was at first a mere geographical expression into a neighborhood, that is to say, a locality with sentiments, traditions, and history of its own. Within this neighborhood the continuity of the historical processes is somehow maintained. The past imposes itself upon the present, and the life of every locality moves on with a certain momentum of its own, more or less independent of the larger circle of life and interests about it. (5-6)

CHAPTER 2

Demographic Dynamism in Los Angeles, Chicago, New York, and Washington, DC

DOWELL MYERS

Demographic dynamism is a term used here to emphasize the fluid dimensions of demographic status that change over a person's lifetime—age, geographic location, duration of residence, and housing or economic careers—in contrast to static demographic characteristics such as gender or race, which are largely invariant over a lifetime. References made to changing demographics usually pertain to a changing population composition made up of different racial groups. Demographic dynamism includes that factor but extends also to the changes experienced *within* the existing population as people grow older and live longer in their current place of residence. Both the changing composition of the city and the longitudinal experience of its residents are important to urban policy.

Los Angeles is often singled out as an urban area undergoing dramatic economic and demographic change. However, other major metropolitan areas may be experiencing similar forces. In this article, I compare Los Angeles with New York, Chicago, and Washington, DC. The principal argument advanced here is that the apparent differences between Los Angeles and the others only accentuate demographic dynamics also present in New York, Chicago, and Washington, DC. Once understood in exaggerated form in Los Angeles, the same factors become visible in the other cities as well.

Perhaps of greater significance is how the major features highlighted in Los Angeles lead us to view the problems of cities differently. Demographic change has been viewed, for the most part, with considerable rigidity and pessimism. Recent

AUTHOR'S NOTE: This chapter is reprinted from "Demographic Dynamism and Metropolitan Change: Comparing Los Angeles, New York, Chicago, and Washington, DC," 1999, *Housing Policy Debate,* Vol. 10, No. 4, pp. 919-954. Copyright © 1999 by Fannie Mae Foundation. Used with permission.

trends have been interpreted as signs of decline and social failure. Once grasped, the lessons to be learned from Los Angeles are more positive. This new evidence reflects a healthy demographic dynamism that should be fostered as a source of solutions to urban problems, not used solely as justification for despair. Nevertheless, certain burdens fall disproportionately on cities in rapid change, which deserve assistance if they are to help their residents achieve the upward mobility this article shows is possible.

Many lessons can be learned by viewing cities through the lens of demographic dynamism. One pertains to a reassessment of the assumption of population stability that links people and place-based policies. The course of people's lives flows through different urban areas and is not contained by a single location for a lifetime. The lessons learned also extend to exposing the black-white paradigm bias that underestimates the significance of growing ethnic diversity. The lessons include the pervasive effects of immigration, not just in its volume, but also in the impact of recency of arrival followed by growing settlement. And the lessons include as well new insights about the prevalence of upward mobility in the city, particularly as illustrated by immigrants. All of these insights are highlighted in the case of Los Angeles, but data for each of the other regions reveal similar dynamics at work in all.

DEMOGRAPHIC DYNAMISM AND URBAN THEORY

State of Urban Theory

Contemporary urban theory emphasizes economic and political dimensions, along with spatial relations, more than it does social behavior and social outcomes. There is good reason for this. The increasing global integration of the economy has unleashed restructuring forces that are remaking urban areas. An international division of labor is leading to polarized job opportunities and spatial rearrangements of jobs and residences in the city. In turn, political interest groups compete for new opportunities and seek to displace new burdens onto others. In this sense, the well-being of urban residents can be viewed as indicating how the benefits and costs of restructuring are distributed.

Much urban theory and policy, coming out of Midwestern- or Eastern-based analyses, is concerned with how a skills/jobs mismatch has led to increasing unemployment of working-class black men who are left behind in deindustrialized inner cities.[1] This framework is stretched to its limits when it is applied to major immigrant-receiving metropolitan areas such as Los Angeles or New York. The immigrant population is a working poor, rather than an underclass.

In contrast to urban theories based on the modern city wracked by deindustrialization and outmigration, an emerging Los Angeles school of thought has pushed urban scholars to look to the complexity of Los Angeles for hints of a new urban reality.[2] In doing so, these scholars have challenged the Rustbelt/Sunbelt, city/

suburb, local/global, industrial/postindustrial, and black/white notions that under-
lie most urban theory and policy. The new Los Angeles school has successfully challenged old assumptions about economic structure and space. Yet these scholars have
yet to incorporate one of the most vital dimensions underlying their city—the
demographic dynamism of a population in flux. The neglect of this dimension amid
the concerted attention to urban restructuring is ironic, for demographic dynamism
may be one of the most vital lessons to be drawn from Los Angeles.

Population Factor

It is well understood that population recomposition has accompanied the
changes in economic activity. What is not understood is how fully integrated these
demographic changes are with the broader forces of restructuring or how much the
demographic changes are embedded in our measurements and interpretations of
social outcomes. The dynamics and consequences of contemporary demographic
changes have simply not been comprehended. Two decades ago, William Alonso[3]
called attention to the population factor and urban structure, emphasizing the role
of demographic change as a driver of other urban changes. He spoke principally
about the aging of the baby boom generation, falling household sizes, and new
migration patterns within the United States.

When Alonso was writing, the major demographic change of the late 20th century—immigration—had yet to make its effects felt. How immigration should be
incorporated is a particular challenge to contemporary urban theory and policy.
More than just adding immigrants to the discussion, the intersection of immigration
with racial change, poverty, and housing problems forces a reconceptualization of
those very issues. As Roger Waldinger,[4] who has studied immigration in both Los
Angeles and New York, has observed: "[I]n a sense, much of the sociological research
on the new immigration to the United States is about people who just happen to live
in cities. Today one could argue that much of urban theory and policy is about cities
who just happen to have people living in them."[5] After a concerted effort to direct
sociologists' and others' attention to ethnic changes in Los Angeles, those who
describe themselves as urban theorists are only beginning to take these factors into
account.[6]

To date, however, Alonso's argument that demographic changes were integral to
changes in urban structure has been largely disregarded, regardless of the extensive
body of social research in cities. In practice, the demographic factor has been
excluded as an important element of urban theory and policy. A current illustration
of this neglect is Robert Fishman's[7] poll of 149 urban specialists regarding the top
ten influences on the American metropolis of the past 50 years. Demographic factors were scarcely visible to these urbanists; instead they highlighted mass-produced
suburban tract housing and the enclosed shopping mall. Similarly, the recent collection on urban theory by Fainstein and Campbell[8] ignored demographics in most
chapters and, when addressing race in only two, focused on black-white differences.
Two other collections of urban theory writings on Los Angeles emphasized a broader

set of ethnic groups,[9] but where attention was given to demographic factors, it was focused on the most static dimensions. Race, gender, and class are personal descriptors that change little, if at all, over a person's lifetime. By contrast, virtually ignored in urban theory are the fluid dimensions of demographic status: age, family status, career trajectories, and for immigrants, increasing duration of residence.

This attention to only the most static of demographic factors is contradictory to the spirit of contemporary urban theory that emphasizes restructuring.[10] Among Los Angeles scholars, many have observed that the "demographic metamorphosis of the region during this period was as dramatic and far-reaching as its industrial restructuring."[11] Others have pointed out that demographic changes and changing life chances may be a more important part of urban restructuring than economic restructuring.[12] Indeed, demographic changes and economic restructuring are closely coupled via a migration process that imports labor to fill expanding occupational niches.[13] Even if economic restructuring is a root cause of demographic change, the latter deserves our special attention because it is through the consequences for people that we typically judge the desirability of economic change.

People Versus Place Orientations

One explanation for why urban theory places little emphasis on demographic change and, at most, addresses only static demographics like race is the choice dilemma posed by the dichotomy between people and place perspectives on urban change. Urban theories and researchers favor a place perspective that emphasizes the conditions of cities and how they change over time. The potential conflict between "place prosperity" and "people prosperity" has long been recognized.[14] The core issue is that a locality's residents do not remain the same over time, and the lifetime trends experienced by residents often diverge markedly from the place trends. Explicit attention to the people being served by planners could also lead to substantial differences in planning policies.

One problem emphasized by Edel[15] is that place-targeting of public programs (such as entitlement zones) is an inaccurate way to target people in need: "[I]nitially ineligible people become beneficiaries by their place of residence, while some intended beneficiaries are excluded for the same reason."[16] In high-growth areas, in particular, newcomers often arrive to take advantage of the place-targeted benefits, displacing the original residents for whom the programs were intended. For example, a study in Atlanta found that the benefits of employment programs intended for local black young adults were often intercepted by the high volume of new migrants, many of them also black.[17]

The longer the period of analysis, the more important the people versus place distinction becomes. Normal processes of mobility can lead to substantial population turnover after a decade or more. Even if the city's population remains constant, new arrivals usually have characteristics systematically different from those who are departing. Or, even if the newcomers resemble those they replace, their newness implies that their situation is unrelated to any benefits or experiences previously provided to residents in that location.

The trends recorded for a place can differ dramatically from the trends experienced by the people themselves. For example, a recent study of upward mobility patterns in Los Angeles found that successive waves of arrivals moved between places as their status increased.[18] At a given point in time, measurement of residents' characteristics includes the most disadvantaged newcomers to a city but not the more advantaged "graduates" from the place. When the influx of disadvantaged newcomers is growing or when the departure of upwardly mobile residents is increasing, the city's average economic status will decline over time. This leads to an odd paradox: The downward trend for the place is the opposite indicator of the upward trend enjoyed by the residents themselves.

There is certainly nothing wrong—and a lot good—with studying places and with using more accessible data. However, urban scholars must always beware of the potential biases of a people-place discordance. If at all possible, we should avoid forming misleading conclusions about the life chances of people when we have studied only the characteristics of residents found in a particular place at a particular time.

Black-White Conceptions of Race

One clear-cut illustration of how demographic change is ignored by urban theory is the maintenance of a black-white conception of race. Even though most sociologists and scholars of ethnicity have now turned to a multiethnic and multifaceted concept of race, urban scholars for the most part retain the view of an earlier time. During the civil rights revolution and urban disturbances of the 1960s, the problem of race in America meant the problem of how to incorporate blacks into white America. The experiences of this decade left a strong and lasting impression on the scholarly and political outlook of today's senior urban scholars.

Since 1970, numerous other racial and ethnic groups have burgeoned in number, because of immigration from Asia, Mexico and Latin America, Africa and the Caribbean, and Europe and the Middle East. These newcomers have not fit easily into the present mold of black-white relations. Africans, West Indians, and Haitians resist being cast as blacks,[19] while Asians resist the model minority label,[20] and Latino leaders are ambivalent about whether their group should be treated as disadvantaged like the black underclass or held up as a model of self-sufficient striving.[21]

Despite the changing ethnic makeup and a consensus among scholars of ethnicity, many urban researchers and policy makers have held to a simpler black-white focus. In part, this is warranted by the persistence of severe black disadvantages and by the continuing black-white makeup of many cities and regions. However, accommodating the new multiethnic urban America requires new thinking, not simply about the meaning of race, but also about the recent origins and dynamic changes accompanying many rapidly growing groups. As will be shown, the old, static black-white paradigm applies poorly in Los Angeles, and it is becoming less useful in other major cities as well.

Life-Cycle Trajectories in the City

An inherent difficulty is that the data used by urban researchers reinforce a place orientation, since data are collected and reported for specific locations at a moment in time. Indeed, the constitutional mandate for conducting the decennial census is to count the population in specific jurisdictions for purposes of political representation by place. Much less often are data assembled for special subject groups of the population (e.g., the elderly), although this can be accomplished by rearranging the place-based data. Most urban analysts remain content to study the more accessible data describing place characteristics instead.

How can we conceptualize change for the individual residents of cities? One strategy is to collect individual life histories that provide deep insights into how life chances interact with the changing structure of opportunity in the city. An excellent example is Rocco,[22] who summarizes the results of extensive ethnographic research and the life histories of 90 Latino families over a number of years. These interviews illustrate in human detail how families' experiences have been shaped by economic restructuring. By its nature this qualitative research is limited in scope, but not in depth. We cannot know how well this limited sample reflects the experience of most Latinos or of other groups. But Rocco's contribution illustrates how much could be learned if a broad-based demographic analysis were coupled with an in-depth qualitative analysis.[23]

An alternative to tracing individual life histories is the cohort longitudinal approach, a means of describing the average trajectory of large groups of people through time.[24] The rates of change within cohorts measure the average life course experience of specific groups of people, tracking net changes for them as they grow older and reside longer in an area. Readily available census data are used to group residents into cohorts defined by their age or by their decade of arrival in the United States. When these cohorts are observed at two points in time, changes can be traced for each group as it grows older, lives longer in the United States, and gains more experience. Differences can also be observed between successive cohorts that are following higher or lower trajectories (such as between those ages 25 to 34 in 1980 and the next cohort entering that age in 1990).

A potential drawback is that cohort measurements risk some bias because of outmigration from an urban area. If attrition from a cohort is substantial and if those who leave the study area are different from those who stay, then the changes observed for cohorts could be biased representations of average experience over time. The most extreme example would be that if all the "failures" left the area, the status of remaining cohort members would rise markedly. More typically, it is the "successes" who depart a locality as part of their upward mobility, leading to underestimates of progress observed among those who remain. In the analysis that follows, the boundaries are drawn to enclose entire regions in the study area, thus capturing the residential mobility between city and suburbs. Nevertheless, the circular migration between Mexico and the United States, for example, could substantially alter the makeup of cohort members remaining over time. Fortunately, as discussed in Myers and Lee,[25] analysis of education trends and other factors within cohorts in the Los Angeles region does not reveal substantial bias over time. Moreover, even if cohort measurements are inevitably biased to some degree, they provide a more accurate and comprehensive depiction of trends than either cross-sectional measurements or locally available life histories.[26]

Urban change transpires not only through the changes recorded as existing cohorts progress forward in time, but also through the compositional change created as new cohorts arrive. New cohorts are formed by the arrival of new groups of people, such as through migration, through birth into childhood, or through maturation into adulthood. When combined with the departure of former residents, whether through outmigration, death, graduation from school, or retirement from the labor force, the total mix of the population (labor force, public school students, etc.) will change through this replacement process. In the case of immigration, a city can see dramatic changes caused by the arrival of new waves with very different characteristics than those of previous residents.

None of the literature on urban theory makes these distinctions about sources of observed change. Instead, for the most part, authors either focus on demographic differences at a single point in time or focus on overall changes recorded across a decade. The danger is that researchers cannot draw a clear interpretation of how residents' experiences may have changed over time. Some of the change in an outcome indicator such as poverty or employment may be due to the impact of restructuring on the overall economy, some may be due to a changing mix of the population residing in the region, and some may be due to the changes in life trajectories of specific population groups. Failing to recognize these possibilities, previous writers have tended to ascribe *all* of the observed differences to one dimension or another. Myers[27] provides a detailed analysis of how policies can be misinformed in this way.

COMPARISON OF FOUR CITIES

Our theories of urban change and our beliefs about good urban policy are rooted in the experiences of particular cities, which may or may not be typical. Chicago has long been the prototype for understanding the large industrial city in 20th century America. This position stems from its place as the site of the Chicago school in sociology and urban studies. New York is also seen as important for its great size and for its role as a financial and media center, and because it serves as a principal gateway for immigrants to America. The Big Apple exemplifies trends toward economic polarization, with pockets of wealthy reinvestment set amidst poverty and the continuing struggle against urban decline.[28] A third city, Washington, DC, exerts a subtle influence on urban policy because it provides the urban experience shared by federal policy makers, against which they informally test their implicit assumptions of urban reality.

Los Angeles is often treated as more exceptional than these other cities. It is perceived as newer, rapidly growing, lower-density (more uniformly "suburban"), and less industrialized. However, Los Angeles is the prototype for a different kind of city, one increasingly prominent in the late 20th century, but not the type of older city facing decline that draws the attention of federal problem solvers. Los Angeles is the paragon of sprawling cities throughout the sunbelt and located even on the growing edge of otherwise large, stagnant northern cities.

Despite the perceived differences, Los Angeles is also treated as similar to the comparison cities. Like New York, Los Angeles is a gateway for immigrants and is ethnically diverse. Like the other cities, it shares problems of poverty and economic polarization, racial segregation, and housing affordability. Both views may be true: Los Angeles can be very different and at the same time have similar problems. But the very nature of those common problems is transformed by the different context of Los Angeles, implying not only different causes and outcomes, but also a different understanding of what the problems mean.

As will be shown, these apparent differences only accentuate features also present in New York, Chicago, and Washington, DC. Once understood in exaggerated form in the case of Los Angeles, the same factors become visible in these other cities as well. In addition, the Los Angeles model already well represents growing cities in both the United States and the developing world, and the changes seen in Los Angeles may be a precursor of changes to come in other cities.

Data and Geographic Definitions

Comparing Los Angeles with New York, Chicago, and Washington, DC, yields important clues, and some surprising findings on the influence of demographic changes. For this comparison, we use both 1980 and 1990 census data, so that we can compare not only differences at one point in time, but also rates of change. The Public Use Microdata Sample (PUMS) data files for 1980 and 1990 permit highly detailed analysis through custom tabulations and provide very large sample sizes for some relatively small groups. More current data, from the Current Population Survey (CPS), have a sample size only about one-hundredth as large. Also, the CPS does not include as consistent a set of variables over time (such as year of immigrant arrival). Pending the release in 2002 of detailed data from the 2000 census, much can be learned from studying the dynamics of change recorded in the last two censuses. Indeed, lessons uncovered here may serve to guide analysis of the 1990 to 2000 period once the necessary data are available.

A basic principle of spatial area analysis is that the smaller and more fine-grained the spatial areas defined, the more extreme the variations among them. Similarly, changes are often much more dramatic in narrowly bounded areas than in large cities or whole regions. In the latter, sharp local variations tend to average out. Thus, a focus on broad regions affords a much more conservative view of urban changes than a focus on selected small communities and neighborhoods. Substantial changes recorded at the metropolitan scale are all the more remarkable for the breadth of the regions involved. The analysis of whole regions also affords a more conservative estimate of demographic dynamism and a more conservative test of the discrepancies between people and place perspectives alleged above.

Each of the four cities is defined as a broad region that approximates a Consolidated Metropolitan Statistical Area (CMSA). An obstacle to defining exact CMSAs with PUMS data is that the geographic building blocks are restricted to areas of at least 100,000 people; hence, it is often necessary to take in larger territories on the periphery of the region than would otherwise be desired. The chief objective in defining city regions is twofold: first, to develop a geographic area delineation for each region that is identical for 1980 and 1990, and second, to make that area large enough to include not only the central city but virtually all of the suburbs. For the most part, I have adopted a set of metropolitan area delineations developed by Ellis, Reibel, and Wright[29] for use with 1980 and 1990 PUMS data. (The Los Angeles region also includes San Diego County.) Whenever the term "cities" is used, it is always meant to imply these PUMS-based greater city regions that resemble CMSAs.

GROWTH AND RACIAL/ ETHNIC COMPOSITION CHANGE

Population Growth

Two of the city regions (New York and Los Angeles) are much larger than the others, but more important is the fact that two of them are growing more rapidly (Washington, DC, and Los Angeles). New York and Chicago barely changed at all in total population between 1980 and 1990, whereas Los Angeles grew by 26.9 percent and Washington, DC, by 16.4 percent. As a context for urban policy making, these differences in growth rate are likely much more important than total population size.

Los Angeles stands out for its high population growth (Table 2.1). None of the four major racial/ethnic groups declined in number: Whites even increased by nearly half a million, while Latinos increased by more than 2 million. In fact, the increase in Latinos is truly exceptional: It is four times greater than the growth of any other racial/ethnic group in any of the four regions. The sources of this exceptional growth are commented on in a later section.

In the Chicago region, total population fell by 0.6 percent, and both white and black populations declined by even greater amounts, 5.8 percent and 2.1 percent, respectively. Similarly, in New York, the white population also fell, by 7.5 percent, but the black population increased. In the other regions, white and black populations increased but by much less than the other groups. In fact, in all four regions, the white population increased less than all other groups. The highest rate of popu-

Table 2.1 Growth of Regional Population by Race-Ethnicity, 1980 to 1990

	Los Angeles Region			*New York Region*		
	1980	*1990*	*Growth (%)*	*1980*	*1990*	*Growth (%)*
White, non-Latino	8,440,940	8,919,490	5.7	12,229,920	11,314,356	−7.5
Black, non-Latino	1,154,480	1,314,951	13.9	2,727,080	2,978,997	9.2
Other	140,540	148,811	5.9	46,900	68,641	46.4
Asian	696,720	1,543,171	121.5	402,320	863,476	114.6
Latino	3,050,520	5,179,175	69.8	2,077,820	2,655,300	27.8
Total	13,483,200	17,105,598	26.9	17,484,040	17,880,770	2.3

	Washington, DC, Region			*Chicago Region*		
	1980	*1990*	*Growth (%)*	*1980*	*1990*	*Growth (%)*
White, non-Latino	2,200,360	2,365,231	7.5	5,526,800	5,207,337	−5.8
Black, non-Latino	875,020	1,026,697	17.3	1,555,220	1,522,753	−2.1
Other	15,860	13,076	−17.6	19,420	18,579	−4.3
Asian	89,340	200,164	124.0	158,480	251,447	58.7
Latino	94,780	208,173	119.6	636,360	852,412	34.0
Total	3,275,360	3,813,341	16.4	7,896,280	7,852,528	−0.6

lation growth in each region was among populations of Asian origin, ranging from 58.7 percent in Chicago to 124.0 percent in Washington, DC. The Latino population grew by 34.0 percent in Chicago and 119.6 percent in Washington, DC. Some of these high percentage increases are distorted by the small base from which the group expanded, however.

Racial/Ethnic Composition

The result of these differential growth rates is a substantial reshaping of the racial composition of the four cities. Figure 2.1 depicts their racial composition in both 1980 and 1990. Three major differences stand out: First, in Los Angeles, the white share of the population has fallen to close to 50 percent, despite growing by nearly half a million persons. In the other cities, the white share did not decline as sharply from 1980 to 1990; nor did it reach as low a level by 1990.

A second difference is that the black share of the population is much lower in Los Angeles, amounting to less than 8 percent. By contrast, the black share in 1990 was 27 percent in Washington, DC, 20 percent in Chicago, and 16 percent in New

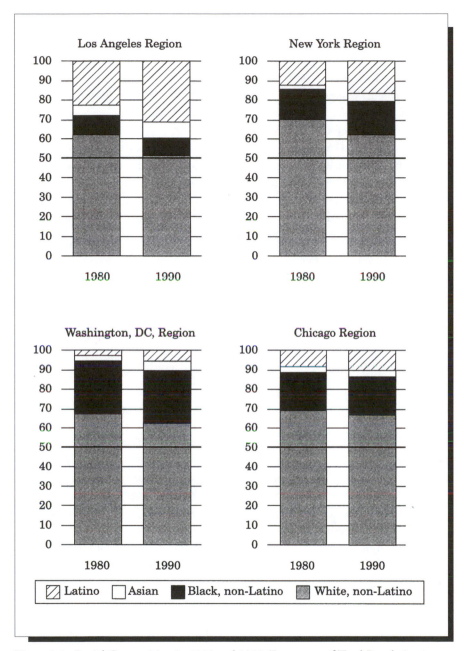

Figure 2.1. Racial Composition in 1980 and 1990 (Percentage of Total Population in Each Racial/Ethnic Group)

York. In fact, the black share of the population in Los Angeles is now the smallest of all four major racial/ethnic groups, exceeded even by that of Asians, who elsewhere are outnumbered by blacks by three to one, or more.

Third, what compresses the other groups to such small shares in Los Angeles is the unusually large and growing number of Latinos, whose share of the population increased from 23 to 30 percent between 1980 and 1990. In the other cities, the next largest Latino share is found in New York, where it is only 15 percent. Waldinger and Bozorgmehr[30] have commented on the relative dominance of this one group (mostly Mexican in origin) in Los Angeles, contrasting it to the more diverse composition found in New York.

Overall, the black-white conception of racial composition fits least well in Los Angeles. Both the small size of the black population and the declining share held by the white population lead to much greater relative significance for the Asian and especially the Latino populations. Yet the growing Asian and Latino populations in the other cities are heading in the same direction, merely lagging behind by a decade or two. As discussed below, the multiethnic balance in Los Angeles creates a different policy context from the black-white dominance of the other cities.

MIGRATION HISTORY

A major unstated premise of urban theory or policy is that the changes observed for cities over time reflect the experiences of their residents over time. The key underlying assumption is that the great majority of residents have lived out their lives in the regions where they now reside, so that their lives have been intertwined with the changing conditions of the places where they live. This assumption implies that most current residents were born and grew up in the region where they now live and that only a relatively small proportion are newcomers. In fact, evidence presented here shows that many residents have moved into their current urban area from other parts of the United States or from other nations. The relative permanence of the population differs between the four cities as well as between racial/ethnic groups. Thus, the discordance discussed above between people and place prosperity is greater in some cases than in others.

As a test of the premise, data for the adult population aged 25 and older in 1990 were assembled. These adults have had at least two decades of life experience, including enough time to relocate from their region of birth and childhood. Local regions of birth are defined somewhat more broadly than the city regions used in the rest of the analysis. Limitations in the place-of-birth variable in the census required that whole states be included, and so the local origins of Los Angeles residents are defined as all of California; local origins of New York residents as the three-state region of New York, New Jersey, and Connecticut; local origins of Chicago residents as the three-state region of Illinois, Indiana, and Wisconsin; and local origins of Washington, DC, residents as the region formed by the District of Columbia, Maryland, and Virginia.

Table 2.2 Place of Birth of 1990 Adult Residents, by Race-Ethnicity (Percentage of All 1990 Residents Aged 25 and Older Who Were Born in Each Location)

Los Angeles Region	Total	White	Black	Asian	Latino
California	27.5	31.7	27.8	9.3	23.2
Other states	42.2	57.5	66.7	6.2	9.8
Other U.S. territories	0.3	0.0	0.2	0.9	0.9
Other nations	30.1	10.8	5.3	83.5	66.1
Total	100	100	100	100	100
	10,497,354	6,268,499	767,362	941,891	2,519,502

New York Region	Total	White	Black	Asian	Latino
NY, NJ, CT	57.6	73.4	37.2	3.9	17.6
Other states	14.0	12.0	37.3	1.9	1.4
Other U.S. territories	4.0	0.1	0.6	0.4	30.0
Other nations	24.5	14.6	25.0	93.9	50.9
Total	100	100	100	100	100
	11,990,269	8,101,113	1,777,948	554,361	1,521,335

Chicago Region	Total	White	Black	Asian	Latino
IL, IN, WI	60.5	71.0	47.4	4.2	19.2
Other states	23.7	19.7	50.5	5.1	9.5
Other U.S. territories	1.1	0.0	0.0	0.2	13.0
Other nations	14.7	9.4	2.0	90.6	58.4
Total	100	100	100	100	100
	5,007,580	3,569,394	857,729	153,628	416,240

Washington, DC, Region	Total	White	Black	Asian	Latino
DC, MD, VA	34.5	32.2	52.5	2.2	4.1
Other states	49.6	59.7	39.1	5.6	13.3
Other U.S. states	0.3	0.0	0.1	0.2	13.0
Other nations	14.7	9.4	2.0	92.0	77.0
Total	100	100	100	100	100
	2,506,195	1,622,766	632,473	125,325	117,347

SOURCE: U.S. Bureau of the Census (1993).
NOTE: Population totals do not include "other" race groups and so may not equal the sum of the four groups shown. Percentage totals may not sum to exactly 100 percent because of rounding.

Total Population

As shown in Table 2.2, only 27.5 percent of Los Angeles adults were born locally, that is, in California. This contrasts to local origins for 57.6 percent of New Yorkers and 60.5 percent of Chicago residents. Among Washington, DC, residents, 34.5 percent were born locally. Not surprisingly, the two high-growth regions have many more migrants from outside the area.

White Residents

Given the ongoing change in racial composition, it seems likely that a higher proportion of whites are native to their current region of residence, while Asians and Latinos are more likely to be newcomers. This supposition is only partially borne out, however. Remarkably, only 31.7 percent of whites in Los Angeles and 32.2 percent in Washington, DC, were born in their current regions of residence (Table 2.2). These figures are little different from the average for all residents in the respective regions. In New York and Chicago, the share of locals among whites is at least 10 percentage points higher than for those regions as a whole. This reflects the fact that white residents have participated more fully in recent migration to Los Angeles and Washington, DC, than to New York and Chicago.

Black Residents

The black population of Los Angeles closely resembles the migration history of white residents: Only 27.8 percent of blacks are native to the region; most have migrated from other states. In Chicago, blacks are much more likely to be natives, but half (50.5 percent) of all Chicago-area blacks were born in other states, versus 19.7 percent of Chicago-area whites. This obviously reflects the great post–World War II northward migration of blacks, whose social and economic consequences are described by Wilson (1987).

In Washington, DC, we see that over half (52.5 percent) of the black adults are native to the region, far surpassing the figure for whites and exceeding the local origins of blacks in any of the four cities. This relative permanence of residency among area blacks is compounded by their unusually large share of the regional population (Figure 2.1) to make that group especially well-established and prominent in the area.

Finally, black residency history in New York is the most complex. Blacks are somewhat evenly divided among locals, migrants from other states, and immigrants from abroad. Fully one quarter of black adults in New York have migrated from outside the United States, and none of the other regions has as substantial a share of foreign borns among the black population. A substantial literature has developed in New York about the unique situation of black immigrants from the West Indies and other areas.[31] The question about whether black immigrants are better off adapting to the norms of native-born blacks in the inner-city neighborhoods where the immigrants reside, or whether they are better off resisting this acculturation has been construed as a challenge to mainstream assimilation theory.

Asian and Latino Newcomers

In contrast to the black population, the great majority of Asian adults in every region are newcomers, mostly from other nations. The proportion of foreign-born Asians ranges from a low 83.5 percent in Los Angeles to a high of 93.9 percent in New York. In fact, only in Los Angeles is there any significant percentage of Asian adults who were born locally (9.3 percent).

Latinos are much more likely to have been born in their current regions of residence, although they also comprise large numbers who were foreign born. As with Asians, the number of locally born Latinos is highest in Los Angeles (23.2 percent) and lowest in Washington, DC (4.1 percent). The foreign-born share is highest in Washington, DC (77.0 percent) and lowest in New York (50.9 percent). However, a large portion of the Latino population of New York is from Puerto Rico, a U.S. territory. Although these residents are not considered foreign born, those who were island born are similar to those who were foreign born. If we add to the foreign-born numbers the 30.0 percent of Latinos who were born in other U.S. territories, the resulting total of 80.9 percent from outside the 50 states is considerable (Table 2.2).

Overall Comparisons of the Four Cities

Despite the distinctive migration histories imprinted on the adult population of the four cities, the evidence supports a common theme. Of greatest significance is the fact that these findings severely challenge the implicit assumption underlying urban policy that residents are permanently linked to their regions of residence. Out of 16 possible combinations of four groups in four cities, in only three instances were half or more of the adults born in their current region of residence. The exceptions are whites in New York and Chicago, and blacks in Washington, DC. In fact, in Los Angeles, less than one-third of the adults in *any* racial/ethnic group were born in their region of residence. In short, the lifetime fortunes of the current residents do not match the trends exhibited in their region of residence.

When viewed in combination with the lingering stereotype of urban policy that assumes black-white dominance of racial composition, the challenge to old assumptions is even more critical. Profound change in population composition at the end of the 20th century is combining with rapid changes in population membership through migration to produce a much more fluid, variegated resident base in cities. Figure 2.2 displays these twin factors in combination. Here, in contrast to the vague unstated assumptions implicit in contemporary urban theory, the actual data for the four regions are represented. The fuzzy assumption is that most of the population is either white or black, with other groups only incidental to the main story. And the

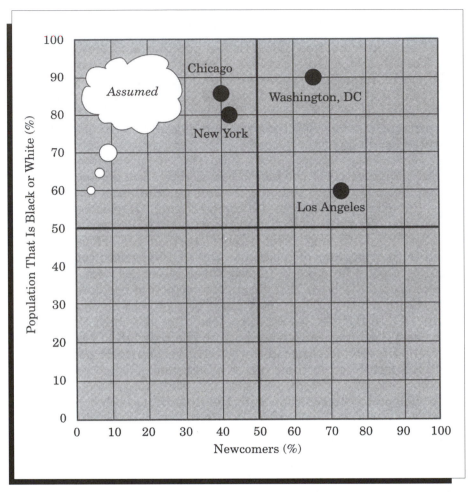

Figure 2.2. Four Regions' Departure From Assumptions of Black-White Dominance and Permanent Residents

implicit assumption is that most residents have lived their lives in the region where they now live, allowing for only a small proportion of newcomers. These twin vague assumptions are represented in the upper left quadrant of Figure 2.2. In fact, we find that the greater regions of Chicago and Washington, DC, and to a slightly lesser extent New York, closely reflect the implicit assumption of black-white dominance. However, Los Angeles and Washington, DC, along with Chicago and New York, all have much greater numbers of newcomers than might be assumed.

Los Angeles emerges as distinctively different from the other cities. Its adult population is characterized both by an extreme degree of non-localness and by a very low degree of black-white dominance. As the composition of other cities continues to change to look more like Los Angeles, it will follow a downward track represented in the diagram by the vector from the implicitly assumed residence base toward that characterized by Los Angeles in 1990. If that city is a harbinger of the future, the unstated biases of urban theory—black-white dominance and lifetimes in one place—will need to be corrected even in places such as Chicago.

Immigration

Immigration is the dominant demographic shift of the late 20th century. Following the major revision of the immigration law in 1965, the number of new immigrants arriving in the United States has approximately doubled each decade (although it is beginning to level off at a high volume in the 1990s). As a result of these newcomers, the total foreign-born population of the United States increased from 4.8 percent of the population in 1970 to 7.9 percent in 1990 (and 9.8 percent in 1998). The new immigrants have been fairly localized, concentrating in gateway regions in a handful of states. The four cities under study here are among the leading immigrant destinations. (Others are Miami, San Francisco, Dallas, and Houston.)

The most obvious overall impact of immigration is its contribution to the total population growth of a region. In the rapid-growth cities, immigration was less important than in slower-growth cities. As shown in Figure 2.3, total population in both New York and Chicago would have *declined* by 5 percent or more between 1980 and 1990 were it not for new immigrant arrivals. By contrast, in Los Angeles and Washington, DC, subtracting the immigrant newcomers would have cut population growth by more than half, but those regions would still have grown in population by 7 to 10 percent. It is reasonable to surmise that the positive benefits of immigration are more greatly appreciated in those slow-growth cities where the newcomers staved off an actual decline in population.

Aside from the total volume of foreign-born population, the most important aspect of immigration is the recency with which immigrants have arrived. Virtually all studies of immigrant incorporation emphasize that newcomers have very different characteristics from those who have lived in the United States for a longer period of time. For example, more settled immigrants are more likely to speak better English, to become U.S. citizens, to have higher incomes, and to become homeowners.[32]

What is most striking about these foreign-born residents of the four cities is how many more of them arrived in the 1980s than in previous decades. Figure 2.4 displays the proportion of total population (foreign born and native born) consisting of immigrants who arrived in different decades. The newest immigrants in these 1990 data are those who arrived in the 1980s, amounting to 13.6 percent of total residents in the Los Angeles region, 8.8 percent in New York, 7.3 percent in Washington, DC, and 4.6 percent in Chicago. In three of the cities, these newcomers are nearly twice as numerous as those who arrived in the 1970s and who are now relatively settled.

The comparison between Los Angeles and Chicago is especially significant. Whereas Chicago has a more evenly balanced proportion of residents in each of the

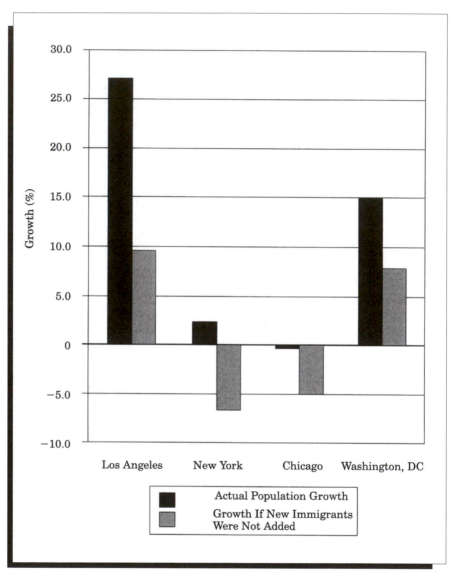

Figure 2.3. Comparison of Regional Population Growth From 1980 to 1990, With and Without the Contribution of Immigrant Arrivals During the 1980s

four arrival periods, the long-settled immigrants in Los Angeles are far less numerous than those who arrived in the 1970s, who are in turn much less numerous than the newcomers of the 1980s. In short, Chicago's immigrants are more mature residents than immigrants who live in Los Angeles (mainly newcomers). The consequence is that Chicago's immigrants may display more advantaged characteristics. In addition, the changes experienced in that region over the 1980s will be less heavily affected by newcomers than in Los Angeles, where the newest wave of arrivals carries more weight.[33]

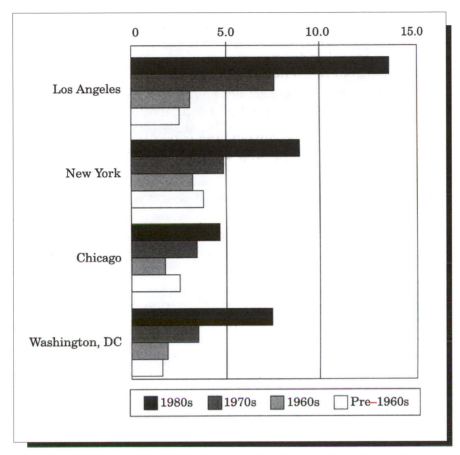

Figure 2.4. Percentage of Total 1990 Population That Had Immigrated to the United States, by Decade of Arrival

Dynamism and Upward Mobility

I now turn from a description of the underlying demographic dynamism in the four cities to an assessment of the urban outcomes. Implicit in demographic dynamism is a strong thrust toward upward mobility by urban residents. Over time, residents in all ethnic groups make advances in both their economic and housing careers. This underlying process deserves to be nurtured and accelerated wherever possible. However, the prevalence of the upward mobility dynamic often goes unrecognized, and urban problems instead are often characterized as reflecting downward mobility. This leads to very different policy interventions.

The force of upward mobility is neglected because it is disguised by the changing composition of the population. New arrivals are frequently from less advantaged ethnic groups, and most are young people who have yet to advance very far in their careers. With a large inflow of such newcomers, the average status of the whole population can be falling downward, even though at the same time each cohort is advancing upward. This dynamic is especially pronounced in selected sub areas of the region, often points of entry for newcomers, because the successful upwardly mobile residents depart for the suburbs and are replaced by less advantaged newcomers.[34]

A second reason that upward mobility is neglected is that urban data comprise a snapshot in time that reveals only current characteristics, not the changes experienced as a cohort grows older and settles in. The cohort approach enables such a longitudinal view to be constructed by using standard census data. For technical reasons, longitudinal changes can be more fully described for immigrants than for native-born residents, and for that reason we highlight them here.[35]

Of course, not everyone experiences upward mobility to the same degree, and immigrants dramatize this process. Nevertheless, it is the arrival of immigrants who are in general relatively disadvantaged that draws so much attention to failing social and economic status in cities, and it is the upward mobility of immigrants that then cuts against that trend.

Upward mobility is measured here by two major outcomes important to both people and the places they live: poverty and homeownership. This is shown most easily by examining the effects of new immigrant arrivals. Initially, they depress the status levels in their regions, especially if they arrive in large numbers, but over time they advance dramatically.

POVERTY RATES

Overall Changes

What is the impact of 1980s immigrants on average changes in poverty observed from 1980 to 1990 for each city region? If the poverty rate in 1990 could be calculated only for residents who were living in an area in 1980, we could learn how much the fortunes of these continuing residents had changed over the decade. Unfortunately, data limitations preclude this, because the census records place of residence only five years earlier for the entire population. However, an alternative to tracing population changes over a full decade is to isolate only new immigrants, because these can be identified by year of arrival, thus permitting us to separate out 1990 residents who immigrated after 1980.[36] On this basis, we can calculate poverty rates including or excluding these recent immigrants. It must be stressed that this is only a hypothetical calculation. In the absence of immigrants, a host of other changes would ensue, including the entry of new disadvantaged residents who would step into the role occupied by immigrants, and the economy would adjust in unknown ways.

As shown in Figure 2.5, the change in overall poverty rates in each city region is altered somewhat if new immigrants are not included in the calculation. The greatest difference is found in Los Angeles, where the actual poverty rate increased by a full percentage point between 1980 and 1990, but where the adjusted rate (absent

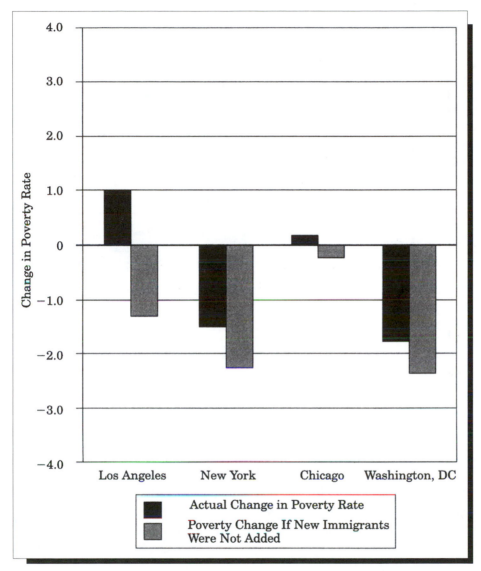

Figure 2.5. Change in Regional Poverty Rate From 1980 to 1990, With and Without the Contribution of New Immigrant Arrivals During the 1980s

new immigrants) *declined* by 1.3 percentage points. In both New York and Washington, DC, the actual poverty rate declined over the decade but would have fallen by half a percentage point more in the absence of new immigrants. In Chicago, the poverty rate was fairly stable, with or without new immigrants. Overall, comparing these four cities, the impact of immigrants appears greatest in the cities where new immigrants made up the largest share of the population (see Figure 2.4).

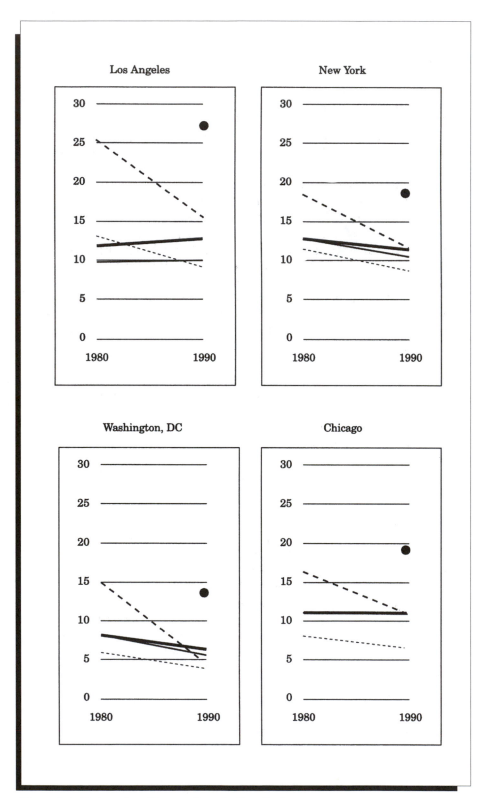

Figure 2.6. Trajectories of Poverty Rates in Four Regions

Underlying Trends

The poverty trends behind these net changes are displayed in Figure 2.6, showing the 1980-1990 changes not only for the total population, but also for native-born residents and for immigrants who arrived in different decades. The black dot depicts the poverty rate observed in 1990 for new immigrant arrivals in each region, a rate far above that of the total population. The heavy dashed line represents the poverty rate of the previous wave of new immigrants in 1980, together with their progress from 1980 to 1990. Generally speaking, those earlier arrivals also began with much higher-than-average poverty, but the rate fell sharply as their residency grew longer. Weaker declines from already lower levels are also observed for immigrants who arrived in the 1960s.

Although poverty rates are highest in Los Angeles and lowest in Washington, DC, the same basic pattern of change is found in all four cities.

Trends for Specific Cohorts by Ethnic Group

Not all new immigrants have fared equally well. Latinos and Asians make up the bulk of the new immigration, and those groups have been found to have very different rates of success, because of differences in economic, human, or social capital. In addition, immigrants of different ages may also fare differently, with younger or elderly immigrants less advantaged than middle-aged ones. Cities with different mixes of residents in their new immigrant populations thus could have very different achievement levels. Accordingly, it makes sense to observe the rate of upward mobility for more detailed cohorts. Figure 2.7 connects the 1980 and 1990 poverty rates of specific birth cohorts of immigrants, tracing their net changes in poverty as they grew 10 years older (passing from the white dot to the black one) and as their residency in the United States extended. These 1970s arrivals were new immigrants in 1980, just as the 1980s arrivals were new in 1990, and their progress can be traced over the ensuing decade.

The overall pattern observable in Figure 2.7 is that poverty declined from 1980 to 1990 for each cohort. The steepest declines were observed among Asians and Los Angeles and Washington, DC, and Asian poverty levels were lower than Latino ones in every city. Nevertheless, upward mobility characterized all cohorts under age 65 in both ethnic groups in all four areas. These trends are very different—even opposite—from the overall trends recorded for places.

HOMEOWNERSHIP RATES

Overall Changes

The impact of 1980s immigrants on average changes in the homeownership rate can be calculated in the same manner as was done for poverty.[37] The change in overall rates in each city region from 1980 to 1990 is larger if new immigrants are not

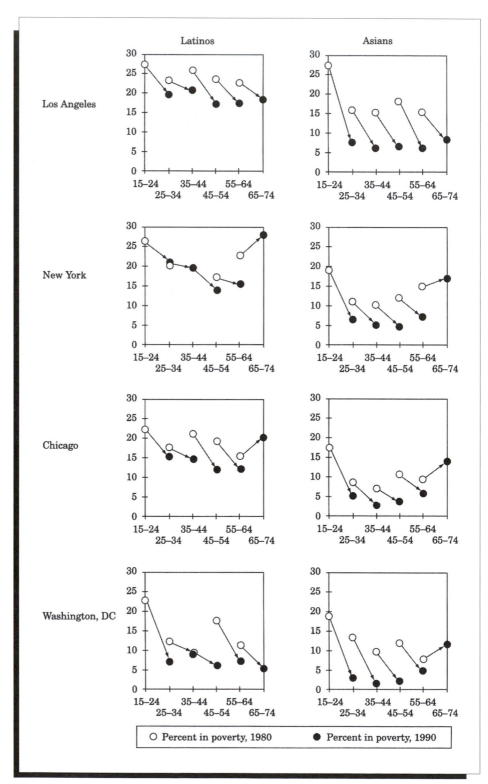

Figure 2.7. Cohort Trajectories of Poverty Change From 1980 to 1990 by 1970s Immigrant Arrivals

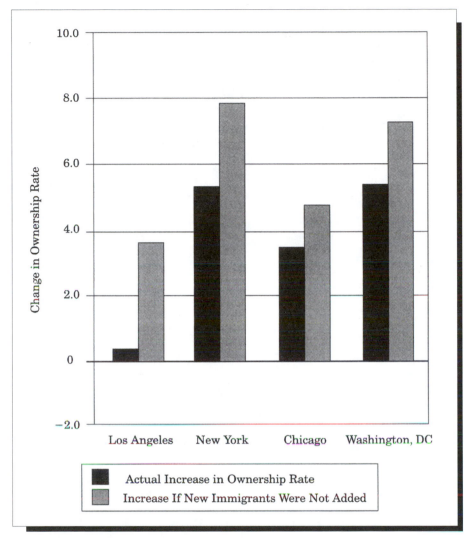

Figure 2.8. Change in Regional Homeownership Rate From 1980 to 1990, With and Without the Contribution of New Immigrant Arrivals During the 1980s

included in the calculation (Figure 2.8). As with poverty, the greatest difference is found in Los Angeles, where the actual homeownership rate increased very little between 1980 and 1990, but where the adjusted rate (absent new immigrants) increased by 3.7 percentage points. In the other three cities, the actual homeownership rate increased substantially between 1980 and 1990, but in all three the rate would have increased by another 1 to 2 percentage points in the absence of new immigrants. Overall, comparing these four cities, the suppressant effect of immigrant arrivals on homeownership appears greatest, as is the case with poverty, in the cities where new immigrants made up the largest share of the population (see Figure 2.4).

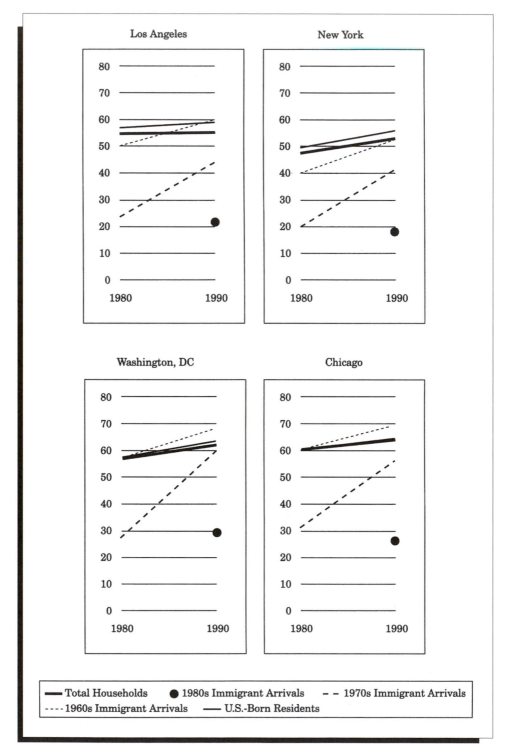

Figure 2.9. Trajectories of Homeownership Rates, 1980 to 1990

Underlying Trends

The homeownership trends behind these net changes are displayed in Figure 2.9, showing the 1980-1990 changes not only for the total population, but also for native-born residents and for immigrants who arrived in different decades. The black dot depicts the homeownership rate observed in 1990 for new immigrant arrivals in each region, a rate far below that of the total population. The upward sloping, heavy dashed line represents the homeownership rate of the previous wave of new immigrants first observed in 1980, showing their progress from 1980 to 1990. Those earlier arrivals also began with much lower-than-average homeownership, but their rate increased steeply as their residency grew. Weaker increases from already high levels are also observed for immigrants who had arrived in the 1960s. A very similar pattern of change is found in all four cities.

Trends for Specific Cohorts by Ethnic Group

Which immigrant cohorts have fared best in their pursuit of homeownership? Cities with higher mixes of certain ethnic groups and age groups in their new immigrant populations might have higher overall achievement levels. Accordingly, it is again necessary to observe the rate of upward mobility for more detailed cohorts. Figure 2.10 connects the 1980 and 1990 homeownership rates of specific birth cohorts of immigrants, tracing their net changes as they grew 10 years older (passing from the white dot to the black one) and as their residency in the United States lengthened.

The overall pattern observable in Figure 2.10 is that homeownership increased from 1980 to 1990 for each cohort. The highest rates and steepest increases were observed among Asians in all four cities. Among Latinos, there is more variability across cities, with the greatest success in Chicago or Washington, DC, and the least in New York. Nevertheless, even in the Latino cohorts with the lowest homeownership in 1980, upward mobility led to a doubling of homeownership among all cohorts under age 45. This finding of steep upward trajectories into homeownership has been reported by other studies, including a detailed analysis that adjusted for differences in income and housing prices across 101 metropolitan areas.[38] This demographic dimension to homeownership attainment is an important illustration of the powerful influence of demographic dynamism.

CONCLUSION

Demographic dynamism is a neglected element of urban structure. Failure to account for the dynamics of population change and the process of upward mobility leads to a flaw in conventional urban theory and policy making. The simplest deficiency is that the lives of people are largely ignored in place-based urban thinking, yet the deeper flaw lies in misinterpretation of demographic change.

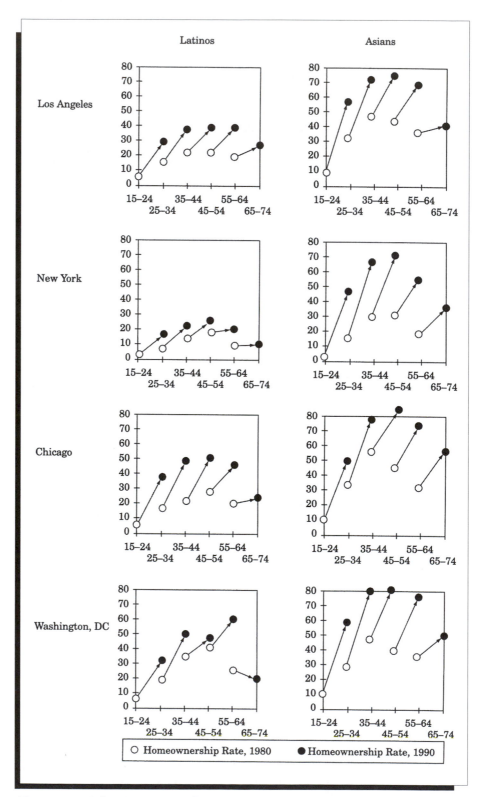

Figure 2.10. Cohort Trajectories of Homeownership Rates From 1980 to 1990 by 1970s Immigrant Arrivals

Demographic dynamism deserves our special attention because it is through the presumed consequences for people that policy makers evaluate the desirability of economic, political, and physical changes in a city. So powerful are the demographic changes in Los Angeles and other cities that they dominate our social indicators of well-being. Yet those same indicators are used to justify one policy instead of another, often on a misguided basis. Failure to clearly grasp the significance of demographic changes can lead to a failure to design effective policies.

Los Angeles has experienced more profound demographic change than any other urban region in recent decades. This is reflected in its high rate of population growth, high percentage of immigrant residents, and rising proportions of Latino and Asian residents. These changes imply distinctly different situations than those at the core of urban theory and policy making.

The black-white paradigm for urban policy analysis assumes one minority group of long-standing residence and past discrimination. When Los Angeles is compared with New York, Chicago, and Washington, DC, it is found to have a far lower share of its population in the black and white racial groups and is truly multiethnic. The implications of this transformation have yet to be incorporated into urban theory, even though other cities are moving in the same direction.

The people versus place assumptions of urban theory emphasize the belief that the history of economic and social conditions in a locality reflects the history experienced by current residents. One of the most surprising findings of this analysis is how few adult residents of Los Angeles were born in the region. Even in Chicago and New York, barely 60 percent of adults were born in their respective regions, and the proportions are much lower for blacks, Latinos, and especially Asians. It is clearly erroneous to cling to the belief that the history of the place and its residents are the same.

The upwardly mobile perspective is far more descriptive of the real experience, with newcomers entering the region, often at low status levels, and achieving rapid improvement with regard to both poverty and homeownership. This upward trajectory is disguised by summary statistics that lump all residents together and allow the disadvantaged status of newcomers to dominate the change in the total.

The distortion imposed by newcomers is greatest when they are most numerous, as clearly illustrated by comparing the four cities. Los Angeles has the highest share of new immigrants in its population, followed by New York, and the impact on poverty and homeownership is greatest in those cases. Thus, the appearance of disadvantaged trends in Los Angeles is created by so many newcomers.

Immigrants should not be blamed for the negative trends that result from their impact on the totals. They are merely the latest group to participate in the upward mobility that is so central to demographic dynamism. Immigrants are often poor when they first arrive, but they surely view their lives as following upward trajectories of opportunity. This is a very different problem perspective than the assumption of the downward mobility of a disadvantaged class.

Of principal concern to policy makers should be the immigrants' fate after they arrive: Do they remain mired in poverty or do they succeed in advancing themselves? It would be small comfort to explain away the negative trends by declaring that a new disadvantaged class of residents was simply distorting the average. Fortunately, the evidence shows that new arrivals do not remain stuck at the bottom. Instead, they advance out of poverty and into homeownership. Their disadvantaged status appears only temporary (although they are replaced by a fresh round of new arrivals who again enter at the bottom).

Local officials understandably have a different perspective. Upward mobility is often accompanied by spatial mobility, with certain communities serving as gateways for the underprivileged and other communities as destinations for the successful. This creates a dilemma for local officials, who are responsible for well-being in only one jurisdiction and want to show positive changes. Elsewhere I have characterized the dilemma: "What is a mayor to do? Take credit for all the successful residents who have moved out of his or her city? Or extol the virtues of less advantaged newcomers who are ready to draw upon the city's services?"[39] The clear policy solution to this dilemma, I argue, is to provide intergovernmental assistance to the gateway communities providing the key human investment services (education, health, and the like) that will enable their residents to become upwardly mobile.[40]

In conclusion, all of the elements of demographic dynamism are more accentuated in the case of Los Angeles than they are in the comparison regions. At the same time, however, all of the elements are also clearly visible in the other regions as well. The conclusion to be drawn is that Los Angeles may be different but that its differences only highlight important commonalities found in New York, Chicago, and Washington, DC. The lesson to be learned from Los Angeles may be the realization of the great importance of demographic dynamism in our urban areas.

NOTES

1. Jargowsky, 1997; Kain, 1992; Kasarda, 1988; Wilson, 1987.
2. Dear, Schockman, and Hise, 1996; Scott and Soja, 1996.
3. Alonso, 1980.
4. Waldinger, 1989.
5. Waldinger, 1989, p. 211.
6. Waldinger and Bozorgmehr, 1996.
7. Fishman, 1999.
8. Fainstein and Campbell, 1996.
9. Dear, Schockman, and Hise, 1996; Scott and Soja, 1996.
10. Soja, 1996.
11. Ong and Blumenfeld, 1996, p. 324.
12. Sandercock, 1998.
13. Scott, 1996.
14. Winnick, 1966.
15. Edel, 1980.
16. Edel, 1980, p. 178.
17. Sawicki and Moody, 1997.
18. Myers, 1999a.
19. Waters, 1994.
20. Cheng and Yang, 1996.

21. Massey, 1993; Skerry, 1993.

22. Rocco, 1996.

23. Cranford, 1999.

24. Myers, 1999b.

25. Myers and Lee, 1998

26. Myers, 1999b.

27. Myers, 1999a.

28. Sassen, 1991.

29. Ellis, Reibel, and Wright, 1997.

30. Waldinger and Bozorgmehr, 1996.

31. Kasinitz, 1992; Waters, 1994.

32. Alba and Logan, 1992; Chiswick and Sullivan, 1995; Jasso and Rosenzweig, 1990; Myers and Lee, 1998.

33. Myers, 1999a.

34. Myers, 1999a.

35. Census data collected from immigrants ask in what year the person came to the United States to live, thus permitting a measure of duration of residence that grows longer between censuses for each arrival cohort. By contrast, for native-born residents, we have data only on place of resident 5 years, not their periods of arrival (10 or 20 years ago) that would permit us to trace cohorts as they settled longer (U.S. Bureau of the Census, 1983, 1993).

36. Although these reported dates of immigrant arrival are subject to some error, observed discrepancies are concentrated in the first years of reported arrival, smoothing out as elapsed time passes five years (Ellis and Wright, 1998).

37. Whereas the poverty rate was calculated as a percentage of all persons, the homeownership rate is calculated as a percentage of all households. The ethnicity, age, and immigration status of households are determined from the household.

38. Myers, Megbolugbe, and Lee, 1998.

39. Myers, 1999a, p. 153.

40. Myers, 1999a.

REFERENCES

Alba, Richard D., and John R. Logan. 1992. Assimilation and Stratification in the Homeownership Patterns of Racial and Ethnic Groups. *International Migration Review* 26:1314-41.

Alonso, William, 1980. The Population Factor and Urban Structure. In *The Prospective City,* ed. Arthur Solomon, 32-51. Cambridge, MA: MIT Press.

Cheng, Lucie, and Phillip Q. Yang. 1996. Asians: The "Model Minority" Deconstructed. In *Ethnic Los Angeles,* ed. Roger Waldinger and Mehdi Bozorgmehr, 305-44. New York: Russell Sage.

Chiswick, Barry R., and Teresa A. Sullivan. 1995. The New Immigrants. In *State of the Union: America in the 1990s.* Volume 2, *Social Trends.* ed. Reynolds Farley, 211-70. New York: Russell Sage Foundation.

Cranford, Cynthia. 1999. Immigration, Economic Restructuring, and Gender Relations at Work: Latina Janitors in Late 20th Century Los Angeles. Ph.D. dissertation, University of Southern California.

Dear, Michael J., H. Eric Schockman, and Greg Hise, eds. 1996. *Rethinking Los Angeles.* Thousand Oaks, CA: Sage.

Edel, Matthew. 1980. People versus Place in Urban Impact Analysis. In *The Urban Impacts of Federal Policies,* ed. Norman J. Glickman, 175-91. Baltimore: Johns Hopkins University Press.

Ellis, Mark, Michael Reibel, and Richard Wright. 1997. *A Procedure for Comparative Metropolitan Area Analysis Using the 1980 and 1990 Census Public Use Microdata Samples.* Los Angeles: University of California, Department of Geography.

Ellis, Mark, and Richard Wright. 1998. When Immigrants Are Not Migrants: Counting Arrivals of the Foreign-Born Using the U.S. Census. *International Migration Review* 32:127-44.

Fainstein, Susan S., and Scott Campbell, eds. 1996. *Readings in Urban Theory.* Cambridge, MA: Blackwell.

Fishman, Robert. 1999. The American Metropolis at Century's End: Past and Future Influences. *Housing Facts & Findings.*

Jargowsky, Paul A. 1997. *Poverty and Place: Ghettos, Barrios, and the American City.* New York: Russell Sage.

Jasso, Guillermina, and Mark R. Rosenzweig. 1990. *The New Chosen People: Immigrants in the United States.* New York: Russell Sage.

Kain, John. 1992. The Spatial Mismatch Hypothesis Three Decades Later. *Housing Policy Debate* 3(2):371-460.

Kasarda, John. 1988. Jobs, Migration, and Emerging Urban Mismatches. In *Urban Change and Poverty,* ed. Laurence E. Lynn, Jr., and Michael G. H. McGeary. Washington, DC: National Academy Press.

Kasinitz, Philip. 1992. *Caribbean New York: Black Immigrants and the Politics of Race.* Ithaca, NY: Cornell University Press.

Massey, Douglas S. 1993. Latinos, Poverty, and the Underclass: A New Agenda for Research. *Hispanic Journal of Behavioral Sciences* 15(4):449-75.

Myers, Dowell. 1999a. Upward Mobility in Space and Time: Lessons from Immigration. In *America's Demographic Tapestry,* ed. James W. Hughes and Joseph J. Seneca, 135-57. New Brunswick, NJ: Rutgers University Press.

Myers, Dowell. 1999b. Cohort Longitudinal Estimation of Housing Careers. *Housing Studies* 14:473-90.

Myers, Dowell, and Seong Woo Lee. 1998. Immigrant Trajectories into Homeownership: A Temporal Analysis of Residential Assimilation. *International Migration Review* 32:593-625.

Myers, Dowell, Isaac Megbolugbe, and Seong Woo Lee. 1998. Cohort Estimation of Homeownership Attainment Among Native-Born and Immigrant Populations. *Journal of Housing Research* 9(2):237-69.

Ong, Paul, and Evelyn Blumenfeld. 1996. Income and Racial Inequality in Los Angeles. In *The City: Los Angeles and Urban Theory at the End of the Twentieth Century,* ed. Allen J. Scott and Edward W. Soja, 311-35. Los Angeles: University of California Press.

Rocco, Raymond A. 1996. Latino Los Angeles: Reframing Boundaries/Borders. In *The City: Los Angeles and Urban Theory at the End of the Twentieth Century,* ed. Allen J. Scott and Edward W. Soja, 365-89. Los Angeles: University of California Press.

Sandercock, Leonie. 1998. *Towards Cosmopolis: Planning for Multicultural Cities.* New York: Wiley.

Sassen, Saskia. 1991. *The Global City: New York, London, and Tokyo.* Princeton, NJ: Princeton University Press.

Sawicki, David S., and Mitch Moody. 1997. The Effects of Intermetropolitan Migration on Labor Force Participation in Poor Communities. *Economic Development Quarterly* 11:45-66.

Scott, Allen J. 1996. The Manufacturing Economy: Ethnic and Gender Divisions of Labor. In *Ethnic Los Angeles,* ed. Roger Waldinger and Mehdi Bozorgmehr, 215-44. New York: Russell Sage.

Scott, Allen J., and Edward W. Soja, eds. 1996. *The City: Los Angeles and Urban Theory at the End of the Twentieth Century.* Los Angeles: University of California Press.

Skerry, Peter. 1993. *Mexican Americans: The Ambivalent Minority.* New York: Free Press.

Soja, Edward W. 1996. Los Angeles, 1965-1992: From Crisis-Generated Restructuring to Restructuring-Generated Crisis. In *The City: Los Angeles and Urban Theory at the End of the Twentieth Century,* eds. Allen J. Scott and Edward W. Soja, 426-62. Los Angeles: University of California Press.

U.S. Bureau of the Census, 1983. *1980 Census of Population and Housing: Public-Use Microdata Samples.* Washington, DC.

U.S. Bureau of the Census. 1993. *1990 Census of Population and Housing: Public-Use Microdata Samples.* Washington, DC.

Waldinger, Roger. 1989. Immigration and Urban Change. *Annual Review of Sociology* 15:211-32.

Waldinger, Roger, and Mehdi Bozorgmehr, eds. 1996. *Ethnic Los Angeles.* New York: Russell Sage.

Waters, Mary C. 1994. Ethnic and Racial Identities of Second-Generation Black Immigrants in New York City. *International Migration Review* 28(4):795-819.

Wilson, William Julius, 1987. *The Truly Disadvantaged: The Inner City, the Underclass, and Public Policy.* Chicago: University of Chicago Press.

Winnick, Louis. 1966. Place Prosperity and People Prosperity: Welfare Considerations in the Geographic Distribution of Economic Activity. In *Essays in Urban Land Economics in Honor of the Sixty-Fifth Birthday of Leo Grebler,* 273-83. Los Angeles: University of California at Los Angeles, Real Estate Research Program.

Los Angeles
as Postmodern Urbanism

EDITOR'S
COMMENTS

The most important chapter in *The City,* at least for my purposes, is E. W. Burgess's "The Growth of the City," in which he outlines the famous concentric zone theory of urban growth and structure. His vision dominated understanding of the city in the twentieth century. In the following extended extract from his chapter, we'll see that Burgess used a most parsimonious set of assumptions to establish the basic logic that produced a dense inner-city core, surrounded by concentric rings of progressively diminishing densities of human activity. Subsequently, he applied this model to explaining Chicago's urban form (see Charts 3.1 and 3.2 on pages 57 and 58 in the following extract).

Burgess imagined what I shall describe as a distinctly modernist characterization of urban process. Its dominant logic is one in which the center molds the urban periphery. As a description of the structure of late-nineteenth- and early-twentieth-century industrial cities, it provides an elegant and altogether plausible explanation of urban development.

The chapter that follows (Dear and Flusty), however, sketches a concept of postmodern urbanism entirely at odds with the intentionalities implicit in the Burgess model. Drawing on empirical evidence from Southern California, the chapter draws a bold analogy between the consequences of the "postmodern turn" in philosophy/social theory and what is happening in contemporary cities.

More specifically, the chapter argues that the tenets of modernist thought (truth, laws, foundationalism, etc.) have been undermined, even discredited; in their place, postmodernity as an era has ushered in a multiplicity of ways of knowing (including feminist and postcolonial thought, for instance). Analogously, in postmodern cities, the logics of previous urbanisms have evaporated, and in their stead, multiple forms of urban (ir)rationalities clamour to fill the vacuum. Hence, although traditional concepts of urban form imagine the city organized around a central core, in postmodern cities the urban peripheries organize what remains of the center.

We replace Burgess's concentric zones diagram with an undifferentiated, decentralized grid. This checkerboard landscape of almost infinite opportunities we term *keno capitalism,* thereby invoking the random, chancelike intentionalities inherent in postmodern urbanism. We claim that our model of urban structure represents a radical break in the way we understand the urban, not only the material conditions that produce the city but also the epistemological conditions through which we see and understand the city. At the same time, however, we offer our view of a postmodern urbanism as a hypothesis, whose veracity can be tested only through extensive comparative analysis with other metropolitan regions throughout the nation and the world.

Readers are cautioned once again that not all contributors to this volume will necessarily concur with the concept of postmodern urbanism presented in this chapter. Only time will tell if the keno grid is to supersede the concentric zones. What seems certain is that our preliminary exegesis of the L.A. School, as set out in Part I of this book, provides the necessary and sufficient conditions to warrant the careful investigations that take up the remainder of this volume.

The typical processes of the expansion of the city can best be illustrated, perhaps, by a series of concentric circles, which may be numbered to designate both the successive zones of urban extension and the types of areas differentiated in the process of expansion. [See Chart 3.1 and Chart 3.2.]

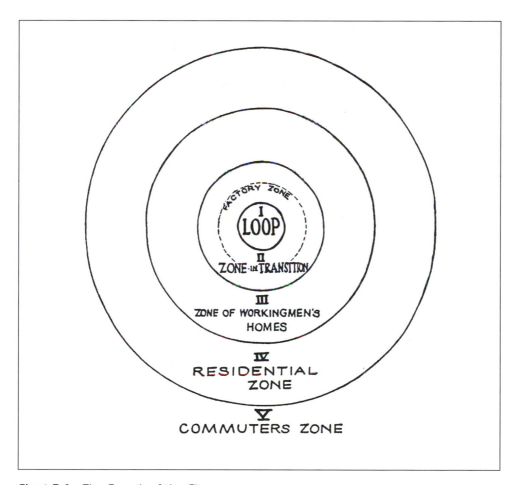

Chart 3.1. The Growth of the City

This chart represents an ideal construction of the tendencies of any town or city to expand radially from its central business district—on the map "The Loop" (I). Encircling the downtown area there is normally an area in transition, which is being invaded by business and light manufacture (II). A third area (III) is inhabited by the workers in industries who have escaped from the area of deterioration (II) but who desire to live within easy access

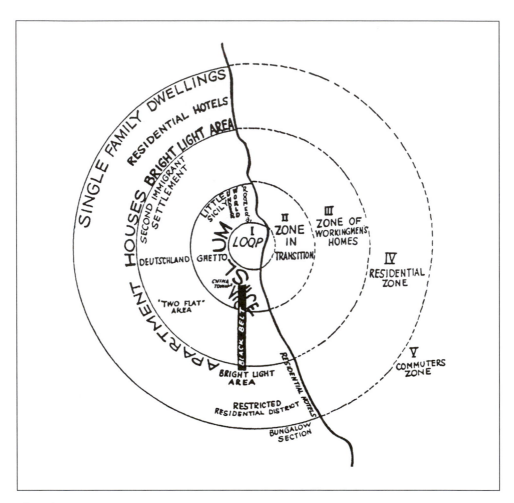

Chart 3.2. Urban Areas

of their work. Beyond this zone is the "residential area" (IV) of high-class apartment build-ings or of exclusive "restricted" districts of single family dwellings. Still farther, out beyond the city limits, is the commuters' zone [V]—suburban areas, or satellite cities—within a thirty- to sixty-minute ride of the central business district.

This chart brings out clearly the main fact of expansion, namely, the tendency of each inner zone to extend its area by the invasion of the next outer zone. This aspect of expan-sion may be called *succession*, a process which has been studied in detail in plant ecol-ogy. If this chart is applied to Chicago, all four of these zones were in its early history included in the circumference of the inner zone, the present business district. The pre-sent boundaries of the area of deterioration were not many years ago those of the zone now inhabited by independent wage-earners, and within the memories of thousands of Chicagoans contained the residences of the "best families." It hardly needs to be added that neither Chicago nor any other city fits perfectly into this ideal scheme. Complications are introduced by the lake front, the Chicago River, railroad lines, historical factors in the location of industry, the relative degree of the resistance of communities to invasion, etc.

Besides extension and succession, the general process of expansion in urban growth involves the antagonistic and yet complementary process of concentration and decentralization. In all cities there is the natural tendency for local and outside transportation to converge in the central business district. In the downtown section of every large city we expect to find the department stores, the skyscraper office buildings, the railroad stations, the great hotels, the theaters, the art museum, and the city hall. Quite naturally, almost inevitably, the economic, cultural, and political life centers here. The relation of centralization to the other processes of city life may be roughly gauged by the fact that over half a million people daily enter and leave Chicago's "loop." More recently sub-business centers have grown up in outlying zones. These "satellite loops" do not, it seems, represent the "hoped for" revival of the neighborhood, but rather a telescoping of several local communities into a large economic unity. The Chicago of yesterday, an agglomeration of country towns and immigrant colonies, is undergoing a process of reorganization into a centralized decentralized system of local communities coalescing into sub-business areas visibly or invisibly dominated by the central business district. The actual processes of what may be called centralized decentralization are now being studied in the development of the chain store, which is only one illustration of the change in the basis of the urban organization.

Expansion, as we have seen, deals with the physical growth of the city, and with the extension of the technical services that have made city life not only livable, but comfortable, even luxurious.

Certain of these basic necessities of urban life are possible only through a tremendous development of communal existence. Three millions of people in Chicago are dependent upon one unified water system, one giant gas company, and one huge electric light plant. Yet, like most of the other aspects of our communal urban life, this economic co-operation is an example of co-operation without a shred of what the "spirit of co-operation" is commonly thought to signify. The great public utilities are a part of the mechanization of life in great cities, and have little or no other meaning for social organization. . . . (50-53)

. . . In what way are individuals incorporated into the life of a city? By what process does a person become an organic part of his society? (53)

Normally the processes of disorganization may be thought of as in reciprocal relationship to each other, and as co-operation in a moving equilibrium of social order toward an end vaguely or definitely regarded as progressive. So far as disorganization points to reorganization and makes for more efficient adjustment, disorganization must be conceived not as pathological, but as normal. Disorganization as preliminary to reorganization of attitudes and conduct is almost invariably the lot of the newcomer to the city, and the discarding of the habitual, and often of what has been to him the moral, is not infrequently accompanied by sharp mental conflict and sense of personal loss. Oftener, perhaps, the change gives sooner or later a feeling of emancipation and an urge toward new goals.

In the expansion of the city a process of distribution takes place which sifts and sorts and relocates individuals and groups by residence and occupation. The resulting differentiation of the cosmopolitan American city into areas is typically all from one pattern with only interesting minor modifications. Within the central business district or on an adjoining street is the "main stem" of "hobohemia," the teeming Rialto of the homeless migratory man of the Middle West. In the zone of deterioration encircling the central business section are always to be found the so-called "slums" and "bad lands," with their submerged regions of poverty, degradation, and disease, and their underworlds of crime and vice. Within a deteriorating area are rooming-house districts, the purgatory of "lost souls." Near by is the Latin Quarter, where creative and rebellious spirits resort. The slums are also crowded to overflowing with immigrant colonies—the Ghetto, Little Sicily, Greektown, Chinatown—fascinatingly combining old world heritages and American adaptations. Wedging out from here is the Black Belt, with its free and disorderly life. The area of deterioration, while essentially one of decay, of stationary or declining population, is also one of regeneration, as witness the mission, the settlement, the artists' colony, radical centers—all obsessed with the vision of a new and better world.

The next zone is also inhabited predominatingly by factory and shop workers, but skilled and thrifty. This is an area of second immigrant settlement, generally of the second generation. It is the region of escape from the slum, the *Deutschland* of the aspiring Ghetto family. For Deutschland (literally "Germany") is the name given, half in envy, half in derision, to that region beyond the Ghetto where successful neighbors appear to be imitating German Jewish standards of living. But the inhabitant of this area in turn looks to the "Promised Land" beyond, to its residential hotels, its apartment-house region, its "satellite loops," and its "bright light" areas.

This differentiation into natural economic and cultural groupings gives form and character to the city. For segregation offers the group, and thereby the individuals who compose the group, a place and a role in the total organization of city life. Segregation limits development in certain directions, but releases it in others. These areas tend to accentuate certain traits, to attract and develop their kind of individuals, and so to become further differentiated.

The division of labor in the city likewise illustrates disorganization reorganization, and increasing differentiation. (54-56)

CHAPTER 3

Los Angeles as Postmodern Urbanism

STEVEN FLUSTY

The problematic of a distinctively postmodern urbanism is based on a simple premise: that just as the central tenets of modernist thought have been undermined, its core evacuated and replaced by a rush of competing epistemologies, so too have the traditional logics of earlier urbanisms evaporated, and in the absence of a single new imperative, multiple urban (ir)rationalities are competing to fill the void. The concretization and localization of these effects is creating the new geographies of postmodern society.

But, what does a postmodern urbanism look like? One of the most prescient pieces anticipating a postmodern vision of the city is Jonathan Raban's *Soft City,* a reading of London's cityscapes.[1] Raban divides the city into *hard* and *soft* elements. The former refers to the material fabric of the built environment—the streets and buildings that frame the lives of city dwellers. The latter, by contrast, is an individualized interpretation of the city, a perceptual orientation created in the mind of every urbanite. The relationship between the two is complex, even indeterminate. The newcomer to a city first confronts the hard city, but soon:

> the city goes soft; it awaits the imprint of an identity. For better or worse, it invites you to remake it, to consolidate it into a shape you can live in. You, too. Decide who you are, and the city will again assume a fixed form around you. Decide what it is, and your own identity will be revealed.[2]

Raban makes no claims to a postmodern consciousness, yet his invocation of the relationship between the cognitive and the real leads to insights that are unmistakably postmodern in their sensitivities. First, he warns of the possibility and consequences of a breakdown in cognitive structures: "so much takes place in the head. So little is known and fixed. Signals, styles, systems of rapid, highly-conventionalized commu-

AUTHORS' NOTE: This chapter was reprinted from "Postmodern Urbanism," 1998, in *Annals of the American Association of Geographers,* Vol. 88, No. 1, pp. 50-72. Copyright © 1998 by Blackwell Publishers. Used by permission.

nication are the life blood of the big city. . . . [But what happens] when these systems break down—when we lose our grasp on the grammar of life . . . ?"[3] To show the consequences, Raban contrasts the organizing visions of nineteenth-century writers with those of present-day urbanists. Nineteenth-century planners, philanthropists and journalists used a metaphor of an encyclopaedia to encapsulate the "special randomness of the city's diversity":

> the logic of the city is not of the kind which lends itself to straightforward narration or to continuous page-by-page reading. At the same time, it does imply that the city is a repository of knowledge, although no single reader or citizen can command the whole of that knowledge.[4]

Contrast this with the perceptual problems presented by the contemporary city, where conventional hierarchies fail:

> The social diversity of the city, which so delighted the eighteenth-century citizen, has, during the course of the twentieth century, multiplied to such an extent . . . that no overview is possible. London now is not so much an encyclopaedia as a maniac's scrapbook.[5]

Raban abandons the search for a general theory, but retains his hold on *place* as a key to understanding the urban, because "place is important; it bears down on us, we mythicize it—often it is our greatest comfort, the one reassuringly solid element in an otherwise soft city."[6]

Ted Relph was one of the first to catalogue the built forms that comprise the places of postmodernity. He describes postmodern urbanism as a selfconscious and selective revival of elements of older styles, though he cautions that postmodernism is not simply a style but also an attitude, a frame of mind.[7] He observes how the coincidence of many trends—gentrification, heritage conservation, architectural fashion, urban design, and participatory planning—has already caused the collapse of the modernist vision of a future city filled with skyscrapers, megastructures and other austere icons of scientific rationalism. The new urbanism is principally distinguishable from the old by its *eclecticism*. Relph warns that arbitrary repetition could result in "a chiaroscuro of increasingly flashy, unrelated and pointless patches, a postmodern, late-modern monotony-in-variety."[8]

Relph's periodization of twentieth-century urbanism involves a *pre-modern transitional period* (up to 1940), an era of *modernist cityscapes* (after 1945), and a period of *postmodern townscapes* (since 1970). The distinction between cityscape and townscape is the crucial to his diagnosis. Modernist cityscapes, he claims, are characterized by five elements[9]:

1. Megastructural bigness (few street entrances to buildings, little architectural detailing, etc.)

2. Straight-space/Prairie space (city center canyons, endless suburban vistas)

3. Rational order and flexibility (the landscapes of total order, verging on bore-dom)

4. Hardness and opacity (including freeways, and the displacement of nature)

5. Discontinuous serial vision (deriving from the dominance of the automo-bile)

Conversely, postmodern townscapes are more detailed, handcrafted and intricate. They celebrate difference, polyculturalism, variety and stylishness.[10] Their elements are:

6. Quaintspace (a deliberate cuteness)

7. Textured facades (aimed at pedestrians, rich in detail, often with an "aged" appearance)

8. Stylishness (appealing to the fashionable, chic, and affluent)

9. Reconnection with the local (involving deliberate historical-geographical re-constructions)

10. Pedestrian-automobile split (to redress the modernist bias toward the car)

The experience of driving through the late-twentieth-century city is, for Relph, one of repetition, where unity is achieved by contiguity and little else. He concludes that the modern urban landscape is a failure, littered with the dreams of Ebenezer Howard, Frank Lloyd Wright, Le Corbusier, and other utopians. But the post-modern townscape may be nothing more than a disguise for an evermore subtle and powerful rationality on the part of government and corporations—a "pretty lie," as Relph calls it.[11] He concludes:

> For all the dramatic modifications that have been made to urban landscapes over the last 100 years I begin to suspect that the only fundamental social advances have been to do with sanitation. All the other changes—skyscrapers, renewal, suburban subdivi-sions, expressways, heritage districts—amount to little more than fantastic imagineering and spectacular window dressing.[12]

A MANIAC'S SCRAPBOOK: CONTEMPORARY SOUTHERN CALIFORNIA

> *This latest mutation in space—postmodern hyperspace—has finally succeeded in transcending the capacities of the human body to locate itself, to organize its immediate surroundings perceptually, and cognitively to map its position in a mappable external world.*
> —Fredric Jameson[13]

Raban's emphasis on the cognitive and Relph's on the concrete underscore the importance of both dimensions in understanding socio-spatial urban process. The

Table 3.1 A Taxonomy of Southern California Urbanisms

Edge Cities	Interdictory Space
Privatopia	Historical Geographies of Restructuring
Cultures of Heteropolis	Fordist/Post-Fordist Regimes of Accumulation/ Regulation
City as Theme Park	Globalization
Fortified City	Politics of Nature

palette of urbanisms that arises from merging the two is thick and multidimensional. We turn now to the task of constructing that palette by examining empirical evidence of recent urban developments in Southern California (Table 3.1). In this review, we take our lead from what exists, rather than what we consider to be a comprehensive urban research agenda. From this, we move quickly to a synthesis that is prefigurative of a proto-postmodern urbanism (Figure 3.1) which we hope will serve as an invitation to a more broadly-based comparative analysis.

Edge Cities

Joel Garreau noted the central significance of Los Angeles in understanding contemporary metropolitan growth in the U.S. He asserts that: "Every single American city that *is* growing, is growing in the fashion of Los Angeles," and refers to L.A. as the "great-grandaddy" of edge cities. (He claims there are 26 of them within a 5-county area in Southern California.[14]) For Garreau, edge cities represent the crucible of America's urban future. The classic location for contemporary edge cities is at the intersection of an urban beltway and a hub-and-spoke lateral road. The central conditions that have propelled such development are the dominance of the automobile and the associated need for parking; the communications revolution; and the entry of women in large numbers into the labor market. Although Garreau agrees with Robert Fishman that "[a]ll new city forms appear in their early stages to be chaotic,"[15] he is able to identify three basic types of edge city. These are: *uptowns* (peripheral pre-automobile settlements that have subsequently been absorbed by urban sprawl); *boomers* (the classic edge cities, located at freeway intersections); and *greenfields* (the current state-of-the-art, "occurring at the intersection of several thousand acres of farmland and one developer's monumental ego").[16]

One essential feature of the edge city is that politics is not yet established there. Into the political vacuum moves a "shadow government"—a privatized protogovernment that is essentially a plutocratic alternative to normal politics. Shadow governments can tax, legislate for, and police their communities, but they are rarely accountable, are responsive primarily to wealth (as opposed to numbers of voters), and subject to few constitutional constraints.[17] Jennifer Wolch has described the rise of the shadow state as part of a society-wide trend toward privatization.[18] In

edge cities, "community" is scarce, occurring not through propinquity but via telephone, fax and private mail service. The walls that typically surround such neighborhoods are social boundaries, but they act as community "recognizers," not community "organizers."[19] In the edge city era, Garreau notes, the term "master-
planned" community is little more than a marketing device.[20] Other studies of
suburbanization in L.A., most notably by Hise[21] and Waldie,[22] provide a basis for
comparing past practices of planned community marketing in Southern California.

Privatopia

Privatopia, perhaps the quintessential edge city residential form, is a private housing development based in common-interest developments (CIDs) and administered
by homeowners associations. There were fewer than 500 such associations in 1964;
by 1992, there were 150,000 associations privately governing approximately 32 million Americans. In 1990, the 11.6 million CID units constituted over 11 percent of
the nation's housing stock.[23] Sustained by an expanding catalogue of covenants,
conditions, and restrictions (or CC&Rs, the proscriptive constitutions formalizing
CID behavioral and aesthetic norms), privatopia has been fueled by a large dose of
privatization, and promoted by an ideology of "hostile privatism."[24] It has provoked
a culture of non-participation.

McKenzie warns that far from being a benign or inconsequential trend, CIDs
already define a new norm for the mass production of housing in the U.S. Equally
importantly, their organizations are now allied through something called the Community Associations Institute, "whose purposes include the standardizing and
professionalizing of CID governance."[25] McKenzie notes how this "secession of the
successful" (the phrase is Robert Reich's) has altered concepts of citizenship, in
which "one's duties consist of satisfying one's obligations to private property."[26] In
her futuristic novel of L.A. wars between walled-community dwellers and those
beyond the walls, Octavia Butler has envisioned a dystopian privatopian future. It
includes a balkanized nation of defended neighborhoods at odds with one another,
where entire communities are wiped out for a handful of fresh lemons or a few cups
of potable water; where torture and murder of one's enemies is common; and where
company-town slavery is attractive to those who are fortunate enough to sell their
services to the hyper-defended enclaves of the very rich.[27]

Cultures of Heteropolis

One of the most prominent sociocultural tendencies in contemporary Southern
California is the rise of minority populations.[28] Provoked to comprehend the causes
and implications of the 1992 civil disturbances in Los Angeles, Charles Jencks[29]
zeroes in on the city's *diversity* as the key to L.A.'s emergent urbanism: "Los Angeles
is a combination of enclaves with high identity, and multienclaves with mixed identity, and, taken as a whole, it is perhaps the most heterogeneous city in the world."[30]
Such ethnic pluralism has given rise to what Jencks calls a *hetero-architecture,* which

has demonstrated that: "there is a great virtue, and pleasure, to be had in mixing categories, transgressing boundaries, inverting customs and adopting the marginal usage."[31] The vigor and imagination underlying these intense cultural dynamics is everywhere evident in the region, from the diversity of ethnic adaptations[32] through the concentration of cultural producers in the region,[33] to the hybrid complexities of emerging cultural forms.[34]

The consequent built environment is characterized by transience, energy, and unplanned vulgarity, in which Hollywood is never far away. Jencks views this improvisational quality as a hopeful sign: "The main point of hetero-architecture is to accept the different voices that create a city, suppress none of them, and make from their interaction some kind of greater dialogue."[35] This is especially important in a city where *minoritization,* "the typical postmodern phenomenon where most of the population forms the 'other,'" is the order of the day, and where most city dwellers feel distanced from the power structure.[36] Despite Jencks' optimism, other analysts have observed that the same Southern California heteropolis has to contend with more than its share of socio-economic polarization, racism, inequality, homelessness, and social unrest.[37] Yet these characteristics are part of a sociocultural dynamic that is also provoking the search for innovative solutions in labor and community organizing,[38] as well as in inter-ethnic relations.[39]

City as Theme Park

California in general, and Los Angeles in particular, have often been promoted as places where the American (suburban) Dream is most easily realised. Its oft-noted qualities of optimism and tolerance coupled with a balmy climate have given rise to an architecture and society fostered by a spirit of experimentation, risk-taking, and hope. Architectural dreamscapes are readily convertible into marketable commodities, i.e., saleable prepackaged landscapes engineered to satisfy fantasies of suburban living.[40] Many writers have used the "theme park" metaphor to describe the emergence of such variegated cityscapes. For instance, Michael Sorkin describes theme parks as places of simulation without end, characterized by aspatiality plus technological and physical surveillance and control.[41] The precedents for this model can be traced back to the World's Fairs, but Sorkin insists that something "wholly new" is now emerging. This is because "the 800 telephone number and the piece of plastic have made time and space obsolete," and these instruments of "artificial adjacency" have eviscerated the traditional politics of propinquity.[42] Sorkin observes that the social order has always been legible in urban form; for example, traditional cities have adjudicated conflicts via the relations of public places such as the agora or piazza. However, in today's "recombinant city," he contends that conventional legibilities have been obscured and/or deliberately mutilated. The phone and modem have rendered the street irrelevant, and the new city threatens an "unimagined sameness" characterized by the loosening of ties to any specific space, rising levels of surveillance, manipulation and segregation, and the city as a theme park. Of this last, Disneyland is the archetype—described by Sorkin as a place of "Taylorized fun," the "Holy See of Creative Geography."[43] What is missing in this new cybernetic suburbia is not a particular building or place, but the spaces between, i.e., the connections that make sense of forms.[44] What is missing, then, is connectivity and community.

In extremis, California dreamscapes become simulacra. Ed Soja identified Orange County as a massive simulation of what a city should be.[45] He describes Orange County as: "a structural fake, and enormous advertisement, yet functionally the finest multipurpose facility of its kind in the country." Calling this assemblage "exopolis," or the city without, Soja asserts that "something new is being born here" based on the hyperrealities of more conventional theme parks such as Disneyland.[46] The exopolis is a simulacrum, an exact copy of an original that never existed, within which image and reality are spectacularly confused. In this "politically-numbed" society, conventional politics is dysfunctional. Orange County has become a "scamscape," notable principally as home of massive mail fraud operations, savings and loan failures, and county government bankruptcy.[47]

Fortified City

The downside of the Southern Californian dream has, of course, been the subject of countless dystopian visions in histories, movies and novels.[48] In one powerful account, Mike Davis noted how Southern Californians' obsession with security has transformed the region into a fortress. This shift is accurately manifested in the physical form of the city, which is divided into fortified cells of affluence and places of terror where police battle the criminalized poor. These urban phenomena, according to Davis, have placed Los Angeles "on the hard edge of postmodernity."[49] The dynamics of fortification involve the omnipresent application of high-tech policing methods to the "high-rent security of gated residential developments" and "panopticon malls." It extends to "space policing," including a proposed satellite observation capacity that would create an invisible Haussmannization of Los Angeles. In the consequent "carceral city," the working poor and destitute are spatially sequestered on the "mean streets," and excluded from the affluent "forbidden cities" through "security by design."

Interdictory Space

Elaborating upon Davis' fortress urbanism, Steven Flusty observed how various types of fortification have extended a canopy of suppression and surveillance across the entire city. His taxonomy of interdictory spaces[50] identifies how spaces are designed to exclude by a combination of their function and cognitive sensibilities. Some spaces are passively aggressive: space concealed by intervening objects or grade changes is "stealthy"; and space that may be reached only by means of interrupted or obfuscated approaches is "slippery." Other spatial configurations are more assertively confrontational: deliberately obstructed "crusty" space surrounded by walls and checkpoints; inhospitable "prickly" spaces featuring unsittable benches in areas devoid of shade; or "jittery" space ostentatiously saturated with surveillance devices. Flusty notes how combinations of interdictory spaces are being introduced "into every facet of the urban environment, generating distinctly unfriendly mutant typologies."[51] Some are indicative of the pervasive infiltration of fear into the home, including the bunker-style "blockhome," affluent palisaded "luxury laager" communities, or low-income residential areas converted into "pocket ghettos" by military-style occupation. Other typological forms betray a fear of the public realm, as with the fortification of commercial facilities into "strongpoints of sale," or the self-contained "world citadel" clusters of defensible office towers.

One consequence of the socio-spatial differentiation described by Davis and Flusty is an acute fragmentation of the urban landscape. Commentators who remark upon the strict division of residential neighborhoods along race and class lines miss the fact that L.A.'s microgeography is incredibly volatile and varied. In many neighborhoods, simply turning a street corner will lead the pedestrian/driver into totally different social and physical configurations. One very important feature of local neighborhood dynamics in the fortified culture of Southern Californian cities is, of course, the presence of street gangs.[52]

Historical Geographies of Restructuring

Historical geographies of Southern California are relatively rare, especially when compared with the number of published accounts of Chicago and New York. For reasons that are unclear, Los Angeles remains, in our judgment, the least studied major city in the United States. Until Mike Davis' *City of Quartz*[53] brought the urban record up to the present, students of Southern California tended to rely principally on Carey McWilliams'[54] seminal general history and Fogelson's *The Fragmented Metropolis*,[55] an urban history of L.A. up to 1930. Other chronicles of the urban evolution of Southern California have focused on transportation,[56] the Mexican/Chicano experience,[57] real estate development and planning,[58] and oil.[59] The political geography of the region is only now being written,[60] but several more broadly-based treatments of Californian politics exist, including excellent studies on art, poetry and politics,[61] railways,[62] and the rise of suburbia.[63]

In his history of Los Angeles between 1965 and 1992, Soja attempts to link the emergent patterns of urban form with underlying social processes.[64] He identified six kinds of *restructuring*, which together define the region's contemporary urban process. In addition to *Exopolis* (noted above), Soja lists: *Flexcities,* associated with the transition to post-Fordism, especially deindustrialization and the rise of the information economy; and *Cosmopolis,* referring to the globalization of Los Angeles both in terms of its emergent world city status and its internal multicultural diversification. According to Soja, peripheralization, post-Fordism, and globalization together define the experience of urban restructuring in Los Angeles. Three specific geographies are consequent upon these dynamics: *Splintered Labyrinth,* which describes the extreme forms of social, economic, and political polarization characteristic of the postmodern city; *Carceral city,* referring to the new "incendiary urban geography" brought about by the amalgam of violence and police surveillance; and *Simcities,* the term Soja uses to describe the new ways of seeing the city that are emerging from the study of Los Angeles—a kind of epistemological restructuring that foregrounds a postmodern perspective.

Fordist vs. Post-Fordist Regimes of Accumulation and Regulation

Many observers agree that one of the most important underlying shifts in the contemporary political economy is from a Fordist to a post-Fordist industrial organization. In a series of important books, Allen Scott and Michael Storper have portrayed the burgeoning urbanism of Southern California as a consequence of this deep-seated structural change in the capitalist political economy.[65] For instance, Scott's basic argument is that there have been two major phases of urbanization in the United States. The first related to an era of Fordist mass production, during which the paradigmatic cities of industrial capitalism (Detroit, Chicago, Pittsburgh, etc.) coalesced around industries that were themselves based upon ideas of mass production. The second phase is associated with the decline of the Fordist era and the rise of a post-Fordist "flexible production." This is a form of industrial activity based on small-size, small-batch units of (typically sub-contracted) production that are nevertheless integrated into clusters of economic activity. Such clusters have been observed in two manifestations: labor-intensive craft forms (in Los Angeles, typically garments and jewelry); and high technology (especially the defense and aerospace industries). According to Scott, these so-called technopoles until recently constituted the principal geographical loci of contemporary (sub)urbanization in Southern California (a development prefigured in Fishman's description of the "technoburb").[66]

Post-Fordist regimes of accumulation are associated with analogous regimes of regulation, or social control. Perhaps the most prominent manifestation of changes in the regime of regulation has been the retreat from the welfare state. The rise of neoconservatism and the privatization ethos has coincided with a period of economic recession and retrenchment which has led many to the brink of poverty just at the time when the social welfare "safety net" is being withdrawn. In Los Angeles, as in many other cities, an acute socio-economic polarization has resulted. In 1984, the city was dubbed the "homeless capital" of the USA because of the concentration of homeless people there.[67]

Globalization

Needless to say, any consideration of the changing nature of industrial production sooner or later must encompass the globalization question.[68] In his reference to the global context of L.A.'s localisms, Mike Davis claims that if L.A. is in any sense paradigmatic, it is because the city condenses the intended and unintended spatial consequences of post-Fordism.[69] He insists that there is no simple master-logic of restructuring, focusing instead on two key localized macro-processes: the over-accumulation in Southern California of bank and real-estate capital principally from the East Asian trade surplus; and the reflux of low-wage manufacturing and labor-intensive service industries following upon immigration from Mexico and Central America. For instance, Davis notes how the City of Los Angeles used tax dollars gleaned from international capital investments to subsidize its downtown (Bunker Hill) urban renewal, a process he refers to as "municipalized land speculation."[70] Through such connections, what happens today in Asia and Central America will tomorrow have an effect in Los Angeles. This global/local dialectic has already become an important (if somewhat imprecise) *leitmotif* of contemporary urban theory.

Politics of Nature

The natural environment of Southern California has been under constant assault since the first colonial settlements. Human habitation on a metropolitan scale has only been possible through a widespread manipulation of nature, especially the control of water resources in the American West.[71] On one hand, Southern Californians tend to hold a grudging respect for nature living as they do adjacent to one of the earth's major geological hazards, and in a desert environment that is prone to flood, landslide and fire.[72] On the other hand, its inhabitants have been energetically, ceaselessly, and sometimes carelessly unrolling the carpet of urbanization over the natural landscape for more than a century. This uninhibited occupation has engendered its own range of environmental problems, most notoriously air pollution, but also issues related to habitat loss and dangerous encounters between humans and other animals.

The force of nature in Southern California has spawned a literature that attempts to incorporate environmental issues into the urban problematic. The politics of environmental regulation have long been studied in many places, including Los Angeles.[73] However, the particular combination of circumstances in Southern California has stimulated an especially political view of nature, focusing both on its emasculation through human intervention[74] and on its potential for political mobilization by grass-roots movements.[75] In addition, Jennifer Wolch's Southern California-based research has led her to outline an alternative vision of biogeography's problematic.[76]

Synthesis: Proto-Postmodern Urbanism

If these observers of the Southern California scene could talk with each other to resolve their differences and reconcile their terminologies, how might they synthesize their visions? At the risk of misrepresenting their work, we suggest a schematic that is powerful yet inevitably incomplete (Figure 3.1). It suggests a "proto-postmodern" urban process, driven by a global restructuring that is permeated and balkanized by a series of interdictory networks; whose populations are socially and

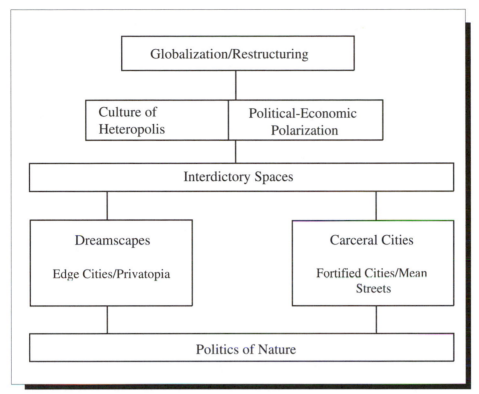

Figure 3.1. A Concept of Proto-Postmodern Urbanism

culturally heterogeneous, but politically and economically polarized; whose residents are educated and persuaded to the consumption of dreamscapes even as the poorest are consigned to carceral cities; whose built environment, reflective of these processes, consists of edge cities, privatopias, and the like; and whose natural environment, also reflective of these processes, is being erased to the point of unlivability while at the same time providing a focus for political action.

POSTMODERN URBANISM

The only theory worth having is that which you
have to fight off, not that which you
speak with profound fluency.

—Stuart Hall[77]

Recognizing that we may have caused some offense by characterizing others' work in this way, let us move swiftly to reconstruct their evidence into a postmodern urban problematic (Table 3.2). We anchor this problematic in the straightforward need to account for the evolution of society over time and space. Such evolution occurs as a

Table 3.2 Elements of Postmodern Urbanism

GLOBAL LATIFUNDIA
HOLSTEINIZATION
PRAEDATORIANISM
FLEXISM
NEW WORLD BIPOLAR DISORDER
Cybergeoisie
Protosurps
MEMETIC CONTAGION
KENO CAPITALISM
CITISTAT
Commudities
Cyburbia
Citidel
In-Beyond
Cyberia
POLLYANNARCHY
DISINFORMATION SUPERHIGHWAY

combination of deep-time (long-term) and present-time (short-term) processes; and it develops over several different scales of human activity (which we may represent summarily as micro-, meso-, and macro-scales).[78] The structuring of the time-space fabric is the result of the interaction among ecologically-situated human agents in relations of production, consumption, and coercion. We do not intend any primacy in this ordering of categories, but instead emphasize their *interdependencies*—all are essential in explaining postmodern human geographies.

Our promiscuous use of neologisms in what follows is quite deliberate.[79] This technique has been used historically to good effect in many instances and disciplines.[80] Neologisms have been used here in circumstances when there were no existing terms to describe adequately the conditions we sought to identify; when neologisms served as metaphors to suggest new insights; when a single term more conveniently substituted for a complex phrase or string of ideas; and when neologistic novelty aided our avowed efforts to rehearse the break. The juxtaposing of postmodern and more traditional categories of modernist urbanism is also an essential piece of our analytical strategy. That there is an overlap between modernist and postmodern categories should surprise no one; we are, inevitably, building on existing urbanisms and epistemologies. The consequent neologistic pastiche may be properly regarded as a tactic of postmodern analysis; others could regard this strategy as analogous to hypothesis-generation, or the practice of dialectics.

Urban Pattern and Process

We begin with the assumption that urbanism is made possible by the exercise of instrumental control over both human and nonhuman ecologies (Figure 3.2). The

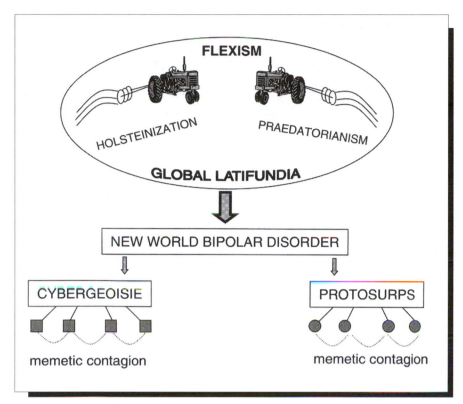

Figure 3.2. Postmodern Urbanism—1

very occupation and utilization of space, as well as the production and distribution of commodities, depend upon an anthropocentric reconfiguration of natural processes and their products. As the scope and scale of, and dependency upon, globally-integrated consumption increases, institutional action converts complex ecologies into monocultured factors of production by simplifying nature into a *global latifundia*. This process includes both homogenizing interventions, as in California agriculture's reliance upon vast expanses of single crops, and forceful interdiction to sustain that intervention against natural feedbacks as in the aerial spraying of pesticides to eradicate fruit-flies attracted to these vast expanses of single crops. Being part of nature, humanity is subjected to analogous dynamics. *Holsteinization* is the process of monoculturing people as consumers so as to facilitate the harvesting of desires, including the decomposition of communities into isolated family units and individuals in order to supplant social networks of mutual support with consumersheds of dependent customers. Resistance is discouraged by means of *praedatorianism,* i.e., the forceful interdiction by a praedatorian guard with varying degrees of legitimacy.

The global latifundia, holsteinization, and praedatorianism are, in one form or another, as old as the global political economy; but the overarching dynamic signaling a break with previous manifestations is *flexism,* a pattern of econo-cultural production and consumption characterized by near-instantaneous delivery and rapid redirectability of resource flows. Flexism's fluidity results from cheaper and faster systems of transportation and telecommunications, globalization of capital markets, and concomitant flexibly-specialized, just-in-time production processes enabling short product- and production-cycles. These result in highly mobile capital and commodity flows able to outmaneuver geographically-fixed labor markets, communities, and bounded nation states. Globalization and rapidity permit capital to evade long-term commitment to place-based socio-economies, thus enabling a crucial social dynamic of flexism: whereas, under Fordism, exploitation is exercised through the alienation of labor in the place of production, flexism may require little or no labor at all from a given locale. Simultaneously, local down-waging and capital concentration operate synergistically to supplant locally-owned enterprises with national and supranational chains, thereby transferring consumer capital and inventory selection ever further away from direct local control.

From these exchange asymmetries emerges a *new world bipolar disorder.* This is a globally-bifurcated social order, many times more complicated than conventional class structures, in which those overseeing the global latifundia enjoy concentrated power. Those who are dependent upon their command-and-control decisions find themselves in progressively weaker positions, pitted against each other globally, and forced to accept shrinking compensation for their efforts (assuming that compensation is offered in the first place). Of the two groups, the *cybergeoisie* reside in the "big house" of the global latifundia, providing indispensable, presently unautomatable command-and-control functions. They are predominantly stockholders, the core employees of thinned-down corporations, and write-your-own-ticket free-lancers (e.g., CEOs, subcontract entrepreneurs, and celebrities). They may also shelter members of marginal creative professions, who comprise a kind of paracybergeoisie. The cybergeoisie enjoy perceived socio-economic security and comparatively long-term horizons in decision-making; consequently their anxieties tend toward unforeseen social disruptions such as market fluctuations and crime. Commanding, controlling, and prodigiously enjoying the fruits of a shared global exchange of goods and information, the cybergeoisie exercise global co-ordination functions that predispose them to a similar ideology and, thus, they are relatively heavily holsteinized.

Protosurps, on the other hand, are the sharecroppers of the global latifundia. They are increasingly marginalized "surplus" labor providing just-in-time services when called upon by flexist production processes, but otherwise alienated from global systems of production (though not of consumption). Protosurps include temporary or day laborers, fire-at-will service workers, a burgeoning class of intra- and international itinerant laborers specializing in pursuing the migrations of fluid investment. True surpdom is a state of superfluity beyond peonage—a vagrancy that is increasingly criminalized through anti-homeless ordinances, welfare-state erosion, and widespread community intolerance (of, for instance, all forms of panhandling). Protosurps are called upon to provide as yet unautomated service functions designed as to be performed by anyone. Subjected to high degrees of uncertainty by the omnipresent threat of instant unemployment, protosurps are prone to clustering into affinity groups for support in the face of adversity. These affinity groups, however, are not exclusive, overlapping in both membership and space, resulting in a class of marginalized indigenous populations and peripheral immigrants who are relatively less holsteinized.

The socio-cultural collisions and intermeshings of protosurp affinity groups, generated by flexist-induced immigration and severe social differentiation, serve to produce wild *memetic contagion.*[81] This is a process by which cultural elements of one individual or group exert cross-over influences upon the culture of another previously unexposed individual/group. Memetic contagion is evidenced in Los Angeles by such hybridized agents and intercultural conflicts as Mexican and Central American practitioners of Afro-Caribbean religion, blue-bandanna'd Thai Crips, or the adjustments prompted by poor African Americans' offense at Korean merchants' disinclination to smile casually.[82] Memetic contagion should not be taken for a mere epiphenomenon of an underlying political economic order, generating colorfully chaotic ornamentation for a flexist regime. Rather, it entails the assemblage of novel ways of seeing and being, from whence new identities, cultures and political alignments emerge. These new social configurations, in turn, may act to force change in existing institutions and structures, and to spawn cognitive conceptions that are incommensurable with, though not necessarily any less valid than, existing models. The inevitable tensions between the anarchic diversification born of memetic contagion and the manipulations of the holsteinization process may yet prove to be the central cultural contradiction of flexism.

With the flexist imposition of global imperatives on local economies and cultures, the spatial logic of Fordism has given way to a new, more dissonant international geographical order. In the absence of conventional communication and transportation imperatives mandating propinquity, the once-standard Chicago School logic has given way to a seemingly haphazard juxtaposition of land uses scattered over the landscape. Worldwide, agricultural lands sprout monocultures of exportable strawberry or broccoli in lieu of diverse staple crops grown for local consumption. Sitting amidst these fields, identical assembly lines produce the same brand of automobile, supplied with parts and managed from distant continents. Expensive condominiums appear amongst squatter slums, indistinguishable in form and occupancy from (and often in direct communication with) luxury housing built atop homeless encampments elsewhere in the world. Yet what in close-up appears to be a fragmentary, collaged polyculture is, from a longer perspective, a geographically-disjoint but hyperspatially-integrated monoculture, i.e., shuffled sames set amidst adaptive and persistent local variations. The result is a landscape not unlike that formed by a keno gamecard. The card itself appears as a numbered grid, with some squares being marked during the course of the game and others not, according to some random draw. The process governing this marking ultimately determines which player will achieve a jackpot-winning pattern; it is, however, determined by a rationalized set of procedures beyond the territory of the card itself. Similarly, the apparently-random development and redevelopment of urban land may be regarded as the outcome of exogenous investment processes inherent to flexism, thus creating the landscapes of *keno capitalism.*

Keno capitalism's contingent mosaic of variegated monocultures renders discussion of "the city" increasingly reductionist. More holistically, the dispersed net of megalopoles may be viewed as a single integrated urban system, or *Citistāt* (Figure 3.3). Citistāt, the collective world city, has emerged from competing urban webs of colonial and post-colonial eras to become a geographically-diffuse hub of an omnipresent periphery, drawing labor and materials from readily-substitutable locations throughout that periphery. Citistāt is both geographically corporeal, in the sense that urban places exist, and yet ageographically ethereal in the sense that communication systems create a virtual space permitting coordination across physical space. Both realms reinforce each another while (re)producing the new world bi-polar disorder.

Materially, Citistāt consists of commudities (commodified cybergeois residential and commercial ecologies), and the in-beyond (internal peripheries simultaneously undergoing but resisting instrumentalization in myriad ways). Virtually, Citistāt consists of cyburbia, the collection of state-of-the-art data-transmission, premium pay-per-use, and interactive services generally reliant upon costly and technologically complex interfaces; and cyberia, an electronic outland of rudimentary communications including basic phone service and telegraphy, interwoven with and preceptorally conditioned by the disinformation superhighway (DSH).

Commudities are commodified communities created expressly to satisfy (and profit from) the habitat preferences of the well-recompensed cybergeoisie. They commonly consist of carefully-manicured residential and commercial ecologies managed through privatopian self-administration, and maintained against internal and external outlaws by a repertoire of interdictory prohibitions. Increasingly, these pre-packaged environments jockey with one another for clientele on the basis of recreational, cultural, security, and educational amenities. Commonly located on difficult-to-access sites like hilltops or urban edges, far from restless populations undergoing conversion to protosurpdom, individual commudities are increasingly teleintegrated to form *cyburbia,*[83] the interactive tollways comprising the high-rent district of Citistāt's hyperspatial electronic shadow. (This process may soon find a geographical analog in the conversion of automotive freeways linking commudities via exclusive tollways.) Teleintegration is already complete (and *de rigueur*) for the *citidels,* which are commercial commudities consisting of highrise corporate towers from which the control and co-ordination of production and distribution in the global latifundia is exercised.

Citistāt's internal periphery and repository of cheap on-call labor lie at the *in-beyond,* comprised of a shifting matrix of protosurp affinity clusters. The in-beyond may be envisioned as a patchwork quilt of variously-defined interest groups (with differing levels of economic, cultural, and street influence), none of which possesses the wherewithal to achieve hegemonic status or to secede. Secession may occur locally to some degree, as in the cases of the publicly-subsidized reconfiguration of L.A.'s Little Tokyo, and the consolidation of Koreatown through the import, adja-

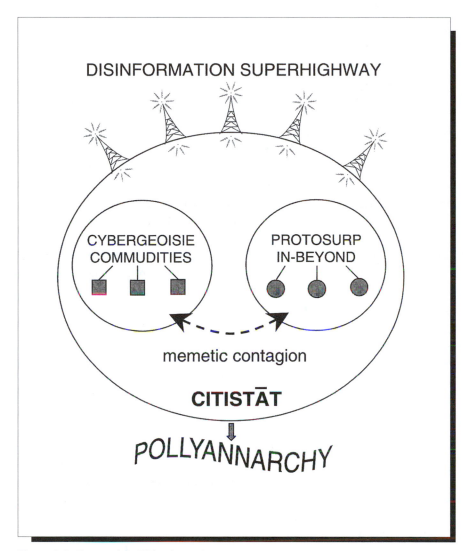

Figure 3.3. Postmodern Urbanism—2

cent extraction, and community re-circulation of capital. The piecemeal diversity of the in-beyond makes it a hotbed of wild memetic contagion. The global connectivity of the in-beyond is considerably less glamorous than that of the cybergeoisie's commudities, but it is no less extensive. Intermittent phone contact and wire-service remittances occur throughout *cyberia*.[84] The pot-holed public streets of Citistāt's virtual twin are augmented by extensive networks of snail mail, personal migration, and the hand-to-hand passage of mediated communications (e.g., cassette tapes). Such contacts occasionally diffuse into commudities.

Political relations in Citistāt tend toward polyanarchy, a politics of grudging tolerance of *difference* that emerges from interactions and accommodations within the in-beyond and between commudities, and less frequently, between in-beyond and commudity. Its more pervasive form is *pollyannarchy*, an exaggerated, manufactured optimism that promotes a self-congratulatory awareness and respect for difference and the asymmetries of power. Pollyannarchy is thus a pathological form of polyanarchy, disempowering those who would challenge the controlling beneficiaries of the new world bi-polar disorder. Pollyannarchy is evident in the continuing spectacle of electoral politics, or in the citywide unity campaign run by corporate sponsors following the 1992 uprising in Los Angeles.

Wired throughout the body of the Citistāt is the *disinformation superhighway* (or DSH), a mass info-tain-mercial media owned by roughly two dozen cybergeoisie institutions. The DSH disseminates holsteinizing ideologies and incentives, creates wants and dreams, and inflates the symbolic value of commodities. At the same time, it serves as the highly-filtered sensory organ through which commudities and the in-beyond perceive the world outside their unmediated daily experiences. The DSH is Citistāt's "consent factory,"[85] engineering memetic contagion to encourage participation in a global latifundia that is represented as both inevitable and desirable. However, since the DSH is a broad-band distributor of information designed primarily to attract and deliver consumers to advertisers, the ultimate reception of messages carried by the DSH is difficult to target and predetermine. Thus, the DSH also serves inadvertently as a vector for memetic contagion, e.g., the conversion of cybergeoisie youth to wannabe gangstas via the dissemination of hip-hop culture over commudity boundaries. The DSH serves as a network of preceptoral control, and is thus distinct from the coercive mechanisms of the praedatorian guard. Overlap between the two is increasingly common, however, as in the case of televised disinfotainment programs like *America's Most Wanted*, in which crimes are dramatically re-enacted and viewers invited to call in and betray alleged perpetrators.

As the cybergeoisie increasingly withdraw from the Fordist redistributive triad of big government, big business and big labor to establish their own micro-nations, the social support functions of the state disintegrate, along with the survivability of less-affluent citizens. The global migrations of work to the lowest-wage locations of the in-beyond, and of consumer capital to the citidels, result in power asymmetries that become so pronounced that even the DSH is at times incapable of obscuring them, leaving protosurps increasingly disinclined to adhere to the remnants of a tattered social contract. This instability in turn creates the potential for violence, pitting Citistāt and cybergeoisie against the protosurp in-beyond, and leading inevitably to a demand for the suppression of protosurp intractability. The *praedatorian guard* thus emerges as the principal remaining vestige of the police powers of the state. This increasingly privatized public/private partnership of mercenary sentries, police expeditionary forces, and their technological extensions (e.g., video cameras, helicopters, criminological data uplinks, etc.) watches over the commudities and minimizes disruptiveness by acting as a force of occupation within the in-beyond. The praedatorian guard achieves control through coercion, even at the international level where asymmetrical trade relations are reinforced by the military and its clientele. It may only be a matter of time before the local and national praedatorians are administratively—and functionally—merged, as exemplified by proposals to deploy military units for policing inner city streets or the U.S.-Mexico border.

AN ALTERNATIVE MODEL
OF URBAN STRUCTURE

We have begun the process of interrogating prior models of urban structure with an alternative model based upon the recent experiences of Los Angeles. We do not pretend to have completed this project, nor claim that the Southern Californian experience is necessarily typical of other metropolitan regions in the United States or the world. Still less would we advocate replacing the old models with a new hegemony. But discourse has to start somewhere, and by now it is clear that the most influential of existing urban models is no longer tenable as a guide to contemporary urbanism. In this first sense, our investigation has uncovered an *epistemological radical break* with past practices, which in itself is sufficient justification for something called a Los Angeles School. The concentric ring structure of the Chicago School was essentially a concept of the city as an organic accretion around a central, organizing core. Instead, we have identified a postmodern urban process in which the urban periphery organizes the center within the context of a globalizing capitalism.

The postmodern urban process remains resolutely capitalist, but the nature of that enterprise is changing in very significant ways, especially through (for instance) the telecommunications revolution, the changing nature of work, and globalization. Thus, in this second sense also we understand that a *radical break* is occurring, this time in the conditions of our *material world*. Contemporary urbanism is a consequence of how local and inter-local flows of material and information (including symbols) intersect in a rapidly-converging globally-integrated economy driven by the imperatives of flexism. Landscapes and peoples are homogenized to facilitate large-scale production and consumption. Highly-mobile capital and commodity flows outmaneuver geographically-fixed labor markets, communities, and nation-states, and cause a globally-bifurcated polarization. The beneficiaries of this system are the cybergeoisie, even as the numbers of permanently-marginalized protosurps grow. In the new global order, socioeconomic polarization and massive, sudden population migrations spawn cultural hybrids through the process of memetic contagion. Cities no longer develop as concentrated loci of population and economic activity, but as fragmented parcels within Citistāt, the collective world city. Materially, the Citistāt consists of commudities (commodified communities) and the in-beyond (the permanently marginalized). Virtually, the Citistāt is composed of cyburbia (those hooked into the electronic world) and cyberia (those who are not). Social order is maintained by the ideological apparatus of the DSH, the Citistāt's consent factory, and by the praedatorian guard, the privatized vestiges of the nation-state's police powers.

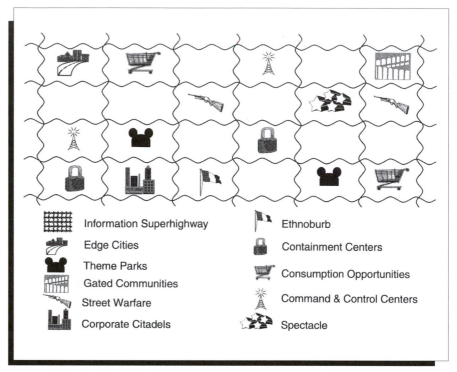

Figure 3.4. Keno Capitalism: A Model of Postmodern Urban Structure

Keno capitalism is the synoptic term that we have adopted to describe the spatial manifestations of the postmodern urban condition (Figure 3.4). Urbanization is occurring on a quasi-random field of opportunities. Capital touches down as if by chance on a parcel of land, ignoring the opportunities on intervening lots, thus sparking the development process. The relationship between development of one parcel and non-development of another is a disjointed, seemingly unrelated affair. While not truly a random process, it is evident that the traditional, center-driven agglomeration economies that have guided urban development in the past no longer apply. Conventional city form, Chicago-style, is sacrificed in favor of a non-contiguous collage of parcelized, consumption-oriented landscapes devoid of conventional centers yet wired into electronic propinquity and nominally unified by the mythologies of the disinformation superhighway. Los Angeles may be a mature form of this postmodern metropolis; Las Vegas comes to mind as a youthful example. The consequent urban aggregate is characterized by acute fragmentation and specialization—a partitioned gaming board subject to perverse laws and peculiarly discrete, disjointed urban outcomes. Given the pervasive presence of crime, corruption, and violence in the global city (not to mention geopolitical transitions, as nation-states give way to micro-nationalisms and transnational mafias), the city as gaming board seems an especially appropriate twenty-first-century successor to the concentrically-ringed city of the early twentieth.

NOTES

1. Raban, J., 1974: *Soft City*. New York: E. P. Dutton.

2. Ibid., p. 11.

3. Ibid., p. 15.

4. Ibid., p. 93.

5. Ibid., p. 129.

6. Ibid., p. 184.

7. Relph, E. C., 1987: *The Modern Urban Landscape*. Baltimore: Johns Hopkins University Press, p. 213.

8. Ibid., p. 237.

9. Ibid., pp. 242-250.

10. Ibid., pp. 252-258.

11. Ibid., p. 259.

12. Ibid., p. 265.

13. Jameson, F., 1991: *Postmodernism, or the Cultural Logic of Late Capitalism*. Durham: Duke University Press, p. 44.

14. Garreau, J., 1991: *Edge City: Life on the New Frontier*. New York: Doubleday, p. 3.

15. Ibid., p. 9.

16. Ibid., p. 116.

17. Ibid., p. 187.

18. Wolch, J., 1990: *The Shadow State: Government and Voluntary Sector in Transition*. New York: The Foundation Center.

19. Garreau, *Edge City*, pp. 275-281.

20. Ibid., p. 301.

21. Hise, G., 1997: *Magnetic Los Angeles: Planning the Twentieth-Century Metropolis*. Baltimore: Johns Hopkins University Press.

22. Waldie, D. J., 1996: *Holy Land: A Suburban Memoir*. New York: W. W. Norton & Company.

23. McKenzie, E., 1994: *Privatopia: Homeowner Associations and the Rise of Residential Private Government*. New Haven: Yale University Press, p. 11.

24. Ibid., p. 19.

25. Ibid., p. 184.

26. Ibid., p. 196.

27. Butler, O. E., 1993: *Parable of the Sower*. New York: Four Walls Eight Windows.

28. Cf. Ong, P., Bonacich, E., and Cheng, L., eds., 1994: *The New Asian Immigration in Los Angeles and Global Restructuring*. Philadelphia: Temple University Press; Roseman, C., Laux, H. D., and Thieme, G., eds., 1996: *EthniCity*. Lanham, MD: Rowman and Littlefield; Waldinger, R., and Bozorgmehr, M., 1996: *Ethnic Los Angeles*. New York: Russell Sage Foundation.

29. Jencks, C., 1993: *Heteropolis: Los Angeles, the Riots and the Strange Beauty of Hetero-Architecture*. London: Academy Editions; Berlin: Ernst & Sohn; New York: St. Martin's Press.

30. Ibid., p. 32.

31. Ibid., p. 123.

32. Park, E., 1996: Our L.A.? Korean Americans in Los Angeles After the Civil Unrest in Dear, M., Schockman, H. E., and Hise, G., eds., 1996: *Rethinking Los Angeles*. Thousand Oaks: Sage Publications.

33. Molotch, H., 1996: L.A. as Design Product: How Art Works in a Regional Economy in A. J. Scott & E. Soja (eds.), *The City: Los Angeles & Urban Theory at the End of the Twentieth Century*. Los Angeles: University of California Press.

34. Boyd, T., 1997: *Am I Black Enough for You?* Indianapolis: University of Indiana Press; Boyd, T., 1996: A Small Introduction to the "G" Funk Era: Gangsta Rap and Black Masculinity in Contemporary Los Angeles, in M. Dear, H. E. Schockman, and G. Hise, eds., *Rethinking Los Angeles.*

35. Jencks (1993), 75.

36. Ibid., p. 84.

37. Cf. Anderson, S., 1996: "A City Called Heaven: Black Enchantment and Despair in Los Angeles" *in A. J. Scott & E. Soja (eds.), The City: Los Angeles & Urban Theory at the End of the Twentieth Century.* Los Angeles: University of California Press; Baldassare, M., ed., 1994: *The Los Angeles Riots.* Boulder, CO: Westview Press; Bullard, R. D., Grigsby, J. E., and Lee, C., 1994: *Residential Apartheid.* Los Angeles: UCLA Center for Afro-American Studies; Gooding-Williams, R., ed., 1993: *Reading Rodney King, Reading Urban Uprising.* New York: Routledge; Rocco, R., 1996: Latino Los Angeles: Reframing Boundaries/Borders in A. J. Scott & E. Soja (eds.), *The City: Los Angeles & Urban Theory at the End of the Twentieth Century.* Los Angeles: University of California Press; Wolch, J., and Dear, M., 1993: *Malign Neglect: Homelessness in an American City.* San Francisco: Jossey-Bass.

38. Pulido, L., 1996: Multiracial Organizing Among Environmental Justice Activists in Los Angeles in M. Dear, H. E. Schockman, and G. Hise, eds., *Rethinking Los Angeles.*

39. Cf. Abelmann, N., and Lie, J., 1995: *Blue Dreams: Korean Americans and the Los Angeles Riots.* Cambridge: Harvard University Press; Martínez, R., 1992: *The Other Side: Notes from the New L.A., Mexico City, and Beyond.* New York: Vintage Books; Yoon, I., 1997: *On My Own: Korean Businesses and Race Relations in America.* Chicago: University of Chicago Press.

40. Such sentiments find echoes in Neil Smith's assessment of the new urban frontier, where expansion is powered by two industries: real estate developers (who package and define value), and the manufacturers of culture (who define taste and consumption preferences), Smith, 1992: New City, New Frontier, in Michael Sorkin, ed., *Variations on a Theme Park:* New York: Hill and Wang, p. 75.

41. Sorkin, M., ed., 1992: *Variations on a Theme Park: The New American City and the End of Public Space.* New York: Hill and Wang.

42. Ibid., p. xi.

43. Ibid., p. 227.

44. Ibid., p. xii.

45. Soja, E., 1992: Inside Exopolis: Scenes from Orange County in M. Sorkin (ed.), *Variations on a Theme Park,* New York: Noonday Press.

46. Ibid., p. 101.

47. Ibid., p. 120.

48. The list of L.A. novels and movies is endless. Typical of the dystopian cinematic vision are *Blade Runner* (Ridley Scott, 1986) and *Chinatown* (Roman Polanski, 1974); and of silly optimism, *L.A. Story* (Mick Jackson, 1991).

49. Davis, M., 1992: Fortress Los Angeles: The Militarization of Urban Space in M. Sorkin (ed.), *Variations on a Theme Park,* New York: Noonday Press, p. 155.

50. Flusty, S., 1994: *Building Paranoia: The Proliferation of Interdictory Space and the Erosion of Spatial Justice.* West Hollywood, CA: Los Angeles Forum for Architecture and Urban Design, (1994), pp. 16-17.

51. Ibid., pp. 21-33.

52. Cf. Klein, M., 1995: *The American Street Gang: Its Nature, Prevalence, and Control.* New York: Oxford University Press; Vigil, J., 1988: *Barrio Gangs: Streetlife and Identity in Southern California.* Austin: University of Texas Press.

53. Davis, M., 1990: *City of Quartz: Excavating the Future in Los Angeles.* New York: Verso.

54. McWilliams, C., 1946: *Southern California: An Island on the Land.* Salt Lake City: Peregrine Smith Books.

55. Folgelson, R. M., 1967: *The Fragmented Metropolis: Los Angeles 1850-1970.* Berkeley: University of California Press.

56. Cf. Bottles, S., 1987: *Los Angeles and the Automobile: The Making of the Modern City.* Los Angeles: University of California Press; Wachs, M., 1996: The Evolution of Transportation Policy in Los Angeles: Images of Past Policies and Future Prospects in A. J. Scott & E. Soja (eds.), *The City: Los Angeles & Urban Theory at the End of the Twentieth Century.* Los Angeles: University of California Press.

57. Del Castillo, R., 1979: *The Los Angeles Barrio, 1850-1890: A Social History.* Los Angeles: University of California Press.

58. Erie, S. P., Forthcoming: *Globalizing L.A.: The Politics of Trade Infrastructure and Regional Development.* Stanford: Stanford University Press; Hise, G., 1997: *Magnetic Los Angeles: Planning the Twentieth-Century Metropolis.* Baltimore: Johns Hopkins University Press; Weiss, M., 1987: *The Rise of the Community Builders: The American Real Estate Industry and Urban Land Planning.* New York: Columbia University Press.

59. Tygiel, J., 1994: *The Great Los Angeles Swindle: Oil, Stocks, and Scandal During the Roaring Twenties.* New York: Oxford University Press.

60. Fulton, W., 1997: *The Reluctant Metropolis: The Politics of Urban Growth in Los Angeles.* Point Arena, CA: Solano Press Books; Sonenshein, R., 1993: *Politics in Black and White: Race and Power in Los Angeles.* Princeton: Princeton University Press.

61. Cándida Smith, R., 1995: *Utopia and Dissent: Art, Poetry, and Politics in California.* Los Angeles: University of California Press.

62. Deverell, W., 1994: *Railroad Crossing: Californians and the Railroad 1850-1910.* Los Angeles: University of California Press.

63. Fishman, R., 1987: *Bourgeois Utopias: The Rise and Fall of Suburbia.* New York: Basic Books, Inc.

64. Soja, E., 1996: Los Angeles 1965-1992: The Six Geographies of Urban Restructuring in A. J. Scott & E. Soja (eds.), *The City: Los Angeles & Urban Theory at the End of the Twentieth Century.* Los Angeles: University of California Press, pp. 426-462.

65. Scott, A. J., 1988a: *New Industrial Spaces: Flexible Production Organization and Regional Development in North America and Western Europe.* London: Pion; Scott, A. J., 1988b: *Metropolis: From the Division of Labor to Urban Form.* Berkeley: University of California Press; Scott, A. J., and Soja, E., eds., 1996: *The City: Los Angeles, and Urban Theory at the End of the Twentieth Century.* Los Angeles: University of California Press; Storper, M., and Walker, R., 1989: *The Capitalist Imperative.* Cambridge: Blackwell.

66. Cf. Fishman, *Bourgeois Utopias;* Castells, M., and Hall, P., 1994: *Technopoles of the World: The Making of the 21st Century Industrial Complexes.* New York: Routledge.

67. Cf. Wolch, *The Shadow State;* Wolch and Dear, *Malign Neglect;* Wolch, J., and Sommer, H., 1997: *Los Angeles in an Era of Welfare Reform: Implications for Poor People and Community Well-Being.* Los Angeles: Liberty Hill Foundation.

68. Cf. Knox, P., and Taylor, P. J., eds., 1995: *World Cities in a World System.* Cambridge: Cambridge University Press.

69. Davis, M., 1992: Chinatown, Revisited? The "Internalization" of Downtown Los Angeles, in D. Reid, ed., *Sex, Death, and God in L.A.* New York: Pantheon.

70. Ibid., p. 26.

71. Cf. Davis, M., 1993: *Rivers in the Desert: William Mulholland and the Inventing of Los Angeles.* New York: Harper Collins; Gottlieb, R., and FitzSimmons, M., 1991: *Thirst for Growth: Water Agencies and Hidden Government in California.* Tucson: University of Arizona Press; Reisner, M., 1993: *Cadillac Desert: The American West and Its Disappearing Water.* New York: Penguin Books.

72. Cf. McPhee, J., 1989: *The Control of Nature.* New York: The Noonday Press; Darlington, D., 1996: *The Mojave: Portrait of the Definitive American Desert.* New York: Henry Holt and Company.

73. FitzSimmons and Gottleib, *Thirst for Growth.*

74. Davis, M., 1996: How Eden Lost Its Garden: A Political History of the Los Angeles Landscape in A. J. Scott & E. Soja (eds.), *The City: Los Angeles & Urban Theory at the End of the Twentieth Century.* Los Angeles: University of California Press.

75. Pulido, Multiracial Organizing.

76. Wolch, J., 1996: From Global to Local: The Rise of Homelessness in Los Angeles During the 1980s in A. J. Scott & E. Soja (eds.), *The City: Los Angeles & Urban Theory at the End of the Twentieth Century.* Los Angeles: University of California Press.

77. Hall, S. 1992, p. 280.

78. Dear, M., 1988; The Postmodern Challenge: Reconstructing Human Geography, *Transactions, Institute of British Geographers,* 13, 262-274.

79. One critic accused us (quite cleverly) of "neologorrhea."

80. Cf. Knox and Taylor, *World Cities.*

81. The term is a combination of Rene Girard's "mimetic contagion" and animal ethologist Richard Dawkin's hypothesis that cultural informations are gene-type units, or "memes," transmitted virus-like from head to head. We here employ the term "hybridized" in recognition of the recency and novelty of the combination, not to assert some prior purity to the component elements forming the hybrid.

82. McGuire, B., and Scrymgeour, D., Forthcoming: Santeria and Curanderismo in Los Angeles, in Clarke, Peter, ed., *New Trends and Developments in African Religion.* Westport: Greenwood Publishing Inc.

83. Dewey, F., and Rugoff, R., 1993: The Floating World, in *The Wild Palms Reader.* New York: St. Martin's Press.

84. Rushkoff, D., 1995: *Cyberia: Life in the Trenches of Hyperspace.* New York: Harper and Collins.

85. Chomsky, N., and Herman, E., 1988: *Manufacturing Consent.* New York: Pantheon Books.

Imagining Postmodern Urbanism

MICHAEL J. DEAR

Borrego Valley, Anza-Borrego Desert State Park, California

I want to imagine what a postmodern urban landscape looks like—how it emerges and matures. I am seeking to describe the physical analogue for an evolving network society, what some refer to as a "city of bits," but which I prefer to call a "postmodern urbanism." Such a city is composed of multiple, differentially interconnected sites, arranged in a decentered, nonhierarchical fashion.

The following text imagines the stages of birth, youth, and maturity in a postmodern metropolis. The accompanying images are intended to invoke the concomitant landscape at each stage. Even though each photograph represents an actual location, these locations should not be understood as a literal representation of postmodern urbanism in that locale. Rather, they should be taken simply as convenient visual analogues of stages in a hypothetical urban history.

Northeast Shore, Salton Sea, California

BIRTH

A. Assume first a *tabula rasa,* an undifferentiated homogenous plain stretching in all directions, each point having the same potential for connectivity to the ubiquitous information superhighway.

Slab City, Imperial County, California

B. *Multicentered nonadjacent parcel development* begins. Sprawl is already characteristic of such development, and because it is unrelated to any conventions of urban core and periphery, it therefore cannot be regarded as traditional suburbanization, edge-city growth, and so forth.

Slab City, Imperial County, California

YOUTH

C. *Keno capitalism* emerges in the form of discrete land use parcels that, although functionally unrelated, tend to become physically adjacent as parcels are successively developed.

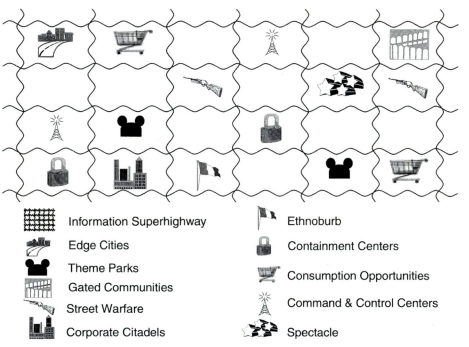

Information Superhighway	Ethnoburb
Edge Cities	Containment Centers
Theme Parks	Consumption Opportunities
Gated Communities	Command & Control Centers
Street Warfare	Spectacle
Corporate Citadels	

Borrego Springs, Anza-Borrego Desert State Park, California

Borrego Springs, Anza-Borrego Desert State Park, California

The proliferation of separate, yet internally homogenous parcels produces a "theme park-ization" of the landscape.

Salvation Mountain, Slab City, California (created by Leonard Knight)

Las Vegas, Nevada, 1930. Photograph courtesy of Ray Cutright Collection, University of Nevada, Las Vegas Library

Photo by W.A. Davis; used by permission.

D. *Infill, agglomeration,* and *densification* begin to manufacture a landscape that is recognizably urban. As proximate land parcels overlap and abut, what appear to be conventional townscapes emerge. Only later is infrastructure added to facilitate the functional integration of the townscapes (including, for example, freeways and "town centers"). However, interparcel connectivity remains rudimentary.

Near Palm Springs, Coachella Valley, California

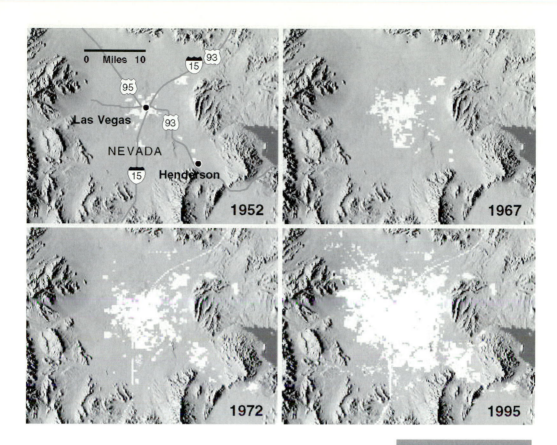

The Mojave Mecca

The Las Vegas metropolitan area is the fastest growing region in the country, and suburban Henderson, Nevada, is the fastest growing city in the nation.
SOURCE: U.S. Census Bureau, U.S. Geological Survey; reprinted by permission from the *New York Times*.

MATURITY

E. *Postmodern urbanism* defines a polycentric metropolis of ubiquitous, apparently limitless, parcelized sprawl. The metropolis remains resolutely ex-urban, in the sense of not being center-related, even though hinterland/core connections *may* occur on a local scale within the multicentered agglomeration. However, just as likely are hinterland connectivities with nonadjacent cores elsewhere in the region, or even at the national and global levels.

Sprawl hits the wall (but then goes around it): the Golden State Freeway (I-5) and Antelope Valley Freeway punch their paths through the San Gabriel Mountains and Angeles National Forest in Northern Los Angeles County.

Stevenson Ranch, Los Angeles County

Near Stevenson Ranch, Los Angeles County

PART 2

City of Industry

Industry and the Landscapes
of Social Reform

EDITOR'S
COMMENTS

Allen Scott, who knows more than most about Southern California's economic geography, tells an excellent story about industry in Los Angeles. Some years ago, Allen had applied to the U.S. National Science Foundation for a grant to study industrial restructuring in the region. One referee flatly rejected the proposal on the grounds that there was no industry to speak of in Southern California—and this is a metropolis that contains municipalities with names such as City of Industry and City of Commerce, which have next to zero residential population!

A similar blind spot appears to have been suffered by Robert Park and his associates. Although they pay lip service to the importance of the urban economy, questions about work, manufacturing, labor, and so on rarely surface in *The City*. It's not clear why this was so. In Chapter 4, Greg Hise suggests that the very centrality of industry in early-twentieth-century Chicago might explain why it was overlooked—as taken for granted as the air the sociologists breathed. Whatever the reasons, we begin our detailed investigations in this book with an important corrective, that is, a focus on L.A.'s industrial history.

In subsequent chapters, Steven Erie focuses on the rise of the twentieth-century industrial city (with particular emphasis on the role played by public works and infrastructure developments), and Allen Scott reviews the process of industrial restructuring in Southern California at the dawn of the twenty-first century. In this chapter, Greg Hise explores the early history of the industrial city, from the late nineteenth century up to 1920. Along the way, Hise engages directly with the legacy of the Chicago School, especially as played out by Emory Bogardus, a 1910 graduate in sociology from the University of Chicago, who went on to become chair of the sociology department at the University of Southern California.

Hise's history reveals the impacts of industry and industrial landscapes in shaping Los Angeles, including the deliberate roles played by developers, city boosters, labor, and urban planners. He argues that Los Angeles began to emerge as the epicenter of a city-centered region in the early part of the twentieth century, but this role quickly slipped away under the impetus of a tidal wave of decentralized urban development that engulfed the entire region. Like everything else, Burgess's model was a product of a particular time and place, Hise concludes, and it is "well past the time to set this model of urbanization aside."

QUOTES FROM
THE CITY

The ancient city was primarily a fortress, a place of refuge in a time of war. The modern city, on the contrary, is primarily a convenience of commerce, and owes its existence to the market place around which it sprang up. Industrial competition and the division of labor, which have probably done most to develop the latent powers of mankind, are possible only upon condition of the existence of markets, of money, and other devices for the facilitation of trade and commerce. . . . (12)

. . . The outstanding fact of modern society is the growth of great cities. Nowhere else have the enormous changes which the machine industry has made in our social life registered themselves with such obviousness as in the cities. (47)

CHAPTER 4

Industry and the Landscapes of Social Reform

GREG HISE

We Must Have a Firm Foundation!

SOURCE: Editorial cartoon courtesy of *Los Angeles Times,* reprinted in Los Angeles Area Chamber of Commerce publication *Southern California Business* in November 1923.

In *The City*, University of Chicago sociologists Robert Park and Ernest Burgess set out to investigate and explain social life and the nature of cultural change in American cities under industrial capitalism. The immigrant newcomer to America and, in these researchers' eyes, a recent arrival to the city, occupied a central position in their study. A considerable portion of their text is devoted to exploring how, or if, these immigrants might negotiate the transition from a traditional folk or peasant culture in their countries of origin to new lives as modern city dwellers in Chicago. Park and Burgess understood these individuals and families as liminal, suspended, as it were, between two seemingly discrete and exclusive states of being, while all around them the certainties of everyday life—folkways, religion, community organization, culture—were in flux. Most of the questions that Park and Burgess pose revolve around one fundamental question: What will become of these people? A quick glance at Park's divisions in his lead chapter is revealing of this inquiry: "Neighborhoods" (What part of the population is floating? How many people live in hotels, apartments, tenements?); "Colonies and segregated areas" (Of what elements are they composed? What is there in clear consciousness, that is, what are its avowed sentiments, doctrines, etc.?); "The church, the school, and the family"; "Commercialized vice and the liquor traffic"; "The moral region"; "Temperament and social contagion"; and so on.[1] Could these newcomers assimilate and become American citizens? Put another way, Park and Burgess repeatedly return to the question of whether these immigrants would remain Poles and Slavs, living in isolated ghettos, cut off from the prospect and promise of a larger participation in American society.

Although they grappled with the scope and gravity of social and cultural uncertainty, these social scientists were quite clear about situating these immigrants unequivocally in an urban "zone of transition," a "slum" and "vice" district surrounding the "loop" or central business district where the habitués of Chinatown, Little Sicily, and the Black Belt roomed in flophouses near the underworld and a host of other unsavory practices and people. For Park and Burgess, this space, imagined as a broad ring bisected by single-use sectors, was liminal, like the people who resided there, and their choice of terminology—a zone of transition—reflected their interpretation. Park and Burgess describe this zone as marginal and heterogeneous, the site for a mix of land uses and activities and an unfortunate, if not threatening, commingling of people. The constant flux that characterized this zone set it apart from the homogeneous districts arrayed in an annular fashion beyond it, those parts of the city where land uses were segregated, where the users were of the "better sort," and where both were fixed, stable, and hence more progressive. The central business district was an anchor of commerce and power at the city's center, but the promised land for immigrants lay out in the single-use zones, first of apartment houses and then of single-family residences. Park's tidy diagram had the lasting effect of setting up an ascendant physical and social gradient. In it, value, status, and prestige increased in proportion to distance traveled away from the center toward the city's periphery.[2]

We know, as Park and Burgess knew, that immigrants came to Chicago and other American cities to work. They performed the difficult, dirty, and dangerous jobs of turning cattle and pigs into beef and pork, stoking the furnaces that fired ore in the city's foundries and mills, moving the goods on its wharves and railroad sidings, and extracting the resources above and below ground in the great northern forests. Industrialists depended on these unskilled and semiskilled laborers for production and trade. But why did immigrants leave an "old world" behind for the "new," especially when the latter seemed to promise so little? What were the push and pull factors that might explain their decision to leave places such as Sicily, Greece, Poland, and Belgium? Why, of all the possible destinations in the United States, did they choose to settle in Chicago? Park and Burgess imply, but never devote sustained attention to, the "why" and "what for" that might explain not only the immigration process itself but also, and more critically, the circumstances, real-life opportunities, and constraints within which these newcomers made choices and acted on their decisions.

Given the centrality of work and manufacturing in "the city" and in the lives of its inhabitants, it is all the more surprising that Park and Burgess were practically silent on the subject. Industrialization, the creation of large manufactories, the transition from artisan to industrial worker—these were the transformative processes of the nineteenth and early twentieth centuries. Yet about these, they have little to say. Moreover, because industrialization was so ubiquitous, an empirical account of social life in an industrial city could only have added to the interest and usefulness both for their contemporaries as well as for later generations of urbanists examining American cities. But there is more at stake here than merely an opportunity missed, given that the research agenda Park and Burgess set out in *The City* has, since its publication, served as *the* model for urban research. Indeed, their omissions have had a shaping influence on the role that industry and manufacturing have had in urban studies as well as in the larger literature on American cities.

My point is not that industry has played a minor role in urban studies, nor that scholars have overlooked or ignored the importance of workplace, industrial districts, unions, and union organizing in the lives of workers and their families and in the creation of working-class and mass culture. Quite the contrary, there is a rich literature devoted to such topics. Instead, I propose a different line of questioning aimed precisely at the silences and omissions in Park and Burgess's texts. This chapter is, therefore, meant as an empirical case study of the urbanization process in Los Angeles during the decades leading up to and including the 1920s. My intent, on one level, is to address lacunae in *The City*. Surprisingly, Burgess's hypothesis regarding a "centralized decentralized system of local communities" turns out to have been a prescient observation, useful for a historical investigation of the urbanization process in Southern California and other American cities.[3] By focusing on industry and industrial location, however, I hope to fill in a critical gap in this seminal work. Just as significant, an attention to industrial geography, industrial capital, and the role that these played in shaping a city such as Los Angeles has more general implications for urban studies. Although there is precious little in the 1925 volume about specific localities and how these were shaped and changed through time, my interest lies precisely in describing how industry and the creation of industrial districts have come to shape specific urban landscapes.

In 1923, Robert Park embarked on a longitudinal study of "all the phases of the problem of the Oriental in the United States" with a primary focus on the Pacific Coast.[4] Park assigned the task of overseeing the West Coast operation to a 1910 graduate in sociology from the University of Chicago, Emory S. Bogardus. Bogardus rose to prominence as a professor of sociology at the University of Southern California and as chair of the unit from 1915 to 1946. Bogardus was a prolific author and a prodigious mentor and, in addition, served as editor of the journal *Sociology and Social Research* for forty-five years (1916-1961). Among his publications are monographs on social groups (*The Mexican in the United States,* 1934), as well as textbooks on the discipline (*Introduction to Sociology,* 1917) and its methods (*Introduction to Social Research,* 1936). In the latter, Bogardus drew from his Chicago training and the survey work that he and his students conducted in Los Angeles. In a chapter on the "ecological approach," he updates the spatial framework he first learned in Chicago. Social problems involving people living in a given area may be viewed to advantage through ecology and call for a consideration of elements such as "population relationships, distances, and pressures. A study of physical location often explains social conflicts."

> People often seem to arrange themselves somewhat like iron filings do under the influence of magnetism. . . . [I]n any local community people are found distributed in spatial relationships somewhat after the manner of the "competitive cooperation" of plant communities. A preliminary examination of the ecology of a social conflict usually reveals natural areas where compatibles and incompatibles live together with boundaries marked off by hills, rivers, railroad tracks and yards, and industrial districts. These natural areas are to be distinguished from administrative and political areas that are set off by unreal and artificial lines on a map.[5]

There were, in effect, "magnetic" forces at work in Los Angeles during the 1910s, 1920s, and 1930s. There was nothing intrinsically "natural" about the urbanization process in this city, however, nor did industrial districts serve as boundaries marking off territory for "compatibles and incompatibles." On the contrary, social reformers and activists viewed the planned dispersion of industry as a means *toward* social uplift and improved living conditions for immigrants and working-class Angelenos.

In a 1907 reform tract, *The Better City,* Dana Bartlett, a Protestant cleric and urban progressive, waxed euphonically about the promise of Los Angeles. From its church-centered founding to the beneficent climate and increasing civic "patriotism," Bartlett cast his eyes on an "American city," where the foreign born "vied with his neighbor in devotion to high ideals," a city poised for greatness and, if residents heeded the social gospel, goodness. In its setting and development, to date, Los Angeles had avoided the blight Bartlett attributed to Chicago, New York, and other eastern cities. "Ugliness," he wrote, "has no commercial or ethical value. The crowded tenement and rookery, a city's ill-kept streets and yards, are not incentives to higher living." Los Angeles, by contrast, was a "city of homes, without slums." There might be "slum people," Bartlett confessed, but "no slums in the sense of vicious, congested districts." Here the "poor live in single cottages, with dividing fences and flowers in the front yard, and oftentimes with vegetables in the back yard." The notable exception, cited to prove the rule, was the house courts along Utah Street, east of the Los Angeles River, occupied by laborers "brought in from Mexico to work on the trolley."[6]

Whether hidden by flowers or open to view, those factories posed a considerable challenge. In Bartlett's lifetime, the "call of the factory whistle [had become] louder and more insistent than the sweet music of the mission bells," as the City of Angels as a "city of homes" steadily gave way to the emerging industrial center. This process was particularly visible in a zone lying between Alameda Street and the Los Angeles River from Ninth Street north to Elysian Park, which came to be known as the East Side Industrial District. In many ways, this moniker was a misnomer because although there were a number of manufacturing concerns in this district, it was a polyglot landscape of the type most urbanists associate with the teeming central area in Chicago and New York. In Los Angeles, this mixed-use zone contained an extraordinary diversity of land uses and activities as well as of people who lived and worked there.

Walking along North Main from Alameda to Sotello streets, Bartlett would have passed by foundries, boiler works, pattern makers' shops, and both Llewellyn and Western iron works. Interspersed among these firms were a Salvation Army store, two groceries, a number of restaurants and saloons, as well as residences ranging from single-family dwellings to apartments and furnished rooms. Writing in 1919, following a survey of this district, the California Commission of Immigration and Housing deduced that "surely life can not be normal in an area so much given over to industry, where there must of necessity be noise, grime, confusion, unpleasant odors, and nothing restful or beautiful to look upon." True to his politics and position, Bartlett imagined this mix of uses and people as an obstacle to be overcome. He shared the progressive vision, advanced by public health professionals, social workers, and advocates for urban improvement and city planning, that the proper solution to this problem was a parceling of land uses, people, and activities to create a more orderly, rational, efficient city.[7]

Danger lurked in the prospect that Los Angeles might come to resemble those eastern cities, and Bartlett feared that "as factories increase in size and number, aliens will be attracted, tenements and house courts will become congested, causing an increase in sickness and crime." Salvation would be ensured if industrialists took up the cause and became architects of the better city. "No modern industrial movement," Bartlett wrote, "means more for the welfare of the working people than the transfer of manufacturing plants from the crowded city to the country where, with better housing conditions, better sanitation, fresh air, greater freedom from temptation, and with flowers and parks and bright work rooms, life seems worth the living."[8] Supporters of urban improvement believed a rational, orderly dispersion of jobs and people would benefit the majority, if not all, Angelenos. In this 1907 tract, then, Bartlett evoked an imaginative geography that would inform city building in

Los Angeles for decades, a vision of manufacturing facilities and working-class residences moving out from the city center and into the surrounding country.[9]

Yet Bartlett was no prophet, and Los Angeles, and other American cities, did not expand along the lines he envisioned. Because of his perceptiveness, however, it is worth considering the ways that industry has shaped, and continues to shape, Los Angeles and Southern California. Even as Park and Burgess were composing their tract on urbanization under industrial capitalism, the 1920s witnessed a new vision for Los Angeles. During this decade, civic elites, entrepreneurs, and workers fixed the coordinates for an industrial region that has structured the pattern of city building and urban life from that time forward, as industrialists, in concert with developers, design professionals, and other city builders, helped shape the precise nature of urban expansion in the region.

In the examination of the creation of industrial Los Angeles as a material artifact, with its particular production landscapes and social patterns, a concomitant creation must also be considered: the construction of industrial Los Angeles in narratives about Southern California. At first glance, this may appear to be an unlikely topic of investigation, one that could offer insights into culture, perhaps, but that might not provide much in the way of explanatory power for questions of lived experience or policy. As recent scholarship has shown, however, cultural practices such as the plotting and dissemination of stories about manufacturing prowess and the spatial reach of local capital are not simply fabrications or passive reflections. Often, these narratives serve as instruments that people leverage as a means toward acting on the world. For this inquiry, we might ask, simply, who told what stories, when, and with what effect or effects.[10]

Finally, a study of industrial Los Angeles during the 1920s should be situated within the expanding literature on the history of the western United States. Such a path of inquiry would contribute to a general reinterpretation of the relationship between financial interests in East Coast and Midwest cities such as Chicago and urban development in the intermountain area and along the Pacific slope. As was the case in the nineteenth century, investments by Chicagoans, New Yorkers, and other capitalists provided the financial wherewithal mandatory for controlling land, creating infrastructure, constructing manufacturing plants, and commanding labor. Just as critical, however, the story of industrial Los Angeles is a regional one. Through time, civic elites, businesspeople, and residents in western and West Coast cities transformed these settlements from mercantile centers dependent on outsiders for goods and the means of exchange to command-and-control centers, with Los Angeles, for example, playing an increasingly important role in international trade and production networks through the twentieth century.

INDUSTRY AND URBAN GROWTH

If we return to Bartlett's tract with these themes in mind, we find that his assessment generates as many questions as it might possibly answer. There are the obvious contradictions, such as his pronouncement that Los Angeles is a city without tenements and slums, poised to be overrun by "aliens" who will then congest the tenements and house courts. His language and terminology do as much to beg further explanation as they do to clarify his argument. To give just one example, what, precisely, would it mean to have a "city" freed of production and manufacturing located in the "country"? Finally, there is an imaginative and idealized coupling of industry and nature; factories with bright workrooms and fresh air surrounded by parks and humble yet uplifting cottages, the latter housing workers and their families who are invited to inhale the "golden smoke" of industry.[11] The contrast between this "vision" and the "reality" that Park and Burgess mapped in Chicago is quite striking. As we shall see, however, the ways in which industry shaped urban development and the actual conditions in Chicago and Los Angeles resembled each other more closely than such a contrast might suggest.

Simply put, Bartlett's proposal called for a spatial fix. His program required a pruning and thinning out in the congested districts to alleviate unhealthy physical conditions such as overcrowding. Out in less densely settled sections of the city, workers could construct single-family dwellings surrounded by open space, light, and air. Here, according to Bartlett, although the "walls may be only the thickness of a single board, [a worker's house] covered in vines and flowers . . . equals in comfort an Eastern palace."[12] Intended to acculturate immigrants through industrial employment and a normative standard of living, Bartlett's description encompasses a part of the Americanizing project. During the subsequent decade, sociologists, health professionals, and housing reformers would offer alternative assessments of conditions in the congested districts, but their prescriptions for change remained consistent with Bartlett's vision. As I will explain, this was a complex process, and the various agents involved articulated different objectives and means for achieving their intentions. Often, the visions of reformers, industrialists, land developers, and workers were contradictory and conflicting, and, at all times, they were engaged in sometimes overt and other times covert contests over the nature and pattern of city building in Los Angeles.

Of course, any chance of realizing some version of Bartlett's vision hinged on the interests of industrialists, particularly their locational decisions, and on a continued expansion of industry in the region. The latter became increasingly critical during the 1920s because during the decade, more and more people chose to move to Greater Los Angeles. Given this fact, it is important to consider the magnitude of industrial expansion in the region in a national context. Contemporary accounts, written to capture the emergence of Los Angeles as a significant center for industry, relied overwhelmingly on quantitative assessments with associated charts and graphs. These graphics displayed an ascending trajectory, intended to suggest that continued expansion was not only expected but inevitable.[13]

This accounting of industrial progress, to use a phrase that boosters trotted out routinely, can never convey the nature and texture of change in Los Angeles during the 1920s. But to a considerable extent, the nature of this change can be traced back to the acres of land developed with the facilities and infrastructure necessary for manufacturing, the increasing number of firms setting up plants in the Southland, the rising employment in industrial production, the innovation in products and production processes, and the enhanced array of goods available from local suppliers, as well as less flattering, and therefore less often noted, attributes such as pollution and an increase in physical and social congestion. Still, it is instructive to review the numbers.

During the decade, the total land area of the city increased by approximately eighty square miles through forty-five annexations, and the population grew from 577,000 to almost 1.24 million. Population in the county increased 240 percent, from just over 900,000 residents in 1920 to more than 2.2 million in 1930, the latter translating into an average of 350 newcomers a day.[14] During these years, civic elites noted with escalating concern that it would require more than tourism, land speculation, and services to provide employment for all the new residents streaming into the Southland. By 1930, the promotion of industrial expansion to meet this perceived shortfall between wage earners and jobs—a call that the Los Angeles Area Chamber of Commerce (LAACC; also known as Los Angeles Chamber of Commerce) first issued in the 1910s as a novel adjunct to the standard promotional litany of year-round sunshine, recreation, and an expropriated Spanish culture—had become the equivalent of a civic mantra.[15]

As Robert Fogelson has shown, the plea for weaning the regional economy off the "tourist crop" and real estate speculation and reorienting it toward industry was advanced with an ever increasing measure of urgency.[16] A *Los Angeles Times* editorial, "Balanced Progress," published November 18, 1923, articulates this particular view of existing conditions by advancing a single vision of the region's future. Los Angeles, the editors declared, "stands at the dawn of a golden tomorrow." But although they gazed out on a city "glittering" with promise and opportunity, the future was "fraught with great problems" because population growth routinely "staggered all power of anticipation." (Keep in mind that this statement was crafted at the beginning of the even greater increases of the 1920s.) According to the newspaper, it was time

> for us to see to it that the various forces that go to make up this terrific expansion are kept working in even and balanced effort. . . . New industries must be established to provide a stable means for the largest possible number of people to make their living. . . . This vast hegira of people who are rushing into Los Angeles must find a way to work and make their living. They can't go on indefinitely supporting themselves by building each other houses and selling lots. As roofs are built to cover their heads, big industries must be developed to give them means to earn money. Whenever population outruns industry, stagnation follows. The principal industry of this city at the present time is building new houses. Other industries of more stable and permanent character must be planted and encouraged.[17]

What would it take to achieve this objective? The *Times* identified a list of needs, the majority of which related to urban infrastructure—water and power, an expanded harbor, solutions for traffic congestion, police protection, schools, and parks. But it also required "men with a large enough vision, prophetic instinct, and practical unselfishness to make these dreams come true." Finally, this vision demanded that the city reach "further into the back country. To get coal and iron and wool and cotton to feed the industries which will grow; we will be compelled to add great areas of tributary country."[18] I will consider much of this inventory but first want to highlight the call for territorial expansion, a project of annexation, whether political, economic, or cultural, that would dominate the agenda of movers and shakers in Los Angeles throughout the decade.

For a comparative statistical assessment of change throughout the decade, I turn to a special report produced by the industrial department of the LAACC for Henry M. Robinson, chairman of the board of Pacific Southwest Trust and Savings. This accounting shows that in eight short years (1919 to 1927), industrial output in the county had increased from just over $400 million to almost $1 billion—an advance of more than 140 percent. Comparable records for the city reveal an increase of almost 500 percent, from $103 million in 1914 to just over $610 million in 1927. In 1929, Los Angeles County, which had begun the decade as the twenty-eighth leading manufacturing center in the nation, had advanced in the rankings to number nine. Between 1925 and 1927, the county was second only to Flint, Michigan, in the percentage increase in value added, fourth behind New York, Flint, and Milwaukee in dollar value of output, and fifth in value added by manufacturing wage earner.[19]

When the LAACC's industrial department handed over its report, Los Angeles County led the nation in motion picture production, was second in the manufacture of automobile tires and tubes, and "leads all cities west of Chicago" in the production of bakery products, canned fish, machine shop products, furniture, ice cream, printing and publishing, pumps, structural and ornamental iron work, wall plaster and wallboard, and window shades and coverings. Notably absent in this account is any explicit analysis and interpretation of how this change came about. Readers are left to assume that the chamber's efforts to set industrial development on a "firm foundation" resulted in the construction of urban infrastructure; the attraction, training, and retention of skilled workers and salaried employees; and the appearance of investment capital in amounts adequate to finance development of this magnitude.[20]

A third source of information provides a timeline that allows us to put the 1920s in longitudinal perspective. In 1937, a New Deal agency, the Federal Housing Administration (FHA), undertook a housing market analysis of Los Angeles city and county. The administration's Division of Economics and Statistics produced a dense statistical portrait of regional development that included their assessment of L.A.'s dramatic growth during the 1920s. They attributed the "upswing" to seven factors: a westward drift in the population; good marketing; climate and soils conducive to specialized agriculture; tourism and retiree resettlement; oil, oil refining, and associated industries; the motion picture industry; and the "rapid expansion of manufacturing industries."[21] FHA surveyors mined the U.S. Department of Commerce's bidecennial census of manufactures for text, graphics, and statistical abstracts that chart the emergence of Los Angeles as an industrial center.

Their findings contextualize the chamber's brief for Robinson using data for the city reaching back to 1899. At that time, the "economic interests of the city were

largely centered upon growing fruit and raising cattle," and the total value of manufactured products recorded for that year amounted to just over $15 million. During
the next five years, that figure increased to almost $35 million (+130 percent) with
meat packing alone adding $4 million in value as well as significant output in print-
ing, foundry and machine shops, flour and grist milling, and planing mill products.
A decade later (1914), production from the city's industries topped $100 million for
the first time, and by 1919, production had increased to $300 million.[22]

The FHA enumerators placed this expansion in industry and output in a state
and national context. Data for 1919 and 1929 show a significant increase for the Los
Angeles industrial area (the same as Los Angeles County) relative to the remainder of
California. This is true concerning the number of wage earners employed (up from
25 percent of the state total in 1919 to 37 percent in 1929), the percentage of the
total number of manufacturing establishments in the state (from 29 percent to 40
percent), and the value of product (21 percent to 40 percent). Included in the
regional market analysis were annual compendia of "important, nationally-known
manufacturers" that established branch factories in Los Angeles. The list for 1929
featured American Brake Shoe & Foundry Co. (Chicago), Bethlehem Steel Corp.
(N.Y.), the Joslyn Company (Chicago), National Lead Co. (N.Y.), Procter & Gam-
ble (Cincinnati), U.S. Steel Corp. (N.Y.), and Willard Storage Battery Co. (Cleveland). The FHA timeline also quantified the effects of the Depression downturn on
Southern California and the relatively rapid return, in most sectors by 1934 to 1935,
to the heights first achieved in the late 1920s. By 1935, Los Angeles had advanced
from ninth to seventh in the national rankings of industrial areas.[23]

What did this statistical evidence of an emergent manufacturing prowess mean
for industrial workers? First, during the decade, their numbers, countywide, grew
from just over 61,000 to almost 106,000.[24] Second, by 1930, 28 percent of Los
Angeles workers received their paychecks from manufacturing, the greatest percentage of any occupational classification.[25] Third, during the decade, a number of these
workers enjoyed an increase in hourly wages. A comparison of city-level aggregate
data reported in the 1919 and 1929 census of manufactures shows that on average,
workers in some of the more significant industrial sectors such as meat packing and
foundry and machine shop products saw hourly wages rise approximately 50 and 75
percent, respectively.[26]

A study conducted by Helen Liggett, a special agent for the Department of
Labor's Bureau of Labor Statistics, provides precise data on wages and hours worked
in select industries from 1915 to 1920. Her findings reveal a wage increase of more
than 75 percent on average, with a notable advance in the skilled trades (+87.5 percent). Although these gains are impressive, they must be considered in light of an
even more robust 107 percent growth in the cost of living. If we compare the wages
Liggett recorded for 1919 with those the chamber provided Robinson in 1930, the
figures point to a slight rise in the hourly wages paid to skilled tradespeople such as
machinists, welders, molders, and structural steel workers, as well as carpenters,
cement finishers, hod carriers, plumbers, and other members of the building trades.
But there is also a notable lack of advance in the wages paid to day laborers and
unskilled workers. Although Liggett did not distinguish differing salary levels

among laborers, the chamber quoted one rate for "unskilled labor, American" (fifty to sixty cents an hour) and another, lower, wage for "unskilled labor, Mexican" (forty-five to fifty cents an hour). As for the cost of living at the end of the decade, when the Works Progress Administration quantified values for fifty-nine cities in 1935 on the basis of family expenditures for food, clothing, housing, and household operation, Los Angeles ranked tenth behind New York, Chicago, Detroit, Boston, Cleveland, and San Francisco.[27]

Although verifiably true, these statistical accounts conceal as much of the story as they reveal. At the time, it seemed that no matter how many new firms set up shop in the region and regardless of how many times existing plants expanded, there apparently would never be enough manufacturing employment to provide jobs for all the newcomers streaming into Southern California. Municipal efficiency expert Clarence Dykstra, who came to Los Angeles following tenure in similar posts in East Coast and Midwest cities, argued that Southern California reversed the "ordinary processes of municipalization. The attractiveness of life in this community draws, as with a magnet, thousands upon thousands each year who beg for a chance to make a living in this nature favored spot." Many of these newcomers worked in agriculture, while increasing numbers tried to "pry their way into industry." The problem, then, was the difficulty of providing an "economic foundation for [this] rapidly accumulating population."[28] At this point, it is important to note that Dykstra, who produced this assessment at about the same time that Park and Burgess were writing *The City*, shared the sociologists' belief that there was a normative, universal, and appropriate pattern for city growth. For Dykstra, economic expansion, and, specifically, industrial expansion, should set the pace and fix the scale for urban growth.

There was no question that Los Angeles, and, for that matter, other cities, would grow. Cities were progressive, and the demographic future was seen as a given. This belief was widespread in the 1920s in fiction, in the popular press, and in the work of pundits and scholars, including Park and Burgess. Dykstra was explicit about the relationship between manufacturing and jobs and makes this the raison d'être for continued urban expansion. Park and Burgess, on the other hand, were silent. If we, further, consider Dykstra's assessment of Los Angeles in light of the sociologists' concentric zone model, what we have, in effect, is a city missing one of its central rings, the "factory zone."

Also absent in presentations of L.A.'s industrial progress were the working poor who, if they were factored in at all, showed up as "all others" or "all other types" on the surveyors' decimally correct charts and graphs, as well as those workers who, by definition, were unemployed, unemployable, or undocumented and who, therefore, went uncounted. Many Angelenos absent in the manufacturing censuses and housing market surveys worked for the railroad and traction companies, in brick, lumber, and cement yards as teamsters and day laborers. These workers, many of them recent immigrants, were counted and their activities analyzed in a series of reports, articles, and theses examining living conditions in the "foreign districts" and the East Side Industrial District, the zone along the Los Angeles River that Bartlett first focused on in 1907.[29]

A "MEXICAN PROBLEM"

Through time, the accounts of residences, home life, and neighborhood along the river and adjacent to the plaza area show a correlation between race (principally Mexican) and place and the emergence of a persistent and virulent imaginative geography in the form of the Mexican slum or generic Sonoratown. During the 1910s, John Kienle, William McEuen, Emory Bogardus, Elizabeth Fuller, G. Bromley Oxnam, and the California Commission of Immigration and Housing found Mexican districts and identified a particular "Mexican problem." For example, in his 1916 study of 854 house courts and 1,202 families, Bogardus found that 298 families, or 25 percent of the total, were Mexican. He classified 32 percent (383) as American. Yet his report, "The House-Court Problem," fixed the dwelling type as only a Mexican problem, while stating that this classification is "of course more or less arbitrary." Fuller, a health care professional and settlement house resident, began her 1920 account by stating simply, "Due to the rapid industrial growth of Los Angeles, thousands of Mexicans are being attracted to [the city] yearly and the housing of these people becomes a current problem. Los Angeles, however, is doing little towards solving it." It is critical to note that although Fuller casts her work as a report on a citywide problem, her fieldwork was limited to six blocks in an area at the edge of the contiguously developed downtown. How could this reductionism be justified? Quite simply, it turns out, because Fuller notes that "instinctively, the Mexicans huddle together in certain districts."[30]

This perceived spatial concentration, however, belied the empirical data. The previous year (1919), the California Commission of Immigration and Housing published "A Community Survey Made in Los Angeles City," a comprehensive, quantitative accounting of eleven districts along both sides of the river. Surveyors recorded people of Mexican descent in each district. Adults from Mexico were the highest number of respondents in four districts and second highest in five. The percentages ranged from fifty-nine in District 11 and fifty-three in District 2 to twelve in District 4 and ten in District 1.[31] Yet Bogardus found a "Mexican house-court problem," and Fuller perceived an instinctive huddling. Their imaginative geographies reveal a conceptual distance that differentiated the reformers' perception of the city in 1920 from that of Dana Bartlett in 1907.

In his report of a 1920 survey of Mexicans in Los Angeles sponsored by the Interchurch World Movement of North America, the cleric and reformer Bromley Oxnam projected a "possible shift in Mexican population" if, or when, the city selected the plaza site for a Union passenger terminal. "This means that between five and ten thousand Mexicans will have to move to other sections of the city." He argued that some of the displaced would move to Palo Verde or cross the river and locate around Stephenson Avenue. "Still another group will seek the new Industrial District just south of the city limits. It will therefore be necessary for the church to look toward [these] sections for possible fields of community development." Oxnam shared Bogardus's and Fuller's perception of Mexican "sections" and a Mexican problem. Thirteen years after Bartlett first proposed a move out from the congested districts to the country, Oxnam renewed this call with a proposal for the "unplanned yet orderly dispersion" of manufacturing and working-class housing from the center city to surrounding zones, a demonstration of the persistence of the spatial fix and a particular imaginative geography.[32]

The "all others" population also appears, somewhat obliquely, in a 1926 survey of workers that Charles S. Johnson conducted for the National Urban League. Johnson, a sociologist trained at the University of Chicago, directed the league's Department of Research and Investigation. He found that many of the racialized attributes ascribed to Mexicans, Mexican Americans, southern Europeans, and African Americans in biased assessments of dwellings and surrounding spaces also prevailed in the workplace. Johnson's transcripts of interviews with business owners and plant managers reveal the ways that unfounded "racial beliefs" and "racial theories" determined not only who might enter plants but also the nature of participation on the shop floor and in the yard, as well as in the general physical and social relationships among white workers and their racialized counterparts.[33]

Johnson surveyed owners and plant managers in 456 industrial firms employing 75,754 workers and found that roughly 3 percent (or 2,239) were African American men. For observation and extended interviews, he selected 104 firms. Fifty-four firms had African American workers, fifty had none. The former included the majority of firms in Los Angeles with more than ten African American employees. Findings such as these subverted long-held stereotypes. For example, he found a distinct lack of specialization—"Whatever is elsewhere evident of the special use of Negroes for special things, the plants which employ them [in Los Angeles] found them adaptable over a rather wide range"—and did not find a significant differential in the wages paid African Americans and whites for similar occupations. He did, however, uncover a remarkable variance in perception, policies, and practices regarding "racial contacts in industry." Popularly held "race theories" were diametrically opposed; some proprietors believed Mexicans were white and white workers accepted them, others held that Mexicans were colored and white workers objected to Mexicans but accepted Negroes. As Johnson put it, "Plants of the same type in the same city declare precisely opposite facts as inherent in Negro nature." Johnson concluded that plant policies designed to address questions of race mixing were based on unsubstantiated beliefs, a majority of which could be traced to plant owners. The standard practice, however, was to limit race mixing, and plants were parsed spatially through the institution of overt and covert policies designed to enforce segregation. These policies, and the imaginative geographies that informed them, meant that most African Americans who worked in industry during the 1920s were employed as members of work crews with discrete tasks and well-defined boundaries that delimited the workplace into zones where they were permitted and those where they were denied.[34]

Now that we have an understanding of how reformers and social scientists envisioned industry, urban expansion, and social patterns in 1920s Los Angeles, we need to consider questions of location and city building. What types of firms were establishing plants in the Los Angeles industrial area? Where did they choose to develop? How did their decisions contribute to the process of urbanization or city building? What type of city had emerged from these decisions?

BRANCH PLANT AND BACKCOUNTRY EMPIRES

If we turn our attention to city boosters, developers, and planners, we find imaginative geographies distinct from those advanced by clerics and social workers. For example, most developers and boosters joined industrialists in articulating boundaries between the races, and their advertisements and sales promoted ownership for white workers. There were considerable overlaps, however, and at least two salient points of intersection. First, both groups shared a belief that industry should be zoned for discrete segments of the city and segregated by type. Second, both encouraged development that surrounded these production landscapes with a complement of residences, services, and community institutions. This pattern, to a degree, agreed with Burgess's assessment in "The Growth of the City," specifically with the approving reference to a study of British conurbations. The pattern described there, however, was of regional agglomeration with remnant "nuclei of denser town growth, most of which represent the central areas of the various towns from which [the conurbation] has grown." Burgess found a similar process under way in New York and Chicago, and although he did not look to California, the same was true in Los Angeles as well as the San Francisco Bay Area.[35] Yet missing from these descriptions and explanations was any causal accounting of the processes through which conurbations were created and the means through which the interstitial zones around existing nuclei were transformed from open space, agricultural production, or low-density settlements into more densely developed parts of the metropolis.

Archives also offer records that illuminate aspects of the urbanization process. One particularly rich source is the minutes of the Los Angeles Area Chamber of Commerce, an association of business owners, financiers and investors, and professionals that formed one of the most powerful private sector institutions active in any American city. The minutes of a January 1922 meeting, for instance, reveal that these boosters and rentiers engaged in a rancorous debate regarding the relative merits of "opening up" San Pedro Street to industry—a move, they duly noted, guaranteed to antagonize voters in Boyle Heights. On one level, this debate focused on the location for Westinghouse's first Los Angeles facility. No one in attendance was opposed to the move itself. On the contrary, the entire board congratulated A. G. Arnoll, a chamber director who had been working six months to persuade Westinghouse to set up shop in their city rather than in Oakland. The only question was where the firm should locate. The proposal before the board called for a site at the corner of Ninth Street and San Pedro. Embedded in the resolution, however, was an implicit proposal to transform San Pedro into a "wholesale district"; as chamber president Weaver noted, "All those who do not believe in it as a wholesale section and who do not want [the construction of additional] grade crossings will be in opposition." The opposition—directors Crandell, Fredericks, and Osterloh—argued for a Vernon location where there is "plenty of vacant ground served by three railroads only twenty minutes from 7th and Broadway."[36]

This inflammatory session witnessed directors opposed to a downtown-adjacent siting making unsavory comparisons with New York, Pittsburgh, and St. Louis and President Weaver arguing that he was all for "giving Los Angeles the advantages those cities have." Although united in principle, these antagonists were drawing precise distinctions between different types of industry, the exact needs of particular firms, the appropriate location for various manufacturing activities, and, most critical, the optimal pattern of land uses in Los Angeles. The geography of industry, as the majority defined it, had retail stores and offices in the central business district, surrounded by warehouses and jobbers serving this downtown core, and production segregated to outlying districts such as Vernon, the Union Pacific's Metropolitan Warehouse and Industrial District, and the Southern Pacific's tracts in present-day Commerce.[37] Note the functional similarity to the Chicago School model.

In *The Fragmented Metropolis,* Robert Fogelson documented the chamber's efforts to set growth in the city and region on a firm industrial foundation. This assessment and similar arguments derive their explanatory power from the stated or implied imposition of external financing and business control.[38] In one sense, the chamber's industrial department had followed a proved strategy, cajoling Eastern and Midwestern industrialists to Southern California, a process similar to the successful appeal for residents to migrate from these regions. One sector, rubber and tire production, can provide some sense of the scale and rapidity of such changes. In 1919, when Goodyear decided to build a Southland plant, only a few independent firms were in operation, producing less than 1 percent of the national output. A decade later, after Firestone, Goodrich, and U.S. Rubber—the nation's number two, three, and four producers—had followed suit, the region's share had grown to 6 percent, which translated into 35,000 tires and 40,000 tubes a day. During that time, employment went from a few hundred workers to more than 5,000, almost 7 percent of the industry total, and annual output reached a value of $56 million. L.A.'s location and transit infrastructure were critical factors for access to raw materials and for the sale of finished goods. Goodyear and Firestone subsidiaries in L.A. supply the intermountain and Pacific states including Alaska and Hawaii.[39]

But as the chamber exchange makes clear, the creation of industrial Los Angeles was just as much a local initiative. As Goodyear and Firestone executives were divvying up the continent into what economist Frank Kidner labeled "branch plant empires," Los Angeles entrepreneurs and civic elites were turning their spatial imaginations to the creation of a "backcountry" empire.[40] Through time, the spatial reach of this trade and the pattern of the branch plant network meant that Los Angeles assumed a more prominent position in the nation's urban system. In other words, the formation of branch plant empires, an endeavor that combined external coordination with local capital and initiative, was part of a dynamic process through which Southern Californian business leaders recast the city and region to their advantage.

In his 1926 article, "Los Angeles, A Miracle City," Edgar Lloyd Hampton imagined the city and its hinterlands in regard to raw materials and resource extraction. "The West," he wrote, "is largely composed of these commodities [and] Los Angeles is especially fortunate." He drew his map to include Mexico and all the states on the arid side of the Rocky Mountains where "almost every known basic metal is on a down-grade haul to Los Angeles harbor." Immodest and imperial, Hampton's vision was, nonetheless, consistent with the principles and strategies that had shaped development in the American West. The novelty was that now Southern California would assume the role of entrepôt, usurping the position that East Coast and Midwest cities had held, to become the control center for western resources and products.[41] Bromley Oxnam envisioned the city's emergent status and asserted it succinctly in a diary entry following his visit to the 1922 Pageant of Progress at Exposition Park: "From the moment one enters . . . to the last, after miles and miles of exhibits, the bewildering progress of manufacturing Los Angeles is before the eyes. A generation ago we bought everything from the East. Today we make our stuff and control the West."[42]

This transition signaled the emergence of Los Angeles as the epicenter of a city-centered region whose entrepreneurs and financiers would exercise influence over dependent territories. It represented enhanced material and symbolic connections in national and international systems of trade and culture as well as an extension of local authority. Like their counterparts in Chicago and New York, Los Angeles entrepreneurs sought to control the hinterlands two ways, as a center for processing and converting resources but also as a center for creating ideas and marketing culture to shape preferences for consumer goods and exchange.[43]

The historical record suggests that Angelenos also perceived the city dichotomously. In 1924, George Law stated boldly in the *Los Angeles Times* that to understand Los Angeles, it was necessary to motor south through the manufacturing district. "The rest of the city, from the winsome foothills to the glittering beaches, when viewed alone does not convey an adequate idea of the true situation. Along with all that it has been in the past, this city is now an industrial entity." A drive from the East Side southward would bring into view what Law imagined as a stage for the newest and biggest act in the great L.A. drama. "The air," he continued, "is filled with industrial haze and queer smells, huge trucks trundle along paved thoroughfares. Here then is the new city; it is not amusements or tourists, it is industrial production."[44]

PLANNING FOR INDUSTRY AND HOUSING

This interpretation can be extended through a consideration of two factors neglected in most studies of urban growth and city building in Southern California, the workplace-residence link and planning. In Los Angeles, as elsewhere, industrialists, investors, planners, and wage earners envisioned a tight and desirable link between the workplace, residence, and local institutions. Design professionals and real estate interests, often acting in concert, devised policy and adopted practices that promoted and supported this form of development. The following section turns to the area east of the Los Angeles River and the Central Manufacturing District (now part of Vernon) to illustrate these points.

In 1925, the Chicago-based engineering firm Kelker, De Leuw & Co. presented a report to the Los Angeles city council and the county board of supervisors with recommendations for a comprehensive rapid transit plan. In the appendixes, four diagrams fix the distribution of residences and the place of work for persons employed in the central business district (27,022 total), the East Side Industrial District (11,080), the Vernon Industrial District (2,507), and the North Side Industrial District (2,184). Contrary to the received narrative regarding traction, residential dispersion, and sprawl (generally presented as the alpha and omega of a Los Angeles growth machine), in 1925, a significant percentage of workers employed in the East Side and North Side industrial districts lived within walking distance to work. Between one fifth and one third of all workers employed in the East Side, Vernon, and North Main districts lived less than two miles from their place of employment. This is the equivalent of the standard distance that urbanists accept as a metric for the preindustrial walking city. It is also contrary to the Chicago School's transit determinism. Although it is not labeled in the concentric zone diagram, their model of "the" city is crisscrossed with a series of radials corresponding to the trolley and streetcar lines that connected the urban periphery with an urban core. In Los Angeles, a three-mile circle captures more than one third of workers in North Main, one half of those employed in Vernon, and three fifths of East Side workers.[45] From this, it is clear that proximity to work was an important consideration for workers located in the established "factory zone."

For many workers, restrictions on employment opportunities, the place of residence, or both determined the physical and social parameters of everyday life. Whether legal or extralegal, these restrictions delineated and configured urban space in 1920s Los Angeles. In 1904, the Los Angeles city council approved an ordinance restricting certain industrial uses in a residential area. This was followed, in 1908 and 1909, by statutes that parsed the city into two residential and seven industrial districts. The next year, a January ordinance designated as residential all city land not falling within the industrial districts. Although designed to protect single-family housing, this legislation promoted dispersed industrial clusters that in turn encouraged manufacturers and developers of these tracts to plan for working-class housing and services in close proximity to employment.[46]

This pattern of development is found in a wedge-shaped segment of the county east of the Los Angeles River between Whittier Boulevard and Gage Avenue extending out to Montebello and then south along the Rio Hondo. This zone encompasses parts of Boyle Heights, East Los Angeles, Commerce, Vernon, and Bell. During the 1920s, it was the site of intensive development, as, within these boundaries, industrial real estate agents such as W. H. Daum leased or sold property to B. F. Goodrich, Samson Tyre and Rubber, Union Iron Works, Truscon Steel, Okeefe and Merritt, Illinois Glass, and Angelus Furniture. Daum began his career as an industrial agent for the Atchison, Topeka, and Santa Fe Railroad and opened his own Los Angeles firm in 1913, where during the next four decades, he helped set the pattern for industrial dispersion in the region. Through a series of holding companies, he managed property in the East Side Industrial District between Central Avenue and the river. At the same time, he was developing sections of Vernon and property along Slauson Avenue. In some cases, Daum leased land in these new industrial tracts to firms such as the Pacific Coast Planing Company, which were moving from parcels he held in the East Side District.[47]

Concomitant with Daum and other real estate agents' industrial programs, firms such as the Janss Investment Company, J. B. Ransom Corporation, Walter H. Leimert and Co., and Carlin G. Smith were promoting residential development in Belvedere Gardens, Samson Park, Bandini, Montebello Park, City Terrace, and Eastmont. Smith noted that Eastmont, his first subdivision on the East Side, was "neighbor to a mighty payroll . . . facing a destined city of factories. The amazing development of the great East Side—teeming with its expanses of moderate priced homes—has become almost overnight one of the most startling features of the city's growth." The Janss Company, better known for Westwood, Holmby Hills, and other exclusive Westside projects, had been developing Belvedere Heights, now part of Boyle Heights, and then Belvedere Gardens since 1905. By 1922, the firm was concentrating on parcels adjacent to the Hostetter Tract, site of Sears-Roebuck's regional distribution center and department store, and adding its voice to calls for street widening to provide for the anticipated 25,000 new residents "who will make their homes in Belvedere Gardens owing to the great industrial program inaugurated for this section."[48]

Walter H. Leimert began his career as a land subdivider in the San Francisco East Bay cities of Oakland and Piedmont, but timing his move to Los Angeles in 1923 to coincide with municipal growth, Leimert coordinated a series of industrial and residential ventures. Although he is best known for Leimert Park (1927), near Baldwin Hills, his first projects in the region were on the East Side, specifically City Industrial Tract along Alhambra Avenue and the adjacent residential district, City Terrace, a "veritable city of working men's homes." Here Leimert's partners included financiers Joseph Sartori, W. G. McAdoo, Irvin Hellman, and Charles Toll. Their sales strategy included a "build your own home campaign" with a single price tag for lot and lumber as well as the option for buyers to set up a tent or other impermanent structure until they could afford to build a permanent dwelling. The Ransom Company's Bandini tract, "The 'Miracle City' of the East Side," and Montebello Park offered lots and houses to workers who wanted to "live in pleasant surroundings, near their work, and yet close to down-town Los Angeles." The Bandini community package included a grade school, proximity to two high schools, and access to the commercial development anticipated along Washington and Atlantic Boulevards.[49]

Through time, the development process varied, and districts took different forms. One type, with obvious parallels in Chicago, is the model industrial satellite. In 1911, Jared Sidney Torrance, an entrepreneur who made his fortune in railroads, real estate, and oil (the Southern California trinity), announced plans for an industrial city. The timing, relative to the bombings at the *Los Angeles Times* and Llewellyn Iron Works and Job Harriman's mayoral bid, was not incidental. Torrance incorporated the Dominguez Land Corporation with financier Joseph J. Sartori (Security Pacific Bank), purchased 2,800 acres in southwest Los Angeles, and hired F. L. Olmsted Jr. and Irving Gill as designers. Olmsted's site plan centered on a transit gateway where visitors and residents disembarked into a civic center with theater, public library, and linear park leading to small, detached, workingmen's cottages. Industrial development was piecemeal, although contemporary accounts lauded the application of protective zoning that attracted "non-speculative ownership in large tracts." In 1916, Dominguez Land donated a 125-acre parcel to the Pacific Electric Railway for its construction and repair yard, a predictable gambit in the internecine politics of urban growth. Union Tool Company, a 25 percent stakeholder in the investment, remained its largest employer into the 1920s. During this decade, Columbia Steel Corporation, Western Sheet Glass, Llewellyn Iron Works, Pacific Metal Products, Hendrie Rubber, and numerous other firms established plants in Torrance.[50]

Promotional materials and publicity photographs for the East Side residential tracts and Torrance's model community depict houses under construction on apparently vacant land. Like other frontiers, the crabgrass frontier on the East Side and in southwest Los Angeles required an imagined and, in some cases, actual removal of particular groups. Advertisements for the small, working-class cottages that took the place of self-built or "makeshift" quarters made it clear that industrialists and land developers envisioned the new "miracle city" as an Anglo-only enclave. In Vernon, for example, the creation of the Central Manufacturing District meant displacing residents from an existing "Mexican village" and tearing down this "colonia" and similar dwellings along Twenty-Sixth Street. In Torrance, zoning excluded "noncaucasians" who were required to live outside the city proper in areas designated "special quarters" on land use maps.[51]

Goodyear, which constructed a $6 million branch plant on Central Avenue at Gage in 1919, an event the *Los Angeles Times* proclaimed as the "most momentous industrial announcement ever made" in the city, provides another variant on the coupling of manufacturing and housing. A follow-up article in the *Times*, "Will Build Model Village," describes the firm's plans for Goodyear Park, an 800-unit, "industrial residential district" sited immediately adjacent to the plant. Here, the company drew lessons from Goodyear Heights, Ohio, company president Frank Sieberling's response to the 1913 strike called by Akron rubber workers. Although the company did not build its model community in Los Angeles, it did take credit for the creation of a satellite industrial district. Goodyear published images showing "Yesterday" and "Today," taken in 1920 and 1928, to illustrate "how the surrounding territory had built up and filled in" and "how industrial development affects city growth."[52]

Other nationally prominent firms, including Swift & Company, Phelps-Dodge, U.S. Steel, Willys-Overland, and Liquid Carbonic, established branch plants in Los Angeles during the 1920s. Swift & Company joined local firms such as Deshell Laboratory, Reo Motor, and Sperry Soap in a 300-acre development planned, constructed, and managed by Chicagoans John Spoor, A. G. Leonard, and Halsey Poronto, prominent members of the syndicate responsible for that city's Central Manufacturing District. In Los Angeles, these entrepreneurs purchased part of the Arcadia Bandini estate, rancho land that had been held in trust and leased for cattle grazing and farming until 1922, and recast the site for modern industry with large, single-story, fireproof buildings; top-of-the-line services and amenities; and low taxes. Apropos of their Chicago venture, the first phase of development centered on a 100-acre livestock market and the construction of a central administration building, a terminal warehouse, and a manufacturers' building with leasable production and storage space for small firms. The remaining acreage they subdivided into 125 parcels with switch track connections for sale or lease to manufacturing firms. The syndicate offered prospective lessees and buyers financing and construction assistance and infrastructure improvements including parkways, landscaping, ornamental street lighting, and the Los Angeles Junction Railway, a beltline with direct connection to all trunk lines entering the city.[53]

Vernon annexed the Central Manufacturing District in 1925. Then, in 1929, the Chicago syndicate sold out to the Atchison, Topeka, & Santa Fe Railroad, which purchased the remaining 2,000 acres of the Bandini estate and extended track and industry west into the remainder of Vernon and east into Commerce. Workers resided in Maywood, Huntington Park, and Bell. The latter, "an island of homes in a sea of industry," was an unincorporated community of 9,000 with direct bus service to the central manufacturing district.[54] By 1930, this configuration had become such a standard that Thomas Coombs, an engineer with the Los Angeles City Planning Commission, could state simply,

> The work shops of the city, the industrial and manufacturing district, should be selected with great care . . . far enough from the residential section . . . but not so located as to make traveling between the two a disadvantage. These areas should be large [with] a small part reserved for a local business center. Before it is possible to intelligently subdivide a city, all these subjects should be given careful consideration and well planned.[55]

How, we might ask, did contemporaries perceive and comprehend this reconfiguration of urban space? In 1922, the Los Angeles County Board of Supervisors sponsored a conference on regional planning. A diagram in the published proceedings offers a model of that city quite different from the Chicago School diagram. These engineers, elected officials, and design professionals found the "whole district crystallizing around natural centers and subcenters. The nucleus is the business center of Los Angeles. Beyond the five or six mile circle we find sub-centers developing, each with its own individual character and identity." In effect, they envisioned a network of villages connected by transit, all forming a dispersed but coherent region. Their diagram represented the expanding metropolis in similar fashion to the British study of conurbations that Burgess quotes in "The Growth of the City," rather than the concentric rings he imagined from the empirical work he and his colleagues conducted. In Los Angeles, the urbanists studying regional development could claim an empirical basis for such findings in Bandini, Inglewood, Hollywood, and Pasadena, to cite examples from each of the geographical sectors, which all functioned as discrete satellites within a comprehensive and comprehensible metropolitan orbit.[56]

If participants in the Pasadena and subsequent conferences had chosen to plot the location of firms engaged in the movie and aircraft industries, the map they produced would have coincided with their diagram of urban growth. Although the initial movie colony settled in Hollywood, by 1915 the chamber of commerce's directory of manufacturers recorded considerable dispersal. Firms existed in Long Beach, Santa Monica, Mount Washington, and multiple districts in between, and there were also significant secondary concentrations. That same year, Thomas Ince established a studio in Harry Culver's new community on the former Rancho Ballona eight miles west of city hall. Within five years, Goldwyn Pictures, the Henry Lehrman Studios, Sanborn Laboratories, and the Maurice Tourneur Film Company had joined the Ince studio in Culver City, making it the "greatest producer of pictures in the world" after Hollywood.[57]

Industrial location for aircraft and parts, a critical sector for understanding industry and urban expansion in Southern California, fits within this model as well. The origins of Southern California's vaunted aircraft (and later aerospace) industry can be traced to small, undercapitalized companies renting office and plant space in warehouses and loft buildings in the East Side Industrial District before acquiring more suitable sites along the then urban fringe. Glenn L. Martin founded the first Los Angeles firm in 1912. Previously, a crew of mechanics under his direction had been assembling biplanes in a Methodist church and later a cannery in Santa Ana, but the company relocated its plant into a three-story former bedding and upholstery shop with a first-floor storefront at 943 South Los Angeles.[58]

In June 1920, Donald Douglas, an engineer and vice president at Martin, opened his own firm, the Douglas-Davis Company, renting the back room of a barber shop at 8817 Pico Boulevard south of Beverly Hills. Five former Martin employees crafted one-off components for a transcontinental plane in a second-floor loft space at Koll Planing Mill, a woodworking shop ten miles east at 421 Colyton near Alameda and Fourth Streets. Finished parts were lowered down an elevator shaft and trucked to the Goodyear Blimp hanger in South Central Los Angeles for final assembly. After securing a contract for three experimental torpedo planes, Douglas, with financial support from Harry Chandler, incorporated as the Douglas Company in July 1921. The following year, forty-two employees relocated to a movie studio on Wilshire Boulevard in Santa Monica, where, between 1922 and 1928, Douglas produced 375 units. A site chosen for its adjacent field, the space proved inadequate for test flights. Completed aircraft were towed to Clover Field. In 1928, the company moved its entire operations to Clover Field, which the city of Santa Monica had purchased two years before. Municipal ownership ensured continuity of operation, the requisite zoning, and eminent domain for expansion. In 1928, the firm opened a subsidiary adjacent to Mines Field, an airstrip that the city of Los Angeles had recently leased for a municipal airport. By the time the city purchased the property in 1937, the district had become a center for prime airframe contractors, subassemblers, and parts and component manufacturers.[59]

During World War II, home builders anticipating an influx of defense workers drawn by these employment centers selected sites in close proximity to community projects. In just three years, four sets of developers converted a five-square-mile parcel owned and master planned by Security Bank into a district for 10,000 residents. A map accompanying advertisements for Westchester in the *Los Angeles Evening Herald and Express* plotted prime contractors and eleven ancillary industries. The copy underscored the district's proximity to a "wide variety of employment," as broadsides attempted to entice potential buyers with promises that they could "live within walking distance to scores of production plants."[60]

HOUSING POLICY AND "SOCIAL AREAS"

When Carey McWilliams surveyed Southern California's immediate postwar landscape for *Harper's Magazine,* he began by asking why the influx of 3 million people during the war years did not result in sheer chaos. His answer revealed the degree to which the decisions and actions that industrialists, planners, and engineers made during the 1920s had informed future patterns. If Los Angeles, he wrote, "had been a compact, centralized city, the migration would have had a devastating impact." Instead, the region's spread-out character

> resulted in a natural, and highly desirable, dispersion of population. Industries are widely scattered in Los Angeles. For the most part growth has taken place round the edge. . . . By an accident, therefore, Los Angeles has become the first modern, widely decentralized industrial city in America.[61]

McWilliams's perceptive account, in many ways an upbeat update of Bartlett's 1907 vision, was exceptional. His exceptionalism missed the mark, however, as he mistook planning for "natural . . . dispersion." Los Angeles's industrial districts had been highly planned regarding location, internal organization, external connections, and ancillary development such as housing. More critical, McWilliams neglected the social implications of what he described as a "natural, and highly desirable, dispersion of population." A map produced for the Haynes Foundation, published in a 1949 study of social areas in Los Angeles by Eshref Shevky and Marilyn Williams, identifies 146 census tracts with high indexes of segregation and plots these as a series of dots in relation to industrial areas delineated in cross-hatching. It is not surprising to find the majority of dots clustered tightly alongside the industrial districts lining the river and extending south and east into Vernon, Montebello, and the more recently incorporated City of Commerce. The remaining dots have a close graphic affinity with dispersed industrial zones of the type outlined in this chapter. The rate of coincidence, even if anticipated, is striking and demands attention.[62]

A partial explanation for the residential segregation that Shevky and Williams recorded may be found in the numbers. The FHA presented its housing market analysis as a straightforward exercise in academic social science. It is intended to be read as a recitation of facts—the text sections are secondary to charts, graphs, and tables. Of course, the numbers were not neutral but were marshaled toward specific effects. Congress endorsed the FHA in 1934 as a means for mitigating the crisis in foreclosures that had plagued the mortgage industry even during the 1920s boom and then threatened to foreclose savings and loans and other segments of the financial markets after 1929. Shoring up these institutions had been the agency's initial mandate. Within a few years time, however, FHA administrators had identified a more proactive and interventionist strategy, and staff began formulating policies and sponsoring programs designed to increase home ownership and extend its perceived benefits to wage earners and workers previously priced out of the market.

In intention and effect, these programs advanced the social and environmental reformers' earlier efforts to alleviate conditions in the congested, mixed-use districts along the river in Los Angeles, southwest of the Loop in Chicago, and in the Lower East Side of Manhattan—what the Chicago School sociologists characterized as "zones of emergence." From the 1910s to the 1930s, and beyond, elected officials, civic elites, philanthropists, and a considerable percentage of citizens have viewed owning one's home as an essential means and criterion for self-improvement, the creation and maintenance of a proper, child-based family setting, and true citizenship.[63]

There are critical distinctions, however, and these have had enormous consequence. Although the social reformers, in Los Angeles and elsewhere, viewed home ownership as one aspect of an Americanization project, a means for acculturating immigrants into shared norms and practices, the FHA followed a course closer to the one based on distinctions and preferences of race and ethnicity set by Los Angeles industrialists and developers. These objectives were explicitly articulated and achieved through instruments and practices that were presented and defended as scientific and race neutral but veiled so thinly that the untutored might see them for what they really were. The former included an active promotion of restrictive covenants for the creation and enhancement of property value, the latter seen in crystalline form in the survey maps that the Home Owners' Loan Corporation (HOLC) drew for major cities. HOLC maps record the population, structures, real estate activity, mortgage financing, and "description and character" of residential districts in American cities. Population, in this case, refers to a quasi-quantitative accounting of class and occupation, the number of "foreign families," nationalities, "Negro," and "shifting or infiltration." "Description and character" is a catchall for everything from terrain and land use to family types and property maintenance.

HOLC surveyors produced one such map for the area between Hawthorne and Torrance in 1939. Although Jared Torrance, industrialists, and residents viewed their city favorably, as orderly and uplifting, HOLC surveyors fixed on the outlying area, shown as a hatched zone on the map, and saw a "suburban farming district" with a "residential character begun less than twenty years ago" and "sketchy zoning" subject to frequent change.

> Under these circumstances it is not surprising that population, improvements and maintenance are extremely heterogeneous. Many Japanese farmers and Mexican laborers are found in the outlying districts and oil well and tank farms occupy adjacent territory to the west. The area is assigned a "medial red" grade.

As damning as the entire assessment was, it is the last sentence that fixed this district's fate. The red pencil and a "Security Grade: 4th" rating meant that the green of capital investment, directed in large measure by the federal government's issuance or withholding of mortgage guarantees, would not venture into this and other similar heterogeneous, industrial, and primarily working-class districts of color in Los Angeles.[64]

At the same time, it is interesting to compare the FHA's mid-1930s assessment of industrial Los Angeles with the accounts of the social reformers and the LAACC in the 1910s and 1920s, respectively. Despite the unmistakable advances in the number of firms, the number of wage earners and salaried employees, the payroll these workers commanded, and the value of output, there remained an explicit and pressing concern. Industry in Southern California remained dependent on tourism and services, the manufacturing that was in place was producing overwhelmingly for a local market, and, more generally, that production was almost exclusively for consumer goods and "light industry" instead of the long-desired heavy industry that would produce "capital goods."[65]

Although the authors of this report noted, begrudgingly, that Los Angeles was "not a one-industry city" and that the Los Angeles industrial area possessed an "extremely high degree of industrial diversification," in their estimation it was the focus on consumer goods that explained why the region had recovered relatively quickly from the Depression. When advancing this case, the authors pointed to Rubber Tire and Tubes, which at the time was ranked fourth in value of product (just more than $34 million) and its percentage of the area total (3.4) and sixth in the number of wage earners employed (3,588) and percentage of the area total (3.5). Adopting a line from the Chamber of Commerce, the FHA pointed out that in just over fifteen years (1919-1934), Los Angeles had risen from a position as one of many local centers for vulcanizing and small-scale tire production to become the second leading center in the country, trailing only Akron, Ohio.

At the groundbreaking for Samson Tyre and Rubber's new East Side plant in 1929, company president Adolf Schleicher claimed that now Los Angeles was the "Akron of the West" and that "soon Akron will be known as the Los Angeles of the East." Despite the bold and imaginative rhetoric, the FHA knew better. Although the production of automobile tires and tubes clearly played an important role in industrial Los Angeles, the agency put this in perspective when it noted that the second place ranking "should not be construed in any way [as implying] that Los Angeles compares with Akron as a rubber center." Statistics from the census of manufactures supported this claim. Los Angeles branch plants employed less than 10 percent of the total wage earners as parent firms in Akron. These workers earned less than 10 percent the aggregate wages paid their counterparts in Akron and produced approximately 10 percent of the value of product.[66]

Organized as an analysis of housing, and intended as an assessment of the housing market, the FHA survey offers researchers a rich statistical abstract of Los Angeles at a particularly critical moment in the city's history. The longitudinal data on mortgages and financing, construction costs, subdivision, building, and real estate activity are packaged with a quantitative accounting of the city and county in population, migration, employment and wages, and the region's "economic background and structure." It appears as if the FHA's Division of Economics and Statistics gave itself the task of taking the city's pulse precisely when manufacturing, commerce, home building, and other business interests had regained the momentum that characterized regional advance during the 1920s, when the area had almost achieved the seemingly dizzying heights of employment and output first reached in 1927, 1928, and 1929.

The FHA enumerators could not have known, however, that reaching that type of milestone, well in advance of other industrial areas in the nation, was actually the end of an era. While the Depression downturn might appear as a pause in the long-range trajectory of manufacturing and city building in industrial Los Angeles, the mid-1930s marked the beginning of a transformation, one that would prove to be just as dynamic as the changes that had occurred during the 1920s. This transformation was precipitated by different factors and furthered by different agents and agencies. The FHA played a central role. It was one of a number of New Deal agencies whose policies—on water and power, road building, aviation, and other infrastructure—laid the groundwork for increased industrial expansion and the emergence, in Southern California, of the type of high-capital, basic, and export-oriented manufacturing that city promoters had longed to attract for decades.[67]

Home builders capitalized on the FHA's mortgage guarantee program to secure financing for projects with a greater number of units. The FHA also endorsed and institutionalized a set of building practices and planning principles that Southern California home builders had hammered out during the 1920s. Housing developments that met these standards, codified loosely as modern community planning, received an FHA stamp of approval that opened up an array of attractive financing options to an expanded pool of potential home buyers.[68] This was but a single aspect of one of the most intense and comprehensive episodes of the exertion of state power in the long history of federal intervention into the West and California.

These New Deal policies and programs for infrastructure and housing were put into service almost immediately with the escalation of armed conflict in Europe and Asia and the entry of the United States as an armed combatant in World War II. The New Deal, the war, and the defense emergency ushered in a qualitatively different moment for Los Angeles and Southern California, and the federal government provided the capital, capacity, and demand mandatory for Southland industrialists and entrepreneurs to create an industrial region comparable with those of the East and

Midwest. Elements of this development were similar to the type of expansion that had occurred during the 1920s and, later, as the region emerged from the Depression downturn in 1934 and 1935. But much of it was qualitatively and quantitatively different.[69] In effect, the creation of post–World War II Los Angeles began in the mid-1930s, and it is here that we must look to find the roots of the city that urban theorists and pundits now trumpet as a prototype for twenty-first-century urbanism.

CONCENTRIC RINGS TO URBAN RENEWAL

As the attention to federal policy suggests, the forces and factors that informed the process of urbanization in Los Angeles and Southern California—from the scale of the decisions and actions of individual workers and their families to the strategies of local institutions to the role of the state and national government—had parallels in other American cities such as Chicago. As Rudolph Vecoli has shown through his study of Italian immigrants and the creation of "Little Italies" across the city limits of turn-of-the-century Chicago—from South Clark Street and the Near North Side out to Kensington (near Lake Calumet) and Terra Cotta (along the North Branch of the Chicago River)—these newcomers did not conform to the concentric ring model. Rather, these sixteen-plus settlements were discrete entities shaped by the residents' place of origin, by their time of arrival, by the skills and capital they brought with them, and, most critically, by Chicago's "industrial ecology," a geography shaped by the lake and the river. The river wards were the site for packinghouses, mills, and factories, and immigrant workers employed in these plants lived in the surrounding residential districts and created communities with distinctive character, reputation, and histories.[70]

So why, then, were the Chicago sociologists so committed to the notion of their city and all other cities as coherent, diagrammatically comprehensible metropolitan areas? It goes without saying that their project, like all intellectual work, was a product of its time. Park and Burgess were conducting fieldwork and developing their interpretative and conceptual framework when the seemingly unprecedented flood of immigrants and migrants to America's cities resulted in severe overcrowding, congestion, and an "undesirable" mixing of races, ethnic groups, and social classes in city centers. At the same time, the dispersion and reconcentration (or "recentralization," to use Burgess's term) of industry, commerce, and housing in the unincorporated urban fringe appeared to contemporaries as unmitigated and unchecked expansion and therefore an equally frightening development. Poised at a moment when the city seemed to be imploding and exploding simultaneously, these scholars and urban pundits strove to mediate this radical recasting of urban space by evoking the traditional ideals of community. The method was scientistic—it involved isolating supposed root causes of phenomena and then applying comprehensive schemes for social change. But the former step, identifying the nature and structure of a problem or problems, was the crux of their enterprise. For these sociologists, a problem defined was a problem solved. Perhaps we can best understand the concentric zone theory and that iconic diagram as a forward-looking model of orderly urban development, an attempt to ensure a stable metropolitan future by keeping the locus of growth and control in the city center at a time when social and economic change was wrenching Chicago and other cities apart. In effect, Park and Burgess's Chicago had to remain fixed—a unified entity and ecological system capable of adapting to any and all external threats and stimuli and eventually assimilating these into an altered, but still recognizable, status quo.

Given this assessment, I am obliged to address the obvious question: Why devote so much intellectual energy to Chicago School sociology and *The City?* This question is especially pertinent if subsequent scholarship reveals that Park and Burgess were, effectively, wrong, and is even more so if this comparative analysis suggests that the supposedly universal insights that these scholars drew from their investigations of Chicago did not translate to Los Angeles, despite the efforts of Bogardus and his students to apply their maxims and templates. Rather than a simple exercise of setting the record straight, this chapter is intended as an update, a critical review of the 1925 volume that points out lacunae and, more important, extends and expands the "suggestions for investigation" that were the primary purpose of the Chicago volume. For good and ill, that book has served as a touchstone for urban research during the past three quarters of a century. The topics, themes, and modes of inquiry set out in that slim volume fixed an agenda, much as their authors hoped, and most likely beyond what they ever imagined. Just as the role of industry in urbanization did not factor into Park and Burgess's account, by and large, the geography of industry remains a largely underexamined topic.

Manufacturing does appear in urban studies. It is a mainstay of urban political economy and a subset of urban theory. But political economy and urban theory operate at the same level as the concentric zone diagram. Each provides general explanations and rules of thumb drawn typically from extensive knowledge of a single locale and then applied uniformly to other sites. Hence we find theories of capital mobility, corporate flight, a transition from manufacturing to a postindustrial or service economy, and the increasingly global organization of capital as latter-day equivalents of the Chicago School's segmentation and sequence of land uses. In this light, the natural pattern of city growth is expansion out from the urban core, and the implied temporal and spatial progression of people and land uses to the leading edge of the metropolitan periphery.

In effect, the Chicago sociologists fixed the immigrant and the factory in the center of the city. In their model of urban growth, progress was measured according to the distance from the core. The concentric rings held different people and were the site for different land uses, both of which were segregated by zones. Each ring was better than the one preceding it, better, in this case, meaning citizenship and privilege, higher status and greater income, quality housing, and access to services—in short, an enhanced social and physical environment. Park and Burgess viewed this progression as a "natural" product of competition within an urban ecological system. The rings appear as a tree's annular growth, and, in this case, the biological analogy is appropriate. For in Park and Burgess's eyes, quality growth was in the new wood, out along the urban periphery. Although they did not use the term, their zone of transition and zone of workingmen's homes were the sites that reformers and urban planners would soon designate as blighted. Here, in diagrammatic form, we have one of the first representations of the American metropolis as a spatial and social unit with a decayed or decaying core and a robust and expanding periphery. Of course, this leitmotif has served as the rationale for everything from policy to punditry from the 1920s forward and has had an enormous, and unfortunately mostly negative, effect on the lives of urban residents in Chicago, Los Angeles, and elsewhere throughout the twentieth century. It is well past the time to set this model of urbanization aside.

NOTES

1. Robert E. Park, "The City: Suggestions for the Investigation of Human Behavior in the Urban Environment," in *The City: Suggestions for Investigation of Human Behavior in the Urban Environment,* by Robert E. Park, Ernest W. Burgess, and Roderick D. McKenzie (Chicago: University of Chicago Press, 1925, 1967; Midway reprint, 1984), 8, 11, 24-25.

2. Park et al., *The City,* 48-58.

3. Park et al., *The City,* 52.

4. Los Angeles City Club, *Bulletin* 5, no. 325 (September 26, 1923). The subsequent edition (vol. 5, no. 326, November 3) reported on Park's visit and his assessment that the "immigrant is doing our Americanization work and the foreign press is playing a large part in this education."

5. Emory S. Bogardus, *Introduction to Social Research: A Text and Reference Study, wherein are presented various methods of social research in a compact, convenient form* (Los Angeles: Suttonhouse, 1936), 28. For biographical and institutional data on Bogardus, see Bogardus, *A History of Sociology at the University of Southern California* (Los Angeles: University of Southern California, 1972).

6. Dana Webster Bartlett, *The Better City: A Sociological Study of a Modern City* (Los Angeles: Neuner Press, 1907), quotes pp. 14, 27, 71-72. Los Angeles as a "slumless" city was the subject of numerous tracts in newspapers as well as the booster and popular press. According to contemporary accounts, when then President Taft was in Los Angeles in October 1909 to dedicate the North Broadway bridge, he asked, "Have you no slum districts?" Note that Taft was less than one half mile from the Ann Street district, which reformers cast as a zone of immigrant "peons or peasants" and a site for disease and disorder. See Gladys Patric, "A Study of the Housing and Social Conditions in the Ann Street District of Los Angeles" (Los Angeles: Society for the Study and Prevention of Tuberculosis, c. 1917). In "Yes, We Have No Smokestacks, and Likewise No Tenements—Latest Figures About the Factories in Our Big Garden Community," *Southern California Business* 11, no. 8 (August 1932): 12-13, R. D. Sangster, manager of the chamber of commerce's industrial department, presented a city with an "utter absence of tenements. . . . Workman's homes are almost entirely single-family on large lots." The Los Angeles newspapers reported a lack of slums along with a purported lack of poverty and the poor and attributed all three to a predominantly American population and their passion for home ownership with stock illustrations and copy noting the miles of artistic bungalows, set in flowers and greenery, along wide, well-paved streets.

7. Los Angeles City Directory Co., Inc., *Los Angeles City Directory, 1905;* California Commission of Immigration and Housing, *A Community Survey Made in Los Angeles* (San Francisco: The Commission, 1919), 23.

8. Bartlett, *Better City,* 191.

9. I have borrowed the concept "imaginative geographies" from Kay Anderson, "The Idea of Chinatown: The Power of Place and Institutional Practice in the Making of a Racial Category," *Annals of the Association of American Geographers* 77, no. 4 (December 1987): 580-598.

10. Robert A. Beauregard, *Voices of Decline: The Postwar Fate of American Cities* (Cambridge: Blackwell, 1993); J. M. Blaut, *The Colonizer's Model of the World: Geographical Diffusionism and Eurocentric History* (New York: Guilford, 1993); William Cronon, "A Place for Stories," *Journal of American History* 78, no. 4 (March 1992): 1347-1376; Alan Mayne, *The Imagined Slum: Newspaper Representation in Three Cities, 1870-1914* (Leicester, England: Leicester University Press, 1993); Denis Wood, *The Power of Maps* (New York: Guilford, 1992).

11. The promotional literature is rife with these tropes; see especially the "Real Estate, Industrial, and Development" section in the Sunday *Los Angeles Times.* I will address this topic in detail in a forthcoming manuscript. For a general introduction to the subject, see the writings collected in William Cronon, ed., *Uncommon Ground: Rethinking the Human Place in Nature* (New York: Norton, 1995).

12. Bartlett, *Better City,* 19-20.

13. The publications, broadsides, and advertisements trumpeting the Southland's industries and emergent industrial prowess are voluminous. Indicative are titles such as "5,100 Factories Now Los Angeles Total; 900 New This Year," *Illustrated Daily News* 15 (December 1923). For similar representations, see the *Los Angeles Times,* especially the Sunday real estate section, as well as LAACC publications such as *Industrial Los Angeles County* and *Southern California Business.*

14. Population and annexation are taken from Robert M. Fogelson, *The Fragmented Metropolis: Los Angeles, 1850-1930* (Berkeley: University of California Press, 1967, 1993), Table 4, p. 78, and Table 24, pp. 226-227, respectively. The LAACC research department noted the change in the Census Bureau's accounting for the metropolitan district in a January 1932 news release: In 1920, the "area extended further to the west [out to Ventura County], today [1930] it omits this western section and extends farther toward the east and southeast to include thickly settled communities, regardless of county boundary lines." Census enumerators noted an increase of 165 percent for this ten-year period in the reconfigured metropolitan area. Report in County of Los Angeles, *Regional Planning Notes,* vol. 2, 1931-1932 (Los Angeles: Regional Planning Commission, 1933).

15. See, for example, the various chamber publications, especially its annual directories of manufacturing, as well as the *Los Angeles Times,* which promoted industry weekly in the Sunday real estate section as well as in the January "Mid-Winter Annual." Other sources include the *Los Angeles Realtor, Southwest Builder and Contractor,* local papers such as the Huntington Park *Daily Signal,* and city biographies such as Carson B. Hubbard, *History of Huntington Park, in 2 Parts* (Huntington Park: A. H. Cawston, 1935). For a contemporary overview, see Robert Glass Cleland and Osgood Hardy, *March of Industry* (Los Angeles: Powell Publishing, 1929). This promotion continued throughout the 1930s, and with considerable flourish after World War II. For an indicative study, see Industrial Department, Los Angeles County Chamber of Commerce, "An Industrial Development Plan for Los Angeles" (n.d./c. 1945).

16. Fogelson, *Fragmented Metropolis,* especially 123-129.

17. Editorial, "Balanced Progress," *Los Angeles Times,* sec. 2.

18. "Balanced Progress."

19. Industrial Department, LAACC, *Special Report to Henry M. Robinson, Chairman of the Board, Security-First National Bank of Los Angeles, California,* 2 vols. (Los Angeles: Industrial Department, 1930).

20. Industrial Department, *Special Report.* Economists Eberle and Riggleman challenged the chamber's glowing assessment in their weekly summary of business conditions. A September 21, 1925, article, "Some Consideration of the Los Angeles Industrial Situation," outlined eight points of concern ranging from the lack of careful planning and the detriments of dispersion to excessive intraregional competition and the low operating efficiencies of established plants. *Eberle & Riggleman Economic Service* 11, no. 28.

21. Federal Housing Administration, Division of Economics and Statistics, *Housing Market Analysis, Los Angeles, California as of December 1, 1937,* two parts and statistical appendix (Washington, D.C.: Government Printing Office, 1938), 3.

22. FHA, *Housing Market Analysis,* Chart 43, p. 251.

23. The U.S. Bureau of the Census introduced the designation "industrial area" in 1929. In Los Angeles, the industrial area was coterminous with the county (FHA, *Housing Market Analysis,* 249). The state comparisons are from Table 68, p. 588; the national rankings can be found in Table 70, p. 590. The aggregate data for the Los Angeles industrial area were reported as two totals, one including and one excluding the motion picture industry. Census enumerators instituted this distinction because the product from this industry was leased rather than sold, which meant actual value could not be calculated as it was for other manufacturing outputs. The figures that included motion pictures factored in the dollar amount for cost of production; compare FHA, *Housing Market Analysis,* 262, for an explanation.

24. FHA, *Housing Market Analysis,* Table 68, p. 588.

25. FHA, *Housing Market Analysis,* 321. The percentage in manufacturing was followed closely by workers in the trades (25.4 percent). No other city in the nation with more than 500,000 population had anywhere near the proximity between these sectors; see Chart 53, p. 322. In 1930, the estimated number of unemployed persons in the county was set at 84,565, while there were 964,436 "gainful workers" (341).

26. U.S. Department of Commerce, Bureau of the Census, *Fourteenth Census of the United States, Manufactures: 1919* (Washington, D.C.: Government Printing Office, 1922), "Cities of 50,000 Inhabitants or More—All Industries Combined and Specified Industries, Los Angeles," 44-49, and *Fifteenth Census of the United States, Manufactures, 1929: State Series, California* (Washington, D.C.: Government Printing Office, 1932), "General Statistics for Important Cities, by Industries: 1929," 17-18.

27. Helen M. Liggett, "The Relation of Wages to the Cost of Living in Los Angeles, 1915 to 1920," *Studies in Sociology* Sociological Monograph no. 19 5/3 (March 1921), Table 12, p. 8 and p. 11; LAACC, "Special Report," n.p.; Works Progress Administration, "Inter-City Differences in the Cost of Living," reported in FHA, *Housing Market Analysis,* Table 92, pp. 621-622.

28. Clarence Dykstra, "The Boulder Dam Project" (n.d.), in Dykstra Collection, UCLA Department of Special Collections, box 2, folder "Addresses or Articles Prior to 1930."

29. On occupation, see William Wilson McEuen, "A Survey of the Mexicans in Los Angeles" (master's thesis, USC, Department of Economics and Sociology, 1914), 49-50, 66; Gladys Patric, M.D., "A Study of the Housing and Social Conditions in the Ann Street District of Los Angeles" (Los Angeles: Society for the Study and Prevention of Tuberculosis, c. 1917), 11-13; G. Bromley Oxnam, "The Mexican in Los Angeles: Los Angeles City Survey" (Los Angeles: Interchurch World Movement of North America, 1920), 14.

30. Elizabeth Fuller, "The Mexican Housing Problem in Los Angeles," *Studies in Sociology,* Sociological Monograph no. 17, 5/1 (November 1920): 1-2; John Emmanuel Kienle, "Housing Conditions Among the Mexican Population of Los Angeles" (master's thesis, USC, Department of Sociology, 1912); Emory S. Bogardus, "The House-Court Problem," *American Journal of Sociology* 22 (November 1919): 391-399; California Commission of Immigra-

tion and Housing, "A Community Survey Made in Los Angeles" (San Francisco: The Commission, 1919).

31. California Commission of Immigration and Housing, "A Community Survey," Table 1, pp. 38-41.

32. Oxnam, "The Mexican in Los Angeles," 23. Stoddard's study of house courts, "The Courts of Sonoratown," appeared in *Charities and the Commons* 15 (December 2, 1905): 295-299.

33. Charles S. Johnson, "Industrial Survey of the Negro Population of Los Angeles, California, Made by the Department of Research and Investigations of the National Urban League" (1926); Johnson, "Negro Workers in Los Angeles Industries," *Opportunity: A Journal of Negro Life* 6 (August 1928): 234-240.

34. Johnson, "Negro Workers," 234-237. Of course, industrialists were not the only ones who gave credence to theories of "racial traditions" as intrinsic social divides. See, for example, USC sociologist Emory S. Bogardus's primer, *Introduction to Social Research* (Los Angeles: Suttonhouse, 1936), as well as articles such as "The Social Explorer," *Journal of Applied Sociology* 9 (1924): 143-147, for discussions of "racial traditions" as "natural barriers" separating people into "compatibles and incompatibles" (146).

35. Ernest W. Burgess, "The Growth of the City: An Introduction to a Research Project," in *The City*, 49.

36. "Manufacturing Committee—Westinghouse Track Connections," in LAACC, *Stenographer's Notes, Board of Directors Meetings,* 1922, pp. 2-5, Chamber of Commerce Collection, box 18, University of Southern California, Department of Special Collections (hereafter, Special Collections, USC).

37. "Manufacturing Committee."

38. Fogelson, *The Fragmented Metropolis,* especially Chapter 6, "Commercial and Industrial Progress."

39. Hugh Allen, *The House of Goodyear* (Akron, OH: Superior Printing, 1936); Goodyear Tire and Rubber Company of California, *Three Dynamic Decades in the Golden State, 1920-1950* in Los Angeles Examiner Collection, Special Collections, USC, photo folder "Goodyear"; Paul Rhode, "California's Emergence as the Second Industrial Belt: The Pacific Coast Tire and Automobile Industries" (unpublished paper, University of North Carolina, Department of Economics, Chapel Hill, September 1994); "Civic Heads, U. P. Officials Aid Ceremony, Los Angeles May Outstrip Akron Soon," *Los Angeles Examiner,* January 24, 1929; "Tire Manufacture a Major Industry Here," *Industrial Los Angeles County* 2, no. 5 (May 1930): 4; "Rubber Industry—Los Angeles County," editorial in *Industrial Los Angeles County* 2, no. 5 (May 1930).

40. Frank L. Kidner and Philip Neff, *An Economic Survey of the Los Angeles Area,* Haynes Foundation Monograph Series 7 (Los Angeles: Haynes Foundation, 1945).

41. Edgar Lloyd Hampton, "Los Angeles, A Miracle City," *Current History* 24, no. 1 (April 1926): 35-42, quote p. 35. See also the discussions in *Los Angeles Today,* May 1, 1916, p. 24; "Los Angeles, The Hub of a Great Empire," *Los Angeles Times,* January 1, 1926, as well as the editorials and commentary in the LAACC publications *Southern California Business* and *Industrial Los Angeles County* and journals such as *California Magazine of the Pacific.*

42. Oxnam diary entry, August 30, 1922, in G. Bromley Oxnam Papers, Madison Building, Library of Congress.

43. Here I am applying an interpretation drawn from Deryck W. Holdsworth's assessment of Chicago in "The Invisible Skyline," *Antipode* 26, no. 2 (April 1994): 141-146.

44. Law quote taken from Perley Poore Sheehan, *Hollywood as a World Center* (Hollywood, Calif.: Hollywood Citizen Press, 1924), 20-21.

45. Plates 14-17 bound as an appendix to *Report and Recommendations on a Comprehensive Rapid Transit Plan for the City and County of Los Angeles* (Chicago: Kelker, De Leuw & Co., 1925).

46. The history of zoning in Los Angeles, and the effect of these regulations for zoning in other cities and national guidelines, has yet to be written. For a contemporary assessment of the significance of these statutes, see Lawrence Veiller, "City Planning in Los Angeles," *The Survey* 26 (July 22, 1911): 599-600. For the district boundaries, see Ordinance N. 17135 (new series, 1908), Ordinance N. 17136 (new series, 1908), and Ordinance N. 19500 (new series, 1909).

47. Author interview with William Daum Jr., June 19, 1996, and clippings in scrapbooks at the Daum office, 123 South Figueroa, Los Angeles.

48. "The Cat's Out of the Bag," six-column advertisement in the *Los Angeles Times,* Sunday, September 10, 1922, pt. V; "Mr. Workingman and Mr. Wage-Earner," tract brochure for Belvedere Gardens, reproduced in Bruce Henstell, *Sunshine and Wealth: Los Angeles in the Twenties and Thirties* (San Francisco: Chronicle Books, 1984); "Bandini: The Model Community on the New East Side" (1926), Huntington Library, Ephemera Collection, F21-B11.

49. "City Industrial Tract," Report for A. G. Arnoll (Los Angeles Area Chamber of Commerce) by H. A. Lafler, Sales Agent, Walter H. Leimert Co. (c. 1923), in LAACC Collection, Special Collections, USC, box 74; John R. Boyd, "Looking Ahead Industrially," *Southern California Business* (August 1924): 14; J. B. Ransom Organization, "Montebello Park: The Model Community of the New East Side" (Los Angeles: J. B. Ransom, 1925).

50. "Torrance, The Model Industrial City," California Ephemera Collection, UCLA Department of Special Collections, box 103, folder "Torrance."

51. This was a continuing process. For a post-World War II account, see "Farewell to 'Manana': Hicks Camp Prepares to Abandon Old Ways," *Los Angeles Times,* May 13, 1949, pt. 3, which describes how an enclave of approximately 150 farmworker families living in "El Monte's bit of old Mexico which has lain sleepily under the California sun for years" was being forced out by a new property owner, Harvey Youngblood, who planned to develop the land as an industrial park for light manufacturing.

52. "Rubber Company to Build Great Factory at Ascot Park," *Los Angeles Times,* June 24, 1919; "Will Build Model Village, Eight Hundred Fine Houses for Workers to Rise at Ascot Park," *Los Angeles Times,* June 24, 1919. For Akron and a company history, see Hugh Allen, *The House of Goodyear* (Akron: Superior Printing, 1936). For the images, see "Los Angeles— 'Queen of Homelands,'" *Industrial Los Angeles County* 2, no. 5 (May 1930) and The Goodyear Tire and Rubber Company of California, "Three Dynamic Decades in the Golden State" (c. 1950), a pamphlet published to commemorate the firm's thirtieth anniversary, in *Los Angeles Examiner* Collection, Special Collections, USC.

53. Central Manufacturing District, Inc., "Central Manufacturing District of Los Angeles: A Book of Descriptive Text, Photographs and Testimonial Letters About the Central Manufacturing District of Los Angeles—'The Great Western Market'" (August 1923), LAACC Collection, Special Collections, USC; "Great Industrial City Here Being Created by the Central Manufacturing District," *Los Angeles Times,* July 15, 1923; "Cabbage Patch to Industrial Paradise," *Santa Fe Magazine* (November 1929): 21-25; H. E. Poronto, "How Chicago Came to Los Angeles Told by Head of Central Manufacturing Dist.," *Southwest Builder and Contractor* 62, no. 2 (July 13, 1923): 34. For an outsider's vantage presented as a photoessay, see Richard Neutra, *Amerika: die Stilbundung des neven bauens in den Vereinigten Stacten; mit 260 abbiblungen* (Vienna, Austria: A. Schroll, 1930).

54. On the sale, see "Los Angeles Holdings Go to Rich Group," March 7, 1928, and "Santa Fe Buys Industrial Hub for $15,000,000," April 11, 1929, both in the *Los Angeles Examiner.* For city biographies of Bell and other incorporated communities, see LAACC, Industrial Department, *Industrial Communities of Los Angeles Metropolitan Area* (Los Angeles: The Chamber, 1925) and *California Real Estate Magazine* 10, no. 9 (June 1930), a special issue devoted to "Growth and Progress of the Golden West."

55. "Subdividing of Land" in Los Angeles Board of City Planning Commissioners, *Annual Report, 1929-1930* (Los Angeles: The Board, 1930): 49.

56. County of Los Angeles, "Proceedings of the First Regional Planning Conference of Los Angeles County" (Los Angeles: Regional Planning Commission, 1922): 6.

57. For firm locations, see the LAACC, Industrial Department publications *Manufacturers' Directory and Commodity Index.* I consulted the second (1915) and fifth (1920) editions. On Harry H. Culver, see a biography ("as of Sept. 1, 1929") in the *Examiner* Collection, Special Collections, USC, and the clippings files in that collection. Culver City was a Better Homes in America site in 1926, and the brochure for that event is in the Seaver Collection, Los Angeles County Museum of Natural History. When enumerators employed by the Works Progress Administration conducted a comprehensive survey of county residents, structures, and land uses, their findings underscored the diversity of manufacturing and its reach. Coded data cards report the tenancy, occupation, place and journey to work, and mode of transit for each household in the county. A summary noted small industrial districts in "almost every municipal and geographic division of Los Angeles as well as in outlying satellite centers." Los Angeles Regional Planning Commission and the Works Progress Administration, *Land Use Analysis: Final Report* (Los Angeles: RPC, 1941).

58. This section is drawn from Greg Hise, *Magnetic Los Angeles: Planning the Twentieth-Century Metropolis* (Baltimore: Johns Hopkins University Press, 1997), Chapter 4, "The Airplane and the Garden City."

59. Don Hansen (McDonnell Douglas, Long Beach) letter to author, June 3, 1994. See also Frank Cunningham, *Skymaster: The Story of Donald Douglas* (Philadelphia: Dorrance, 1943), and Crosby Maynard, *Flight Plan for Tomorrow: The Douglas Story, A Condensed History* (Santa Monica, Calif.: Douglas Aircraft Co., 1962).

60. "Finest Community Development in 20 Years" and "Typical Homes in Westchester District," *Los Angeles Evening Herald and Express,* March 28, 1942. See also "City Planners Flock to Study Westchester," *Los Angeles Daily News,* May 8, 1942, and the low-altitude oblique aerials of this development in the Spence and Fairchild Aerial Photo Collections in the Department of Geography at the University of California, Los Angeles.

61. "Look What's Happened to California," *Harper's Magazine* 199, no. 1193 (October 1949): 21-29, quote p. 28.

62. Eshref Shevky and Marilyn Williams, *The Social Areas of Los Angeles: Analysis and Typology,* published for the John Randolph Haynes and Dora Haynes Foundation (Berkeley: University of California Press, 1949): Figure 18, opposite p. 56.

63. Park et al., *The City,* especially "The Growth of the City: An Introduction to a Research Project"; U.S. Department of Commerce, *How to Own Your Home: A Handbook for Prospective Home Owners,* prepared by John M. Gries and James S. Taylor (Washington, D.C.: Government Printing Office, 1923).

64. "Southern Hawthorne and Suburbs, Area No. D-44" (March 17, 1939), HOLC City Survey files, National Archives, Record Group 195. Richard Harris (McMaster University) supplied me with copies of these documents. On the HOLC, restrictive covenants, and redlining, see Kenneth T. Jackson, "Race, Ethnicity, and Real Estate Appraisal: The Home Owners' Loan Corporation and the Federal Housing Administration," *Journal of Urban History* 6 (August 1980): 419-452.

65. FHA, *Housing Market Analysis,* 331. In their report, the authors pointed to aviation as an emergent sector with the potential to become an export industry capable of generating ancillary capital goods manufacturing and thereby setting the region firmly on a foundation of industrial progress (252-257).

66. FHA, *Housing Market Analysis,* 270-271; "Civic Heads, U.P. Officials Aid Ceremony, Los Angeles May Outstrip Akron Soon, Samson Corporation Head Says in Keynote Talk," *Los Angeles Examiner,* January 24, 1929.

67. The obvious example is Kaiser's steel plant in Fontana, but during the defense emergency, industrialists and entrepreneurs, with financial and material assistance from the federal government, coordinated the development of an extraordinary complex of chemical, power, and technology concerns that became the basis for postwar advances in aviation and other sectors. The government invested more than $800 million in more than 5,000 industrial plants in the region between 1940 and 1943. See Hise, *Magnetic Los Angeles,* as well as Carey McWilliams, *Southern California: An Island on the Land* (Salt Lake City, Utah: Peregrine Smith Books, 1946/1990), especially the epilogue in which McWilliams states that during the war, Los Angeles became an important industrial area "overnight . . . preoccupied not with tourists and climate alone, but with such problems as 'smog' and 'smoke' and 'strikes'" (371).

68. For an extended discussion of the FHA's role in transforming home building and home buying during the 1930s in Los Angeles and the rise of modern community planning, see Hise, *Magnetic Los Angeles,* Chapters 1, 2, and 4. On the FHA more generally, see Gertrude Fish, ed., *The Story of Housing* (New York: Macmillan, 1979), and Nathaniel S. Keith, *Politics and the Housing Crisis Since 1930* (New York: Universe Books, 1979).

69. Industrial Department, LAACC, "Statistical Record of Los Angeles County Industrial Development: Summary, on an Annual Basis, for Years 1929-44" (1945).

70. Rudolph J. Vecoli, "The Formation of Chicago's 'Little Italies,'" *Journal of American Ethnic History* 2 (spring 1983): 5-20.

Los Angeles as a Developmental City-State

EDITOR'S
COMMENTS

The enormous significance of "political interests" in the rise of Los Angeles is revealed in Steven P. Erie's history of infrastructure investment in the region during the twentieth century. In effect, L.A.'s emergence as a world city and capital of America's Pacific Rim was made possible through a deliberate politics of public works investments, especially water and power, and harbor and airport facilities—the region's "crown jewels," in Erie's terminology.

Erie points out bluntly that the Burgess model was a market-based growth dynamic that did not incorporate the role of public goods or of federal and local states as engines of economic development, or the rise of city-states as global market competitors. In a plea to "bring the state back in" to urban theory, Erie shows how in the early years of the twenty-first century, Los Angeles is once again reinventing itself with another round of massive public infrastructure investments.

QUOTE FROM
THE CITY

The city is not, however, merely a geographical and ecological unit; it is at the same time an economic unit. The economic organization of the city is based on the division of labor. The multiplication of occupations and professions within the limits of the urban population is one of the most striking and least understood aspects of modern city life. From this point of view, we may, if we choose, think of the city, that is to say, the place and the people, with all the machinery and administrative devices that go with them, as organically related; a kind of psychophysical mechanism in and through which private and political interest find not merely a collective but a corporate expression. (2)

CHAPTER 5

Los Angeles as a Developmental City-State

STEVEN P. ERIE

The Chicago School's famed concentric zone theory of urban growth is, at base, a market model of development. That is, forces of supply and demand are depicted as generating a distinctive spatial patterning for the city, separating commercial from residential areas and inner-city working-class residential districts from affluent suburban neighborhoods. In such a model, there is little role for state-directed growth, and public policies such as zoning merely reflect and ratify inexorable market-driven forces.[1]

The school's market-based theory well may have described Chicago growth in the 1920s when the model was constructed. In those days, local government's planning and zoning responsibilities were limited or nonexistent, while city politicians concentrated on distributing divisible benefits, for example, patronage jobs, rather than providing public goods. Only in the 1950s, when Mayor Richard Daley assumed power and massive urban redevelopment and public housing projects were launched, would the Democratic machine (which consolidated power in the 1930s) turn to the provision of public goods. As a result, collective goods were late arriving in the Windy City.

Yet a model that may explain pre–machine-era Chicago expansion cannot adequately account for L.A.'s improbable yet explosive twentieth-century growth. Despite L.A.'s reputation as another Sunbelt city run by newspaper publishers and real estate developers, such private development had to be complemented with massive public investments. In particular, Southern California lacked the requisite infrastructure, for example, water, power, and a harbor, for large-scale growth. In response, turn-of-the-century Angelenos created a powerful local state apparatus—under the direction of "reform" bureaucracies rather than party machines—to provide needed public goods. Los Angeles strategically used its infrastructure to dramatically expand its boundaries and population and to ensure economic dominion over Southern California and much of the Southwest. Today, in back-to-the-future fashion, Los Angeles is once again reinventing itself with massive public infrastructure investments. Aspiring to be an American Singapore (a global center for trade and

Port of Los Angeles
Photograph by Michael J. Dear.

transshipment), Los Angeles is planning multi-billion-dollar port, rail, and airport projects to ensure its status as the nation's leading Pacific Rim gateway.

Central to an emerging L.A. School perspective must be an account of the role of a powerful local state in shaping the region's early growth, successive economic restructurings, and global future. The purpose of this chapter is to "bring the local state back in" by examining the city of L.A.'s so-called crown jewels—its proprietary or independent Water and Power (DWP), Harbor, and Airports Departments and the facilities they manage—and the roles they have played in the twentieth-century political economy of city and region.

Five arguments are advanced here. (1) The Los Angeles case demonstrates the role of the local state as potent stimulus for an emerging "city-states" paradigm examining how regions can compete in the global economy. (2) Except for the well-told story of bringing water to Los Angeles, the conventional narrative of how Southern California grew largely ignores the provision of local public goods. As argued here, the local state served as necessary catalyst for the emergence of modern Los Angeles and indeed Southern California. (3) The California constitutional framework was critical to the building of L.A.'s local state apparatus. The Golden State's early embrace of municipal home rule gave the city the autonomy and fiscal capacity needed to build and finance its ambitious water, power, harbor, and airport projects. Within this enabling state legal framework, Los Angeles led the nation in

Wind Farm, San Gorgonio Pass, near Palm Springs. Energy and water supplies are the largest infrastructural constraints on Southern California's future. Photograph by Michael J. Dear.

Castaic Lake Reservoir, northern Los Angeles County. The story of water supply undergirds L.A.'s past, present, and future. Without a plentiful supply of water, there will be no city. Photograph by Michael J. Dear.

Sepulveda Dam and Flood Control Basin, San Fernando Valley, County of Los Angeles. Too much water can also be a problem. Heavy winter rains cause catastrophic flash flooding. The 710-foot high Sepulveda Dam (left foreground) was completed in 1941 to protect downstream cities in L.A. County. It permits the 1,335-acre basin to be flooded during sustained downpours. Photograph by Michael J. Dear.

devising innovative growth-inducing public debt and pricing strategies. (4) Strong and effective bureaucracies were also a product of both local constitutional design and agency leadership. Unlike Chicago and its powerful machine, L.A.'s city charter gave the proprietary departments independence from city hall politicians. Visionary public entrepreneurs such as the DWP's William Mulholland crafted strategies of electoral mobilization and interest group alliance to build political support for their agencies and projects. (5) Despite past successes, L.A.'s crown jewels—and the global future of the city and region—lay at an uncertain crossroads in the 1990s. A series of challenges in the form of a fiscal crisis, community and environmental opposition, and deregulation and market competition threatened the proprietary departments' ambitious expansion and restructuring plans.

Just as the Chicago School once used that city as a paradigm for spatial patterns of urban growth, so can Los Angeles serve as a vital laboratory for state-centered theories of urban development and new understandings of how local government structures can confer regional advantage in the domestic and world economies.

FROM CITY LIMITS TO CITY-STATES: LOS ANGELES AS AN IDEAL TYPE

The 1990s were witness to a paradigm shift in the way we understand cities and regions and their ability to compete in the global economy. In the 1970s and 1980s, despite recognition that growth was the central dynamic of urban politics, the conventional "city limits" wisdom held that cities could do little independently to shape their economic fortunes. They either were viewed as hostages of mobile private capital, which adeptly played municipalities off against one another for tax, subsidy, or regulatory advantage, or were seen as supplicants of the federal government, seeking financial assistance for redevelopment and restructuring. In the received account, economic actors—businesses and rentier interests—and federal officials set the fundamental contours of urban development policy and outcomes. In an age of multinational corporations and a postindustrial service economy, cities were depicted as politically democratic but economically dependent—held in thrall of supermobile multinational corporations yet hoping to exploit the federal counterbalance to the power of national and international capital.[2]

Today, however, in a globalized economy, free trade and floating currency exchange rates sharply limit the ability of nation-states to macromanage their economic affairs. In domestic politics, a balanced budget agreement, policy devolution to subnational governments, and the prospect of divided government mean that at the national level, little can be done for cities. With the apparent "withering away" of the nation-state, new understandings of the global potency of cities and regions are emerging. Despite grandiose claims by some futurists that modern information-based economies render place irrelevant, there is growing evidence that cities and regions may matter more than ever in the world economy.

Nowhere does this seem to be more true than in so-called world cities. Saskia Sassen, for example, details the bloodcurdling triumph of late-twentieth-century finance capital located in a handful of global metropoles—New York, London, and Tokyo. For Sassen, the postindustrial thesis of a shift to a service economy and the multinational thesis of the triumph of transnational corporations fail to capture the more recent global concentration of economic power in a few world cities that function as highly specialized international financial markets built around the provision of producer services, for example, and speculative investment markets, real estate, insurance, legal services, accounting, advertising, and management consulting. Located at the apex of a hierarchy of world cities, these metropoles function as corporate and financial command-and-control centers directing worldwide investment flows and production processes.[3]

Nonetheless, smaller metropoles increasingly refuse to behave as mere satellites of the so-called command centers. As investment, industry, technology, and consumption become more global in orientation, what Kenichi Ohmae calls "region states," which form natural "business units," have arisen throughout the world to become the new engines of global prosperity in a borderless economy. In similar fashion, Neal Peirce and Rosabeth Moss Kanter trace the rise of regionally articulated and globally integrated "citistates" such as Seattle, Boston, and Miami that use their comparative advantages—location, infrastructure, human capital, and regulatory and tax policies—to lure foreign trade and investment. According to this emerging city-states or new regionalism paradigm, metropolitan areas are becoming pivotal actors in the global economy.[4]

City-states proponents claim that how regions (and particularly their central cities) are organized for governance and policy making have important effects on global competitiveness. Yet their concept of governance remains incomplete. Although the notion of city-states reminds us of the once powerful Renaissance centers of global commerce and finance in Venice and Amsterdam, today the concept prosaically refers to informal public-private partnerships fostering regional cooperation and policy making in the general absence of metropolitan-wide government. As with the city limits paradigm, the new approach depicts businesses, not local government, as the chief architects of global strategies. Scant attention is paid to local state structure and capacity—that is, to formal governmental institutions and powers.

As such, the emerging city-states perspective discounts the role of local development bureaucracies and infrastructure in shaping a region's global competitiveness. Yet there is growing evidence that what local governments do locally matters globally. International ports and airports, for example, give grassroots governments considerable leverage over regional trade flows. Although conventional wisdom holds that international trade flows are primarily shaped by global trade agreements and currency markets, national trade and fiscal policies, and corporate sourcing decisions, little appreciation is given to the stimulus provided by a superior import-export infrastructure that facilitates the movement of global goods through the regional economy. Cities are becoming intermodal transportation centers speeding the flow of people, goods, information, and finance through the world economy.

Regions with the capacity to build a global transportation infrastructure strengthen their competitive advantage enormously and build barriers to the entry of competing regions.[5]

As scholarly work on the role of government in less developed countries attests, state structure—particularly powerful development bureaucracies—can decisively shape patterns of growth and global competitiveness. Peter Evans, for example, contrasts what he terms predatory and developmental states to explain the different growth trajectories of African and East Asian countries. In predatory African states, such as the former Zaire, rent-seeking politicians and bureaucrats have siphoned off private capital for personal use, thereby substantially reducing incentives for business investment.[6]

According to Evans, developmental states share three essential features. First, strong meritocratic state bureaucracies under civil service rules direct the development process. Second, these bureaucracies possess the requisite resources—legal, financial, and political—necessary to play a transformative role in the economy. Third, such bureaucracies have "embedded autonomy" vis-à-vis economic actors. Public servants are more than mere instruments of the business community, instead possessing the political capacity to mobilize private sector actors and resources behind state development projects. Chalmers Johnson's work treats Japan—and its powerful Ministry of International Trade and Industry—as the prototypical bureaucratic-centered developmental state. Stephan Haggard's comparative analysis of the political determinants of industrial development in East Asia and Latin America emphasizes the role of East Asian state capacity and insulation from interest group and class pressures in shaping postwar export-oriented development policies.[7]

The concept of developmental states can be fruitfully applied to the United States, and particularly to its local governments. In economic policy making, the United States is a weak national state. In his study of American foreign materials investment policy, Stephen Krasner argues that federalism and strong interest groups sharply limit the national government's ability to make coherent economic policy. In contrast, Peter Eisinger argues that state and local governments have greater capacity to fashion coherent development mandates because of their smaller size and greater homogeneity of economic interests, thus reducing collective action problems. For Eisinger, subnational governments function as entrepreneurial states when they creatively mobilize and deploy the public and private resources needed for development.[8]

Metropolitan areas, characterized by more coherent economies, greater homogeneity, and fewer actors, appear to have strong incentives to create developmental state structures. Not surprisingly, then, the nation's strongest development bureaucracies have formed at the grass roots. These normally take the form of independent public authorities addressing regionwide problems. For example, New York is famed for its powerful triborough and port authorities operating under the stewardship of public entrepreneurs such as Robert Moses and Austin Tobin. In Chicago, the machine informally centralizes power, whereas much formal power is parceled out to ten regional agencies such as the sanitary district.

Unlike New York, Chicago, and other big cities that rely primarily on regional public authorities for infrastructure provision, in Los Angeles the port, airport, water, and power systems all are agencies of central city government. Here, functioning as part of general purpose municipal governments (in contrast to fragmented, limited-purpose regional authorities), and under the nominal control of mayors and city councils, city bureaucracies can serve as coherent instruments of municipal policies involving central-city development, regional dominion, and global competitiveness.[9]

Los Angeles, more so than New York, Chicago, or other major cities, offers the most fruitful application of the concept of a local developmental state. In explaining both early population growth and industrialization and recent transformation into one of the world's great trade and transshipment centers, Los Angeles represents a Weberian ideal-typical case of local state-assisted development. Like postwar East Asian countries, Los Angeles early in the twentieth century transformed itself into a prodigious public growth machine to jump-start a backward regional economy. Los Angeles city government features strong meritocratic bureaucracies with ample resources for economic transformation and substantial capacity for "embedded autonomy" relative to private sector actors.

Although Los Angeles government plans, regulates, and promotes business (staples of East Asian states), its core development function involves the provision of public goods. At the heart of municipal Los Angeles lie the three powerful proprietary or semiautonomous Water and Power, Harbor, and Airports Departments. These mammoth public enterprises accounted for nearly one half of the city's $9 billion budget and more than three quarters of its $12.5 billion debt in 1996-1997. No other major city devotes such a large share of its municipal budget and debt to public enterprise. Although other cities resort to regional public authorities for infrastructure provision, Los Angeles has made infrastructure the centerpiece of municipal governance. No other major American city has all four of these functions under the aegis of city government.[10]

L.A.'s proprietary departments manage the city's historic crown jewels—its municipal water and power systems (the nation's largest municipal utility); the Port of Los Angeles (the nation's second largest container port after Long Beach which, combined, is the world's third largest container facility); and Los Angeles International Airport (LAX; the world's fourth busiest passenger airport and second busiest air cargo facility). Spawned during the Progressive era, when California home rule constitutional provisions gave local governments the legal autonomy and fiscal capacity to act as veritable city-states, L.A.'s crown jewels have played crucial (and largely underrecognized) roles in L.A.'s—indeed all of Southern California's—unparalleled twentieth-century population growth, early industrialization, and recent metamorphosis into the nation's leading center for global trade. In no small part due to the efforts of the city's enterprising bureaucrats, Los Angeles has grown into the nation's second largest city (3.7 million inhabitants), anchoring a 16 million population, $500 billion metropolitan economy—the world's twelfth largest, larger than South Korea's.[11]

Balanced against their stimulus role, however, the operations of L.A.'s powerful public growth machines also raise serious normative concerns about democratic accountability, efficiency, and regional quality of life. Critics charge that the crown jewels are bloated empire-building bureaucracies relentlessly pursuing growth at the expense of community and the environment. Although Ted Lowi coined the phrase "bureaucratic machines" to refer to New York's 1960s-era ungovernable post-Tammany Hall bureaucracies, the concept is even more aptly applied to L.A.'s Progressive-era reform bureaucracies. Early on, the DWP was widely considered to be the real government of Los Angeles. Later, the Los Angeles Police Department became known as one of the nation's leading rogue bureaucracies, unanswerable to the mayor, city council, and voters. In the 1960s and 1970s, as LAX dramatically expanded through the wholesale condemnation and eminent domain acquisition of nearby residential neighborhoods, the Department of Airports joined the list of so-called imperial bureaucracies.[12]

In the 1990s, charges of bureaucratic inefficiency replaced unaccountability, as the mayor and city council ordered critical audits of the DWP and the Harbor Department, charging them with being complacent monopolists tolerating waste and mismanagement. Critics also claim to have documented a massive trail of community and environmental destruction. The litany of alleged bureaucratic ruin includes the so-called rape of the Owens Valley, where Los Angeles supposedly stole water from valley farmers and left a shrinking Mono Lake and huge dust storms created by a dry Owens Lake; the forced removal of thousands of Westchester and Playa del Rey residents to facilitate LAX expansion; and, most recently, the sizable air pollution generated by heavy commercial airplane and vessel traffic in the nation's smoggiest air basin.

UNRAVELING THE ENIGMA OF L.A.'S GROWTH: BRINGING THE LOCAL STATE BACK IN

Modern Los Angeles is a city that should not be. Were paleontologist Stephen Jay Gould to discover a Burgess Shale containing the fossil remains of late-nineteenth-century America, the small City of the Angels would have been considered a most unlikely candidate for growth. In 1890, the city numbered but 50,000 inhabitants, its economy still reeling from the collapse of a speculative land boom. Besides sunshine and a temperate year-round climate, the area possessed few comparative advantages. Unlike Chicago and St. Louis, its isolated geography placed it thousands of miles from major markets. Unlike New York and San Francisco, it had no natural deep-water harbor. The Los Angeles River and nearby artesian wells could support a population of only 300,000. Before the discovery of oil, there were few local energy sources. At twenty-eight square miles, Los Angeles was only one half the size of rival San Francisco, and city boundaries lay a distant sixteen miles from the Pacific Ocean. Given these multiple disadvantages, Los Angeles appeared destined for the scrap heap of history.[13]

Yet grow it did, undergoing what historian Robert Fogelson has described as the most extraordinary urban expansion in American history. By 1930, as the city's population mushroomed to 1.2 million, Los Angeles ranked fifth in population, second in territory (442 square miles, because of annexation), and ninth in manufacturing among the nation's cities. In the short span of two generations, improbable Los Angeles had become the Colossus of the West and Southwest, surpassing in size San Francisco, San Diego, Seattle, Portland, Denver, Phoenix, Houston, Dallas, and San Antonio. Compared with these regional rivals, Los Angeles by 1930 had already industrialized, with automobile and tire branch plants and thriving aircraft and petrochemical industries. World War II military spending—a prime catalyst for Sunbelt urban growth elsewhere—merely solidified L.A.'s position as the leading manufacturing center of the West and Southwest.[14]

In the postwar era, the astonishing pace of growth continued as the region became the world's leading aerospace center. By the early 1980s, as the city's population surpassed 3 million, Los Angeles replaced Chicago as the nation's Second City. Hosting its second Olympic Games in 1984, Los Angeles appeared ready to challenge New York as the nation's premier metropolis. The five-county Los Angeles metropolitan area approached Greater New York in population. No longer just capital to the entertainment industry, Los Angeles outranked New York as the nation's leading manufacturing center. Los Angeles also served as the beachhead for Pacific Rim investment and trade. Fully one half of Japan's leading banks headquartered their American operations in Los Angeles. Driven by burgeoning East Asian trade, Los Angeles supplanted New York as the nation's leading trade center.[15]

The 1990s, however, appeared to mark the end of L.A.'s remarkable ascendancy. As the Cold War ended, military cutbacks decimated the country's most defense-dependent economy. With Los Angeles County alone losing 200,000 aerospace jobs, the region's historically low unemployment rate climbed to 50 percent above the national average. As Stephen Cohen observed, "L.A. is the hole in the [national] bucket. Twenty seven percent of the nation's entire 1990-92 job loss took place in Greater Los Angeles." In the midst of the deepest downturn in the region's economy since the Great Depression, the 1992 riots erupted. The nation's worst twentieth-century urban disorder resulted in a three-day toll of fifty-five deaths, upwards of $1 billion in property damage, more than 700 businesses destroyed, and 10,000 jobs lost. Nature only compounded man-made disaster with the 1994 Northridge earthquake, which produced more than $20 billion in property losses, the nation's most costly temblor.[16]

Could the fallen City of the Angels find new formulas for growth? Answering this question requires an understanding of how this improbable city had grown in the first place. The conventional wisdom of L.A.'s twentieth-century development draws on two general models of urban growth—one rooted in the forces of the market, the other in the state. An entrepreneurial account, consistent with the Chicago School perspective, gives primacy to private sector actors and private development strategies. This model figures prominently in Todd Swanstrom's study of the historical roots of Cleveland's postwar crisis of growth politics, whereby, before the New

Deal, American cities generally pursued market-based strategies of development. The business community represented the chief motor of investment, and a minimalist philosophy of government prevailed. As inducements for business location and investment, municipalities offered a lean menu of low taxes and caretaker services.[17]

This entrepreneurial model seems to best fit Sunbelt cities of the West and Southwest. In Stephen Elkin's study of Dallas, for example, business elites energetically pursued private growth strategies while confining local government's role to low taxes and limited planning, zoning, and service provision. Houston is considered an even more quintessentially free enterprise city guided by a powerful business elite and a laissez-faire philosophy of government. The major historical departures from Sunbelt entrepreneurialism have been federal investments—river and harbor projects, New Deal public works, and World War II defense spending.[18]

State-centered theories represent a second general model of urban development, emphasizing the role of government actors, institutions, and policies in shaping growth. The model originally was fashioned to explain Frostbelt urban redevelopment. In the postwar era, older Eastern cities such as New York, Chicago, New Haven, and Cleveland faced the imperatives of revitalizing decaying downtowns, rebuilding deteriorating infrastructures, restructuring shrinking manufacturing bases, and resolving growing municipal fiscal crises. For such cities, revitalization has been a state-driven process involving federal urban renewal and community development programs and financing.

John Mollenkopf, a leading proponent of a state-centered model of urban redevelopment, argues that in pluralistic fashion, big-city mayors and bureaucrats served as innovative public entrepreneurs, assembling public-private coalitions and using federal redevelopment monies to rebuild decaying downtowns. In contrast to this pluralist model of state-directed redevelopment, neo-Marxians invoke two variants of a theory of state capitalism—that local economic elites instrumentally use redevelopment projects for their benefit and, when public entrepreneurs appear to prevail, that hegemonic capitalist accumulation imperatives structurally constrain all forms of state action.[19]

State-centered theories now are being applied to Sunbelt cities. In a pluralist vein, Heywood Sanders argues that seemingly entrepreneurial Sunbelt cities such as Houston, San Antonio, and San Jose actually grew " 'the old fashioned way' . . . through a massive expansion in the local public fisc, with an enormous growth of debt and public capital investment [for] streets, sewers, water supply, airports, ports, parks and libraries." In a neo-Marxian account, Joe Feagin furnishes a valuable case study of early state-assisted capitalism in "free enterprise" Houston. During the Progressive era, Houston's business elite energetically pursued federal funding for ship channel dredging and port expansion designed to link the city to the world economy.[20]

The two models have been used to explain different stages of L.A.'s twentieth-century development. An entrepreneurial account is the leading explanation of the city's pre-1930s growth. It depicts early Los Angeles as a West Coast Dallas or Houston controlled by a powerful business elite and laissez-faire philosophy. For the post-

1930 period, a state-centered approach is offered. It characterizes Los Angeles not as a Pacific Rim candidate ripe for redevelopment—like highly politicized New York— but as one of the nation's leading martial metropolises.

Much of L.A.'s early development appears to fit the entrepreneurial paradigm. Historian Robert Fogelson, a leading chronicler of early Los Angeles, emphasizes the overweening power of the business community in shaping the region's pre-New Deal growth. In the late nineteenth century, the coming of the railroad jump-started the region's economy. Harrison Gray Otis and Harry Chandler, owners of the *Los Angeles Times,* spearheaded projects ranging from San Fernando Valley land development to lobbying Eastern manufacturers to establish branch plants in Southern California. The Los Angeles Chamber of Commerce, one of the nation's most powerful local business organizations, launched its famous "land of sunshine" national advertising campaign exploiting what Thorstein Veblen called, in a different context, the "advantages of backwardness." The chamber's advertising emphasized leisure, not work; consumption, not production; and the single-family residence, not the industrial park.[21]

Recent studies have highlighted the catalytic role of private developers such as Henry E. Huntington, early L.A.'s master builder and the region's private sector equivalent to New York's Robert Moses. While Moses used public authority to shape an entire metropolitan area, Huntington used private authority to similar effect. Huntington's private development empire started with trolleys but quickly graduated to real estate and utilities. L.A.'s master tycoon constructed a vast radial trolley network extending from downtown to the suburbanizing periphery. In tandem, his land company subdivided the property along the rail lines for residential development. Finally, his privately owned electrical power firm supplied energy both for his trolley lines and for residential customers. More than any other private individual, Huntington shaped the region's decentralized pattern of spatial development.[22]

This received account of L.A.'s supposed entrepreneurial growth regime suggests that the real estate market represented the chief motor of early regional development. Although real estate developers have historically shaped urban growth, nowhere did this appear to be more evident than in Los Angeles. In 1930, the city was home to 7 percent of the nation's 240,000 real estate agents and developers, as one seventh of the city's workforce was employed in real estate and construction. Given massive obstacles to export-based growth strategies—transportation and capital barriers and the absence of a hinterland market in the sparsely settled West— L.A.'s economic elite, in the conventional account, turned to national advertising to encourage settlement and inflate the real estate market.[23]

Notwithstanding the vaunted power of L.A.'s real estate industry, a state-centered explanation for the city's post-Progressive era growth depicts Los Angeles as a martial metropolis rather than a free enterprise city. Offered as a general account of Sunbelt urban development in the World War II era, this theory views federal military spending as a prime catalyst for cities such as Los Angeles. Yet on the West Coast, as historian Roger Lotchin argues, the martial metropolis traces its roots even further back to World War I. As that war ended, the military faced the threat of massive demobilization and desperately needed new budget-building bases and civilian constituencies. In turn, rapidly growing California cities such as Los Angeles had fragile real-estate-based boom-and-bust economies. These cities had only begun to industrialize. For local civic boosters, military payrolls and projects represented municipal Keynesianism at work.[24]

These structural forces created powerful incentives for an early "city-and-the-sword" alliance between local boosters and the military that helped make World War II-era Los Angeles the nation's second leading arsenal of democracy, trailing only Detroit. By 1938, fully 60 percent of the nation's aircraft industry had settled in Southern California. World War II militarized the region's entire manufacturing base. In the postwar era, federal funding continued to drive the local economy and allowed Southern California to prosper and partially insulate itself from the national business cycle. In the early 1990s, as the Cold War ended, defense cutbacks, not surprisingly, resulted in the region's worst economic downturn since the Depression.[25]

As attractive as these two theories are for explaining particular stages of L.A.'s development, each lacks a crucial catalytic ingredient—the region's comprehensive program of local public works. More so than any other major metropolitan area, Greater Los Angeles had to be invented with public works. Except for sunshine and a temperate climate, nature was not kind to Southern California, so government—city, county, special district, state, and federal—had to supply what nature could not. Greater L.A.'s development—both past and projected—is far more publicly shaped than the entrepreneurial account suggests. Water is only part—and certainly not the whole—of L.A.'s ambitious local state-based strategy of growth. A series of extraordinary *public* decisions and investments built modern Los Angeles and Southern California. From the turn of the century onward, the construction of a vast system of public works opened up the undeveloped region to market forces and provided the necessary template for industrialization and, later, a defense-based economy.

The five-county economy of metropolitan Los Angeles rests on an $85 billion public investment (in 1998 dollars) in infrastructure—water, power, ports, airports, freeways, streets, rail lines, subways, sewers, and flood control. Spending on Greater L.A.'s public capital stock rivals that for the New York metropolitan area. Public infrastructure investments such as L.A.'s represent both a complementary input and initiating factor for private development, generating regional growth in four ways: as public works construction activity, as a production subsidy, as a household consumption good, and as inducement for migrating households and firms.[26]

Modern Los Angeles has taken four great economic leaps forward: (1) in the late nineteenth century, with railroads and real estate; (2) 1900 to 1940, with territorial expansion, population growth, and industrialization; (3) 1940 to 1990, with federal military spending; and (4) beginning in the 1970s, and accelerating since 1990, with international trade. Yet massive infrastructure investments were needed for each of these transformations to occur.

Southern California has been called "Reagan Country," but not because of its growth, which has violated all laissez-faire principles of Reaganomics. Starting in the late nineteenth century, Los Angeles voters paid a king's ransom—5 percent of the county's assessed valuation (equivalent to $25 billion in 1996 dollars)—to bring the Southern Pacific railroad to Los Angeles. In the early twentieth century, the DWP (created in 1902) and Harbor Department (1909) became the cornerstones of modern Los Angeles. The Los Angeles Aqueduct, public power, and the man-made harbor at San Pedro-Wilmington underwrote the city's relentless territorial expansion, population growth, and pre-World War II industrialization. In particular, the DWP's hydroelectric plants generated the cheap and abundant energy needed to attract Eastern industry, while the Port of Los Angeles served as a key conduit for raw materials needed by the region's fast-growing automobile and tire branch plants. Later, the DWP played a central role in creating regional water and power projects and agencies—Hoover Dam, the Colorado Aqueduct, and the Metropolitan Water District of Southern California (MWD)—allowing the larger metropolitan area to grow and industrialize.

The pre-World War II era also saw the origins of the L.A. municipal airport system, beginning with Mines Field (later to become LAX) in 1928. In 1947, the Department of Airports would become the city's third crown jewel with voter approval of its new status as a semiautonomous proprietary department. In the 1960s, the department would blossom into a de facto regional airport authority with the acquisition of Ontario and Palmdale Airports. Along with downtown redevelopment, the expansion of the Port of Los Angeles and LAX would be the postwar capstones of L.A.'s public development strategy. Since the 1970s, the region's ports and airports have made global trade a major element of the region's economy.

FORGING L.A.'S DEVELOPMENTAL CITY-STATE: HOME RULE AND INNOVATIVE FINANCING

One must be careful, however, when "bringing the state back in." Although it has become fashionable to call for more state-centered interpretations of urban political economy, few have attempted to define the term more precisely. The crucial distinction between entrepreneurial and statist growth regimes is relative, not absolute. This difference lies in the relative autonomy and influence of private sector versus public sector actors in shaping urban growth and the relative importance of private versus public development strategies.[27]

Late-nineteenth-century Los Angeles was a classic entrepreneurial growth regime. It featured business hegemony, a low-tax and low-spending caretaker government, and primary reliance on booster advertising and real estate to generate growth. Yet a business-led laissez-faire regime was not devoid of state action. Thus, in the 1860s, Yankees used the legal system to wrest control of the Spanish land grants from the native ranchero class. In the 1870s, the business community skillfully orchestrated voter approval of the huge public subsidy needed to bring the Southern Pacific railroad to Los Angeles. These political interventions by the local business community, although significant, had an ad hoc and episodic quality. The laissez-faire state was not systematically organized to direct the process of development.

L.A.'s twentieth-century developmental state was, however, so organized. It featured massive public bureaucracies and infrastructure projects as the centerpiece of a more public-centered growth strategy. With the construction of the municipal water, power, and harbor systems, public bureaucrats began challenging the longstanding hegemony of the business community. A more state-centered growth regime, however, was not without entrepreneurial force. The Los Angeles Chamber of Commerce continued to wield significant power. With the advent of a more statist growth regime, the city's power structure was pluralized and public development strategies complemented private ones.

L.A.'s version of state-assisted capitalism displayed increasing independence from the business community. Although an instrumentalist theory (wherein economic elites control government) best describes the initial stages of local state building, a more autonomous model better describes the behavior of the city's development bureaucracies after World War I. Powerful public agencies such as the DWP fashioned alliances with politicians and voters to extend successfully the city's water and power systems (and the department's authority) in the face of strong opposition from private utilities, the powerful and then archconservative *Los Angeles Times,* and the antiunion Merchants and Manufacturing Association. The city's experience with bureaucratic machines such as the DWP suggests that the state cannot always be reduced to instrumental terms. In the final analysis, however, the dynamics of a market economy structurally constrained the city's development bureaucrats.[28]

Unlike Chicago's patronage-based machine politics, the building of powerful public bureaucracies in Los Angeles required the elimination of the patronage system. In Los Angeles, a turn-of-the-century reform movement wrested control of city government from a formidable bipartisan "interest group" machine controlled by the Southern Pacific railroad. Reforms such as a civil service system, approved by city voters in 1902, were needed to shield the city's fledgling public enterprises and their public works projects from rent-seeking politicians. Under L.A.'s civil service system, 5,000 municipal workers were hired to build the Los Angeles Aqueduct between 1906 and 1913. The merit system largely eliminated opportunities for graft and corruption.[29]

Yet L.A.'s developmental state apparatus could not have been constructed without the wide legal and financial latitude granted to cities by the California Constitution. In 1879, California was the second state in the nation to authorize municipal home rule, and in 1889, Los Angeles was the state's first city (and the nation's second, after St. Louis) to have voters approve a home rule charter. California also gave its local governments the fiscal capacity needed to finance large-scale infrastructure projects. The state's debt ceiling for municipal borrowing was 15 percent of assessed valuation—double the national average. These extensive borrowing powers largely went unused under L.A.'s early entrepreneurial growth regime. After the turn of the century, however, these powers were invoked to the fullest to finance the city's expensive projects. Between 1905 and 1932, the city of Los Angeles and MWD marketed $412 million in water, power, and harbor bonds (equivalent to $4.3 billion in 1996 dollars) with a considerably smaller and poorer population than today.[30]

Powerful Progressive-era municipal governments were a Western phenomenon, where urbanization preceded state building. In 1870, for example, San Francisco represented one half of California's population. Thus, Western cities were able to control state constitutional conventions and legislatures and secure laws serving urban interests. In the East, where state building preceded urbanization, cities confronted rural-dominated state constitutional conventions and legislatures. As a result, Eastern cities suffered from state interference such as tax and debt ceiling limits.[31]

Armed with home rule and extensive borrowing powers, Progressive-era Los Angeles could operate as a developmental city-state. Los Angeles is a prime example of what economist Joseph Schumpeter has called an "entrepreneurial state" that goes into business for itself, building and operating revenue- and growth-generating public enterprises such as Hoover Dam, the Tennessee Valley Authority, and L.A.'s proprietary departments.[32] In its role as entrepreneurial state, Los Angeles became a national innovator in public finance. Although the California Constitution—in a Lockean provision designed to protect property interests and deter excessive debt—required two-thirds voter approval for general obligation bonds backed by the "full faith and credit" of the city, L.A.'s proprietary departments repeatedly built the extraordinary voter majorities needed for project financing.

The City of the Angels also became a national innovator at targeting municipal debt for revenue- and growth-generating projects. Early on, the city charter earmarked 80 percent of L.A.'s total bonded indebtedness for the revenue-producing proprietary departments. In contrast, no other city in the nation targeted as much as 50 percent of its general obligation debt for such projects. Los Angeles strategically annexed surrounding areas to increase the city's assessed valuation (and thus bonding capacity) and reduce per capita tax burdens. Special districts such as the MWD of Southern California were created as debt-pyramiding schemes because their debt did not count against municipal borrowing ceilings. Starting in the 1930s, as the politics of hard times made voter approval of general obligation bonds difficult, Los Angeles led the nation's cities in shifting infrastructure financing to revenue bonds, which did not require voter approval.[33]

Los Angeles also pioneered developmental pricing strategies, offering the nation's lowest water, power, harbor, and airport charges before World War II. Developmental pricing (a low-bid strategy intended to increase business volume) produced growth sufficient to cover operating expenses and retire debt but left little cash available for new projects. As a result, the city's proprietary departments were continually conducting bond elections to raise new project capital.

In the postwar era, however, as the city's public enterprises shifted to revenue bond financing, a new higher rate structure was installed. To receive favorable bond ratings (thus lowering borrowing costs), L.A.'s crown jewels began raising their user fees to create self-sustaining project revenue yields. More recently, the Port of Los Angeles has chosen a higher pricing strategy—monopoly rent-seeking, which builds ample cash reserves funneled back into facility modernization and expansion. Monopoly pricing has downside risks, however. The port risked losing market share to its lower-priced competitors at the Port of Long Beach. It also encouraged the city's elected officials to divert cash reserves targeted for port improvements into the city's general fund to pay for popular items with voters, such as more police.[34]

BUILDING POWERFUL BUREAUCRACIES: LEGAL FRAMEWORK, AGENCY LEADERSHIP, AND POLITICAL STRATEGIES

Although crown jewels normally serve as ceremonial objects of sovereignty, L.A.'s water, power, port, and airport facilities are industrial-grade gems driving the engines of economic development. They power three of the region's—indeed the nation's—most powerful and effective development bureaucracies. In Southern California, their political influence and economic impact are rivaled only by the mammoth MWD (which the DWP helped to create), the city's Community Redevelopment Agency (responsible for the postwar rebuilding of downtown Los Angeles), the Port of Long Beach, and the recently created and conflict-plagued Metropolitan Transportation Authority. In contrast, L.A.'s city Planning Department has neither the political influence nor transformative capacity of the three proprietary departments.

The local constitution, or city charter, is key to explaining the crown jewels' political autonomy and transformative capacity. Although city agencies, the proprietary departments historically have approached the independence and influence of public authorities such as New York's famed port and triborough authorities. In L.A.'s decentralized governance, where commission-run bureaucracies share power with the mayor and city council, the crown jewels are first among bureaucratic equals. Under the charter, they are semiautonomous departments with broad formal powers (particularly over their budgets) and are not subject to the types of controls that Congress exercises over federal agencies that are creatures of congressional statute and delegated authority. L.A.'s city charter, not the city council, is the primary source of authority for the proprietary departments, limiting the mayor's and city council's ability to control these departments.[35]

The crown jewels, however, are not rogue bureaucracies unanswerable to voters and elected officials. By simple majority vote, the electorate can approve charter amendments, rewriting the rules of the bureaucratic game. Departments are managed by five-member boards of commissioners appointed by the mayor with council approval. Under a voter-approved 1995 charter amendment, for instance, the mayor can hire and fire managers with council approval, and, under a 1992 charter amendment, the fifteen-member council can overturn board decisions by a two-thirds vote.

The council also must give its approval to board-proposed rates, revenue bond offerings, major contracts, and long-term leases. Both the city council and the city administrative officer (who reports to the mayor and council) have broad investigatory powers over bureaucracy. Yet the mayor and council have little direct authority over the proprietary department's budgets and capital spending. In this fashion, the charter maintains a delicate balance between political oversight and agency independence.

This constitutional balance reflects that these are public businesses responsible for economic development. Yet providing public goods while charging user fees means that these government enterprises function in the dual and conflicting arenas of market and democracy. As such, they face the inevitable trade-off between market efficiency and democratic accountability. To achieve such efficiency, public enterprises must be free of interference from rent-seeking politicians. Such political autonomy can yield enormous economic benefit. In the short run, agencies can respond to changing market conditions quickly, ensuring cost recovery and profitability; in the long run, autonomy encourages public enterprises to undertake major capital investments that promise long-term yield. Long-term project horizons also closely match professional civil servants' lengthy thirty- to forty-year careers.

In contrast, the city's elected officials face short career horizons under voter-approved term limits of two four-year terms. As a result, office seekers favor current expenditures popular with voters over long-term capital investments with little immediate political payoff. Because L.A.'s city charter recognizes these different budgetary priorities, proprietary departments have their own special revenue funds that are shielded from periodic raids by the mayor and city council.

The charter also provides for democratic accountability, meaning that elected officials and voters can influence bureaucratic decision making. Since 1990, there has been a shift in the local constitutional balance between efficiency and accountability. From 1925 through the 1980s, the charter enshrined efficiency. In the early 1990s, voter-approved charter amendments made the city's bureaucracies more responsive to the mayor and council. In 1999, a new city charter approved by the voters strengthened the mayor's powers while reaffirming the semiautonomous nature of the proprietary departments.[36]

Yet in forging the autonomy central to the early history of the proprietary departments, public entrepreneurs sought to insulate their agencies and capital projects from meddling politicians and business notables. These public entrepreneurs—unheralded public servants who have served neither as mere handmaidens of the business community, as the entrepreneurial model would suggest, nor as passive agents of the mayor and city council—quickly developed three political strategies for bureaucratic empowerment and project development: mastering ballot-box growth; cultivating their clientele; and developing city, state, and federal influence.

The crown jewels became acknowledged masters of ballot-box growth. Until recently, cities financed their infrastructure projects with voter-approved general obligation bonds rather than, as now, with revenue bonds. To obtain necessary voter approval, L.A.'s proprietary departments transformed themselves into powerful ballot-box machines. Departmental staff mapped out campaign strategies and created dummy support organizations, while agency employees served as precinct workers in bond elections. Interest group alliances were essential to bond campaign strategy, with support from local business and civic organizations only enhancing the prospects of voter approval.

Once created, L.A.'s bureaucratic bond machines began behaving like their party counterparts—slating and campaigning for friendly candidates, pressing for voter passage of charter amendments, and enhancing departmental powers and autonomy. In the 1920s and 1930s, the nation's most powerful local bureaucratic electoral machine was L.A.'s DWP, which the *Los Angeles Times* accused of running city hall. In particular, the *Times* pointed to long-serving DWP Commissioner John Randolph Haynes (who it claimed was the "chief architect" of the 1925 city charter, enshrining the independence of the proprietary departments) and to DWP's Ezra Scattergood, who allegedly created a political machine (with city employees) to run public power bond elections and slate candidates for city office.[37]

To achieve their objectives at city hall, the crown jewels have also forged strong alliances with their clientele. The Harbor Department regularly uses the lobbying muscle (and campaign contributions) of the shipping industry to secure council approval of proposed fees, leasing arrangements, and capital projects. The Department of Airports has developed a close working relationship with the airline industry to pressure city hall into low landing fees and favorable terminal lease arrangements. With the advent of revenue bond financing, new allies have appeared: municipal security traders and bondholders. Bond covenants are a potent tool preventing meddling by elected officials in departmental finances. Yet strong interest group ties have led to charges that L.A.'s development bureaucracies have become captives of their clientele.

The proprietary departments have also become acknowledged masters of city hall. Under L.A.'s district system of city council elections, council members representing San Pedro-Wilmington (the harbor) and Westchester (LAX) are first among equals in port and airport matters. Offering generous side payments—such as neighborhood projects—the Harbor and Airports Departments have assiduously courted, and often co-opted, local council members. Civil servants also try to make mayoral-appointed commissioners department-friendly. Similar to processes described by Hugh Heclo at the federal level, career professionals encourage board members to "go native" by identifying with the agency's self-defined mission rather than with the mayor's agenda.[38]

Finally, the crown jewels also lobby state and federal officials for needed assistance. L.A.'s bureaucrats have developed close working relationships with such agencies as the U.S. Bureau of Reclamation, the Army Corps of Engineers, the Federal Aviation Administration, federal and state environmental protection agencies, the California Coastal Commission, and the state Department of Transportation. Such alliances have allowed L.A.'s public entrepreneurs to project their voices into state legislative and congressional decision making. State legislation, for example, allowed Los Angeles to annex the harbor cities of San Pedro and Wilmington, to capture the tidelands from railroad control, and to create the MWD to build the Colorado Aqueduct. Federal assistance made the Los Angeles Aqueduct, the harbor breakwater, Hoover Dam, and LAX expansion all possible.

Notwithstanding the focus here on the crown jewels, other city departments have played important development roles—two in particular. The first, interestingly enough, is the Los Angeles Police Department. Because the city's business elite agreed on the need for cheap labor to compete with unionized, high-wage San Francisco, from the turn of the century onward a draconian labor policy formed an essential component of a state-centered growth strategy. Business leaders enlisted the city's police in a bloody, twenty-year-long antiunion crusade that made Los Angeles "the citadel of the open shop." By the 1920s, however, a downsized and domesticated labor movement had been incorporated into (and survived as part of) the DWP-led growth coalition. The second agency worthy of mention is the Community Redevelopment Agency. The agency (created in 1948), which in partnership with the downtown business community oversaw the Bunker Hill redevelopment project—the nation's largest urban renewal effort—deserves further study.[39]

LOS ANGELES AT THE GLOBAL CROSSROADS

In the 1990s, L.A.'s crown jewels and the global future of the city and region lay at an uncertain crossroads. Rebounding from the deep recession, Los Angeles planners drew up ambitious plans to expand dramatically the region's global gateways—its international ports, airports, and rail lines—to ensure its future as one of the world's great trade and transshipment centers. But a municipal fiscal crisis and environmental and community challenges threatened to frustrate the region's promise as an American Singapore or Hong Kong.

Responding to the challenges of the global economy, the region's public investment priorities since the 1970s have shifted to trade and transportation. Leaders such as former L.A. Mayor Tom Bradley envisioned the region as the premier Pacific Rim gateway, strenuously pushing port and airport expansion. Billions of dollars were spent to expand and modernize the Ports of Los Angeles and Long Beach and to build international terminal and air cargo facilities at LAX. This investment strategy paid off handsomely.

By the 1990s, the San Pedro Bay ports had become the world's third largest container facility, handling more than 25 percent of the nation's international waterborne commerce. LAX had become the world's second busiest air cargo facility. Because of San Diego's inadequate port and airport facilities, L.A.'s global gateways carried nearly two thirds of California's international trade, from San Luis Obispo to the Mexican border.

Because of its superior import-export infrastructure and strategic Pacific Rim location, Los Angeles experienced remarkable trade growth. In 1996, with $216 billion in merchandise trade—one seventh of the nation's total—the Los Angeles Customs District far surpassed New York, with $155 billion, as the nation's leading trade center. Within the short span of twenty-five years, the trade fortunes of the nation's two largest metropolises had dramatically reversed. Between 1972 and 1996, L.A.'s share of total U.S. global trade climbed from 6 to 15 percent while New York's share plummeted from 21 to 11 percent. By 1996, 20 percent of Greater L.A.'s five-county (Los Angeles, Orange, Ventura, San Bernardino, and Riverside) gross regional product depended on international trade, up from 13 percent in 1972. The San Pedro Bay ports and LAX had become the most important public engines of regional development. Together, they generated $90 billion in regional economic activity and more than 1 million jobs.[40]

But Los Angeles fast was becoming a victim of its trade success, with unprecedented congestion threatening its ports, airports, and rail and highway systems. More than 50 percent of the world's economic growth, 1995 to 2015, was projected to occur in East Asian countries such as China, Japan, Taiwan, and South Korea—the region's leading trade partners—while post-NAFTA Mexican trade opportunities placed even further demands on the region's transportation system. As a result, L.A.'s already crowded ports and airports faced a doubling, even tripling, of demand by 2020.

To meet rising demand and head off West Coast rivals eager to capitalize on the region's inability to manage it, Los Angeles officials prepared ambitious port, rail, and airport expansion plans: (a) the $4 billion program of Los Angeles and Long Beach port development, 1995 to 2020; (b) the $2 billion Alameda Corridor rail project, 1995 to 2001, designed to facilitate the movement of goods from the ports to the downtown railheads; and (c) the LAX Master Plan, and a projected $10 to $12 billion in outlays, 1995 to 2015, for new facilities at LAX and Ontario International Airport. Representing the largest capital spending program for trade infrastructure of any metropolitan area in the country, it far surpassed the capital spending plans of L.A.'s chief trade rivals—San Francisco-Oakland, Seattle-Tacoma, and New York. If implemented in timely fashion, L.A.'s trade projects promised to generate more than one fifth of the metropolitan area's projected 3.6 million new jobs, 1994 to 2015.[41]

Yet L.A.'s ambitious global plans were placed in double jeopardy by a municipal fiscal crisis and a breakdown in the region's long-standing growth consensus. The tandem effects of Proposition 13, the property tax initiative passed by California voters in 1978, and subsequent state raids on local revenues coupled with the 1990s recession sharply reduced municipal revenues, creating enormous budget-balancing pressures. City officials turned to the three revenue-producing proprietary departments to resolve the budget crisis. Los Angeles Mayor Richard Riordan's proposed $4 billion fiscal year 1996-1997 general fund budget tapped heavily into the funds of the crown jewels to close a $240 million budget shortfall and pay for more police. The Riordan administration's strategy of milking these so-called cash cows had netted nearly $400 million, 1994 to 1996, and yielded another $170 million for fiscal year 1996-1997. Despite such laudable goals as a balanced budget, no additional taxes, and 3,000 more police, revenue diversions had a long-term cost: a less competitive infrastructure unable to meet the challenges of a global, deregulated marketplace. The costs of these hefty revenue diversions would be borne in the form of higher user charges and project financing charges, resulting in reduced growth potential.[42]

Consider the case of Los Angeles International Airport. LAX is one of the most important public assets in North America, generating $43 billion in regional economic activity—nearly 10 percent of the metropolitan area's gross regional product. As the state's only true international airport south of the Bay Area, an overcrowded LAX desperately needed to expand to meet a doubling of Southern California passenger demand and a tripling of air cargo demand—both chiefly driven by international traffic—by the year 2015. The long-delayed LAX Master Plan attempted to address these needs, and expansion promised to create 370,000 new regional jobs—in transportation, tourism, manufacturing, and services—and $37 billion in new regional economic activity by 2015.[43]

Yet city hall's attempted revenue diversions threatened these expansion plans. Mayor Riordan's controversial 1993 quadrupling of LAX aircraft landing fees—the subject of a bitter legal dispute with the airlines and a planned first step in airport revenue diversion to the general fund—made the airport cash-rich but less competitive. LAX landing fees were now twice as high as those at rival airports in San Francisco, Las Vegas, Phoenix, and Seattle; LAX passenger charges were 50 percent higher. Thwarted by federal regulators from diverting landing fees and passenger charges to the city's general fund, the mayor demanded an additional $30 million—in aircraft fuel taxes or repayment of ancient loans—from the airport. The mayor's policies appeared to take their toll. The airlines viewed LAX as expensive, overcrowded, adversarial, and inconvenient. In 1996, the Bay Area—with three international airports, lower fees, limited revenue diversion, and the Silicon Valley benefits of a semiconductor agreement with Japan—surpassed Los Angeles, for the first time ever, in global air cargo value.[44]

Things were worse at the Port of Los Angeles. The port's ambitious $2 billion expansion program (similar in size to Long Beach's) was threatened by a 150 percent increase in city service charges. On the basis of a city hall-ordered audit, which examined port contributions to the city's general fund, the Harbor Department was billed an additional $68 million for putative service underpayments, primarily for fire service, dating to 1977. Yet hefty revenue transfers resulted in higher port development costs by reducing pay-as-you-go financing and forcing greater reliance on debt financing. If revenue diversions continued, the ocean carriers, fearing fee hikes, threatened to divert discretionary cargo to rival West Coast ports. Already, the Port of Los Angeles was losing market share to the Port of Long Beach. In 1995, Long Beach's container business grew by 11 percent, compared with L.A.'s 2 percent.[45]

At greatest risk from the mayor's revenue diversion efforts was the storied DWP. Faced with deregulation and competing for customers with investor-owned utilities such as Southern California Edison, the DWP was unable to pay down its massive debt or lower its high industrial and commercial rates. Since 1993, all DWP net income and cost savings had been transferred as a "surplus" to the city's general fund. DWP's exposure to market forces could result in a death spiral as business customers might flee and residential users—whose rates were highly subsidized by vote-seeking city council members—would be forced to pay sharply higher utility bills. Continued revenue transfers and an inability to restructure rates could force the nation's largest municipal utility to privatize.[46]

The crown jewels had faced fiscal raids before—in the 1930s—but had been able to beat them back with the hardy growth consensus of the interwar years, which they themselves, along with the chamber of commerce, had actively nurtured. Yet by the 1980s, that consensus was breaking down. Symptomatic of the collapse, the crown jewels in the 1990s faced substantial environmental and community opposition to their ambitious development plans. The California Coastal Commission imposed lengthy permitting delays on the dredging and pier development projects of the Port of Los Angeles. The smaller cities along the path of the Alameda Corridor railroad project filed lawsuits to mitigate the traffic congestion generated by port development and to increase their voice in project decision making, resulting in project delays. Issued in 1994, the proposed Federal Implementation Plan threatened to impose stiff federal regional air quality standards and emissions fines on ships, locomotives, and commercial aircraft. In response to the LAX Master Plan, the neighboring communities of Westchester and El Segundo organized to oppose the airport's expansion. Finally, the DWP faced threats to the city's Owens Valley water supply as environmental and community groups halted L.A.'s water diversions from the Mono Lake basin and forced DWP to partially reirrigate dry Owens Lake for the purpose of dust abatement.

For L.A.'s storied crown jewels, the real catalysts of the region's improbable twentieth-century development, the 1990s were both the best and worst of times. Economically, they were never more necessary to the revitalization of a sluggish economy. Never had the regional trade benefits of harbor and airport expansion been more evident. Yet at the same time, the crown jewels faced serious threats to their expansion and restructuring plans and, in the case of DWP, to its very existence.

Yet with passage of state electricity deregulation in 1996, there has been a dramatic turnaround in DWP fortunes. With a flawed deregulation scheme, soaring energy demand, and price gouging and market manipulation by energy generators, it was the state's investor-owned utilities that were pushed to the brink of bankruptcy. DWP wisely shunned deregulation. By 2000, DWP's customers basked in low electricity rates and a large energy surplus. Selling surplus power to other utilities, DWP has managed to pay down its once massive debt by more than one half since 1996. Thus, a seemingly uncompetitive DWP has emerged as the unexpected hero in a deregulated electricity market.[47]

CONCLUSION

Los Angeles offers a most instructive case of how local state structures can drive regional development and global competitiveness. Alone among major American cities, Los Angeles has incorporated water, power, harbor, and airports into municipal government rather than into regional authorities or private enterprise. No large city devotes as great a share of its budget and debt to public enterprise as does Los Angeles. Central to an L.A. School perspective must be an account of this powerful local state apparatus. Unlike Eastern and Midwestern cities such as New York and Chicago, infrastructure provision in Los Angeles was centralized rather than decentralized, guided by city bureaucrats rather than state and regionally elected and appointed officials or party bosses.

Los Angeles could not have transformed itself into a veritable developmental city-state without the extensive legal and fiscal powers granted under the California Constitution's home rule provisions. For the proprietary departments, bureaucratic autonomy and fiscal capacity were further institutionalized by the city charter. Visionary public entrepreneurs enhanced these formal powers with political strategies involving the ballot box, clientele alliances, and public sector lobbying. The result was the capacity to plan, finance, and build world-scale public works projects such as the Los Angeles Aqueduct, the Port of Los Angeles, and LAX. Developmental pricing strategies for these facilities furnished significant comparative advantage relative to regional competitors.

These massive public infrastructure investments were crucial to the city's and region's twentieth-century development. If the stimulus role of public enterprise is ignored, explanations of L.A.'s dramatic transformation from frontier town to regional imperium to Pacific Rim gateway will remain incomplete. Yet at the dawn of the new millennium, the City of the Angels finds itself again at a crossroads with fiscal, community, and environmental challenges to its ambitious trade infrastructure projects.

NOTES

1. See the chapters by Ernest W. Burgess, "The Growth of the City: An Introduction to a Research Project," and Roderick D. McKenzie, "The Ecological Approach to the Study of the Human Community," in *The City: Suggestions for Investigation of Human Behavior in the Urban Environment,* by Robert E. Park, Ernest W. Burgess, and Roderick D. McKenzie (Chicago: University of Chicago Press, 1925, 1967; Midway reprint, 1984), 47-62 and 63-79.

2. Regarding the conventional "city limits" wisdom, see Paul E. Peterson, *City Limits* (Chicago: University of Chicago Press, 1981); John H. Mollenkopf, *The Contested City* (Princeton, N.J.: Princeton University Press, 1983); John R. Logan and Harvey L. Molotch, *Urban Fortunes: The Political Economy of Place* (Berkeley: University of California Press, 1987); Paul Kantor, *The Dependent City Revisited* (Boulder, Colo.: Westview Press, 1995).

3. Saskia Sassen, *The Global City: New York, London, Tokyo* (Princeton, N.J.: Princeton University Press, 1991).

4. Kenichi Ohmae, *The End of the Nation State: The Rise of Regional Economies* (New York: Free Press, 1995); Neal R. Peirce, *Citistates: How Urban America Can Prosper in a Competitive World* (Washington, D.C.: Seven Locks Press, 1993); Rosabeth Moss Kanter, *World Class: Thriving Locally in the Global Economy* (New York: Simon & Schuster, 1995); William R. Dodge, *Regional Excellence: Governing Together to Compete Globally and Flourish Locally* (Washington, D.C.: National League of Cities, 1996).

5. David J. Keeling, "Transport and the World City Paradigm," in Paul L. Knox and Peter J. Taylor, eds., *World Cities in a World-System* (New York: Cambridge University Press, 1995), 115-131; Nigel Harris, "The Emerging Global City: Transport," *Cities* 11, no. 5 (October 1994): 332-336.

6. Peter Evans, *Embedded Autonomy: States and Industrial Transformation* (Princeton, N.J.: Princeton University Press, 1995); Evans, "Predatory, Developmental, and Other Apparatuses: A Comparative Political Economy Perspective on the Third World State," *Sociological Forum* 4, no. 4 (1989): 561-587.

7. Chalmers Johnson, *MITI and the Japanese Miracle: The Growth of Industrial Policy* (Stanford, Calif.: Stanford University Press, 1982); Johnson, *Japan: Who Governs? The Rise of the Developmental State* (New York: Norton, 1995); Stephan Haggard, *Pathways From the Periphery: The Politics of Growth in the Newly Industrializing Countries* (Ithaca, N.Y.: Cornell University Press, 1990).

8. Stephen D. Krasner, *Defending the National Interest: Raw Materials Investments and U.S. Foreign Policy* (Princeton, N.J.: Princeton University Press, 1978); Peter K. Eisinger, *The Rise of the Entrepreneurial State: State and Local Economic Development Policy in the United States* (Madison: University of Wisconsin Press, 1988).

9. Robert A. Caro, *The Power Broker: Robert Moses and the Fall of New York* (New York: Random House, 1974); Jameson W. Doig, "To Claim the Seas and the Skies: Austin Tobin and the Port of New York Authority," in Jameson W. Doig and Erwin C. Hargrove, *Leadership and Innovation: Entrepreneurs in Government* (Baltimore: Johns Hopkins University Press, 1990), 89-138; Doig, "Progressivism as Regional Planning: The Politics of Efficiency at the Port of New York," *Studies in American Political Development* 7, no. 2 (fall 1993): 316-370; Doig, *Empire on the Hudson: Entrepreneurial Vision and Political Power at the Port of New York Authority* (New York: Columbia University Press, 2001).

10. City of Los Angeles, *Budget for the Fiscal Year 1996-97* (as proposed by Mayor Richard J. Riordan), pp. v, 221-225, 231-234, 243-254; Office of the City Administrative Officer, "Net Debt of the City of Los Angeles as of December 1, 1996" (n.d.), 1 p.; Steven P. Erie, "Building and Rebuilding Los Angeles: How the City's Development Agencies Shape Regional Growth," Ninth Annual John C. Bollens/John C. Ries Lecture, April 28, 1993, University of California, Los Angeles, 1-24.

11. Center for Continuing Study of the California Economy, *California Economic Growth: 1996/97 Edition* (Palo Alto, Calif.: CCSCE, 1997), p. 8-2; "The Los Angeles Economy: Bigger Than South Korea," *The Economist* (February 4, 1995): 25-26.

12. Theodore J. Lowi, "Machine Politics—Old and New," *Public Interest* 9 (fall 1967): 83-92.

13. David L. Clark, "Los Angeles: Improbable Los Angeles," in Richard M. Bernard and Bradley R. Rice, eds., *Sunbelt Cities: Politics and Growth Since World War Two* (Austin: University of Texas Press, 1983), 268-308.

14. Robert M. Fogelson, *The Fragmented Metropolis: Los Angeles, 1850-1930* (Berkeley: University of California Press, 1967), 1, 78; Martin J. Schiesl, "Airplanes to Aerospace: Defense Spending and Economic Growth in the Los Angeles Region," in *The Martial Metropolis: U.S. Cities in War and Peace,* ed. Roger W. Lotchin (New York: Praeger, 1984), 135-149; Carl Abbott, *The New Urban America: Growth and Politics in Sunbelt Cities* (Chapel Hill: University of North Carolina Press, 1987), 101-122.

15. Miles Kahler, "Cities and the International System: International Strategy and Urban Fortunes" (paper prepared for the Metropolitan Dominance Working Group, Social Science Research Council, November 1988), 20-21; 26 pp.; Joel Kotkin and Yoriko Kishimoto, "The Japanese Are Banking on Los Angeles," *Los Angeles Times Magazine,* July 28, 1976; Charles Lockwood and Christopher B. Leinberger, "Los Angeles Comes of Age," *Atlantic Monthly,*

January 1988; Evelyn Iritani, "L.A. Surpasses New York City as Top Trade Hub in 1994," *Los Angeles Times,* March 17, 1995, pp. D1, D2.

16. Stephen Cohen, "L.A. Is the Hole in the [National] Bucket," *Los Angeles Times,* March 7, 1993, p. B7.

17. Todd Swanstrom, *The Crisis of Growth Politics: Cleveland, Kucinich, and the Challenge of Urban Populism* (Philadelphia: Temple University Press, 1985).

18. Stephen L. Elkin, *City and Regime in the American Republic* (Chicago: University of Chicago Press, 1987); Joe Feagin, *Free Enterprise City: Houston in Political and Economic Perspective* (New Brunswick, N.J.: Rutgers University Press, 1988). Also see Peter A. Lupsha and William J. Siembieda, "The Poverty of Public Services in the Land of Plenty: An Analysis and Interpretation," in *The Rise of Sunbelt Cities,* ed. David C. Perry and Alfred J. Watkins, (Beverly Hills, Calif.: Sage, 1977), 169-190.

19. Mollenkopf, *Contested City.* For neo-Marxian accounts, see Ralph Miliband, *The State in Capitalist Society* (London: Weidenfield and Nicholson, 1969); James O'Connor, *The Fiscal Crisis of the State* (New York: St. Martin's Press, 1973); Susan Fainstein et al., eds., *Restructuring the City: The Political Economy of Urban Redevelopment* (New York: Longman, 1983).

20. Heywood T. Sanders, "The Political Economy of Sunbelt Urban Development: Building the Public Sector" (paper delivered at the annual meeting of the American Political Science Association, Washington, D.C., September 2-5, 1993), 1; Feagin, *Free Enterprise City,* 50-69.

21. Fogelson, *Fragmented Metropolis,* 85-136; Kevin Starr, *Inventing the Dream: California Through the Progressive Era* (New York: Oxford University Press, 1985), 45-61, 75-89.

22. William B. Friedricks, *Henry E. Huntington and the Creation of Southern California* (Columbus: Ohio State University Press, 1992).

23. Marc Weiss, *The Rise of the Community Builders: The American Real Estate Industry and Urban Land Planning* (New York: Columbia University Press, 1987), especially 79-106 on the L.A. Realty Board; U.S. Bureau of the Census, *Census of Population,* vol. 4, Tables 3, 4; vol. 5, Table 3 (Washington, D.C.: Government Printing Office, 1933).

24. Abbott, *New Urban America,* 101-122; Roger W. Lotchin, *Fortress California, 1910-1961: From Warfare to Welfare* (New York: Oxford University Press, 1992), 3-22.

25. Lotchin, *Fortress California,* 64-130, 206-259.

26. David Brodsly, *L.A. Freeway: An Appreciative Essay* (Berkeley: University of California Press, 1981); Randall W. Eberts, "Public Infrastructure and Regional Economic Development," *Economic Review* 26, no. 1 (1990): 15-27; Eberts, "Some Empirical Evidence on the Linkage Between Public Infrastructure and Local Economic Development," in *Industry Location and Public Policy,* ed. Henry W. Herzog Jr. and Alan Schlottman (Austin: University of Texas Press, 1991), 83-96; David C. Perry, ed., *Building the Public City: The Politics, Governance, and Finance of Public Infrastructure* (Thousand Oaks, Calif.: Sage, 1995).

27. Theda Skocpol, "Bringing the State Back In: Strategies of Analysis in Current Research," in *Bringing the State Back In,* ed. Peter B. Evans et al. (Cambridge: Cambridge University Press, 1985), 3-37; Gordon L. Clark and Michael Dear, *State Apparatus: Structures and Language of Legitimacy* (Boston: Allen and Unwin, 1984); Terrence J. McDonald, "The Burdens of Urban History: The Theory of the State in Recent American Social History," *Studies in American Political Development* 3 (1989): 3-29.

28. Fred Block, "The Ruling Class Does Not Rule," *Socialist Review* 7 (1977): 6-28; Margaret Weir and Theda Skocpol, "State Structures and the Possibilities for 'Keynesian' Responses to the Great Depression in Sweden, Britain, and the United States," in *Bringing the State Back In,* ed. Peter B. Evans et al. (Cambridge: Cambridge University Press, 1985), 107-168.

29. Burt A. Heinley, "Los Angeles—A City in Business," *National Municipal Review* 3 (1914): 97-102; Fogelson, *Fragmented Metropolis*, 205-228.

30. Carl Brent Swisher, *Motivation and Political Technique in the California Constitutional Convention of 1878-1879* (1930; New York: Da Capo Press, 1969); E. P. Oberholtzer, *The Referendum in America* (New York: Charles Scribner's, 1912); Lane W. Lancaster, "State Limitations on Local Indebtedness," *The Municipal Year Book* 3 (1936): 313-327; Steven P. Erie, "How the Urban West Was Won: The Local State and Economic Growth in Los Angeles, 1880-1932," *Urban Affairs Quarterly* 27, no. 4 (June 1992): 522-524. Regarding the importance of local public financing in late-nineteenth- and early-twentieth-century cities, see Eric H. Monkkonen, *The Local State: Public Money and American Cities* (Stanford, Calif.: Stanford University Press, 1995).

31. Erie, "How the Urban West Was Won."

32. Richard Swedberg, ed., *Joseph A. Schumpeter: The Economics and Sociology of Capitalism* (Princeton, N.J.: Princeton University Press, 1991), 3. For an analysis of the rise and functioning of public enterprise, see Annmarie Hauck Walsh, *The Public's Business: The Politics and Practices of Government Corporations* (Cambridge: MIT Press, 1978).

33. Regarding the importance of the municipal bond market to infrastructure provision and regional development, see Albert M. Hillhouse, *Municipal Bonds: A Century of Experience* (New York: Prentice-Hall, 1936); Alberta M. Sbragia, ed., *The Municipal Money Chase: The Politics of Local Government Finance* (Boulder, Colo.: Westview Press, 1983); Heywood T. Sanders, "Building a New Urban Infrastructure: The Creation of Postwar San Antonio," in *Urban Texas: Politics and Development,* ed. Clem Miller and Heywood T. Sanders (College Station: Texas A&M University Press, 1990), 154-173. Regarding Los Angeles debt use, see Erie, "How the Urban West Was Won," 547-550.

34. For a discussion of Port of Los Angeles pricing strategies, see Michael Denning and David J. Olson, "Comparative Analysis of West Coast Ports" (unpublished manuscript, University of Washington, 1988), 98-100.

35. Office of the City Attorney, *Charter of the City of Los Angeles,* 1990 Edition, Revised (Los Angeles: Brackett Publishing, 1993), Articles XI, XXII, XXIV, 157-198, 341-399, 405-436; Edward C. Banfield, *Big City Politics* (New York: Random House, 1965), 83; Francis M. Carney, "The Decentralized Politics of Los Angeles," *Annals of the American Academy of Political and Social Science* 353 (May 1964): 112.

36. Steven P. Erie and James Warren Ingram III, "History of Los Angeles Charter Reform" (research report prepared for the Los Angeles Business Advisors, Santa Monica, Calif.: RAND, 1997), 45 pp.

37. Erie, "How the Urban West Was Won," 538-547.

38. Hugh A. Heclo, *A Government of Strangers: Executive Politics in Washington* (Washington, D.C.: Brookings Institution, 1977).

39. See Carey McWilliams, *Southern California Country: An Island on the Land* (1946; Salt Lake City, Utah: Peregrine Smith, 1983), 274-283; Joe Domanick, *To Protect and to Serve: The LAPD's Century of War in the City of Dreams* (New York: Pocket Books, 1994), 38-39, 64-68; Susan E. Clarke, "The Effectiveness of Entrepreneurial Downtown Development Strategies: A Comparative Analysis" (paper presented at the International Geographical Union Meetings, Melbourne, Australia, August 1988), 22 pp.; Mara Marks, "Shifting Ground: Bureaucratic Politics and Redevelopment in Los Angeles, 1948-1998" (Ph.D. diss., UCLA, 1999).

40. U.S. Bureau of the Census, FT920 Series, "U.S. Merchandise Trade: Selected Highlights, 1995 and 1996"; Bureau of the Census, FT990 Series, "Highlights of U.S. Import and Export Trade, 1972-1987"; Evelyn Iritani, "L.A. Surpasses New York City as Top Trade Hub in 1994," *Los Angeles Times,* March 17, 1995, pp. D1, D2.

41. Steven P. Erie, *International Trade and Job Creation in Southern California: Facilitating Los Angeles/Long Beach Port, Rail, and Airport Development* (Berkeley: California Policy Seminar, 1996), 3-4, 66-67.

42. Jean Merl, "City Reliance on Profitable Departments Threatened," *Los Angeles Times,* March 25, 1996, pp. B1, B3; Steven P. Erie, "The Recession Obsession," *Los Angeles Times,* May 23, 1993, pp. M1, M6; Erie, "Why Southern California May Be Unprepared for Its Destiny," *Los Angeles Times,* January 28, 1996, p. M6; Erie, "A Budget That Pays Today's Bills With L.A.'s Future Growth," *Los Angeles Times,* May 19, 1996, p. M6.

43. Erie, *International Trade and Job Creation in Southern California,* 57-65; Dan Garcia and Steven P. Erie, "Does Region's Future Depend on 6th Runway?" *Los Angeles Times,* December 15, 1996, p. M5.

44. Steven P. Erie, "Riordan Beats the Airlines at City's Long-Term Expense," *Los Angeles Times,* December 5, 1993, pp. M1, M3; Erie, "A Budget That Pays Today's Bills With L.A.'s Future Growth."

45. Erie, "A Budget That Pays Today's Bills With L.A.'s Future Growth."

46. Robert V. Phillips and Steven P. Erie, "Political Piracy at the Expense of DWP Customers," *Los Angeles Times,* April 4, 1995, pp. M1, M3; Phillips and Erie, "Why Utility Deregulation Won't Benefit L.A. Rate Payers," *Los Angeles Times,* December 24, 1995, p. M6; Michael E. Tennenbaum, "Privatize to Eliminate a $2-Billion Problem," *Los Angeles Times,* April 8, 1997, p. B9.

47. Douglas P. Shuit and Joe Mozingo, "By Luck or Skill, DWP Gets the Last Laugh," *Los Angeles Times,* August 3, 2000, pp. A1, A26; Steven P. Erie and Robert V. Phillips, "The Unexpected Hero in a Deregulated Electricity Market," *Los Angeles Times,* September 10, 2000, p. M6.

Industrial Urbanism in Late-Twentieth-Century Southern California

EDITOR'S
COMMENTS

Roderick McKenzie's article on "The Ecological Approach to the Study of Human Community" (Chapter 3 in *The City*) advances a taxonomy of urban places based essentially on their economic functions: "primary service community," based in extractive industries such as agriculture and mining; "commercial community," that is, one that collects and distributes basic materials being produced elsewhere; "industrial town," the locus for the manufacture of commodities; and communities "lacking in a specific economic base," not involved directly in the production and distribution of economies but more concerned with what we would today identify as service industries (McKenzie gives the examples of recreational resorts, educational centers, etc.). Most interesting about this classification, of course, is the fourth category, because service industries dominated the emerging economies of late-twentieth-century cities.

Equally interesting, however, is that Southern California is today one of the world's largest manufacturing agglomerations. As Allen J. Scott reveals, this industrial complex is based in two main sectors: labor-intensive craft industries and high technology. The recent growth of business and financial services is also especially noteworthy. The principal dynamic in Southern California's historical economic geography during the twentieth century was the shift from a Fordist to a post-Fordist mode of production. The former is associated with large-scale, integrated assembly line industries such as auto manufacturing; the latter with a much smaller-scale "flexible production" organization that has its roots (in Southern California, at least) in the motion picture and aircraft production industries. The post-Fordist regime typically gives rise to regional "technopoles," in Scott's terminology, which themselves are important determinants of a concomitant decentralized urban structure.

Scott concludes that the rise of an L.A. School is necessary at this time to solve the "enigma" posed by Southern California. An associated group of scholars is trying to invent a vocabulary to explain the region, in much the same way as the Chicago School of urban sociology "came into being at an earlier time in response to the puzzle of Chicago."

QUOTES FROM
THE CITY

Far from being an arbitrary clustering of people and buildings, the city is the nucleus of a wider zone of activity from which it draws its resources and over which it exerts its influence. The city and its hinterland represent two phases of the same mechanism, which may be analyzed from various points of view.

Just as Galpin, in his *Social Anatomy of Rural Community,* was able to determine the limits of the community by means of the area over which its trade routes extend, so the city may be delimited by the extent of its trading area. From the simpler area around it the city gathers the raw materials, part of which are essential to sustain the life of its inhabitants, and another part of which are transformed by the technique of the city population into finished products which flow out again to the surrounding territory, sometimes over a relatively larger expanse than the region of their origin. From another point of view the city sends out its tentacles to the remotest corners of the world to gather those sources of supply which are not available in the immediate vicinity, only to retail them to its own population and the rural region about it. Again, the city might be regarded as the distributor of wealth, an important economic role which has become institutionalized in a complex financial system. (182-183)

CHAPTER 6

Industrial Urbanism in Late-Twentieth-Century Southern California

ALLEN J. SCOTT

Patterns of industrialization and urbanization have, since the very beginning of capitalism, been closely intertwined, just as they have also been jointly subject to periodic restructuring. One distinctive expression of these phenomena was seen in Britain in the early nineteenth century where dense urban concentrations of workshops, mills, and manual workers developed in response to the factory system in places like Birmingham, Bradford, Leeds, Manchester, and Sheffield. Another expression can be found in the Northeast of the United States in the decades following World War I, with Chicago and Detroit as its typical cases, where a hugely successful Fordist mass production system created the basis of the American Dream. Yet another is discernible in the U.S. Sunbelt today where cities such as Dallas-Fort Worth, Denver, Houston, Phoenix, and the great megalopolis of Southern California have grown on the basis of a very different kind of capitalist industrialization from that which shaped the earlier urban centers of the Northeast. The cases mentioned represent peculiar conjunctures in the historical geography of capitalism; they can be seen as particularly intense distillations of economic order and ways of life that have prevailed at different times and places over the last two centuries.

This chapter investigates the version of these phenomena that is currently found in Southern California. This region constitutes a single extended metropolitan area made up of the central county of Los Angeles, together with the four surrounding counties of Orange, Riverside, San Bernardino, and Ventura. It is one of the largest urban agglomerations in the world; and it is almost certainly the largest manufacturing center. Its economy is based on a mix of manufacturing and service activities, with no clear dividing line between the two. I shall deal mostly with the manufacturing end of this continuum, since this remains a basic and centrally significant component of the whole urban system of Southern California, though I shall seek also to bring the service sector into the discussion.

AUTHOR'S NOTE: This chapter is reprinted from "Industrial Urbanism in Southern California: Post-Fordist Civic Dilemmas and Opportunities," *Contention*, Vol. 5, No. 1 (1995), pp. 39-65. Reprinted by permission.

Manufacturing in Southern California is represented by a diverse set of activities and sectors, with two major classes of industry being dominant. These are labor-intensive, craft-based industries (such as clothing and motion pictures) and high technology industries producing mainly aerospace-electronics outputs for defense. In addition, Southern California is a leading business and financial services center with strong connections to similar centers around the Pacific Rim. It is characterized by a social structure that divides sharply into two tiers; one consists of highly paid and privileged workers while the other is composed of low-income workers, most of whom belong to distinct ethnic and immigrant groups. At the same time, the economic and social character of Southern California is closely bound to the region's status as the hub of a vigorous, demotic, entertainment/fashion/ideological products industry whose outputs have come to function as important cultural bulwarks of global capitalism.

How did this complex of industrial-urban activities and relationships come into being? What is its inner logic of growth and development? How might it evolve in the future? What critical political issues does it raise, both locally and nationally? What are its strengths and weaknesses, and how might the latter be dealt with?

FROM CHICAGO AND DETROIT TO LOS ANGELES

Fordist Mass Production and Urbanization

For much of [the twentieth] century, capital-intensive mass production was seen as the royal road to high levels of productivity and competitiveness in manufacturing enterprise, especially when coupled with "Fordist" labor relations and corporate forms of business organization. Irrespective of the degree to which mass production actually penetrated the U.S. economy (about which there is now much debate), it was widely interpreted as representing a historical tendency to which all production sectors aspired, even if many of them were still using more "archaic" operating principles. Giedion captured the essence of this form of industrialization in the formula: "The symptom of full mechanization is the assembly line, wherein the entire factory is consolidated into a synchronous organism,"[1] and it was full mechanization that accounted for the success of industries such as petrochemicals, steel, cars, domestic appliances, packaged foods, and toiletries. Though many industries were only partially reorganizable in this way, and others thoroughly resistant to it, prevailing managerial ideologies tended to view these recalcitrant cases as being in due course susceptible to modernization *qua* "full mechanization." In the immediate prewar period, as Hounshell writes:

> Businessmen and social thinkers . . . saw unprecedented opportunity in the productive efficiency of the assembly line. . . . Despite the implications of the annual model change, some observers continued to see mass production as . . . a panacea for the industrial and business ills of all nations on both hemispheres. . . . America of the late 1920s and early 1930s was pervaded by an ethos of mass production.[2]

Banham, among others, pinned an entire design aesthetic on the mass replication of identical products, including a celebration of Corbusier-style city planning, the last word in standardized, modernist, modular urban utopias.[3] Small-scale, labor-intensive, and craft forms of industry and associated patterns of urban life were widely seen as anachronisms that would in due course be swept away by technological progress.

The great allure of mass production is that it can in theory deliver endless productivity gains via continual technological upgrading and the pursuit of internal economic of scale.[4] At least, it can deliver in this manner so long as markets are expanding and consumer demands can be made to reflect uniform tastes for standardized goods. From the close of the Second World War to the end of the 1960s these conditions were realized in the United States to an extent never previously achieved. In this manner, many of the central ingredients of the "American Dream" were put into place.

Those industrial sectors that shifted most decisively into Fordist mass production tended to form what Perroux called "growth poles."[5] The lead plants in these sectors commonly constituted the nuclei of dense industrial regions that emerged because producers tend to converge toward their common center of gravity to take advantage of agglomeration. Detroit is the archetypical case of the mass production era industrial metropolis, though it was Chicago with its meatpacking, machinery, steel, and other heavy industries that gave birth to the school of sociology that defined the hegemonic urban theory from the 1920s to the 1970s.

The Chicago School of Urban Sociology, as it came to be known, focused its attention on the characteristics of *residential* space within the large industrial metropolis.[6] Residential space was seen as the site of a struggle for survival among the heterogeneous social groups drawn into the orbit of urban life: congeries of distinct neighborhoods differentiated by social class and cultural identity. At the core of the city is the central business district, surrounded by a "zone of transition" characterized by a multitude of urban pathologies (prostitution, crime, dereliction, homelessness, and so on). Around this is an inner city zone comprising neighborhoods housing mainly an immigrant population and differentiated by national, ethnic, and racial identity. The inner city zone fades off into a further zone made up chiefly of the residences of second and third generation American blue-collar families. Finally, the outermost areas are dominated by the residences of white-collar and professional families. In his seminal essay, "Urbanism as a Way of Life," Wirth gave expression to the Chicago School's view of the city, painting it as a desolate terrain of intergroup competition, isolation, and anomie.[7] The Chicago School [adherents] paid scant attention in their urban theory to relations between industrialization and urbanization. Instead, they developed a Darwinian, "ecological" view of urban space, which expressed the rich sociogeographical texture of the large industrial metropolis in America in the 1920s and 1930s, but which remained largely oblivious to the underlying production system that was generating so much of the change in the large cities of that time.

In the early decades of the present century, this system started to shift in significant ways into a Fordist mass production configuration accompanied by massive rounds of urban growth and in-migration. Whereas many contemporary observers felt that mass production represented a basic developmental tendency in capitalism, we can now see with the wisdom of hindsight that this view depreciated the continued existence (and eventual resurgence) of an alternative pattern of industrialization based on networks of small-scale producers and their location in dense industrial districts. Some of Marshall's followers in Britain had continued to emphasize this kind of industry and its occurrence in many urban areas, and in the United States it was forcefully described by Haig in his work for the New York Regional Plan.[8] Over the 1950s and 1960s, occasional references were made to the enduring presence of small-scale industry in urban areas, but by and large theorists understandably continued to put high emphasis on the most visible motors of urban and regional development, that is, Fordist mass production and its corollary in growth pole forms of economic and spatial organization.

By the early 1970s, the mass production system in North America began to falter, as reflected in the economic decay of the cities of the Manufacturing Belt. Moreover, a dramatic revitalization of industrial sectors based on small to medium-sized establishments was becoming apparent in several parts of the world, and these sectors were starting to drive much economic growth. In the 1980s, many analysts began to suggest that a new pathway of industrialization and urban development was opening up, that a break with the old model of Fordist mass production was occurring. In many respects, the sharpness of the break was exaggerated, though there could be little doubt that a new form of industrialization and urbanization was now making its appearance in the United States, and that its *locus classicus* was in the Sunbelt.

Post-Fordist Industry and Urbanization

The factors underlying the crisis of Fordist mass production in North America are still far from being fully deciphered, though the saturation of mass markets in the 1970s, insistent competition from cheaper foreign producers, and the rise of new and highly differentiated niche markets certainly played an important role.

The crisis was not so much the harbinger of the postindustrial society that Bell had proclaimed,[9] though to be sure industrial capitalism was becoming ever more service-intensive. It was rather a sign of the ascent (or re-ascent) of another trajectory of industrial development in capitalism, one based primarily on what has subsequently, and inadequately, been labeled "flexible production." Southern California, along with certain other regions, was in a particularly favorable position to capitalize on this trend, for even in the heyday of American Fordist mass production after the Second World War, its manufacturing economy was strikingly different from the established norm. In Southern California, two main species of this model of post-Fordist industrialization have been in evidence in the last few decades. The first is represented mainly by labor-intensive and design-intensive craft industries, like textiles, apparel, furniture, jewelry, and motion picture production, though it can also be observed in a number of high technology sectors, like some forms of electronics production or medical instruments. Here, the industrial apparatus consists primarily of groups of small and medium-sized producers linked together in shifting networks of externalized transactions. The second is represented by high technology industry, and by the aerospace-defense industry in particular. This second type is also a network form of production with many small and medium-sized producers; however, these networks are structured around large systems houses at the pinnacle of a many-tiered production hierarchy. Systems houses are usually concerned with the production of small batches of enormously complex products like aircraft, space equipment, and communication satellites; they take on the responsibility for overall design, engineering, and final assembly of such artifacts while subcontracting out many elements of actual production.

Both species of the flexible production model that prevails in Southern California exhibit an intense agglomeration of producers in localized industrial districts, even though many of these producers also have strong national and international business connections. Together, they have also been one of the major factors underlying the emergence of a system of local labor markets in the region that is deeply segmented, and from which much of the traditional, unionized, blue-collar American working class has been eradicated.[10]

FROM HOLLYWOOD TO ORANGE COUNTY

A Brief Conspectus of Southern California's Industrial Geography

Even though services now employ more people than manufacturing in Southern California, manufacturing in the narrow sense remains a principal underpinning of the local economy, employing 1.26 million workers in the five counties in 1990. As suggested, much of the region's existing industrial base can be decomposed into a set of labor-intensive craft industries on the one side, and a set of high technology industries on the other. In addition, there is an important group of flexible production sectors (in both the craft and high technology categories) focused on metallurgical and machinery production, and composed of small flexible firms that provide a diversity of products and services to other industries. Mass production was never strongly developed in the region, and what now remains is almost moribund.

The broad geographical distribution of these industries in Southern California is depicted in Figure 6.1. The figure stresses the propensity of manufacturing establishments to cluster together in specialized industrial districts, which occur at widely varying locations over the metropolitan area. These districts owe their origins to external/agglomeration economies that flow from the complex organizational interrelations between the different producers caught up within the urban production system.[11] In the case of the region's craft industries, these districts are located in the immediate vicinity of the central city area of Los Angeles. The high technology

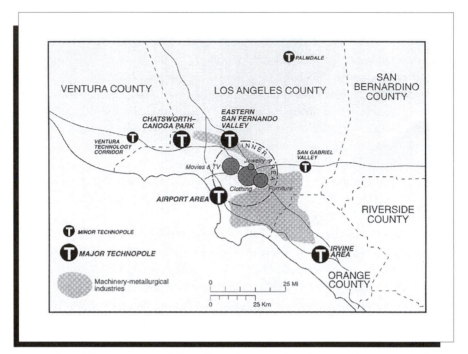

Figure 6.1. Schematic View of the Industrial Geography of Metropolitan Los Angeles

industrial districts, or technopoles, are mainly distributed over the outer fringes of the metropolitan area. The Orange County technopole (focused on Irvine) is the most dynamic at present, followed by the Chatsworth-Canoga Park area in the San Fernando Valley. The metallurgical-machinery complex, together with what is left of the mass production group, is largely confined to the older industrial quarters of Los Angeles.

Considerable deindustrialization has occurred in these quarters over the last three decades, but distinct localized peaks of industrial land use continue to occur in particular areas. We should note that much of the region's service economy is also spatially organized in a system of identifiable agglomerations, with the central business district forming the core cluster.

The Historical Emergence of Southern California's Distinctive Industrial Landscape

The roots of Southern California's craft and high technology industrial complexes can be traced back to the early decades of [the twentieth] century. Two industries, in particular, helped to initiate and shape the region's subsequent industrial trajectory, namely, motion pictures and aircraft.

The motion picture industry in the pre-World War II years was concentrated in large vertically integrated studios that incorporated almost all of the myriad functions needed to produce films. Each studio maintained a stable of stars, and each typically turned out 20 to 40 films a year.[12] As an economic phenomenon, the star system helped to standardize final products, to create a captive audience, and thus to mitigate market fluctuations.

In the case of the aircraft industry, too, production was concentrated in large manufacturing units, and these lay at the center of extensive and many-tiered networks of subcontractors and input providers. The aircraft industry started to boom in Southern California over the 1930s as technologies improved and as markets expanded. Two major technological breakthroughs by local firms were of special meaning in establishing the region as the main center of the industry; these were the development of the L10 Electra by Lockheed in 1933 and the DC-3 by Douglas in 1935.

Both the motion picture and the aircraft industries in the 1930s and 1940s were heavily influenced in their managerial practices and outlook by the successes of Fordist mass production. Both industries introduced limited Taylorization of work routines, and during World War II, one aircraft factory in Los Angeles installed a powered assembly line. However, the two industries were caught up in various technological, organizational, and employment structures that effectively impeded transformation of their operations in conformity with the logic of mass production, and the large movie studios and aircraft assembly plants in the region in the prewar years are more properly thought of as systems houses than as something akin to a typical car assembly plant.

The full analytical story of how these industries came to be established and to prosper in Southern California has not been laid out. However, it would almost certainly conform to a generalized locational scenario comprising four main stages:

1. *A chaotic series of initiating events* involving industry pioneers, where they happened to be at any given time, and many other fortuitous circumstances (such as the activities of the New York "movie trust" after 1909, or the early history of the peripatetic aircraft industry pioneer Donald Douglas)

2. *The activities of local power brokers* (such as Harry Chandler and the Merchants and Manufacturers Association in Los Angeles), especially where these are able to mobilize critical resources in support of local economic growth

3. *A breakthrough moment* when manufacturers begin to capitalize on a developing complex of cultural and technological sensitivities and skills, and when their products begin to rise to ascendancy on wider markets

4. *Consolidation of the local production complex* as a result of the growth of networks of secondary input providers and the development of multifaceted local labor markets

Note that this account radically downplays the role of climate in the original location of the motion picture and aircraft industries in Los Angeles. In fact, in the early years of [the twentieth] century, when climate presumably mattered most to both of them, they were for the most part located in the Northeast.

During World War II, the motion picture and aircraft industries were finally consolidated in the region as both in their different ways were dragooned into the war effort. Then, in the immediate postwar years both industries went through dramatic transformations that affected the entire future of the region. The motion picture industry was completely restructured over the 1950s and early 1960s. One triggering event was the antitrust decision of the U.S. Supreme Court in 1948, which forced the major studios to divest themselves of their theater chains. Another was the advent of television. Both events created much turbulence and instability for the industry, and led to wholesale vertical disintegration.[13] Thus, while the major studios continued to exert a decisive influence over financing and marketing, production to an increasing degree occurred within networks of small specialized firms, subcontractors, consultants, and independent creative and crafts workers. At the same time, the motion picture industry encouraged the parallel growth of related and derivative sectors making products for popular entertainment, including what were becoming globally dominant television and music-recording industries.

The aircraft industry, for its part, experienced a deep slump after 1945. It once more began to expand apace with the outbreak of the Korean War in 1950, however, and continued to grow for much of the ensuing Cold War period. At the same time, the aircraft industry stimulated the development of two other major industries in the region, namely, missile production (and later the production of space equipment in general), and electronics, especially communication systems and navigation devices. The missile industry grew, in part, out of the basic research carried out in the 1930s and 1940s under Von Karman at the Jet Propulsion Laboratory in Pasadena, and it was brought to practical realization in large local aircraft firms like Consolidated-Vultee, Douglas, and Lockheed.

By the mid-1950s, the industrial geography of Southern California was starting to approach something of the shape that characterizes the central part of Figure 6.1. At this time, there was a set of inner city craft industrial districts, dominated by Hollywood, and composed of dense agglomerations of small producers. Two major technopoles had also made their appearance, one in the Burbank-Glendale area in the eastern San Fernando Valley, the other centered on the El Segundo area. Each consisted of a number of large systems houses surrounded by constellations of smaller subcontractors and input providers. In addition, in the area that has recently been described by Davis as the "empty quarter,"[14] the formerly flourishing industrial suburbs to the east and south of downtown Los Angeles, the metallurgical-machinery industries were actively at work serving the aerospace-defense sector as well as the small mass production complex that was now reaching its zenith.

Industrialization and Urbanization
in Southern California Today

In 1960, the population of the five counties of Southern California stood at 7.8 million, of which 8.8% was foreign-born. Census data also tell us that in this year, 6.4% of the total population was African American. By 1990, the population of the five counties had expanded to 14.5 million, of which 27.1% was foreign-born. The African American population accounted for 8.5% of the total population in 1990 but had now essentially stopped growing or was even declining slightly. By contrast, there has been explosive growth of Hispanic groups since the 1960s, and they now account for 32.9% of the total population. The Asian population, too, has grown with great rapidity, and in 1990 made up 9.2% of the population.

Much—though by no means all—of this demographic upheaval goes hand-in-hand with a number of far-reaching developments in the local economy. Two phenomena are especially important for the effects they have had on urban form. One is the explosive economic growth of the region over much of the postwar period, which created the conditions for vigorous population expansion and high levels of in-migration. The other is the steady segmentation of local labor markets, leading to ever-increasing polarization of the urban society of Southern California.[15] Thus, in the region's manufacturing and service sectors alike we can observe a widening divide (in incomes, entitlements, and expectations) between, on the one hand, a highly paid cadre of professional, managerial, creative, and technical workers, and on the other hand, a huge stratum of low-paid, low-skilled manual workers, a very large proportion of whom are immigrants. This lower stratum has been growing more rapidly than the upper, and since the 1960s, the region has seen the rise of a great underbelly of sweatshop industries with an insatiable appetite for cheap labor. These events have been associated with declining rates of unionization and declining real wage rates in manufacturing industry over the last couple of decades. By 1990, too, the manufacturing labor force of Southern California had become significantly more feminized, with women comprising 33.7% of the total, as contrasted with 23.9% in 1950. All of this ferment is deeply etched on the industrial-urban landscape of Southern California, and some further elucidation of its meaning is now in order.

The Labor-Intensive Craft Industries

While the different sectors in this group are much alike in terms of underlying structure and organization, they also exhibit widely varying evolutionary paths. Consider the contrasting fortunes of the motion picture industry and the furniture industry in the region.

The motion picture industry has remained the most dynamic and prosperous of all the craft industries in Southern California. Despite the far-reaching reorganization of the industry after 1948, and its reconstitution as a predominantly small firm sector, its global range continues to expand, and levels of worker remuneration are very high on average. In part, the latter circumstance can be explained by the industry's need for skilled labor; and in part, it can be explained by the persistence of powerful labor guilds and unions in the industry which have managed to restrict the flow of cheap immigrant workers into the bottom reaches of the labor market.

At the other end of the spectrum is the furniture industry. This sector has become increasingly locked into a cost-squeezing competitive strategy focused on the employment of non-union, low-wage, immigrant (mainly Hispanic) workers. But this strategy is likely in the end to prove to be self-defeating, and it seems improbable that the furniture industry of Los Angeles will be able to compete indefinitely against cheaper Third World producers. Nor, given the erosion of skills in the industry, can it compete against the world's high-priced but high-quality producers like Germany, Italy, and Scandinavia. As a result of these pressures, the industry has been losing ground in recent years, and many producers have attempted to survive by moving facilities to low-wage and under-regulated *maquiladora* locations in Mexico.

Between the two extremes of the motion picture industry and the furniture industry are arrayed a number of other sectors like textiles, apparel, toys, jewelry, and leather goods. The labor-intensive craft industries of the region thus vary greatly in terms of their competitive strategies and energies. At one end there is a substantial sweatshop sector, and, at the other, an immensely successful set of industries punctuating the economic landscape of the region with a few notable islands of prosperity. The products of these latter industries are susceptible to creative design innovation and are pregnant with cultural meanings. Such industries constitute the foundations of a commercial-*cum*-cultural milieu that constantly creates and recreates an identifiable range of images and sensations. The motion picture industry is traditionally the prime motor of this phenomenon, but other sectors also contribute in important ways to keep it alive and in a constant state of flux. Among these are the television industry, the music industry, and elements of the clothing industry; we should also include in this list activities like advertising, theme parts, tourism, and even architecture.

Los Angeles has become an international capital of interpenetrating design-based and fashion-oriented cultural products industries that both forge and reflect popular taste on a global scale. The iconic powers of these industries are based on their ability to capture and project images and life-styles—real or imagined—of Southern California. The resulting regional "industrial atmosphere" is a potent economic resource that is continually tapped and re-made by many different industries. Moreover, almost every major car manufacturer in North America, Europe, and Japan has established a design studio in Southern California, presumably in an effort to capture emerging trends in styling and automotive fashion. The region now ranks as probably the world's major center of automobile design activities.

The High Technology Industries and the Dynamics of Urban Form

From the early 1950s to the late 1980s, the high technology industries of Southern California have been one of the mainstays of the region's economy. High technology industrial development has found spatial expression in discrete technopoles representing clustered networks of defense-oriented systems houses together with large numbers of smaller establishments. Despite the imbrications of these smaller establishments in structures of high technology industrial production, many of them are actually sweatshops employing low-wage immigrant and female workers, with working conditions that are often even inferior (because of high levels of toxic emissions) to those that can be found in the labor-intensive craft industries.

The geography of the region's technopoles is the result of an ordered spatiotemporal process. The analytics of the process are of some complexity, and they have been described elsewhere;[16] in what follows I shall simply adumbrate their outlines. Note that the discussion applies in principle to the spatiotemporal development of many different types of economic activity, though it is presented here specifically as a story about high technology industry because this has long been so important in Southern California. Five main points are now developed for an imaginary city in which high technology industry has started to grow.

1. At some historical point (the 1920s and 1930s in the case of Los Angeles) agglomeration economies and local labor market pressures bring about the formation of an initial technopole, or proto-technopole, close to the city center.

2. As this proto-technopole grows, land prices and labor costs rise, inducing decentralization of production units toward cheaper suburban sites.

3. Eventually, the gravitational pull of agglomeration economies induces these decentralizing units to form incipient technopoles in suburban areas.

4. The new suburban technopoles begin to grow rapidly as industrial expansion proceeds, and in due course, the central technopole may begin to atrophy when agglomeration diseconomies and rising land prices pass a certain threshold.

5. So long as industrial growth continues, this cycle of events will repeat itself, with new technopoles breaking off from the old and recurring yet further out in the urban field. Meanwhile, those technopoles that had previously been identifiable as "suburban" now lie well within the frontiers of outward urban expansion.

Figure 6.2 provides a sketch of this idealized pattern of development counterposed against a second sketch indicating how the technopoles of Southern California really emerged historically and geographically. The actual pattern is a diminished version of the ideal, perhaps because the overall expansion of high technology industry in the postwar years was not sufficient to sustain the full-blown spatiotemporal sequence of development as identified in the ideal case. The realized pattern can be decomposed into three main generations of technopoles, as indicated in Figure 6.2. Each technopole, as it comes into existence, functions as the spatial focus of new rounds of local urban development, residential growth, and also (because of its local labor market effects) of intensified social differentiation in the surrounding area. Soja, in his explorations of "exopolis," has claimed that the outer cities that have grown in this manner in Southern California are also distinguishable by their

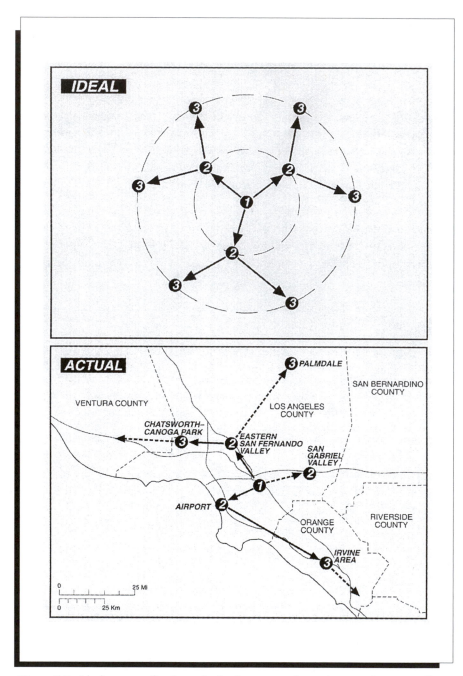

Figure 6.2. Ideal pattern of technopole development and actual pattern in metropolitan Los Angeles. Numbers in circles indicate generations of technopole development.

postmodern landscapes and social order, as epitomized by their pervasive architectural ambiguity and factitious expressiveness, and rootlessness.[17]

These phases of technopole development have coincided with major surges in federal defense procurements. By the same token, in the present conjuncture of international détente and severe cutting of the federal arms budget, the onward march of the process of technopole development in the region has been significantly slowed down, if not altogether arrested. Between 1988 and 1991 the labor force in the aerospace-defense industries of Southern California shrank from 375,000 to 314,500, yielding a net loss of 60,500 jobs. If we make the usual assumption that the employment multiplier associated with these jobs ranges from 1.5 to 2.5, then the 60,500 jobs lost in the core aerospace-defense sectors are likely to have engendered an additional loss of between 90,800 and 151,300 jobs in other sectors of the local economy. Job losses continued apace over 1992 and 1993, making high technology industry one of the weakest segments of the Southern California economy today, and helping to prolong a severe economic and social crisis.

Patterns of Socio-Spatial Differentiation

The urban landscape of Southern California is a complex tissue of economic locations, dominated by a multifaceted congeries of industrial districts. But it is also an assemblage of socially differentiated neighborhoods. These two phenomena are deeply interconnected.

Southern California is today a diverse, multicultural, and multiethnic metropolis in which a still dominantly Anglo population is rapidly giving way to a variety of other groups.[18] These non-Anglo groups tend to form distinctive neighborhoods in urban social space, as shown in Figure 6.3. Three major elements stand out in the figure. The first is represented by the main area of African American residential settlement, that is, a tract of land coinciding with much of South Central Los Angeles. The second consists of an area of Hispanic neighborhoods circling around the eastern and southern sides of downtown Los Angeles, with an outlier in San Fernando to the north, and another in Santa Ana to the south. The third is a series of multiple nuclei in which the Asian population is concentrated, each with a specific identity like Koreatown, Old Chinatown, New Chinatown, Little Saigon, and so on. The overall pattern of social segregation revealed by Figure 6.3 is reminiscent of Chicago in the 1920s, though the immigrant populations of Southern California today have their origins in radically different parts of the world. What has also changed greatly is the degree of social bifurcation, as marked by the virtual disappearance of a middle stratum of skilled and semi-skilled blue-collar workers, and the rise of an overgrown sweatshop sector alongside a core of high-performance employers. Moreover, as the attacks on the welfare state over the Reagan-Bush years have had deeper and deeper effect, a marked resurgence of the old Chicago School "zone of transition" has occurred, with accumulating numbers of permanently marginalized and homeless individuals concentrated in and around the central business district of Los Angeles.

As things stand, Southern California is a hotbed of social predicaments and tensions brought on by the manifest inequalities and social breakdowns alluded to above. Already, in August 1965, when the African American population of Watts

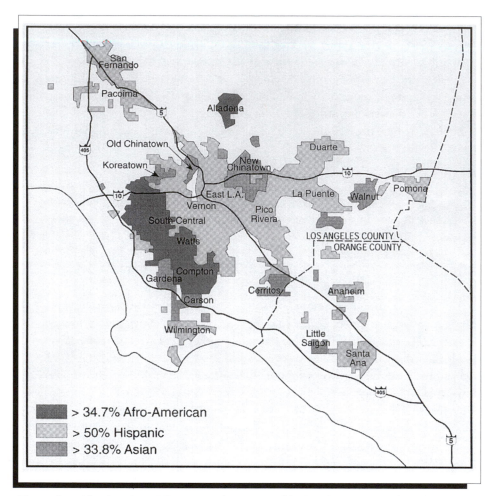

Figure 6.3. Afro-American, Hispanic, and Asian Neighborhoods in Los Angeles and Orange Counties

rioted in the streets, the explosive nature of the situation in Los Angeles was apparent. Since then, the problems have intensified, leading to further social conflicts and disturbances, and culminating in the tumultuous riots of South-Central Los Angeles in the last days of April 1992. South-Central has become a point of multiple social collisions where African Americans, Hispanics, and to a lesser extent Asians, find themselves in increasing competition for housing and political representation, and, more than anything else, in competition for scarce jobs.

According to Soja, the area lost more than 75,000 jobs due to plant closings and layoffs between 1978 and 1982 alone.[19] These circumstances have had a heavy impact on the African American population, for whom rates of unemployment are more than double the metropolitan average. The spark setting off the riots of 1992 was widespread indignation among African Americans over the verdict in the Rodney King trial, but what began as spontaneous African American street protests escalated rapidly into a rampage of the dispossessed and socially-marginalized, with total property destruction exceeding one billion dollars. In the aftermath of the riots, a prestigious Rebuild LA Committee was set up in an effort to find some answers to the city's underlying problems, but despite the committee's good intentions, little has yet been accomplished by way of durable solutions.[20]

The Post-Fordist Industrial Metropolis

The Fordist industrial cities that dominated the American urban scene some decades ago can be described in ideal-typical terms as growing out of an industrial base anchored in mass production, populated largely by unionized, blue-collar workers and their families (constituting the best-paid working class in the world), and offering considerable upward mobility into mainstream society. The terminal point of this process of assimilation was achieved with the attainment of suburban residential status, combined with conspicuous consumption of the material benefits made possible by Fordist mass production.

The ideal-type of the *post*-Fordist industrial metropolis in America today has many similar characteristics, but it also displays a number of notable contrasts. These can be identified in terms of an urban economic base comprising diverse flexible production sectors; a concomitant re-polarization of occupational structures; and rapidly expanding numbers of low-skill, low-wage jobs, which act as a magnet for immigrants from Third World countries. As a corollary, this metropolis is also typically the site of resurgent social marginalization, and—as opposed to the assimilationist pressures that prevailed in an earlier era—of a new-found emphasis on ethnic self-assertion and multiculturalism. To an increasing extent, as well, the archetypical post-Fordist industrial metropolis is caught up not just in its own localized patterns of work and life but also in wider networks of relationships that span the entire globe. In the case of Southern California, the latter feature is incarnated in almost all aspects of the economy but most dramatically in its cultural products and defense industries.

So perplexing is the enigma posed by Los Angeles that a distinctive "Los Angeles School" of urban studies has been forged as scholars have tried to reconstruct a vocabulary and a set of concepts to deal with it, much as the Chicago School of Urban Sociology came into being at an earlier time in response to the puzzle of Chicago.[21] But if Los Angeles is the paradigmatic case of the post-Fordist metropolis in America—or at least one important version of it—it is also a version that seems destined to rapid demise in the absence of bold political measures to offset its internal disarray. As we have seen, much of the economy of the region is faltering badly and its social fabric is unstable and predisposed to violent explosions. These weaknesses are not just temporary aberrations due to the current recession; they represent problems that are embedded in the very structural makeup of the region, and they are apt to endure over a considerable period unless decisive action is taken. They stem, in part, from the long-term downturn in federal defense expenditures and severe job loss in the region; but equally important, they also grow out of the propensity of many key sectors in the region's economy to shift into sweatshop forms of production, thus sustaining a downward spiral of wage cutting, a shrinking skills base, and increasing vulnerability of many sectors that might otherwise be much more competitive. Moreover, a survey carried out a few years ago revealed that much of Southern California's flexible economy displays a huge deficit of precisely the kinds of institutional infrastructures and forms of collaborative interaction that in countries like Germany, Italy, and Japan have proven to be important factors in the construction of regional competitive advantage.[22] A slow but persistent enervation of the social and economic fabric of Southern California, punctuated by occasional turbulent upheavals, is occurring as a result of these different but interrelated crosscurrents. If left unchecked, this trend threatens to take Southern California straight toward the bleak "Blade Runner" scenario that Davis has so eloquently invoked.[23]

NOTES

1. Siegfried Giedion, *Mechanization Takes Command* (New York: Oxford University Press, 1948), 5.

2. D. A. Hounshell, *From the American System to Mass Production, 1800-1932* (Baltimore: Johns Hopkins University Press, 1984), 304-305.

3. Reyner Banham, *Theory and Design in the First Machine Age* (London: Architectural Press, 1960).

4. A. D. Chandler, *Strategy and Structure* (Cambridge: MIT Press, 1962); John K. Galbraith, *The New Industrial Estate* (London: Hamish Hamilton, 1967).

5. F. Perroux, *L'Économie du XXe Siècle* (Paris: Presses Universitaires de France, 1961).

6. R. E. Park, E. W. Burgess, and R. D. McKenzie, *The City* (Chicago: University of Chicago Press, 1925).

7. L. Wirth, "Urbanism as a Way of Life," *American Journal of Sociology* 44 (1938): 1-24.

8. G. C. Allen, *The Industrial Development of Birmingham and the Black Country, 1860-1907* (Hemel Hempstead, Herts.: Allen and Unwin, 1929); P. S. Florence, *Investment, Location, and Size of Plant* (Cambridge: Cambridge University Press, 1948); R. M. Haig, *Major Economic Factors in Metropolitan Growth and Arrangement* (New York: Regional Plan of New York and its Environs, 1927).

9. D. Bell, *The Coming of Postindustrial Society* (New York: Basic Books, 1973).

10. A. Kourchid, *L'Autre Modèle Californien* (Paris: Méridiens Klincksieck, 1992).

11. A. J. Scott, *New Industrial Spaces: Flexible Production and Regional Development in North America and Western Europe* (London: Pion, 1988).

12. M. Storper and S. Christopherson, "Flexible Specialization and Regional Industrial Agglomerations: The Case of the US Motion Picture Industry," *Annals of the Association of American Geographers* 77 (1987): 104-117.

13. M. Storper, "The Transition to Flexible Specialization in the US Film Industry: External Economies, the Division of Labour, and the Crossing of Industrial Divides," *Cambridge Journal of Economics* 13 (1989): 273-305.

14. M. Davis, "The Empty Quarter," in D. Reid, ed., *Sex, Death, and God in L.A.* (New York: Pantheon, 1992), 54-71.

15. P. Ong et al., *The Widening Divide: Income Inequality and Poverty in Los Angeles* (Graduate School of Architecture and Urban Planning, University of California, Los Angeles: The Research Group on the Los Angeles Economy, 1989).

16. A. J. Scott, "High-technology Industry in the San Fernando Valley and Ventura County: Observations on Economic Growth and the Evolution of Urban Form," in A. J. Scott and E. Soja, eds., *The City: Los Angeles and Urban Theory at the End of the Twentieth Century* (Berkeley and Los Angeles: University of California Press, 1998).

17. E. Soja, "Inside Exopolis: Themes Screened in Orange County," in M. Sorkin, ed., *Variations on a Theme Park: The New American City and the End of Public Space* (New York: Hill and Wang, 1992), 94-122.

18. B. Marchand, *The Emergence of Los Angeles: Population and Housing in the City of Dreams, 1940-1970* (London: Pion, 1986); Z. Pearlstone, *Ethnic L.A.* (Beverly Hills, CA: Hillcrest Press, 1990).

19. E. Soja, *Postmodern Geographies: The Reassertion of Space in Critical Social Theory* (London: Verso, 1989).

20. M.-R. Jackson, J. H. Johnson, and W. C. Farrell, "After the Smoke Has Cleared: An Analysis of Selected Responses to the Los Angeles Civil Unrest of 1992," *Contention* 3 (Spring 1994): 3-21.

21. M. Cenzatti, *Los Angeles and the L.A. School: Postmodernism and Urban Studies* (West Hollywood Forum for Architecture and Urban Design, Forum Publication No. 10, 1993); C. Jencks, *Heteropolis: Los Angeles, the Riots, and the Strange Beauty of Hetero-Architecture* (London: Academy Editions, 1993).

22. A. J. Scott and A. S. Paul, "Collective Order and Economic Regulation in Industrial Agglomerations: The Technopoles of Southern California," *Environment and Planning, C: Government and Policy* 8 (1990): 179-193.

23. M. Davis, *City of Quartz* (London: Verso, 1990).

PART 3

Reconsidering Community

From Immigrants in the City, to Immigrant City

EDITOR'S
COMMENTS

With a primary focus on what they called "human ecology," the Chicago School researchers devoted a great deal of time and effort to the study of community. "Man," as they used to say, is a social being, even if he was demonstrably inept at certain social graces! The communities that subsequently developed from human interaction were an agglomeration of people, institutions, and places. When these institutions floundered, trouble began because community ties were thereby weakened. The great threats to community stability, according to the Chicago School, included the automobile ("connected with more seductions than happen otherwise in cities altogether," mobility, motion pictures, newspapers, and so on. As Park ruefully observed, "Apparently anything that makes life interesting is dangerous to the social order." "Social disorganization" and "cultural decadence" were understood to follow inevitably upon weakened community ties.

Our focus in Part III of this book is on community. First, in Chapter 7, Jerome Straughan and Pierrette Hondagneu-Sotelo examine immigration, perhaps the single most significant factor in the construction of community in contemporary Southern California. Then, Madeleine R. Stoner (Chapter 8) and Cheryl L. Maxson and Malcolm W. Klein (Chapter 9) address the Chicago School themes of hobos and juvenile delinquents, expanding their concerns to consider the contemporary crisis of homelessness and the rise of the street gangs in U.S. cities. The last two chapters in this section consider important pieces of contemporary communities that were not anticipated by the Chicago School: Donald Miller considers the renaissance of religion in urban areas (Chapter 10), and J. Dallas Dishman examines the advent of communities in cyberspace (Chapter 11).

California in general and Los Angeles in particular have always been demographically diverse (see Chapter 2, this volume). For most of the nineteenth century, San Francisco was already the most diverse city on the West Coast. The growing racial and ethnic diversity of American cities was given a strong push by revisions in U.S. immigration laws, which (beginning in the 1960s) shifted the emphasis in international immigration away from traditional European sources. In addition, the nation's southern border became the focus of large-scale immigration (sometimes illegal) from Central and South American countries.

It is impossible to overestimate the significance of immigration in Southern California. Immigrants arrive in all shapes, sizes, and colors, with incredible variations in education, skills, and financial resources. They generally get along with each other, but sometimes they don't. One distressingly familiar error committed by observers from beyond Southern California is that politics in the region can be understood by the black-white conflicts that characterize cities elsewhere in the nation. To the contrary, there is now a brown (Latino) majority in many California cities, although Latinos may not yet hold a plurality. Brown communities are being joined in community politics by increasingly vociferous Asian American populations.

In this chapter, Jerome Straughan and Pierrette Hondagneu-Sotelo consider the legacy of the Chicago School in immigration studies and how Los Angeles departs from such traditions. Several important themes could not have been anticipated by these traditions, including transnationalism, identity politics, and gender issues. Straughan and Hondagneu-Sotelo conclude that things are different now and that Los Angeles may give us a glimpse of our collective futures.

QUOTES FROM
THE CITY

In view of the fact that man is so manifestly—as Aristotle described him—a political animal, predestined to live in association with, and dependence upon, his fellows, it is strange and interesting to discover, as we are compelled to do, now and again, how utterly unfitted by nature man is for life in society.

It is true, no doubt, that man is the most gregarious of animals, but it is nevertheless true that the thing of which he still knows the least is the business of carrying on an associated existence. . . . (99)

. . . [T]here was something fundamentally diabolical in human nature, a view which found expression in the well-known doctrine of the "natural depravity of man."

One reason why human beings, in contrast with the lower animals, seem to be so ill-adapted to the world in which they are born is that the environment in which human beings live is so largely made up of the experience and memories and the acquired habits of the people who have preceded them.

This experience and these memories—crystallized and embodied in tradition, in custom, and in folk-ways—constitute the social, as distinguished from the biological, environment; for man is not merely an individual with certain native and inherited biological traits, but he is at the same time a person with manners, sentiments, attitudes, and ambitions.

It is the social environment to which the person, as distinguished from the individual, responds; and it is these responses of the person to his environment that eventually define his personality and give to the individual a character that can be described in moral terms. . . . (100)

The community, then, is the name that we give to this larger and most inclusive social milieu, outside of ourselves, our family, and our immediate neighborhood, in which the individual maintains not merely his existence as an individual, but his life as a person.

The community, including the family, with its wider interests, its larger purposes, and its more deliberate aims, surrounds us, encloses us, and compels us to conform; not by mere pressure from without, not by the fear of censure merely, but by the sense of our interest in, and responsibility to, certain interests not our own.

The sources of our actions are, no doubt, in the organic impulses of the individual man; but actual conduct is determined more or less by public opinion, by custom, and by a code that exists outside of us in the family, in the neighborhood, and in the community. This community, however, with its less immediate purposes and its more deliberate aim, is always more or less outside of, and alien to us; much more so than the family, for example, or any other congenial group. This is to such an extent true that certain sociological writers have conceived society as having an existence quite independent of the individuals who compose it at any given time. Under these circumstances the natural condition of the individual in society is one of conflict; conflict with other individuals, to be sure, but particularly conflict with the conventions and regulations of the social group of which he is a member. Personal freedom—self-expression, as we have learned to call it in recent years—is, therefore, if not a fruitless, still a never ending, quest. . . . (104-105)

While I [Park] was on the Pacific Coast a few months ago, studying what we have called "race relations," I was impressed by the marked differences, as between immigrant groups, with respect to their ability to accommodate themselves to the American environment and, within the limitations imposed upon them by our customs and our laws, to provide for all the interests of life.

Immigrant communities are likely to include within the circle of their interests and their organizations all the interests of life. Every immigrant's community will have a religious organization—a synagogue, a temple or a church—with its related, often dependent, mutual aid and welfare organizations. It will have also its own business enterprises, its clubs, lodges, coffee houses, restaurants and gathering places, and a press. Every immigrant community is likely to have its press in America even if it did not have one in the home country. The immigrant colony is frequently nothing more than a transplanted village, for America actually has been colonized not by races or by nationalities, but by villages. (119)

CHAPTER 7

From Immigrants in the City, to Immigrant City

JEROME STRAUGHAN
PIERRETTE HONDAGNEU-SOTELO

Is Los Angeles one sprawling, massive federation of transplanted villages? Newcomers to Southern California might think so if they exit USC, passing successively through Central American, Mexican, and African American neighborhoods as they head north on Vermont, until finally reaching Koreatown. Navigating the radio and television waves in Los Angeles leaves us with the same impression. L.A.'s airwaves provide an array of Chinese, Vietnamese, Korean, and the especially popular Spanish-language soap operas, news programs, and variety shows. Ethnically organized social clubs and Mexican hometown associations are popular, and immigrant temples and churches, ranging from the fledgling Evangelical storefronts attended largely by Central American and Mexican immigrants to the more imposing Islamic mosques or Armenian Orthodox churches, dot the religious landscape. Newcomers to the region express shock as they take in the "English spoken here" signs posted outside shop windows. On the surface, Robert Park's metaphor of the transplanted village seems to fit contemporary Los Angeles, but move in for a closer look, and things begin to appear a little differently.

As Dowell Myers showed in Chapter 2, immigrants to Los Angeles today are far more diverse than the European immigrants who flooded into Chicago in the early twentieth century, and that diversity, together with a differently structured economy and a proliferation of new technologies, means that immigrant neighborhoods are no longer necessarily defined by territory. Today's immigrants come from Latin America and Asia, and they include not only labor migrants but also professionals and entrepreneurs. Their differential economic incorporation into Los Angeles, together with new transportation and communications technology, has had profound implications for the ways that community is constituted.

Together, Salvadoran, Guatemalan, and Mexican immigrants account for about half of all post-1965 adult immigrants to Los Angeles, and like earlier generations of European immigrants to Chicago, they toil at low-wage, manual labor that many U.S.-born workers reject.[1] Unlike their working-class immigrant predecessors in

Border Fence Separating Tijuana and San Diego
Photograph by Michael J. Dear.

Chicago, these workers toil less in foundries and factories and more in the myriad of low-wage, low-skilled jobs in the service, construction, trucking, packing, and deskilled assembly sectors. Meanwhile, other immigrant groups populate the professions and business world. Indian doctors, Filipina nurses, and highly capitalized Hong Kong entrepreneurs, all of whom enter the United States with high levels of what economists refer to as "human capital," enjoy a different reality from that of their low-wage counterparts. Their substantial economic and occupational resources allow them a wider range of residential choices, loosening them from the spatially bounded nuclei of ethnic enclaves, which are still common among labor migrants. Evidence suggests that immigrant professionals and entrepreneurs may have to work hard to imaginatively devise and create new institutions comparable with those that immigrant neighborhoods provide.[2]

Even working-class Latino immigrants are no longer as place-bound as in previous generations. Today, Mexican immigrants settle all over Los Angeles—not just in the old East Side.[3] Many Central American and Mexican immigrants do remain anchored in poor, crime-ridden, inner-city neighborhoods, but Latino immigrant newcomers use these neighborhoods as launchpads, whereas others bypass the central city altogether, settling, instead, in the San Gabriel and San Fernando Valleys. For working-class and middle-class professional immigrants alike, L.A.'s conglomeration of multiple centers and its largely suburbanized landscape lead to residential

Crosses on the U.S.-Mexican Border Fence Identifying People Who Died Trying to Reach *El Norte*
Photograph by Michael J. Dear.

settlement patterns quite different from those posited by the Chicago School's ecological model of urban concentric circles.

The widespread dispersion of new technologies has also changed the character of immigrant communities. The automobile and the freeway—those iconic L.A. symbols—function as the dominant means of transportation, even among poor, laboring immigrants. Jet plane travel, international telephone communications, and even e-mail have allowed immigrants in Los Angeles to better constitute community ties "back home" in their countries of origin. Increasingly, when we speak of immigrant communities, we are speaking of communities constituted across national boundaries. Families and households, political associations, and even sports teams now defy the traditional boundaries of geography and of nation-state.

During the past twenty-five years, as the United States once again became a country of immigrants, Los Angeles emerged as the metropolitan area of choice for new residents and workers.[4] For this reason, Los Angeles has quickly become a multiracial and multilinguistic world center. By 1990, Los Angeles was already home to 3.9 million immigrants, who constituted slightly more than one third of Los Angeles County's total population. If one calculates the children of immigrants into these figures, the magnitude of this recent immigration is truly impressive: By 1997, immigrants and their children accounted for 62 percent of metropolitan L.A.'s population.[5] Although the Asian and Latin American predominance of post-1965 immigration is generalized throughout the United States, L.A.'s proximity to the U.S.-Mexican border and geographical placement on the Pacific Coast have yielded even greater concentrations of Mexicans and various Asian immigrant groups in the area. Numerically, however, Mexicans far outpace all other groups. With 40 percent of the entire population—both U.S.- and foreign-born—claiming Mexican origin, Los Angeles, in an ironic turn of events, is once again becoming a Mexican city.[6] Mexican migration to the United States remains the largest and longest-running migration anywhere in the world, and its effects are particularly concentrated in Southern California.

In this chapter, we assess the Chicago School's influence on immigration research and review contemporary theories of immigration. We examine the Chicago School's contributions to several key immigration themes, and on the basis of the case of Los Angeles and of recent developments in immigration studies, we suggest future directions for scholarly work. We begin with comments about immigrants and urban life made by some of the key figures of the Chicago School and then turn to what we take to be the plurality expressed in contemporary immigration theory.

THE CHICAGO SCHOOL AND THE STUDY OF IMMIGRATION

Chicago School scholars shared in a continuing interest with the internal dynamics of city life, as, for example, those sociologists who studied immigrants examined how illiterate or semiliterate European peasants were adapting to urban American life.[7] Coming primarily from poor, rural areas of southern and eastern Europe, these immigrants received a much less hospitable reception than did the "old immigrants" who had preceded them from England, Germany, and Ireland. Although Chicago School participants saw social life proceeding on a more or less linear progression from rural to urban life, from immigrants' villages to Chicago neighborhoods, most—with the exception of Robert Redfield—focused on the dynamics of lived, urban experiences, distinguishing them from earlier European social theorists.

Influenced by German thought on Western urban life, Robert Park brought to the Chicago School both social theory and a substantial exposure to nonacademic pursuits. Prior to arriving at Chicago, Park had served as Booker T. Washington's speechwriter and travel companion, worked as a newspaper reporter, and also studied at Harvard and later in Germany with Georg Simmel.[8] Although his thinking never led to a solely authored book, he wrote a number of important articles and was perhaps most influential in inspiring his graduate students to look at the various social strata of Chicago—to study taxi dancers, hobos, immigrants, and other societal "others." Further, he is responsible for pushing his students to empirical examination of lived experiences and social institutions, to approach the neighborhood as a "natural area," and to develop social theory connected to the details of daily urban life.

The classic Chicago School text on immigrant life is *The Polish Peasant,* a five-volume study published between 1918 and 1920. In it, William I. Thomas and Florian Znaniecki pursue a phenomenological inquiry into the immigrant life experienced by former peasants in the city of Chicago. Relying on diverse sources, including life histories, letters exchanged between Poles in Chicago and their kin in Poland, and oral history and testimonials, the authors sought to capture historical social change and subjective experience in the lives of these immigrants. In the historical trajectory of social science research, their efforts were significant because they were among the first to focus on social groups and the implicit social rules, meanings, and relationships that hold them together. Although locked into an overtly modernist bipolar theoretical model consisting of a more or less linear trajectory from rural, traditional backgrounds to urban, modern settings, they offered many important insights and method that are still relevant today.

Thomas and Znaniecki use the term *social disorganization* in referring to the diminished social bonds between nuclear families (which they termed *marriage groups*). They, like Louis Wirth, who would follow them, viewed ethnic neighborhood associations, voluntary groups, and clubs as viable social organizations that would, through time, come to replace family bonds weakened by the changes brought on by migration. Such social disorganization would, they concluded, be alleviated by immigrant participation in instrumental, rational, voluntary groups. Implicit to this bipolar model is the presumed conflict between secondary associations, ethnicity, and individualism on the one hand and primary groups on the other. Given the weakness of affectual, primary groups, Thomas and Znaniecki believed that these secondary groups, with their emphasis on specific goals, objectives, or purposes, would lead immigrants toward assimilation. In these scholars' estimation, adaptation, acculturation, and assimilation function as a type of salvation for immigrant newcomers who might otherwise be led into a destructive and disorderly process of migrant transience and anomie.

In "Human Migration and the Marginal Man," first published in 1928, Park even compared the social disruption caused by migration with full-blown revolution:

> The first and most obvious difference between revolution and migration is that in migration the breakdown of the social order is initiated by the impact of an invading population, and completed by the contact and fusion of alien with native peoples.[9]

Park was obsessed with the pathological, "changed type of personality" created by migration and the breakdown process, but he also believed that marginalized immigrants who belonged fully neither to the society of origin nor to the new society of destination were also possessed of sharpened vision and sensibilities.

But more than Park, it was his student Louis Wirth who hypothesized that specific urban features, including the physical separation of work from community, created a unique "urban culture." In "Urbanism as a Way of Life," Wirth described city life "as consisting of the substitution of secondary for primary contacts, the weakening of bonds of kinship and the declining social significance of the family, the disap-

pearance of the neighborhood and the undermining of the traditional basis of solidarity."[10] This transformation results in social breakdown and, again, anomie,
whereas again, redemption arrives with the formation of clubs, instrumental associations, and voluntary groups that offer members a sense of belonging and shared
purpose.

Oscar Handlin's Pulitzer prize-winning history of nineteenth-century European immigration to the United States, *The Uprooted*, offers evidence of the mid-
twentieth-century legacy of the Chicago School. It is here, in the curious metaphor
of gardening, that the breakdown view of migrant adaptation to urban industrial life
finds its most graphic expression. Written during the 1930s and 1940s and originally published in the 1950s, Handlin's book reflects, as Eli Zaretsky has pointed
out, both the optimism of the United States in the era marked by the New Deal and
by the beginnings of the early civil rights movement and the celebration of American
individualism.[11] Handlin deplored the disruptive adjustment period of migrant
adaptation, the effects of which would continue to be felt by the second generation:

> The immigrants lived in crisis because they were uprooted. In transplantation, while
> the old roots were sundered, before the new were established, the immigrants existed
> in an extreme situation. The shock, and the effects of the shock, persisted for many
> years; and their influence reached down to generations which themselves never paid
> the cost of crossing.[12]

Like the Chicago School participants, Handlin believed that neighborhood associa-
tional life would help speed individual upward mobility and assimilation. Familial
breakdown and poverty would be alleviated by time and ethnic succession. In the
second half of the twentieth century, Milton Gordon also extended Robert Park's
concept of assimilation, distinguishing between cultural assimilation, which involves language and cultural practices, and structural assimilation, which occurs
when the newcomers and their children are fully incorporated and accepted
throughout social institutions.[13]

CONTEMPORARY IMMIGRATION THEORIES

The current theoretical debates about immigration go far beyond the widely dissem-
inated restrictionist and advocacy immigration stances and have moved past the narrow parameters of assimilation and adjustment put forth by the Chicago School. To
underscore the wide range of theoretical developments that immigration theory has
recently undergone, we employ the outlines of a theoretical taxonomy introduced by
Portes and Bach. This includes four groupings of theoretical debates: (1) the origins
of immigration, (2) the stability of migrant flows through time, (3) migrant labor
and its uses, and (4) social and cultural adaptation.[14] We find this particular system
useful to begin a discussion of contemporary immigration theory. Because we see the

contents of each area slightly differently than do Portes and Bach, however, we will also offer some revision to their taxonomy.

The Origins of Migration

Derived from neoclassical economics and congruent with modernization theory, the orthodox perspective—alternately called the equilibrium or "push-pull" theory—best approaches what passes as common sense in our society today. This model portrays migration as an individual response to negative "push" factors in the society of origin and positive "pull" factors in the society of destination.[15] The key explanation here involves the wage gap and monetary incentives and disincentives for migration. In the most extreme versions of this approach, the individual migrant becomes a purely self-interested economic agent who coldly compares present income with potential earnings in alternative locations. This type of theoretical framework generally yields studies characterized by a one-dimensional, reductionist view of human action, in which complex social processes are flattened into a random selection of generic, individual calculations. Moreover, the voluntarist assumptions embedded in this paradigm ignore the social structural factors that shape migration, so that individual calculus occurs in a historical and political economic vacuum. The conditions that give rise to push and pull factors remain uninvestigated and are simply assumed to derive from distinct, unconnected societies.

Many of the assumptions of the neoclassical model were modified in the 1980s by scholars working in anthropology, sociology, and economics who shifted the focus from the individual to the household.[16] Recognizing that people see their actions in relation to larger groupings with whom they are associated, the household approach considers how individuals in households diversify the allocation of households resources, such as family labor. In some versions, this household model approaches Gary Becker's "new household economics," with all its rational choice assumptions, whereby households are posited as units that assume the agency to "send" household members elsewhere for monetary remittances to guard the family unit against crop price fluctuations.[17] Massey and colleagues refer to this approach as "the new economics of migration."[18]

Yet these theoretical approaches remain flawed by several unexamined assumptions. First, proponents of the household model generally view the household as a clearly bounded and unified collectivity, in which social solidarity, altruism, and a sharing ethic are said to characterize household social relations. Yet this view comes at the expense of seeing the sometimes divergent and conflicting interests within families and glosses over the influence of gender and generation difference on migration. The household model ignores the social relations internal to families and treats the household through the prism of individualism. Moreover, such research generally portrays migration as a reactive response pursued when household economic necessities outstrip locally available income and resources. Finally, the model assumes that strategies based on deliberate householdwide calculation drive migration, regardless of whether people migrate as individuals or as family units. The claim that "migration is not an individual decision, but one taken by the whole household" typifies this perspective.[19]

But a look inside the household reveals that discussions on migration are often contentious, so an examination of gender and generational dynamics may better explain how people respond to broader economic pressures and opportunities.[20] More recently, Portes proposes what he calls an "economic sociology of immigration" to address the social underpinnings of economic actions associated with immigration.[21] In this perspective, attention to social networks, social capital, and collective resources forces us to reconsider the notion that immigration is a purely economic action, but strong tones of economic rationality shade this perspective.

Macrostructural approaches to the study of migration developed in opposition to the neoclassical model, rooted as it is in economics, have redirected research toward the structural and historical factors that make labor migration possible. More eclectic than the competing framework, the macrostructural (or macropolitical) approaches, developed primarily by sociologists, appear in a variety of models that emphasize the political economy of immigration. Some explanations have focused, for example, on how foreign investment in Third World nations disrupts established economic structures and generates emigration and on how capital mobility from "core" to "periphery"—to use modern world-systems theory vernacular—induces labor migration in the opposite direction. Others emphasize the significance of labor migration for capital accumulation in the societies of immigrant destination or how the presence of U.S. military bases and foreign policy interventions prompt U.S.-bound migration, whereas still others emphasize patterns of regional political and economic development. As Massey et al. note, this perspective owes much to Immanuel Wallerstein, whose modern world-systems model focuses on the structural knitting of dense global markets since sixteenth-century European colonialism.[22] It also owes much to Lenin's theory of imperialism, whereby representatives of advanced industrialized nations seek higher profits and new markets in less industrialized societies that then become colonies.

Research informed by macrostructural approaches illuminates how broad structural factors induce and support migration, offering a necessary corrective to the orthodox view by providing the missing big-picture focus. Yet in explaining the origins of migration and the functions that labor migration plays in the development and maintenance of modern capitalism, the social dimensions of immigration are all too often neglected. Conspicuously absent from the macrostructural perspective is any sense of human agency or subjectivity. Immigrants are portrayed not as human beings but as homogeneous, nondifferentiated objects responding mechanically and uniformly to the same set of structural forces.

Stability of Migration Through Time

Finding an explanation for the persistence of migration through time and space spawned a good deal of immigration research in the second half of the twentieth century. In the orthodox view, the stability of immigration corresponds to the pressures of economic pulls and pushes. Accordingly, immigration restrictionist legislation may focus on employer sanctions against hiring undocumented immigrant workers. The most recent example of this theory is the Immigration Reform and Control Act of 1986, whereby employer sanctions served as the centerpiece of restrictionist efforts. Although the intent of employer sanctions is to stop the pull factors, such sanctioning has had only a modest effect in deterring undocumented migration. In other renditions of the orthodox view, the ebb and flow of migration may be controlled by the state through special guest worker programs, the largest U.S. experiment in this regard being the Bracero Program, a contract labor scheme designed to meet World War II labor shortages. Between 1942 and 1964, nearly 5 million labor contracts were issued to Mexican citizens. But as many subsequent observers have noted, the designers of the project had not anticipated the extent to which the program would stimulate more immigration and settlement. Like the guest worker programs in Europe, the Bracero Program is generally credited for stimulating flows of undocumented and permanent settlement migration.

We opt for a more social perspective of immigration flows, focused not solely on simplistic economic pulls and pushes or legislative efforts but instead on the key social networks that facilitate migration. According to this thinking, the maturation of social networks among immigrants propels more migration. As better-established immigrants help their friends and relations relocate, a new social infrastructure of migration takes shape, and migration gains momentum independent of job demand in the place of destination. Massey and colleagues refer to this process of migration inertia as *cumulative causation.*[23]

Uses of Immigrant Labor

Economic downturns in the United States spark nativism and anti-immigrant campaigns. Historically, the rhetoric of anti-immigrant movements has targeted immigrants with allegations of labor displacement and wage depression. This is not altogether surprising, as the majority of foreign-born persons who have come to the United States have come as labor migrants. The confluence of labor migration and the labor-based rhetoric of various xenophobic campaigns has driven many contemporary empirical researchers to examine the uses of immigrant labor to determine if immigrants are a net economic benefit or cost to the United States. Much of this research has focused on the Los Angeles economy, and, like studies on this question conducted elsewhere, the conclusions are mixed. A series of studies based on 1990 U.S. census data in Los Angeles, compiled by UCLA researchers in the book *Ethnic Los Angeles,* inconclusively suggest that contemporary immigrant labor may have a deleterious effect on Chicano and African American workers in specific areas and industries.[24] Yet another recent study, based on collaborative survey research by demographers at USC and El Cologio de la Frontera Norte in Tijuana, suggests that undocumented Mexican immigrant workers in the Los Angeles economy may actually raise wages for U.S.-born workers of Mexican ancestry.[25]

Although there are various, discernible theoretical perspectives in this field of immigration studies—that is, theories of labor scarcity, split labor markets, and ethnic enclaves—we focus in this section on recent trends in xenophobic movements and immigrant labor in California and Los Angeles. As recently as the early 1980s, immigration restrictionists argued that undocumented immigrants were stealing jobs and depressing wages of U.S. citizens. This view, representative of public opinion and fueling many studies, casts immigrant workers—especially Mexicans—as unfair labor competition. Intensifying during California's recession of the early 1980s, plant closures, unemployment, and the declining number of manufacturing jobs made immigrant workers an easy scapegoat in the public's eye. Yet by the 1990s, although the cry of unfair economic competition faded, xenophobic restrictionists recast their fears by shifting attention from immigrant Mexican workers to their families, claiming that undocumented immigrants and their children were depleting the welfare system and "draining public resources."[26]

Why the switch from "depressing wages" to "draining public resources"? By the 1990s, California politicians readily acknowledged that most new immigrant jobs—in the lower end of garment manufacturing, food processing, construction, services, and agriculture—were not the jobs that the voting public desired. The switch in rhetoric reflected more than expedient ploys by political consultants and desperate politicians, however. It was a muted acknowledgment that reflected the profound historical transformation in Mexican migration from a predominantly sojourner or temporary pattern to the establishment of permanent settlement communities throughout California.

Immigrant labor, especially Mexican immigrant labor, has become a fundamental part of California's and L.A.'s diverse economy. Similarly, Asian immigrant labor and capital are now important features of L.A.'s heralded Pacific Rim economy. The creation of permanent occupational niches for these workers helps explain the emergence of established immigrant communities throughout rural, urban, and suburban California and the concentration of these communities in Los Angeles.

Yet it is instructive to recall that the earliest Asian immigrants and Mexican immigrants to enter the California economy did so under coercive labor conditions. The concept of "internal colonization," first introduced by Stokely Carmichael and later popularized by sociologist Robert Blauner, describes the incorporation of non-European, foreign-born workers into the United States through coercive labor schemes that resembled traditional colonization.[27] Chinese, Japanese, and Filipino men were initially brought to work in western agriculture as contracted laborers, and exclusions laws were deliberately set in place to restrict the migration of women and entire families. Similarly, Mexican workers came to the United States under a series of contract labor systems, the largest and most recent one being the already mentioned Bracero Program (in effect from 1942 until 1964). These work stints required long family separations, ranging from months to years and even decades, interspersed with brief visits. Eventually, these men used their developing social contacts to seek jobs in the growing cities and suburbs of postwar California, which increasingly relied on the labor of these male Mexican workers. These men were subsequently joined in commercial and residential areas by Mexican women, who also found jobs in various occupational niches. As more immigrants settle, their consumption needs generally create greater job demand at both ends of the occupational hierarchy. Today, Asian and Latino immigrant labor and capital are the bedrock of the contemporary Los Angeles economy.

Contrasting the Chicago School With Contemporary Currents

Sociological studies of immigrants have traditionally focused on immigrant responses to the new social environment in the country of destination.[28] In this regard, much of the research has been grounded in and limited to the language of assimilation and adaptation. Although these concepts improved on earlier eugenic notions that proclaimed the biological inferiority of immigrants, the sociological imagination was confined to examining only how immigrants fail or succeed in becoming more like dominant U.S.-born groups. We turn our attention to these frameworks, developed through studies conducted by the Chicago School sociologists, to describe them in relation to current immigration scholarship. Relying on several themes to organize our discussion—the approach to social research, transnationalism and place, ethnicity and identity, relations of gender and generation in families, and the economy—we hope to illuminate some of the influences as well as breaks between the Chicago School sociologists and contemporary immigration scholars.

Although the field of urban studies claims the Chicago School for its origins as a discipline, the Chicago School was also central to the development of field studies and qualitative methods in urban sociology. Participants in the Chicago School, however, adhered to different ideas about how empirical inquiry should be approached. If we understand empiricism to be related to a positivist, prescriptive research agenda that is guided by the belief that the social world is made up of positive, observable, empirical facts that simply need to be collected and measured to obtain the "laws" guiding social behavior, then Chicago School adherents were not strictly empiricist. Moreover, many of the Chicago School faculty of that era, including Albion Small, William I. Thomas, George Herbert Mead, and Ellsworth Faris, engaged with fundamental questions about how people make meaning from their social worlds and pursued community projects and service as part of their work.[29]

Thomas and Znaniecki examined historical and structural changes in Poland and the United States, but they were concerned primarily with meaning, understandings, and subjectivity. They relied on existent primary materials—using study participants' letters, for example—for glimpses into this world. More concerned with behavioral, individual aspects, Robert Park, in some ways, tried to emulate natural sciences, focusing on "instincts" and "natural ecologies." Unlike Thomas, Park had faith that through detachment, he and his students could discover an objective truth "out there" and that this expert knowledge could then help inform policy. Park believed that social workers and reformers would never obtain the objectivity necessary for social science research. As one commentator has observed in a discussion of the Chicago School researchers and their study of ethnic groups, "Detachment came readily to those who were essentially complacent with the course of human events."[30]

At the University of Chicago, Park was part of the push to make social science more professionalized, aimed more at producing experts rather than radical reformers, leading some contemporary commentators to condemn academic social sciences that were increasingly divorced from social action. By contrast, the women trained as social scientists and associated with Hull House—the Chicago settlement house that served as a center for the city's women reformers—wanted to link empirical data with social action. Unlike most of his colleagues, Thomas frequently lectured and dined at Hull House and was politically active in women's suffrage, prostitution reform, and civil liberties. Like the Hull House women, Thomas was skeptical of government-sponsored reforms, believing that such changes had to originate in the community, rather than be created by experts who fall outside its boundaries. Although he maintained a modernist's belief in evolutionist progress, he remained a staunch opponent of social engineering from above.

Today, the split between contemporary immigration scholars and their empiricist counterparts survives. A 1995 review article by John Lie in *Contemporary Sociology* describes it in this way:

> The historical and the ethnographic impulse of *The Polish Peasant*—and most glaringly the place of personal narratives—has largely sunk with only a few traces. . . . In pursuing scientific rigor, most sociologists have consigned individual voices to the academic periphery—the marginalia of Americana. *International Migration Review* (IMR), the flagship journal of migration studies in the United States, exemplifies this trend. . . . [Its articles] focus on the questions of socioeconomic and cultural accommodation and assimilation and rely predominantly on survey and census data.[31]

We share John Lie's lament that the contemporary impact of the Chicago School is a theoretical approach more adequate for understanding European immigration in the early twentieth century than what has followed.[32]

A good deal of the North American immigration literature remains descriptive and empirical, concerned with measuring migration flows and migrant characteristics. These studies may count immigrants and make conclusions about assimilation on the basis of indicators of education, language acquisition, and occupation but rarely engage with current theoretical debates. This research seldom acknowledges that social science is, itself, a social construct, with inquiry and methods shaped by relations of power, history, dominant ideologies, and official experts. Some projects seem more driven to test theory, to develop explanation. Two review articles cowritten by six authors, for example, bemoan the absence of a single, systematic theory of international migration.[33] In one article, the authors conclude that "sorting out the relative empirical support for each of the theoretical schemes and integrating them in light of that evaluation will be among the most important tasks carried out by social scientists in ensuing years."[34]

A revival of the ethnographic tradition as pioneered by the Chicago School would be a welcome addition to contemporary scholarship. The sprawling megalopolis of Los Angeles, like other large cities, contains many distinct cities inside its often fuzzy boundaries. We are tempted to call them "natural areas," ignoring that they are not naturally produced but socially manufactured. These areas are each characterized by particular immigrant relations and may be studied through a variety of research methods, including qualitative ethnography. Research that seeks to capture the nuanced meanings of everyday social life in these communities can be powerful when coupled with structural analysis.

Transnationalism and Place

In *The Polish Peasant,* Thomas and Znaniecki looked carefully at the social relationships between Poles in Chicago and Poland. They examined letters written between Polish immigrants in Chicago and kin back home, written primarily by and to men—sons, husbands, and fathers—referring to them as "bowing letters" because they typically opened with formal greetings that "manifest the persistence of familial solidarity in spite of the separation."[35] In a discussion of the immigrant political idealist in *Old World Traits Transplanted,* Thomas hints at these transnational ties and nationalist-oriented political aspirations and orientations on the part of those back home.

> Consequently they wish first of all to save their members from Americanization, to send them home with unspoiled loyalty, or to keep them a permanent patriotic asset working here for the cause of home. They regard America as merely the instrument of their nationalistic wishes. Their leaders wish also to get recognition at home for their patriotic activities here, and superior status on their return. They speak of the penetration of America by their own culture.[36]

Yet in Ernest W. Burgess's chapter in *The City,* "Can Neighborhood Work Have a Scientific Basis?" we find a striking contrast to today's immigrant transnational communities that defy territoriality by spanning international borders. In Burgess's view, immigrant culture is an amalgam of old and new, containing the cultural experience of two places:

> The immigrant colony in an American city possesses a culture unmistakably not indigenous but transplanted from the Old World. The telling fact, however, is not that the immigrant colony maintains i0ts old-world cultural organization, but that in its new environment it mediates a cultural adjustment to its new situation. How basically culture is dependent upon place is suggested by the following expressions, "New England conscience," "southern hospitality," "Scottish thrift," "Kansas is not a geographical location so much as a state of mind."[37]

In contrast to the Chicago School paradigm, however, immigration scholarship has taken a transnational turn. Inspired by postcolonial, postmodern anthropology, the transnational view explicitly challenges the bipolar model of "old country" and "new world," of "back home" and "new home." Scholars such as Roger Rouse, Prema Kurien, Michael Kearney, Luis E. Guarnizo, and particularly Linda Basch, Nina Glick Schiller, and Cristina Szanton Blanc in their book *Nations Unbound* argue that the circulation of people, goods, and ideas creates new transnational cultures that become autonomous social spheres transcending national borders.[38]

Immigration in the late twentieth century is contextualized by different infrastructure than was early-twentieth-century European migration to Chicago. New technologies of communication and transportation now allow people in geographically distant areas to function as one community. Although acknowledgment of how these new technologies facilitate global ties is central to the transnational perspectives of immigration, a contemporary study of these types of immigrant communication remains to be written.

Will cyberspace create new transnational spheres? In early 1996, Belize Telecommunication Limited began offering Internet and World Wide Web access to Belizeans in Belize. As Belizean Web pages popped up on the Web, Belizeans abroad began contacting their homes. For one of us (Straughan), a Belizean American living in Los Angeles, awareness of high-tech transnationalism was heightened through participation in a Los Angeles-based Belizean educational network and cyberspace. The Belizean Web pages offer news and information about Belize, including a listing of Belizean e-mail addresses of Belizeans at home and abroad. Belizeans may connect with individuals whom they have not seen for a long time.

In addition to acknowledging the potential of the Internet to create new communities, it is also important to recognize its limitations related especially to access. At that time, the e-mail names and addresses of Belizeans at home consisted primarily of prominent Belizeans, higher-income Belizeans, and those associated with businesses, whereas the e-mail names and addresses of Belizeans abroad appear to be primarily middle-class university students. Nevertheless, the potential for immigrants to articulate a sense of transnationalism in cyberspace will increase as the technology becomes more affordable and accessible.

This example of recent cyberspace explorations suggests that these emerging forms of community also have an important political dimension. Belizean students' forays into cyberspace were initially prompted by concern for absentee voters. Because the political elites in nations as diverse as Grenada, the Philippines, Haiti, and Mexico recognize (to varying degrees) that substantial portions of their populations have settled abroad, these politicians are approaching political mobilization in ways that transcend nation-state boundaries. As Linda Basch, Glick Schiller, and Szanton Blanc note, "Migrants and political leaders in the country of origin are engaged in constructing an ideology that envisions migrants as loyal citizens of their ancestral nation-state."[39] In their book, Basch and colleagues note that it is usually some sort of political crisis back home that draws transmigrants into open discussions with their home government that then allows for the reconstitution of their identities.

Home governments often play a critical role in such exchanges. Turkey and the former Yugoslavia, for example, traditionally sponsored immigrant organizations in

Western Europe that addressed immigrants' legal, social, educational, and cultural needs. Because of these efforts, Western European immigrant communities came to resemble immigrant exclaves more than enclaves, as the organizations strengthened immigrants' ties to social and political institutions in their home countries.[40] These institutional ties reinforce the plausibility of return migration and lead to less permanent and rigid settlement patterns.

Although Los Angeles holds the third largest concentration of Mexicans in the world, the Mexican government has not traditionally sponsored popular organizations for emigrants. Instead, regional and hometown organizations—many of which are organized into federations representing constituents of Mexican states, such as the *Federacion de Jaliciences,* which is made up of approximately thirty-four clubs in hometowns and in Southern California—soccer clubs, and more informal transnational social network ties connect Mexican immigrants to Mexico. The electoral challenges faced by the PRI, Mexico's ruling political party from the early twentieth century until 2000, prompted the Mexican government to take a more interventionist, activist role on behalf of Mexican nationals living in the United States. Since 1988, the Mexican consuls have aggressively defended Mexican immigrants who find themselves to be targets of hate crimes or police brutality, have supported regional and hometown clubs, and have actively promoted and committed resources to literacy programs and bilingual education.[41] In Los Angeles, Mexican Consul General José Angel Pescador Osuña voiced opposition to Proposition 187 and the 1996 legislation passed by the House of Representatives to eliminate education and health care for the children of undocumented immigrant parents; spoke out against the practices documented in the videotaped beating of Mexican nationals by Riverside County sheriff's deputies; and supported new, dual citizenship provisions for Mexicans, who, historically, have the lowest naturalization figures. President Vicente Fox, the first non-PRI candidate to win a presidential election in Mexico's recent history, promises to pursue an even more aggressive transnational immigration policy.

The "transnationalists"—we will use this term for shorthand, although it probably implies more consensus than is accurate—have raised important issues for the study of immigration. They have challenged the view that immigration involves the crossing of rigid, territorial national boundaries and have instead posited the emergence of new bicultural spheres and identities. They have taken the basically unchallenged but sometimes overlooked observation of back-and-forth migration and reinterrogated how bidirectional movement and distinct spatial referents construct new ways of living and new identities. In some ways, the new transnationalists revisit themes from the Chicago School (recall their emphasis on immigrant letters, politics, and newspapers). The Chicago School participants, however, identified the city and dominant U.S. culture as the primary agents of influence. Contemporary transnationalists, on the other hand, might argue that the hinterland no longer exists but is meshed together with Los Angeles in one shared sphere of perpetual circulation and transmutation. This assessment downplays some of the material and legal barriers that intervene in these processes, which encourage people to experience different places as distinct social spheres, and the transnationalist perspective too often adopts a celebratory tone, with incidents of transnational culture and social relations taken as "resistance" to nation-states. The transnationalist turn, however, has raised important questions and perspectives for the study of contemporary immigration. For the future, attention to transnational factors, as well as to the political and economic context of reception, will be important.

Ethnicity and Identity

The assimilation of southern and eastern European immigrants and their offspring became a focal point of interest for the Chicago School participants. Robert E. Park proposed that these immigrants who entered the United States during the early twentieth century and their subsequent generations would, through time, move through phases of conflict and accommodation, eventually arriving at assimilation. With time, residential and occupational segregation would disappear. Today, it is impossible to assess the accuracy of this hypothesis, given that Jews and Italians, for example, were often racialized, discriminated against, and confined to urban ethnic ghettos, yet the impact of these theories of assimilation on current "common sense" views of immigrant life is undeniable. Assimilationist constructs and contrasting views of cultural pluralism, however, are no longer the only ways of understanding immigrant adaptation, the mid-twentieth-century publication of *Beyond the Melting Pot* by Nathan Glazer and Daniel Patrick Moynihan constituting the last great pitch for assimilation. In a more recent requiem article titled "Is Assimilation Dead?" Glazer ponders the decline of the positive popular attitude toward assimilation, as well as its virtual obliteration in social science.[42] He explains the death of assimilation theories as linked to their failure to explain the strength of racism toward African Americans.

Post-1965 immigration from Latin America, Asia, and the Caribbean has prompted new inquiries into emergent racial-ethnic identities and relations. Identity and ethnicity are now treated as fluid, socially constructed categories, and not as primordial ties that diminish, linearly, through time. In this constructionist view, ethnicity is renegotiated and revitalized through interaction with group members, as well as with outsiders. The focus on group boundaries by anthropologist Fredrik Barth and, more recently, sociologist Joane Nagel acknowledges that ethnic boundaries shift and are shaped by social, political, and economic forces, as well as by group members' own volition and interests.[43] Do Mexican immigrants assimilate, do they become "ethnic" Mexican Americans and Chicanos, or do they come to feel themselves more Mexican than they did prior to migration? Note that the second and third alternatives would never have been voiced by the Chicago School participants. Do Belizean immigrants of African heritage identify with African Americans or with Central Americans, or do they form their own distinctive identity? Although on the surface these questions may seem straightforward, finding answers to them can be complex indeed.

An important arena for future research and theory involves attention to intra- and intergroup relations of immigrants and relations between immigrants and established communities. As Bach puts it, "For many immigrants who live in communities in which the primary, dominant group is Chicano or African American, Anglo conformity, long considered the reference point for assimilation, is simply no longer salient."[44] This recognition requires that we move beyond concepts of assimilation to an acknowledgment of dynamic social relations. Questions, particularly about what kinds of ties newcomers form with more established communities, are quite complex, given that in cities such as Los Angeles, whites constitute a diminishing proportion of the population. Regarding an important trend also in immigrant cities such as Miami and New York City, sociologist Alejandro Portes has introduced the concept of "segmented assimilation" to capture the diverse cultural and social realities to which immigrant youth must adapt.

Relations of Gender and Generation

Although the Chicago School sociologists focused some analytic attention on women and youth, they did not turn their attention directly to gender and generation as key relations that structure social life.[45] If we translate the Chicago School "breakdown" perspective to traditional gender relations and contrast it with social historians' views, two clear alternative theoretical traditions to immigrant gender relations emerge: one positing the disintegration of traditional gender relations once immigrants are immersed in the new urban society, and the other asserting that these relations remain intact.

Feminist scholarship has shown that gender—that is, the social and cultural ideals, displays, and practices of masculinity and femininity—organizes and shapes our opportunities and life chances. In recent years, feminist scholarship on immigration has moved far beyond debates focusing on the transformation of gender relations in immigrant communities to the examination of gender as an outcome or a variable constitutive of migration patterns and migrant labor recruitment.[46] Still, research strategies that fully incorporate this observation are rare, gender often being taken into consideration only when women are the focus of study (as if men were without gender).

Research strategies similarly undertheorize and neglect generational relations. Although research on the new "second generations" in immigrant communities is apparently well funded and vigorous, constituting a virtual growth industry in immigration scholarship, generational relations have received less attention. This appears to be a direct legacy of the Chicago School efforts, where the focus was on youth, not generation. In a chapter in *The City*, for example, Burgess noted the corruption of youth that comes about with migration, as youth are released from the close ties of family and community into what he perceived as disorienting urban "cultural decadence":

> The cultural controls over conduct disintegrate; impulses and wishes take random and wild expression. The result is immorality and delinquency; in short, personal and social disorganization. An illustration of cultural decadence as a result of movement is

the excessively high rate of juvenile delinquency among the children of immigrant parents. . . . In the village type of neighborhood, where everyone knows everyone else, the social relationships of the young people were safeguarded by the primary controls of group opinion. But in the public dance hall, where young people are drawn from all parts of the city, this old primary control breaks down. Is not this the basic reason why social workers find the dance hall so recurring a factor in personal disorganization and delinquency?[47]

Future immigration research will be enhanced by considering the gendered and generational aspects of both macrostructural arrangements and quotidian living arrangements as they are actually experienced by immigrant women, men, and children. By following this route, research will continue to unveil how gender and generational hierarchies within households, and through larger political and economic structures, shape immigration, involving, among other things, conceptualizing men as gendered actors.

Economy

Not unlike rational choice theorists today, Thomas and Znaniecki always described the research participants in *The Polish Peasant* as individual economic actors, as the immigrants moved, for the first time, into a "full-fledged money economy." Although social relations back home in Poland were said to be characterized by primary, affectual ties in which familial control and solidarity prevailed, Thomas and Znaniecki believed that in the "new world," individualistic principles led immigrants either to opportunities for individual autonomy—which they speculated might be positive and liberating—or to social crises, such as juvenile delinquency and family breakdown.

But Thomas and Znaniecki assume that because relations of production in Poland were not fully capitalist, they were ruled by consensus and harmony. In the United States, they observe the commodification of previously shared services and items, especially those used for productive purposes, constituting the introduction of exchange values where kinship-sharing values had once prevailed. As Eli Zaretsky has pointed out, however, these scholars overlook the presence of significant economic inequalities between landlords and peasants in Poland and also ignore the trade unions through which Poles were attempting to define and improve their situations through collective action.[48] With hindsight, we can see that the Poles and other southern and eastern European immigrants of the early twentieth century were entering the United States at a particular moment of industrial history when flourishing factories meant production jobs that would provide the means of upward social mobility for many immigrants, and especially for their offspring.[49]

A recent study by Sarah J. Mahler, *American Dreaming: Immigrant Life on the Margins,* carries forth Thomas and Znaniecki's thesis that immigration provokes the "substitution of the principles of exchange for the principles of help."[50] Studying Salvadoran and South American immigrants in suburban Long Island, Mahler found these immigrants struggling to eke out a living on the margins of society by exploiting newcomer greenhorns. The need for income during the early stages of resettlement causes tremendous financial urgencies that, according to Mahler, lead to the deterioration of social mores. By preying on newcomers—selling simple favors, services, and information that their peers might take for granted in other contexts—the more well-established immigrants find modest upward social mobility at the expense of their more recently arrived counterparts. Mahler argues that suburban residential segregation, racism, job exploitation, and the language and legal status barriers all work to create this climate of greed, and she implicitly assumes that social relations in their Central and South American countries of origin were guided by principles of reciprocity and nonmarket civility. El Salvador, Chile, Colombia, and Peru, however, are countries with capitalist market economies that have produced considerable public upheaval in recent years. Although Mahler's analysis does place more importance on the political economy and context of reception, it is still reminiscent of the Chicago School approaches.

New scholarship on citizenship adds greater complexity to inquiries of immigrants and the economy. The proliferation of undocumented immigrants who are homeowners, taxpayers, school attendees, and small-business owners presents a challenge to the traditional dichotomous fashion in which we think about citizens and "illegal aliens." The label "illegal alien" denotes not only unlawful, criminal activities but also marginal involvement in societal institutions. Undocumented immigrants who are integrated into social and economic life in the United States and who have developed strong, sometimes irreversible ties to their new home areas cannot be equated with newcomer undocumented migrant workers, although both are technically of the same legal status. Given the current political and historical context, the critical category is no longer citizenship, but membership. Questions of membership concern persons already well integrated into the economic, social, and cultural life in the territory but excluded from the rights and obligations of citizenship and legal permanent residency. Like settlement, membership is not a neat category but develops through time as immigrants establish ties while living and working in a particular country.[51]

LOS ANGELES: IMMIGRANT CITY OF THE FUTURE?

Is immigration to Los Angeles different from or the same as that facing other U.S. cities? One way to answer this question is through a historical comparison, in broad strokes, with early-twentieth-century Chicago. The class composition of immigrants is fundamentally different in Los Angeles than in turn-of-the-century Chicago. In Chicago, no immigrant group was as well endowed with capital and valued skills as are some of today's Korean, Indian, Iranian, and Chinese immigrants. Similarly, no immigrant groups remained consistently at the bottom of the occupational and income hierarchy after several generations of immigration, such as is the case with Mexican migrants. By contrast, Los Angeles has a bifurcated immigrant population that contains not only highly educated, high-income immigrants, who work as professionals, managers, and entrepreneurs, and who may have entered with extensive capital resources, but also poorly educated, low-income, manual workers. L.A.'s immigrants are, now, both workers and professionals.

Another recent development concerns the strong ties developed between today's immigrants and organizations in their countries of origin. The ties that Asian immigrant entrepreneurs maintain with economic partners in Asia, and the political bonds maintained between Mexican immigrants and Mexican government officials, are much stronger than the social ties examined by Thomas and Znaniecki in *The Polish Peasant*. Telecommunications and transportation technology help explain these developments. Today, Mexican governors of major immigrant-sending states travel regularly to Los Angeles to meet with conationals, Central American courier services transport goods and money that immigrants send back home, and Asian entrepreneurs travel and trade regularly with business partners in their home countries.

The mobility structures available to European immigrants in Chicago in an earlier period have all but vanished. Because of the immigrants' common European origin, the assimilation trajectory posited by Chicago School writers fails to account for how these immigrants' mobility was predicated on economic structures particular to their time as well as on patterns of racial reception. Conversely, although poor immigrants continue to work in L.A.'s manufacturing sector, these jobs have been downgraded and no longer hold the promise of upward mobility into steady, well-paying, unionized jobs. Already numerically dominant in Los Angeles and overrepresented in these low-paying manufacturing jobs, many Mexican immigrant workers shift to the service or informal sectors. This economic structure of employment and particularly of the absence of mobility is critical, as it may signify a near permanent form of social and economic subordination for many immigrant groups. Let us hope that for the sake of the U.S.'s increasing immigrant population, Los Angeles can offer valuable insights into our current demise rather than simply providing a glimpse into an increasingly difficult future.

NOTES

1. Waldinger and Bozorgmehr, 1996, p. 14.

2. Sociologist Prema Kurien (1999) finds that Indian Hindu immigrants residing in Southern California, most of whom are professionals living outside ethnically homogeneous neighborhoods, organize associations of religious worship, which require hours of freeway travel for them to attend.

3. Raymond Rocco (1997) examines the reconfiguration of the new Latino Los Angeles, and the lifetime recollections from one of his interview participants speak volumes about Latino demographic growth and dispersion throughout Los Angeles:

> I think that probably the biggest change is that now we are everywhere. When I was growing up in the fifties, you knew where the Mexican areas were, and when you wandered out of those you saw very few of us in places like Santa Monica or the westside.

... I wouldn't see any Mexicans at all. But now, hell, I feel at home almost everywhere because I know there is going to be somebody that looks like me, that talks like me, no matter where I am (in L.A.). (102)

4. For the 1992 fiscal year, 129,669 legal immigrants stated that the Los Angeles-Long Beach metropolitan area was their intended area of residence. This is more than the number that stated the New York metropolitan area as intended residence, and when the respondents listing Anaheim-Santa Ana—part of the Southern California metropolis—are added, the total comes to 164,192. This figure is more than four times greater than the third largest metropolitan area drawing new legal immigrants, Chicago.

5. See Rumbaut, 1998. The figures are based on Rumbaut's calculations using the 1997 Current Population Survey data file and the March 1996 census data.

6. See Waldinger and Bozorgmehr, 1996.

7. Although many European social theorists—including Spengler, Simmel, Weber, Toennies, and Durkheim—were concerned with the city, they understood city life only in contrast to rural life. Toennies, for example, referred to the dichotomization of rural-traditional-community versus urban-modern-society as *gemeinschaft* and *gesellschaft,* positing that in the latter, social life became more superficial, functional, and transitory. Durkheim focused on the division of labor in society, positing that traditional preindustrial society is characterized by mechanical solidarity, strong interpersonal bonds, and shared beliefs. By contrast, modern society is characterized by organic solidarity, greater job specialization, increasing social differentiation, societal interdependence, and nonenduring obligations. For Weber, the character of city life was the result of modern capitalism that had replaced traditional modes of authority with legal, bureaucratic authority.

8. Coser, 1994, p. 4.

9. Park, 1928, quoted in Sennett, 1969, pp. 134-135.

10. Wirth, 1938, p. 14.

11. Zaretsky, 1984, p. 33.

12. Handlin, 1973, p. 6.

13. Gordon, 1964.

14. Portes and Bach, 1985. All these theoretical arenas are primarily concerned with labor migration, not with movements of political refugees or highly educated professionals.

15. Borjas, 1990; Lee, 1966; Todaro, 1969.

16. Wood, 1982; Dinerman, 1978.

17. Becker, 1981.

18. Massey et al., 1993, 1994.

19. Selby and Murphy, 1982, p. 9.

20. Hondagneu-Sotelo, 1994.

21. Portes, 1995.

22. Massey et al., 1993, 1994; Wallerstein, 1974.

23. Massey et al., 1994.

24. See Waldinger and Bozorgmehr, eds., 1996.

25. See Marcelli and Heer's 1997 USC Population Research Laboratory study.

26. For a more developed version of this argument, see Hondagneu-Sotelo, 1995.

27. Carmichael and Hamilton, 1967; Blauner, 1972.

28. For historical monographs on migrants in the city, see Thompson, 1966; Yans-McLaughlin, 1977; Gutman, 1977.

29. Persons, 1987, p. 29.

30. Persons, 1987, p. 30.

31. Lie, 1995, p. 303.

32. In the same review article, Lie points to new publishing outlets for new transnational perspectives, such as the journals *Diaspora* (published by the Oxford University Press) and

Public Culture (published by the University of Chicago Press for the Society for Transnational Cultural Studies).

A contemporary journal that is similar in orientation is *Identities: Global Studies in Culture and Power.* Formerly known as *Ethnic Groups,* this journal, although it is not limited to immigration scholarship, became a publishing home for a certain type of immigration literature. In the inaugural issue of *Identities* in 1994, editor Nina Glick Schiller, an anthropologist and primary innovator of transnational perspectives on immigration, defines the new journal's problematic as an inquiry into globalization and the relationship between representations of culture and power. Gramsci, Foucault, and the critique of the modernist paradigm are invoked, and there is a clear statement that scholarship is never socially or politically disinterested.

33. Massey et al., 1993, 1994.
34. Massey et al., 1993, p. 463.
35. Thomas and Znaniecki, 1984, p. 98.
36. W. I. Thomas in Park and Miller, 1921, p. 97.
37. Burgess [1925/1967], Midway reprint, 1984, p. 146.
38. Rouse, 1995a, 1995b; Kurien, 1999; Kearney, 1995; Smith and Guarnizo, 1998; Basch, Glick Schiller, and Szanton Blanc, 1994.
39. Basch et al., 1994, p. 3.
40. Heisler, 1986.
41. Gutierrez, 1993.
42. Glazer, 1993.
43. Barth, 1969; Nagel, 1996; Olzak and Nagel, 1986.
44. Bach, 1993, p. 158.
45. Women and children were viewed as conduits of traditional social relations. Robert E. Park saw immigrant women and children as extraordinarily well situated for involvement in creating community. In a chapter in *The City* called "Community Organization and the Romantic Temper," Park positively valorizes the community-building contributions of women, children, and immigrants who cannot speak English, all of whom he refers to as "incompetent persons." He notes that "competent persons," by which he meant professionals involved in public life outside their neighborhood, were most poorly situated for community life:

> Women, particularly women without professional training, and immigrants who are locally segregated and immured within the invisible walls of an alien language are bound to have some sort of interest in their neighbors. Children in great cities, who necessarily live close to the ground, however, are the real neighbors. (113)

46. Grasmuck and Pessar, 1991; Hondagneu-Sotelo, 1994; Repak, 1995.
47. Burgess [1925/1967], Midway reprint, 1984, pp. 150-151.
48. Zaretsky, 1984, pp. 20-22.
49. Bodnar, Simon, and Weber, 1982.
50. Mahler, 1995.
51. Brubaker, 1989.

REFERENCES

Bach, Robert L. 1993. Recrafting the common good: Immigration and community. In Interminority Affairs in the U.S.: Pluralism at the Crossroads (special issue), ed. Peter I. Rose, *Annals of the American Academy of Political and Social Science* 530 (November): 155-170.

Barth, Fredrik. 1969. *Ethnic groups and boundaries: The social organization of culture differences.* Boston: Little, Brown.

Basch, Linda, Nina Glick Schiller, and Cristina Szanton Blanc, eds. 1994. *Nations unbound: Transnational projects, postcolonial predicaments, and deterritorialized nation-states.* Langhorne, Pa.: Gordon and Breach Science Publishers.

Becker, Gary. 1981. *A treatise on the family.* Cambridge, Mass.: Harvard University Press.

Blauner, Robert. 1972. *Racial oppression in America.* New York: Harper & Row.

Bodnar, John, Roger Simon, and Michael P. Weber. 1982. *Lives of their own: Blacks, Italians, and Poles in Pittsburgh 1900-1960.* Urbana: University of Illinois Press.

Borjas, George. 1990. *Friends or strangers: The impact of immigrants on the U.S. economy.* New York: Basic Books.

Brubaker, William, R., ed. 1989. *Immigration and the politics of citizenship in Europe and North America.* Lanham, Md.: University Press of America.

Burgess, Ernest W. 1925, 1967. Can neighborhood work have a scientific basis? In *The city: Suggestions for investigation of human behavior in the urban environment,* by Robert E. Park, Ernest W. Burgess, and Roderick D. McKenzie (pp. 142-155). Chicago: University of Chicago Press, Midway reprint, 1984.

Carmichael, Stokely, and Charles V. Hamilton. 1967. *Black power: The politics of liberation in America.* New York: Vintage.

Coser, Lewis A. 1994. Introduction. In *Everett C. Hughes: On work, race, and the sociological imagination,* ed. Lewis A. Coser (pp. 1-17). Chicago: University of Chicago Press.

Dinerman, Ina R. 1978. Patterns of adaptation among households of U.S.-bound migrants from Michoacan, Mexico. *International Migration Review* 12: 485-501.

Glazer, Nathan. 1993. Is assimilation dead? In Interminority affairs in the U.S.: Pluralism at the crossroads (special issue), ed. Peter I. Rose. *Annals of the American Academy of Political and Social Science* 530 (November): 122-136.

Glazer, Nathan, and Daniel Patrick Moynihan. 1963. *Beyond the melting pot.* Cambridge: MIT Press and Harvard University Press.

Gordon, Milton M. 1964. *Assimilation in American life: The role of race, religion, and national origins.* New York: Oxford University Press.

Grasmuck, Sherri, and Patricia R. Pessar. 1991. *Between two islands: Dominican international migration.* Berkeley: University of California Press.

Gutierrez, Carlos Gonzalez. 1993. The Mexican diaspora in California: Limits and possibilities for the Mexican government. In *The California-Mexico connection,* ed. Abraham F. Lowenthal and Katrina Burgess (pp. 221-235). Stanford, Calif.: Stanford University Press.

Gutman, Herbert G. 1977. *Work, culture and society in industrializing America.* New York: Vintage.

Handlin, Oscar. 1973. *The uprooted,* 2nd ed. Boston: Little, Brown.

Heisler, Martin O., and Barbara Schmitter, eds. 1986. From foreign workers to settlers? Transnational migration and the emergence of new minorities (special issue). *Annals of the American Academy of Political and Social Science* 485 (May).

Hondagneu-Sotelo, Pierrette. 1994. *Gendered transitions: Mexican experiences of immigration.* Berkeley: University of California Press.

Hondagneu-Sotelo, Pierrette. 1995. Women and children first: New directions in anti-immigrant politics. *Socialist Review* 25: 169-190.

Kearney, Michael. 1995. The effects of transnational culture, economy, and migration on Mixtec identity in Oaxacalifornia. In *The bubbling cauldron: Race, ethnicity, and the urban crisis,* ed. Michael Peter Smith and Joe R. Feagin (pp. 226-243). Minneapolis: University of Minnesota Press.

Kurien, Prema. 1999. Gendered ethnicity: Creating a Hindu Indian identity in the United States. *American Behavioral Scientist* 42, no. 4 (January): 648-670.

Lee, Everett S. 1966. A theory of migration. *Demography* 3: 47-57.

Lie, John. 1995. From international migration to transnational diaspora. *Contemporary Sociology* 24, no. 4 (July): 303-306.

Mahler, Sarah J. 1995. *American dreaming: Immigrant life on the margins.* Princeton, N.J.: Princeton University Press.

Marcelli, Enrico A., and David Heer. 1997. Unauthorized Mexican workers on the 1990 Los Angeles County labor force. *International Migration* 35, no. 1: 59-83.

Massey, Douglas S., with Joaquin Arango, Graeme Hugo, Ali Kouaouci, Adela Pellegrino, and J. Edward Taylor. 1993. Theories of international migration: A review and appraisal. *Population and Development Review* 19, no. 3 (September): 431-465.

Massey, Douglas S., with Joaquin Arango, Graeme Hugo, Ali Kouaouci, Adela Pellegrino, and J. Edward Taylor. 1994. An evaluation of international migration theory: The North American case. *Population and Development Review* 20, no. 4 (December): 699-751.

Nagel, Joane. 1996. *American Indian ethnic renewal: Red power and the resurgence of identity and culture.* New York: Oxford University Press.

Olzak, Susan, and Joane Nagel, eds. 1986. *Competitive ethnic relations.* Orlando, Fla.: Academic Press.

Park, Robert E. 1925, 1967. Community organization and the romantic temper. In *The city: Suggestions for investigation of human behavior in the urban environment,* by Robert E. Park, Ernest W. Burgess, and Roderick D. McKenzie (pp. 113-122). Chicago: Chicago University Press, Midway reprint, 1984.

Park, Robert E. 1928. Human migration and the marginal man. *American Journal of Sociology* 33: 881-893.

Park, Robert E., and Herbert A. Miller. 1921. *Old world traits transplanted.* New York: Harper and Brothers.

Persons, Stow. 1987. *Ethnic studies at Chicago, 1905-45.* Urbana and Chicago: University of Illinois Press.

Portes, Alejandro. 1995. *The economic sociology of immigration: Essays on networks, ethnicity, and entrepreneurship.* New York: Russell Sage Foundation.

Portes, Alejandro, and Robert L. Bach. 1985. *Latin journey: Cuban and Mexican immigrants in the United States.* Berkeley: University of California Press.

Repak, Terry A. 1995. *Waiting on Washington: Central American workers in the nation's capital.* Philadelphia: Temple University Press.

Rocco, Raymond. 1997. Citizenship, culture and community: Restructuring in Southeast Los Angeles. In *Latino cultural citizenship: Claiming identity, space and rights,* ed. William Flores and Rita Benmayor (pp. 97-123). Boston: Beacon.

Rocco, Raymond. 1999. The formation of Latino citizenship in Southeast Los Angeles. *Citizenship Studies* 3, no. 2 (July): 253-266.

Rouse, Roger. 1995a. Questions of identity: Personhood and collectivity in transnational migration to the United States. *Critique of Anthropology* 15, no. 4 (December): 351-380.

Rouse, Roger. 1995b. Thinking through transnationalism: Notes on the cultural politics of class relations in the contemporary United States. *Public Culture* 7, no. 2 (winter): 353-402.

Rumbaut, Ruben G. 1998. Transformations: The post-immigrant generation in an age of diversity. Paper presented at the American Diversity: Past, Present and Future annual meeting of the Eastern Sociological Society, Philadelphia, March 21.

Selby, Henry A., and Arthur D. Murphy. 1982. *The Mexican urban household and the decision to migrate to the United States.* ISHI Occasional Papers in Social Change, no. 4. Philadelphia: Institute for the Study of Human Issues.

Sennett, Richard. 1969. *Classic essays on the culture of cities.* New York: Appleton-Century-Crofts.

Smith, Michael Peter, and Luis Eduardo Guarnizo, eds. 1998. *Transnationalism from below.* New Brunswick, N.J.: Transaction Publishers.

Thomas, William I., and Florian Znaniecki. 1927. *The Polish peasant in Europe and America.* Boston: Knopf.

Thomas, William I., and Florian Znaniecki. 1984. *The Polish peasant in Europe and America,* ed. and abridged by Eli Zaretsky. Vols. 1-5 first published between 1918 and 1920. Urbana and Chicago: University of Illinois Press.

Thompson, E. P. 1966. *The making of the English working class.* New York: Vintage.

Todaro, Michael P. 1969. A model of labor migration and urban unemployment in less-developed countries. *American Economic Review* 59: 138-148.

Waldinger, Roger, and Mehdi Bozorgmehr. 1996. The making of a multicultural metropolis. In *Ethnic Los Angeles,* ed. Roger Waldinger and Mehdi Bozorgmehr (pp. 3-37). New York: Russell Sage Foundation.

Waldinger, Roger, and Mehdi Bozorgmehr, eds. 1996. *Ethnic Los Angeles.* New York: Russell Sage Foundation.

Wallerstein, Immanuel. 1974. *Capitalist agriculture and the origins of the European world-economy in the sixteenth century.* New York: Academic Press.

Wirth, Louis. 1938. Urbanism as a way of life. *American Journal of Sociology* 44: 1-24.

Wood, Charles. 1982. Equilibrium and historical-structural perspectives in migration. *International Migration Review* 16: 298-319.

Yans-McLaughlin, Virginia. 1977. *Family and community: Italian immigrants in Buffalo, 1880-1930.* Ithaca, N.Y.: Cornell University Press.

Zaretsky, Eli, ed. 1984. Editor's introduction. In *The Polish peasant in Europe and America,* by William I. Thomas and Florian Znaniecki (pp. 1-53). Vols. 1-5 first published between 1918 and 1920. Urbana and Chicago: University of Illinois Press.

The Globalization
of Urban Homelessness

EDITOR'S
COMMENTS

On the edges of Chicago's downtown business area, there was what Robert Park caustically referred to as a "human junk heap," people who had been scrapped by the "march of industrial progress." These people overlapped with, but differed from, the true "hobo." For Park, the hobo was a "belated frontiersman," driven by wanderlust and lacking a vocation in life. He was not only a homeless man but "a man without a cause and without a country."

In this chapter, Madeleine R. Stoner explains how we got from "hobohemia" to a global crisis of homelessness in advanced industrialized nations. (Nonindustrialized nations have endured such an epidemic for much longer periods.) Stoner emphasizes the striking concatenation of events that have led to this crisis, including economic restructuring on a global scale and the retreat from the welfare state in the United States and other countries. She draws intriguing parallels and contrasts between the experiences of Los Angeles and other places in the nation and the world.

The global connectedness of homelessness in advanced industrialized nations is clearly more than a coincidence, but a great deal more effort is necessary to understand these connections and to alleviate the enormous human suffering endured by homeless people. From a different time and era, Robert Park certainly hit the nail on the head when he wrote, "We who are presumably normal have very little understanding of the struggles of the physically or mentally handicapped to accommodate themselves to a world to which they are constitutionally not adapted."

QUOTES FROM
THE CITY

Our great cities, as those who have studied them have learned, are full of junk, much of it human, i.e., men and women who, for some reason or other, have fallen out of line in the march of industrial progress and have been scrapped by the industrial organization of which they were once a part.

A recent study by Nels Anderson of what he calls "Hobohemia," an area in Chicago just outside the "Loop," that is to say, the downtown business area, which is almost wholly inhabited by homeless men, is a study of such a human junk heap. In fact, the slum areas that invariably grow up just on the edge of the business areas of great cities, areas of deteriorated houses, of poverty, vice, and crime, are areas of social junk. . . . (109)

. . . The trouble with the hobo mind is not lack of experience, but lack of a vocation. The hobo is, to be sure, always on the move, but he has not destination, and naturally he never arrives. Wanderlust, which is the most elementary expression of the romantic temperament and the romantic interest in life, has assumed for him, as for so many others, the character of a vice. He has gained his freedom, but he has lost his direction. Locomotion and change of scene have had for him no ulterior significance. It is locomotion for its own sake. Restlessness and the impulse to escape from the routine of ordinary life, which in the case of others frequently marks the beginning of some new enterprise, spends itself for him in movements that are expressive merely. The hobo seeks change solely for the sake of change; it is a habit, and, like the drug habit, moves in a vicious circle. The more he wanders, the more he must. It is merely putting the matter in another way to say that the trouble with the hobo . . . is that he is an individualist. He has sacrificed the human need of association and organization to a romantic passion for individual freedom. Society is, to be sure, made up of independent, locomoting individuals. It is this fact of locomotion, as I have said, that defines the very nature of society. But in order that there may be permanence and progress in society the individuals who compose it must be located; they must be located, for one thing, in order to maintain communication, for it is only through communication that the moving equilibrium which we call society can be maintained. . . . (158-159)

. . . The hobo, who begins his career by breaking the local ties that bound him to his family and his neighborhood, has ended by breaking all other associations. He is not only a "homeless man," but a man without a cause and without a country; and this emphasizes the significance, however futile, of the efforts of men like James Eads How to establish hobo colleges in different parts of the country. . . . (159)

. . . [M]odern industry is organized in a way which tends inevitably to the casualization of labor. It is due, in part, to the fact that the hobo, in so far as he is a congenital type, finds in casual and seasonal labor a kind of occupation congenial to his temperament, for the hobo is the bohemian in the ranks of common labor. He has the artistic temperament. Aside from the indispensable labor of his hands, the only important contribution which we call our culture has been his poetry. . . . The hobo is, in fact, merely a belated frontiersman, a frontiersman at a time and in a place when the frontier is passing or no longer exists. (160)

CHAPTER 8

The Globalization of Urban Homelessness

MADELEINE R. STONER

Robert Park's portrayal of the "hobo" misrepresents homeless people by romanticizing them as "bohemians" and the "last frontiersmen." This view, fortified by pseudoscientific explanations of vegetative and intellectual processes, lacks a conceptual grounding in the history of homelessness in the United States and, of greater importance, bears no resemblance to the situation and processes of homelessness at the beginning of the twenty-first century. In this chapter, I describe Park's view of the hobo in the United States and compare it with contemporary perspectives on homelessness to reveal generalizable themes about the Chicago and Los Angeles Schools in consideration of homelessness. Such a comparison, I believe, will allow us to see homelessness as a structural rather than an individual problem, global rather than local in scale, and to view persons who are homeless as part of a complex urban environment, rather than as simply "hobos" looking to satisfy a frontier "wanderlust."[1] Finally, I argue that homelessness confronts urban societies at the beginning of the twenty-first century with fundamental questions about the nature of the social contract and the relationships between institutions, the society of citizens, and the poor.

THE CHICAGO SCHOOL
AND THE HISTORY OF HOMELESSNESS

Park's characterization of the hobo is vastly different from the realities of today's homeless population. Park mistakenly claimed that skid row hobos were generally alcoholic and marginally employed, offering ungrounded explanatory theory of human behavior to support his description. He questioned the hobo's mind-set and viewed him as lacking a vocation or destination and forsaking any need for local or personal association. Park romanticized the hobo as a free spirit, dwelling in "hobohemia," a final urban frontier. Suggesting that its inhabitants were belated frontiersmen, even poets, lacking a sense of place and driven by wanderlust, he attempted to describe their resistance to social organization. Park went so far as to

Street Encampment of Homeless People, Towne Avenue, Los Angeles
Photograph by Michael J. Dear.

recommend the establishment of hobo colleges scattered in places where hobos congregated so that they could exchange experiences and develop their own forms of social cohesion.[2] Park's description of hobohemia not only relies on a misplaced romanticization of hobos but also fits the linear model of the Chicago School's configuration of the city as providing differentiated spaces for people differently placed in the social hierarchy.

Historical interpretations of homeless people identify both new and old explanations for homelessness.[3] In the former, homeless persons were characterized as the undeserving poor under the Elizabethan Poor Laws, and, in later periods, equally stigmatizing explanations attributed homelessness to personal flaws of character. Park's views reflect these earlier interpretations of homelessness.

The earliest settlements of the American colonies reflected the Elizabethan Poor Laws of England, which distinguished between *neighbors* and *strangers*. Communities were obligated to assist permanent residents, whereas poor strangers were deported to their place of origin. Because this division was a product of a stable agrarian society, however, it soon lost credibility in an increasingly mobile industrial society. The earlier distinction between neighbors and strangers gave way to new distinctions between the *undeserving, able-bodied poor* and the *deserving, disabled poor* that eliminated the former from the public relief rolls.[4] This codification ensured that poverty would be viewed as "the willful product of sinfulness, laziness, and immorality—rather than social or economic misfortune."[5]

Tree House of Homeless Person, South Central Los Angeles
Photographs by Michael J. Dear.

The appearance of hundreds of thousands of "tramps" after the Civil War terrified most Americans, who viewed their presence as a harbinger of the collapse of civilized society. Most of the tramps were young, unmarried men who had chosen or been forced to take up life on the road by the social disruption of the war years, large-scale immigration from Europe, and the economic depression of 1873. Even charitable organizations of the time described the tramp as "a lazy, shiftless, incorrigible, cowardly, utterly depraved savage . . . having no moral sense."[6]

When prosperity and its accompanying stability returned to the United States in the late 1870s, some of these wandering men found permanent jobs and homes, but hundreds of thousands remained migratory laborers. These workers began to congregate in neighborhoods that emerged in cities designed to house them and provide them with other basic services. By the 1930s, these neighborhoods were being called "skid rows," the name referring to the waterfront district of Seattle, where timber was skidded along log roads until it reached the water, where it could be floated to sawmills.

By the twentieth century, skid rows diminished in size and changed in character. They became associated in the public mind with a more or less permanent core of alcoholics and derelicts who were a population of older white men considered by most to be responsible for their own poverty[7]—the selfsame hobos romanticized by Park.

The Great Depression, which ushered in new waves of homelessness, challenged these assumptions. The connections between the rise in unemployment and homelessness became clear, as poverty forced people from their homes and into the application to charities and local government for shelter, food, and money. Those who could not obtain charitable help set up homeless encampments, or Hoovervilles, across the nation. Although the policies and programs of the New Deal did not end the Depression, they did identify poverty as a structural, rather than an individual, problem. Nevertheless, the skid row hobos fit no more easily into New Deal interpretations of poverty and, therefore, remained misfits in the eyes of the general public, the private social welfare establishment, and the institutions of the emerging welfare state.

The 1950s, arguably the period of greatest prosperity in the United States, made it possible for American public opinion and policy to virtually ignore the existence of poverty and to return to the image of homeless people as aging, white, male alcoholics. Skid row neighborhoods shrank, and with the homeless population generally believed to have shrunk by half and on the verge of possible disappearance, Park's vision of hobohemia once again became the accepted norm.

Yet by the early 1980s, mass homelessness emerged again as an issue of major concern and debate in the United States, and the division between structural and individual explanations of homelessness rose in public consciousness. Structural explanations attributed homelessness to the combination of high unemployment and inflation in the late 1970s coupled with the impact of the Reagan presidency's cuts in social programs on the lives of poor Americans. Individual explanations of homelessness were, familiarly, grounded in individual flaws, echoing Park's view that homeless people deliberately choose lives of substance abuse, an unwillingness to work, and (believe it or not) mental illness.

Contemporary explanations for the structural roots of the growth of homelessness draw a crucial connection between an increase in poverty and a corresponding decline in the availability of affordable housing.[8] Homelessness is viewed as a predictable consequence of the widening gap between the number of low-income housing units and the number of households that require such units.[9]

The interpretations of homelessness associated with disability (mental illness, substance abuse, domestic violence, and poor health) are controversial. Some analysts resist all efforts to attribute homelessness to personal vulnerability, relying, instead, on the more systemic aspects of poverty. Nevertheless, the lack of housing and services for vulnerable people can be a logical precursor to homelessness.

Clearly, a complex combination of poverty, a lack of low-income housing, and personal vulnerability explains contemporary homelessness. Today's homeless persons include men, women, and children, predominantly people of color, often those who are severely and persistently mentally ill, and substance abusers.[10] They are people who have lost housing, jobs with adequate pay, services, and care. Their severe marginalization has placed them below all social safety nets, and it is doubtful whether any form of social contract has applied to them during the past two decades. They are the faces of extreme poverty and cycles of systemic disadvantage in postmodern society.

Yet despite the dramatic contrast between the hobos of 1925 and the homeless persons of today, these two populations do share some characteristics. They are both severely marginalized and little understood by mainstream society, their connection to productive labor is tenuous at best, they tend to be disaffiliated from their early associations and locations, and yet they are also interested in re-creating new associations and personal spaces.[11] Despite the linguistic change since 1981, when the term *homeless* replaced *hobo* in the public consciousness, our new vocabulary is no less endowed with a similar mystique.

HOMELESSNESS IN LOS ANGELES

The Los Angeles response to homelessness stands as an exemplar of homeless policies in large urban areas. Its policies are particularly significant because the city and surrounding county contain the second largest concentration of homeless persons in the United States, and the five-county Southern California region is the second largest metropolis in the nation. Estimates of the homeless population in Los Angeles for 1993-1994 were 84,300 individuals on any given night, and 236,400 individuals at some time during the year. The largest factor associated with homelessness in Los Angeles is the limited supply of affordable housing. The number of persons "precariously housed"—those with incomes 50 percent or less than the median county income and whose housing payment requires 50 percent or more of that income—is three times that of other cities in the United States.[12]

Although municipal responses to homelessness have varied in their emphasis on public or private sector responsibility, they have all been guided by common institutional interests. Cities share the goal of creating a favorable economic climate for business and residence, seeking to gain the greatest economic good as they compete with other cities for revenue. For reasons of self-preservation, they must respond to homelessness because it is bad for business and creates concerns for public safety.[13] Many municipal responses have focused on obtaining external funding from federal and state government, as well as assistance from the voluntary sector, to provide shelter and services, even as a corresponding set of responses has attempted to criminalize the public behavior of homeless people.

Two main obstacles have blocked comprehensive programming for homeless services in Los Angeles. First, conflict between the city and the county governments about jurisdiction has dominated decisions concerning homeless persons. Although the city is responsible for housing, the county carries responsibility for the provision of health, welfare, and social services. Second, although the city and county both have espoused a preference for public-private partnerships for service delivery, they rely mainly on the private voluntary sector. Los Angeles homeless policies, therefore, reflect the city's and county's historical distrust of the public sector.[14]

The factor contributing to homelessness unique to Los Angeles is its shortage of affordable housing and the large number of its residents who are "precariously housed." Public housing in Los Angeles never received the support that it did in other large American cities, and, consequently, low-income renters have relied mainly on the private market or federally subsidized Section 8 housing vouchers to gain shelter. With the third most expensive rental market in the United States, following San Francisco and Boston, approximately 35 percent of homeless persons in the city and county are employed but cannot afford to pay for housing. A mayoral commission found that one of every four renters in the city was paying more than half of his or her monthly income for rent; that rent had more than doubled between 1980 and 1988; and that by 1991, a worker needed to earn $14.37 per hour to rent a two-bedroom apartment in Los Angeles.[15] Calling the housing situation in Los Angeles "the affordability crisis," Wolch and Dear[16] argue that affordability problems affect both owners and renters, the typical homeowner spending more than twice the national average on housing.[17] L.A.'s affordability crisis has resulted in a fierce competition for the least expensive housing. By the end of the 1980s, more than four public assistance households were competing for each unit renting at $200 or less, and this situation is compounded by the number of low-wage workers who compete for the same housing.[18] In the strong economy of 1999-2000, this scarcity escalated as landlords increased rents in the face of demand or removed their housing from federal subsidies altogether to compete in the private market.

Wolch and Dear's characterization of the homeless problem in Los Angeles as "malign neglect"[19] accurately describes the three key trends that have emerged in this context: (1) Los Angeles city and county spend none of their general revenues on programs for homeless people; (2) they concentrate most homeless resources in one regional center (the Skid Row area east of the central city business district) and, to a lesser extent, Hollywood; and (3) most recently, the city and county have sought to criminalize homeless people.

Funding Patterns

Despite large expenditures for homeless services, most of the funding comes from nonlocal sources. The county provides the largest amount of funding for shelter and services because of its statutory responsibility. Yet prior to its replacement by the

Temporary Assistance to Needy Families federal workfare program and General
Relief programs, most of its expenditures came from the Department of Public
Social Services' federal allocations for the Aid to Families With Dependent Children
and General Relief programs. It also administers the federal Community Development Block Grant, which has included homeless programs. The city and county
have also received Stewart B. McKinney Homeless Assistance funds and Department of Housing and Urban Development special allocations, and their policies
reflect a strong reliance on these external sources.

At the city level, $1 million in general fund monies was allocated to homeless ser-
vices and programs by the late 1980s. But by the early 1990s, the city had eliminated
most of its local funding. Its Community Redevelopment Agency receives separate
financing through tax increments and is mandated to spend 20 percent of its revenues on low-income housing. This became the city's showcase for homeless services.
The agency spent $39 million on homeless programs, including housing, between
1977 and 1986.[20] It located most of these services in Skid Row, however. Only two
other cities in Los Angeles County (Santa Monica and Long Beach) formulated
homeless policies, advocating the provision of food, adequate housing, and medical
services. They also called on Los Angeles County to fulfill its responsibility to provide public welfare.

Despite the size of the homeless population in Los Angeles city and county and
the magnitude of its problem, homeless expenditures remain a relatively small percentage of the total budgets. This policy of relying on nonlocal funds promises,
through time, to erode in the face of domestic spending budget cuts for services to
poor and disadvantaged populations by the federal government.

Containment

Applying rational principles of efficient multiservice integration, L.A.'s policy of
containing its homeless services has also served to contain the homeless population.
Undoubtedly, there is much to be said in support of locating a wide range of services
in a single geographical space. This facilitates referral, information, and coordination of services. It reduces client confusion and maximizes access to services. There
have also been serious efforts to create a sense of community on Skid Row replete
with opportunities for recreation and social support reminiscent of Park's
hobohemia. Nevertheless, the containment policy draws disturbing parallels with
nineteenth-century responses to social problems that built institutions designed to
keep problem populations out of sight and out of mind.

The critical problem with the containment policy rests on injustices in the geographical distribution of these social services. Agencies equipped to provide social
coping and long-term stabilization tend to be located in the more affluent neighborhoods. In contrast, gatekeeper services such as emergency food and shelter programs
are consistently located in the poorest of neighborhoods. This has been the case in
Los Angeles, where most of the Skid Row services perform gatekeeper functions: emergency food, shelter, and health and mental health care. The Community

Redevelopment Agency has built more than a dozen single room occupancy hotels on Skid Row, but their location on the row clearly demonstrates an intent to contain a cohort of extremely poor people. Moreover, this containment policy blocks easy access to the longer-term stabilization coping services so vital to many homeless people.[21]

Skid Row Privatopia

The Los Angeles Skid Row containment zone is a powerful analogue to the *privatopia*—based on common interest developments described by Dear and Flusty[22]—which has no connection to other communities and is fortified by the Southern California obsession with security. Los Angeles has, in effect, created a fortress on Skid Row that serves less to protect its inhabitants against the hardships of homelessness than to guard those outside the fortress from those inside. Although the general concept of *privatopia* designates a form of private housing for the "secession of the successful," devoted to satisfying their obligations to private property,[23] the strategy of geographically separating discrete populations by status is a central response to managing urban diversity. The spatial containment of homeless people in Skid Row fits neatly into this separation pattern to the point that it has become a common interest development privatopia.

Privatopias naturally lend themselves to the transformation of an urban region into the type of fortress described by Mike Davis, where spatial containment has emerged, in effect, as a "place of terror where police battle the criminalized poor."[24] A number of urban phenomena identified by Davis as having placed Los Angeles "on the hard edge of postmodernity"[25] characterize the spaces occupied by homeless people in contrast to those set aside for the affluent. These phenomena, identified by Dear and Flusty,[26] are as follows:

1. The destruction of public space—a central concern for homeless people who live their private lives in public and have been increasingly subject to criminal charges and harassment for doing so: In effect, local governments are attempting to destroy public spaces as arenas for homeless people. The National Law Center for Homelessness and Poverty identified fifty-two antihomeless policies or laws enacted in forty-nine American cities.[27]

2. The creation of forbidden cities (sealed fortresses that exclude the poor): Although judicial decisions have clearly specified constitutional protections for homeless people to travel, to be free of unreasonable searches and seizures, and to have freedom of speech, local governments are making continuous headway in a movement to prohibit homeless people from their properties.

3. Mean streets (where the homeless are deliberately contained): This describes the central function of Skid Row containment zones.

4. Sequestering of the poor: Reflecting the logic of containment, sequestering is the contemporary analogue to earlier indoor relief policies that compelled public relief recipients to live in work- or almshouses.

5. Space police (advanced high-tech policing methods that have led to "invisible Haussmannization" of Los Angeles): The ratio of police to the population in areas where homeless people are contained is probably higher than in any other areas of the city.

6. Carceral city (the proliferation of microprisons): The containment of homeless people on Skid Row raises the possibility of viewing the area as a microprison. Moreover, its proximity to the central jail serves as a reminder that the jail is an integral component of the multiservice arrangement of containment. Many persons on Skid Row frequent the jail, and its presence reinforces the threat of criminal charges against homeless people.

As "perhaps the most heterogeneous city in the world," Los Angeles is "a combination of enclaves . . . where minoritization . . . is the order of the day."[28] Its homeless containment policy has produced an enclave exclusively for distancing the "other" from the power structure. Perhaps Park's assessment of hobos as individuals incapable of independent locomotion reflects the intent of the contemporary Los Angeles Skid Row multiservice enclave—to keep the homeless incapable of movement. It may also serve to isolate the inhabitants of Skid Row from gaining any larger access to the social contract.

THE LOS ANGELES SCHOOL AND
HOMELESSNESS IN THE POSTMODERN CITY

Societal explanations, and any solutions that may flow from them, need to be evaluated through symbolic meanings and patterns linking the functional and cultural dimensions of social reality.[29] At the beginning of the twenty-first century, the social world presents sociology and society with new functional and cultural problems that cannot be reduced to one another. With them, compelling new modes of adaptation emerge to deal with these two sets of problems and their mutual and sometimes overlapping influence at different levels and scales. Foremost among these adaptations are urbanization, the proliferation of fragile economies that offer little in the way of security or tenure, changes in family and social support patterns, and an exponential expansion in the number of groups that make claims of entitlement against social institutions.

The Urbanization of Homelessness

By the year 2000, the urban population of the world was expected to account for 50 percent of the total population; it was 48 percent in 1995. Forecasters anticipated that by 2000, there would be twenty-seven megalopolises (cities with 8 million inhabitants or more) worldwide—twenty-one of which were predicted in developing countries where there were none in 1950 and fourteen in 1990.[30] This new world of an urban citizenry will be dealt with according to the normative standards created in and for "the city" and its symbolic meaning and patterns. Indeed, the essential boundary separating modern and postmodern change may lie in urban transformation.[31]

This perspective on urban life frames homelessness as a global problem. In the postmodern city, homelessness appears to be increasingly related to the very constitution of the city, with its ruptures between a normative system and the institutional multilevel and multiscale management by which it functions, between institutions and the citizenry they serve, and between citizens and the poor. Rossi and colleagues observe the failure of institutions to effectively address extreme poverty and the extent to which the poor are increasingly being set apart from the society of citizens.[32] They, as well as Snow and Anderson,[33] found mental illness to be a questionable correlate of homelessness. As little as 10 percent of their samples indicated mental disability in the growth of extreme poverty among homeless people.

Although poverty is undoubtedly extensive in rural areas, it is far more concentrated in cities. In the United States, the National League of Cities reported that increasing numbers of poor people live in neighborhoods in which at least 40 percent of the residents are below the official poverty line,[34] and this increasing spatial concentration of poverty has been well documented. In the 100 largest cities in the United States, the percentage of people living in extreme poverty more than doubled between 1970 and 1990, from an average of 5.2 percent to 10.7 percent per census tract.[35]

De Bernart assesses homelessness in the postmodern Italian city against this background.[36] The number of citizens has grown to such an extent that institutions have difficulty adequately responding to their claimants. Still connected to general housing deprivation, homelessness has been transformed from a problem of disadvantaged families and of people who emigrated from the South to the North in the 1960s and 1970s into a problem that affects mostly individuals who meet with precariousness—often and increasingly young people and immigrants who began to arrive in the 1990s, largely after the demise of the Soviet Union. Labos conducted an inquiry on homelessness in Rome, demonstrating that precarious events precipitating individual or family homelessness cannot be placed in standard categories.[37] The way that events such as loss of a job, rent problems, family disruption, mental illness, personal problems, or illness combine with each other varies with each life story up to the extreme limit when the homeless person renounces his or her citizenship rights and begins to perceive him- or herself as no longer a citizen, outside its official bounds. Although the reverse is true for immigrants, the consequences are similar. Homelessness among the postmodern Italian citizenry, of which 72 percent are homeowners, has come to be regarded as a growing kaleidoscope of marginal people and group problems ranging from mental illness to ethnic and cultural differences, rather than an overall social phenomenon.

Likewise, Wolch and Dear's[38] study of homelessness in Los Angeles demonstrates that the problem is, indeed, an extension of poverty that includes the most economically marginal people. Their work illustrates the failure of institutional responses and adds a note of irony by documenting that solutions and responsibility have been largely turned over to cities and local communities in the United States. The problem has been localized as one that belongs to the cities, demanding local solutions to what are societal problems. The passing off of responsibility to the cities in the United States creates a paradox wherein those governments least able, and, frequently, least willing, to help are continuously handed more of the responsibility for developing institutional responses to a global problem. This combination of extreme poverty and homelessness and the localization of these problems have only emphasized the institutional failure to respond.

Economic Insecurity

Because homelessness has been identified increasingly with extreme poverty, an understanding of the constitutive role played by global economic restructuring is essential to an analysis of the larger dimensions of the problem. The changed employment and wage structures in developed countries hold special significance for analyzing homelessness as a problem of extreme poverty and neglectful institutional responses to it. The lack of affordable housing has been a partial result of declining incomes. This explanation is complicated because each of the nations in the European Community and the United States reports a decline in the number of people living below the poverty line. The number of extremely poor persons in those nations who cannot afford a decent dwelling is increasing, however, and the gap between the rich and the poor has grown dramatically, as the economic recoveries in the second half of the 1980s and the latter part of the 1990s had their greatest impact at the upper ends of the wage and wealth spectrum.

By contrast, those who have fallen into the lowest wage pools have become marginalized workers whose job tenure is highly fragile. The decline of low-skill manufacturing and service jobs in postindustrial economies may mean that those at greatest risk of homelessness and unemployment are equally at the greatest risk of long-term unemployment. Linking homelessness with chronic unemployment brings together several important issues concerning social relationships between homeless persons, citizens, and institutions. Even the most advanced welfare nations favor workers whose claims to social rights hold the greatest legitimacy. As more homeless persons fall out of the workforce, their social and civil claims diminish, despite their citizenship, and they, then, need to compete in a large and growing institutional arena in which many other groups have established moral justification for their claims against those institutions. Among those other groups are retired persons, disabled persons, disadvantaged minorities, those uprooted by political forces and natural disasters, and other groups of marginalized people.[39]

The exponential growth of claims making has led to social policies that address target categories. Yet this change in the categorization of claims has not incorporated the changing patterns and processes that lead to homelessness. Homeless people and those at risk of homelessness remain targeted in more traditional categories that may not grant benefits either to prevent homelessness or to help people exit from it. Moreover, their claims are frequently considered less important than those of other priority populations that capture public sentiment, such as displaced refugees. England even targeted homeless assistance to families rather than individuals, as did New York City, although the majority of homeless persons are single adults. In other words, homeless single adults with a fragile hold on income from wages have become the new "undeserving poor" among competing claims makers.

Given this situation, administrative categories have become the primary shapers of the "culture of homelessness." De Bernart has observed that the shifting scenario from granting social rights to workers to granting the more general rights and choices to consumers has left a part of the population behind.[40] Between the normative system and its institutional implementation, the categorization of people and the stigmatization of sanctionable acts are commonplace. Moreover, at the institutional level, the normative systems and their local implementation are seldom designed to be user-friendly for the poorest claimants. Procedural problems, linguistic confusions, and space-time organization, frequently difficult to negotiate, render both the normative systems and their implementation a Byzantine maze for homeless persons that remains unresponsive to the complexity of their condition.

Between institutions and the society of citizens, there needs to be a growing acknowledgment of the equality of claimants. Between the society of citizens and those who are poor, more attention needs to be paid to the reality that few institutional interventions address homeless people and their needs. Although postindustrial economies have shaped new normative social systems that feature conflicting and competing cultures, the challenge is to create a social and built environment that supports the coexistence of mainstream and marginal citizens at global and local levels.

Sociodemographic Changes

The function of homelessness in the Netherlands suggests a broad perspective that has implications for the rest of Europe and the United States. In the Netherlands, homelessness is frequently defined as a sociopsychological problem, rather than as a problem of poverty or a welfare phenomenon. This is particularly important to consider for a nation with extensive social insurance and a reasonable supply of affordable housing, including rent subsidies. In the Netherlands, homelessness is viewed as a "situation of societal and social vulnerability, when functional and meaningful relationships no longer exist, and when the steady physical and social conditions in which they live are lost."[41] This concept evolved from poverty debates that identified "new poverty" as characterized by social isolation, an accumulation of problems, and permanent state dependency. Dutch analysts have concluded not that homeless people lack social skills or contacts but that they are cautious with their contacts because they are usually not in a position to support mutual relationships with friends, family, and acquaintances. Greshof and Deben and their colleagues relate homelessness to modern society wherein personal problems are a reflection of public problems. They characterize modern society as featuring unemployment, individualism, ethnic and racial diversity, more diverse gender relationships, and the dysfunctional bureaucracy of the contemporary welfare state, in which professional relationships tend to displace personal ties.

These sociodemographic changes have been universally observed in other nations, but their implications for homelessness have been less visible than the decline of welfare, employment, and adequate and affordable housing. Yet on closer inspection, they appear to play an increasingly important role in determining who becomes homeless. As in the Netherlands, the most important sociodemographic changes in other European countries and the United States during the past three decades have transformed family relationships and household dynamics. These changes include declining numbers of children born to couples; a decrease in the marriage rate and in the number of remarriages; an increase in the divorce rate and in consensual unions, single households, and single-parent families; and changing patterns of young adults leaving home. On a macrolevel, the salient features of these changes can be summarized as an increase in the variety of living arrangements and increased variation through the life cycle, with feminization and aging of households as outcomes of the interaction between demographics and socioeconomic-cultural factors.[42]

These tendencies, although they may be universally true, vary among countries. Curiously, they may be more the product of prosperous economies and more advantaged social groups than of their less affluent counterparts, as states of disadvantage may actually hinder or delay the evolution of a greater variety of living arrangements. The average household size is higher in southern European countries and Ireland, where the least prosperous prevail. These countries have a higher share of households with five or more members and a lower share of single households. Such data raise the possibility that high national poverty rates may sustain certain forms of social cohesion.

The complexity of processes that transform households includes both new phenomena and their long-term implications and a variety of processes amenable to short-term solutions. The feminization and aging of households, along with the high frequency of female-headed households at younger ages, are phenomena with long-term implications, whereas the pattern of young people leaving home is more susceptible to short-term solutions. Changes in the public allocation of resources, for instance, may have an impact on the timing of transitions and reversibility of passages from one household form to another for young adults, and numerous proposed reforms in family assistance programs have addressed this phenomenon in the United States. In the long term, there is general agreement that societies will have to accommodate changing household needs, especially of aged people, single families, and single parents. These changes imply increased need for social support for households of older persons, especially at the end of the life cycle. There is more consensus about the impact of rising expectations and the multiplication of opportunities for the more affluent citizens, however, than there is about the etiology and responsibility for the social condition of those who are extremely poor. The sociodemographic changes described here have fundamentally altered the social contract between institutions and citizens and between citizens and the poor.

The most immediate and visible consequences of these recent changes in household and family patterns are their effects on consumption, particularly in the housing market. Although the increase in the number of new dwellings has exceeded population growth, it has generally lagged behind household growth, with the exception of Greece, Spain, Portugal, and Ireland, the poorest nations in Europe. The structural discrepancy between available housing and increasing demand varies among countries but is marked in the Mediterranean countries. It is moderate in Denmark, Ireland, and the United Kingdom, while four European countries—Belgium, Germany, Luxembourg, and the Netherlands—have a shortage of more than 1 million registered dwelling units. The housing stock in the United States is marked by the same discrepancy between supply and demand found in Europe.[43]

But where the housing stock has grown, it has not kept pace with the changing composition of households. There is a universal shortage of small apartments. In those countries with the highest share of single households—Belgium, Denmark, Germany, France, the Netherlands, and the United States—an average of three of ten households have shortages of two- and three-room apartments. In the United States, an additional factor has been the general loss of single room occupancy hotels, once the cheapest form of housing available across the nation. Most of the welfare states have exacerbated the misfit between new socioeconomic demography and the housing supply by opting out of public and social housing and deregulating the housing market. This has led to an "affordability crisis" found nearly everywhere, as intervention by public housing authorities has shifted from construction to targeted individual aid.

IMPORTANT LESSONS FROM LOS ANGELES

These sociodemographic changes have dramatically altered the character of homelessness well beyond Park's vision of individualists in hobohemia. Homelessness is now a structural issue that is global and urban in scale and causality. Its pervasiveness has prompted powerful value judgments with serious implications for social policy. Although one major thrust has been to decry these changes and advocate policies to force reversals in social trends, these proposals tend to seek a return to past values in the form of misplaced nostalgia and a romanticized version of the hobo, such as is the case with the American "family values" movement. It is also possible that the communitarian movement with its altruistic agenda for the "good society" reflects a similar longing for the past.

This analysis makes no attempt to judge contemporary normative systems. Its intent is to explore operating norms and raise new questions about the efficacy of institutional responses to normative social systems and their implications for the universal proliferation of homelessness. Policy agendas must address the new structural dynamics in postmodern society that have fundamentally altered the social contract between governing institutions and citizens, and between citizens and marginalized poor people, which has produced homelessness. The convergence of urbanization and extreme poverty suggests that cities have clearly become the nexus for homelessness and that attention must therefore focus on cities and their relationships with their citizens, and between their citizens and the very poor.

One important direction for achieving change lies in the equalization of claimants against institutions. This could take the form of changing or eliminating the categorization of claimants, so that the claims of nonworkers become far more legitimized in the claims-making process. This promises to be a monumental task, given public hostility to claimants who are not connected to the workforce. The contemporary American workfare welfare reform agenda reflects the difficulty that lies ahead on this front.

Changing socioeconomic demographics require a redesigned housing supply and built environment to reverse the social isolation of contemporary single and small households. The human environment also needs to develop formal social supports to augment the numerous informal systems of support currently operating and to rebalance the human and built environment to challenge the fortress mentality of privatopias.

Yet the ultimate question facing global urban societies at the beginning of this century demands a reevaluation of the nature of the social contract between institutions, citizens, and those who are poor. Varying degrees of declining resources and altered public sentiment have rejected the social contract that has prevailed since the establishment of national welfare states after World War II. This has occurred in the midst of dramatic social and economic changes that have contributed to the polarization of wealth, poverty, opportunity, and equality against a backdrop of increasing claims making and entitlement. Because the poorest members of society have lost credibility among the constellation of claimants, there is a need to consider new paradigms for meting out justice.

This has led to the recent policy agendas designed to re-create a civil society, compelling political centrists to question the theory of justice proposed by John Rawls, which contends that a rational person will accept some inequalities to ensure an egalitarian society.[44] Rawlsian justice demonstrates how rational individuals would choose distributive mechanisms that worked to the benefit of the least advantaged members of a society, thus providing a justification for the welfare state based on subjective opinion rather than logic. Bellah et al. have argued that the Great Society did not translate to the Good Society.[45] Objecting to Rawls's preference for the right over the good, communitarians argue that we must transform the social institutions that shape our lives to reflect a sense of social commitment and collective responsibility rather than the American preoccupation with the individual ethos. Writing in the shadow of Rawls, Margalit poses a vision of a decent society that does not humiliate its citizens and respects their self-esteem.[46] He shifts the discussion away from Rawls's notion of justice as fairness and believes that the goal of a social contract should be a society containing institutions that avoid humiliating human beings who are both individuals and members of groups.

The growing debate about the morality and ethics of equality and the institutional arrangements needed to implement it will be central to this century. It signifies serious concern that the inequality explosion undermines not only the quality of life but global politics, and the globalization of homelessness in urban centers stands as a bold reminder of the social polarization that characterizes our contemporary world.

NOTES

1. Park [1925/1967], Midway reprint, 1984, p. 159.
2. Park, Burgess, and McKenzie [925/1967], Midway reprint, 1984.
3. Hoch and Slayton, 1989.
4. Katz, 1989.
5. Fantasia and Isserman, 1994, p. 4.
6. Fantasia and Isserman, 1994, p. 4.
7. Bahr, 1973.
8. McChesney, 1990; Shinn and Gillespie, 1994; Stern, 1984.
9. Snow and Bradford, 1994, p. 457.
10. Baker, 1994, pp. 476-504.
11. Baker, 1994.
12. Wolch and Sommer, 1997.
13. Blau, 1992, pp. 110-111.
14. Blau, 1992, pp. 123-124.
15. Fantasia and Isserman, 1994, pp. 110-111.
16. Wolch and Dear, 1993, p. 73.
17. Wolch and Dear, 1993, p. 78.
18. Wolch and Dear, 1993, p. 80.
19. Wolch and Dear, 1993.
20. Law and Wolch, 1993, p. 12.
21. Wolch and Dear, 1993, pp. 167-176.
22. Dear and Flusty, 1995.
23. Quoted in Dear and Flusty, 1995, p. 11.
24. Davis, 1994, p. 155.
25. Davis, 1994, p. 155.
26. Dear and Flusty, 1995, p. 14.
27. Stoner, 1994.
28. Jencks, 1992, quoted in Dear and Flusty, 1995, p. 14 (see Chapter 3, this volume).
29. Donati, 1993; Munch and Smelser, 1992.
30. United Nations, 1992; Zlotnick, 1993.
31. de Bernart, 1994.
32. Rossi, Fisher, and Willis, 1986.
33. Snow and Anderson, 1993.
34. Fantasia and Isserman, 1994.
35. Quigley, 1994.
36. de Bernart, 1994.
37. Labos, 1988.

38. Wolch and Dear, 1993.
39. Drover and Kerans, 1993.
40. de Bernart, 1994.
41. Greshof and Deben, 1994.
42. Avramov, 1994.
43. Schwartz, Ferlauto, and Hoffman, 1988.
44. Rawls, 1971.
45. Bellah et al., 1991.
46. Margalit, 1996.

REFERENCES

Avramov, D. 1994. Homelessness: A condition or a social process? Paper presented at the 13th World Congress of Sociology, Bielefeld, Germany, July. Mimeograph.

Bahr, H. 1973. *Skid row.* Oxford: Oxford University Press.

Baker, S. G. 1994. Gender, ethnicity, and homelessness. *American Behavioral Scientist* 37, no. 4: 476-504.

Bellah, R. N., R. M. Madsen, W. M. Sullivan, A. Swidler, and S. M. Tipton. 1991. *The good society.* New York: Knopf.

Blau, J. 1992. *The visible poor: Homelessness in the United States.* New York: Oxford University Press.

Davis, M. 1994. The empty quarter. In *Sex, death, and God in L.A.,* ed. D. Reid. Berkeley: University of California Press.

Dear, M. J., and S. Flusty. 1995. Postmodern urbanism or, the spatial logic of global capitalism. Paper presented at a Theory, Culture, Society Conference, Berlin. Reprint, 1998. Postmodern urbanism. *Annals of the American Association of Geographers* 88, no. 1: 50-72 (see Chapter 3, this volume).

de Bernart, M. 1994. The reality and culture of homelessness in the post-modern city. Paper presented at the 13th World Congress of Sociology, Bielefeld, Germany, July. Mimeograph.

Donati, P. 1993. *La cittadinanza.* Rome: Lazera.

Drover, G., and T. Kerans, eds. 1993. *New approaches to welfare theory.* Aldershot, England, and Brookfield, Vt.: Edward Elgar.

Fantasia, R., and M. Isserman. 1994. *Homelessness: A source book.* New York: Facts on File.

Greshof, D., and L. Deben. 1994. Homeless careers in Amsterdam: A longitudinal research project. Paper presented at the 13th World Congress of Sociology, Bielefeld, Germany, July. Unpaginated mimeograph.

Hoch, C., and R. Slayton. 1989. *New homeless and old: The community and the skid row hotel.* Philadelphia: Temple University Press.

Katz, M. B. 1989. *The undeserving poor: From the war on poverty to the war on welfare.* New York: Pantheon.

Labos (Laboratorio per le politiche sociali). 1988. *Essere barboni a Roma.* Rome: TER.

Law, R., and J. Wolch. 1993. Homelessness and the cities: Local government policies and practices in Southern California. Working paper 44, Los Angeles Homelessness Project. Los Angeles: University of Southern California, Department of Geography.

Margalit, A. 1996. *The decent society.* Cambridge, Mass.: Harvard University Press.

McChesney, K. Y. 1990. Family homelessness: A systemic problem. *Journal of Social Issues* 46, no. 4: 191-295.

Munch, R., and N. J. Smelser. 1992. *Theory of culture.* Berkeley and Los Angeles: University of California Press.

Park, R. E. 1925, 1967. The mind of the hobo: Reflections upon the relations between mentality and locomotion. In *The city: Suggestions for investigation of human behavior in the urban environment,* by R. E. Park, E. W. Burgess, and R. D. McKenzie. Chicago: University of Chicago Press, Midway reprint, 1984.

Park, R. E., E. W. Burgess, and R. D. McKenzie. 1925, 1967. *The city: Suggestions for investigation of human behavior in the urban environment.* Chicago: University of Chicago Press, Midway reprint, 1984.

Quigley, J. M. 1994. New directions in urban policy. *Housing Policy Debate* 51: 97-106.

Rawls, J. 1971. *A theory of justice.* Cambridge, Mass.: Harvard University Press.

Rossi, P. H., G. A. Fisher, and G. Willis. 1986. *The condition of homelessness in Chicago: A report based on surveys conducted in 1985 and 1986.* Amherst and Chicago: University of Massachusetts-Amherst, Demographic Research Institute, and National Opinion Research Center.

Schwartz, D. C., R. C. Ferlauto, and D. N. Hoffman. 1988. *A new housing policy for America: Recapturing the American dream.* Philadelphia: Temple University Press.

Shinn, M., and C. Gillespie. 1994. The roles of housing and poverty in the origins of homelessness. *American Behavioral Scientist* 34: 505-521.

Snow, D., and L. Anderson. 1993. *Down on their luck: A case study of homeless street people.* Berkeley: University of California Press.

Snow, D., and M. G. Bradford, eds. 1994. Broadening perspectives on homelessness (special issue). *American Behavioral Scientist* 37, no. 4 (February).

Stern, M. 1984. The emergence of homelessness as a public problem. *Social Service Review* 582: 291-301.

Stoner, M. R. 1994. *The civil rights of homeless people: Law, social policy and social work practice.* New York: Aldine de Gruyter.

United Nations. 1992. *World urbanization prospects: The 1992 revision.* New York: United Nations Publications.

Wolch, J., and M. J. Dear. 1993. *Malign neglect: Homelessness in an American city.* San Francisco: Jossey-Bass.

Wolch, J., and H. Sommer. 1997. *Los Angeles in an era of welfare reform: Implications for poor people and community well-being.* Los Angeles: Human Services Network, Liberty Hill Foundation.

Zlotnick, H. 1993. Population distribution and migration: The emerging issues. Santa Cruz, Calif. Mimeograph.

"Play Groups" No Longer
Urban Street Gangs in the Los Angeles Region

EDITOR'S
COMMENTS

Briefly alluding to what was to become Frederic Thrasher's seminal work on more than 1,000 "boys' gangs" in Chicago, Robert Park noted the gangs' connection with juvenile delinquency and adolescent crime. Youthful rebellion, he went on, is something to be expected, but delinquency was a measure of the breakdown of community institutions. The associated social dislocation was a consequence of mobility (especially the car), newspapers, motion picture shows, and similar distractions.

Park can be forgiven for not foreseeing the staggering rise in urban street gangs nationwide, which is the subject of a careful analysis by Cheryl L. Maxson and Malcolm W. Klein in this chapter. Suggesting that the Los Angeles region has become the epitome of the urban street gang phenomenon, Maxson and Klein attribute the rise and diffusion of gang culture in the United States to increased poverty among youth and the pervasive nature of media coverage of the phenomenon. But they also uncover important connectives to popular wisdom on gangs, in particular the exaggerated notions of gangs' relation to crime and violence. The very size of the gang population in Los Angeles, its diverse demographics, and the peculiarities of the region's urban spatial structure are factors that create unique patterns of gang formation in Los Angeles, as well as a need for novel public policy responses.

QUOTES FROM
THE CITY

Only gradually, as he succeeds in accommodating himself to the life of the larger group, incorporating into the specific purposes and ambitions of his own life the larger and calmer purposes of the society in which he lives, does the individual man find himself quite at home in the community of which he is a part.

If this is true of mankind as a whole, it is still more true of the younger person. The natural impulses of the child are inevitably so far from conforming to the social situation in which he finds himself that his relations to the community seem to be almost completely defined in a series of "don'ts." Under these circumstances juvenile delinquency is, within certain age-limits at least, not merely something to be expected; it may almost be said to be normal. . . . (105)

In the family and in the neighborhood such organization as exists is based upon custom and tradition, and is fixed in what Sumner calls the folk-ways and the mores. At this stage, society is a purely natural product; a product of the spontaneous and unreflective responses of individuals living together in intimate, personal, and face-to-face relations. Under such circumstances conscious efforts to discipline the individual and enforce the social code are directed merely by intuition and common sense.

In the large social unit, the community, where social relations are more formal and less intimate, the situation is different. It is in the community, rather than in the family or the neighborhood, that formal organizations like the church, the school, and the courts come into existence and get their separate functions defined. With the advent of these institutions, and through their mediation, the community is able to supplement, and to some extent supplant, the family and the neighborhood as a means for the discipline and control of the individual. However, neither the orphan asylum nor any other agency has thus far succeeded in providing a wholly satisfactory substitute for the home. The evidence of this is that they have no alumni association. They create no memories and traditions that those who graduate from them are disposed to cherish and keep alive.

It is in this community with its various organizations and its rational, rather than traditional, schemes of control, and not elsewhere, that we have delinquency. Delinquency is, in fact, in some sense the measure of the failure of our community organizations to function. . . . (105-106)

The mobility of city life, with its increase in the number and intensity of stimulations, tends inevitably to confuse and demoralize the person. For an essential element in the mores and in personal morality is consistency, consistency of the type that is natural in the social control of the primary group. Where mobility is the greatest, and where in consequence primary controls break down completely, as in the zone of deterioration in the modern city, there develop areas of demoralization, of promiscuity, and of vice.

In our studies of the city it is found that areas of mobility are also the regions in which are found juvenile delinquency, boys' gangs, crime, poverty, wife desertion, divorce, abandoned infants, vice. . . . (59)

It is probable that the most deadly and the most demoralizing single instrumentality of present-day civilization is the automobile. The automobile bandit, operating in our great cities, is much more successful and more dangerous than the romantic stage robber of fifty years ago. The connection of the automobile with vice is notorious. "The automobile is connected with more seductions than happen otherwise in cities altogether."

The newspaper and the motion picture show, while not so deadly, are almost as demoralizing. If I were to attempt to enumerate all the social forces that have contributed to the disorganization of modern society I should probably be compelled to make a catalogue of everything that has introduced any new and striking change into the otherwise dull routine of our daily life. Apparently anything that makes life interesting is dangerous to the existing order. (107-108)

CHAPTER 9

"Play Groups" No Longer
Urban Street Gangs in the Los Angeles Region

CHERYL L. MAXSON

MALCOLM W. KLEIN

Writing in the first quarter of the twentieth century, Park and Burgess provided a rare glimpse of urban dynamics in a period of accelerating change. They and, more generally, the Chicago School of sociology, were concerned about urban ills that seemed endemic to urban growth. Included among these urban ills were crime, delinquency, and (with only the briefest hint of interest) urban gangs, concerns yet untouched by modern social science. In Chapter 5 of *The City*, Park alludes in a single paragraph to "the play group," noting that "Mr. Frederic Thrasher has recently been studying the boys' gangs in Chicago." Indeed, Thrasher's report became the first, classic study of urban gangs in America, a required citation and reverent reference for virtually all gang scholars in the seven decades to follow.[1] Yet the Chicago scholars could not have foreseen, nor could even Thrasher have foretold, what courses gang development would take in these intervening years.

Chicago's gangs—its urban or street gangs, not the mobs of the Prohibition era—grew slowly and, in the process, developed a set of unique patterns in size, in organization, and in political entanglements, as well as in their attention from gang scholars. Indeed, they became so unique as to endanger any reasonable generalization to gangs elsewhere. Meanwhile, starting a bit later, the street gangs of Los Angeles emerged in Mexican American communities in East L.A. prior to World War II and, following the war, grew to multiethnic proportions and patterns far more descriptive of gangs that would emerge nationwide toward the end of the century. The gangs of Los Angeles, not Chicago, have come to epitomize the urban street gang phenomenon.

In this chapter, we use Park's Chapter 5 material as a springboard to describe and discuss the street gangs of the Los Angeles region. We examine four interconnected concerns: (1) the context of Los Angeles gangs and of gang research generally, (2) the social construction of street gangs, (3) patterns of gang structure and migration, and (4) responses to gangs, especially in view of Park's prediction of a "new social science."

LOS ANGELES GANGS IN CONTEXT

Prevalence

Responsibility for gathering information on street gangs in Los Angeles has, for years, been lodged in a special unit of the Los Angeles County Sheriff's Department. In a series of funded research projects, we have gathered additional information on gang prevalence and crime. Together, these sources provide a disheartening picture. It is estimated that within this one county alone, as many as 1,350 named street gangs with a total of perhaps 150,000 gang members now exist. We estimate that this may account for one quarter of all active gangs and gang members across the country. Chicago, having the next largest aggregation, is nonetheless far behind this Los Angeles growth. Further, of the seventy-four municipal jurisdictions surveyed within the county in 1992, all but thirteen municipalities reported street gangs indigenous to their communities.[2] Thus, the problem is no longer urban in any narrow sense; it is suburban, and even rural in a few instances. These jurisdictions range in size from the city of Los Angeles with its roughly 3.5 million people to Hawaiian Gardens with a population of less than 14,000.

This proliferation mirrors the pattern reported for the nation as a whole. Although gang-involved jurisdictions increased linearly from the 1950s to 1980, the rate of acceleration increased starting in the 1980s to the point that our 1992 list of documented gang cities stood at nearly 800. Beyond that, we used a sample of additional towns and cities yielding a combined estimate of more than 1,100 such locations by 1992, whereas federal surveys started in 1995, using a far broader population base, have put the likely number of cities, towns, and counties with street gangs at more than 4,700.[3] With only the minutest number of these being subject to research, the Los Angeles region has become a reasonable microcosm for gathering gang knowledge.

Yet neither public concern nor scholarly interest has been triggered solely by the proliferation of gangs. Gang crime and, in particular, gang-related homicide have captured public attention. Our data documented more than 2,000 gang-related killings in 1991, a third of them occurring in Los Angeles County alone. Between 1980, an earlier peak year, and 1998, the year of our last count, almost 9,500 gang homicides had occurred in the county (see Figure 9.1). For the last several years, roughly 40 percent of all homicides in the county could be laid at the gang door. Homicides, however, account for a minuscule percentage of the crimes committed by gang members. Thus, gang crime has become, unfortunately, one of the prime urban signatures of this region. Los Angeles and its setting stand alone in this regard, throughout the nation and world.

If we are to understand future American cities through the lens of Los Angeles, its street gangs stand as a peculiar marker for what is to come. We say this not because we expect to see other urban centers mirror the gang picture of Los Angeles but because of what the gang problem represents about urban centers. It is critical to consider that street gangs are the by-products of their settings. Elsewhere, we have

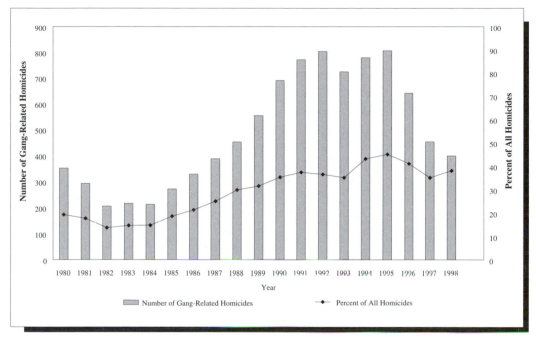

Figure 9.1. Gang-Related Homicides in Los Angeles County (1980-1998)

suggested two factors that more than others have led to the current state of gang pro-liferation: the post-1980 intensification of the urban underclass and the diffusion of gang culture through the media.[4] Both factors increasingly encompass not only the inner city but suburban areas and relatively isolated towns. The concentric circles of Park and Burgess no longer apply, as we shall explain in greater detail later.

The State of the Field

Park's almost offhand mention of gangs in Chicago and his reference to the pio-neering work undertaken there by Thrasher presaged an era in which Chicago gang research became the hallmark of gang research generally. The Chicago School of so-ciology set the stage. The development by Shaw and McKay of the Chicago Area Projects demonstrated much in the way of community-based approaches to gang prevention and the role of street-level gang workers in particular. The styles of research undertaken—field observation and surveys, close liaison between research-ers and community agencies—would be mirrored in the later prestigious work of Albert Cohen, of James F. Short Jr. and his colleagues, of Hans Mattick and his research group, and of Irving Spergel—all of them in Chicago.

From this base, often serving explicitly as research models, other gang researchers in the 1950s through the mid-1970s carried out field studies in Boston, New York, San Francisco, and Seattle, as well as in the separate black and Latino communities of Los Angeles. Common pictures of the street gang emerged from common methodologies almost irrespective of the city involved. Gangs were large, youthful, struc-tured in age-graded subgroups, primarily males of color, explicitly territorial, and principally located in deprived, inner-city areas. Their behaviors were diverse, as were their criminal activities. Yet unlike many of Thrasher's rather playful gangs, those of the postwar era were composed of alienated, combative, and, to an extent, considerably self-destructive, juveniles, isolated from mainstream America.

Throughout the 1970s, because of reduced research funding and the emergence of other pressing social problems, the attention to gangs flagged.[5] As a result, it was thought that gang activity itself had decreased, but recent studies suggest that this was not true. Indeed, at a rather steady rate, the number of cities experiencing gang problems increased until by 1980, there were approximately 200 American cities with gang problems. The cities were there, and the gangs were there, but with few notable exceptions, the researchers were not.[6]

But a radical increase in gang problems commencing in the 1980s changed this situation nationally, as well as in the Los Angeles region. The proliferation of gang-involved cities forced renewed attention, as did insistent reports of increased gang violence and a greater lethality of weapons used. Zip guns and tire irons had been replaced by semiautomatic handguns and drive-by shootings. After periods of denial by local officials across the nation, the 1980s also increased law enforcement con-cern with gang problems in hundreds of jurisdictions, and eventually among federal agencies as well. This enhanced concern led to a new and continuing round of sup-port for gang research, but now of two types. The earlier ethnographic and field sur-veys were again undertaken, but now in far more locations.[7] In addition, the increased enforcement concern led to the collection of data seldom seen before, and these data have had major effects on gang research.

In most cities, the police are the only agency with a broad data collection man-date in the gang arena. Police intelligence on gangs—formerly weak to abysmal—has intensified to enhance enforcement operations and prosecutorial success. By the mid-1980s and increasingly since then, police gang specialists in many cities have been gathering information on the number of active gangs and gang members and on the extensiveness of the more serious forms of gang crime. Gang researchers have, understandably, sought access to these police data.[8] Thus, within the past few years, far more information has become available on the proliferation of gangs across the country and on certain aspects of gang crime involvement. A national picture is now emerging that simply was not available before, and it is being filled in, in piecemeal fashion, by more local field studies. It has now become possible for researchers to do surveys of police experts in hundreds of cities about issues not recorded as part of official police statistics. Patterns of gang structure, ethnicity, the migration of gang members, patterns of gang violence and involvement in drug sales, gang prevention and control programs, and the relationships of all these to the city are now receiving close research scrutiny.

Nowhere has this been truer than in the two major hubs of gang activity, Chicago and Los Angeles. In Chicago, Irving Spergel and his associates, a group headed by George Knox, and the team of Carolyn and Richard Block have emerged as major contributors to the "new" gang research (Spergel having been active since the 1960s). In Los Angeles, in addition to our studies, the works of Joan Moore and James Diego Vigil have taken advantage of the data sources in the region to keep research abreast of the gang activity in Los Angeles.

The field is at a critical point now. Ethnographic and field surveys are well-tested procedures for understanding local gang situations. Enforcement data are rapidly becoming sufficient to permit regional and national depictions. Expert surveys yield data on the middle ground—data not routinely collected yet retrievable if done so with care. Researchers should be concerned with the melding of these research technologies, not with arguments about preferences for one over another.

SOCIAL CONSTRUCTION OF GANGS

This promising data situation has also forced to the surface, among a number of gang scholars, epistemological issues that have, heretofore, received only occasional comment, and seldom with much support. We have selected three of these topics for discussion.

Definitional Issues

Street gangs—and for that matter, gangs of most types—are informal groups without membership lists. Who is or is not a member lies in the eye of the beholder, and there are many beholders. This is especially true of those toward the gang's periphery, where disagreement about membership is common. Members themselves are often uncertain of the status of many of their peers; police and social agencies can (if they will) name those only with whom they have contact, plus a few whose reputations are passed along, and the same is true of school personnel. This situation is complicated by errors of omission (failing to note some members) and errors of overinclusion (counting former members and peer associates who more properly ought not to be counted). Researchers, beyond their own observations using generally vague inclusionary and exclusionary criteria, often rely heavily on agency (social or enforcement) designations of gang members, or on gang members themselves. New youth join, others pass in and out, irregularly, and others simply fade away.

Given this ambiguity of status, the rapidity of turnover, and the constancy of recruitment and retirement, one research finding has emerged with considerable reliability and construct validity—self-nominated gang membership is surprisingly robust. When young people in a known gang setting are asked by researchers whether they are gang members, the admitters and the deniers are consistently different on a number of gang-relevant factors, most particularly on type and amount of illegal behaviors.[9] In other words, neighborhood youth have a rather clear image of gang membership. If this were not true, the robust differences emerging from the research would simply not be reliable. But they are.

Yet if gang members are relatively forthcoming about their status to researchers, they are often far less so to agency personnel—police, social and health workers, teachers, and counselors. In our own research in cities scattered across the nation, we have found that social and enforcement agency gang experts can differ radically on gang size, gang members, and related issues. Only the police, if anyone, can regularly provide citywide information, and one has to be careful about the questions asked of them. The police normally think relative to crime patterns and describe gangs first and foremost in those terms. They are able to report gang locations and ethnicities but usually fall short on gang structures, leadership, female participants, nonindex crimes (nonserious or most property crimes), and noncriminal life histories and activities of gang members.

If gang membership is unclear, how do we, then, find a clear definition of a gang? One answer, of course, is that a public stereotype has evolved, heavily influenced by the limited scope of police exposure and the exaggerated versions provided by the media and entertainment industry. This stereotype usually emphasizes a tightly cohesive gang, a gang with strong hierarchical leadership, a gang clearly delineated by special clothing and other symbols, a gang dedicated to criminal pursuits and especially violence, and a gang totally alienated from the mainstream. In every one of these particulars, the stereotype is very much in error. The public image of gangs has been almost totally unaffected by research carried out during the past century.

If this public image is derived as suggested from police, media, and entertainment sources, then it seems clear that these sources, too, have been relatively unaffected by research data. Widely noted definitions or descriptions of gangs by scholars who have spent years in the field are almost unknown to these sources.[10] Gang "experts" who appear on behalf of the prosecution in court, usually police officers, are often quite knowledgeable about the gangs under their individual surveillance but not about the variety of gangs within which theirs could be located.

In Chapter 13 of this volume, Vasishth and Sloane distinguish between a Darwinian or essentialist approach to defining categories and a population approach. The former defines street gangs by what they have in common, as a type, the latter by boundaries between types (allowing for much variability within a category). We find this population approach more useful in characterizing various forms of street gangs and separating them from other types of groups.

Sources of Information

We have noted the general predominance of law enforcement and the media in providing gang information, but let's be a bit more precise. First, only the police generate jurisdiction-wide data on gang presence and activity. With gangs defined partially or wholly by their criminal acts, it is not surprising that others turn to them for "official" information on gangs. Also, because the police often seek help in controlling gangs, they disseminate their beliefs, as well as their knowledge, through meetings, briefings, seminars, and lectures to schools, PTAs, business groups, and of course to media representatives. In the Los Angeles region, the sheriff's department is charged with collecting gang data from all police jurisdictions and maintains a countywide roster of gangs and gang members. Thus the sheriff's spokespersons are, ipso facto, the experts in the county, with Los Angeles Police Department representatives close behind.

The media—the news media particularly—rely on the police and occasionally other informants to present their gang picture. Thus, to produce newsworthy items that will provide headlines, the print and broadcast media principally offer reports on gang violence, innocent victims, and conspiracies (e.g., drug distribution or intergang warfare). Although the basic data come from the police, this information is further selected and filtered for newsworthiness. In a parallel world, the entertainment industry, always ready to take advantage of public interests, creates its own stylized gang images, distorted for entertainment value. Movies such as *The Wild One, Colors, Boyz in the Hood,* and *New Jack City* provide drama and distortions of reality that frame the public image. Commercial television has contributed its share to media images as well, most often by providing instantaneous, repetitive, and national dissemination of the presumed cultural signs of gang membership: baggy pants (or pressed chinos), Pendleton shirts (or pressed T-shirts), colored bandannas (or shoelaces), sports caps (or beanies) turned backwards (or to the side), special hand signs (or tattoos), and special gang argot (or "inner-city" language patterns). In other words, gang culture and youth culture become intermixed, at the mercy of culture purveyors, with the result, first, that gangs seem omnipresent and, second, that virtually every adolescent in America has been taught how to look, walk, talk, and act like someone's image of gang members. Not surprisingly, many do, and the media help concretize the constructed image of gangs and spread it to towns large and small.

Finally, there are local agencies—usually small but occasionally citywide—that take it upon themselves to prevent or redirect gang energies. They, too, have an image of gang membership that includes violence and predation, but it is generally softened by the belief in youthful malleability and potential for betterment. Their image of an energetic but misguided gang member, often the product of unfair social conditions but potentially redeemable, is an image of romantic street corners and dedicated personnel believing in prevention and salvation. It is an image as valid as that provided by the police, but it has barely survived the 1980s and 1990s era of suppression. It is not the image that captures the public, although it did from the time of Thrasher through the mid-1960s.

Darnell Hunt's depiction of the "mediated reality" of Los Angeles (see Chapter 12, this volume) applies equally well to the mediated reality of street gangs. Part of our modernist approach is to connect that mediated reality to a research-elicited database on street gangs. In the case of gangs, this is particularly important because the mediated reality is heavily dependent on the images framed by law enforcement, which, themselves, are highly reflective of the restricted views and goals of the law enforcement community.

A Scholarly Construction of Gangs

If the public has accepted the general image of gangs described earlier—organized, violent, purposefully criminal—we present a contrasting scholarly image, realizing that scholars differ among themselves, having carried out their research at different times, in different places, with different methods, and from different perspectives. Nonetheless, a general description does emerge that largely differs from that generally available to the public. It includes the following six elements (all of which apply to the Los Angeles region as to most other settings).

1. Street gangs exist as a broad class of groups within a broader category of groups also often labeled "gangs." Other forms of gangs include prison, terrorist, and motorcycle gangs, as well as supremacist groups such as skinheads. These, in turn, comprise but a portion of a far larger enumeration of groups that Miller refers to as "law violating groups."[11] Scholars are in general but not complete agreement that street gangs are sufficiently different from these other groups that they should be conceptualized, however ambiguously, as different in type.

2. The category "street gangs" also contains a considerable variety of forms. Best known and most thoroughly studied in research dating to the 1950s are the large, territorial groups often called "traditional" gangs. They generally number in the hundreds of members at any given time and are typically broken into subgroups or cliques based on age or location. They have existed in urban centers for decades through constant self-regeneration. Typically black or Latino—more often the latter—they are found disproportionately in the Los Angeles region, among others.

Far less common, but of late given great media attention, are specialty gangs, groups whose general goal is to reap the profits of specific forms of crime. They may be concerned principally with burglary, auto theft, or graffiti, but the ones getting most police and media attention are the drug gangs oriented principally to the distribution and sale of narcotics. Drug gangs tend to be small, typically with two or three dozen members, quite tightly organized around their "business." Their specialized criminal focus helps distinguish them from the other, more criminally versatile, gangs described here. The press and many enforcement officials often fail to appreciate the significant differences between drug gangs and other types. Much of this failure has originated in selected police agencies in the Los Angeles region, where the explosion of crack cocaine sales in the 1980s was mistakenly overattributed to black street gangs.

The past ten to fifteen years have seen the emergence of a different form of gang, usually referred to as "taggers," tagger crews, and tagger posses. They tend to be young, Latino or white, small, less versatile in crime than traditional gangs, and known principally for their sometimes playful yet destructive penchant for stylized forms of graffiti. They are not usually territorial, preferring to write or paint their groups' and individual symbols in as many locations as possible and taking particular pride in placing the symbols in the most unlikely, difficult to reach, and visible locations. These gangs are usually not very criminally oriented but are occasionally transformed into more typical gang forms as a result of forming intergroup rivalries. Taggers are common throughout the Los Angeles region.

Recently labeled "compressed gangs," are, by far, the most common form of street gang, although this is somewhat truer nationally than in the Los Angeles area. Smaller than traditional yet larger than specialty gangs, compressed gangs have a short history—typically under ten years—and versatile crime patterns, with less emphasis than many on territoriality. They are called compressed because they contain no clear subgroups based on age or location but are comparatively age homogeneous. These gangs are less predominant in Los Angeles because they have appeared more often in the emergent gang cities that have proliferated in and since the 1980s—a newer form in newer gang cities. Descriptions of such gangs in Kansas City (Missouri), Louisville, New Orleans, Toledo, Torrance (California), and many other jurisdictions in which we have carried out our interviews make us cautious about generalizing too far from traditional big-city gangs. But we can say that Los Angeles provides a less unique pattern than does Chicago. The former contains a mixture of the gang types just described; even the infamous Bloods and Crips are less genuine confederations than shifting alliances in name, tending to obscure common and intense rivalries, with Crips battling Crips and Bloods battling Bloods in addition to the more publicized Crip-Blood confrontations.

Chicago gangs, in contrast, have, through several decades, developed into large-scale, organized confederations of what had already been called supergangs. Such gangs numbered membership in the thousands and then aligned themselves under even more inclusive banners, the People and the Folks.[12] Such gangs and gang "nations" have produced constitutions, received large federal and private grants, tied themselves to political leaders, and in one case, even dabbled in international arms sales. The danger in evaluating any research emanating from Chicago lies in underestimating the uniqueness of its context.

3. A reasonable consensus among gang scholars has also been reached with regard to gang internal structure. Although popular images stress cohesive, well-structured groups with clear—and tough—leaders, gang research offers a far more varied picture. More often than not, researchers have been impressed by a lower level of gang cohesiveness distinguished by the wax and wane of activity, distribution of labor among numerous individuals, and the surprisingly weak norms or codes of conduct (although the normative rhetoric would lead one to believe otherwise).[13]

4. The image of gang behavior often portrayed in public descriptions is of groups who are criminally oriented and engaged principally in the most violent of crimes—assaults, drive-by shootings, homicides, and rapes. This is an image all too often employed by politicians for their own purposes. Yet with great consistency, and with the exception of the relatively small number of specialty gangs, research has shown gang member behavior to consist, first and foremost, of noncriminal activity.[14] Members sleep, eat, attend school or work, hang around in various locations

with each other, and lead a boring and desultory life. When they do engage in delinquent or criminal behavior, once or a few times a day in some instances but often
more rarely, the bulk of this behavior is minor—vandalism, graffiti writing, petty
theft, joy riding, and drinking (with a lesser amount of minor drug use). Of the total
delinquent and criminal acts, a minor portion—perhaps 5 to 10 percent—can be
described as serious. Included in this small portion will be auto theft, burglary, theft
of valuable items, perhaps robbery, various forms of assault, and disorganized drug
sales. Homicide, the most serious offense, is the most rare.

This picture provides three basic points: (1) Most gang activity is noncriminal,
(2) most criminal gang behavior is nonserious, and (3) most gangs are involved in a
wide variety of illegal behavior. Furthermore, with respect to the violence that most
disturbs the public, it has become clear that for any gang, this too waxes and wanes.
It is highly variable across gangs, with most gangs participating in relatively little
violence and a small number being quite heavily involved. In gang intervention, it is
well to know which type of gang is being targeted.

5. Just as street gangs vary in structure and behavior pattern, so, too, they vary in
many other dimensions. Ethnicity, for instance, is determined more by local population characteristics and minority status than by any "cultural" predilections. Nationally, Latino and black gangs are about equally predominant, although regional
differences are common. White and Asian gangs are far less common (in the days of
Thrasher and the Chicago School writers, white ethnic gangs predominated).

Gender differences are major. Gangs are primarily male but clearly not exclusively so. Ten males to one female or less are common, but often four-to-one, two-
to-one, and even one-to-one ratios have been reported. Independent, fully autonomous female gangs have been and remain fairly rare, but otherwise the form of
female involvement, from auxiliary groups to full integration, has shown considerable variety.

Similarly with age, both average age and the range from youngest to oldest member have been found to be highly variable. There are gangs of adolescents with age
ranges of only one to three years, and there are young adult gangs with age ranges
closer to five or ten years. Among gangs of the traditional, multigenerational form,
members may average eighteen to twenty years of age, yet the range of ages in such a
gang may extend from ten or younger to over forty.

With the proliferation of gangs in medium-size and small communities, the
social class level has become more varied and has become more obvious in recent
years. No longer are gangs confined to lower- or working-class areas. Although gangs
are still ethnically marginalized and located in relatively segregated areas, they now,
more often than in the past, include memberships drawn from suburban areas as
well as those unconnected to metropolitan regions. Although each such area reports
a small number of gangs and gang members, usually exhibiting minor levels of criminal behavior as seen from the big-city perspective, they are street gangs nonetheless.

Within Los Angeles County alone (with apologies to readers unfamiliar with the
area), smaller jurisdictions facing gang problems include Bellflower (population

65,000; four gangs, 600 members); Lawndale (population 27,000; nine gangs, 500 members); Culver City (population: 39,000; two gangs, 16 members); Santa Monica (population 87,000; eight gangs, 250 or more members); Palmdale (population 69,000; twenty-five gangs, 850 members); and San Fernando (population 23,000; fifteen gangs, 500 members). These figures, reported by police during our survey in 1992, are illustrative of similar towns across the country, as the list includes both traditional (gang onset in the 1960s) and emergent (onset in the 1980s) gang cities. Few people in Los Angeles think of these as inner-city areas as, elsewhere in the country, most would not describe Beloit (Wis.), Tyler (Texas), Jackson (Miss.), Arlington (Va.), Bellingham (Wash.), or Napa (Calif.)—all with gang problems—as inner-city jurisdictions.

6. Finally, and not unrelated to this demographic picture, it is not uncommon to think of gang areas of a city as gang controlled, overrun with gang members, abandoned by residents to lounging hordes of gang youth. We have studied, worked in, and observed numerous gang-involved areas throughout Los Angeles and have visited others in the country. We have yet to observe a gang area that "belongs" to the gangs. Although some gang areas can indeed make one feel quite uncomfortable, the majority of residents are not gang members. Indeed, in most such areas, gang membership constitutes a small portion of the gang-aged youth—variously estimated at less than 5 to 10 percent of such youth in most instances. Living in a gang area does not require gang membership (although an alert eye is recommended). When told we were about to engage in an intensive research project in a famous gang area in East L.A., we were warned by an experienced gang "expert" in the police department that "every kid down in there is a gang member—every one." During a year and a half, we found, among several thousand gang-aged youth, 110 members belonging to our target gang, and perhaps 50 resident youth who belonged to rival gangs, or approximately 5 percent. In four other areas studied in South Central Los Angeles, we found a high of 6 percent youth involvement. No area is so gang infested as to be unapproachable for intervention. No area is so bereft of nongang residents that local, informal social control of gangs is impossible. Missing, often, is not the capacity but the will and the resources. Yet both of these can be built.

COMMUNITY ISSUES IN GANG RESEARCH

Street gangs are spawned within communities and occasionally branch out beyond their own spawning grounds. Understanding gangs requires attention to their community foundations, an understanding that is far too complex and extensive to be covered here.[15] Within this community context, however, we will cover three basic concerns: (1) the Los Angeles situation, (2) the migration of gang members beyond their home territories, and (3) Los Angeles and Chicago, in particular, as sources of national gang imagery via gang member migration. These issues are directly connected to that of the community spawning ground.

Los Angeles, Generalizable and Unique

Understanding the Los Angeles street gang situation within its own setting is one thing; fitting it into the broader national scene is quite another. Los Angeles is neither so similar to other areas nor so unique that definitive statements of "gang truths" come easily here. We'll look first at three issues: (1) community structures, (2) the enormity of the Los Angeles problem, and (3) gang structures, here and elsewhere.

First, the founders of the Chicago School of sociology made a prescient and enduring discovery about their city and many others, namely, that one could understand much about an urban area's growth and change by adopting the concentric circle model described by Burgess in Chapter 2 of *The City*. This was an ecological model that illustrated zones of residential movement from the factory-based core of the city to a "transitional zone" through which moved a succession of immigrant populations to, successively, a working-class zone, a residential zone, and finally a commuter zone.

For gang research purposes, there are at least two vital elements to this model. First, it is immigrant or minority status that places one in the transitional and most socially troubled zone, regardless of which immigrant or minority group is involved. That these new groups were Catholic, Jewish, Irish, Polish, Latino, or black was far less important than their ecological niche. It was not a given ethnicity, nationality, or race but that group's marginalized status that spawned gangs. Second, this model made little distinction between the groups based on the reasons for their marginality or for their eventual mobility. Another way of saying this is that the model did not sufficiently allow for differential discrimination on the part of the dominant majority (which, incidentally, would later come to include the earlier transitioning minority or immigrant groups).

The Los Angeles situation reveals the problems with the two Chicago-based elements of the model, the concentric circle depiction and demographic succession expectation. Regarding the first, Los Angeles has for years been described by its many centers, as opposed to its one civic center. Greg Hise (Chapter 4) describes L.A.'s mixed-use, industrial-residential clusters as satellite centers within a metropolitan orbit and notes the network of urban villages envisioned by the board of supervisors in the early 1920s. "Los Angeles" is, variously, its civic center, South Central, East L.A., the San Fernando Valley, the San Gabriel Valley, Pasadena, Hollywood, the Harbor area, West L.A., the Beach Cities, and so on. Multinuclei theory is, therefore, more appropriate to describing and analyzing the region.

This pattern has implications for many aspects of community development, including those that affect gang presence. The first is that the succession of immigrant and minority groups has not followed the Chicago pattern. Second, gangs have originated not simply in one zone of transition but rather independently in many segregated, minority districts through the region. According to police respondents and our own work in various Los Angeles County jurisdictions, street gang onset took place prior to 1960 in such widespread locations as Arcadia,

Azusa, Compton, Gardena, Glendale, Hawaiian Gardens, Los Angeles proper, Paramount, San Fernando, and Whittier, among about eighteen such locations. Outside Los Angeles County, other nearby locations included Oxnard, San Bernardino, Santa Ana, Placentia, and Riverside. This was due not to minority succession but to independent evolution of gangs in similarly deprived and segregated minority areas.

Furthermore, despite the existence of many community names, Los Angeles has not been the site of many communities, as was the case in Chicago (or Boston, or New York, or Philadelphia). The Chicago area projects were predicated on and made use of clear community identities—felt and perceived areas of common background, experience, and even destinies. Los Angeles has few such communities. When a strongly community-based gang intervention program was transferred to Los Angeles from Philadelphia, some predicted that it would either fail or have to fully transform itself to suit the amorphous structure of Los Angeles. Both predictions have been borne out. Community Youth Gang Services, as it was called, found little by way of community identities on which to build.

In neighborhoods that spawn gangs but lack sufficient community cohesion to control them, gang control is relinquished to public authorities—the justice system in general and, in particular, the police. In the absence of effective informal social control at the community level, the region has called on its law enforcement agencies. Accordingly, in 1980, the county district attorney developed a large unit devoted solely to the prosecution of gang members. The city attorney followed suit later, with special emphasis on the use of civil injunctions to prohibit certain forms of gang activity. The Los Angeles police and sheriff's departments independently developed large gang units, with many scores of officers, to crack down on gangs and to develop a countywide gang intelligence and roster system within the sheriff's unit. Both the county probation and the state parole systems instigated gang surveillance units whose basic goal was to return gang members to incarceration for violating probation or parole provisions.

These efforts have amounted to an enormous crackdown on gangs, with virtually no attention given to the wellsprings of gang formation within the affected neighborhoods. Throughout this county and others, the pattern has been copied, often with relish.[16] Thus, the absence of effective local control does not mean no control, but it may lead to a shift in the locus of control whereby the operant value is not prevention but suppression.[17]

All the above stems from aspects of L.A.'s social structure and the absence of Chicago-like city growth patterns as described by Park and Burgess. The Chicago School was also marked by its implicit acceptance of minority succession, regardless of the minorities involved. Chicago and most eastern cities with similar migration patterns absorbed large numbers of European immigrants—Poles, Germans, Irish, Swedes, Italians, eastern Europeans and Jews, and so on. Each of these groups slowly but steadily assimilated into mainstream society. Although many of them spawned street gangs—minority street gangs because of their immigrant background—such gangs largely disappeared with the assimilation of their forebears.

American social values have not extended the same open hand offered to their European counterparts to the blacks and Latinos who, increasingly, came to and have remained in inner cities. The demographic succession described by the Chicago scholars has been stalled for both blacks and Latinos; they have not been permitted the same level of assimilation, and the vast majority of street gangs proliferating throughout the Los Angeles region and the United States are black and Latino. Thus, although one might have predicted a reduction in urban street gangs prior to the 1950s, we have seen just the opposite. Segregated areas of cities large and small have increasingly become mostly black and Latino (mostly Puerto Rican and Mexican, but now showing increases in other Caribbean and Central American populations).

Nationally, street gangs are roughly equally black or Latino, with far smaller proportions of Asians, whites, and mixed groups. The Los Angeles region, prior to World War II, contained mostly Latino gangs. Wartime and postwar migration of blacks from the South and Southwest balanced the picture considerably, while the racial disturbances and rock cocaine sales in South Central Los Angeles gave special weight to the image of black gangs. Nonetheless, Latino gangs, in both traditional and compressed forms, are more widespread in the region. Racism, patterns of segregation, and political inattention to the requirements of lower- and working-class black and Latino neighborhoods provide little optimism for gang reduction.

Second, as mentioned earlier, perhaps the most unique feature of the Los Angeles gang situation is, unfortunately, its immensity. We noted in the first pages of this chapter that sixty-one of seventy-four reporting jurisdictions in the county of Los Angeles had become gang cities by 1992. This does not mean, of course, that the majority of the residents in sixty-one cities are aware of, are threatened by, or care much about their gangs. Quite the opposite: The majority of such residents may feel little concern because gangs are limited to small geographic territories within these cities. For most residents, it is not gang members who burglarize their homes, steal their cars, bother their children, or steal from their stores and businesses but the far larger population of nongang delinquents and criminals.

Clearly, the city of Los Angeles has the worst problem; it reports approximately 400 gangs with gang membership set at about 56,000. If these figures are correct, this means more than 100 members per gang, a sure sign of a high proportion of traditional gang structures. Twelve Los Angeles-area cities sampled and reporting in 1995 on their gang structures report no specialty gangs, 24 percent compressed gangs (vs. 39 percent nationally), and 74 percent traditional or neotraditional gangs with established subgroups (vs. 35 percent nationally). Thus, Los Angeles is far more involved with these large established gangs than are most cities, the bulk of which showed gang onset after 1980. Los Angeles is not typical, but it may well illustrate the gang forms that other cities will see in the future.

How extensive is the Los Angeles street gang problem? The two measures most commonly used are the numbers of gangs and gang members and the numbers of gang-related homicides. As we noted earlier, the sheriff's department estimates about 1,350 gangs and 150,000 gang members for the county as a whole. Our own

1992 survey of all the jurisdictions in the county yielded totals of 1,400 listed gangs and 137,500 gang member residents. Whichever estimate is taken, the numbers are enormous. Using our larger national survey, we find Los Angeles County to be home to perhaps a quarter of the gangs and an even larger proportion of gang members in the country (Los Angeles gangs being larger, on average, than those elsewhere).

If gang activity now were similar to that of the 1950s and 1960s, even these large numbers might not be cause for major social and political concern. Gang predation used to be relatively minor, and the greater social damage was to the gang members themselves in both physical harm and costs to successful entry into mainstream adult life. In other words, in prior times, it was common to "write off" the damage that accompanied gang life. But nationally, and most particularly in a few larger cities such as Los Angeles, such a cavalier attitude has become harder to sustain because of the nature of gang violence. Easy access to lethal weapons and a gang culture that increasingly validates intergang hostilities—symbolized in the public's mind by the stereotypical drive-by shooting—have forced an altered view of the consequences of gang presence.[18]

In Los Angeles County, gang-related killings, broadly defined, climbed to a peak of 351 cases in 1980 (see Figure 9.1).[19] This heretofore unheard-of escalation in gang violence triggered a whole series of countermeasures by established and newly formed intervention and control agencies. By the time these went into effect, however, gang killing had subsided by 40 percent within two years. Although various politicians and agencies inappropriately claimed credit for this reduction, nothing had been done to deal with the causes of gang violence.[20] Starting in 1983, a slow but steady linear increase in gang homicides was recorded through 1992, whereupon a four-year plateau was reached. The highest figure was reached in 1995, when 807 gang-related homicides were recorded, although the following year, the number of gang incidents decreased dramatically to 614 and plunged subsequently to 400 in 1998. Starting in the year before the earlier 1980 peak, the county has now registered more than 9,500 gang-related deaths. For the past several years, about 40 percent of all homicides in the county have been gang-related, the vast majority by way of firearms (mostly handguns). All the above figures except this last would be considerably larger, were we to include the five-county region in which Los Angeles is situated.

Third, the enormity of the problem makes Los Angeles unique. Only Chicago and its surrounding jurisdictions can begin to compare. Yet this does not prevent one from generalizing the gang phenomenon in Los Angeles to other areas. The massive figures are aggregated from more than seventy local jurisdictions. Most of these are cities and towns that are similar to those found throughout the nation, and it is the multiple nucleated character of Los Angeles, not the older concentric circles model, that makes the Los Angeles experience and Los Angeles gang data relevant elsewhere.

One way to approach the application of Los Angeles data—and this becomes a proposal for future research—is to concentrate on the various forms of gang structure and the community differences associated with them. Nationally, we have identified five basic street gang structures (in addition to tagger crews), including the traditional, compressed, and specialty structures described briefly in this chapter.[21] Each is to be found in the Los Angeles region, although traditional gangs are overrepresented in Los Angeles. Indeed, in comparing Chicago with Los Angeles, it seems clear from the available literature that generalization from Chicago would be a major error. That city is the progenitor not only of supergangs such as the Vicelords, Gangster Disciples, Latin Kings, and Blackstone Rangers (later called Black P. Stone Nation and then El Ruk'n) but also of the overarching gang nations known as the People and the Folks. These are enormous confederations with intricate political connections, written constitutions, and formalized behavior norms that put other street gang organizations to shame.[22] Although one can find gangs in other cities called Gangster Disciples and Latin Kings, one must not assume they are branches of the Chicago confederations. In most cases, they are not, nor are the Crips and Bloods found across the nation simply branches of Los Angeles gangs. In this respect, it is important to understand something of the general nature of gang migration before our discussion returns to the Los Angeles and Chicago situations.

General Patterns of Gang Migration

Our surveys of law enforcement personnel in about 1,000 cities and towns across the United States suggest that the movement of gang members from one city to another is quite common. By the early 1990s, more than 700 cities were destinations for gang members from elsewhere. These cities spanned the geographic reaches of the country, with slightly more prominence in the West (see Figure 9.2), gang member migration occurring rarely in the Northeast. Cities of all population sizes are affected, with nearly 100 towns with populations under 10,000 receiving gang migrants. Most cities experienced relatively little migration, however, with just fewer than half reporting the arrival of ten or fewer migrants in the year prior to the survey. To examine the nature of gang migration and its impact on these receiving cities, we conducted lengthy telephone interviews with police gang experts in a random sample of 211 cities that reported the arrival of at least ten gang migrants in the prior year. These interviews revealed several patterns related to distance traveled, reason for relocation, and impact on local crime situations.[23] We conclude this section with a brief discussion of the diffusion of gang culture.

Most Angelenos are quite familiar with media reports of Los Angeles gang members fanning out across the nation's highways and flyways to distant cities such as Shreveport, Kansas City, and Seattle to peddle crack cocaine. This reputation is something we share with Chicagoans. Leaving the particular examples of these two cities aside for the moment, we find that our data suggest patterns in travel distance that contrast markedly with the media-driven image. When we plotted on a map of the United States the 700 cities that reported migration, patterns of both widespread dispersion and focused clustering were evident. The visible clusters were not really surprising—the Bay area of northern California, the Chicago area, Boston, southern Florida, and the western portion of Southern California. Mileage calculations of the

Figure 9.2. Cities With Migrant Gang Members in 1992

distance between the 211 migration cities with which we conducted interviews and the city representing the primary source of migration suggested that gang migrants generally do not travel far. About 60 percent of our police respondents identified a primary departure city within 100 miles of their jurisdiction. Primary source cities more than 1,000 miles away were by far the exception; only 12 percent of the respondents cited a city of such distance as the major departure point of their gang migrants.

We can also assess the spatial distribution of migration by looking for migrant source city clusters. If three or more gang migration sources were cited, the coding staff determined whether a majority (60 percent) were located within a thirty-mile radius of the center of a cluster. Regional clustering of migration sources was identified for seventy-three cities, about one third of all migration cities in our sample but just less than half of cities with three or more migration sources. More than three fourths of these destination cities were located within the area represented by departure city clusters. Taken as a whole, these data suggest that city officials concerned about gang migration might more profitably look in their own backyards rather than casting blame cross-country.

Our use of the term *migration* is different from the immigration concerns as seen by Straughan and Hondagneu-Sotelo (Chapter 7, this volume), but it is associated closely with the "push-pull" concept that derives from early immigration theory described by those authors. For gang migrants, the pushes and pulls may come from issues related to the justice system or to broader social concerns (see below). Where Straughan and Hondagneu-Sotelo discuss "transnational" immigrants who form transnational cultures or communities, some gang migrants (including Vietnamese) might be thought of as transjurisdictional immigrants framing transjurisdictional or transstate gang cultures (aided by the media). Thus we have "Crip and Blood" cultures well beyond the Los Angeles area, as far away as the Hague and San Salvador.

According to police, although gang members move to new cities for a variety of reasons, expansion of drug sale territories was not at the top of the list. When asked to name the single reason that accounts for most of the gang member migration to their cities, interviewees frequently indicated family migration. When combined with stays with relatives and friends, such reasons were cited by nearly 60 percent of respondents. Drug-motivated moves were identified as the primary reason in just one fifth of the cities, clearly debunking the popular media image. The 1997 survey data gathered by the National Youth Gang Center confirm this pattern in a nationally representative sample of U.S. cities.

Given that a focal concern of law enforcement is crime, it is hardly surprising that most respondents felt that gang migrants contributed to local crime rates—primarily increases in theft, robberies, other violent crimes, and, to a lesser extent, drug sales. Also attributed to gang migrants were increased use of firearms and more sophisticated weapons. Our interviews with gang migrants in three cities selected as case studies, however, suggest a different pattern. Most gang migrants reported that their levels of criminal activity had decreased since their relocation to new cities. It stands to reason that such moves disrupt commitments to gang affiliations as migrants experience a period of adjustment to new communities. Social service providers appear to be missing the opportunity to intervene at a time when gang members may be most receptive to positive change.

Perhaps the greatest concern about gang migration for policymakers stems from the perceived role of gang migration as a catalyst for the proliferation of gangs nationwide. We have described migration as a broad yet shallow phenomenon insofar as many cities experience migration but at relatively low levels. Our research does not support the idea of migrants as major culprits in the proliferation question, yet migrants can be viewed as direct bearers of established urban gang culture to less exposed communities.[24] Our interviews were rife with anecdotal comments in this vein, but statements about the influence of the media and the entertainment industry were also common. Three fourths of the respondents felt that the media have helped spread gang culture to their communities. As suggested earlier, the social construction of gangs from the cultural imagery transmitted through the media is at great odds with scholarly work, but there can be little question about which source has the greatest influence on youths. Young people vulnerable—perhaps because of the diminished conditions of their own neighborhoods and communities—to the seduction of excitement, toughness, and camaraderie of the gang mythology need only to turn on a television to experience gang culture.

Gang Migration From Los Angeles and Chicago

In one regard, media portrayals of gang migration are accurate: Los Angeles and Chicago are by far the most common sources of gang migrants. Los Angeles-area cities (within thirty miles) were mentioned as points of departure by two thirds of respondents and Chicago-area cities by one third. Detroit was a distant third, at about 10 percent, with many cities identifying several sources. Mentions of both Los Angeles and Chicago occurred in just 17 percent, Los Angeles but not Chicago in 46 percent, and Chicago but not Los Angeles in another 17 percent of interviews. Just one fifth of cities cited neither Chicago- nor Los Angeles-area cities as sources of gang migrants.

We have already described aspects by which Chicago and Los Angeles gangs are thought to differ and also suggested that the Los Angeles situation may be the better fit for many other gang cities across the country. Limiting our attention to just the primary source of gang migration allows us to assess whether the nature of gang migration from these two areas might also differ—seventy-five cities (35 percent) identified the Los Angeles area as the primary source, whereas the Chicago area was cited by thirty-two cities (15 percent). Consistent with the earlier discussion about distances traveled, cities with mostly Los Angeles migrants were most often located in the West (77 percent), occasionally in the South (15 percent), and rarely in the Midwestern (8 percent) region. Nearly all the cities whose migrants primarily hail from Chicago are located in the Midwest (91 percent), and the remainder are Southern cities. This minor difference is reflected in the distance between departure and destination cities. Half of the cities with L.A. migrants are within eighty miles of the area, whereas half of the Chicago migrant cities are forty miles away or less. In each case, about three fourths of the cities identified three or more source cities, the majority of which formed a regional cluster.

These data suggest that, in general, the geographic reach of Los Angeles and Chicago gangs is not nearly as far as one might expect. Given some of the differences in the gang patterns of the two cities, we can anticipate that the character of migration from them would vary as well. This is not the case, however. In particular, we would expect that expansion of drug operations would be more of a motivating factor for gang migration from Chicago, but social reasons predominate in both types of cities. There is no discernable difference between cities with Los Angeles or Chicago migrants with regard to the reasons for gang member relocation. On arrival, Chicago gang migrants appear more likely to establish branches for their old gangs, whereas Los Angeles migrants join existing gangs, establish branches, or limit their gang activity to their original gangs at similar levels, but these differences are not statistically significant. Similarly, a greater perception of Chicago gang migrant influence on local gang recruiting methods is not a stable difference from Los Angeles migrant cities.

In the past several years, Chicago and Los Angeles have each experienced dramatic demographic changes and high emigration among some population groups. High levels of gang activity in both cities leave little doubt that some of the individuals leaving these cities are gang members and that they carry with them gang experiences and cultural exposures that influence young people in the cities to which they travel. The range of this direct impact, however, is often regional, rather than national. The anticipated differences between Los Angeles and Chicago gang migration did not emerge. Perhaps street gangs in these two cities are more similar than they are sometimes portrayed, or perhaps the migration process acts to blur the distinctions between the two cities.

RESPONSES TO URBAN STREET GANGS

Communities respond to their gang situations in a variety of ways, ranging from outright denial of the problem to downright suppression. Some responses are comprehensive, as in the Chicago Area Projects launched by Shaw and McKay, or the multifaceted law enforcement suppression approach found in the Los Angeles region. Others are local and/or piecemeal, based in one agency or targeted at one gang, for instance. To capture how far this multiplicity of approaches has gone beyond what Park's Chapter 5 of *The City* originally envisioned, we turn in this last section to three issues: (1) Park's notion of a "new social science," (2) some obstacles presented by characteristics of contemporary gangs, and (3) some questions about gang intervention in the next century.

Social Science and Social Intervention

Park and Burgess wrote independently about the uses of social science (most specifically, sociology) to guide intervention into remediable social conditions in urban settings. In Chapter 5 of *The City,* Park declared, "A new social science is coming into existence." In an era when sociology and social work were far less independent disciplines than is now the case, Park envisioned an interaction between community experimentation carried out by social agencies and the development of empirical knowledge. This interaction

> will presently enable us to interpret these experiments, redefine the problem, and eventually gain a deeper insight into the social conditions and the social processes under which not merely juvenile delinquency but other forms of personal and social disorganization occur.

This prediction was made under the heading "The Gang and the Local Community."[25]

Burgess, however, seemed less sanguine about the possibilities. Writing in Chapter 8 of *The City,* he noted at the time that the social sciences—again, referring specifically to sociology—"had little to offer as a scientific basis for social work" and that little of what was available could be used in practice. He also noted something that has since constantly been reported by gang scholars—that is, "the recalcitrance of the boys' gang" and its endemic opposition to attempts at intervention. In assessing the potential for a social scientific base to social intervention, Burgess posed two questions and gave answers that, taken in their generic form, strike us as most apt: "Can neighborhood work have a scientific basis? It can have a scientific foundation if it will base its activities upon a study of social forces," and "Is neighborhood work prepared to base its justification for existence upon facts rather than upon sentiment?"[26]

If we simply transform these queries to apply to gang intervention in any form (including prevention through local law enforcement), we can fairly conclude that despite Park's prediction of the "new social science," we have not come very far during the last three quarters of a century. New scientific data and principals are now available, but their application to gang intervention is little advanced since those early days in Chicago.

One of the more useful descriptions of approaches to gang intervention has been provided by Irving Spergel and his associates, who worked out of Chicago but used surveys of dozens of gang programs throughout the nation (with rather heavy input from Los Angeles).[27] Spergel and Curry outline five basic approaches.

Community Organization. Represented, first, by the Chicago Area Projects and copied in various forms elsewhere, this approach emphasizes empowering community residents to reassert informal social controls on neighborhood youth. This is generally done in collaboration with or through leadership from local social agencies, churches, and other community groups. Street gang workers were originally an important component of this approach.

Opportunities Provision. This approach rests on the assumption that gang members (or potential members) can be weaned away from the gang only through offering alternative activities and the training that would allow members to use those activities. Local communities have employed job training and opportunities, educational tutoring and counseling, recreation, and formal programs such as Head Start, Job Corps, and CETA.

Social Intervention. This involves attempts to bring community and gang members into better connection with each other, the major mechanism being the street gang worker noted under the heading "Community Organization." The aim of street workers or "detached workers" (detached from their agency offices and assigned to work with gang members at the latter's "offices," i.e., street corners, parks, homes) is to transform the values of gang members, reduce their criminal involvement, and lessen their dependence on the gang structure. Using their one-to-one relationships, workers employed an eclectic mix of methods in which counseling, group work, and opportunities provision were paramount.

Suppression. This is the approach taken by law enforcement agencies, principally the police but in many instances prosecution and corrections agencies as well. Suppression here means more than normal law enforcement and includes extra efforts designed specifically to crack down on gangs as units and gang members as individuals. The techniques include police sweeps of gang areas, reduced correctional caseloads for gang members, special gang prosecution units within district and city attorney offices, and legislation that enhances gang member convictions and sentences.

Organizational Change. Here, the strategy is to alter or energize components of social institutions to make them more responsive to gang problems. Typical targets include schools, which often prefer to ignore gang students; recreational agencies that prohibit gang members from using their facilities; businesses and unions that close their doors to gang members; and the criminal justice system, which tends to stereotype rather than individuate its gang clients. The notion is that institutional change must proceed to allow for change in gang member behavior.

Overall, surprisingly few careful, independent evaluations have been carried out on these different approaches.[28] One clear statement can be made, however: Precious few of the programs encompassing any of the five approaches described above have been built on research findings about gang development, gang members, gang behavior, or their community contexts. The social science predicted by Park has not significantly evolved because program developers have relied on their own beliefs and values or their own personal and work experiences. Community organizational approaches tend to be based on social work principles that do not accommodate to the peculiar characteristics of street gangs. Individual counseling and provision of opportunities for youth seldom deal with the counteracting dynamics of gang membership. Street work programs—sound data exist to support this conclusion—inadvertently reinforce gang cohesiveness, thereby extending gang life and increasing gang activity. Attempts at institutional change have proved far weaker than bureaucratic resistance to the targeted institutions (schools, local political organizations, the justice system, etc.). Finally, gang suppression attempts via enhanced law enforcement, uniformly unevaluated, nonetheless seem to be associated with continuing or increasing levels of gang activity (perhaps mirroring the cohesion-building results of street work programs).

Examples of all these approaches have been, at one time or another, implemented in Los Angeles (city, county, and region), yet little in the way of serious attempts at evaluation has happened since the 1960s. Nothing in the increased patterns of gang activity suggests success for such programs. In addition, these programs of prevention, intervention, and suppression have been almost completely uncoordinated.

The Office of Juvenile Justice and Delinquency Prevention (OJJDP), an arm of the U.S. Department of Justice, has recently raised questions about the effectiveness of a possible coordinated, comprehensive program. Seeking an exemplar of a comprehensive approach, OJJDP took a close look at the Los Angeles system and recognized the multiplicity of approaches that remained uncoordinated. Thereafter, OJJDP allocated funds to Irving Spergel to undertake a national survey of gang interventions, with an emphasis on suppressive approaches, to develop a comprehensive model.

The results of that work, including the fivefold categorization noted earlier, have led to a pilot project in the Little Village section of Chicago and the award of program funds to five jurisdictions elsewhere to develop comprehensive gang programs.[29] As of this writing, those model programs are in their third years. It is OJJDP's stated intention to see their implementation as a test of their use in reducing gang programs. Broadly viewed, this could mean the confirmation of Park's social science prediction, more than seventy-five years later.

Obstacles Presented by the Gang Situation

One implication of the proliferation of street gangs across the country despite efforts to control them is that gangs may now be more resistant to intervention than was the case in earlier decades. There are several reasons to suspect that gangs have become a more recalcitrant problem. Among these are the change in gang ethnicity, the increase of the urban underclass, the diffusion of gang culture, and the effects of lethal weaponry.

As noted earlier, gang populations nationally have become primarily black or Latino, with far smaller numbers of whites and Asians. For the most part, people of color are the least accepted by the white majority in this nation, where racism remains a dominant social factor. Likewise in Los Angeles, gang membership is predominantly black and Latino. Latino gang members are primarily of Mexican heritage, although, more recently, Central American (principally Salvadoran) gang membership has increased. Among Asian gangs in the area, one finds a great diversity, including Chinese, Japanese, Korean, Vietnamese, Cambodian, Filipino, and Samoan. Black, Latino, and Asian populations have proved to be least assimilated by a larger white society. The results in discrimination, as seen in jobs, schooling, and provision of health and social resources, are the very results that breed the alienation and sense of hopelessness that pervade communities spawning gangs. Street gangs are a product, in this sense, of ethnic and racial origin in a context where ethnic and racial origin is a matter of some consequence. The importance of skin color to whites, and what skin color symbolizes to whites, will continue to furrow the ground in which gangs grow.

Closely related to this have been the spread and intensification of the urban underclass in America—the "pervasive and persistent poverty" that accompanies racial discrimination and segregation. When skeptics note the proliferation of gangs to smaller and smaller jurisdictions, we counter with the demonstration that this mirrors the occurrence of segregated black and Latino areas within these jurisdictions, and, predictably, black and Latino gangs emerge in the most segregated black and Latino areas of town. Segregation is not a big-city problem but a problem wherever a sufficient minority population exists.

Especially since the early 1980s, we have seen an increasing gap between the haves and the have-nots, and from the latter, urban street gangs develop. Only two "hopeful" developments occur to us. First, there will be a self-limiting component to the spread of the urban underclass. As it plateaus, so gang proliferation may also plateau. Second, in some areas including Los Angeles, minorities will in time become the majority. Then, within such jurisdictions, it will be poverty or social class alone, not class plus racism, that yields social problems such as gangs. This, too, should provide a brake to gang growth.

A third obstacle to gang control is the increasing spread of gang culture into mainstream youth culture. Twenty years ago, targeted attacks on youth exhibiting gang clothing or argot might have had some limited effect. But now, these styles are youth styles—the sagging pants, earrings, tattoos, styles of address, and the rest are shared by many youth through exposure to the media, movies, music, and antigang programs in school. Through the media, we have taught American teens how to talk, walk, and act like gang members. Yet culture is hard to outlaw, and behaviors common to gang and many nongang youth alike cannot be forbidden or punished without also affecting the wrong targets. In one sense, and certainly inadvertently, gangs are mainstreaming. Because the mainstream in a democracy, by definition, is a protected population, wider youth acceptance of the accoutrements of gang styles provides the protective coloring within which gang members can now more successfully hide.

The fourth obstacle to gang control is, oddly, the instrument that most forcefully requires that control, namely, the sophisticated and deadly weaponry now accessible to gang members. Despite numerous public comments to the effect that gang killings by firearms are driven principally by the drug business, the primary target of gang shooters is other, mostly rival, gang members. The obstacle to gang control is created by at least two interacting factors, the unwillingness to implement gun control in the United States and the "demand character" of gun-based violence. The first of these will be obvious to the reader, but the second perhaps less so.

In prior decades, intergang fighting was accomplished principally with nonlethal weapons—fists, sticks, knives, tire irons, and chains, as well as zip guns and other only occasionally effective single-shot firearms. Although the stated gang norms required retaliation for rival gang attacks, the norms were as often broken as not. Injuries were seldom fatal and could often be either ignored, accepted, or "avenged" by an equally ineffective retaliation or show of force.

With the advent of today's sophisticated weaponry, however, surefire semiautomatic handguns being the most common, the demand character of each confrontation increases—it calls for an equal and opposite response. The death or serious wounding of a fellow gang member is not easily ignored and is too public and obvious an affront to be merely accumulated as part of a tally of grievances; it more commonly "demands" a response. Rivalry feeds on itself in the type of rhetoric that resists efforts at rational control or peacemaking. Ironically, in some recent gang truces, successful, if temporary, reductions in violence have followed only in the wake of excessive killings (an oxymoron in most contexts). These are internal reactions among and between gangs, not generally engineered by adult control agents. In the absence of a truly significant reduction in firearm availability, it is difficult to foresee any form of social control that might overwhelm gang rivalry; the rival gang is the first and foremost source of gang cohesiveness, and gangs can maintain themselves only by feeding their own cohesion. Lethal guns provide ideal fodder in such situations.

Gangs in the Twenty-First Century

In this chapter, we have intended to portray the current gang picture in pessimistic tones. Having followed the gang situation for many years and having participated in various attempts at gang prevention and control, we do not see the next decade as anything but continuation of the current, deteriorating trends. For the reader seeking or needing a more positive outlook, we emphasize three concerns. These concerns must be addressed both in Los Angeles as a microcosm of the gang world at large and in the nation as a whole, where the patterns of Los Angeles have much room to grow if they are not interrupted.

First, if gangs are to be controlled, we cannot simply attack them in the naive hope that some sort of magical deterrence of potential gang members will take place. The urban street gang does not emerge and sustain itself in a vacuum but is, rather, a by-product of its community. Although enforcement procedures should be aimed at keeping a lid on serious gang offending and at reinforcing the limits of acceptable behavior, and attempts to limit firearm accessibility should continue, the heavy work must take place within gang-involved communities. In the near future, we expect to find more attention being paid to developing and reinforcing local community control—informal social control—in collaboration with law, welfare, educational, and employment institutions. Park's expectations for a "new social science" would be better realized if valid data on the risk and protective factors in gang development and gang enlistment were integrated into both current and new forms of community-based social intervention.

Second, we urge that more concentrated attention be paid to the group dynamics that characterize gangs. We must understand the requirements of gang cohesiveness, the oppositional culture that develops, and the self-reinforcing nature of gang values in the context of community alienation to overcome them.[30] Most gang intervention procedures, we believe, inadvertently strengthen gang bonds. To avoid reinforcement of such bonds, we need to better grasp the dynamics of this process. In the face of failure, simply pouring more resources into what we have already been doing is hardly rational. Understanding precedes effective social engineering.

Finally, some directions for further gang research need further encouragement. Recent descriptions of the major forms of gang structure need confirmation and then must be carefully correlated with different forms of intervention.[31] Increasing work on ethnic and gender differences in gang functioning similarly calls for investigation of the practical implications. We need more research on how gang members "mature out" of their involvement and become integrated into the mainstream of the community. This research includes determining what types of gang members benefit from suppression (such as periods of incarceration at various life stages) and what types of members become further entrenched in criminal styles following suppression efforts.

Because most gang ethnographies are carried out at times and in locations convenient to the researchers, and because individual gang ethnographers tend to ask different questions or to employ differing procedures, there is an urgent need for systematic ethnographies. These would, in addition to following through on idiosyncratic interests and situations, undertake to study questions determined a priori by a consortium of interested scholars. This process could yield far more generalizable information about such issues as gang member characteristics, gang structures, gang member behavior, community characteristics, and gang responses to attempts at intervention.

Each of these suggested research questions responds to Park's expectations for the new social science that would drive and improve community organization. Although Park was not speaking specifically to gang issues, it seems highly likely that he would have, had gang issues in his time taken on the forms and proportions that we know to be the case today. Gang understanding is first and foremost a community concern. The difference now is that we have social science methods appropriate to the task and an increasing store of gang-specific knowledge to provide hope for rational applications of those methods.

NOTES

1. Frederic M. Thrasher, *The Gang: A Study of 1,313 Gangs in Chicago* (Chicago: University of Chicago Press, 1927).

2. Many of the data reported throughout this chapter are derived from studies funded by the National Institute of Justice (91-IJ-CX-K004 and 93-IJ-CX-0044). Points of view or opinions expressed herein are our own and do not necessarily represent the official position of the U.S. Department of Justice.

3. Malcolm W. Klein, *The American Street Gang: Its Nature, Prevalence and Control* (New York: Oxford University Press, 1995); John P. Moore and Craig P. Terrett, *Highlights of the 1997 National Youth Gang Survey* (Washington, D.C.: Office of Juvenile Justice and Delinquency Prevention, 1999).

4. Klein, *The American Street Gang.*

5. Hedy Bookin-Weiner and Ruth Horowitz, "The End of the Youth Gang: Fad or Fact," *Criminology* 21 (fall 1983): 585-601.

6. Joan W. Moore, *Homeboys: Gangs, Drugs and Prison in the Barrios of Los Angeles* (Philadelphia: Temple University Press, 1978); James Diego Vigil, *Barrio Gangs: Street Life and Identity in Southern California* (Houston: University of Texas Press, 1988).

7. Among these have been Chicago, Philadelphia, New York, Boston, Los Angeles, San Francisco, San Diego, Milwaukee, Columbus, Cleveland, Kenosha, St. Louis, Phoenix, Kansas City, Detroit, Denver, Rochester, Honolulu, San Jose, San Antonio, and Long Beach.

8. Some researchers more than others are hesitant to work with the police or to trust their information. Police data, almost inevitably, manifest problems of validity that require careful attention from the research community.

9. Cheryl L. Maxson, Monica L. Whitlock, and Malcolm W. Klein, "Vulnerability to Street Gang Membership: Implications for Practice," *Social Service Review* 72 (1998): 70-91; Jeffrey Fagan, "The Social Organization of Drug Use and Drug Dealing Among Urban Gangs," *Criminology* 27 (1989): 633-669; Terence B. Thornberry, Marvin D. Krohn, Alan J. Lizotte, and Deborah Chard-Wierschem, "The Role of Juvenile Gangs in Facilitating Delinquent Behavior," *Journal of Research in Crime and Delinquency* 30 (1993): 55-87; Finn-Aage L. Esbensen and David Huizinga, "Gangs, Drugs, and Delinquency in a Survey of Urban Youth," *Criminology* 31 (1993): 565-589; L. Thomas Winfree Jr., Kathy Fuller, Teresa Vigil, and G. Larry Mays, "The Definition and Measurement of Gang Status: Policy Implications for Juvenile Justice," *Juvenile and Family Court Journal* 42 (1992): 29-37.

10. Walter B. Miller, "Lower Class Culture as a Generating Milieu of Gang Delinquency," *Journal of Social Issues* 14 (1958): 5-19; Malcolm W. Klein, *Street Gangs and Street Workers* (Englewood Cliffs, N.J.: Prentice-Hall, 1971); Joan W. Moore, *Going Down to the Barrio* (Philadelphia: Temple University Press, 1991); Thrasher, *The Gang;* Fagan, "The Social Organization of Drug Use and Drug Dealing Among Urban Gangs"; Irving A. Spergel, *Racketville, Slumtown, Haulberg* (Chicago: University of Chicago Press, 1964).

11. Walter B. Miller, "Gangs, Groups, and Serious Youth Crime," in *Critical Issues in Juvenile Delinquency,* ed. David Schichor and Delos H. Kelly (Lexington, Mass.: D. C. Heath, 1980), 115-138.

12. Irving A. Spergel, *The Youth Gang Problem: A Community Approach* (New York: Oxford University Press, 1995); John M. Hagedorn, *People and Folks: Gangs, Crime and the Underclass in a Rustbelt City* (Chicago: Lake View Press, 1988); George Knox, *An Introduction to Gangs* (Berrien Springs, Mich.: Van de Vere, 1991); Carolyn Rebecca Block and Richard Block, "Street Gang Crime in Chicago," in *The Modern Gang Reader,* ed. Malcolm W. Klein, Cheryl L. Maxson, and Jody Miller (Los Angeles: Roxbury, 1995), 202-210.

13. Malcolm W. Klein and Lois Y. Crawford, "Groups, Gangs, and Cohesiveness," *Journal of Research in Crime and Delinquency* 30 (1967): 75-85; Hagedorn, *People and Folks;* Scott Decker and Barrik Van Winkle, *Life in the Gang* (New York: Cambridge University Press, 1996).

14. Klein, *Street Gangs and Street Workers;* James F. Short Jr. and Fred L. Strodtbeck, *Group Process and Gang Delinquency* (Chicago: University of Chicago Press, 1965, 1974); Decker and Van Winkle, *Life in the Gang.*

15. See Spergel, *The Youth Gang Problem,* for a detailed discussion of this issue.

16. A description of an Orange County program is provided by Douglas R. Kent and Peggy Smith, "The Tri-Agency Resource Gang Enforcement Team: A Selective Approach to Reduce Gang Crime," in *The Modern Gang Reader,* ed. Malcolm W. Klein, Cheryl L. Maxson, and Jody Miller (Los Angeles: Roxbury, 1995), 292-296.

17. Societal-level responses to gang issues provide a stark contrast with Madeleine Stoner's description (Chapter 8, this volume) of the slow evolution of perspectives on the homeless as becoming more sympathetic, yielding widespread social service responses. This portrayal differs markedly from the gang image evolution during the recent past, as gangs—equally featured in the media and in political circles—have become demonized and subjected to suppression rather than social service. Yet both are widely acknowledged as resulting from social *structural* problems even more than personal inadequacies, and both are often placed in an urban underclass context of understanding those problems. Both are featured by strong components of *marginalization* (albeit of different types). Finally, both issues present particular challenges to Los Angeles: Stoner notes that Los Angeles encompasses the second largest concentration of homeless people in the country, and it clearly ranks first in the size of its gang population.

18. For analyses of drive-by shootings, see William B. Sanders, *Gangbangs and Drivebys: Grounded Culture and Juvenile Gang Violence* (New York: Aldine de Gruyter, 1994) and H.

Range Hutson, Dierdre Anglin, and M. J. Pratts, "Adolescents and Children Injured or Killed in Drive-by Shootings in Los Angeles," *New England Journal of Medicine* 330 (1994): 324-327.

19. For extended discussions of approaches to defining gang homicide, see Cheryl L. Maxson and Malcolm W. Klein, "Defining Gang Homicide: An Updated Look at Member and Motive Approaches," in *Gangs in America,* 2nd ed., ed. C. Ronald Huff (Thousand Oaks, Calif.: Sage, 1996), 3-20; Cheryl L. Maxson and Malcolm W. Klein, "Street Gang Violence: Twice as Great or Half as Great?" in *Gangs in America,* 1st ed., ed. C. Ronald Huff (Newbury Park, Calif.: Sage, 1990), 71-102; Cheryl L. Maxson, "Gang Homicide," in *Homicide Studies: A Sourcebook of Social Research,* ed. M. Dwayne Smith and Margaret A. Zahn (Thousand Oaks, Calif.: Sage, 1999).

20. Malcolm W. Klein, "Street Gang Cycles," in *Crime,* ed. James Q. Wilson and Joan Petersilia (San Francisco: Institute for Contemporary Studies, 1995), 217-236.

21. Malcolm W. Klein and Cheryl L. Maxson, "Gang Structures, Crime Patterns, and Police Responses," report submitted to the National Institute of Justice, 1996.

22. Knox, *An Introduction to Gangs;* Chicago Crime Commission, "Public Enemy Number One" (Chicago: Chicago Crime Commission, 1995).

23. Cheryl L. Maxson, "Gang Members on the Move: The Role of Migration in the Proliferation of Street Gangs in the U.S.," *OJJDP Bulletin* (Washington, D.C.: Office of Justice Programs, October 1998); Cheryl L. Maxson, Kristi J. Woods, and Malcolm W. Klein, "Street Gang Migration: How Big a Threat?" *National Institute of Justice Journal* 230 (February 1996): 26-31.

24. Cheryl L. Maxson, "Gang Members on the Move."

25. Robert E. Park, "Community Organization and Juvenile Delinquency," in *The City: Suggestions for Investigation of Human Behavior in the Urban Environment,* by Robert E. Park, Ernest W. Burgess, and Roderick D. McKenzie (Chicago: University of Chicago Press, 1925, 1967; Midway reprint, 1984), 110-111.

26. Ernest W. Burgess, "Can Neighborhood Work Have a Scientific Basis?" in *The City: Suggestions for Investigation of Human Behavior in the Urban Environment,* by Robert E. Park, Ernest W. Burgess, and Roderick D. McKenzie (Chicago: University of Chicago Press, 1925, 1967; Midway reprint, 1984), 142, 154.

27. Irving A. Spergel and G. David Curry, "Strategies and Perceived Agency Effectiveness in Dealing With the Youth Gang Problem," in *Gangs in America,* 1st ed., ed. C. Ronald Huff (Newbury Park, Calif.: Sage, 1990), 288-309.

28. But see Klein, *The American Street Gang,* and Spergel, *The Youth Gang Problem.*

29. These funds have been awarded to Tucson and Mesa, Arizona; Riverside, California; Bloomington, Illinois; and San Antonio, Texas.

30. For a discussion of oppositional culture, see Joan Moore and James Diego Vigil, "Chicano Gangs: Group Norms and Individual Factors Relating to Adult Criminality," *Atzlan* 18 (1989): 31.

31. Klein and Maxson, "Gang Structures, Crime Patterns, and Police Responses."

Religion in Los Angeles
Patterns of Spiritual Practice
in a Postmodern City

EDITOR'S
COMMENTS

The place of religion in American community life is a hotly contested topic. Scholars and social commentators have long predicted the slow but persistent decline of religious beliefs and practices in industrialized societies. Yet as Donald E. Miller discovers in this chapter, the numbers of religious adherents in the United States are growing steadily. This trend may be driven by myriad factors, not the least of which are the high rates of international immigration from countries with a strong faith base (e.g., Roman Catholics from Mexico) and the proliferation of New Age religious communities.

At the same time, religious communities have become increasingly called on to provide essential human services to the needy, largely as a consequence of the retreat from the formal welfare state. In addition, many churches, synagogues, and mosques have begun to adopt aggressive stances on advocacy issues pertaining to human rights, labor contracts, immigration, and so on. Miller suggests that a renaissance of religion, founded in an incredible diversity of peoples, is characteristic of postmodern urbanism.

In *The City*, three chapters by Park and by Burgess confirm the role of religion in community life, but Park, most notably, emphasizes its continuous readjustment to the evolving conditions in great cities, especially since the printed page has "so largely taken the place of the pulpit in the interpretation of life." Yet still, religious belief is one factor in the creation of the "moral regions" so characteristic of great cities. (Analogous processes give rise to "vice districts" and other spatial expressions of social affiliations.)

In the unfolding "mentality" of city life, Park draws particular attention to the role of "magic" in individual and collective behaviors. In this context, magic is perhaps best understood as congeries of diverse belief systems, superstitions, and moral constructs that exist in stark contrast with the precepts of "rational thought." For Park, the city is a crucible of reason. But in drawing this distinction between magic and rational thought, Park readily concedes that many areas of human experience have not yet been "fully rationalized," most notably, the fields of medicine and religion.

QUOTES FROM
THE CITY

The city, and particularly the great city, in which more than elsewhere human relations are likely to be impersonal and rational, defined in terms of interest and in terms of cash, is in a very real sense a laboratory for the investigation of collective behavior. Strikes and minor revolutionary movements are endemic in the urban environment. Cities, and particularly the great cities, are in unstable equilibrium. The result is that the vast casual and mobile aggregations which constitute our urban populations are in a state of perpetual agitation, swept by every new wind of doctrine, subject to constant alarms, and in consequence the community is in a chronic condition of crisis. . . (22)

. . . In the great city, where the population is unstable, where parents and children are employed out of the house and often in distant parts of the city, where thousands of people live side by side for years without so much as a bowing acquaintance, these intimate relationships of the primary group are weakened and the moral order which rested upon them is gradually dissolved.

Under the disintegrating influences of city life most of our traditional institutions, the church, the school, and the family, have been greatly modified. . . . The church . . . which has lost much of its influence since the printed page has so largely taken the place of the pulpit in the interpretation of life, seems at present to be in process of readjustment to the new conditions. . . . (24)

Great cities have always been the melting-pots of races and of cultures. Out of the vivid and subtle interactions of which they have been the centers, there have come the newer breeds and the newer social types. The great cities of the United States, for example, have drawn from isolation of their native villages great masses of rural populations of Europe and America. Under the shock of the new contacts the latent energies of these primitive peoples have been released, and the subtler processes of interaction have brought into existence not merely vocational, but temperamental, types. . . . (40)

. . . It is inevitable that individuals who seek the same forms of excitement, whether that excitement be furnished by a horse race or by grand opera, should find themselves from time to time in the same places. The result of this is that in the organization which city life spontaneously assumes the population tends to segregate itself, not merely in accordance with its interests, but in accordance with its tastes or its temperaments. The resulting distribution of the population is likely to be quite different from that brought about by occupational interests or economic conditions.

Every neighborhood, under the influences which tend to distribute and segregate city populations, may assume the character of a "moral region." Such, for example, are the vice districts, which are found in most cities. A moral region is not necessarily a place of abode. It may be a mere rendezvous, a place of resort. . . . (43)

We must then accept these "moral regions" and the more or less eccentric and exceptional people who inhabit them, in a sense, at least, as part of the natural, if not the normal, life of a city. . . . (45)

Because of the opportunity it offers, particularly to the exceptional and abnormal types of man, a great city tends to spread out and lay bare to the public view in a massive manner all the human characters and traits which are ordinarily obscured and suppressed in smaller communities. The city, in short, shows the good and evil in human nature in excess. It is this fact, perhaps, more than any other, which justifies the view that would make of the city a laboratory or clinic in which human nature and social processes may be conveniently and profitably studied. . . . (45-46)

The reason the modern man is a more rational animal than his more primitive ancestor is possibly because he lives in a city, where most of the interests and values of life have been rationalized, reduced to measurable units, and even made objects of barter and sale. In the city—and particularly in great cities—the external conditions of existence are so evidently contrived to meet man's clearly recognized needs that the least intellectual of peoples are inevitably led to think in deterministic and mechanistic terms. . . . (130)

In fact, if we define them strictly, . . . we may say that reason and reflective thinking were born in the city. . . . (130)

Magic may be regarded, therefore, as an index, a rough way, not merely of the mentality, but of the general cultural level of races, peoples, and classes. It is even possible that a more thorough-going analysis of the mental processes involved in magic and rational thought will permit us to measure the mentalities of social groups with as much precision, at least, as we now measure and grade . . . the intelligence of individuals. At least we should know in this case what we were measuring, namely, the extent and degree to which a given group or class had acquired the ability and the habit of thinking in rational rather than magical terms. . . . (131)

It is evident that we are not to assume, as otherwise we might, that there is no area of the experience in which primitive or preliterate people think realistically and rationally. On the other hand, in contrasting primitive mentality with that of civilized man, we need not assume—except for the sake of the contrast—that the thinking of civilized man is always and everywhere either rational or scientific. As a matter of fact, there are still wide areas of our experience that have not as yet been fully rationalized, notably the fields of medicine and religion. (140)

Friday Prayer at Masjid Umar Ibn-Al Khattab, Los Angeles, 1999
Photograph by Jerry Berndt. Used by permission of the USC Center for Religion and Civic Culture.

CHAPTER 10

**Religion in Los
Angeles**
Patterns of Spiritual
Practice in a
Postmodern City

DONALD E. MILLER

Los Angeles is the most diverse religious population in the world, as well as one of the most fluid, dynamic, and entrepreneurial. All the major world traditions have representation in Los Angeles, and it has incubated many new religious movements. Although Southern California is viewed as a haven for New Age spiritual movements, most residents of Los Angeles identify with the Judeo-Christian tradition. In so doing, however, they exhibit an individualistic spirit that distinguishes them from other regions of the country, forging personal religious identities that often depart from their childhood upbringing.

In the Yellow Pages listings of religious groups for the 213 telephone area code—which includes only Central Los Angeles and none of the outlying areas of Los Angeles County—there are 2,276 congregations or groups. Not included in this list are numerous storefront churches and groups that elect not to pay for inclusion in the Yellow Pages and the hundreds of quasi-religious groups (e.g., meditation courses and palm readers) that constitute a large part of the spiritual ferment of Los Angeles. I conservatively estimate that there are 10,000 religious congregations, fellowships, and formalized groups in Los Angeles County. Some of these groups are historic denominations, but there are also many religions that were brought by immigrants to the region and serve important roles in mediating between the "old country" and their new culture.

Particularly revealing is a street-by-street assessment of the religious ecology of urban neighborhoods in Los Angeles. In the 90018 zip code near the USC campus are eighty-three religious groups in a 3.3 square mile area, far outnumbering, for example, the number of liquor stores in this low-income neighborhood. Within this small area is an enormous diversity of faith traditions, including Catholic, Baptist, Methodist, Presbyterian, Lutheran, Seventh-Day Adventist, Jehovah's Witnesses, Foursquare, Church of God in Christ, Rastafarian, and Islamic, as well as numerous Pentecostal and independent churches. In addition, there are churches whose client base is primarily African American, Latino, or Korean. There are congregations that have 10,000 members attending weekly, as well as storefronts with a dozen participants. From a marketing standpoint, there is something for everyone.

Nationally, it is estimated that there are approximately 350,000 congregations in the United States, each serving multiple functions. For example, religion is one of the primary institutions through which people experience community. It is also one of the most important locations where political debate and moral discourse occur. It is a place where children can be nurtured, life cycle crises negotiated, and inspiration found for confronting the difficulties of an urban environment. In 1992, Americans gave $57 billion in support of religion, $9 billion more than the movie industry's total revenues and fourteen times the combined amount spent on professional baseball, football, and basketball.[1]

THE CHICAGO SCHOOL

If Robert Park were to visit Los Angeles at the beginning of the twenty-first century, he would undoubtedly be surprised by the level of religious activity. In his chapter in *The City,* "Magic, Mentality, and City Life," the underlying assumptions are that (a) religion is being replaced by science, (b) only "primitive" people are tempted by the magic of religion, and (c) city life requires a rational and empirical approach that precludes religious commitment.[2] In this regard, he was mirroring the perspective of many sociologists of the time who accepted the inevitability of growing secularization. Theorists such as Karl Marx, Max Weber, Émile Durkheim, and Sigmund Freud were captives of an Enlightenment worldview that uncritically accepted the conflict between religion and science as one that would inevitably result in the triumph of science. Although some theorists, such as Max Weber, had more nuanced interpretations—believing that science could never answer Tolstoy's question, "What shall we do and how shall we live?"—nevertheless, there was an implicit assumption that religion was a doomed institution given the progressive routinization and bureaucratization of human life.[3] Somewhat in jest, Robert Park suggests that the only place religion might survive in the future would be on the golf course and in coping with the unpredictable twists and turns of the stock market. For him, religion is magical thinking that "savages" and "primitives" employ in coping with the unknown. Religion is an escapist, fear-based, childlike response to the world. Unlike a theorist such as William James, he had little appreciation of the role of religion as a source of inspiration, moral guidance, and affirmation of those transcendent mysteries of life that add depth and meaning to human experience.[4]

Reality is sometimes difficult to cope with, even for sociologists. Nevertheless, in the last decade, an increasing number of sociologists have disagreed with the secularization hypothesis as articulated by the founding fathers of their discipline.[5] When people kept attending church or synagogue—including those who were well educated and middle class—and when religion failed to decrease in saliency as a variable in explaining people's voting behavior and lifestyle choices, then sociologists were forced to reconcile their theories with people's behavior—even if they, themselves, were not committing personal resources to religion. Hence, from the perspective of many contemporary sociologists, Robert Park's observations on religion seem outdated and without nuance. On the other hand, the methods of the Chicago School—especially the emphasis on field research and neighborhood case studies— have a newfound appreciation among sociologists of religion.[6] Qualitative studies of congregations and religious movements are viewed as helpful complements to statis- tical analysis of religious behavior. Recently, there is revived interest in an ecological approach in which religious institutions are seen as one asset among many within a neighborhood.

NATIONAL GALLUP POLL DATA

Although the religious ecology continually changes, there is little evidence to sup- port the generalization that religion is declining in the United States. Despite the mythology surrounding the view that religious freedom was the reason for the founding of this country, church attendance rates in the mid-1700s were a fraction of today's figures. In 1995, 43 percent of the respondents surveyed said that they had attended religious services within the past seven days, and this figure has held relatively constant since the question was first asked by the Gallup organization in 1939.[7] In contrast, it is estimated that church attendance in the early years of this nation's history was less than half the current amount.[8]

As one might expect, Gallup surveys reveal that membership in religious organi- zations is substantially higher than weekly attendance. For example, in 1995, more than two thirds (69 percent) of respondents were members of a church or syna- gogue. On matters of belief, Americans are highly religious: 83 percent in 1995 believe that there is a God, and another 12 percent believe in a spirit or life force. Americans are also rather orthodox in their beliefs, with 84 percent believing that Jesus Christ is God or the Son of God.[9]

Regarding religious preference, 58 percent of respondents in a national Gallup poll in 1995 indicated that they were Protestant, 25 percent were Roman Catholic, 2 percent were Jewish, and a surprising 2 percent said they were Mormon.[10] These different religious populations, however, attend religious services at different rates. For example, African Americans are more religious than the general population on many measures; they attend church more frequently (50 percent said they attended last week), attesting that religion is important in their own lives (82 percent vs. 58 percent for the general population), and 82 percent say that they are church mem- bers (vs. 69 percent for all respondents). Historically, Roman Catholics have attended worship services at a higher rate than Protestants, but current rates are nearly identical, representing a slide for Catholics of about 20 percentage points from the pre-Vatican II era. Jews, traditionally, have attended services at about half the rate of Protestants and Catholics.

In a comparison of attendance on different demographic variables, some sur- prises do not fit common stereotypes. For example, people with annual incomes greater than $50,000 are as likely to attend church or synagogue as people earning less than $30,000. People who went to college are as likely to attend religious services as those who did not. Less surprisingly, older people are more likely to attend religious services on a weekly basis; 34 percent of those under thirty years of age attended church or synagogue, in comparison with 40 percent of people thirty to forty-nine years of age, 46 percent who were fifty to sixty-four, and 53 percent of those sixty-five and older.

According to Gallup surveys, people living in the western United States are least likely to attend church or synagogue (35 percent); individuals living on the East Coast are the next least likely (41 percent), followed by those in the Midwest (45 percent), while those living in the South are the most likely (47 percent). These differences are even more exaggerated when comparing membership statistics: Only 53 percent of those living in the West are members of a church or synagogue, in comparison with 69 percent in the East, 72 percent in the Midwest, and 77 percent in the South.

Many of these regional differences continue to be evident when respondents reply to the question, "How important would you say religion is in your own life?" (See Table 10.1.)

Although those living in the West value religion less than the rest of the U.S. population, 80 percent of respondents claim that religion is either *fairly important* or *very important,* which scarcely supports the secularization hypothesis. Furthermore, although there are differences between urban and rural respondents, surveys do not support Robert Park's view that city life will lead to the diminution of religion (see Table 10.2). People living in urban areas are slightly more likely to state that religion is *not very important* in their lives, but the difference between those living in cities (14 percent), suburbs (12 percent), and in rural regions (8 percent) is relatively modest.

Perhaps it is not surprising that 90 percent of those surveyed say they believe in heaven, whereas only 73 percent believe in hell, and that although 96 percent believe in God, only 65 percent believe in the devil. Given the recent spate of movies featuring angels, it may also be unsurprising that 72 percent say they believe in angelic beings and 79 percent affirm their belief in miracles. What seems more contradictory, however, especially considering that all but a few people identify with the Judeo-Christian tradition, is that 27 percent of the respondents indicate that they believe in reincarnation and 23 percent believe in astrology, neither of which is consistent with orthodox Christianity or Judaism. Also, persons under thirty years of age were much more likely to believe in angels than those older than fifty years; the same is true with respect to belief in miracles. Religion is not necessarily tied to church or synagogue attendance. Rather, there is a new distinction present in the vocabulary of the younger generation whereby "spirituality" is viewed as positive, while they reject "religion," which they associate with institutional expressions.

RELIGIOUS TRENDS IN CALIFORNIA

In comparing California with three other states—North Carolina, Ohio, and Massachusetts—some important differences emerge, as revealed in the following table

Table 10.1 The Regional Importance of Religion

Region	Very Important	Fairly Important	Not Very Important
East	51%	35%	13%
Midwest	58%	31%	10%
South	69%	22%	8%
West	48%	32%	19%

Table 10.2 Urban and Rural Variations in the Importance of Religion

Region	Very Important	Fairly Important	Not Very Important
Urban	57%	29%	14%
Suburban	54%	33%	12%
Rural	66%	25%	8%

from Phillip Hammond's *Religion and Personal Autonomy* (see Table 10.3).[11] California has the lowest percentage of people claiming a religious preference (80.9 percent). There are several religious populations, with an almost equal number of Roman Catholics (31.7 percent) and conservative Protestants (32.4 percent). Furthermore, if one combines moderate and liberal Protestants (totaling 22.5 percent), there is another distinct grouping, revealing a rather fragmented religious state made up of substantial numbers of Roman Catholics, conservative Protestants, and moderate/liberal Protestants. In addition, California's heterogeneity allows for more than twice as many people outside the Judeo-Christian fold as the three other states. When asked whether one practices a meditation technique "like those taught by Transcendental Meditation, Zen, etc.," 21 percent of the California respondents indicated that they did, a substantially higher percentage than in any other state (North Carolina, 6 percent; Ohio, 11 percent; and Massachusetts, 13 percent). That a fifth of the Californians claim to practice meditation is quite remarkable given that the examples cited (Transcendental Meditation and Zen) lie outside either the Jewish or Christian traditions. Also, perhaps predictably, the California sample was higher in its belief in reincarnation (30 percent).

One other trend distinguishes California from the other three states: It has the highest percentage of people who have ceased church attendance for two or more years (59 percent), which contrasts with 35 percent for North Carolina, 44 percent for Ohio, and 51 percent for Massachusetts. Hence, Californians demonstrate a capacity to make decisions about their religious life that may involve terminating unsatisfactory commitments to organized religion, but this does not mean that they are uninterested in spiritual matters. Summarizing the various characteristics of Cal-

Table 10.3 Religious Preferences in North Carolina, Ohio, Massachusetts, and California

	N.C.	*Ohio*	*Mass.*	*Calif.*
(% Claiming a Preference)	94.0	90.9	82.4	80.9
Liberal Protestant	3.3	6.2	13.3	10.0
Moderate Protestant	1.8	20.1	5.4	12.5
Conservative Protestant	74.2	34.0	15.2	32.4
Black Protestant	13.1	6.8	1.9	7.2
Roman Catholic	6.2	30.6	57.9	31.7
Jewish	0.7	1.1	4.4	2.8
Other Religion	0.7	1.2	1.9	3.4
	100%	100%	100%	100%

SOURCE: From Phillip E. Hammond, *Religion and Personal Autonomy: The Third Disestablishment in America* (Columbia: University of South Carolina Press, 1992).

ifornia respondents and comparing them with those from Massachusetts, Hammond states:

> Californians are somewhat more likely to have decreased their parish involvement (or dropped out altogether), but they are quite a bit more likely to assign some importance to religion, to engage in pious practices (including unorthodox meditation), and to hold more to both orthodox Christian doctrines and the one heterodox doctrine we asked about [i.e., meditation]. California compared to Massachusetts, in other words, is religiously more active; it is more religiously interested.[12]

Californians are much more prone to switch from the denominational family of their upbringings than are residents of the other three states. For example, only half of those raised as either liberal or moderate Protestants remained in that denominational family. Even Catholics lost three of ten members to other faiths, with many of the defectors eventually going to conservative Protestant churches. In all states, it is conservative Protestantism that tends to gain in the switching game. In contrast, when people switch from liberal Protestantism, it is usually to drop out of organized religion altogether, rather than to become a conservative Christian.

California illustrates a growing religious trend in America. Religious affiliation is something that people choose, rather than adopt as a matter of obligation. Simply because one comes from three generations of Presbyterians does not mean that one will raise his or her children as Presbyterians or even elect to affiliate with institutional religion at all.[13] The focus is not on religious tradition or tribal loyalty so much as on the religious group or philosophy that serves one's personal needs. Individuals feel increasingly free to switch religions, or even to invent one that combines elements from several traditions. Practicing Buddhist or Hindu-derived meditation techniques during the week and attending mass on Sunday morning is not an oxymoron. Many people view themselves as deeply spiritual, although they hold no formal membership in a church or synagogue.[14] In California, more than most other states, the locus of authority has been transferred from the institution to the individual. Although this may result in somewhat lower church attendance figures in a place such as Los Angeles, it does not mean that people are not serious about religion—especially when defined as spirituality.

RELIGION IN SOUTHERN CALIFORNIA

Southern California has a long-standing reputation for birthing new religious movements and being a haven for unconventional or exotic expressions of the spiritual quest. Three factors account for this fertile religious climate. First, people who moved west were often seeking a chance to start over, and, by leaving relatives and traditions behind in other states, they were free to make new religious associations—or none at all. Second, as the home of the entertainment industry, Los Angeles often attracts people who pride themselves on innovation and putting ideas and images together in novel ways. Third, Southern California is the recipient of hundreds of immigrant groups, all of which bring their religion and culture with them, introducing new patterns of thought and behavior and creating a complex reservoir of religious symbols and practices from which rootless individuals can choose to create their own bricolage of beliefs.

Groups that have found Southern California to be hospitable include several branches of the Theosophical Society, the Anthroposophical Society, the Church of Light, the Coptic Fellowship, the Church of Scientology, the Prosperos, Wicca, 3HO (associated with the guru Yogi Bhajan), Tenrikyo, Nichiren Shoshu, the Unification Church, the International Society for Krishna Consciousness, and the Vendanta Society.[15] All these groups are religiously innovative and are supplemented by more conventional imports from other countries, such as various branches of Buddhism, Hinduism, the Sikh religion, and Islam.

Southern California has also contributed to the birth of several religiously innovative Christian movements: in particular, Pentecostalism that flowered on Azusa Street in Los Angeles in 1906[16] and the Foursquare Gospel denomination that was founded by the flamboyant and colorful Aimee Semple McPherson.[17] More recently, Southern California has given rise to three movements that started in the 1960s and 1970s: Calvary Chapel, the Vineyard Christian Fellowship, and Hope Chapel, which today, collectively number more than a thousand churches, including many megachurches with memberships exceeding several thousand people.[18] Indeed, California has twenty-five of the largest 100 churches in America, and most of these are in the Southland. Southern California is also host to the Crystal Cathedral, a church that pioneered televangelism as well as the drive-in church.[19] Hollywood is the international headquarters for the Church of Scientology, which has a presence in 122 countries.

A Baptism in a Pool at Mosaic, a Southern Baptist Church, Los Angeles, 1999
Photograph by Jerry Berndt. Used by permission of the USC Center for Religion and Civic Culture.

Roman Catholicism is the single largest denomination in Southern California, with 3.6 million communicants in the archdiocese of Los Angeles. Approximately 60 percent of this membership is Latino, 5 percent African American, and 10 percent Asian (including many Filipinos).[20] Serving this population are 284 parish churches, including churches such as St. Thomas the Apostle, which has a Friday night charismatic mass that overflows the interior of the church, requiring loudspeakers for those in the parking lot. This church, as well as nearby St. Vincent's—a beautiful cathedral-like church that in the 1920s served the millionaires living on Adams Boulevard near the USC campus—is home to the thousands of Guatemalans, Salvadorans, and Mexicans who live in the neighborhood. In contrast to the Latino majorities of St. Thomas and St. Vincent's, St. Basil's (located on Wilshire Boulevard) is a multiethnic congregation whose largest contingent is 1,200 Koreans who worship separately from the Anglo, Latino, and black communicants.

Although Los Angeles is the largest archdiocese in the nation, there is a considerable transfer of people who were born Catholic but are switching to Protestant Evangelical and Pentecostal churches.[21] One explanation for this shift is that people accustomed to the familial spirit of Latino culture prefer smaller and more intimate congregational settings in contrast to the more impersonal climate of most large Catholic parish churches. But it is also true that in a free market economy, the Protestant "sects," as Catholic officials tend to label them, are simply more aggres-

Palm Sunday at St. Thomas the Apostle Catholic Church, Los Angeles, 1996
Photograph by Jerry Berndt. Used by permission of the USC Center for Religion and Civic Culture.

sive in their marketing (as well as service) to potential members. Furthermore, alienation by members from the institutional hierarchy must be considered as cause for defection.

A 1993 Gallup Poll showed that 58 percent of Catholics surveyed believed that abortion should be allowed under some circumstances, 63 percent thought that women should be ordained as priests, 75 percent believed priests should be permitted to marry, and 84 percent favored artificial methods of birth control—all these attitudes being in sharp contrast with official church teaching. Perhaps even more surprising, a *Los Angeles Times* poll found that 59 percent of priests and 66 percent of nuns believe that priests should marry, and 44 percent of priests and 57 percent of nuns believe that women should be ordained as priests. Hence, it is not simply the laity, but even the clergy, who disagree with the church hierarchy.[22]

There is little doubt that the Catholic Church is undergoing dramatic changes, fueled, in part, by what is projected to be a serious shortage of clergy. At the end of the 1960s, the church was ordaining 1,000 new priests a year, nationally. Today, that figure is down to 600, despite a substantial increase in the number of Catholics.[23] Nuns appear to be a dying institution in America, with the median age (according to a 1994 study) at sixty-five; only 3 percent were forty or younger. In 1993, there were 94,022 nuns in the United States, compared with nearly double that number in 1966.[24]

The headline story among Protestant denominations in Los Angeles is that the older, more established mainstream churches, with few notable exceptions, are declining, while the conservative Evangelical and Pentecostal churches and their denominations continue to grow. Nationally, liberal denominations such as the Episcopalians, Presbyterians, and Methodists have had membership declines of 20 to 30 percent in the past several decades.[25] In contrast, many conservative churches are growing, including "postdenominational" churches that are independent and exist in networking relationships but do not have centralized bureaucracies, seminaries, or standardized curricular materials. Exceptions to this declining mainstream are churches such as All Saints Episcopal Church in Pasadena, which has a vital social outreach ministry to the community. This church, with its outspoken record on gay rights, support of a woman's right to terminate pregnancy, and criticism of military intervention, demonstrates that there is a market for liberal theology—so long as it is anchored in life-transforming worship. Nevertheless, the biggest draws in attendance are Protestant churches that offer a conservative theology teamed with contemporary worship and support groups dealing with issues ranging from divorce recovery to coping with teenage children and managing money responsibly.

African American religion is robust in Los Angeles, with three congregations that have memberships exceeding 10,000 members. Former Los Angeles Mayor Richard Riordan states that the second most powerful religious spokesperson in Los Angeles, after Cardinal Mahony, is Bishop Charles E. Blake, pastor of the 24,000-member West Angeles Church of God in Christ. Several blocks away, the First African Methodist Episcopal Church (First AME) is led by the charismatic Reverend Cecil (Chip) Murray, who appeared regularly in the media interpreting the April 1992 riots in Los Angeles. His 17,000-member congregation has spawned seven nonprofit corporations that are involved in social ministries in the community, including the construction of $35 million worth of low-income housing, a loan program to assist minority-owned businesses, various entrepreneurial training programs, and a job placement service. Members of this church have closed down every crack house in the neighborhood and were also an important presence during the riots, forming a wall around a black-owned insurance corporation that was threatened by fires.[26] A half dozen miles from both First AME and West Angeles Church of God in Christ, Pastor Fred Price leads the Crenshaw Christian Center, which is focused less on community outreach but whose television programs beam their message of gospel-based financial prosperity across the nation. The theater-in-the-round church on the former campus of Pepperdine University seats more than 9,000. Although smaller in size, Holman Methodist Church, under the prophetic leadership of Pastor James Lawson, has been very active in civil rights issues as well as in advocating for a "living wage" for poor people and immigrants working in Los Angeles.

A 1990 survey by the Barna Research Group in Glendale found that blacks are much more likely to be involved in religious activities than are whites and Latinos, showing that in any given week, 58 percent of African Americans living in Los Angeles County report attending church, compared with 28 percent of whites and 37 percent of Latinos. In various measures of religiosity, such as Bible reading, blacks were much higher than whites or Latinos. Paralleling the drift of Catholics to Protes-

Via Crucis on Good Friday in the Wilshire Center Neighborhood Around Immanuel Presbyterian Church, Los Angeles, 1999
Photograph by Jerry Berndt. Used by permission of the USC Center for Religion and Civic Culture.

tantism, black churches in Los Angeles have lost some members to the Nation of Islam, which provides a highly structured and disciplined lifestyle along with a well-articulated ideology. Scholar Lawrence Mamiya argues that prisons are a prime recruiting ground for the Nation of Islam, offering an alternative to gang life and gang protection within prisons.[27] The appeal is more generic than this, however. One individual who had attended black Baptist churches his entire life said that when he visited a Nation of Islam meeting for the first time, he heard a message that named, definitively, his experience of racism in American society—or, perhaps more important, posed a methodology for responding to it.

A growing number of African Americans are also joining orthodox Muslim congregations. For example, approximately 10 percent of the audience of the mosque across the street from the USC campus (on the corner of Exposition and Vermont) is black. Farther up Vermont, the Islamic Center of Los Angeles has a thousand active members. There are fifty-five masjids (mosques) in Southern California, with approximately 11,858 people attending Friday midday prayers.[28] Nationally, there are more than a thousand Muslim congregations, most having been formed in the last quarter century. If Islam continues to grow at its current rate of about 125,000 people a year, the Muslim population will surpass the number of Jews in the United States by the year 2010. Currently, Southern California has the third highest number of masjids in the country, after New York City with ninety-eight and the Chicago metropolitan area with sixty.[29]

A growing presence in Southern California is the Church of Jesus Christ of Latter-Day Saints, more popularly known as the Mormon Church. Currently, approximately 800,000 active Mormons live in California, with approximately 250,000 in the Los Angeles area. Sixty percent of those being baptized in Southern California are nonwhite. For example, there are five Spanish stakes (i.e., districts), with approximately six to thirteen local congregations per stake. But there is also an increasing number of converts who are Chinese, Laotian, Cambodian, Vietnamese, Japanese, Tongan, and Samoan.[30] Southern California is experiencing a larger gain in Mormons than any other region in the United States. Worldwide, Mormons are growing at a rate of approximately 30 percent a decade and are fast becoming a major world religion.[31] In Southern California, Mormons have made a point of being socially active, especially giving leadership to youth-oriented programs such as the Boy Scouts and Girl Scouts.

Although estimates vary, approximately a half million Jews live in Los Angeles County, with the largest concentrations in Brentwood, Beverly Hills, and West-wood, which are currently 83 percent Jewish.[32] Orange County numbers an additional 90,000 to 100,000 Jews, but only about 15 percent are affiliated with a synagogue, one of the lower rates in the country.[33] A considerable threat to Judaism is intermarriage, with an estimated 52 percent of Jews marrying Gentiles. Nationally, American Judaism is composed of three main bodies: 47 percent identifying with the Conservative movement, 36 percent Reform, and 11 percent Orthodox.[34] Los Angeles hosts two major seminaries for these traditions—the University of Judaism (Conservative) and Hebrew Union College (Reform).

Listing all the various ethnic and national religions represented in Los Angeles would involve a long compendium. For example, there are well-established "Orthodox" churches associated with the Greeks, Russians, and Armenians. St. Sophia Greek Orthodox Church is an architectural landmark in Los Angeles and on Good Friday is filled late into the night with several thousand worshipers from all over Southern California. The 300,000 Armenian immigrants to Los Angeles gather in a number of branches of several Christian traditions: Armenian Apostolic (Orthodox), Protestant, and Catholic. The church one attends often says a great deal about where one immigrated from and one's political commitments. For Armenians, as with many immigrant groups, the church not only serves as a bridge between the new and old culture but also is a conduit for sending charitable contributions back to the country of origin. In this regard, churches are transnational organizations that enable people to maintain dual identities. Furthermore, clergy play multiple roles for immigrants: They link newcomers to jobs, social services, and emergency assistance; they organize citizenship classes; sermons inform immigrants what behavior is expected of them if they are to be respected in their host country; and liturgy and religious practice are carriers of tradition from the country one has left, including language and custom.

Asians are extraordinarily diverse in their religious commitments. For example, in Little Tokyo in downtown Los Angeles, temples represent several traditions of Buddhism. Services tend to be in Japanese, although there is some attempt to cater to second- and third-generation Japanese immigrants who have lost fluency with their

Services at the Khemara Buddhikaram, a Cambodian Buddhist Temple, Long Beach, 1999
Photograph by Jerry Berndt. Used by permission of the USC Center for Religion and Civic Culture.

native tongue. An extraordinary Buddhist temple (Hsi Lai Temple) located in Hacienda Heights attracts thousands of visitors each year. In addition, Los Angeles has several active Zen centers, representing different traditions. Koreans have two highly visible congregations in Los Angeles, the Oriental Mission and Young Nak Presbyterian Church, both of which number several thousand members. There are dozens, if not hundreds, of smaller Korean congregations, however. For example, one 2 by 1.5 square mile area adjoining Wilshire Boulevard has twelve Korean churches.

In sum, the Glenmary Research Center confirms the dominance of Catholicism in the religious ecology of Los Angeles County.[35] The twelve denominations or faith groups with the largest number of adherents in 1990 are shown in Table 10.4. In the number of actual churches or synagogues in Los Angeles County, however, groups such as the Mormon, Assembly of God, and Foursquare denominations rival the number of Catholic churches, as shown in Table 10.5.

Los Angeles County statistics parallel Orange County, San Diego, and San Francisco, but there are also a few distinctions.[36] Table 10.6 lists only a few of the larger groupings of religious traditions. Catholics represent the largest single denomination in each of the four counties, which perhaps is not surprising. These counties, however, have a higher percentage of people without a religious identity than is the case in the rest of the country (7.5 percent in the United States, in contrast to 20.1 percent in San Francisco, 12.9 percent in San Diego, 12.8 percent in L.A., and 11.6 percent in Orange County). Many of the western states have a disproportionate

Table 10.4 The Twelve Largest Denominations and Faith Groups in Los Angeles County

Denomination	Number of Adherents, 1990
1. Catholic	3,077,114
2. Jews	501,700
3. Black Baptist	268,605
4. Southern Baptist	128,895
5. Mormon	103,286
6. American Baptist	76,010
7. United Methodist	70,590
8. Foursquare	65,280
9. Presbyterian	64,168
10. Episcopal	60,674
11. Assembly of God	55,107
12. Seventh-Day Adventists	54,514

number of persons without religious preferences, led by California (13 percent), Colorado (11.4 percent), and Montana (10.2 percent), which are all above the national average (7.5 percent).[37] Hence, although religion is still a major factor in the lives of people in the West, in a free market of religious choice, some people do not identify with an institutional expression of religion.

RELIGION AND SOCIAL CAPITAL IN LOS ANGELES

In several hundred interviews conducted after the 1992 riots, staff at USC's Center for Religion and Civic Culture discovered an enormous amount of social activism across the theological and religious spectrum. Black churches in America have traditionally played an important role in addressing the needs of residents in their neighborhoods, and this spirit continues in churches such as the First AME, West Angeles Church of God in Christ, and Second Baptist. Liberal Protestant churches have a strong history of launching social programs related to homelessness, AIDS, health care, and community violence. More recently, however, many of these mainstream churches are struggling with internal funding problems, having failed to maintain or attract younger members. In their place, a number of more conservative churches, such as First Nazarene, have expanded youth and community development programs. Some of the Pentecostal churches seek to change their communities by transforming persons, one at a time, and Jewish congregations throughout Los Angeles continue to sustain one of the most well-organized responses to human need in the city. Finally, Catholic churches in Los Angeles play an important role in immigrant

Table 10.5 Number of Churches and Synagogues in Los Angeles County

Faith Group	Number
1. Catholic	272 churches
2. Mormon	271 churches
3. Assembly of God	231 churches
4. Foursquare	231 churches
5. Southern Baptist	226 churches
6. American Baptist	202 churches
7. United Methodist	186 churches
8. Presbyterian	170 churches
9. Jewish	145 synagogues
10. Lutheran (ELCA)	132 churches
11. Seventh-Day Adventist	123 churches
12. Church of Christ	114 churches

Table 10.6 The Largest Religious Groupings in the Counties of Los Angeles, Orange, San Diego, and San Francisco

	L.A. Co.	Orange Co.	San Diego Co.	San Francisco Co.
Catholic	31.5%	29.3%	27.6%	33.5%
Baptist	11.9	6.2	9.9	6.4
Methodist	3.1	4.1	6.9	3.7
Lutheran	3.5	5.0	4.1	2.8
Presbyterian	2.2	4.6	2.9	3.5
Mormon	1.8	3.2	1.7	0.8
Jewish	3.9	2.7	1.9	4.1
No religion	12.8	11.6	12.9	20.1

rights, gang prevention, and basic social services. In Los Angeles, no one group or tradition has a monopoly on social activism.

Nevertheless, my colleagues and I have encountered four basic forms of faith-based activism in our research. First are those that emphasize individual services—providing food, clothing, emergency shelter, and medical assistance to people. Second are the community and economic development programs that provide literacy skills, job training, job placement, courses in entrepreneurship, and risk capital for

Torah Reading
at Temple
Emanuel,
Beverly Hills,
1999

Photograph by Jerry
Berndt. Used by
permission of the
USC Center for
Religion and Civic
Culture.

starting new businesses. Third are highly successful programs, such as those developed by the Industrial Areas Foundation, that use community organizing strategies intended to register people to vote and otherwise appropriate political power. Fourth, a burgeoning number of groups—for example, Victory Outreach—attempt to address intractable problems such as drug abuse and gang membership through religious conversion.

The complex religious ecology of Los Angeles also exhibits a high degree of interfaith cooperation, even if different faith traditions and orientations dictate different forms of social activism. Hence, in Pasadena, a Catholic, an Episcopal, and a black Baptist church joined together in an 800-person-strong march against violence in the city. For several years, a group of Catholics, Protestants, Mormons, Muslims, Jews, and Buddhists struggled together after the 1992 riots as members of the Interfaith Coalition to Heal L.A. In Los Angeles, a new "in-the-trenches" style of interfaith cooperation is quite different from previous patterns of ecumenical dialogue that led to discussions of beliefs rather than to the pursuit of a collective mission to serve the residents of the city.

In addition to such forms of cooperation, we are also witnessing new partnerships between the faith community and foundations, corporations, and publicly funded agencies. Indeed, there are several reasons why faith-based programs have become a "good investment": (a) Churches and synagogues already have facilities in place, removing the need for new capital expenditures; (b) they are strategically located throughout cities and communities; (c) they have committed volunteers who can multiply the efforts of paid staff; (d) they have a donor base that allows them to raise funds from foundations, corporations, and public agencies; (e) they already have leadership, accounting systems, and staff; (f) clergy know the needs of the neighborhoods they serve; (g) religious leadership is driven by vision; and (h) people within faith-based programs talk unashamedly about moral accountability, meaning, and human purpose, which are often absent from more bureaucratic approaches to human service.

Although many of the persons in faith-based projects in Los Angeles are overworked and their programs underfunded, an enormous reservoir of hope and optimism seems to drive their response to people's needs. These people's lives are rooted in daily spiritual practice, liturgy, and worship that renew their vision, and they refuse to accept cynicism, despair, and inequality as appropriate conditions of the human community. Week after week, clergy stand before their congregations, sharing a vision of human possibility that allows people to imagine the impossible. Sociologically, this role is essential to the health of urban America. In Los Angeles, new partners are collaborating in this vision: Buddhists, Muslims, Hindus, and even members of some New Age congregations.

Several forces are converging to fuel this interest in faith-based activism. First, we are in the midst of a crisis in public order in urban America that includes unacceptable levels of violence, a growing gap between rich and poor, a drug problem that produces too many victims, families that do a poor job of nurturing children, and levels of interracial conflict that deny human dignity. Second, the disappearance of

Song and Celebration at First AME Church, Los Angeles, 1996
Photograph by Jerry Berndt. Used by permission of the USC Center for Religion and Civic Culture.

the public safety net is thrusting more and more people on to the private sector, with churches and synagogues serving for many as the last court of appeal. Third, many of the adults who were touched by the activist 1960s are drawn to commitments that move beyond a purely self-centered quest for fulfillment. Indeed, they are inspired by the view that personal meaning is linked to communal responsibility. Finally, religious institutions are among the few trusted institutions in many communities.

CONCLUSION

Robert Park's assumption that religion would diminish in importance has not occurred. Although there have been changes in the religious ecology, with some groups gaining in influence and other groups declining, religion is still important for most people. The traditional model of secularization, articulated by theorists such as Peter L. Berger, portrays religion as strongest where there is a religious monopoly.[38] Yet recent work indicates exactly the opposite: Religious commitment is highest when many groups are competing with each other.[39] Competition results in niche marketing, where because not everyone has the same religious needs or desires and with more options from which to choose, interest in and commitment to religion increase. Furthermore, in countries where there is a religious monopoly, clergy tend to become lax. There are fewer reasons to innovate or serve the client population because people have no other religious options. Hence, despite factors that might dampen religious involvement in a city such as Los Angeles, the multiplicity of options leads to relatively high levels of involvement. Indeed, if one were to include all the quasi-religious practices in Los Angeles County, then Los Angeles would be as religious as any region of the country.

Another theory challenged by Los Angeles data is that religion does not seem to stimulate assimilation of various ethnic groups in the ways articulated by some observers of religion's role in producing the "melting pot."[40] Instead, although religion serves as an important bridge to immigrant people entering the region, many churches primarily serve homogeneous racial, ethnic, and national populations. Hence, religion may help maintain ethnic and racial affiliation rather than promote assimilation. Religious institutions, thus, allow for a type of "dual citizenship" that political organizations, or even labor unions, would not permit. I believe that this *transnational* character of churches and synagogues in Los Angeles is a topic that deserves continuing research.

Finally, a new religious identity that has not been documented may be increasingly prevalent in Los Angeles, namely, people who simultaneously maintain several religious identities. For example, a person may have been born Catholic—and continue to claim this heritage—but may currently attend a Protestant church. This person might also practice yoga on a regular basis and attend Wiccan gatherings on various neopagan holidays. Novel about this "religious schizophrenia" is the apparent absence of guilt or need for a coherent philosophy. After all, given an experience of the world that lacks coherence, why should religious practice be so constrained? This attitude clearly reveals a loss of authority for religious institutions and corresponding increases in *personal authority* to choose religious practices that meet one's needs and experience. Although this change in the locus of authority may threaten the custodians of church institutions, there is no reason to imagine that it will lead to the demise of religion. Instead, this may be the spirit undergirding religious innovation.

NOTES

1. These statistics were cited in comments made by Robert Wuthnow (Princeton University) at the annual meeting of the Society for the Scientific Study of Religion, 1996.

2. Robert E. Park, "Magic, Mentality, and City Life," in *The City: Suggestions for Investigation of Human Behavior in the Urban Environment,* by Robert E. Park, Ernest W. Burgess, and Roderick D. McKenzie (Chicago: University of Chicago Press, 1925, 1967; Midway reprint, 1984).

3. Max Weber, "Science as a Vocation," in *Max Weber: Essays in Sociology,* trans. and ed. H. H. Gerth and C. Wright Mills (New York: Oxford University Press, 1946), 143.

4. See William James, *Varieties of Religious Experience: A Study in Human Nature* (New York: Collier Books, 1961).

5. The secularization hypothesis was challenged in an influential book by Andrew Greeley, *Unsecular Man* (New York: Schocken Books, 1972), but this was merely the beginning of an avalanche of critical commentary. See, for example, the volume edited by Phillip E. Hammond, *The Sacred in a Secular Age: Toward Revision in the Scientific Study of Religion* (Berkeley: University of California Press, 1985).

6. For examples of field research studies, consult the two major journals in the sociology of religion: *Journal for the Scientific Study of Religion* and *Sociology of Religion.* For an excellent ethnographic monograph, see Lynn Davidman, *Tradition in a Rootless World: Women Turn to Orthodox Judaism* (Berkeley: University of California Press, 1991).

7. All Gallup Poll data for 1995 are drawn from *Religion in America: 1996 Report* (Princeton, N.J.: Princeton Religion Research Center, 1996).

8. See Roger Finke and Laurence R. Iannaccone, "Supply-Side Explanations for Religious Change," in *Religion in the Nineties,* ed. Wade Clark Roof, *Annals of American Academy of Political and Social Science* 527 (1993): 27-39.

9. Americans are more religious as measured by church attendance and orthodox beliefs than are most Europeans. For example, less than 15 percent of those surveyed in Great Britain report that they attended religious services in the past seven days, and church attendance in many of the Scandinavian countries is less than 5 percent.

10. No comparable survey has been done for Los Angeles County as a whole, but a *Los Angeles Times* survey done in 1991 of residents of the San Fernando Valley indicated that 32 percent were Protestant; 28 percent were Catholic; 20 percent had no religion; 10 percent were Jewish; 5 percent claimed no part of other Christian religions; 4 percent identified with non-Christian religions, such as Islam, Hinduism, or Buddhism; 1 percent were Eastern Orthodox; and 1 percent stated they didn't know what religion they were. In a 1991 *Los Angeles Times* poll of Orange County residents, 49 percent were Protestant, 28 percent Catholics, 3 percent Mormon, 1 percent Eastern Orthodox, 2 percent Jewish, 4 percent other religions, and 13 percent of the respondents said that they had no religious preference (*Los Angeles Times,* Orange County Edition, December 17, 1991, p. A1).

11. Phillip E. Hammond, *Religion and Personal Autonomy: The Third Disestablishment in America* (Columbia: University of South Carolina Press, 1992).

12. Hammond, *Religion and Personal Autonomy,* 134.

13. See the study by Dean R. Hoge, Benton Johnson, and Donald A. Luidens, *Vanishing Boundaries: The Religion of Mainline Protestant Baby Boomers* (Louisville, Ky.: Westminster/ Knox Press, 1994).

14. See Wade Clark Roof, *A Generation of Seekers: Baby Boomers and the Quest for a Spiritual Style* (San Francisco: HarperSanFrancisco, 1993).

15. See Robert S. Ellwood and Donald E. Miller, "Eastern Religions and New Spiritual Movements," in *The Religious Heritage of Southern California: A Bicentennial Survey,* ed. Francis J. Weber (Los Angeles: Interreligious Council of Southern California, 1976), 99-117.

16. For a history of American Pentecostalism, see Robert Mapes Anderson, *Vision of the Disinherited: The Making of American Pentecostalism* (Peabody, Mass.: Hendrickson, 1979).

17. See Edith L. Blumhoffer, *Aimee Semple McPherson: Everybody's Sister* (Grand Rapids, Mich.: Eerdmans, 1993).

18. See the study of Calvary, Vineyard, and Hope Chapel by Donald E. Miller, *Reinventing American Protestantism* (Berkeley: University of California Press, 1997).

19. For commentary on the Crystal Cathedral and other megachurches in Southern California, see Tammerlin Drummond, "The Super-Church: A Little Something for Everyone," *Los Angeles Times,* Orange County Edition, December 19, 1991, p. A1.

20. This information is based on a telephone interview with Father Gregory at the Los Angeles Archdiocese office on January 3, 1997.

21. See "More Anglos Leave Church," *Los Angeles Times,* Valley Edition, January 5, 1992, p. A25.

22. Stanley Meisler, "Pope Visits Amid Growing Disagreement With U.S. Flock," *Los Angeles Times,* Home Edition, October 4, 1995, p. A14.

23. Meisler, "Pope Visits."

24. *Los Angeles Times,* February 21, 1994, p. A22.

25. See Wade Clark Roof and William McKinney, *American Mainline Religion: Its Changing Shape and Future* (New Brunswick, N.J.: Rutgers University Press, 1987).

26. See the recent dissertation by Brent A. Wood, *First AME Church and Its Social Intervention in South East Los Angeles,* University of Southern California, 1997.

27. See C. Eric Lincoln and Lawrence H. Mamiya, *The Black Church in the African American Experience* (Durham, N.C.: Duke University Press, 1990), 389-390.

28. See John Dart, "A Closer Look at Islam in the West," *Los Angeles Times,* Home Edition, December 10, 1994, Metro section, p. B4.

29. Dart, "A Closer Look at Islam."

30. These statistics are based on personal correspondence on January 2, 1997, with Keith J. Atkinson, director, Southern California Public Affairs, Church of Jesus Christ of Latter-Day Saints.

31. See Rodney Stark, "Modernization, Secularization, and Mormon Success," in *In Gods We Trust: New Patterns of Religious Pluralism in America,* ed. Thomas Robbins and Dick Anthony (New Brunswick, N.J.: Transaction Publishers, 1990).

32. See the article by Stephen Games discussing recent demographic studies of Jews in Los Angeles, "A Counter of Culture," *Jewish Journal,* no. 9 (April 22-28, 1994): 8. Also see Jack Wertheimer, "Recent Trends in American Judaism," in *American Jewish Year Book, 1989,* ed. David Singer and Ruth R. Seldin (Philadelphia: Jewish Publication Society, 1990), 63-84.

33. John Dart, "The Times Poll: Organized Religion's Hold on Valley Residents Weak," *Los Angeles Times,* Valley Edition, January 5, 1992, p. A1.

34. *Los Angeles Times,* Orange County Edition, December 17, 1991, p. A1.

35. *Churches and Church Membership in the United States, 1990* (Atlanta, Ga.: Glenmary Research Center, 1992).

36. Barry Kosmin and Seymour P. Lachman, *One Nation Under God: Religion in Contemporary American Society* (New York: Harmony Books, 1993).

37. Kosmin and Lachman, *One Nation Under God,* 88-89.

38. Peter Berger, *The Sacred Canopy: Elements of a Sociological Theory of Religion* (Garden City, N.Y.: Doubleday, 1967).

39. See R. Stephen Warner, "Work in Progress Toward a New Paradigm for the Sociological Study of Religion in the United States," *American Journal of Sociology* 98 (1993): 1044-1093; Roger Finke and Rodney Stark, "Religious Economies and Sacred Canopies: Religious Mobilization in American Cities," *American Sociological Review* 53 (1988): 41-49; and Roger Finke and Rodney Stark, "How the Upstart Sects Won America: 1776-1850," *Journal for the Scientific Study of Religion* 28 (1989): 27-44.

40. See, for example, Will Herberg, *Protestant, Catholic, Jew: An Essay in American Religious Sociology* (Garden City, N.Y.: Doubleday, 1960).

Ecologies of Cyberspace
Gay Communities on the Internet

EDITOR'S
COMMENTS

In today's world, the Internet is inescapable, although it is far from universally available. A digital divide has already sprung up to separate those who are wired from those who are not. It's impossible to say just how important the new technology is, but I believe the information revolution will have consequences on human society at least as profound as the industrial revolution. The Internet is a vital dynamic in the trend toward a postmodern society.

There are many ways to consider the impact of telecommunications on contemporary society, not the least of which is how they will change the way we construct human settlements (cf. Chapter 3, this volume). For present purposes, we will stick with the Chicago School's obsession with community and explore the way the Internet is changing the nature of community, identity, and spaces.

Our point of departure in this chapter is the discussion by Ernest Burgess of Evelyn Buchan's study on girl delinquency. As elsewhere in *The City*, mobility is the crucial variable in the breakdown of traditional mores. In particular, Buchan's work portrays how mobility fosters promiscuity in young girls. This is most likely to occur when partners come from two communities and make contact in a third extracommunity space (such as the dance hall)— hence, Buchan's concept of the "promiscuity triangle," referring to the three spaces essential to the promotion of promiscuity.

In this chapter, J. Dallas Dishman introduces "virtual space" into this calculus, not to explore variations on the promiscuity theme but instead to examine how the Internet plays a role in creating communities in cyberspace among gay men. Dishman reveals how virtual communities reflect many of the strengths (and drawbacks) of traditional place-based communities, except of course that the virtual communities have no particular locus. This does not prevent many men from seeking real-world meetings with other cyberspace community members. Dishman concludes that the Internet is already altering the way we think about community, space, and identity.

QUOTES FROM
THE CITY

On the other hand, our leisure is now mainly a restless search for excitement. It is the romantic impulse, the desire to escape the dull routine of life at home and in the local community, that drives us abroad in search of adventure. This romantic quest, which finds its most outrageous expressions in the dance halls and jazz parlors, is characteristic of almost every other expression of modern life. Political revolution and social reform are themselves often merely expressions of this same romantic impulse. Millennialism in religion, the missionary enterprises, particularly those that are limited to "regions beyond," are manifestations of this same wish to escape reality. . . . (117)

We are everywhere hunting the bluebird of romance, and we are hunting it with automobiles and flying machines. The new devices of locomotion have permitted millions of people to realize, in actual life, flights of which they have only dreamed previously. But this physical mobility is but the reflection of a corresponding mental instability.

This restlessness and thirst for adventure is, for the most part, barren and illusory, because it is uncreative. We are seeking to escape from a dull world instead of turning back upon it to transform it.

Art, religion, and politics are still the means through which we participate in the common life, but they have ceased to be our chief concern. As leisure-time activities they must now compete for attention with livelier forms of recreation. It is in the improvident use of our leisure, I suspect, that the greatest wastes in American life occur. . . . (117-118)

. . . Movement in the person, as from one social location to another, or any sudden change as caused by an invention, carries with it the possibility of cultural decadence. The cultural controls over conduct disintegrate; impulses and wishes take random and wild expression. The result is immorality and delinquency; in short, personal and social disorganization. . . . (150)

These changes taking place in community life may be observed in a dramatic form in commercialized recreation. The day of the neighborhood public dance hall and the neighborhood motion picture show has passed, or at least is passing. Young people are deserting the neighborhood recreation centers and are thronging to centers outside the local community, to the high-class, magnificent dance gardens and palaces, and to the so-called "wonder" theaters of the "bright light" areas. . . . (151)

A map of the residences of dance hall patrons which shows both the disappearance of the small public dance hall from the neighborhood and the concentration of large dance halls in "bright light" areas is all the more significant because it portrays the phenomenon of promiscuity. By promiscuity is meant primary and intimate behavior upon the basis of secondary contacts. In the village type of neighborhood, where everyone knows everyone else, the social relationships of the young people were safeguarded by the primary controls of group opinion. But in the public dance hall, where young people are drawn from all parts of the city, this old primary control breaks down. . . . (151)

A study by Miss Evelyn Buchan of girl delinquency shows the effect of the increasing mobility and promiscuity of city life upon the behavior of youth, and suggests an interesting method of study. To bring into clearer relief the role of mobility and promiscuity as factors in behavior, a device called "the delinquency triangle" was employed. The three points of the triangle were located by spotting the home of the girl, the home of her male companion, and the place of delinquency. Three typical forms of the triangle soon appeared. [See Figure 11.1, page 298.]

Form 1 represents the traditional form of sex delinquency, where all three points of the triangle are within the community. This may be called the "neighborhood triangle." In this case the intimacy of the boy and girl might be old-world folkways, but without the protection for the girl in subsequent marriage which the European peasant mores afford.

Form 2, which is "the mobility triangle," stands for delinquency of the type related to increased freedom of movement, where two points of the triangle or its base, formed by the homes of the girl and the boy, lie within the same community, but where its apex, or the place of delinquency, is situated outside. In this case the bright-light area becomes a place of freedom from the narrower, distant controls of the home and the neighborhood.

In Form 3, delinquency is of the type of promiscuity, because here all the points of the triangle lie in different communities. The intimacy developing from the casual acquaintance of the metal worker from the steel mills with the girl from the West Side whom he "picked up" at an amusement park may be so transient that neither knows the family name or the address of the other.

The total effect of forces of city life, like mobility and promiscuity, upon the neighborhood and upon our traditional culture seems to be subversive and disorganizing. Particularly is this true of deteriorating areas, where neighborhood work originated, and where it is still, in any completely developed state, for the most part confined. . . . [T]he zone of deterioration and the areas of the greatest mobility in the city have the greatest concentration of poverty, vice, crime, juvenile delinquency, divorce, desertion, abandoned infants, murder, and suicide. (152-153)

CHAPTER 11

Ecologies of Cyberspace
Gay Communities
on the Internet

J. DALLAS DISHMAN

In *The City*,[1] the complex interplay of individuals, neighborhoods, and communities was understood, in part, through Evelyn Buchan's studies of delinquent girls and their relationship to local and distant communities. Buchan introduced the concept of *triangles of delinquency* to explain the web of connections that mobile (and, conversely, immobile) people use to create relationships and communities. Common in all three triangles is the notion of propinquity as a dynamic in the development of relationships. Yet recent decades have given rise to nonpropinquitous communities, where proximity does not dictate the boundaries of relationship formation. Although nonpropinquitous communities take a variety of forms, the development and outcomes of gay Internet communities present a unique opportunity to explore how and why digital communities form and how they may build on Buchan's triangles.

The establishment of real-world gay communities (such as the Castro District in San Francisco, Greenwich Village and Park Slope in New York, and West Hollywood in Los Angeles) reflects a well-documented ghettoization of gay men and lesbians across space and time.[2] The virtual communities that have developed on the Internet, however, are only now beginning to be understood as a hyperghettoization of gays into viable nonpropinquitous communities. The lives of gay men online offer insight into the formation of a new form of electronic gay culture that is highly motivated by the social, sexual, and political conditions of real-world environments. This chapter undertakes the exploration of gay virtual communities and the recasting of triangles of delinquency as the "pink triangles" of the gay Internet.

The aims of this chapter are to (a) theorize community formation on the Internet; (b) understand how and why the social lives of gay men are affected by the formation of gay Internet communities; (c) determine the extent to which Internet communities supplement real-world communities or, in some cases, supplant them entirely; and (d) identify those outcomes that most clearly affect the lives of the gay men who choose to go online. This chapter is not intended to be an exhaustive examination of gay Internet communities. Rather, it represents an effort to establish a dialogue about some key facets of gay men's lives online.

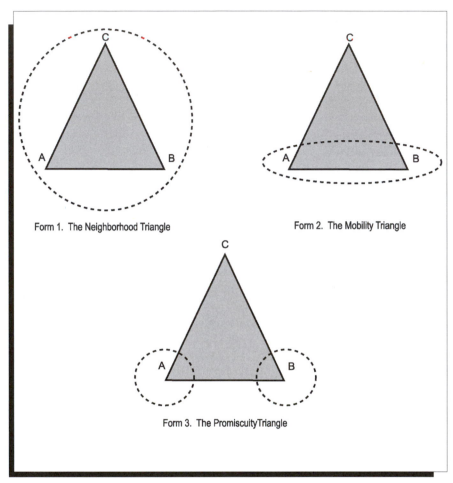

Figure 11.1. Triangles of Delinquency
Adapted from Ernest W. Burgess, "Can Neighborhood Work Have a Scientific Basis," pp. 152-153, in R. E. Park, E. W. Burgess, and R. D. McKenzie, *The City*. Chicago: University of Chicago Press. Copyright © 1925, 1967 by The University of Chicago. All rights reserved. Midway Reprint 1984. Used by permission.

THE BASIS OF ECOLOGICAL TRIANGLES AND THE INTERNET

Buchan hypothesized that the relationship of delinquent girls to communities took one of three principal forms—three triangles (see Figure 11.1). In each case, the triangles consisted of two points of origin, which represented the local communities (and homes) of the youth being observed (points A and B, respectively). Points A and B constituted the local environments of the youth and formed the base of the triangle. A third point (C) served as the triangle's apex, a third community where neither of the youth resided. This scheme forms what Buchan called "triangles of delinquency."

In Form 1, the neighborhood triangle, Buchan depicts traditional relationships in which connections between individuals (in her case delinquent girls) are confined to a single local community. Form 1 depicts a simple, single community-based relationship, a localized type of community. The youth in this model live in and interact in the same community.

On the other hand, in Form 2, the mobility triangle, individuals are depicted as residing in a common community at sites A and B but moving outside their local community to meet and interact at site C. This triangle is intended to connote an increasing ability of residents in a community to move outside their local environments to interact with others.

Through time, increasing access to transportation (both public and private) has allowed for greater mobility within both local and distant communities. This greater mobility, which tends to prevail in industrialized nations, has given rise to a third type of triangle, Form 3, in which the promiscuity triangle's relationships develop in multiple communities of origin and activity. Neither of the participants lives in the community where their relationship/interactions take place, nor do they live in the same local community—meeting and developing their relationships, instead, in a third, independent community. Although Buchan's study deals with delinquent youth (hence her use of the term *delinquency triangle*), her general thesis applies to the understanding of a wide range of communities. Although triangles of delinquency are in many ways a conceptual mismatch for gay Internet communities, they serve as a heuristic point from which to begin to explore the development of these communities.

If we reconsider Buchan's triangles, we need only add a virtual apex to create fourth form, a doppelgänger triangle (see Figure 11.2). The doppelgänger triangle offers a new virtual space, area D, where individuals can develop and maintain relationships and virtual communities. In this recasting of Buchan's triangles, individuals can come from and be interacting in any possible combination of local or distant communities, both real and virtual. An area (i.e., area D), rather than a point or apex (i.e., point C), represents virtual space because of its fluid nature. Virtual communities shift and flow from data point to data point in electronic transmissions—being loosed from the restrictions of physical space. In the real world, it is easy to point to a community or area and say, "that's it, the community is there." In a virtual world, it is impossible to pinpoint an electronic community or, for that matter, to actually *see* the community. Virtual communities exist in words, data bits, minds, and emotions, rather than in physical spaces. Using Buchan's models of community formation as a starting point, we can begin to understand the importance of virtual communities and their impacts on the real world.

The first step toward a clearer understanding of Internet communities begins with learning to think outside the conventional definitions of space, place, identity, and community. We must necessarily move toward accepting fluid definitions of who, what, where, and even when, if we are to understand these new and emerging forms of community.

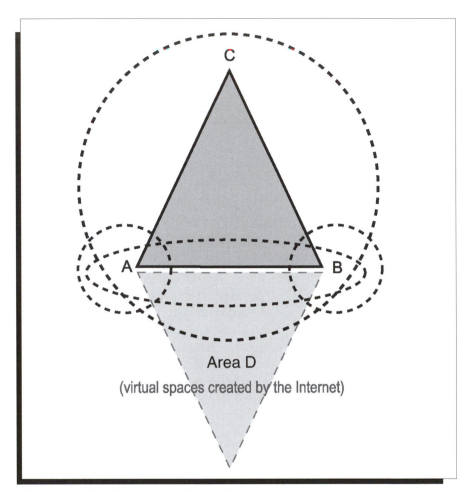

Figure 11.2. The Doppelgänger Triangle Formed by the Internet

Technically speaking, the Internet is the proper name for the global computer-moderated communications network that developed as an outgrowth of a U.S. military project to create a global, multinodal, redundant, computer-moderated communications network (the ARPANET). The Internet has become not only a tool for communication but also the subject of a number of science fiction writers, including William Gibson. In 1984, Gibson published one of the first widely read and perhaps the most influential works of science fiction to deal with the Internet, *Neuromancer.* In this novel, Gibson coined and introduced the world to the term *cyberspace,* referring to the aspatial, nonphysical dimensions of computer-moderated communications forums.

These aspatial environments are *virtual environments,* cyberspace communities that do not exist in the same physical sense that they do in Buchan's model. Instead, they are digitally produced spaces, contained entirely within computer systems—hence, *virtual* communities. In the minds of many computer users, however, these virtual environments are not unreal—quite the opposite. To say that they are not real neglects the real-world exchanges of goods, services, information, and emotions that occur in these virtual environments and disregards the consequences of online interactions in virtual communities. Although cyberspace, virtual space, and the Internet are technically not the same thing, their definitions have been co-opted within popular culture and have essentially become synonymous. As such, the terms are used interchangeably in this text. In the context of this chapter, *community* has been loosely defined as a socially bound network of individuals who are not necessarily in close geographical proximity.[3] In a manner that builds on this definition of community, electronic communities are constructed through consistent computer-mediated communication, be it in the form of extensive or casual conversation. Electronic communities are not restricted to or by propinquity.

VIRTUAL COMMUNITIES

The Origins of Cyberspace

Cyberspace evades easy definition. Indeed, there is no single metaphor that can completely convey either the nature or the complexity of cyberspace. Gibson posits that although cyberspace is not physical, it is very much a "real" conceptual space where computer-mediated communication and interactions occur.[4] According to Michael Benedikt,[5] these virtual communities have evolved through four communications epochs:

1. Mid-1600s to 19th century: Texts (e.g., books, magazines, and other printed materials)

2. 1900 to 1960: Electronic communications and entertainment media (e.g., telegraph, telephone, and television)

3. 1960 to 1984: Information technologies (e.g., personal computer)

4. 1984 to present: Virtual reality and cyberspace (e.g., Internet)

The quantity of information and the manner of exchange have changed significantly during each period. Briefly defined, epoch 1 is characterized by a quasi one-to-one communications system wherein written text was used to communicate through books and other printed media. This period also witnessed the collapse of many geographical barriers, as fewer constraints were placed on the distances across which one could transmit information, ideas, and feelings.

During epoch 2, some of the earliest nonpropinquitous communities appeared, including the emergence of communities based on participation in radio programs and television audiences. Making an ideological leap forward, people began thinking about presence and community in new ways.[6] These communities were limited, however, by their "one-to-many" characteristic—one person transmitting and many people receiving a communication of one form or another. Not until the 1970s, during epoch 3, did the emergence of a "many-to-many" communications medium appear in the form of online electronic bulletin board systems (BBSs). With the development and widespread use of home computers, BBSs began popping up across the country and around the globe, allowing many people to communicate with many others simultaneously, although they remained geographically distant. San Francisco programmer and visionary thinker John James proposed that the BBS was a fully functioning virtual community—a novel concept for the time. Indeed, James was right on the mark in describing the BBS as a catalyst for changing the ways that people think about communications and communities.[7]

The fourth epoch, coinciding with Gibson's *Neuromancer,*[8] is marked not so much by a technological shift as by a shift in ways of seeing and thinking about technology, cyberspace, and society. With the publication of *Neuromancer* and other novels like it, people began to redefine the way they thought about space and their role in the rise of digital cultures and communities. To paraphrase Benedikt, at this point the idea of a new type of virtual community crystallized.

In *City of Bits,* William Mitchell anticipates the continued collapse of spatial barriers in contemporary society. "The efficient delivery of bits [computer-moderated information and communication] to domestic space will continue to collapse many of the spatial and temporal separations of activities that we long have taken for granted—for instance work and pastimes will be multiplexed and overlaid."[9] As telecommunications (computer-moderated communications) further replace the physical movements of the body, spatial linkages between the physical spaces that currently exist will continue to loosen.[10] Many activities that formerly required some form of physical presence to accomplish a task can now be augmented or replaced by technology, further eroding the necessity for propinquity. According to Benedikt, this process has already begun via the familiar virtual spaces of online communications—telephones, e-mail, news groups, and so on.[11] Computer-mediated communications offer unrestricted freedom of expression and personal contact with far less hierarchy than is found in the primary social world (i.e., the real world). With this shift, the apexes of Buchan's triangles of delinquency and their respective effects on community formation must necessarily be reconsidered to accommodate the ever increasing rise of virtual communities. What are the roles and effects of emerging virtual communities in people's lives?

Identity in Cyberspace and the Real World

The concept of identity is intimately tied to place. In everyday life, identity, the self, and conceptions of the other are tied to our interactions with people and the places around us. In the real world, we partition our lives in ways that inscribe spaces with meanings and establish and maintain boundaries around place-based social norms and mores. In daily life, we have neighborhoods, men's and women's rest rooms, prisons, colleges, day care centers, retirement homes, psychiatric institutions, houses of parliament, theaters, schools, parks, zoos, and so on that allow us to partition space and define and constrain what we do and who we are across space and time.

In virtual space, identity[12] is formed as a result of a complex interplay of real-world *and* virtual relationships and places. Cyberspaces allow people to experience events, things, and people that they might not be able to or allow themselves to experience in the real world. The "instabilities and ambiguities" of cyberspace therefore challenge traditional ways of representing social distinction and socialization,[13] such as those described by Buchan. Urry, emphasizing the extent to which identity is inextricably bound to place in multiple and contradictory ways, argues that much of our current notion of place is tied to the technologies that we employ—essentially that identity is bound to place and place is mediated by technology.[14] In virtual communities, every space has the potential to become a penetrable and contested space, and every virtual community exists as part of a fluid architecture of data bits and digital communications.

Community Creation

How closely does the formation of online communities adhere to the various models that we employ to make sense of the real world? We know from the work of Wirth and Redfield that the organization of space, mainly in its scale and density, produces a corresponding social pattern.[15] Because virtual spaces lack these traditional measures, however, we cannot predict how social patterns will typically form. Even in the real world, it is difficult, at best, to anticipate exactly how sociospatial interactions will develop. The increasing use of technology promises to further complicate our efforts to understand how and why communities form—perhaps even what constitutes a community.

Our increasing reliance on technology also diminishes our need for direct human interdependence in daily life as we move closer to a hyperautonomous state.[16] Our daily routines testify to the increasing metaphorical and literal distances that separate us. For example, many of us now feel inclined to conduct our affairs through machines rather than standing in lines with other people; we use the drive-through windows at restaurants to speed the delivery of food and limit our interaction with others; we use voice mail and electronic answering services to take and screen telephone messages; we use e-mail to avoid voice conversation entirely. With each new device, each technological advance, we retreat further from direct human contact, becoming a culture of autonomies.

Rheingold has suggested that one reason for the formation of virtual communities is "the hunger for community that grows . . . as more and more informal public space disappears from our real lives."[17] Arguably, the formation of online communities is driven, in part, by the lack of real-world public spaces in which to gather for conversation and communion and by the waning sense of connection and community that comes with the disappearance of communal space. Yet the disappearance of real-world agoras has led to the formation of their electronic counterparts. The local park, barber shop, grocery stores, block party, and even the county fair—spaces where "the structure of shared experience beyond that offered by family, job and passive consumerism is small and dwindling"[18]—are being replaced by the virtual spaces of modern technology.

Many people, including gay men, have sought to replace the disappearing public spaces of the real world with virtual environments and cybercommunities. Although great varieties of public spaces in which to meet and socialize with others still exist, these spaces are most frequently heteronormative and can be alienating or even threatening for gay men. As a result, many gay men have made a strategic retreat from many real-world spaces to create homonormative real-world and virtual gay communities.

THEORIZING GAY COMMUNITY FORMATION

Simone LeVay has suggested that a desire to address sexual yearning compels homosexuals to form communities.[19] Although this is at least partially true, the formation of gay communities is also a direct response to the stigmatization experienced by most gays and a desire to end their social isolation. The result is a complex abdication of spaces that are largely heterosexually defined and maintained. In their retreat from heterosexually dominated spaces, homosexuals do not form homogeneous communities; there is as much diversity in the gay community as there is anywhere else. The gay community is split by race, ethnicity, age, phenotype, and sexual proclivity,[20] and yet there is an overriding sense of a larger inclusive gay community with which most gays identify. The need for acceptance and a desire to feel safe drive many gays to seek the comfort that comes with being with other gays.[21] To paraphrase Erving Goffman,[22] it is a chance—finally—to be at least as good as the other members of your community.

> What holds our [gay] community together, more than sexual desire or gender nonconformity, is a sense of being different. Too often this sense of difference is confused with homophobia. Stigmatization can make a difference into a disease, certainly, and that has happened all too often with homosexuality but removing the stigmatization does not remove the difference, it only removes the pathology. Many gays and lesbians recall having felt different at a very early age. Not oppressed or victimized—that came later if at all—but simply different, in a way that they typically find hard to verbalize. Different from their sisters or brothers, different from their parents' expectations, different perhaps from their own wishes for themselves. More self-aware, more inner-directed, lesbians and gay men develop apart from the regular world, not just in matters of sex but in every sphere of life. They look at the world from the outside, not with the bitterness of loners, but with the irony and sympathy of commentators, artists, helpers, and mediators.[23]

A sense of being different drives many gay men (and lesbians alike) to form communities in the real world. These same feelings of difference and a desire to connect with other gay men who share similar life experiences compel a number of gay men to seek out and even create virtual gay communities.

Motivated by a desire to better understand the virtual gay experience, I interviewed fourteen gay men in detail about their experiences in gay cyberspaces and gay virtual communities. The quotations contained in this chapter are those of fourteen self-identified gay men who were participating in gay virtual communities in Los Angeles County in 1996, when I conducted this research. The comments, obtained during semistructured interviews, are intended to be read as cultural texts that have been distilled to offer insight into the possible formation, maintenance, and relevance of gay virtual communities in gay men's lives in Los Angeles. Fictitious names have been used throughout this chapter to protect informants' privacy.

Getting Online and Forming Communities

The first step to forming an online community is getting online. The transition from the real world to virtual environments takes place in a number of locations. For some men, this transition occurs as a part of the regular workday. But by far, the majority of users make the transition to virtual spaces in the privacy of their homes during their free time. This first step in a three-stage typology (formation, process, and outcomes) explores some of the motivations for gay men to establish a presence online and to create virtual communities. Each of the men brought with him a specific set of expectations as he went online and revisited those expectations once there. For George, a local architect, getting online was a way of connecting with his local gay community—a way to form a smaller electronic community. As a result of his time online, George has developed a number of ties to his local gay community and also a significant long-distance relationship:

Well, that's how I keep in touch with everyone else that I know. I have moved into the gay community online in Santa Monica. I used the key words, gay and Santa Monica, and I came up with a list of like 20 entries. So, I sent e-mail to those people, seeing what they were up to, where they live, and I met a lot of them, like 5 or 6. And we are friends now. We've been sky diving together and all that sort of things. They've been pretty good friends to be in touch with. . . . And then after my last breakup in December or November, I used the "Heart to Heart" section to look at the personals. I never answered them, but I looked at them, and that's pretty much it. I have a cyberlover from Boston. And we talk to each other about three times a week or maybe more. And every time that I go out of town I go into the gay sections online and I post something saying, "What's up there? What's to see?" I've made friends that way from Boston, New York, and Florida, anywhere that people would just go and pick me up and take me around. Whenever I see a post of someone coming this way, I try to do the same. Yeah, there are lots of people that I know that way. I have friends in Hawaii that I've never met and we just talk to each other on e-mail. Fortunately, [my service] allows me to send photographs as well as text and stuff like that. We've been sharing anything from porn to recipes and pictures and stuff. It's been really wonderful.

Not surprisingly, the varieties of exchanges that occur online give rise to the development of differing types of relationships.

Access From a Spatial Perspective

There is a clear distinction between where men access the Internet and the types of activities and relationships in which they participate. Generally, the men I spoke with retained their conceptions of a public-private dichotomy after shifting to virtual environments. George, like the other men, remains guarded while online in public environments, such as cybercafes or at work:

> I've used [a cybercafe] to go to chat rooms online. But I had to stop because there were people behind me, and that wasn't the right place to do it.

Another user, Bruce, accesses exclusively from home and spends up to twenty hours a week online, mostly in a gay chat room called Enigma. Bruce, who works in a local arts institution, found the freedom and anonymity of online culture to be a tremendous pull that helped establish and maintain his interest in becoming part of the Enigma community:

> I'm more outgoing online than I am in real life. And they really like me. And it's given me confidence. It's very ego satisfying. In fact, Enigma has a World Wide Web page where you can post your picture. So, there are a number of people who have their pictures placed on that. So, I did mine, and I was getting hit on left and right.

Bruce's motivations are not dissimilar to those of many gay men online. Furthermore, like most of the men I've spoken with, he preferred to access the Internet from the privacy of his own home.

Paradoxically, it is while retreating to the private spaces of the home and going online that many gay men escape their sense of social isolation, their outsiderness, and find a sense of community and connection. Although Los Angeles has a number of thriving gay communities, all the interviewees exhibited varying degrees of isolation from the existing L.A. gay communities. Although not universal among all gay men, experiences of social isolation, to a greater or lesser extent, are common among most gay men.

Paul, who lives in the city of West Hollywood,[24] typifies the dissociation and isolation expressed by many gay men who go online:

> I'm not really involved with anything socially. And I don't really frequent the bars or anything like that. I think the most that I do is go to [a local, predominantly gay gym], which every other gay man goes to. And I don't really go there and talk to anyone. So, I sort of feel like I'm there, but not really.

Paul's comments belie a sense of isolation in his everyday life. Although he lives in the predominantly gay community of West Hollywood, he does not actually feel "a part of it, a connection, a sense of belonging."

Unfortunately, Paul is not alone. A significant percentage of gay men seldom, if ever, fully engage or connect with gay communities (for any number of possible reasons). Although all the men I interviewed loosely identified with the L.A. gay community, only a few were actively involved in community-building activities in the real world. For many gay men, going online is part of a complex abdication from real-world communities. Part of the reason that gay men (and presumably others like them) participate in online communities is a need to feel a connection to a larger identifiable community. Hence, they seek connections to clearly identified gay communities online.

The accessibility of online communities contributes to their attraction as an alternative to the real world for gay men. Arthur spoke enthusiastically of the extent of online communities:

> There is this entire gay community out there. It's amazing. I think it's incredible, actually. Especially for people who are not living in West Hollywood, living in the middle of "dog patch." It's amazing. Anyway, I think that's where the power lies.

The formation of gay electronic communities and the access that they provide to additional resources are key factors in the decisions of many men to participate in online communities. Joe, reflecting on his early experiences online, said,

> I think it's a fairly safe way for inexperienced people to meet other gay people and find out about yourself. That's another big theory about what you find out about in these chat rooms: You don't really meet people; what you are really exploring is yourself. That's what I think is so incredibly seductive.

Through the development of online relationships and the resulting self-reflection, gay men quickly form cohesive groups online.

From Connection to Commitment

Generally speaking, the degree of commitment required of gay men to be a part of a virtual community is considerably less than in the real world. Partially because of increasing time constraints and a rising fragmentation in many men's real-world lives, online users frequently express a desire to easily access, engage, and disengage with diverse communities. The ability to easily find and connect with other gay men, without considerable effort or fear for safety or loss of personal anonymity, attracts many gay men to the Internet and has given rise to an increasing number of virtual gay communities. The shift away from the local gay community development toward virtual community development, coupled with the lack of physical presence, both of which are essential referential points in Buchan's triangles of delinquency, warrants the closer examination of virtual communities.

The ebb and flow of virtual community development makes greater fluidity and passivity possible. This should not, however, be misinterpreted as a lack of commitment and personal investment. Some individuals are as emotionally committed to their online communities as they are to their real-world communities. The lack of restraints and requirements imposed by virtual communities sometimes garners a higher level of commitment from individuals than they exhibit in their real-world communities—in effect, for some gay men, virtual communities become more important in their lives than real-world communities.

The majority of gay men who are part of online communities, however, simultaneously manage memberships in virtual and real-world communities—weighing options and balancing individual needs against community participation in both worlds. Tacit connections persist in almost every case between the real and virtual worlds. It is rare that gay men online give up their connections to their real-world communities entirely. Some factors, such as fear and accessibility, make virtual communities more attractive. But they can't entirely replace the real world.

Fear as a Contributing Factor in Daily Life

Fear (stemming from prejudices and biases against same-sex sexual orientation/ preference) has been, and remains, a potent force in the daily geographies of many, if not most, gay men. When asked how being "out" (i.e., publicly self-identifying as a gay man) was different online from their experiences in the real world, most of the gay men quickly turn to the issue of personal safety. Although he has never been physically attacked, Ken, a recent graduate of a major West Coast university, has been verbally assaulted several times because he is gay. His experiences online, however, were quite different from his real-world experiences:

> In the online world, you don't have a face to go with a name. You simply have [the] characterization of an online personality, which can be constructed and visualized in as many sundry different ways as there are people that view your responses and communicate with you online. Whereas if you come out in the real world, they have a certain face, a certain name, a certain gait, a certain style of dress that is specific and individual to that person. And there is much less individual interpretation of that online. Your personality can be as solid, as immune, or as capricious as you wish it to be. You can play with a full spectrum of how you want to present yourself in any number of online groups. In the real world, you are much more limited by having a physical presence.

Similarly, Joe, a part-time writer, saw a difference between being out on the Internet and being out in the real world, drawing a clear distinction between the virtual and the real experiences of being out:

> I see a lot of people on [the Net] who probably wouldn't be out at all in the real world. Some people seem very fearful. There are a lot of people on there who never or rarely have sex, but they will have a lot of online sex. They will talk about sex, and they will be very campy when talking to gay people, but you realize that they would never do that [in the real-world]. And those are the people that I always, at first, feel paternal [toward], but then eventually I want to slap them and say: Go to a bar, go meet somebody, have a *real* experience.

For Joe, the safety provided by the Internet creates a false sense of self. Safety becomes a double-edged sword. Although the Internet provides a safe space in which to publicly self-identify as gay, it can also rob people of the real-world experiences of being gay. Gay men become trapped in a doppelgänger world where they are essentially deprived of real-world experiences and relationships and, ultimately, those vital parts of identity that are derived from the being part of a physical world. The very spaces of retreat can become virtual prisons, robbing these men of real-world experiences *as* gay men.

SOME *OUT*COMES OF LIVING ONLINE

The Managed Self Online and Off-Line

Although all the men I interviewed are relatively comfortable that they are gay, each of them also demonstrates (to varying degrees) a spatial and temporal partitioning of his daily life to conceal his sexual identity. As part of the coming-out process, whereby an individual begins to publicly self-identify as homosexual, gay men become keenly aware of when and where it is safe to be openly gay. This practice of spatial and temporal partitioning begins with the realization of otherness and the imperative to identify strategies to avoid possible conflict and/or rejection on a daily basis. This process is not entirely dissimilar to the realizations and daily practices of other marked groups who are in some way set apart from the dominant culture around them (e.g., sexual, racial, and ethnic minorities, among others).

The Internet challenges traditional ways that gay men think about their otherness, as well as the ways in which gay men are actually coming out as gay (or any other form of otherness). Phillip, a young Latino entertainment industry worker, had gone through the coming-out process while actively participating in a virtual community:

> I started going to the gay and lesbian room on [my Internet service provider] to talk. And [the participants] were so funny and so bright and they had such wit about them. They were so fun with each other. I wanted to get to know them. And I got to know the oldest guy in the group. I've never met any of the people, not one of them. But we all talk. And I sort of got the rap as being the young kid on the block and they were all older and we would all tease each other. I would say, "Hey aren't you guys supposed to be in bed by now?" And they would say, "Isn't it past your curfew?" We just had fun. I was really young, like 22, and that was really young as far as people who were on the Net at that point. So, yeah, it did help me come out. Just talking to them about what it was like for me; they were very helpful and supportive, and besides that, it was just great to see people who were working, just having really normal lives. And that helped me to deal with things. Being gay—it was just a part of who they were.

As Buchan demonstrates in *The City*, personal relationships form the basis of community. This is as true for online communities as it is for real-world communities. The intensity and speed with which communities form online help explain why virtual communities are able to develop so spontaneously and quickly. The emotional intensity of online relationships and the freer discussions that result from their safety and anonymity, together, create fertile ground for communities of common interest to form. Phillip explained how the Internet affected his relationships:

> It really quickly lets me get to know somebody by the exchange of facts and getting to talk to them. It's easy to figure out a common interest, because we're in the same room; the icebreaker is already set up for you. You both have a computer, and I have this idea that the person on the Internet is usually pretty intelligent, usually technologically astute, and that's something that I like.

Phillip's comments point to the spatial partitioning of the Internet. The typology of the Internet is based on the creation of virtual spaces that steer conversations toward general or sometime specific topics. People are in the common space because they share a common interest. Although this is not unlike meeting someone in a real-world public or private space (such as a bar, park, or dinner party), it more closely mimics highly specialized and segregated environments (e.g., a dinner party of music librarians). The spatial containment provides a predefined community with common interests—*a spatially and temporally defined special interest community.* A particularly attractive facet of online communities is their ability to mediate managed identities.

"Odd Man" No Longer

Stigmatization and alienation are common experiences for gays in society.[25] A sense of alienation and the desire to avoid stigma drive many gay men to seek out virtual gay spaces where they can participate more fully and equally while maintaining a self-regulated degree of anonymity. In the virtual spaces that gay men create, they are not, as Arthur put it, the "odd man out in society." The sense of connection offered by the Internet compensates for the real-world isolation that gay men experience. In an effort to reduce loneliness, the men focus their online activities primarily on gay communities and gay issues. Bruce clearly draws on the virtual gay community's ability to provide communion:

> These connections with other people out there are very un-isolating. I think of [these contacts] as quite real.

Although Arthur experienced a similar decrease in his feelings of isolation as a result of going online, he also expressed a concern frequently voiced by critics of virtual community:

> From an objective point of view, I would imagine everyone is off in their own little corners playing with their computers and not talking to each other.

The waning sense of isolation was intoxicating and pervasive. But these men seemed to be well grounded in their real-world lives. As Ken expressed it,

[The real-world] is the one that ultimately matters. The computer can go down tomorrow, but the real-world is still going to be here.

Victor, like most gay men, approaches the Internet in a very pragmatic manner:

It sort of bothers me in the sense that I have less time to read. And it's a very distracting feature in this apartment right now. In terms of communication, I can see where your so-called computer geeks can be occupied by whatever they see online and be totally involved in that. But that shouldn't be the ultimate way of communication. So, that's why I've been trying to limit my time on it. . . . It's taking away from my regular life. Although I did get a second phone line installed in this apartment expressly for it.

The Internet has become a potent force in the lives of men who found that it fosters a growing sense of connection and community among themselves and other like-minded gay dissidents. These "odd men" have banded together, formed communities of digital dissidents, and, in doing so, discarded their odd man labels. The Internet has become an integral part of their daily lives, radically altering the way that these men negotiate everyday life.

Cyberspace Sexuality

Virtual environments provide a space that allows for an increased sense of personal freedom around and being more vocal about issues of sexuality and sexual orientation. Generally, gay men feel much freer to speak while online, to address sensitive issues (e.g., homophobia and coming out) and desires (e.g., the need for companionship and sex) that they do not share as readily in the real world. In some instances, being more vocal online has led to real changes in the real-world day-to-day lives of cybercitizens. Although by no means the totality of virtual interactions, sexual expression is a major part of virtual life on the Internet.

Examinations of online sexuality reveal it to be a decisive way to augment and in some cases supplant real-world expressions of sexual desire. These expressions of online sexuality vary in form and intensity. For Joe, the capacity of the Net to recreate the sexual energy of a sex club was an attractive feature:

Even though I'm no longer having virtual sex, there is still this sexual energy, like going to a sex club. I love the environment of a sex club, and in cyberspace it's very similar. You can go in a room and see who's there, and what they look like, and you know what they will do with you. And if there is no action, you just go some place else. I haven't done that in a while, but there is always this sexual, illicit energy there that I certainly enjoy.

The sexual energy that is available online is undoubtedly a draw for many people (of all sexual orientations). For others, it is an opportunity to experiment with sexuality in new ways. In Victor's case, at some point his virtual world crossed the doppelgänger boundary into his real world:

I've met people who have introduced me off-line to areas that I would not necessarily have gone into had I not been online . . . because there are a lot of people who are kinky online. . . . Off-line you would not access it as readily as you can online. . . . When we met, we did it off-line. That goes with game playing. It's not necessarily me, I just explored it for curiosity.

Sexual experimentation online, although not a universal, is not uncommon. The online world allows for safe sexual exploration at a time when sexual liberation can be complicated by sometimes life-threatening sexually transmitted diseases (STDs). For Shane, online communities provide a place to express sexual desires, a space somewhat free from his real-world fears of STDs (particularly HIV):

We all know it's safer. No one is touching anyone, there is no risk of transmission [of STDs] over the computer. So yeah, there is a correlation between the possibility of HIV transmission in the real world and an increase in online sex, that and phone sex; all those very anonymous, nonphysical kinds of things.

Joe also commented on the connection between HIV and online sex, describing how the presence of HIV in the gay community and in the lives of two of his friends affected their online sex lives:

The two of my friends who have been most sexually intense and most addicted to Enigma are HIV-positive; and it is much less complicated for them to have virtual sex than to have real sex.

Although most gay men acknowledge the connections between real-world gay communities and the HIV-AIDS epidemic, only about half of the men in the study saw links between gay virtual communities and HIV-AIDS. That trend is undoubtedly changing, however, as the Internet becomes increasingly used to transmit information about HIV-AIDS, including up-to-date information on possible treatments and vaccines. The anonymity and safety of the Internet appear to remove online concerns about the sexual risk-taking behaviors of some gay men—and not just as it relates to STDs.

For Joe and Daniel, online sex allows for experimentation with power relations. Joe says,

Yeah, I would be more dominant—butch it up. Be kind of mean, which I would never do in real life, sort of S&M sort of things. Although I don't think I ever did, I could probably see doing stuff that I really wouldn't be interested in doing in the real-world—things that are slightly more exotic.

For Daniel, the virtual environment is a psychological playground, permitting him to interactively satisfy his fantasies through words and images, rather than physical acts:

I am into water sports, and [my lover] is as well, but not to the extent that I am. Some of the heavier stuff, for me, is psychologically exciting; physically they are not as exciting. Dominance and submission are both psychologically and physically exciting to me. And I would partake of in the real world. But with my relationship with [my lover], it's a relationship based on equality. So, I don't.

Although Daniel is excited by some expressions of online sexuality, his real-world relationship could not satisfy all his desires. Similarly, because he is interested in some of the activities only mentally and not physically, the real world does not meet those needs. Virtual environments, however, can meet his psychological desires without compromising his physical person (e.g., no risk from STDs or physically abusive situations). Online communities provide gay men with a multitude of outlets for repressed desires, from sexuality to simply just fitting in, and offer a way to redress the real-world oppressions and suppressions felt by so many gay men.

CREATING A BETTER PLACE FOR GAY MEN VIA THE INTERNET: IMPLICATIONS FOR REVISIONING URBAN THEORY

Online environments offer participants a way to redress the fear and restraint they experience in their everyday off-line lives. For many men, the online environment offers a way to express feelings and ideas in a safe and convivial forum as well as a way to address a variety of issues that, for whatever reason, have been stifled in their real-world lives. Inasmuch as these men are able to participate in a continuing dialogue, without fear of violence or rejection, they are building loosely formed communities of common interest.

Going online is a complex abdication of the real world. In an effort to escape a censoring real-world environment (censored by both the self and others), gay men go online to express and, in some cases, to develop, their gay identities. The crossover to virtual communities provides them with an arena in which to safely express themselves *as* gay men.

The myriad of relationships that develop online result in men being better informed about gay identity, community, rights and advocacy, and sexual expression in real and virtual worlds. Gay men become increasingly vocal and expressive as they grow more comfortable in the gay communities that form online, and, through time, what begins as a simple online interaction can congeal and give rise to new types of communities—virtual communities.

The outcomes of community formation are both diverse and far-reaching. Online communities provide outlets for previously suppressed selves. Users who are motivated by a desire to connect with and communicate with others generally find the Internet to be an ideal environment in which to forge a new type of community, a virtual community. Virtual communities have noticeably affected gay men. They are often much more expressive and better informed as a result of their participation in virtual communities.

The formation of virtual communities also compels the addition of a fourth triangle to Buchan's model of community and relationship development (Figure

11.2). Although her earlier models are still applicable to many types of communities, virtual communities require a reconsideration of conceptions of an individual's connection to his or her community. The virtual connections between people situated in communities A and B can now occur in cyberspace's virtual communities, as in the case of the gay men's virtual community experiences discussed in this chapter. In this new conceptualization of community formation, virtual relationships and communities are indicated by the dotted lines, which symbolize the digital nature of those connections. Area D represents the virtual community. Virtual communities are frequently doppelgänger communities, mirroring real-world communities in form and development. They can also be radically different from their real-world counterparts, however. Ultimately, the real world is augmented by the virtual world. Needs, desires, and emotions that are not or cannot be expressed in the real world are expressed online, providing a crucial outlet for virtual community citizens.

The emergence of virtual communities in cyberspace could not have been predicted at the time *The City* was originally published. Although many of the conventions employed by Buchan are still useful when thinking about community formation, the Internet and the rise of virtual communities necessitates that researchers revisit many of the assumptions about space, place, and community put forward in *The City*. This chapter is a step toward reconceptualizing space, place, and community in light of the increasing use of the Internet and the continued emergence of virtual communities. This chapter does not present any rigid conclusions about the coming virtual world, nor does it make any hegemonic claims as to the significance of virtual communities in Los Angeles, California, or the United States. But it does present one of many paths to begin discussions about the impacts of virtual communities on real-world lives.

Unlike some of the other observations provided in this book, this chapter is not about experiences unique to Los Angeles, or even experiences in which Los Angeles has been a trendsetter. Virtual communities, gay and otherwise, are not derivatives of the Los Angeles urban experience. It is not only possible but also probable that virtual gay communities play an even larger role in the lives of gay men in isolated and more conservative parts of the country—places where real-world gay communities are not readily accessible. The same can be said for the various types of virtual communities that form when people of diverse experiences, backgrounds, and physical locations come together to form virtual communities that are bound by their common interests.

The rise of Internet communities is neither novel nor negligible, but it is an increasingly powerful cultural phenomenon that must be reckoned with. Just as the other chapters in this volume have urged a reconsideration of a variety of urban phenomena, the readers of this chapter are invited to reconsider how and why these new types of communities are growing in number and popularity. Ultimately, we must begin to address the serious question of how virtual communities are affecting real-world communities in Los Angeles and elsewhere.

NOTES

1. Park, Burgess, and McKenzie [1925/1967], Midway reprint, 1984.
2. See Brown, 1997; Ingram, Bouthillette, and Retter, 1997; Valentine and Bell, 1995; Chauncey, 1994.
3. Johnston, 1994, p. 61.
4. Gibson, 1984.
5. Benedikt, 1992, p. 85.
6. Benedikt, 1992.
7. Benedikt, 1992.
8. Gibson, 1984.
9. Mitchell, 1995, p. 100.
10. Mitchell, 1995.
11. Benedikt, 1992.
12. See, for example, Stone, 1995, and Turkle, 1996a, 1996b.
13. Mitchell, 1995.
14. Urry, 1995.
15. R. Redfield and L. Wirth, in Urry, 1995.
16. Benedikt, 1992.
17. Rheingold, 1993, p. 6.
18. Rheingold, 1993, p. 25.
19. LeVay and Nonas, 1995.
20. LeVay and Nonas, 1995; Browning, 1996.
21. Myslik, 1996.
22. Goffman, 1963.
23. LeVay and Nonas, 1995, p. 400.
24. See Forest, 1995, and Geltmaker, 1992, for discussions of the importance and symbolic nature of the city of West Hollywood for L.A.'s gay communities.
25. See, for example, Goffman, 1963; Chauncey, 1994; Browning, 1996; Ingram et al., 1997.

REFERENCES

Benedikt, M., ed. 1992. *Cyberspace first steps.* Cambridge: MIT Press.

Brown, M. P. 1997. *RePlacing citizenship: AIDS activism and radical democracy.* New York: Guilford.

Browning, F. 1996. *A queer geography: Journeys toward a sexual self.* New York: Crown.

Chauncey, G. 1994. *Gay New York: Gender and urban culture, and the making of the gay male world 1890-1940.* New York: HarperCollins.

Forest, B. 1995. West Hollywood as symbol: The significance of place in the construction of a gay identity. *Environment and Planning D: Society & Space* 13, 133-157.

Geltmaker, T. 1992. The queer nation acts up: Health care, politics, and sexual diversity in the County of Angels. *Environment and Planning D: Society & Space* 10, 609-650.

Gibson, W. 1984. *Neuromancer.* New York: Ace.

Goffman, E. 1963. *Stigma: Notes on the management of spoiled identity.* Englewood Cliffs, N.J.: Prentice Hall.

Ingram, G. B., Anne-Marie Bouthillette, and Yolanda Retter, eds. 1997. *Queers in space: Communities, public places, sites of resistance.* Seattle, Wash.: Bay Press.

Johnston, R. J., ed. 1994. *The dictionary of human geography.* Cambridge, Mass.: Blackwell.

LeVay, S., and E. Nonas. 1995. *City of friends: A portrait of the gay and lesbian community in America.* Cambridge: MIT Press.

Mitchell, W. J. 1995. *City of bits: Space, place, and the infobahn.* Cambridge: MIT Press.

Myslik, W. D. 1996. Renegotiating the social/sexual identities of places: Gay communities as safe havens or sites of resistance? In *BodySpace: Destabilising geographies of gender and sexuality,* ed. Nancy Duncan. London and New York: Routledge.

Park, Robert E., Ernest W. Burgess, and Roderick D. McKenzie. 1925, 1967. *The city: Suggestions for investigation of human behavior in the urban environment.* Chicago: University of Chicago Press, Midway reprint, 1984.

Rheingold, H. 1993. *The virtual community: Homesteading on the electronic frontier.* New York: HarperPerennial.

Stone, A. R. 1995. *The ware of desire and technology at the close of the mechanical age.* Cambridge: MIT Press.

Turkle, S. 1996a. Who am we? *Wired,* January, 149-199.

Turkle, S. 1996b. Quoted in Sex, lies, and avatars, by Pamela McCorduck. *Wired,* April, 106-165.

Urry, J. 1995. *Consuming places.* New York: Routledge.

Valentine, G., and David Bell, eds. 1995. *Mapping desire.* New York: Routledge.

PART 4

Revisioning Urban Theory

Representing "Los Angeles"
Media, Space, and Place

This final part of the book is intended to open up a conversation about the Los Angeles School, avoiding closure in any conventional sense of the word. The four chapters in Part IV in different ways address these questions: How do we come to know the city? How can we adequately represent what we purport to know? These are tough issues in the realms of epistemology and ontology, and they lie at the heart of debates about postmodern thought and the existence and viability of an L.A. School. As our contributors begin to formulate answers to these questions, they simultaneously provide a first cut on a research agenda for a revisioned urban theory.

In Chapter 12, media expert Darnell M. Hunt takes his lead from *The City*, most especially Park's chapter on "The Natural History of the Newspaper." Park noted how the newspaper was, for better or worse, the mainstay of community intelligence in the early part of the twentieth century. This did not prevent newspapers from being gossipy, vulgar, or sensationalist—sometimes all three at once! Park thought that the public got the newspapers they deserved and that improvements would occur only if the public demanded them.

Hunt considers the "reporting," or representations, of Los Angeles at the beginning of the media-saturated twenty-first century. Multimedia representations mirror an acute fragmentation in the collected stories being told about the city; they axiomatically provide multiple ways of seeing. How, then, could we possibly arrive at shared meanings or understandings about the place, and our position in it? Or about collective social action? Hunt suggests that the cornucopia of mental maps in Los Angeles (born from a decentralized, multicultural, multi-identity metropolis) must somehow all be brought into play if we are to really know a place and adequately re-present our knowledge.

In subsequent chapters, Vasishth and Sloane resurrect The Chicago School's concept of urban ecology (Chapter 13), while Wolch, Pincetl, and Pulido take the Chicago protagonists to task for ignoring urban environmental issues (Chapter 14). Finally, Ethington and Meeker make their case for combining the Chicago and L.A. Schools (Chapter 15), and Dear attempts to assess the implications of the book's arguments (Chapter 16).

QUOTES FROM
THE CITY

The newspaper is the great medium of communication within the city, and it is on the basis of the information which it supplies that public opinion rests. The first function which a newspaper supplies is that which formerly was performed by the village gossip.

In spite, however, of the industry with which newspapers pursue facts of personal intelligence and human interest, they cannot compete with the village gossip as a means of social control. . . . In small communities there is a perfectly amazing amount of personal information afloat among the individuals who compose them.

The absence of this in the city is what, in large part, makes the city what it is. . . . (39)

The newspaper has a history; but it has, likewise, a natural history. The press, as it exists, is not, as our moralists sometimes seem to assume, the willful product of any little group of living men. On the contrary, it is the outcome of a historic process in which many individuals participated without foreseeing what the ultimate product of their labors was to be.

The newspaper, like the modern city, is not wholly a rational product. No one sought to make it just what it is. In spite of all efforts of individual men and generations of men to control it and make it something after their own heart, it has continued to grow and change in its own incalculable ways. . . . (80)

. . . Humanly speaking, the present newspapers are about as good as they can be. If the newspapers are to be improved, it will come through the education of the people and the organization of political information and intelligence. . . . (97)

The real reason that the ordinary newspaper accounts of the incidents of ordinary life are so sensational is because we know so little of human life that we are not able to interpret the events of life when we read them. It is safe to say that when anything shocks us, we do not understand it. (98)

CHAPTER 12

Representing "Los Angeles"
Media, Space, and Place

DARNELL M. HUNT

Throughout this volume, my colleagues journey from a variety of theoretical locations to (re)visit "Los Angeles" as a common object of inquiry. Their goal, in short, is to engage modern and postmodern conceptions of the city and city life and to assess the degree to which Los Angeles stands as an exemplar of contemporary urban processes. Surveying the Los Angeles landscape, for example, in Chapter 3, Dear and Flusty find patterns (and the lack thereof) that lead them to make generalizations about four primary forces behind postmodern urbanism. Similarly, Straughan and Hondagneu-Sotelo focus on the recent flood of immigrants into Los Angeles to highlight the shortcomings of both classical economic and macromodels of immigration (Chapter 7). Other contributors focus on Los Angeles phenomena as divergent as religion, homelessness, and gangs in their journeys to advance our understanding of the contemporary urban condition.

Undergirding each of these journeys, it seems, is some basic image of just what Los Angeles is—or is not. In a few cases, these images largely coincide, whereas in others, they barely overlap. By interrogating basic images such as the ones implicit in my colleagues' contributions, I hope to foreground what I see as the epistemological question that precedes those questions about what the city is—that is, how do we come to *know* "the city"? Moreover, how might this knowledge shape the urban processes that students of the city endeavor to understand? I explore these questions by problematizing Los Angeles as our common object of inquiry.

WHAT *IS* LOS ANGELES?

Commonsense knowledge first tells us that Los Angeles is a *place,* a geographic location cradled by mountains to the north and east and by the Pacific Ocean to the west. This physical space extends for hundreds of square miles, is engulfed in a desert climate, and is dotted with palm trees. But we also know Los Angeles as an urban environment[1] where masses of people live, work, and die. To many observers, this particular environment seems blessed with sunshine but cursed with fires, mudslides, and earthquakes. Its store of images includes the Lakers, several prominent universities, and Hollywood. It boasts one of the most racially and ethnically diverse populations in the world, one that is typically divided by freeways, socio-economic status, and political access. It has been blemished in recent years by civil unrest, crime, and polarization but has also been celebrated in Olympic Games, marathons, and film locations. Given these apparent complexities and contradictions, how are we to understand the nature of what is commonly referred to as Los Angeles?

The U.S. Bureau of the Census, for example, offers three rather divergent answers to the Los Angeles question. The first identifies an area known as the central city that in 1992 consisted of 469.3 square miles, had a population of 3.5 million, and was designated the largest single "place"[2] in the Los Angeles-Long Beach Primary Metropolitan Statistical Area (PMSA).[3] Meanwhile, the Census Bureau also defines this latter area as a "large urbanized county or cluster of counties that demonstrates very strong internal economic and social links, in addition to close ties to other portions of the larger area," with a population of 9.1 million in 1992.[4] Finally, the Census Bureau identifies a metropolitan area with a population between the third largest such area in the United States (Chicago at 8.4 million) and the largest (New York at 19.7 million). The Los Angeles/Riverside/Orange County Consolidated Metropolitan Area—the "larger area" of which the Los Angeles/Long Beach PMSA is a part—had a population of 15.0 million in 1992.[5] Implicit in these definitions are issues of physical space, social relationships, and economic exchange patterns. Yet as these patterns have changed through the years, so too have official definitions of Los Angeles.

But what of *popular* definitions? What does Los Angeles *mean* to those within and outside its boundaries? Modern conceptualizations of the city present it as a bounded, knowable object composed not only of pavement and buildings but of people and their day-to-day activities. Indeed, in the Chicago School's classic treatise on the city, Louis Wirth[6] outlined five discrete dimensions on which we might come to know the city: first, a geographic dimension, one defined by site, situation, topography, and density; second, a historical dimension identified by political status, title, and law; third, a statistical dimension establishing the parameters of the city with the type of census data and definitions I described above; fourth, a dimension rendering the city as an economic unit in which exchanges regularly occurred between a multitude of interdependent buyers and sellers; and fifth, a dimension revealing the sociological core of the city, from which residents become "conscious of their membership in some larger group known as the city."[7] This final dimension comes closest to addressing what Los Angeles might mean to its inhabitants. From this vantage point, we might understand Los Angeles as

a state of mind, a body of customs and traditions, and of the organized attitudes and sentiments that inhere in these customs and are transmitted with this tradition. [Los Angeles] is not, in other words, merely a physical mechanism and an artificial construction. It is involved in the vital processes of the people who compose it; it is a product of nature, and particularly of human nature.[8]

In other words, real people interact with and shape a real object they know as the city, and this activity is somehow patterned by the meanings people associate with an identifiable geographic and social center.

But postmodern analyses suggest that the center no longer stands as a referent. The city is instead conceptualized as an amalgamation of differentiated spaces held together primarily by structures of thought that work to pattern action but offer little closure. Los Angeles—often portrayed as the prototypical postmodern city—is the embodiment of these observations. Who can point to the center of Los Angeles? Is it marked by the downtown skyline? The theme building at Los Angeles International Airport? The Hollywood sign? Disneyland? Or is it better represented by Watts, Little Tokyo, Koreatown, East L.A., or Beverly Hills? Where should the boundaries of Los Angeles be drawn, and what do they mean? Indeed, Baudrillard[9] advances the provocative argument that Los Angeles *as place* is no longer real. Instead, it has become a third-order simulation[10] that relies on the explicitly imaginary nature of surrounding tourist attractions such as Disneyland and Magic Mountain to make us *believe* in its reality:

> Disneyland is presented as imaginary in order to make us believe that the rest is real, when in fact all of Los Angeles and the America surrounding it are no longer real, but of the order of the hyperreal and of simulation. It is no longer a question of a false representation of reality (ideology), but of concealing the fact that the real is no longer real, and thus of saving the reality principle.[11]

But Los Angeles is all too real. Although postmodern observations about the lack of center and closure sound compelling,[12] blanket denials of reality discount the day-to-day experiences and memories of real people,[13] blunt modernist attacks on normative structures,[14] and, by default, serve conservative agendas. At the same time, however, classic conceptualizations of the city also seem to fall short. Born of conquest in 1781 and nourished on real estate speculation and boosterism,[15] the phenomenal growth of Los Angeles through the years is no more a "product of nature" or "human nature" than is any other social construction.[16]

To the degree that Los Angeles is knowable, I propose that it is so as a *collective representation,*[17] or a commonsense, public understanding and explanation for the physical space, social relationships, and economic exchanges associated with the *place* in question. In other words, it is not that a real Los Angeles does not exist, it is that real people are engaged in a continuing struggle over what it is and how to represent it. Thus, although Los Angeles is (re)constructed by official definitions such as those of the Census Bureau, it is also simultaneously implicitly shaped by people's day-to-day experiences with it. We might usefully think of these experiences as either *direct* or *mediated*—the former including intensive, in-person encounters so central to classic understandings of community,[18] the latter based on encounters with various print or electronic media discourses. In today's increasingly mediated world,[19] however, the line between the two has arguably blurred as, more than ever, our understanding of "reality" is filtered through our encounters with media discourses. As Fiske puts it,

> There is a nondiscursive reality, but it has no terms of its own through which we can access it; it has no essential identity or meaning in itself: we can access this reality only through discourse, and the discourse that we use determines our sense of the real.[20]

Accordingly, the remainder of this chapter aims at outlining the *process* by which people actively represent Los Angeles through their encounters with media and experience it as a real *place*. To do this, I will review classic and contemporary statements about important interconnections between media, space, and place and conclude by proposing a model and research agenda for exploring the contours of Los Angeles as both contested space and mediated place.

MEDIA, SPACE, AND PLACE

It is hardly an accident that Robert Park, Ernest Burgess, and Roderick McKenzie are generally considered the "forerunners of mass communication, media, and audience research."[21] Their early investigations quickly revealed the growing importance of mass communication to urban life—how people are influenced and modified in the city through their media encounters. Through the years, several scholars have made similar observations, uncovering, in the process, critical links between media, space, and place.

In an early theoretical piece, for example, Lippman[22] acknowledges the independent reality of a material environment but argues that our understanding of it in modern times is largely filtered through media. Indeed, he juxtaposes the "isolated rural township"[23] of the past with urbanized society to make this point. In the former, "one could assume . . . a homogenous code of morals" and "take its supply of information for granted." That is, face-to-face contact in self-contained communities made it possible for individuals to know their environment more directly. In the latter, however, the "real environment" had become too complicated and massive for any one individual to experience and know directly:

> For the real environment is altogether too big, too complex, and too fleeting for direct acquaintance. We are not equipped to deal with so much subtlety, so much variety, so many permutations and combinations. And although we have to act in that environment, we have to reconstruct it on a simpler model before we can manage with it.[24]

For Lippman, then, what people think they know about the modern environment— "the pictures in our heads"[25]—was necessarily mediated, based largely on stereotypes from news media.

Contemporary media scholars have recirculated this basic insight by taking the argument one step further. Hartley,[26] for example, refers to the nation as an "invisible fiction" constructed by media, while Gans[27] argues that both nation and society are "social constructs which, for all practical purposes, do not exist until someone acts or speaks for them."[28] That is, the media are "constructors of nation and society"[29] and participate in the creation of what Sorlin calls a "symbolic proximity."[30]

Park's[31] early treatise on the metropolitan newspaper is concerned, centrally, with the "symbolic proximity" known as the city. Like Lippman,[32] he presents media as playing a prominent role in the construction of community. Unlike later conceptualizations,[33] he describes the newspaper as a "natural" emergence whose growth follows the basic societal trend from rural community to urban settlement. The "motive" of the metropolitan newspaper was, he explains, to "reproduce, as far as possible, in the city the conditions of life in the village."[34] Although that earlier form of settlement featured gossip and public opinion as forms of social control, city life is marked by high degrees of atomization and the impossibility of a meeting of the whole. Thus the metropolitan press—"with its persistent search in the drab episodes of city life for the romantic and the picturesque, its dramatic accounts of vice and crime, and its unflagging interest in the movements of personages of a more or less mythical high society"[35]—emerges as a common cultural forum. As such, newspaper representations of the city—be they crime stories, reports on city hall, or department store advertisements—serve an important integrative function for its inhabitants.

Later scholars, to be sure, had much to say about this classic premise. For example, Alexander[36] echoes Park, affirming the integrative function performed by media, their status in modern society "a functional substitute for concrete group contact."[37] Although he affirms this integrative role for media, Schudson questions its functionalist logic.[38] He acknowledges the role that media play "in the cultural construction of American nationhood and cityhoods and communityhoods across the land,"[39] yet in his earlier work,[40] he critiques Park's[41] natural history-evolutionary approach as one that ignores the role of interests and agency in the shaping of markets, media forms, and modes of use.

For critical scholars, media, interests, and markets are intricately connected. Adorno describes "mass culture" as a "system of signals that signals itself,"[42] which ultimately blurs the distinction between image and reality for a "resistanceless" audience[43]—that is, as consumers lose their memories to the "abstract present,"[44] a "canon of synthetically produced modes of behaviour"[45] controls them. This rather dismal perspective rests firmly on a basic image of urbanized society as a "mass" of atomized individuals. Adorno assumes that increasing divisions of labor and specialization reinforce the importance of the marketplace, decrease the need for social solidarity, and thus create fertile ground for media manipulation. Indeed, the metropolitan newspaper becomes a powerful tool of the "culture industry," integrating its audience from above—by constructing needs, modes of behavior, and a community of consumers.

Mills[46] stops just short of Adorno's[47] mass society thesis but nonetheless argues that media have played a prominent role in reshaping the nature of community in the United States. For Mills, a "community of publics" represents the democratic ideal whereby "virtually as many people express opinions as receive them."[48] A mass society, in contrast, is one in which fewer people express opinions than receive them, where the dominant type of communication is the formal media, and where the publics become *media markets*. Mills argues that U.S. society has moved closer to becoming such a mass society. Echoing Lippman's[49] observations of some thirty years earlier, Mills underscores what he sees as the central role that media play in the construction of the social environment:

> Very little of what we think we know of the social realities of the world have we found out firsthand. Most of the pictures "in our heads" we have gained from these media—even to the point where we often do not really believe what we see before us until we read about it in the paper or hear about it on the radio. The media not only give us information; they guide our very experiences. Our standards of credulity, our standards of reality, tend to be set by these media rather than our own fragmentary experience.[50]

Although earlier conceptualizations of the relationship between media, space, and place tended to concentrate on media content, McLuhan turns his attention, instead, to media *as technology*. For McLuhan, the medium—as an extension of our senses—*is* the message. Indeed, the electronic media, principally, extend our reach, thus eliminating space as "a main factor in social arrangements."[51] McLuhan, like Park, seems to understand community in evolutionary terms: The city emerges to remake "man into a more suitable form than his nomadic ancestors,"[52] but as the proliferation of electronic media remakes the entire globe into "a single consciousness," the city *as space* becomes increasingly "irrelevant":

> Metropolitan space is equally irrelevant for the telephone, the telegraph, the radio, and television. What the town planners call "the human scale" in discussing ideal urban spaces is equally unrelated to these electric forms. Our electric extensions of ourselves simply by-pass time and space, and create problems of human involvement and organization for which there is no precedent.[53]

Recent works on media and space have picked up on this theme, arguing that the technology of electronic media (i.e., instantaneous transmission) has contributed to "placelessness," to the decoupling of experience from physical location.[54]

By recentering the role of audiences, however, other studies demonstrate the shortcomings of the placelessness perspective. Morley, for example, criticizes postmodern visions of emergent placelessness as overstated claims based on little empirical evidence.[55] Indeed, these theories typically present globalization as a one-way process, whereby "the 'local' is itself often produced by means of the 'indigenization' of global resources and inputs."[56] Newcomb and Hirsch also acknowledge the integrative function performed by media (i.e., their reliance on a degree of shared meanings) but argue that the process is unstable—television being, for example, a "cultural forum" in which viewers struggle to make their own meanings from media, where "metaphoric 'fault lines' . . . are expressed and worked out."[57] Place, therefore, retains significance because the particulars of various localities (e.g., pressing social, political, and economic issues) influence the way that social actors decode media texts. Moreover, these same media encounters are routinely put to use by people as they attempt to navigate the particular localities in which they live:

> If everyday life is comprised of various procedures for negotiating places and producing paths and spaces, then "audience" becomes a way of considering how, when, and where certain technologies (television, radio, books) and techniques (viewing, listening, reading) are deployed to produce contexts, relations among sites, and networks.[58]

Ritual models of media acknowledge these audience activities, understanding communication as a process by which social actors (re)affirm, (re)enact, and celebrate community and their place in it.[59]

Returning, now, to our central problematic—what is Los Angeles, and how can we know it?—we see a considerable history of scholarly explorations into the various connections between media, space, and place. These links ultimately trace the process by which real people—including students of the city—come to know Los Angeles. In this sense, they are also essential to the social processes that continually shape life in the city. Below I flesh out these connections.

LOS ANGELES AS CONTESTED SPACE AND MEDIATED PLACE

Synthesizing postmodern insights about the decentered nature of "the real," critical understandings of power, and cultural concerns about meaning construction, I propose a model that conceptualizes Los Angeles *as representation*. Previous scholars of the city have tended to treat it either as concrete and empirically bounded[60] or as a rather abstract concept that suggests few clues for *how* one might engage in the practical work of actually mapping the social terrain that people experience.[61] The proposed model, by contrast, depicts Los Angeles as a mediated place whose reality ultimately depends on the meaning-making activities of social actors there as well as in other places. In other words, the reality of Los Angeles can be accessed and evaluated only through the discourses circulating at any given moment, discourses that are and have been produced by socially situated people to be consumed by others who are no less socially situated. As we shall see, this basic conceptualization expands the horizon of research questions that ought to be asked about our object of inquiry, as well as the empirical methods that might be brought to bear on it.

Figure 12.1 presents what is necessarily an oversimplified schematic of the proposed model. In two-dimensional space, it describes a complex, iterative process in which the material context influences a host of social factors that interact with one another to (re)shape and/or (re)produce that context. In short, the material context (1) constrains and patterns the types of social action (2) that are likely to take place in the city; this meaningful action provides the inputs for intertextual memory, (3) which, in turn, informs commonsense understandings of Los Angeles (4) (i.e, Los Angeles-as-representation); media workers encode these understandings into media

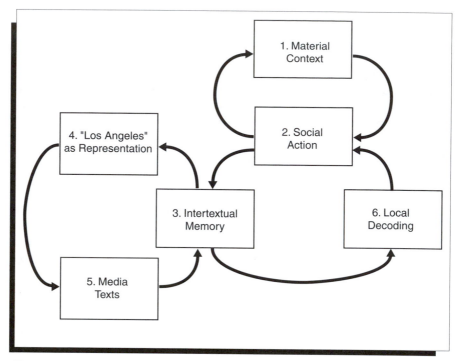

Figure 12.1. Representing Los Angeles: A Conceptual Model

texts (5), which necessarily pass through the filter of intertextual memory (3) as they are decoded (6) by differently situated social actors; the model comes full circle as these actors' local decodings pattern successive social actions, thereby (re)shaping and/or (re)producing the material context.

An important conceptual note is in order here. Despite my ordering of factors numerically (for narrative purposes), I conceive of the process as one without temporal beginning or end. The factors and related concepts, however, *are* ordered regarding their direct and indirect connections. The factors that directly construct Los Angeles as "contested space(s)" occupy the top third of the model (1 and 2) and are defined by the intersection of material factors (e.g., scarce resources) and the social actions of divergent groups. The middle third (3 and 6) includes factors that directly contribute to the formation of "community(ies)" such as the social groups that coalesce and splinter as people attempt to secure and justify their access to the scarce resources available within the material context. Factors that directly work to anchor and objectify "place(s)" in Los Angeles[62] compose the bottom third (4 and 5), particularly the struggle between intertextual memories and media representations of Los Angeles that work to integrate/cultivate the Los Angeles media market from above.[63] This model is designed to help us explicitly connect the various factors without losing sight of any particular link—as so often occurs in scholarly explorations into the city. Next, I offer an expanded discussion of the six factors and give examples for how each might contribute to the process by which Los Angeles is represented.

Material Context

By material context, I mean the objectively unknowable but nonetheless "real" array of ecological and economic factors that sustain and constrain life in the space(s) we refer to as Los Angeles. These factors include variables such as climate, population density, food supply, job market characteristics, and geographies of transportation and architecture, as well as, more generally, standards of living. Although modernist tropes often compare the workings of the city to the metabolism of organisms, treating them as objectively measurable developments of natural, evolutionary processes,[64] I understand the city as the subjective product of human consciousness and agency. Indeed, the forerunners to the later, radically positivist Chicago School shared similar understandings: As Ethington and Meeker note in this volume, scholars such as W. I. Thomas and George Herbert Mead were social constructionists who in the early twentieth century believed that what we see as the material world is necessarily suspended in symbolic communication.[65] Decades later, Blumer, describing symbolic interactionism, expresses the same insight, commenting that "objects have no fixed status except as their meaning is sustained through indications and definitions that people make of objects."[66] Yet in their rush to foreground the role that meaning plays in our knowledge of material contexts, symbolic interactionism and other forms of social constructivism often privilege microactivities to the exclusion of macroprocesses.

The concept of hegemony bridges this gap by combining the insights of social constructivism with notions of power, struggle, and discourse. Gramsci[67] describes it as an unstable equilibrium in the social order maintained through coercion and consent (undoubtedly the inspiration for Dear and Flusty's conceptualization of "praedatorianism" and "holsteinization" in Chapter 3, this volume). True to his Marxist roots, Gramsci views hegemony as the outgrowth of a struggle waged on many fronts between two opposing classes. Organic consciousness becomes an important object of inquiry, affecting the level of consent—a critical ingredient for the maintenance of any social order.

In a useful revision of Gramsci's work, Laclau and Mouffe define hegemony as "a political type of relationship" between a multitude of antagonistic forces that through discourse continually struggle to articulate their preferred views of social reality.[68] From time to time, Gramsci's "historical blocs" emerge, but these unifications of social and political space revolve around not only class but also distinct cores of interests, ideas, and identities. Moreover, Laclau and Mouffe depict hegemony as an unstable process that defies closure, one in which the identity of opponents is never fixed. In the end, the process works to overdetermine the material context through the prism of competing discursive fields.

> The fact that every object is constituted as an object of discourse has *nothing to do* with whether there is a world external to thought, or with the realism/idealism opposition. An earthquake or the falling of a brick is an event that certainly exists, in the sense that it occurs here and now, independently of my will. But whether their specificity as objects is constructed in terms of "natural phenomena" or "expression of the wrath of

God," depends upon the structuring of a discursive field. What is denied is not that such objects exist externally to thought, but the rather different assertion that they could constitute themselves as objects outside any discursive condition of emergence.[69]

In other words, we can gain access to the material context only through the meanings we produce about it in the course of symbolic interaction. Shaped by competing discourses, these meanings, in turn, (re)produce the material context by informing the actions of social agents who work within it.

For example, the spectacular growth of Los Angeles during the past century can be traced directly to this complex interaction between meaning and agency. Early growth in this region resulted from real estate speculation and boosterism that attracted millions of Midwesterners to the region. Images of sunshine, beaches, and affordable housing undoubtedly danced in the heads of these migrants, while railroad tycoons, land developers, and building contractors enjoyed skyrocketing profits. These meanings of Los Angeles were undoubtedly produced in conjunction with prominent discourses about health and material success and informed actions that actually changed the material context.

Similarly, we can attribute more recent Los Angeles growth largely to immigrants who were "pushed" out of their country of origin by relatively poor conditions and "pulled" into the region by relatively favorable ones. These factors exerted their force through peoples' understandings of their situations and their expectations about the better life that awaited them in Los Angeles. Yet as Straughan and Hondagneu-Sotelo point out in Chapter 7, classical economic accounts of immigration fail to explore the underlying conditions (e.g., the movement of global capital) that give rise to these factors in the first place. Accordingly, these classical models echo Parkian views of the city, and immigration acquires an almost natural, self-regulating quality. But push and pull factors are no more explained by natural process than are stock market fluctuations explained by Adam Smith's invisible hand.

Underlying the microdecisions made by immigrants are macrolevel issues of structure. Structure, of course, raises important issues concerning status, access, and power that microlevel analyses often gloss over. Unfortunately, however, macrolevel analyses frequently commit comparable sins by ignoring human agency altogether. It is as if structures emerge and exist in a vacuum, when in actuality they are the dynamic products of real people acting on the basis of meanings formed in specific social, political, and economic discourses. In other words, social action and the structures that pattern the material context are always mutually dependent spheres.[70]

Social Action

I define social action as significant action that is based on expectations about or in consideration of the consequences of that action. Immigration constitutes social action, as do crime, voting, working, and choosing which route to take home or which neighborhood to live in. Each of these activities depend, in the first instance, on actors' understanding of the situations that confront them and their relationship (actual or desired) to these situations. In other words, a necessary precursor to social action is thought, which is informed by important cultural elements such as values, norms, expectations, beliefs, and commonsense explanations—or representations. To a degree unprecedented in history, these representations are, today, continually circulated through media to social actors.

For example, my own research suggests that popular discourses surrounding the 1992 Los Angeles uprisings often depicted them as the result of black-white antagonisms. The *Los Angeles Times* thus described "the attack on Reginald Denny" as "the flip side of the attack on King—the unofficial, black-on-white answer to the official, white-on-black beating.[71] Within hours Los Angeles would plummet into chaos."[72] Indeed, offering the black-white explanation, early television news coverage of the events generally relied on and cultivated a prevailing racial common sense. First, the King beating verdicts—involving the beating of a black man by white police officers who were charged with use of excessive force and assault with a deadly weapon but acquitted by a white jury—were typically offered in isolation as *the* cause of the events. One local television station, for example, framed its entire coverage of the events the first evening with a graphic that read, "Cops on Trial: The Rodney King Case." Other causes that might have explained (or even acknowledged and considered) the involvement of Latinos, whites, and Asians thus went unexamined.[73] Moreover, the origins of the events were typically located in "South Central Los Angeles," an area that the media routinely associated with African Americans (especially African American gangs)—despite recent census representations that depict it as roughly half black and half Latino.[74] The same local television station that framed the events solely by the verdicts also reduced the boundaries of the "riot areas" to Watts, the flash point of the 1965 Los Angeles uprisings. Both Watts and South Central, of course, were similarly distorting as geographic indicators in that the events occurred in a number of places, from Long Beach to downtown Los Angeles, to Hollywood and beyond. Not surprisingly, perhaps, my interviews with both white and black informants suggested that they generally embraced the standard media representation of the events as black-white antagonism. Moreover, mirroring the tendency of local news media to seek out black officials and "community leaders" for comments, most informants understood blacks as the event insiders.

At the same time, however, racial common sense seemed to divide informants by how they interpreted and *used* this representation of the events. White informants generally viewed the events as crime, whereas black informants usually spoke of the events as an unfortunate yet necessary attempt by the oppressed to be heard. Although I lack conclusive data, it is quite conceivable that these images of the events—as those in Watts twenty-seven years earlier—have (re)shaped and/or (re)produced for social actors the mental maps outlining the "desirable" and "safe" places to live in Los Angeles. When acted on, these images directly affect the material context by deflating housing values in "undesirable" areas and constraining the wealth-producing possibilities of those who own homes in those communities.[75]

Intertextual Memory

Different social groups may make use of the same media representation in radically different ways, reflecting the power of memory to inflect our understanding of the situations that confront us. I define intertextual memory as the fluid reservoir of prior direct and mediated experiences or prior meaning-making processes. Although this memory is invoked by individual actors as a precursor to social action, it is not something that actors develop in isolation; rather it is (re)negotiated through time as social actors interact with one another and encounter new situations. Gabriel, for example, explains how the conditions confronted by marginalized groups result in the formation of a "collective memory" that often deviates from "official history."[76] Indeed, this memory "decisively frames the production and reception of commercial culture" for these groups,[77] and despite efforts to privilege certain meanings, society is never "sutured."[78] Accordingly, the places that constitute society's landscape are also contingent, the product of intertextual memories, never objectively knowable:

> Places are fragmentary and inward-looking histories, pasts that others are not allowed to read, accumulated times that can be unfolded like stories held in reserve, remaining in an enigmatic state, symbolizations encysted in the pain or pleasure of the body.[79]

In the 1992 Los Angeles uprisings, social actors likely activated strikingly different memories of the events when engaging television news images of fire and mayhem. Moreover, these memories may have inflected, for the moment at least, understandings of their "place" in Los Angeles. For example, one black informant who lived near the infamous intersection of Florence and Normandie[80] recalled, with fondness, a feeling of community that emerged among her neighbors the first night:

> It was like a campfire and everybody was outside, you know. Cooking and feasting together, for real. You see, it shows you how everybody, the whole neighborhood, the whole street just started cooking and everybody sharing food and all that.

In contrast, the same images prompted a white informant from West Los Angeles to remember the climate of fear that he and his companions endured that night:

> I smelled the flames and everything . . . and the whole air is like, there's like this cloud covering the sky or something. And you could smell the ashes everywhere you went. It was really bad. We were scared.

These memories, of course, fed into the process by which the informants made meanings from the news text, how they used and interpreted the representations of Los Angeles.

Los Angeles-as-Representation

By Los Angeles-as-representation, I mean the commonsense meanings that social actors there and in other places attribute to Los Angeles and its sociospatial characteristics. In other words, *as a representation,* Los Angeles becomes a conventionalized object that is classified and categorized along with other cities, urban areas, and metropolises such as New York, Philadelphia, or Chicago. As such, the unfamiliar or unknowable aspects of Los Angeles are made familiar and knowable. Indeed, the abstract notion of Los Angeles as city, urban area, or metropolis is made into something nearly concrete, a place that exists in the physical world—an object that can be measured, reported, and understood.[81] As Milgram puts it,

> The social representations of the city are more than disembodied maps; they are mechanisms whereby the bricks, streets, and physical geography of a place are endowed with social meaning. Such urban representations, therefore, help define the social order of the city, and the individual's place in it.[82]

But Los Angeles-as-representation is also prescriptive; that is, it imposes itself on us with irresistible force and provides a language for us to communicate what we think we already know about this place. Indeed, it is through the continual use of this representation in day-to-day discourse that the representation is hegemonically (re)shaped and (re)produced through time. As Moscovici points out, this process has accelerated greatly in today's increasingly complex and diverse material context.[83] The media's ever more available depictions of the environment have led to the continual (re)adjustment and (re)constitution of commonsense explanations, of the representations we rely on to make sense of our world. This function of media is particularly pertinent to Los Angeles as contested space.

For example, U.S. census representations of Los Angeles suggest that it is one of the most racially and ethnically diverse places in the world. Whether one looks at city, county, or metropolitan area population statistics, one finds that there is no majority group. Moreover, Los Angeles contains areas in which people from more than 140 nations reside, where more than eighty languages and dialects are used by county court interpreters.[84] The broad array of local media reflects this diversity, with at least ten ethnic and fourteen foreign language newspapers.[85] Each of these media works to (re)affirm, (re)enact, and celebrate life in relatively bounded area communities. As an index of their function, perhaps, the circulation of the largest area newspaper, the *Los Angeles Times,* has actually decreased in recent years while the population continues to grow.[86]

Nonetheless, mainstream media such as the *Los Angeles Times* continue to dominate the media market, circulating many of the representations that saturate the area. As is the case with media throughout the nation,[87] upper-middle-class white males are highly overrepresented in key decision-making positions in Los Angeles media. Indeed, all but one of the news directors at the mainstream television stations were white males in 1993. Accordingly, these and other mainstream media tend to privilege a white and middle-class view of Los Angeles. The area's diversity and complexity are typically presented as a form of surveillance that represents communities of color as threats to the established (white) order. Media coverage of these communities routinely zooms in on crime stories or other occurrences that fit with and fuel negative stereotypes[88] to the exclusion of other stories that might more fully portray the range of experiences in those areas. The Los Angeles-based Multicultural Collaborative expressed its concerns about such coverage in this way:

> The media wields a double-edged sword when it comes to race relations in Los Angeles and other communities. It has the potential to contribute powerfully to the understanding of complexities and the bridging of differences, and in some cases has begun to attempt such an effort. . . . But the media is also among those institutions perpetuating notions feeding the roots of racial conflict. For both the media as a profession and the products it generates, there are miles to go to abolish the exclusion, exploitation and misrepresentation of people of color.[89]

These concerns about how local media could/should represent diversity in Los Angeles echo the ritual model of media[90] and underscore the role played by the media in the contestation and construction of space, place, and community.

Media Texts

Los Angeles-as-representation, of course, is (re)shaped, (re)produced, and (re)circulated through a proliferation of media texts. Broadly defined, media *text* describes any construction of image, written word, and/or sound composed to convey certain privileged discourses. By *discourse,* I mean a network of ideas and statements constructed from key representations and normative expressions of commonsense understandings. In the case of Los Angeles-as-representation, media texts might employ disparate items as signifiers of place, including area maps (city, county, region); famous landmarks (city hall, the Coliseum, the Hollywood sign); background murals for local television news programs (the downtown skyline); topographical features (palm trees, mountains, ocean); area labels (South Central, Beverly Hills, East L.A., Watts); census data (statistics on population density, immigration, and income distribution); public officials (the mayor, city council members, the police chief); and styles (casual dress, gang attire, college sweatshirts). In Hay's words, "Places are designated and mediated discursively. They become signified and signifying frames of reference for social subjects."[91]

In Los Angeles, of course, media texts continually circulate in what is the second largest media market in the United States. The Los Angeles Designated Market Area covers twenty-two television stations in the cities of Los Angeles, Anaheim, Barstow, Corona, Huntington Beach, Ontario, Riverside, San Bernardino, Santa Ana, and Ventura.[92] The Los Angeles Arbitron Metro Market includes eighty-one radio stations from Anaheim to West Covina.[93] The Los Angeles Area of Dominant Influence is served by 251 daily and weekly newspapers—only nine of which carry Los Angeles on their nameplate.[94] Finally, hundreds of area studios and production facilities create countless film and television texts that circulate representations of Los

Angeles throughout the region and beyond. Although most of these media purport to serve the interests and needs of some community, all are beholden to the logic of the marketplace, all attempting to amass and cultivate the largest possible audience for sale to advertisers or for the sale of tickets. This continuing process sets many of the parameters by which Los Angeles is (re)constructed as place.

Local Decoding

Nonetheless, before media texts can contribute to the (re)construction of Los Angeles as place, they must be decoded at the local level by real people. Local decoding denotes the microprocess by which social actors make meanings from their encounters with media texts. This definition is, of course, informed by a vast body of literature that suggests that people are not passively duped by the media[95] but that they are active constructors of the symbolic universe surrounding them.[96] Thus, when real actors receive a media text, they consider not only the discourses and representations privileged by the text but also the meanings arising from their past experiences and their past encounters with other texts. In short, no text is ever self-contained—intertextuality is a given.[97] Moreover, local decoding is necessarily a social process. Social actors do not exist in a vacuum but are embedded in networks of social actors who are all continually encountering and making meanings from texts. These social connections inflect how people find meaning in texts, even when individual social actors encounter these texts alone. The resulting meaning-making process contributes daily to people's basic images of the place in which they live. Indeed, this "mapping helps secure an individual or group's relation to place, in part, by excluding or marginalizing other ways of imaging/imagining a relation to place."[98]

REPRESENTING LOS ANGELES: AN AGENDA FOR RESEARCH

> The growth of great cities has enormously increased the size of the reading public. Reading, a luxury in the country, has become a necessity in the city. In the urban environment, literacy is almost as much a necessity as speech itself.[99]

Three quarters of a century ago, Robert Park wrote about the newspaper because he correctly understood how reading it was central to city life. Yet so much has changed since then. Today, newspapers are just one among many popular media forms that circulate texts in and about the city, texts that are read by people both there and in other places. Moreover, the social geography of the city, shaped by a never-ending circulation of media texts, today has become a forever open, empirical question. Still, much remains the same. As Park discovered through his explorations into the function of the urban newspaper, today's broad array of newer media also acts as a cultural forum in which the meanings of life in the city are debated and negotiated. Students of the city, in my view, have heretofore underestimated the degree to which this process influences how we all come to know the city.

As I have argued throughout this chapter, we can best understand Los Angeles as representation. Yet I have suggested ways in which representations of this place might conflict and cut across issues of space and community. To understand how real people make sense of and *experience* Los Angeles, we need to empirically examine the mental maps that they use to navigate this space and their place in it. Only by entering this discursive realm can the reality of Los Angeles become an object of inquiry. As an initial stop on our intellectual journey, then, we need to amass audience ethnographies in Los Angeles and in other places so that we might begin to understand the process by which they negotiate the city—how real people interpret and act on representations of Los Angeles. Consider a questionnaire such as the following:

1. Where are you now (i.e., location in Los Angeles)?

2. Briefly describe the route you took to get here from your previous location.

3. Why did you make this journey?

4. Circle all that apply. Are you now
   a. listening to radio?
   b. watching television?
   c. reading a book or magazine?
   d. using a computer?
   e. listening to CDs, tapes, or other recorded music sources?
   f. participating in other types of communication?

5. Briefly describe the nature (or subject matter) of the activities you circled in question number 4.

Something such as this questionnaire could be periodically administered to a diverse sample of Los Angeles residents using a technique known as experience sampling. Informants would be outfitted with beepers or other devices that signal them at randomly chosen intervals to stop whatever they are doing and complete the brief questionnaire. The informant logs created from this sampling would then be used to jog the memory of each informant during an in-depth interview phase of the study, interrogating the links that informants make between the places in which they find themselves from time to time, their *social* locations (e.g., race, class, gender, and sexuality), and salient representations. Consequently, four of the five items in the proposed questionnaire are open-ended (if not polysemic) so that informants' own immediate interpretations of each situation can be used to actually drive the subsequent analyses.

A critical issue, of course, concerns how to link these individual maps (microlevel) to group and community maps and concerns (macrolevel), which brings us to the second stop on our journey. The tools of network analysis might be used to construct a sociogram[100] that fleshes out links between informants and centrally located social groups. Public statements made by representatives of the groups and other group literature would be textually analyzed to uncover each group's mental map of

Los Angeles. What patterns are evident in the distribution of maps across groups? Which maps predominate?

But these audience exercises would, of course, be incomplete. We would also need to learn more about the domain of representations in which the audiences' meaning-making activity occurs. The third stop on our journey would, therefore, take us to those who produce and circulate media texts in and about Los Angeles. That is, we need a systematic analysis of how the media texts that saturate the area (and other localities) work to construct Los Angeles as place. This analysis would also involve surveying official accounts of the material context (e.g., physical resources, population, industry, employment statistics, and so on), data used by people in Los Angeles and other places to make sense of life in the city. Although these texts are crucial in establishing the representational boundaries of this place, participation in their creation is far from equal. As Milgram notes,

> Social representations are the product of a multitude of persons. Not all of those persons, of course, need play an equal part in the formation of the urban image. Those occupying dominant positions in society have greater influence, prestige, and access to the media than poorer elements of society. They are therefore in a better position to impose their own conception of what is desirable and what must be avoided.[101]

In other words, we would need to know something about the context—economic, political, and ideological—in which representations are constructed, activated, and circulated. By using the individual and group analyses outlined above as a road map, we could identify salient texts (and/or communication technologies) and subject them to such an analysis. By whom were these texts created? For what purpose? What representations are embedded in them? Do they tend to privilege certain ideological understandings of this place? If so, what are the social, economic, and political implications?

In the final analysis, only by empirically exploring the intersection of real people and texts, of meaning making and power, can we truly begin to understand the process by which the city is represented and continually (re)constructed. That is, we must look beyond the "illusion of opaqueness" where "spatiality is reduced to physical objects and forms," beyond the "illusion of transparency" where "spatiality is reduced to mental construct alone,"[102] to the points where the substances of these illusions interact and mutually construct one another. This chapter offers but a few considerations that may, I hope, increase the range of empirical tools at our disposal and, more fundamentally, the range of questions we ask.

NOTES

1. Park [1925a/1967], Midway reprint, 1984, p. 1.
2. The Census Bureau (1992) defines *places* as either incorporated areas or "Census designated" places: "densely settled concentrations of population that are identifiable by name, but not legally incorporated places" (pp. A9-A10).
3. See U.S. Bureau of the Census, 1994-1995, Table 46.

4. U.S. Bureau of the Census, 1992, p. A9; see U.S. Bureau of the Census, 1994-1995, Table 42.

5. See U.S. Bureau of the Census, 1994-1995, Table 42.

6. Wirth [1925/1967], Midway reprint, 1984, p. 163.

7. Wirth [1925/1967], Midway reprint, 1984, p. 169.

8. Park [1925a/1967], Midway reprint, 1984, p. 1.

9. Baudrillard, 1993.

10. Baudrillard (1993) identifies four "successive phases" of the image: first, "it is a re-flection of a basic reality"; second, "it masks and perverts a basic reality"; third, "it masks the absence of a basic reality"; and fourth, "it bears no relation to any reality whatever: it is its own pure simulacrum" (pp. 346-347).

11. Baudrillard, 1993, p. 352.

12. See Lyotard, 1993.

13. Lipsitz, 1990.

14. Habermas, 1993.

15. Soja, 1989; Davis, 1990.

16. For example, the Chicago School's classic statement on the city assumed an ecologi-cal model that understood growth and development as a series of natural or evolutionary pro-gressions. This basic model is implicit in Burgess's (1925/1967) concentric circles and Park's (1950) race relations cycle.

17. Farr and Moscovici, 1984.

18. For example, Wirth, 1995.

19. Ewen and Ewen, 1992.

20. Fiske, 1994, p. 4.

21. Hay, 1996, p. 365.

22. Lippman, 1922.

23. Lippman, 1922, p. 171.

24. Lippman, 1922, p. 11.

25. Lippman, 1922, p. 3.

26. Hartley, 1989, p. 227.

27. Gans, 1979.

28. Gans, 1979, p. 298.

29. Gans, 1979, p. 297.

30. Sorlin, 1994, p. 55.

31. Park [1925b/1967], Midway reprint, 1984.

32. Lippman, 1922.

33. For example, Gans, 1979; Sorlin, 1994.

34. Park [1925b/1967], Midway reprint, 1984, p. 84.

35. Park [1925b/1967], Midway reprint, 1984, p. 94.

36. Alexander, 1981.

37. Park [1925a/1967], Midway reprint, 1984, p. 18.

38. Schudson, 1995.

39. Schudson, 1995, p. 42.

40. For example, Schudson, 1978.

41. Park [1925b/1967], Midway reprint, 1984.

42. Adorno, 1991, p. 71.

43. Adorno, 1991, p. 62.

44. Adorno, 1991, p. 60.

45. Adorno, 1991, p. 78.

46. Mills, 1956.

47. Adorno, 1991.

48. Mills, 1956, pp. 303-304.
49. Lippman, 1922.
50. Lippman, 1922, p. 311.
51. McLuhan, 1964, p. 95.
52. McLuhan, 1964, p. 67.
53. McLuhan, 1964, pp. 103-104.
54. For example, see Meyrowitz, 1985.
55. Morley, 1991.
56. Morley, 1991, p. 10.
57. Newcomb and Hirsch, 1994, pp. 511-512.
58. Hay, 1996, p. 369.
59. See Carey, 1989; Schudson, 1995.
60. For example, Burgess [1925/1967], Midway reprint, 1984.
61. For example, Soja, 1989.
62. Compare Moscovici, 1984.
63. Compare Adorno, 1991.
64. Park, Burgess, and McKenzie [1925/1967], Midway reprint, 1984.
65. Compare Chapter 15 of this volume.
66. Blumer, 1969, p. 12.
67. Gramsci, 1971.
68. Laclau and Mouffe, 1985, p. 138.
69. Laclau and Mouffe, 1985, p. 108.
70. Giddens, 1993; Fine and Kleinman, 1983.
71. Reginald Denny is the white trucker who was pulled from his truck by black youth and beaten in the middle of a South Central Los Angeles intersection during the earlier hours of the events.
72. Coffey, 1992, p. 45; Hunt, 1997.
73. Media might have alternatively portrayed the events as an unfortunate but necessary wake-up call for the government, an important societal agent that had neglected inner-city needs for years (cf. Johnson et al., 1992). Or they might have depicted the events in more systemic terms, as emblematic of struggles between haves and have-nots in a classist and racist society (cf. Robinson, 1993).
74. Johnson et al., 1992.
75. Oliver and Shapiro, 1995.
76. Gabriel, 1988, p. 70.
77. Lipsitz, 1990, p. vii.
78. Laclau and Mouffe, 1985, p. 111.
79. de Certeau, 1984, p. 108.
80. Most media accounts depicted the intersection of Florence and Normandie as the flash point of the events.
81. Moscovici (1984) calls this process—wherein unfamiliar objects are categorized and, thereby, given relatively stable meanings—"anchoring"; "objectifying" is the complementary process by which these categorized objects are made concrete, by which "what is perceived replaces what is conceived" (p. 40).
82. Milgram, 1984, p. 309.
83. Moscovici, 1984.
84. Pearlstone, 1990.
85. *Working Press of the Nation,* 1996.
86. From analysis of *Los Angeles Times* mastheads through time.
87. Wilson and Gutierrez, 1995.

88. Interviews with Los Angeles-based community advocacy groups and media watch-dog groups. See also Wilson and Gutierrez (1995).

89. Dowell, 1996, p. 71.

90. Compare Carey, 1989; Schudson, 1995.

91. Hay, 1996, p. 372.

92. *Working Press of the Nation,* 1996.

93. *Working Press of the Nation,* 1996.

94. *Working Press of the Nation,* 1996.

95. For example, see Garfinkel, 1967; de Certeau, 1984; Fiske, 1987, 1989.

96. For example, see Berger and Luckmann, 1966.

97. See Fiske (1987) for a cogent discussion of horizontal and vertical intertextuality. The first involves common axes such as genre and character, whereas the second refers to specific references in one or more texts to another.

98. Hay, 1996, p. 375.

99. Park [1925b/1967], Midway reprint, 1984, p. 81.

100. Compare Knoke and Kuklinski, 1982; Wellman and Berkowitz, 1988.

101. Milgram, 1984, pp. 308-309.

102. Soja, 1989, pp. 122-125.

REFERENCES

Adorno, Theodor. 1991. The schema of mass culture. In *The culture industry: Selected essays on mass culture,* ed. J. M. Bernstein. London: Routledge.

Alexander, Jeffrey C. 1981. The mass media in systemic, historical and comparative perspective. In *Mass media and social change,* ed. E. Katz and T. Szesko. Beverly Hills, Calif.: Sage.

Baudrillard, Jean. 1993. The precession of simulacra. In *A postmodern reader,* ed. J. Natoli and L. Hutcheon. Albany: State University of New York Press.

Berger, Peter L., and Thomas Luckmann. 1966. *The social construction of reality: A treatise in the sociology of knowledge.* New York: Anchor.

Blumer, Herbert. 1969. *Symbolic interactionism: Perspective and method.* Berkeley: University of California Press.

Burgess, Ernest W. 1925, 1967. The growth of the city: An introduction to a research project. In *The city: Suggestions for investigation of human behavior in the urban environment,* by R. E. Park, E. W. Burgess, and R. D. McKenzie. Chicago: University of Chicago Press, Midway reprint, 1984.

Carey, James. 1989. *Communication as culture.* Boston: Unwin Hyman.

Coffey, Shelby, III, ed. 1992. *Understanding the riots: Los Angeles before and after the Rodney King case.* Los Angeles: Los Angeles Times.

Davis, Mike. 1990. *City of quartz: Excavating the future in Los Angeles.* London: Vintage.

de Certeau, Michel. 1984. *The practice of everyday life.* Berkeley: University of California Press.

Dowell, Carol. 1996. The media machine. In *Race, power and promise in Los Angeles: An assessment of responses to human relations conflict.* Los Angeles: Multicultural Collaborative.

Ewen, Stuart, and Elizabeth Ewen. 1992. *Channels of desire: Mass images and the shaping of American consciousness.* Minneapolis: University of Minnesota Press.

Farr, Robert M., and Serge Moscovici. 1984. *Social representations.* Cambridge: Cambridge University Press.

Fine, Gary Alan, and Sherryl Kleinman. 1983. Network and meaning: An interactionist approach to structure. *Symbolic Interaction* 6: 97-110.

Fiske, John. 1987. *Television culture.* London: Routledge.

Fiske, John. 1989. *Understanding popular culture.* Boston: Unwin Hyman.

Fiske, John. 1994. *Media matters: Everyday culture and political change.* Minneapolis: University of Minnesota Press.

Gabriel, Teshome H. 1988. Thoughts on nomadic aesthetics and the black independent cinema: Traces of a journey. In *Blackframes: Critical perspectives on black independent cinema,* ed. M. B. Cham and C. Andrade-Watkins. Cambridge: MIT Press.

Gans, Herbert. 1979. *Deciding what's news.* New York: Pantheon.

Garfinkel, Harold. 1967. *Studies in ethnomethodology.* Cambridge, Mass.: Polity.

Giddens, Anthony. 1993. Problems of action and structure. In *The Giddens reader,* ed. P. Cassell. Stanford, Calif.: Stanford University Press.

Gramsci, Antonio. 1971. *Selections from the prison notebooks.* New York: International Publishers.

Habermas, Jürgen. 1993. Modernity versus postmodernity. In *A postmodern reader,* ed. J. Natoli and L. Hutcheon. Albany: State University of New York Press.

Hartley, John. 1989. Invisible fictions: Television audiences, paedocracy, pleasure. In *Television studies: Textual analysis,* ed. G. Burns and R. J. Thompson. New York: Praeger.

Hay, James. 1996. Afterword: The place of the audience: Beyond audience studies. In *The audience and its landscape,* ed. J. Hay, L. Grossberg, and E. Wartella. Boulder, Colo.: Westview.

Hunt, Darnell M. 1997. *Screening the Los Angeles riots: Race, seeing and resistance.* Cambridge: Cambridge University Press.

Johnson, James H., Cloyzelle K. Jones, Walter C. Farrell Jr., and Melvin L. Oliver. 1992. The Los Angeles rebellion, 1992: A preliminary assessment from ground zero. UCLA Center for the Study of Urban Poverty Occasional Working Paper Series. Los Angeles: UCLA Institute for Social Science Research.

Knoke, David, and James H. Kuklinski. 1982. *Network analysis.* London: Sage.

Laclau, Ernesto, and Chantal Mouffe. 1985. *Hegemony and socialist strategy: Towards a radical democratic politics.* London: Verso.

Lippman, Walter. 1922. *Public opinion.* New York: Free Press.

Lipsitz, George. 1990. *Time passages: Collective memory and American popular culture.* Minneapolis: University of Minnesota Press.

Lyotard, Jean-François. 1993. Excerpts from *The postmodern condition: A report on knowledge.* In *A postmodern reader,* ed. J. Natoli and L. Hutcheon. Albany: State University of New York Press.

McLuhan, Marshall. 1964. *Understanding media: The extensions of man.* New York: McGraw-Hill.

Meyrowitz, Joshua. 1985. *No sense of place.* Oxford, England: Oxford University Press.

Milgram, Stanley. 1984. Cities as social representations. In *Social representations,* ed. R. M. Farr and S. Moscovici. Cambridge: Cambridge University Press.

Mills, C. Wright. 1956. *The power elite.* London: Oxford University Press.

Morley, David. 1991. Where the global meets the local: Notes from the sitting room. *Screen* 32, no. 1 (spring): 1-15.

Moscovici, Serge. 1984. The phenomenon of social representations. In *Social representations,* ed. R. M. Farr and S. Moscovici. Cambridge: Cambridge University Press.

Newcomb, Horace, and Paul M. Hirsch. 1994. Television as a cultural forum. In *Television: The critical view,* 5th ed., ed. H. Newcomb. Oxford, England: Oxford University Press.

Oliver, Melvin L., and Thomas M. Shapiro. 1995. *Black wealth, white wealth: A new perspective on racial inequality.* New York: Routledge.

Park, Robert E. 1925a, 1967. The city: Suggestions for the investigation of human behavior in the urban environment. In *The city: Suggestions for investigation of human behavior in the urban environment,* by R. E. Park, E. W. Burgess, and R. D. McKenzie. Chicago: University of Chicago Press, Midway reprint, 1984.

Park, Robert E. 1925b, 1967. The natural history of the newspaper. In *The city: Suggestions for investigation of human behavior in the urban environment,* by R. E. Park, E. W. Burgess, and R. D. McKenzie. Chicago: University of Chicago Press, Midway reprint, 1984.

Park, Robert E. 1950. *Race and culture.* Glencoe, Ill.: Free Press.

Park, Robert E., Ernest W. Burgess, and Roderick D. McKenzie. 1925, 1967. *The city: Suggestions for investigation of human behavior in the urban environment.* Chicago: University of Chicago Press, Midway reprint, 1984.

Pearlstone, Zena. 1990. *Ethnic L.A.* Beverly Hills, Calif.: Hillcrest Press.

Robinson, Cedric J. 1993. Race, capitalism, and the anti-democracy. In *Reading Rodney King, reading urban uprising,* ed. R. Gooding-Williams. New York: Routledge.

Schudson, Michael. 1978. *Discovering the news: A social history of American newspapers.* New York: Basic Books.

Schudson, Michael. 1995. *The power of news.* Cambridge, Mass.: Harvard University Press.

Soja, Edward W. 1989. *Postmodern geographies: The reassertion of space in critical social theory.* London: Verso.

Sorlin, Pierre. 1994. *Mass media: Key ideas.* London: Routledge.

U.S. Bureau of the Census. 1992. *Public use microdata samples U.S. technical documentation.* Washington, D.C.: Author.

U.S. Bureau of the Census. 1994-1995. *American almanac: Statistical abstract of the United States.* Washington, D.C.: Government Printing Office.

Wellman, Barry, and S. D. Berkowitz. 1988. *Social structures: A network approach.* Cambridge: Cambridge University Press.

Wilson, Clint C., II, and Felix Gutierrez. 1995. *Race, multiculturalism, and the media: From mass to class communication,* 2nd ed. Thousand Oaks, Calif.: Sage.

Wirth, Louis. 1925, 1967. A bibliography of the urban community. In *The city: Suggestions for investigation of human behavior in the urban environment,* by R. E. Park, E. W. Burgess, and R. D. McKenzie. Chicago: University of Chicago Press, Midway reprint, 1984.

Wirth, Louis. 1995. Urbanism as a way of life. In *Seeing ourselves: Classic, contemporary, and cross-cultural readings in sociology,* ed. J. J. Macionis and N. V. Benokraitis. Englewood Cliffs, N.J.: Prentice Hall.

Working press of the nation. 1996. Chicago: National Research Bureau.

Returning to Ecology
An Ecosystem Approach
to Understanding the City

EDITOR'S
COMMENTS

In *The City,* the chapters by McKenzie and Burgess consistently return to the central ecological metaphor of the Chicago School. In the following extracts, they draw strongly on lessons of plant ecology (including notions of invasion, succession, etc.) to account for the growth of urban communities. In this chapter, Ashwani Vasishth and David Sloane reconsider human ecology and discover merit in a scale-sensitive ecosystem approach to understanding and planning the city. From a stout defense of the Chicago School's legacy, they argue that fundamental categories (such as organism, population, and community) retain their significance. In addition, the ecosystem approach retains the emphasis on place, and thus brings the environment back into consideration.

QUOTES FROM *THE CITY*

In the process of community growth there is a development from the simple to the complex, from the general to the specialized; first to increasing centralization and later to a decentralization process. In the small town or village the primary universal needs are satisfied by a few general stores and a few simple institutions such as church, school, and home. As the community increases in size specialization takes place both in the type of service provided and in the location of the place of service. The sequence of development may be somewhat as follows: first the grocery store, sometimes carrying a few of the more staple dry goods, then the restaurant, poolroom, barber shop, drug store, dry-goods store, and later bank, haberdashery, millinery, and other specialized lines of service.

The axial or skeletal structure of a community is determined by the course of the first routes of travel and traffic. . . . The point of junction or crossing of two main highways, as a rule, serves as the initial center of the community.

As the community grows there is not merely a multiplication of houses and roads but a process of differentiation and segregation takes place as well. Residences and institutions spread out in centrifugal fashion from the central point of the community, while business concentrates more and more around the spot of highest land values. Each cyclic increase of population is accompanied by greater differentiation in both service and location. There is a struggle among utilities for the vantage-points of position. This makes for increasing value of land and increasing height of buildings at the geographic center of the community. As competition for advantageous sites becomes keener with the growth of population, the first and economically weaker types of utilities are forced out to less accessible and lower-priced areas. By the time the community has reached a population of about ten or twelve thousand, a fairly well-differentiated structure is attained. . . . (73-74)

The structural growth of community takes place in successional sequence not unlike the successional stages in the development of the plant formation. . . . [J]ust as in plant communities successions are the products of invasion, so also in the human community the formations, segregations, and associations that appear constitute the outcome of a series of invasions. . . . (74)

The general effect of the continuous processes of invasions and accommodations is to give to the developed community well-defined areas, each having its own peculiar selective and cultural characteristics. Such units of communal life may be termed "natural areas," or formations, to use the term of the plant ecologist. . . . It has been suggested that these natural areas or formations may be defined in terms of land values, the point of highest land value representing the center or head of the formation (not necessarily the geographic center but the economic or cultural center), while the points of lowest land value represent the periphery of the formation or boundary line between two adjacent formations. . . . (77-78)

. . . [C]ommunity life, as conditioned by the distribution of individuals and institutions over an area, has at least three quite different aspects.

First of all, there is the community viewed almost exclusively in terms of location and movement. . . . (144) This apparently "natural" organization of the human community, so similar in the formation of plant and animal communities, may be called the "ecological community." . . . (145)

In the second place, the community may be conceived in terms of the effects of communal life in a given area upon the formation or the maintenance of a local culture. Local culture includes those sentiments, forms of conduct, attachments, and ceremonies which are characteristic of a locality, which have either originated in the area or have become identified with it. This aspect of local life may be called "the cultural community." . . . (145)

There remains a third standpoint from which the relation of a local area to group life may be stated. In what ways and to what extent does the fact of common residence in a locality compel or invite its inhabitants to act together? . . . This is the community of the community organization worker and of the politician, and may be described as "the political community." (146)

CHAPTER 13

Returning to Ecology
An Ecosystem Approach
to Understanding the City

ASHWANI VASISHTH
DAVID C. SLOANE

RETHINKING RAIN IN LOS ANGELES

When people think of rain, they don't think of sunny Southern California, and if they do, they're only remembering the most recent drought. Because the paucity of rainfall is foremost in people's minds in a drought-prone region, related issues such as storms receive relatively short shrift in urban policy and planning. As with many ecological processes, however, the particulars make a difference. On average, about half of Southern California's total annual precipitation is concentrated in a handful of storms that occur during a couple of months.[1] Because of this disproportionate intensity in downpour, issues related to urban storm water drains and beach debris provide a simple example of the need to rethink urban environmental planning in a way that recognizes the functional scales of natural processes.

The city of Los Angeles, along with most of the cities in Los Angeles County, has an extensive system of storm water drains that run directly into the ocean without any pretreatment. For most of the year, these drains are dry, accumulating trash from city streets. When the rains come, tons of trash are carried out to the ocean, tidal action returning between 50 to 75 percent of this garbage to coastal beaches. Well over half of all debris found on Southern California's beaches may have originated in inland cities and towns.[2]

Under conventional public planning and policy decision-making structures, "local" concerns are prioritized over "global" concerns. At each level of decision making—city, county, state, nation—administrative units treat their boundaries as natural delimiters of responsibility. The difference between what is local and global, however, is not always obvious. If, for instance, the city decided for budgetary reasons to reduce the number of downtown trash cans and the frequency of trash collection and street-cleaning operations,[3] this "local" decision might save the city's taxpayers money and have only a marginal impact on the appearance of downtown Los Angeles. From an ecological standpoint, however, the cutbacks would quickly increase the amount of trash deposited on the beaches of Santa Monica Bay. The city of Santa Monica would, then, be forced to either increase its beach sanitation expenditures or abrogate its civic responsibility. From such an ecological view, which may require drawing different boundaries, what does it mean to speak of "the city"?

A different response to such environmental and community issues might be to take an ecosystem approach to decision making in urban planning and policy. Then, the city could be seen as a conceptual label given to layered, overlapped, and nested arrangements of subsystems, systems, and suprasystems organized in scale-hierarchic rather than rank-hierarchic arrangements. We would better treat the patterns we observe in the city as tangible but abstract representations of intangible but actual processes and functions. Once urban planners and policymakers begin to take such an ecosystem approach, words such as *local* and *global* are transformed. They are no longer robust natural categories but simply stereotypes providing first approximations, awaiting refinement and the insertion of functional and perspectival meaning.

Yet making such a transition requires confronting three quarters of a century of social theory building. The early direction of this enterprise was set by founders of the Chicago School of sociology, who derived their urban theory from their conceptions of science and nature, particularly ecology and evolution. Robert E. Park, Ernest W. Burgess, and Roderick D. McKenzie adopted the then current vegetation ecology model of population dynamics and successional change in plant communities, as proposed by Frederic Clements, to draw a theory of urban organization and change. They also used work from animal ecology and cell physiology to understand the role of competition and cooperation as mechanisms for evolutionary change and progress. These examples became the foundation for their subsequent efforts to empirically measure and map urban patterns and processes and, more generally, to ecologize the study of society.[4]

Many conventional critiques of the Chicago sociologists ignore the historical moment of their activity, and so underrate the transformative aspects of their ecological leanings. As ecologists have moved beyond these primitive, prototypical models of natural organization and occurrence to develop more sophisticated notions of ecosystem dynamics that take account of patchiness and perturbation,[5] the short-comings and errors embedded in those early models become easy to detect. More recently, neo-Marxist and postmodern theorists have suggested that the city—through a globalizing economy and post-Fordist production—has so radically transformed from turn-of-the-century cities caricatured by the Chicago model that the "concentric circles" model has lost both descriptive and explanatory power and must be completely replaced.

Yet a closer examination of the writings of Burgess, Park, and McKenzie suggests that contemporary efforts to understand urban social systems might benefit more by building on the work of these early Chicago sociologists than by rejecting it entirely. Therefore, we suggest that the turn to ecology initiated by the Chicago urban theorists still provides a sound foundation for urban research.[6] Discarding the confounding effects of the then prevalent organismic frame and the notion of progress as ceaseless improvement, and introducing a natural organization and occurrence approach from ecosystem ecology, we argue that the scale-hierarchic ecosystem concept provides a rich and versatile frame for urban inquiry. Moreover, such an ecosystem approach, by centralizing historic, purposive, and perspectival contingency, makes room for subjective as well as objective modes of knowing.

THE CHICAGO SCHOOL AND THE CITY

The Chicago School of sociology, prior to World War II, represents the first institutionalized and systematic effort to take an ecological approach to social theory and to look for ways to study community as an emergent entity. This school's work represents a turning point in the place of cities, communities, urban phenomena, and social facts, as distinct from social analysis, as special objects of study in social theory. Park, Burgess, McKenzie, and other early human ecologists are conventionally credited with institutionalizing, if not establishing, sociology as a science. They are also criticized for their overly empiricist and idealized approach to the study of society. Yet the temper of their time and the momentum of ideas that enabled their work in the first place were such that both the institutionalization and empiricization were, perhaps, inevitable.

Social theorists such as Émile Durkheim, Ferdinand Toennies, and Georg Simmel centrally informed the Chicago School sociologists, as they did turn-of-the-century Americans.[7] They took from John Dewey and George Herbert Mead the principle that social research be directed by a concern for effecting improvement in prevailing social conditions.[8] In particular, Albion Small played no small role in shaping the direction and research of Chicago's Department of Sociology.[9] He pushed systematically for an empirical, research-driven social theory instead of the armchair theorizing that had become so typical in the United States[10] and made a concerted effort to incorporate the work of European theorists into the curriculum.[11] Small was instrumental in sociology's shift away from the study of patterns and toward the analysis of processes.[12]

Finally, the Chicago schools of pragmatism and sociology were influenced by the city of Chicago itself. In it, the Chicago social scientists saw patterns of rapid and dynamic growth driven by migration, and their recognition of migration as a formative pressure on patterns of urbanization conditioned the tools they crafted, the techniques they developed, and the concepts they evoked in their models. The particulars of urban change—the waves of immigrants, arriving, concentrating, and dispersing in patterned succession—and of ecological processes—invasion, assimilation, adaptation, cooperation, competition, and local migration—shaped their theoretical structures and the questions they asked in their research.

ECOLOGY AND SOCIAL THEORY

Three dialectical histories of ideas in social thought converge to give direction, shape, and meaning to the work of the Chicago sociologists: ideas about the relationship between individual and community, or entity and environment; the nature and meaning of progress, equilibrium, and climax; and the relationship between pattern and process, structure and function, and organization and occurrence. These three themes have centrally shaped and polarized debates in social theory.[13]

From at least Auguste Comte's efforts in the mid-1850s to articulate a positive methodology, and Herbert Spencer's efforts to lay out a more prescriptive sociology of structure and function, conceptions in social theory have been grounded firmly in ideas about individual organisms—particularly as they affect assumptions about progress, equilibrium, and climax.[14] Both social theorists and scientists of nature have persistently projected characteristics of individual organisms on community and society by the use of organismic analogies.[15] But much as this organicism may have helped explorations of organization by providing the reductionist tools necessary for inquiry, it obscured at least some of what could be known, even then, about natural occurrence.

Although knowledge of organisms has always informed our understanding of nature, this organicism became more problematic with the turn-of-the-century transition from a population to a community view. Levine[16] suggests that although Durkheim was opposed to the use of organismic analogy to understand community, his refinements to the understanding of patterns and processes in society rest on ideas of a self-maintaining social organism. The efforts of Clements to organize ideas about successional change in vegetative communities are also schematically driven by the idea of community as superorganism.[17] At least some of the critiques of Chicago sociology in planning might more accurately be leveled at the limitations of organicism in explaining community-level phenomena.

Individual and Community

Views of the relationship between individuals and community reveal a deep-rooted division in social theory. Is community (society) knowable as an additive agglomeration of individuals and events, or is community (society) a thing apart, always more than any aggregation of individuals? Can we sufficiently explain group interactions by examining the individuals who compose a group, or, as Durkheim had it, are individuals themselves the products of community? If community is no more than some summing of its individual members, then data on individuals will explain community. More important for urban studies, community-level patterns can be used to map individual-level processes. But if community is more than merely the sum of its individual members, then community must be described at its own level of organization. This way, we can see community-level patterns and processes as distinct from patterns and processes in populations of individuals.

In tracing the use of spatial metaphors in social theory, Silber points to Durkheim's

> attention to the "external," constraining reality of social facts, the boundedness of social wholes, the statistical distribution and density of social phenomena within the territory of the nation-state, and, perhaps best known, the ritual enforcement of physical and other boundaries between sacred and profane.[18]

Following from the work of social theorists such as Simmel, Durkheim, and Toennies, an increasing acceptance of such an environmental, contextual frame accompanies the emergence of a community view of natural organization.

Organicism and Evolution

The confounding influence of organicism on evolutionary thought rests on the assumption that the process of change in individual organisms is, generally speaking, a good thing. This assumption is based, for example, on the idea that an organism's ability to maintain a fairly constant internal state in the face of environmental stress produces equilibrium in nature. The life cycle of an organism, from embryo to infant to youth to maturity to death and decay, therefore, becomes a plausible model for successional change in levels of organization other than the individual.[19] The improvements apparent in the human condition—the increases in knowledge and technology and cultural refinement so evident through the life span of even a single generation—reinforce the idea of evolutionary progress as increasing improvement. But deep and persistent divisions pervade discussions of equilibrium, progress, and succession and are particularly relevant in the context of the Chicago urban sociologists and the ways in which these ideas are incorporated in their models of urban patterns and processes.

From early on, natural and social scientists accepted the idea that nature moves toward equilibrium in response to changing external conditions, and organismic metaphors were used extensively even in medieval times.[20] Hippocrates, the Greek physician, pressed the idea of homeostasis in hypothesizing the tendency of organisms and their organs to return to health after disruption or disease.[21] But only after theorists began to see the limits of this typological view did an individual or population view begin to emerge and knowledge of organisms begin to find application in generating explanatory and instrumental models that went beyond mere analogy. Only after this transition—associated as it was with the rise of a Darwinian model— was a concept of dynamic equilibrium and homeostasis legitimized. Organismic conceptions of evolutionary change began to be applied in different ways to social theory, influencing the emergence of sociology as a science, in the work of Comte, Spencer, and Durkheim.[22]

From Types to Populations

Both Comte and Spencer began their efforts to formulate a science of society and social development from a conception of dynamic equilibrium, of the tendency toward harmony and balance and fit between organisms and their changing environment, where a "failure to maintain this harmony or balance—failure on the part of the organism either to modify its form in response to changes in the environment or (in the case of man) to modify the environment itself—would result in the death of the organism."[23] This is the property they then extend to society, seeing it as, itself, an organism:

> Life for the organism, as we have seen, depends on the maintenance of equilibrium between organism and environment—a maintenance achieved through the mutual interaction of organic functions. Similarly, the social organism maintained itself through interrelation among its constituent parts. As in healthy animal organisms no question could arise of conflict or competition among parts, so the tendency to cooperation rather than dissidence characterized the social organism as well.[24]

But although Comte and Spencer share this common ground,[25] their arguments develop in opposition to one another,[26] and at least some of the tension between them derives from their different ideas of progress.[27] For Comte, evolutionary progress was little more than a manifestation of a perpetually responsive adaptation by organisms to shifts in their environment, leaving a world that was, at any given moment, "as good as it could be." Spencer began similarly, by taking progress to be driven by adaptive responses, but instead posited some final, ideal state toward which this progress was inexorably driven. For Spencer, evolutionary change was little more than a transitional phase, one that would terminate in a single, perfect ultimate state.[28]

But the subsequent Durkheimian project of transferring the organismic frame from individuals to community and society[29] remained problematic and limited in application until the emergence of some operational conception of group evolution. The work of botanists and plant geographers provided just such a conception, marked in most accounts by Eugenius Warming's efforts to systematize knowledge of plant communities and of the patterns and processes of "communal life." In 1866, Ernst Haeckel coined the word *ecology*, and this later body of work synthesizing the organismic conceptions of community with the conceptions of landscape by geographers gave shape and substance to ecology as a science.[30]

From Population to Community

This transition from a population view of nature to a community view marks the start of the ecological moment, although preconceptions of organismic behavior and development remain entrenched and buried deep in early conceptions of community. The turn-of-the-century work of plant ecologists and plant geographers such as Henry C. Cowles[31] and Frederic E. Clements,[32] following from Warming's operational outline in 1895 of the ecology of plant communities, generated many of the instrumental sociological conceptions of community organization and occurrence. Ironically, these ideas of developmental succession and of climax states, which themselves derived from early organismic social theories,[33] reinforced the applications of an organismic frame in the study of community—even as they allowed theorists and scientists alike to transcend the population view of nature.

But it was Clements's conception of community as a superorganism and of monoclimax—the development of communities in a fixed pattern of successional stages from inception through to some single ultimate climax state—that provides the keystone for the empirical, although admittedly organismic, study of both ecological and social community. As Golley points out,

> Clements' concept of the vegetation as a superorganism is appealing since we can readily develop the analogy from our personal knowledge of individuals. . . . The (vegetative) formation "arises, grows, matures, and dies." Thus, the community and formation have unique emergent properties which are greater than the sum of the properties of the parts.[34]

Although Clements's postulation of vegetative patterns and processes proved central to the enterprise of both ecology and social theory, his theory of successional development was intended more as an idealized frame for structuring inquiry than as any product of systematic observation. Within ecology, his ideas of succession toward a climatically determined monoclimax were quickly challenged[35] but never quite displaced until the more recent transition in ecology to an ecosystem view.[36]

Clements's Spencerian conception of nature was formatively influenced by his own experience of the pioneering settlement of the North American prairie by white Europeans and also explicitly by Frederick Jackson Turner's 1893 account of the evolutionary life history of frontier society.[37]

> In a 1935 essay, for example, [Clements] explicitly compared the development of vegetation with the pattern of settlement on the frontier of the Middle West. The progression of plants in a habitat follows a process of pioneering and settlement, just as man's advance was doing on the prairie. The stages of civilization formed their own kind of sere: first trapper, then hunter, pioneer, homesteader, and finally urbanite.[38]

Admixtures of these core conceptions—of community as superorganism, of orderly successional stages of development toward some preferred or ideal state, of self-regulating equilibrium, of progress as improvement and civilization, of change as organismic and comparable to individual life histories, and the notions of association, interdependence, cooperation and pioneering invasion—limit the sorts of tools conceptually available to the Chicago sociologists in developing an empirical science of society. These forces, bound by the insights and prejudices of the time, mark the ecological moment of Chicago urban sociology in their transition from an individual to a community frame.

The Ecological Turn

A key driver in this ecological turn was an emerging awareness of the distinction between pattern and process. In the study both of nature and of society, there was a growing recognition that the structures, forms, and patterns most apparent to direct observation were merely material manifestations of underlying processes and functions. These processes and relationships were the true constitutive forces in nature and society, and thus the proper objects of inquiry, while the patterns they generated were indexes that allowed one to "get at" the processes behind them, providing the tools by which to change nature and society.

The Burgess zonal hypothesis is likely the most widely known and probably the most narrowly understood concept of the Chicago urban sociologists. The fact of urban expansion was well recognized by the turn of the century, particularly in America, and the conception of metropolitan areas extending well beyond a city's political boundaries had already taken shape.[39] With the rise of urban planning as a discipline, particularly infrastructure planning, the desire to anticipate and direct these patterns of expansion generated questions about the processes of urban expansion. On the basis of extensive efforts to empirically measure processes and functions within the city of Chicago and to map the patterns generated by these processes, Burgess sought to express an ecological pattern he saw emerging from their data, a pattern he believed to be as natural, inevitable, and universal to city development as Clements's proposed pattern of successional development in plant communities.

Burgess proposed that this pattern of urban expansion took the form of functionally differentiated zones, radiating spatially outward from the city's central business district. His diagram of four concentric circles illustrated his primary hypothesis about "the tendency of each inner zone to extend its area by the invasion of the next outer zone."[40] What made these patterns ecological for the Chicago urban sociologists was their recognition that urban expansion was neither arbitrary nor haphazard but strongly controlled by community-level forces such as land values, zoning ordinances, landscape features, circulation corridors, and historical contingency. The patterns that emerged were ecological because they emerged not from chance or human intent but rather from the "natural" actions of "the selective, distributive, and accommodative forces of the environment" on the "spatial and temporal relations of human beings."[41] Their method of inquiry was ecological, we argue, because they sought to derive patterns from a study of processes, rather than to ascribe processes to observed patterns. Their conception of urban development processes and the patterns they saw emerge are strongly reminiscent of Clements's ideas of plant community development.[42]

In the years following presentation of the concentric rings model, a number of studies attempted to support or refute the model. Many critiques of the zonal hypothesis erred, however—as, indeed, did many supporters of the hypothesis—in taking the ideogram of four concentric rings to be some literal spatial expression of reality, rather than seeing it, more properly, as an ecological conceptualization. Quinn points to many such cases that attempt to present "a concrete test of the validity of the Burgess hypothesis," drawing circles on half-mile units around cities and then seeing if those zones matched Burgess's ideogram. Failure to find correspondence between these spatially constructed zones and the functional boundaries of social data and cultural processes, however, says little about the validity or failure of the Chicago model.[43] As McKenzie reminds us,

> Ecological distance is a measure of fluidity. It is a time-cost concept rather than a unit of space. It is measured by minutes and cents rather than by yards and miles. By time-cost measurement the distance from A to B may be farther than from B to A, provided B is upgrade from A.[44]

Under such a definition of distance, everyday spatially geometric concepts such as circles and squares become abstractions, rather than any literal depictions of reality.

Undoubtedly, the particular views of progress, nature, and monoclimactic end states held by the Chicago urban theorists distorted their model, forcing them to interpret the city in certain ways. But the shape of their worldview is a result of their understanding of the best science available to them, and they set in place a move *away from the pattern realism of entity and place and toward the process actuality of function and scale.*

RETURNING TO ECOLOGY: ORGANIZATION AND OCCURRENCE

The ecological turn produced by the Chicago sociologists sets the foundation for the development of an ecosystems approach to social theory and urban planning. In such places as Los Angeles, we can apply alternative conceptions of boundaries and scale that allow us to better and differently understand the relationship between issues that are now viewed separately in policy discussions. Default planning practice usually takes organization to be linear and rank ordered, boundaries to be inherent, and scales to be topographical and chronological. Thus, we often represent intangible relationships and processes with "boxes and arrows"—boxes standing for the real and significant objects of concern and arrows symbolizing conceptual constructs.[45]

Ecosystem ecology, however, takes organization to be nested and overlapping, boundaries to be contingent with respect to purpose and perspective, and scale to be directly attached to processes and functions.[46] In such an ecosystem approach, in which systems are seen to be driven by relationships and processes, the arrows are taken as the real and significant objects of concern, whereas the boxes represent conceptual constructs deriving from the particulars of our purpose and helping us understand the functions and flows we properly care about.[47]

Within such an ecological conception of organization and occurrence, nature and society reflect multiple and simultaneous realities, because we know that the reality we see is contingent on (a) the perspective, purpose, and point of view we elect to take; (b) the levels of organization we consider significant and within which we situate ourselves for observation; (c) the boundaries we choose and maintain or change during description; and (d) the scales by which we choose to give these descriptions.

Contingent Boundaries: Mugu Lagoon

The case of Mugu Lagoon in Ventura County, California, illustrates the problem of naming and choosing boundaries. Located at the southern end of the county coastline, Mugu Lagoon is one of the few remaining links in the Pacific flyway, providing vital resting, feeding, and nesting habitat for a variety of migratory birds. Although its location inside the boundaries of a naval air base leaves it, at present, well protected, the lagoon has historically been subjected to intense internal and external stresses and pressures, and a strong case has been made for its management.[48] It is a fascinating case, with distinct hydrologic, atmospheric, biologic, technologic, and administrative dimensions. Each area of concern brings with it its own functionally derived set of boundaries.

To further complicate matters, none of these boundaries will stay put, whether because of perturbation and pulsing, changing interactions between its biotic and abiotic subsystems, or changes in land use or other regulatory regimes. In such cases, management efforts—particularly those aimed at either preserving the lagoon in some "natural" state or conserving some "natural" functions—become particularly problematic because the lagoon will not sit still. Tectonic activity is ceaselessly changing topographies in Southern California, and ocean levels themselves change through geologic time.[49] Two thousand years ago, the present site of the lagoon was under the Pacific Ocean. Two hundred years ago, it was a saltwater lagoon, with virtually no surface (fresh) water inputs. But with the growth of settlements in the late 1800s and flood control in adjoining basins and plains, runoff from surrounding areas was channeled into the lagoon, turning it into an estuarine (mixed salt- and freshwater) lagoon.

With the growth of agriculture, surface runoff began to change, both in toxicity and in turbidity (sedimentation). Although siltation has been increasing through time, turning more of the lagoon into wetlands and marsh, dredging to restore depth and through-flow may call for unacceptable trade-offs because the layers of silt clogging the lagoon have trapped within and beneath them significant amounts of DDT and other pesticides from surrounding agricultural lands, as well as toxic chemicals from the naval base. Regional meteorological conditions and wind patterns, coupled with the atmospheric chemistry of oxides of nitrogen generated by air pollution in the Los Angeles and Ventura air basins, have also taken their toll in the form of increased acid rain.

Rapid suburbanization as far as fifty miles inland, including Simi Valley and Thousand Oaks, has had its own impact. The increase in paved surfaces and roof areas, when combined with a pattern of infrequent but intense rainfall and a soil structure unable to absorb more than four inches of rain at any time, has increased surface runoff throughout the extensive watershed and dramatically altered the physical parameters of the lagoon by increasing siltation rates.[50]

Nature, too, adds its own pressures. During the past two decades, a two-week period of storms has completely altered its depth profiles, radically changing the mix of species that the lagoon can support. Even now, tidal action, partially modified by the construction of breakwaters to protect beachfront properties a few miles north, is cutting a submarine canyon near the mouth of the lagoon, sucking the very coast-line away from around it.[51]

Depending on which aspects we concern ourselves with, we find different sets and sorts of boundaries: the lagoon at low tide, the lagoon at high tide, the lagoon and its wetlands, the lagoon and its watershed, the lagoon and its catchment, the lagoon and its air basin, the lagoon and the Pacific flyway extending from Canada to South America, the lagoon and endangered species, the lagoon and adjacent land use, and the lagoon and administrative agencies. Each of these boundaries varies considerably from all others, and none is inherently more useful (or even independently robust) for purposes of management. Efforts to treat the lagoon as a place with some inherent state that demands preservation or conservation naturalize the lagoon in quite unnatural ways.

Functional Scales: Lead Paint

Ecosystem ecology is concerned primarily with relationships and connections linked to processes and functions in natural systems, and only secondarily with the morphology of individuals, communities of organisms, events, and landscapes. In urban environmental planning, such is the case with lead abatement. Lead is widely recognized as a highly toxic substance, with both acute and chronic health effects. Exposure leads to neurological and immune system damage and often results in reproductive and developmental disorders.[52] Many cities have instituted intensive lead abatement programs. But the picture of lead in an urban setting is contingent on whether we think of lead as a thing, attached to other things (such as electrodes on batteries or paint on buildings), or whether we think of lead as constituted by processes and functions of exchange and transformation. For example, much of the effort in lead abatement programs has focused on (and often stops at) finding products with substantial lead content and removing or containing them—a morphological, point-source mitigation approach to lead abatement that does little to recognize how the presence of lead relates, functionally, to other processes.

But urban ecological studies begun in Baltimore and Minnesota during the 1980s tell a different story.[53] Recognizing that lead is a persistent substance that tends to accumulate in the soil, these studies use what atmospheric scientists call a lifetime-and-fate approach, shifting focus away from the physical and morphologic incidence and distribution of lead-containing objects and toward the flows and concentrations of lead within the urban system through time. Once lead is physically released into an urban environment, much of it tends to accumulate in the soil. These ecological studies found little correspondence between the density distributions of lead-containing objects (such as old neighborhoods with painted wooden houses) and densities of lead in the soil. Instead, we can best describe long-term, accumulative densities of lead in urban areas through atmospheric and geophysical processes.

At the scale of the building, for instance, lead concentrations are independent of whether the building was unpainted (brick) or painted (wood). Even around a building, lead will be disproportionately concentrated in soils on its upwind and road-facing sides. At the scale of the city, too, concentrations of lead in the soil are linked more closely to particulate behavior within thermal processes than to present-day patterns of emission or to the incidence of buildings with lead-based paint. The studies found that lead accumulation in urban soils within a city corresponded most closely to the presence of heat islands such as high-density downtowns (even those that never had any lead-based paint buildings), to atmospheric dust such as in areas with little erosion-controlling ground cover, or to high volumes of diesel-fueled vehicular traffic. Any concern with the health effects of lead in urban settings requires descriptions at multiple levels of organization that use multiple scales derived from chemical, biological, geological, meteorological, industrial, and mechanical processes and functions.[54]

AN ECOSYSTEM APPROACH TO SCALE IN PLANNING

Spatial scales will always be important to urban and environmental planning. Simply put, place matters. Humans are spatial creatures, and much of the business of our existence occurs in the tangible, morphologic, topographic world. Landscapes, organisms, and entities are what we sense and interact with most directly, allowing us to manipulate the world. Besides, biotic and abiotic entities have physical form and take up space, and so natural and social community is contingent on territorial organization.

Ecosystem ecologists argue, however, that organisms, entities, and landscapes are most usefully treated as manifestations of not so obvious processes and functions—that is, exchanges of matter, energy, and information—and that these processes and functions are the proper and fundamental ways that natural organization and occurrence should be conceptualized.[55] Ecosystem ecology begins with the premise that all systems, including ecosystems, are theoretical constructs rather than real things and thus demand a much richer conception of scale. Scale has spatial, temporal, and organizational dimensions, which are contingent on the location of the observer, and can be functionally derived and become significant only after we explain our purpose in choosing it.

Furthermore, there are certain classes of things (problems, situations, phenomena, issues, social facts) that are fundamentally ecological in their organization and occurrence. Such ecological things are not "things in themselves," singular entities with agreeable boundaries and reconcilable properties. Instead, they have no inherent boundaries and exhibit multiple and pragmatically distinct levels of organization. Each level requires its own set of scales for description, and descriptions of patterns and processes at one level of organization may tell us little about organization or occurrence at another.

We must draw distinctions between problems that can be treated as closed systems and those that are most usefully viewed as open systems. In Rittel and Webber's characterization, "tame" problems, however complicated, can always be solved, whereas "wicked" problems, conversely, show no logical starting point and no computable end.[56] Rittel and Webber formulate a series of "properties" for such wicked problems. They defy definitive description and can always be multiply described. Moreover, every formulation of such a problem may lead to a different solution. Models or predictions of future states, therefore, become contingent on problem formulation, as well as on what one imagines the original state to be. Wicked problems, as open systems, have no logical stopping point, no inherent end state that allows one to claim to have solved the problem. Nor, because of this, do they show any natural stage at which implemented solutions can definitively be tested for success or failure. Furthermore, "every wicked problem can be considered a symptom of another problem."[57]

In the scale-hierarchic approach in ecosystem ecology, whereby a phenomenon or circumstance at one level of integration may have functional connections with its supra- and subsystems, what is taken to be a problem at one level may well be beneficial or even essential at another and perhaps a whole different sort of problem at some other scale of description. Finally, for purpose of this discussion, every wicked problem is unique. This, taken along with the absence of clear starting and end points, means that the method of trial and error, which rests most on the building of experiential learning, becomes less reliable and must at least be relocated within the methodological repertoire for planning with open systems.[58]

Such ecological *things,* we argue, can be usefully described only by using an ecosystem approach. Setting such an ecosystem approach apart from past and conventional efforts at ecological description both in ecology and in urban planning-related social sciences are scale-hierarchic description and an evolutionary frame. Ecology and an ecosystem approach, importantly, shift the focus of attention in planning.

Briefly, a scale-hierarchic approach in ecology holds, first, that all ecological systems are conceptually bounded by the pragmatics of purpose, exhibiting distinct, functionally nested levels of organization.[59] In ecology, for instance, individual, population, community, and ecosystem represent useful levels of organization. Each level of organization needs to be explicitly recognized in description, and each level of organization relevant to purpose may need to be described at more than just one or two functional scales. These levels of organization are linked by (indeed constituted by) processes and functions, and each level of organization interacts with its sub- and suprasystems in particular and variable ways. So there are rules we can discover by following processes and functions across levels of organization.

An ecological phenomenon requires description at more than one level of organization, with each level demanding its own set of particularized tools and scales, because observations of occurrence at one level of organization may have little to tell us about responses at other levels.[60] In an ecological view, the world, in its organization and its occurrence, appears differently at different levels of organization and at different scales of description, where what one can see of it is sometimes dramatically contingent on the boundaries chosen in the first place.

The core conception behind the ecosystem approach from process-function ecology is that of a nested, scale-hierarchic arrangement of complex, self-organizing set of systems and subsystems nested within and around each other. Conceptually, any system of concern emerges from the relationships among its constitutive subsystems and relates responsively with other systems to constitute some wider suprasystem. We know the complexity of any particular system by the quantity and quality of *relationships* it contains, rather than simply and trivially by the *number* of its components.

We suggest that such an ecological approach to description offers planning—particularly in nature management and community planning—useful tools for organizing and resolving apparent contradictions in analysis and assessment. The significance and difficulty of separating pattern from process, structure from function, and organization from occurrence and also the telling apart of ontogenic and phylogenic (individual and group) evolutionary processes are likely to be large.[61] Space, whether geographic, administrative, or temporal, becomes a necessary but insufficient measure for telling the differences between structures and functions. Although there are, undoubtedly, significant structures to be identified in describing social and natural phenomena, these structures take more of their shape from processual relationships than from simple sequences and proximities. Even when we do find and bound such structures and find them to be durable through time, we can never take for granted their circumstantial and perspectival contingency.

A pragmatic approach to planning no doubt requires that we make models of the world. But these models are intentional and provisional, and the structures and functions we ascribe to the world for any particular purpose—the boxes and arrows we draw on it—are always contingent and open to revision.[62] When we are dealing with open systems that defy agreeable reduction, the descriptions we make require particular attention and demand at least the explicit testing of spatial, administrative, and temporal scales.

A central challenge in an ecosystem approach to planning and its concern with managing open systems lies in this seeking out and questioning traditionally accepted definitions in our conceptions of organization, boundaries, and scale—definitions that, in the absence of careful attention, inevitably permeate the descriptions we make of the natural and social world we seek to control. In such cases, the idea that we should "think globally, act locally" becomes less than adequate, and we may need to settle for some less catchy but more pragmatic version—perhaps one that says this: Think at the scales that matter, and act at the levels that count.

NOTES

1. Onuf, 1987.
2. Bierce and Debenham, 1990.
3. Rainey, 1993.
4. Park, Burgess, and McKenzie [1925/1967], Midway reprint, 1984.
5. Odum, 1969; Pickett and McDonnell, 1989; Pickett, 1985.
6. Quinn, 1940; Duncan, 1961; Catton, 1993, 1994; Smith, 1995.
7. Kurtz, 1984, p. 17.
8. Kurtz, 1984, p. 8.
9. Russett, 1966, pp. 61-74; Kurtz, 1984, p. 93.
10. Faris (1970) cites Lester F. Ward, William G. Sumner, Franklin H. Giddings, and Edward A. Ross among those American pioneers who "had a strong disposition to discover, mainly by reflection, one or a few fundamental and simple principles that would serve as explanation of all human behavior" (p. 4).
11. Kurtz, 1984, outlines this influence, pointing out that

European social thought figured prominently in their teaching and research, and in articles by Simmel, Toennies, and Durkheim translated and published in the early issues of the [*American Journal of Sociology*, which was then largely controlled by the Chicago sociologists]. Simmel's influence was pronounced in early American sociology, thanks largely to Small's efforts. Small was at the University of Berlin while Simmel was himself a student there. (p. 17)

Furthermore, Faris (1970) argues that Park, who had studied under Simmel while traveling in Europe, received from him the concept of social distance and that Park later "suggested to Bogardus that the latter devise a social-distance scale as a statistical basis for the life-history materials in this field" (p. 108).

12. Russett, 1966, p. 67.
13. Russett, 1966; Davison, 1983; Mitman, 1992; Cittadino, 1993; Levine, 1995; Silber, 1995.
14. Russett, 1966.
15. Levine, 1995.
16. Levine, 1995, p. 254.
17. Although Clements's (1916) notions of successional stages culminating in some climatically determined mono-climax were quickly challenged and problematized within ecology (Gleason, 1917; Tansley, 1935), "the concept became a central tenet of range condition analysis used by the USDA for range management . . . and is still used today even though it is recognized as conceptually flawed" (Gibson, 1996, pp. 135-136).
18. Silber, 1995, p. 329.
19. Gould, 1977.
20. Berlin, 1965, pp. 50-51.
21. Russett, 1966, p. 19.
22. Russett, 1966; Levine, 1995.
23. Russett, 1966, p. 30. The claim that the ability to modify the environment as an adaptive strategy is unique to humans rests on a rather narrow definition of what it means to modify the environment. The work of James Lovelock and Lynn Margulis (1974) supports a recognition that all biotic entities and some abiotic processes do indeed modify their environment by the very activities of their own existence.
24. Russett, 1966, p. 33.
25. Russett (1966, p. 28) points out that the two men, although contemporaries, never met each other.

26. Russett (1966, p. 28) shows some of the oppositional consequences of Comte's background in mathematics and adoption of biological knowledge and Spencer's background in engineering and adoption of the knowledge of mechanics.

27. Berlin (1965, p. 82) argues that the notion of a steady progress, at least in human history, was one of three well-established myths of the eighteenth century—the other two being the myth of one culture's innate superiority over others, and the myth of a classic, sunlit culture of the past (whether Gallo-Roman or pagan). Not until a century later did knowledge of life and evolution grow to a stage where the idea of progress began to affect organismic conceptions.

28. In problematizing the conventional history of ideas about progress, one that dominated until fairly recently, Hull (1988) says,

> According to the traditional view, no one throughout human history found the idea of progress either in nature or in the course of human affairs plausible or appealing until the Renaissance. The ancient Greeks and later Romans viewed the world in terms of eternal cycles, while Christian theology portrayed human history as a period of tribulation between Adam's fall and the Second Coming. Not until the sixteenth century did intellectuals in the West begin to think that possibly human history as well as nature at large might be progressive. (p. 27)

Although Hull proceeds to formulate an alternative history, these two positions can perhaps be taken as representative of some broad division in social thought. Certainly, the versions of evolution and progress elaborated by Comte and Spencer appear generally to divide along similar lines.

29. Durkheim [1898], 1974.

30. Worster, 1977, p. 198; Allen & Hoekstra, 1992, p. 130.

31. Cowles, 1899.

32. Clements, 1916.

33. The notion of succession as an orderly and repeating pattern of social change, akin to the life cycles of organisms, was used in social theory before it appeared in ecology. The phrase "sociological succession," to denote some version of orderly displacement in social groupings, was used at least as early as Comte. In ecology, the term *plant sociology* was almost interchangeably with *plant ecology* at least until the 1950s (Whittaker, 1953). More generally, the term *sociology* was commonly used to "designate the study of patterned associations among and between different non-human species of organisms" (Catton, 1993, p. 74).

34. Golley, 1977, p. 181.

35. Gleason, 1917, 1926; Tansley, 1935.

36. See Odum, 1960, 1969. For a comprehensive review of the early ecological literature on succession and climax theories, in both the United States and Europe, see Whittaker (1953).

37. Although the influence of Turner's frontier hypothesis (1893/1994) and of the pioneering settlement process shows clearly in Clements's work, surely other forces may have been as formative. After all, Warming, who lived and worked in Copenhagen, appears to have outlined a theory of successional development that can reasonably be seen as a precedent to Clements's version. Certainly, Clements was not working *tabula rasa* but participating in a more painstaking process of knowledge building. In addition, the frontier hypothesis would have at least reinforced already, and differently, emerging understandings of nature and society. But there may have been no great leap in insight, no singular paradigm shift, rather a patchy and sporadic transformation of ideas and conceptions as diverse ways of knowing came together and went their own ways.

38. Worster, 1977, pp. 218-219.

39. Burgess [1925/1967], Midway reprint, 1984, pp. 48-50.

40. Burgess [1925/1967], Midway reprint, 1984, p. 50.

41. McKenzie [1924], 1968, pp. 14-17; McKenzie, [1926] 1968, pp. 20-21.

42. For all that Clements's conception of community as superorganism was a prerequisite for the Chicago urban theorists' efforts to find a scientific basis for sociology, the sources they drew from were considerably richer.

43. Quinn, 1940, p. 212.

44. McKenzie [1926], 1968, p. 22.

45. Verma, 1993.

46. Allen and Starr, 1982; O'Neill et al., 1986; Allen and Hoekstra, 1992.

47. Verma (1993) argues that this is the "savvy" version of any systems approach.

48. Onuf, 1987; Soil Conservation Service, 1994.

49. Onuf, 1987.

50. Williams, 1993.

51. Weiss, 1994.

52. Winder, 1993; Folinsbee, 1993; Goyer, 1993.

53. Mielke, 1994.

54. Cernak and Thompson, 1977; Mielke, 1994.

55. O'Neill et al., 1986; Allen and Hoekstra, 1992.

56. Rittel and Webber, 1973.

57. Rittel and Webber, 1973, p. 165.

58. Holling and Goldberg, 1971; Holling, 1986.

59. Functional nesting is not necessarily analogous to, and certainly not commensurate with, morphological or spatial nesting (e.g., the "boxes within boxes" model). Getting at processes and functions directly, in both ecology and social theory, is made imperative because functions (processes) don't map reliably from structures (patterns).

60. Checkland, 1981.

61. Levin (1992) has argued that this matter of telling pattern from process remains as *the* challenge for ecosystem ecologists.

62. Krieger, 1989.

REFERENCES

Allen, Timothy F. H., and Thomas W. Hoekstra. 1992. *Toward a unified ecology.* New York: Columbia University Press.

Allen, Timothy F. H., and Thomas B. Starr. 1982. *Hierarchy: Perspectives for ecological complexity.* Chicago: Chicago University Press.

Berlin, Isaiah. 1965. Herder and the Enlightenment. In *Aspects of the eighteenth century,* ed. Earl R. Wasserman (pp. 47-104). Baltimore: Johns Hopkins University Press.

Bierce, R., and P. Debenham. 1990. *California marine debris action plan.* San Francisco: Center for Marine Conservation.

Burgess, Ernest W. 1925, 1967. The growth of the city: An introduction to a research program. In *The city: Suggestions for investigation of human behavior in the urban environment,* by Robert E. Park, Ernest W. Burgess, and Roderick D. McKenzie (pp. 47-62). Chicago: University of Chicago Press, Midway reprint, 1984. Reprinted from *Publications of the American Sociological Society* 18 (annual 1924): 85-97.

Catton, William R., Jr. 1993. Sociology as an ecological science. In *Human ecology: Crossing boundaries,* ed. Scott D. Wright, Thomas Dietz, Richard Borden, Gerald Young, and Gregory Guagnano (pp. 74-86). Fort Collins, Colo.: Society for Human Ecology.

Catton, William R., Jr. 1994. Foundations of human ecology. *Sociological Perspectives* 37, no. 1: 75-95.

Cernak, J. E., and R. S. Thompson. 1977. Urban planning. In *Lead in the environment,* ed. William R. Boggess and Bobby G. Wixson (pp. 229-239). Prepared for the National Science Foundation. Washington, D.C.: Government Printing Office.

Checkland, Peter. 1981. *Systems thinking, systems practice.* Chichester, England: Wiley.

Cittadino, Eugene. 1993. The failed promise of human ecology. In *Science and nature: Essays in the history of the environmental sciences,* ed. Michael Shortland (pp. 251-283). Oxford, England: British Society for the History of Science.

Clements, Frederic E. 1916. *Plant succession: An analysis of the development of vegetation.* Carnegie Institute of Washington Publication No. 242. Washington, D.C.: Carnegie Institute.

Cowles, H. C. 1899. The ecological relations of the vegetation on the sand dunes of Lake Michigan. I. Geographical relations of the dune floras. *Botanical Gazette* 27, nos. 2, 3, 4, 5: 95-117, 167-202, 281-308, 361-391.

Davie, Maurice R. 1937. The pattern of urban growth. In *Studies in the science of society,* ed. George P. Murdock (pp. 133-161). New Haven, Conn.: Yale University Press.

Davison, Graeme. 1983. The city as a natural system: Theories of urban society in early nineteenth-century Britain. In *The pursuit of urban history,* ed. Derek Fraser and Anthony Sutcliffe. London: Edward Arnold.

Duncan, Otis Dudley. 1961. From social system to ecosystem. *Sociological Inquiry* 31 (spring): 140-149.

Durkheim, Émile. [1898] 1974. Individual and collective representations. Reprinted in *Sociology and philosophy,* by Émile Durkheim, trans. D. F. Pocock. New York: Free Press.

Faris, Robert E. L. 1970. *Chicago sociology: 1920-1932.* Chicago and London: University of Chicago Press.

Folinsbee, L. J. 1993. Human health-effects of air-pollution. *Environmental Health Perspectives* 100 (April): 45-56.

Gibson, David J. 1996. Textbook misconceptions: The climax concept of succession. *American Biology Teacher* 58, no. 3 (March): 135-140.

Gleason, H. A. 1917. The structure and development of the plant association. *Bulletin of the Torrey Botanical Club* 44, no. 10: 463-481.

Gleason, H. A. 1926. The individualistic concept of the plant association. *Bulletin of the Torrey Botanical Club* 53, no. 1: 7-26.

Golley, Frank B., ed. 1977. *Ecological succession.* Benchmark Papers in Ecology, vol. 5. Stroudsburg, Pa.: Dowden, Hutchinson and Ross.

Gould, Stephen J. 1977. *Ontogeny and phylogeny.* Cambridge, Mass.: Harvard University Press, Belknap Press.

Goyer, R. A. 1993. Lead toxicity: Current concerns. *Environmental Health Perspectives* 100 (April): 177-187.

Holling, Crawford S. 1986. The resilience of terrestrial ecosystems: Local surprise and global change. In *Sustainable development of the biosphere,* ed. William C. Clark and R. E. Munn (pp. 292-317). Cambridge: Cambridge University Press.

Holling, Crawford S., and Michael A. Goldberg. 1971. Ecology and planning. *AIP Journal* [now *JAPA*] (July): 221-230.

Hull, David L. 1988. Progress in ideas of progress. In *Evolutionary progress,* ed. Matthew H. Nitecki (pp. 27-48). Chicago: University of Chicago Press.

Krieger, Martin H. 1989. *Marginalism and discontinuity: Tools for the crafts of knowledge and decision.* New York: Russell Sage Foundation.

Kurtz, Lester R. 1984. *Evaluating Chicago sociology: A guide to the literature, with an annotated bibliography.* Foreword by Morris Janowitz. Chicago and London: University of Chicago Press.

Levin, Simon A. 1992. The problem of pattern and scale in ecology. *Ecology* 73, no. 6 (December): 1943-1967.

Levine, Donald N. 1995. The organismic metaphor in sociology. *Social Research* 62, no. 2 (summer): 239-265.

Lovelock, James, and Lynn Margulis. 1974. Atmospheric homeostasis by and for the biosphere: The gaia hypothesis. *Tellus* 26, nos. 1-2: 2-10.

McKenzie, Roderick D. [1924] 1968. The ecological approach to the study of the human community. *American Journal of Sociology* 30, no. 3 (November): 287-301. Reprinted in *Roderick D. McKenzie on human ecology: Selected writings,* ed. Amos H. Hawley (pp. 3-18). Chicago: University of Chicago Press.

McKenzie, Roderick D. [1926] 1968. The scope of human ecology. *American Journal of Sociology* 32, no. 1, pt. 2 (July): 141-154. Reprinted in *Roderick D. McKenzie on human ecology: Selected writings,* ed. Amos H. Hawley (pp. 19-32). Chicago: University of Chicago Press.

Mielke, Howard W. 1994. The automobile as a toxic substance delivery system. In *The environment: Global problems, local solutions,* ed. James E. Hickey Jr. and Linda A. Longmire. Westport, Conn.: Greenwood.

Mitman, Gregg. 1992. *The state of nature: Ecology, community, and American social thought, 1900-1950.* Chicago and London: University of Chicago Press.

Odum, Eugene P. [1960] 1977. Organic production and turnover in old field succession. *Ecology* 41, no. 1: 34-49. Reprinted in *Ecological succession,* ed. Frank B. Golley. Benchmark Papers in Ecology, vol. 5 (pp. 102-117). Stroudsburg, Pa.: Dowden, Hutchinson and Ross.

Odum, Eugene P. 1969. The strategy of ecosystem development. *Science* 164 (April 18): 262-270.

O'Neill, R. V., D. L. DeAngelis, J. B. Waide, and T. F. H. Allen. 1986. *A hierarchical concept of ecosystems.* Princeton, N.J.: Princeton University Press.

Onuf, Christopher P. 1987. *The ecology of Mugu Lagoon, California: An estuarine profile.* Biological Report 85 (7-15). Slidell, La.: U.S. Department of the Interior, Fish and Wildlife Service, National Wetlands Research Center.

Park, Robert E., Ernest W. Burgess, and Roderick D. McKenzie. 1925, 1967. *The city: Suggestions for investigation of human behavior in the urban environment.* Chicago: University of Chicago Press, Midway reprint, 1984.

Pickett, Stewart T. A. 1985. Patch dynamics: A synthesis. In *The ecology of natural disturbance and patch dynamics,* ed. Stewart T. A. Pickett and P. S. White. Orlando, Fla.: Academic Press.

Pickett, Stewart T. A., and M. J. McDonnell. 1989. Changing perspectives in community dynamics: A theory of successional forces. *Journal of Evolutionary Ecology* 4, no. 8 (August): 241-245.

Quinn, James A. 1940. The Burgess zonal hypothesis and its critics. *American Sociological Review* 5, no. 2: 210-218.

Rainey, James. 1993. Bradley budget cuts draw fire; council panel attacks mayor's proposal to eliminate city trash cans, anti-graffiti crews. *Los Angeles Times,* April 30, p. B1.

Rittel, Horst W. J., and Melvin M. Webber. 1973. Dilemmas in a general theory of planning. *Policy Sciences* 4, no. 2 (June): 155-169.

Russett, Cynthia Eagle. 1966. *The concept of equilibrium in American social thought.* New Haven, Conn., and London: Yale University Press.

Silber, Ilana Freidrich. 1995. Space, fields, boundaries: The rise of spatial metaphors in contemporary sociological theory. *Social Research* 62, no. 2 (summer): 323-355.

Smith, David A. 1995. The new urban sociology meets the old: Rereading some classical human ecology. *Urban Affairs Review* 30, no. 3 (January): 432-457.

Soil Conservation Service. 1994. *Calleguas Creek watershed erosion and sediment control plan for Mugu Lagoon.* Draft report prepared by the U.S. Department of Agriculture, Soil Conservation Service, Davis, Calif.

Tansley, Sir Arthur G. 1935. The use and abuse of vegetational concepts and terms. *Ecology* 16, no. 3 (July): 284-307.

Turner, Frederick Jackson. [1893] 1994. The significance of the frontier in American history. In *Rereading Frederick Jackson Turner: The significance of the frontier in American history and other essays* (with commentary by John Mack Faragher) (pp. 31-60). New York: Henry Holt.

Verma, Niraj. 1993. Boxes and arrows as models of systems. Paper presented at the meeting of the International Society for the Systems Sciences, Asilomar, Calif., October 3-5.

Weiss, K. R. 1994. Mugu Lagoon losing itself in sediment. *Los Angeles Times,* November 30, p. A3.

Whittaker, R. H. 1953. A consideration of climax theory: The climax as a population and pattern. *Ecological Monographs* 23: 41-78. Reprinted 1977 in *Ecological Succession,* ed. Frank B. Golley, Benchmark Papers in Ecology, vol. 5 (pp. 240-277). Stroudsburg, Pa.: Dowden, Hutchinson and Ross.

Williams, Michael J. 1993. An exceptionally powerful biotic factor. In *Humans as components of ecosystems: The ecology of subtle human effects and populated areas,* ed. Mark J. McDonnell and Steward T. A. Pickett. New York: Springer-Verlag.

Winder, C. 1993. Lead, reproduction and development. *Neurotoxicology* 14, nos. 2-3 (summer-fall): 303-318.

Worster, Donald. 1977. *Nature's economy: The roots of ecology.* San Francisco: Sierra Club Books.

Urban Nature and the Nature of Urbanism

EDITOR'S
COMMENTS

Nowhere in *The City* is the connection with the natural environment clearer than in Roderick McKenzie's chapter, "The Ecological Approach to the Study of the Human Community." Yet as Jennifer Wolch, Stephanie Pincetl, and Laura Pulido persuasively argue in this chapter, despite the school's reliance on the lexicon of ecology, the nonhuman ecology of urban areas rarely entered the writings of its advocates. Absent from the texts of *The City* are issues relating to the appropriation of ecosystems for urban expansion, the consequences of the erasure of plant and animal habitats, sustainability, environmental degradation, and so on.

Wolch and her colleagues set out to create an ambitious alternative version of urban studies—one that focuses on the relationships among humans, plants, and animals in the city. At the core of this revitalized urban paradigm lies the notion of *zoöpolis,* a city in which humans and nonhuman life forms coexist to their mutual benefits. Drawing on experiences from the remarkable natural environments of Southern California, Wolch, Pincetl, and Pulido show how environmental awareness is reshaping natural and human behaviors throughout the region. Their chapter is one more example of an important connective to the (absent) conventions of the Chicago School. They insist that to know the city requires that we invent a transspecies urban theory. The enormous ramifications of this theory for the reconceptualization of the urban are demonstrated by the authors' considerations of nonhuman life in cities, the political dynamics of urbanization, natural hazards, environmental justice, and human-animal relations in Southern California.

QUOTES FROM
THE CITY

In the absence of any precedent let us tentatively define human ecology as a study of the spatial and temporal relations of human beings as affected by the selective, distributive, and accommodative forces of the environment. Human ecology is fundamentally interested in the effect of *position,* in both time and space, upon human institutions and human behavior. . . . These spatial relationships of human beings are the products of competition and selection, and are continuously in process of change as new factors enter to disturb the competitive relations or to facilitate mobility. Human institutions and human nature itself become accommodated to certain spatial relationships of human beings. As these spatial relationships change, the physical basis of social relations is altered, thereby producing social and political problems.

A great deal has been written about the biological, economic, and social aspects of competition and selection, but little attention has been given to the distributive and spatial aspects of these processes. . . . (63-64)

The essential difference between the plant and animal organism is that the animal has the power of locomotion which enables it to gather nutriment from a wider environment, but, in addition to the power to move in space, the human animal has the ability to contrive and adapt the environment to his needs. In a word, the human community differs from the plant community in the two dominant characteristics of mobility and purpose, that is, in the power to select a habitat and in the ability to control or modify the conditions of the habitat. (64-65)

CHAPTER 14

Urban Nature and the Nature of Urbanism

It is in vain to dream of a wildness distant from ourselves. There is none such. It is the bog in our brain and bowels, the primitive vigor of Nature in us, that inspires that dream.

—Henry David Thoreau[1]

JENNIFER WOLCH
STEPHANIE PINCETL
LAURA PULIDO

The Chicago School of urban sociology was intellectually grounded on ideas derived from ecology, with concepts such as competition, invasion, succession, segregation, and equilibrium infusing their discussions of urban social structure, process, and problems.[2] Not coincidentally, human geographers on the Chicago faculty worked closely with Park, Burgess, and other Chicago sociologists, promulgating the type of environmental determinism typical of geography at that time and shaping conceptualizations developed by their colleagues in urban sociology.[3] This reliance on ecological concepts and biological analogy imbued studies by Park, Burgess, McKenzie, and their coworkers with a pervasive organicism that today stands as one of the primary hallmarks of the Chicago School.[4] Yet naturalizing the process of urbanization also removed human agency from city growth and development and depoliticized processes of local decision making. Moreover, apart from a recognition that cities rely on natural resources, the book is silent about the appropriation of ecosystems for urban expansion, the impacts of urbanization on the quality of the natural environment and availability of wildlife habitat, the urban politics of nature preservation, natural hazards, and environmental degradation. This is despite the reliance of Chicago's development trajectory on a tremendous transformation and appropriation of nature and the generation by its industrialization of environmental hazards and toxic pollution of unprecedented proportions.[5]

Coyote in Santa Monica Backyard
Photograph by Michael J. Dear.

Since *The City* was published, urban ecological questions have continued to be ignored by urban sociology and geography, as well as by urban theory.[6] Although Logan and Molotch's well-known growth machine theory explains how "growth has obvious negative consequences for the physical environment,"[7] the environment itself remains static, acted on (rather than acting), an object of struggle. Similarly, Harvey's recent attempt to more explicitly link urbanization with environmental questions objectifies nature.[8] Although many of his questions are crucial—power, production, and exploitation—space is essentially the product of human creation, and hence nature itself becomes an empty category.

Questions of urban ecology have, therefore, been left to scholars outside the social sciences, such as conservation biologists and landscape ecologists. Although such work still objectifies nature, it does reveal the fundamental role of urbanization in ecosystem appropriation, which in turn, limits the life chances of many plants and animals. The world's 744 largest cities with 20 percent of the world's population, for example, have been estimated to appropriate 25 percent of productive marine ecosystems. They also claim between 100 and 300 percent of total forest carbon absorption or C sink capacity. These estimates do not even account for issues of waste assimilation beyond nitrogen, phosphorus, and carbon dioxide.[9] Within the immediate environs of cities, urban ecological research has documented the wholesale denaturalization of wild or rural habitat slated for homes, offices, and factories.[10] Specifically, urban development causes vast and multifaceted changes in soils,[11] hydrology,[12] climate,[13] ambient air and water quality,[14] and vegetation.[15] Besides leading to the extinction, endangerment, or precipitous drop in native plant and animal populations, these changes also threaten humans and affect local economies, neighborhoods, and development patterns.

In its early years, the putative Los Angeles School of urbanism[16] largely ignored urban environmental questions, instead emphasizing social and economic issues such as urban restructuring and social polarization. Interest in environmental questions has been largely confined to the ways in which peripheral urbanization served as a defining feature of the region, how urbanization engendered new perceptions and definitions of nature, or the re-creation of "Nature" in the form of theme parks, gardens, and reserves.[17] Once again, nature was seen as a passive entity, seldom recognized as fuel for urbanization or as constitutive of urban form itself.

During the past decade, however, a distinctively ecological orientation has emerged among a small group of scholars associated with the L.A. School. This work draws on larger theoretical strands (including growth regime frameworks, antiracist theory, ecofeminism, etc.), the history of growth and associated denaturing of Southern California, and contemporary conflicts about environmental quality in Los Angeles. A basic contention in this scholarship is that the history of a city is partly bound up in its nature and that patterns of urban development and population well-being reflect not only social processes but also the natural environment (both real and perceived). Several specific themes of this branch of the L.A. School are by now apparent. They include the urban appropriation of nature and its politics;[18] the interconnections between urbanization and natural hazards, and the politics of environmental risk in Los Angeles;[19] environmental racism and the redefinitions of *environment* and *race* shaping environmental justice struggles;[20] and the question of how diverse animals and people negotiate the extensive nature-culture borderlands in Southern California.[21]

In this chapter, we seek to provide an exegesis of the Los Angeles School's approach to urban ecology. We have five specific goals. First, to contextualize our discussion, we provide a highly abbreviated account of the ways in which urbanization affects environmental quality and the possibilities for human and nonhuman life in cities. Second, we focus on the political dynamics of urbanization. Urbanization and the politics of habitat planning for endangered species of Orange County provide an empirical example of this work. Third, we turn to environmental hazards and the political economy of hazard mitigation in different parts of the city, using the example of fire. Fourth, we discuss environmental justice movements and show how such movements have arisen in the context of increasing racial/ethnic and class polarization and identity politics, industrial restructuring, and deteriorating public services. We examine the Bus Riders' Union/*Sindicato de Pasajeros* as an example of how environmental justice is reframing urban environmentalism. Fifth, we attend to the question of human-animal relations in the contemporary metropolis. The "animal question" finds expression in fierce philosophical and class-based debates about urban wildlife management, cross-cultural conflicts over animal practices, and efforts to reclaim space for animals in the city involving rights for domestic animals and an everyday politics of care for nonhumans affected by urbanization.

Our conviction is that urban ecology must be reclaimed as a primary focus for urban theory and analysis, although certainly not as viewed through the lens of the Chicago School. Thus we close with a short agenda for urban ecological research suggested by the emergent L.A. School of urbanism and informed by the premise that just as there is no clear separation between culture and nature, socially constructed distinctions between city and country are no longer tenable. Ideas about urban structure, processes, and problems need to account for nature-society relations and how they shape the dynamics and possibilities for urban life.

NATURE AND THE MAKING OF LOS ANGELES

The Southern California environment is astoundingly varied, complex, and extreme—a highly improbable site for an urban region of more than 14 million people.[22] The region's climate, physical geography, and geological structure are perhaps unique in the world. The sole example of a Mediterranean climatic regime in North America, Southern California weather is characterized by long, hot, dry summers and stormy winters. Temperature differentials can be extreme (up to forty degrees Fahrenheit),[23] and wind conditions include annual hot, searing winds from the southeast called Santa Anas. Precipitation averages fifteen inches per year in downtown Los Angeles but can range widely not only from year to year but from place to place within the region. The coastal *bajada,* on which much of the urban area is built, has alluvium more than 14,000 feet deep and seventy-five miles wide, built up through millions of years by flooding and meandering of the region's three major rivers (Los Angeles, San Gabriel, and Santa Ana). Beneath the coastal plain lies a complicated system of faults created by the collision of two major tectonic plates moving in opposite directions (the Pacific plate moving north, the North American plate moving west). Some of the steepest mountains in the world surround the *bajada.* These block-fault ranges, also resulting from the region's underlying tectonics, include the Transverse Ranges (including, from west to east, the Santa Monicas, the San Gabriels, and the San Bernardinos) and the Peninsular Ranges (including, from north to south, the San Jacintos, Santa Rosas, Lagunas, and, to the west, the Santa Anas). Because these mountains create a rain shadow effect, the eastern portions of the region are semiarid; moreover, the mountains create a major barrier to offshore air currents, causing inversion layers that trap air contaminants within the L.A. basin.

Together, the climatic regime and topographic features of the region create a complex series of distinctive biotic zones. These include diverse chaparral and scrub communities at the lower elevations, yellow pine and lodgepole forests at the upper elevations, and pinyon-juniper and Joshua tree woodlands east of the mountains, with scattered remnant southern oak and riparian habitats. These plant communities, adapted to low rainfall and temperature extremes, have low levels of biomass productivity and are thus food-poor ecosystems. Nevertheless, they support an amazing array of animate life forms.

Few if any regions in North America face the prospect of so many extreme geophysical events as Southern California, including earthquakes, floods, wildfires, landslides and debris flows, and even hurricanes. Since the 1930s, there have been four earthquakes registering 6.0 or greater on the Richter scale. The fire ecology of the region is intimately linked to its chaparral communities, whose species not only are fire adapted but may have volatile oil coatings or require fire to germinate, thus ensuring periodic wildfires even in the absence of human occupation. Slopes of the young, steep mountains surrounding the region are extraordinarily prone to failure, making debris flows and landslides common. Fire not only removes vegetation but coats topsoils with impermeable ash, increasing overland flows.[24] Although the region has never been identified with meteorological events such as cyclones (or funnel clouds), they have nonetheless been surprisingly regular throughout the past century.

Transformations of L.A.'s Nature

From the outset of Anglo occupation in the mid-nineteenth century, urbanization of the Los Angeles region proceeded under the assumption that technology could overcome natural barriers to development.[25] Control of nature was itself naturalized as a basis for Southern Californian growth, as seen in the region's vast engineering works. The Los Angeles Aqueduct brought water from the distant Owens Valley to the city, only the first of many regressive water piracy schemes promoting the development of Los Angeles as an "infinite suburb."[26] The Los Angeles Drainage Area Project, with its seventeen debris basins, three major flood control dams, forty-eight miles of channels, and more than 100 bridges kept flood waters at bay and allowed development of the foothills. A storm drain system more than 1,100 miles long—the nation's largest—shunted an ever increasing volume of urban surface runoff into the Pacific Ocean.[27]

Ironically, urbanization and rapid population expansion were themselves catalyzed by a profoundly antiurban vision for the region. This vision, shared by both the civic elite and general populace, involved a gardenlike, horizontal settlement free of the perceived evils of dense Eastern and Midwestern cities that was ensured not only by a strict limit on building heights but by the early development of the largest public transit system in the nation. This system linked the far corners of the region to its core, promoting a suburbanization only intensified by the arrival of the automobile and freeway subsidies, cheap suburban mortgage credit, and a decentralized distribution of blue-collar manufacturing jobs. The result was the rapid disappearance of wild landscapes, especially valleys and hills (Table 14.1).[28]

The loss of wilderness in the region was accompanied by a thorough fragmentation of remaining wildlands, especially by freeways and vast suburban tract develop-

Table 14.1 Disappearance of Southern California Landscapes

Ecological Zone	Percentage in Aboriginal Wild Landscape		
	1769	1959	1995
A. Coastal	11%	3%	1%
B. Valleys and Hills	50%	8%	3%
C. Interior Uplands	39%	22%	12%
I. Wild Landscape	100%	33%	16%
II. Urban Landscape	0%	67%	84%

SOURCE: Mike Davis, 1996, p. 179, Table 6.3; Davis's table is based on Homer Aschmann, "The Evolution of a Wild Landscape and Its Persistence in Southern California," in *Man, Time and Space in Southern California: A Symposium,* ed. W. L. Thomas Jr., *Annals of the Association of American Geographers,* Supplement 49, no. 3 (1959): 2-55.

ments on the urban fringe. Entire habitat types were virtually eliminated or are now on the brink of extinction. Such extensive habitat loss and fragmentation decimated local wildlife populations. Freeways cut through the Transverse and Peninsular Ranges, not only opening up new areas for development but also blocking wildlife movement corridors. These barriers prevented mobility entirely for some species, increased the incidence of roadkills for others, and put plant and animal communities at risk because of other deleterious effects of fragmentation. Coming on the heels of nineteenth- and early-twentieth-century market hunting of antelope, deer, waterfowl, and fish and relentless pursuit of bountied predators such as cougars and coyotes, the effects of habitat loss and fragmentation were exacerbated by worsening pollution, and Southern California's biodiversity plummeted. Coastal sage scrub habitats in the state are home to more than 100 animal and plant species considered rare, sensitive, threatened, or endangered by either state or federal wildlife agencies.[29] In Los Angeles County alone, there are twenty-two animals and nineteen plants on either state or federal threatened/endangered species lists or proposed for listing.[30]

Degradation of the ambient environment has also been severe, as a result of industrialization, vehicular traffic, and profligate consumption of energy and water.[31] Despite significant reductions in both mobile and point-source emissions, the South Coast Air Basin remains the most polluted in the nation and has a particular problem with pollution hot spots, especially near large-scale refineries and chemical plants. Moreover, the region appropriates massive amounts of energy from other regions to keep air conditioners and other equipment going, simultaneously exporting its air pollution. Widespread fears about drinking water safety and groundwater contamination arose in the late 1970s and early 1980s in response to the discovery of contaminated wells in San Fernando and San Gabriel Valleys—so contaminated that they were eventually declared federal Superfund sites. Of 3,426 wells in Southern California, 40 percent are contaminated. L.A. County's seventeen landfills handle 50,000 tons of garbage per day, creating both groundwater pollution and air pollution from escaping gases. Illegal dumping and seepage of toxic wastes from industrial facilities or obsolete storage tanks contaminate groundwater and soils at numerous sites throughout the region, rendering them "brownfields" that, because of costly cleanup, sit vacant.

The city of Los Angeles alone supports 6,500 miles of sewers, delivering 1 billion gallons a day of wastewater to treatment plants. Frequent violation of pretreatment standards means that a ton of zinc, half a ton of copper and chrome, plus sixty pounds of arsenic enter the area's sewage treatment plants each day. Deadly agricultural and urban garden runoff from earlier periods, polluted with DDT, contaminates certain parts of the coast (such as the offshore zone along the Palos Verdes Peninsula), along with other industrial effluents such as polychlorinated biphenyls, polycyclic aromatic hydrocarbons, and heavy metals, as well as bacteria and viruses.

Physicians surveyed as early as the mid-1950s recognized the health dangers posed by poor air quality. By the late 1980s, health effects studies demonstrated that failure to meet federal standards for ozone and fine particulates cost the region $9.4 billion in health-related expenses annually. Virtually everyone living in the air basin was exposed to unhealthful air; 1,600 deaths were attributed annually to air pollution, with people of color (especially African Americans and Latinos) most vulnerable. Children raised in the air basin were particularly vulnerable (10 to 15 percent suffer decreased lung capacity), being disproportionately affected by ozone exposure.

Poor air and water quality has also severely damaged the region's plant and animal communities. For example, many native plants in the San Bernardino Mountains, especially Ponderosa pines, white fir, and Jeffrey pines, are weakened by ozone, suffer from chloritic decline, and become susceptible to bark beetles, resulting in high mortality rates. California black oaks are also affected, as are lichen species within the coastal sage scrub assemblage. Through biomagnification, parts of the food chain (especially white croaker, corbina, queenfish, surfperches, and scorpion fish) have become contaminated, leading to the near extinction of brown pelicans. In addition, dumping of household plastics has led to many gruesome deaths among marine mammals that have either ingested or become fatally entangled in these castoffs of a disposable society.

Having reviewed the geography of the Southern California region and identified some of the key impacts of urbanization, we now explore some of the research on the urban environment undertaken by scholars of the L.A. School. We begin with two key sets of issues: the politics and ecology of urban growth control.

LOCAL GOVERNANCE AND THE LOSS OF NATURE IN SOUTHERN CALIFORNIA

Land use planning and management in Southern California are responsible for the region's contemporary urban form, as well as a major share of environmental degradation and sociospatial inequality. Land use decision making takes place at the local level. Except for the national forests in the major mountain ranges that surround the vast Los Angeles basin, most of the land lies in private property ownership, subject to local government regulatory jurisdiction and decision making. Two major and interrelated themes emerge with respect to land use control and the relationship to nature in Southern California: first, the fundamental lack of democratic process and participation in land use planning, despite its localization and theoretical accessibility of locally elected officials responsible for decision making; and second, the fragmentation of governance at the local level and how it affects nature. Each of these themes is linked to larger issues—the structure of land use planning itself, private property rights in America, the ideology of nature, and the relationship of nature and the city.

Land Use Planning and the Coastal Sage Scrub Gnatcatcher

In Orange County, structures of land use control have evolved to protect large-scale development interests—Logan and Molotch's growth machine—with changes in land use planning techniques preserving the symbiotic relationship between the county and land developers.[32] As a result, Orange County has witnessed a dramatic upsurge in land development during the past two decades, leading to the swift conversion of previously rural and agricultural lands into new towns. Much of this development has been carried out by the Irvine Ranch Company (IRC) and the Santa Margarita Ranch Company. The IRC, enjoying a reputation of careful and deliberate land use, continues to control about one sixth of total county land and has developed a sophisticated lobbying and public relations machine that operates at the county, state, and federal levels. The IRC and the county have a long-standing cooperative relationship—the county relies on the planning expertise of the IRC and its ability to generate economic growth for the county, and the IRC depends on the county for favorable land use decisions.

With the passage of the 1978 property tax initiative, Proposition 13, and precipitous decline in municipal revenues, local governments began to examine much more closely how the leading resource of local governments (land) was being used. As a consequence, land use planning increasingly has become an exercise in financial planning, fueling ever more growth and development without which local budgets might find themselves stagnant and unable to meet expenses. Orange County was no exception, approving new development on IRC and Santa Margarita lands. But the pace of growth and ensuing traffic congestion also eroded the county's quality of life. A series of successful but ineffectual city-level initiatives left localities unable to address the interjurisdictional spillover effects of growth such as increased traffic, zoning that de facto does not provide for sufficient employee housing, and lack of open space. Likewise, such efforts could not slow the rate at which the county approved proposed development projects. This situation was exacerbated by Orange County itself, which encouraged large-scale IRC development plans that created negative externalities for local cities legally powerless to fight the powerful IRC-county growth coalition. So, in 1988, local residents placed a countywide growth control initiative on the ballot.

Because of widespread support, the 1988 growth control initiative was predicted to win easily.[33] The Building Industry Association, in conjunction with the IRC, responded by spending more than $2.6 million to defeat it.[34] Still, uncertain of success, the IRC hedged its bets by working with the county to create and pass a series of development agreements (DAs) that would allow local jurisdictions to enter into long-term (up to thirty-year) contracts with development for certain land uses.

At this point, it might be useful to take a little detour into the world of developer agreements because they have become an important tool in the developer's arsenal to force their progrowth plans on municipal agendas. DAs provide a way for local jurisdictions to grant certainty in land use in exchange for concessions provided by the developer—such as agreeing to build a road. A DA has to be consistent with the jurisdiction's general plan, but once approved, such an agreement is immune to change by the local jurisdiction for its duration.[35] Because Proposition 13 took important tax revenue away from local municipalities after 1978, they had far less capital to invest in infrastructure (roads, schools, etc.) and other improvements. These local jurisdictions, looking to make up their shortfalls in tax revenue, were compelled to use DAs to get developers to foot the bill for expensive infrastructure improvements and repair, if only they would surrender control of local land use to these developers. DAs more easily escape the increasingly narrow definition imposed by the courts of a demonstrable nexus between what a jurisdiction asks for from a developer and the fiscal impact of the new development because DAs operate for such a long period.[36] Although most planning projects go through a series of public hearings, first at the planning commission level, then in front of locally elected officials required to take public comments into consideration, by contrast, most DAs are negotiated behind closed doors between developers and planning departments, and little or no public input takes place during hearings; they are voted either up or down by the city council or board of supervisors.

The IRC, encouraged by a county hungry for additional tax revenues, advanced twelve DAs for approximately 60,000 houses in exchange for a significant open space set-aside using DAs to secure their "right" to build ahead of the election. This open space would later be purchased by the county (a concession to long-standing pressure from local environmentalists), along with the county's agreement to float bonds for a highly contested series of toll roads that would relieve traffic congestion. Opponents of the DAs lacked time and money to halt these agreements, and the DAs were passed, allowing for substantial new development during the following twenty-five years. In the spring of 1989, the growth control initiative failed.

Clearly, approval of the DAs by the Orange County Board of Supervisors violated the spirit of democratic local self-rule and the electoral process, even if their passage was legal. By circumventing the election process, the county effectively preempted residents who were trying to control growth. This action, combined with a sophisticated and an expensive public relations campaign by the Building Industry Association, prevented county residents from genuinely engaging in the issues raised by development and land planning. The Building Industry Association cleverly aimed its progrowth campaign at the populated and poorer cities of the northern part of the county, claiming that slowing growth would bring higher taxes—an entirely disingenuous claim. As this example illustrates, private and fiscal imperatives have come to dominate local planning, and jurisdictional fragmentation has had a negative environmental impact on adjacent communities that local residents have no political power to hinder or halt.

Soon after the defeat of countywide growth control and the passage of twelve DAs, a tiny songbird—the gnatcatcher—arrived on the scene. The gnatcatcher, which lives in the coastal sage scrub ecosystem of Orange County, was nominated for protection under the Federal Endangered Species Act by the Natural Resources Defense Council and other environmental groups. Part of the gnatcatcher's habitat, however, overlapped with the open space that the Irvine Ranch Company had agreed to put aside. Preserving a species that is nearly extinct requires drastic last-minute intervention, and in the context of a rapidly urbanizing region with extremely valuable real estate (land was valued at between $4,000 and $200,000 an acre), the economic stakes were high indeed.[37] Thus, although an endangered species listing could have indefinitely halted land development in the entire county while the arcane and difficult Endangered Species Act process unfolded, the IRC once again circumvented the regulatory process.

The IRC's tactic was to propose an alternative conservation strategy to Governor Pete Wilson's Resources Agency that was ultimately implemented by the state—the Natural Communities Conservation Planning (NCCP).[38] The NCCP is a voluntary process by which all stakeholders come to the table to negotiate habitat conservation. It is predicated on the willingness of landowners to determine what lands they are willing to set aside for habitat protection in perpetuity; landowners thus drive the process. Ideally, endangered habitats coincide with the lands that private owners are willing to forgo developing, but this is not always the case, particularly with the intense competition between humans, plants, and animals for landscapes such as coastal sage scrub. In addition to such inevitable disagreements, requirements for public participation are weak and vary widely. Nominally, the process encourages the participation of "all stakeholders," yet even this approach undermines a genuine public involvement because of its narrow definition of *stakeholders*. Thus participants are reduced to predictable categories such as environmentalists and developers, although at stake is the very future of an ecosystem and of human-environment relations. Although the NCCP's single advantage is that it can transcend jurisdictional boundaries and in best-case circumstances bring numerous parties to the table, in practice it more commonly undermines democratic land use planning by narrowing it to immediately interested parties and by giving property owners the upper hand. Further, the NCCP process, unlike conventional planning, is voluntary, and, therefore, public hearings and input depend on the local municipal culture.

In central Orange County, the IRC offered its already dedicated open space as well as 2,500 additional acres to preserve a coherent coastal sage scrub habitat area. This habitat, however, was also slated to be shared with the promised toll roads.

Moreover, the NCCP process was stalemated because of the unwillingness of the Santa Margarita Company to set lands aside on a permanent basis, resisting any control over its property. Although the county has been the lead agency on the NCCP, it has offered little leadership. Indeed, because of its historic alliance with the IRC and other land developers, the county joined the Building Industry Association in its opposition to the gnatcatcher as an endangered species. The NCCP process, furthermore, offers no guarantees of objective scientific review of habitat designation. In central Orange County, the IRC hired its own scientists to determine which lands were suitable and sufficient habitat for the gnatcatcher. Their findings were contested by environmental groups and ultimately negotiated. In southern Orange County, the Santa Margarita Company remains unwilling even to enter into discussion with environmental groups over questions of scientific analysis of habitat or of habitat designation.[39]

Struggles over growth and the preservation of nature in Orange County show the tenuous character of democratic accountability in local governments and the enduring power of vested economic interests. This influence has grown for local jurisdictions with shrinking revenues and expanding fiscal responsibilities. Although residential development rarely pays for itself, the general attitude of local government has not changed. Local jurisdictions engage in a continual search for capital to finance infrastructure once provided through property taxes. Local residents, torn between wanting low taxes and the preservation of their quality of life—intimately tied to low-density development and low traffic levels—use the only tools they have available, that is, the initiative and local elections. But these are ineffectual in the face of powerful economic interests, private property rights, and the fiscal crises of local government. Democratic accountability is undermined and environmental degradation continues apace while new structures evolve (such as DAs) to perpetuate the status quo.

Although the California Environmental Quality Act and various state and federal laws require consideration of the environmental impacts of development, these approaches epitomize a piecemeal, fragmented view of nature that fails to account for interrelations and interdependencies among ecosystems and human beings. Environmental impact reports, written about specific developments, are strictly limited to a specific piece of land—although it is but a fragment of a larger natural system and place of human settlement.

The Case of the California Spotted Owl

Fragmentation has plagued efforts to preserve habitat corridors in Southern California.[40] The lines of fragmentation run between jurisdictions (as in the Orange County case) but also between humans and nature and between wilderness and the rest. The rapid urbanization of the Southland has decimated riparian corridors and traditional circulation paths of many species, from cougars to spotted owls. Although most of the region's mountains were set aside in the late nineteenth century for watershed management purposes and are within national forests, the paths

California Spotted Owl
Photograph courtesy of the State of California.

of connection among the mountains and between the mountains and the sea have been either entirely urbanized or nearly so. Such loss of landscape-level connectivity poses serious survival problems for a number of species whose habitat goes beyond the confines of the mountains themselves or whose long-term viability depends on being able to mate with species from adjoining mountain ranges.

Nearly one quarter of the state's spotted owl population (*Strix occidentalis occidentalis*) lives in the mountain ranges of Southern California. Owls inhabit Southern California mountain habitat "islands," surrounded by unsuitable habitat of desert, chaparral, and urban development. Much of this splintered distribution comes from human activity. Land between the mountain ranges has been swallowed by urban and suburban development and road building. Thus, successful movement by owls between separate Southern California populations has become increasingly difficult, if not impossible.[41] Owls' increasing inability to move from one range to another means that the existing populations are potentially subject to extinction as the genetic pool is increasingly restricted. This situation is compounded by the human-engendered transformations of the forest habitat, including (a) increased mountain-water mining by foothill cities; (b) the Forest Service's restricted ability to restore a "natural" fire regime in the mountains to improve its resistance to catastrophic fire; and (c) the rise in recreational use of the mountains.

Owl habitat is doubly affected by air pollution, which weakens their tree habitat and increases the potential for the catastrophic fires (resulting from decades of fire suppression) that kill roosting trees. Fire suppression puts the Forest Service in an impossible situation, caught between the equally pressing imperatives of reintroducing a more natural fire regime and of the reduction of air pollution. The South Coast Air Quality Management District (SCAQMD), in response to the high levels of air pollution endemic to urban areas, severely restricts burn days available to the Forest Service because forest fires can pollute significantly and normally coincide with the high levels of air pollution in the Los Angeles basin in the fall. But the forest ecosystem responds best to burning in the fall. Consequently, after a century of artificial fire suppression, just as the Forest Service is trying to reintroduce a more natural fire regime (also artificial), it cannot do so because of urbanization-driven air pollution—the same air pollution killing the remaining old growth tree habitat for spotted owls. To make matters worse, the Forest Service is also restricted in its ability to burn because of encroaching urbanization. As suburbs creep up mountain foothills, homeowners fear fires and resent ashes from fires on adjoining forest lands. Although they may have purchased their property for its proximity to nature, they are unwilling to accept the costs of maintaining that nature. The Forest Service is thus reluctant to burn in urban-adjacent areas because it is liable for property damage if fires escape control.

Riparian corridors, which provided migration pathways for owls, have through time mostly disappeared from the Southland—paved over for flood control and freeways, converted to golf courses, and sucked dry by water diversion for urban uses. Drought in the late 1980s only accelerated the desiccation of these corridors. As local municipalities dug deeper wells or went (often illegally) to water sources in the mountains, they provoked a further series of linked changes in the local ecosystems. For the owl, the reduction of water meant that rodents, on which owls prey, no longer had sufficient food because there was not enough water for the plants that rodent populations depended on for survival. Reduction in prey caused owl numbers to decline precipitously.[42] Migration corridors disappeared, preventing owls from moving easily from one mountain range to another. The remaining riparian corridors near and within the national forests were also desiccated and altered by increased urbanization.

Owls are only one of many species that are on the road to extinction in Southern California as a result of the complex mix of environmental changes caused by urbanization. But the owls' vulnerability reveals both how urbanization can cause extinction and how current governance structures fail to address the effects of urbanization on natural systems. This inability stems from their bounded land use jurisdictions, land use planning processes, local fiscal needs, and the rights of private property. The narrow boundaries of local jurisdictions lead to the cutting up of habitat corridors for municipal expedience, each piece becoming the planning domain of different local governments. A river's watershed, for example, may come under the planning jurisdiction of dozens of local governments, each planning for its own fiscal advantage, none required to take the watershed, itself, into account. For owls and many other mobile species that follow life cycles defined by boundaries other than those laid out by local government jurisdictions, this can be nothing short of catastrophic.

These incremental land use decisions by local jurisdictions remain largely out of public democratic deliberation. Although local jurisdictions are required to make environmental impact reports, they are responsible only for their small pieces of the natural system, and, therefore, natural systems are splintered by the fragmentation of jurisdictional authority. Even if an environmental impact report is made, the prerogatives of private property ownership allow land to be used for financial gain and largely ignore that the land is part of a larger ecosystem. Once again, the collective resource of nature is devalued at the hands of individual property.

The dialectical relationship between the city and nature is invisible, yet, as the owl example shows, invisibility does not make it inconsequential. The ideologies of nature that undergird U.S. land use planning are based on a division of space—domestic, private property is regulated by local governments, whereas nature lies in the preferably humanless "wild" of the public domain. This approach creates a spatial division of labor in which "nature" is governed by public concerns, whereas in urban areas, considerations about the public good of the health of nature are abandoned in favor of individual property rights. This division is a fiction, of course, because nature is ubiquitous. The air we breathe; the water we drink; the soil we build on; and the millions of plants, animals, and microorganisms that inhabit the space around us are all nature. But it is a convenient fiction, which allows for the persistent privatization of nature and an illusion of local democratic control over local land uses.

THE URBAN POLITICAL ECONOMY
OF ENVIRONMENTAL HAZARD

Local jokesters often quip that Los Angeles has only four kinds of weather: earthquake, flood, fire, and riot. But the link between environmental hazards and urban social conditions is closer than we might realize—a consideration few if any urbanists have seriously entertained. Building on John McPhee's[43] brilliant analyses of relations between local residents and debris flows, Mike Davis[44] has explored the Angeleno penchant for seeking to control nature in the pursuit of profit and political gain. In the process, wealthy residents seeking to live near the region's wildlands, while avoiding the associated risks, are heavily subsidized by taxpayers, whereas poor inner-city tenement dwellers, facing different sorts of environmental risks, are often left to pay the (ultimate) burden on their own. The resulting urbanization patterns thus not only shape the region's landscapes but also create deep social inequalities. Davis's work connects nature, environmental policy, city politics, and urban space. He not only debunks the social construction of hazards such as fires and floods as natural but reveals how the urban political economy works to simultaneously eradicate wildlands and wildlife, engender unsustainable settlement patterns, and endanger the city's economically marginalized residents.

The Urban Politics of Fire

McPhee's long chapter, "Los Angeles Against the Mountains," was a precursor to Davis's work on urban environmental hazards. It is a classic tale of what happens when people forget the constraints imposed by their environment and how governments at various levels collude in spreading the notion that nature can be controlled via fancy engineering "solutions." As suburb after suburb sprung up in Los Angeles, covering vast tracts of the region's alluvial plain, development eventually hit the base of the San Gabriel Mountains. There, confronted by deadly environmental hazards in the form of mass movements such as landslides and debris flows, suburbanites hunkered down and persuaded their local governments to build elaborate fortifications to defend them against the mountains.

Although McPhee focuses on the fundamental folly of living along the San Gabriel front, Davis, by contrast, uses the case of fire policy to reveal a deeper political and economic logic. This logic, which naturalizes the environmental hazards produced by suburban development, leads to enormous, regressive public investments to protect private property on the urban-wildland interface. It also leaves shamefully inadequate public safety investments for protecting the lives of inner-city residents. Thus, Davis argues "the case for letting Malibu burn."

Fires are a major environmental hazard in Southern California, directly affecting people, property, and wildlife and also triggering costly floods and mass movements. The federal approach to dealing with such fires comes from the U.S. Forest Service's experience of suppressing fires in wildland areas. Historically, the system hinged on rapid detection (using fire lookouts, for example) and extinguishing of fires, often at large public expense. This fire suppression policy became a major source of controversy as, increasingly, ecologists realized that fire suppression ran contrary to natural fire regimes and led to far more severe fires because suppression allowed fuel buildup. Adjustments have led to the present federal policy whereby each fire is evaluated and managed by either extinguishing, containing, or confining it (allowing it to burn as long as it is within a range of acceptable fire behaviors). The latest U.S. Forest Service policy on wildfires mandates the reintroduction of wildfires into ecosystems on federal lands and forests (through prescribed or controlled burns). But prescribed burns near urban areas or where wildlands are interspersed with housing, like much of L.A.'s mountains, are difficult to control. A recent report estimates that since 1985, the federal government alone spent $300 million to protect this wildland-urban interface zone. Urban expansion and jurisdictional fragmentation have only deepened the problem.

Property owners believe that insurance companies and public sector disaster assistance will cover their losses and that the government should protect them from environmental hazards. The federal government reports that neither public education nor prevention efforts have had much impact, even among those most at risk. The public relies on fire prevention agencies to suppress fire, and insurance companies do not charge sufficiently proportionate rates for those living in fire zones. Conditioned to ignore fire risk, residents are unwilling to take responsibility for living in fire hazard zones.

As Davis explains, the Malibu coast of Southern California offers a defining case of urban fringe fire suppression policy and politics. Native Californians (the Chumash and Gabrielinos) set fires every year to keep the brush down and the plants and animals flourishing, augmenting the effects of naturally lit fires (e.g., fires caused by lightning). Throughout the nineteenth century, however, Spanish/Mexican governments imposed restrictions on native Californians' annual burning practices, leading to regular firestorms along the coast. Consequently, from the nineteenth century onward, Malibu became the wildfire capital of North America and perhaps the world, where a large fire (100+ acres) occurs on average every 2.5 years.

Malibu's policy of total fire suppression guarantees that under the right weather conditions, any fire is apt to become a conflagration that costs large sums of public monies. Southern California is at its most dangerous when, after a dry summer, Santa Ana winds, originating in the Mojave Desert, push the temperature up. The Malibu canyons, protected from fire for years, often store up to forty tons of fuel per acre (in the form of leaf litter, dead scrub vegetation, etc.), and, again because of fire suppression, canyon chaparral cover is old and far more flammable than younger vegetation. A Malibu firestorm can create the heat equivalent of 3 million barrels of crude oil burning at 2,000 degrees. Essentially, the Malibu zone has became a distinctive fire regime or fire ecology characterized by a lethal mixture of homeowners and brush buildups, or what Davis calls "suburb plus chaparral." During the 1950s, Malibu fire policy took on national political significance as Cold War fears of nuclear disaster spilled over to influence fire policy. If federal planners could not deal with wild firestorms in Malibu, how could they possibly deal with a nuclear fire-storm? According to fire historian Stephen Pyne, the Eisenhower administration identified the 1956 Malibu fire as "the first major fire disaster of national scope," triggering a debate in Congress about how to provide "complete fire prevention and protection in Southern California."[45]

With Eisenhower's declaration of Malibu as a federal disaster area, Malibu and other areas struck by wildfires in the future became eligible for tax relief, preferential low-interest loans, and other subsidies. In effect, the nation's citizenry began to sub-sidize the fire-suburbs, treating these fires as "natural hazards." The result was more and more upscale building in Malibu. In 1962, the Los Angeles County Board of Supervisors approved a 1,400 percent increase in the Malibu area population—from 7,900 in 1960 to a projected 117,000 in 1980. State coastal protection legislation prevented this large an expansion, but the population has grown rapidly and spread into the chaparral canyons. Property was not zoned according to fire risk, and the availability of disaster relief kept homeowner insurance rates artificially low. But in 1970, fire erupted again, setting the Pacific Coast Highway ablaze, killing ten per-sons and destroying more than 400 homes. Property owners, many of whom were wealthy, powerful, and active in national politics, were furious at the government for failing to save their homes and demanded more technology to combat the fires, which they promptly received. Yet more fires inevitably followed—in 1978, 1982, 1985, 1993, and 1995, the 1993 blaze carrying a hefty taxpayer price tag of $1 bil-lion.

Davis contrasts the Malibu case with local government's responses to tenement fires in downtown Los Angeles. Communities such as Westlake and Skid Row near downtown, known for their relentless stretches of asphalt and concrete rather than their trees or gardens, also have a specific fire ecology, which, given the inadequate public response to fires in these areas, is far more deadly than Malibu's. But unlike the case of Malibu fires, downtown's "fire tenements" are not the result of criminal behavior or political extremism; rather, fires are naturalized and portrayed as an endemic and inevitable condition of the inner-city environment. Westlake and adja-cent areas of downtown Los Angeles, for instance, have the highest incidence of urban fire in the nation, some buildings in the area having burned repeatedly. As Malibu burned in 1993, Westlake's Burlington apartments caught fire. Although the building was less than ten years old, its owners had been repeatedly cited for fail-ure to repair smoke detectors, fire doors, and so forth and for housing residents in extremely crowded conditions. Prior to the fire, inspectors had discovered people living in closets and found that fire doors had been nailed open, making them use-less. They ordered an emergency twenty-four-hour fire watch until violations were corrected, but the property owners refused to comply and were not prosecuted. Two weeks later, the building was engulfed in flames, and ten people burned to death.

Yet if between 1947 and 1993, there were thirteen tenement building fires that left almost 120 people dead, why do residents of these downtown communities con-tinue to face such a high risk from fire? The answer lies in a deadly political economy of inner-city fire policy in which apartment owners play power politics with public officials, while residents—poor people of color and, increasingly, immigrants—are left to take the heat (literally). Arson in pursuit of insurance dollars plays its role, but more critical are the weak fire codes and equally weak local politicians unwilling to act against developers and the absentee property owners. Code enforcement is lax and often simply ignored by property owners. A 1993 city study, for example, found that more than half of all required fire inspections had not been made, and more than 60 percent of buildings were in violation of fire codes. A later study by the fire department itself found that structures in affluent areas of the city were three times as likely to be inspected than in poor communities. Further, unlike national agencies that can fight Malibu "wild" fires and then simply bill Congress, local government pays for urban fire protection from general fund revenues. Not surprisingly, fire services have been severely underfunded since Proposition 13, and continuous and deadly fires are the result.

Fire protection policies and expenditures in Malibu and similar Southern California communities are rarely if ever put in the context of urban fire protection. Compared with the expense of fighting a wildfire, inner-city buildings could be retrofitted, adequate inspection and enforcement systems established, and community residents far better protected for a fraction of the cost. But such trade-offs are never debated, and the political interests of the powerful, whether they are Malibu homeowners or Westlake slumlords, continue to be served at the expense of life and limb in poor inner-city communities. These interests are served by characterizing Malibu fires as natural hazards rather than as the result of a particular form of suburban development whose costs could more readily be compared with those of other forms of urban development. This artful elision between nature and culture perpetuates deep-seated patterns of social injustice in Los Angeles and reveals how nature—as social construction and objective reality—shapes both social relations and urban form in the city.

ENVIRONMENTAL RACISM AND STRUGGLES FOR ENVIRONMENTAL JUSTICE IN LOS ANGELES

Despite the existence of environmental racism and an environmental justice movement rooted in many of the transformations and issues central to the L.A. School, such as social polarization, the topic has not received significant scholarly attention. Nonetheless, the rise of the environmental justice movement has challenged how we think about the environment and environmental policy making by rearticulating traditional questions of urbanization and nature in light of social justice. In this section, we outline the contours of the Los Angeles environmental justice movement, focusing on why the movement has become prominent in the region. In addition, we consider how environmental justice reframes conventional approaches to the environment, urbanization, and social justice by focusing on one recent campaign, the Bus Riders' Union/*Sindicato de Pasajeros*.

Los Angeles as a Site of Environmental Justice Struggle

Although L.A.'s environmental policy overwhelmingly reflects corporate interests, the region has emerged as a key city on the national environmental justice map. This is hardly surprising in view of the transformations that Los Angeles has undergone in recent years—many of which have intensified environmental justice struggles, particularly social, racial, and spatial polarization. For instance, L.A.'s extreme racial segregation and the spatiality of income inequality are key elements of environmental inequality.[46] To date, all major studies have found that communities of color, and in particular, working-class Chicanos/Latinos, bear a large and disproportionate toxic burden—in the distributions of abandoned hazardous waste sites,[47] of facilities emitting toxic air emissions,[48] and of the geography of air toxins by size,[49] as well as in the number of facilities that handle hazardous waste.[50] Such findings corroborate other studies indicating that urban industrial hazards, in addition to being located near communities of color, are also associated with industrial land use,[51] and L.A.'s racial inequality further reinforces the urgency for versions of environmental justice that account for environmental racism.

As of 1990, Los Angeles County was roughly 40 percent Anglo, 40 percent Latino, 10 percent Asian/Pacific Islander, and 10 percent Black. The racial diversity of Southern California has been coupled with a long history of white racism—a history that frames contemporary events.[52] Accordingly, when the city of Los Angeles tried to build the first in a series of waste-to-energy incinerators in South Central, local residents, primarily African American women, saw the plan as a clear case of environmental racism. Likewise, when the Mothers of East L.A. identified the city of Vernon's plan to build an incinerator adjacent to Boyle Heights as racism, their claims resonated not only with Latinos throughout the region but also with other racially subordinated groups.

Another key factor contributing to L.A.'s prominence in the environmental justice movement is its role as a leading manufacturing county in the nation, resulting in vast amounts of pollution and waste. In addition to L.A. smog, residents face chemical explosions and oil spills. Efforts to solve these problems offer another window into environmental justice through the process of environmental regulation. Although policymakers traditionally have been concerned with the technical aspects of waste disposal and pollution control, environmental justice activists have demanded not only that their voices be heard but that the social justice implications of environmental policy be considered.

When considering why Chicanos/Latinos are so vulnerable to toxic exposure, we must first recognize their close connection to the city's manufacturing sector, where they constitute the bulk of L.A.'s working class.[53] Latino overrepresentation in manufacturing is partly due to immigration but also to racist social structures that keep Latinos working at the bottom of L.A.'s labor pool. Latino exposure is also a product of the spatial division and density of labor. Although most industries are located in industrial zones with limited residential units, many Latinos live immediately adjacent to these areas.[54] Because of the poverty of this population, particularly among immigrants, the overall residential densities are quite high. Finally, whites' withdrawal from industrial zones of the harbor and central city has only intensified these areas' transformation into all-nonwhite neighborhoods of poor immigrant workers of color with little or no political clout to change government decisions regarding pollutants.

The distribution of environmental quality or lack thereof (environmental racism) is deeply rooted in larger processes of restructuring, which have, in turn, produced a fertile ground for environmental justice activism. Activists have effectively linked urban, environmental, and social justice issues because they approach these issues as marginalized citizens. We can see this broad, integrated redefinition of the environment in the recent campaign of the Bus Riders' Union/*Sindicato de Pasajeros*.

The Bus Riders' Union/*Sindicato de Pasajeros* and Environmental Justice Policy

The Bus Riders' Union (BRU), an arm of the Labor/Community Strategy Center, seeks to force the Metropolitan Transportation Authority (MTA) to be more responsive to the transit needs of low-income and nonwhite bus riders. Although the BRU is a path-breaking civil rights struggle, its historical development allows us to see how the framing of environmental issues has changed, with important consequences for the city as a whole. The Labor/Community Strategy Center was established in the early 1980s in an effort to keep the General Motors Van Nuys automotive plant open. After waging an intense battle that kept the Van Nuys plant running a decade longer than GM had planned, organizers became increasingly concerned with environmental issues and felt the need for a more progressive response to mainstream environmentalism. This resulted in the Watchdog campaign, which emphasized corporate accountability (particularly for the petrochemical industry) and forced the SCAQMD to prioritize public health concerns. Throughout the late 1980s and early 1990s, the Strategy Center became an active voice for environmental justice by winning a number of impressive victories.[55]

The center, however, began to shift its attention to mass transit. Despite the severity of air toxins (emitted from stationary sources), the majority of Southern California's smog comes from vehicles. But at the same time that the SCAQMD was grappling with air pollution, the MTA was planning a vast subway and light rail system to serve the outlying suburbs that they touted as a solution to L.A.'s polluted air: getting suburbanites out of their cars and onto rail for their daily commutes. Although many attacked the plan as inefficient and expensive, few bothered to ask who would pay for this great public works project. When the Strategy Center began to examine this question, it became clear that, unbeknownst to them, the city's overwhelmingly nonsuburban, working-class bus riders would be forced to foot the bill.

Although the largest in the country, L.A.'s bus system has never been stellar. Despite overcrowding, rising bus fares, and continual breakdowns, the MTA board intended to further decimate the bus system to subsidize its rail operation. Its plans called for both fare hikes and a reduction in bus service. This might make sense if

Bus Riders Union/Sindicato de Pasajeros demonstration in front of Los Angeles City Hall, 1996. (Labor/Community Strategy Center, used with permission).
Photograph by Geoff Ray.

rail served the majority of the MTA's passengers. But such was not the case. The rail system serves 26,000 riders daily, while the bus carries 350,000. Moreover, rail passengers are predominantly white, suburban, and affluent—a striking contrast to the 80 percent of the bus riders who are urban dwellers of color and 60 percent of whom have family incomes less than $15,000. In effect, the MTA was meeting the needs of 10 percent of its ridership on the backs of the other 90 percent.[56]

Although the agency catered to a relatively elite constituency, it brought millions of dollars to the construction industry while undermining the well-being of already poor and politically weak populations. With this in mind, the BRU charged the MTA with "transit racism." Under Title VI of the 1964 Civil Rights Act, it is illegal for an entity receiving federal monies to discriminate on the basis of race. Given that the MTA was subsidizing each rail ride by $20, versus each bus ride at $0.33, the BRU felt it had a strong case when it charged the MTA with operating two separate and unequal mass transit systems.

In its first move, the BRU challenged the MTA's effort in the fall of 1994 to eliminate the monthly pass. After the BRU obtained a restraining order prohibiting the MTA from doing away with the pass and preventing a rate hike, the NAACP Legal Defense Fund agreed to take on the BRU's case. Since then, BRU organizers have been riding the buses, drawing new members and educating the public about the inequities of transit policy. At present, the BRU has more than 1,500 dues-paying members and a whopping 35,000 bus riders who consider themselves affiliated with the union. Although the initial objective of the BRU was a lawsuit, the judge ordered the plaintiffs and the MTA to pursue mediation. This effort resulted in the consent decree agreement reached by both parties, outlining a whole series of transit goals, including the establishment of a joint working group—consisting of four BRU members and four MTA staffers—to oversee the implementation of these changes during the next ten years. Some of the key provisions of the decree are (a) retention of and a reduction in the price of the monthly pass; (b) commitment to purchase 152 new buses, a percentage of which had to be clean-fuel burning; and (c) a commitment to alleviate overcrowding.

Besides creating very real material changes in Los Angeles and the lives of all its residents, the BRU's "Billions for Buses" campaign is an excellent example of reframing and expanding environmental concerns as part of a larger social justice agenda. In no way is it solely about air quality. The environment is not even the primary concern. The BRU is challenging not only the racist and class-biased policies of an agency committed to large-scale public works projects but also the historical accumulation or "sedimentation of racial inequality" inscribed in the landscape of the city.[57] By reframing environmental justice concerns in this way, activists not only reshape the city along more humane outlines but also revise traditional notions of the relationship between the environment and urbanization.

NEGOTIATING HUMAN-ANIMAL
BORDERLANDS IN SOUTHERN CALIFORNIA

Among urban theorists trying to understand Los Angeles, the idea that Southern California—epitomized by all things artificial, plastic, and fake—could be home to anyone besides its human inhabitants seldom arises. Oblivious to this view, however, animals have persistently inserted themselves into everyday social and political life in Southern California. Wild, domestic, and commensal animals are part and parcel of a wide variety of neighborhoods and communities stemming from the sociospatial structure of the place itself. Los Angeles, with the longest urban-wildland interface of any city outside the tropics,[58] contains miles of canyon-dominated urban edge that routinely bring people into contact with wild animals. Demographic changes and the growth of childless households partly explain an enlarged social role for domestic "pets" and an assertion of their right to space in the city. Economic polarization has led not only to deteriorating housing but also to a proliferation of "pest" animals. The rise of a popular biocentrism, challenging the region's bedrock control-of-nature ideology, means that demands for coexistence are displacing older practices of exclusion or extermination. At the same time, globalization and international migration to the region mean that both traditional anthropocentric and newer biocentric ideologies must confront alien patterns of human-animal interaction among the region's diverse population—confrontations that are not always peaceful.

A small body of work by scholars of the L.A. School has begun to bring animals, especially wildlife, into focus as a vital part of the urban environment. Several issues arise from this research, each related to dominant concerns of the L.A. School (such as spatial fragmentation, economic restructuring, and population diversity). They include ideological and class-based conflicts over wildlife management as traditional anthropocentric ideologies are challenged by more biocentric philosophies; social conflict and racialization arising from controversial animal practices linked to cultural diversity; and the politics of resistance to the neglect, persecution, and exclusion of animals from the city.

Negotiating the Wild in Los Angeles

Following World War II, the L.A. growth machine fueled the rapid expansion of the metropolis, covering the coastal plain with single-family subdivisions, garden apartment developments, and neighborhood strip commercial centers. Residential development spread into the canyons and foothills of local mountains, expelling many animals from the city and bringing endemic species to the brink of extinction. Legitimized by an anthropocentric ideology highlighting the overarching benefits of economic growth, suburban expansion, and the single-family home, as well as a pervasive belief in the city as an exclusively human habitat, few Angelenos questioned the disappearance of wild animals from their midst.

In the wake of the 1970s environmental movement, however, a more biocentric consciousness emerged, particularly among the urban middle and upper-middle classes. During the 1980s, the rise of the animal rights movement led to a questioning of many assumptions basic to the ideology of growth and nonstop urbanization. The results of these ideological shifts have been bitter conflicts over wildlife management, and not just over endangered species. Indeed, far more common local animals were the subject of concern and debate. These conflicts hinged not only on scientific disputes about wildlife populations or best management practices but also on class-based differences in attitudes toward nature among Angelenos.

Both news media coverage and a few systematic analyses reveal that the debates over the management of wild animals in Los Angeles—even dangerous predators—have shifted, especially along the expanding urban edge.[59] Recently, a black bear was discovered relaxing in a suburban hot tub in middle-class Monrovia. Tranquilized and removed by state wildlife officials, the bear was slated for euthanasia. But a major protest of local residents demanding that the bear's sentence be reprieved led Governor Pete Wilson to personally announce that a permanent home for the bear—now named Samson—would be established in an existing zoo. Local residents responded by embarking on a zealous fund-raising campaign, selling T-shirts and stuffed bears, with proceeds going to the rapid construction of a cozy enclosure for the bear to live out his days.

Coyotes, too, have been a source of conflict, pitting animal rights activists against fearful suburban residents angry at animal control officers for failing to control the highly adaptable canines. Despite repeated extermination campaigns, coyotes remained numerous not only along the urban edge but also in relatively built-up areas. Public animal regulation units came under mounting attack over urban coyote management during the late 1980s and early 1990s when the long drought of this period reduced access to water and drove animals into the city in search of food and water. Residents whose neighborhoods had been "invaded" by coyotes demanded relief from this predatory threat. In working-class districts of the San Fernando Valley, for example, angry residents demanded municipal action against the "scum animals" who they claimed had "no reason to live." At the same time, however, animal rights advocates gained increasing presence on animal control commissions in the region. They fought against the use of leg-hold traps and routine practices of urban coyote extermination (perfectly legal given the coyote's listing as a so-called pest species). Instead, they argued for public education to alter what Davis terms the "pet-and-garbage ecology of the suburbs" and thus minimize danger of attack.[60] Most coyote ecologists supported this approach because coyote births invariably rose following exterminations because of increased food supplies available to remaining animals. And simple measures such as covering garbage cans securely, keeping small pets inside at night, and feeding pets indoors effectively discourage coyotes from frequenting residential areas. Moreover, concerns about liability also emerged after an Orange County incident that resulted in an injury and ultimately a successful lawsuit against the county; eventually, the city of Los Angeles decided that removal of coyotes from private premises was not within their legitimate purview. Thus ended more than two centuries of unremitting attack on Angelenos of a coyote persuasion.

Cultural Diversity and the Politics of Animal Practices

Human-animal interactions can also become highly politicized in culturally diverse cities such as Los Angeles and can, in turn, initiate processes of social exclusion and racialization. Such practices have thus far been ignored by urban theories of race and ethnicity, given their focus on human interactions alone. Animal practices, however, are extraordinarily powerful as a basis for creating difference and, hence, racialization because such practices serve as defining moments in the social construction of the human-animal divide—that shifting metaphorical line built up on the basis of human-animal interaction patterns, ideas about hierarchies of living things, and the symbolic roles played by animals in society.[61] Certain animals (such as pets and primates) are positioned on the human side of the line, and must be treated as such, whereas harmful practices directed at other sorts of animals are normalized and legitimated, despite the pain and suffering such practices may involve. Those who violate such culture-specific standards of treatment, for example, by eating animals considered quasi-human, are axiomatically defined as beastly and barbaric. In some cases, violation of standards arises not because of the type of animal practice per se (e.g., eating shellfish) but because it occurs in the "wrong" site or situation (e.g., eating an endangered shellfish stripped from an environmentally fragile tide pool). But codes of animal practice and thus definitions of the human-animal divide are far from universal. In a rapidly globalizing city such as Los Angeles, where more than a quarter of the population is foreign born and people come from all over the world, cultural differences can strike at deeply rooted belief systems around the definitions of *human* and *animal.*

For example, in 1989, two Long Beach men were charged with cruelty to animals for allegedly killing a German shepherd puppy and eating the dog for dinner. An L.A.-area judge ruled that there was no law against eating dogs and that the animal had not been killed in an inhumane fashion, and the charges were dropped. The case did not die but rather spurred passage of a state law making the eating of dogs or cats a criminal misdemeanor. It seemed that eating a dog or cat is too close to cannibalism for comfort, given their quasi-human status in the United States. Significantly, the two Long Beach puppy-eaters were not U.S. born—but refugees from Cambodia. Trying to minimize the backlash against his community, the head of the Cambodia Association of America claimed that "Cambodians don't eat dogs," but it is widely known that many people from various parts of Asia do. Dogs and cats are specialty meats, often considered a delicacy. Although most people see nothing wrong with eating many animals for food (including baby animals) and even taboo animals under conditions of duress, killing a supposedly cute, helpless puppy for a *luxury meal* is another story. Thus, although the pet protection bill was amended in the face of protests by Asian civic organizations to include a wider variety of animals, the legislation was largely seen as anti-Asian; according to one editorialist, the law implied that "the yellow horde is at it again, that the eating habits of South East Asians . . . are out of control."[62]

The divisive politics of animal practices deepens marginalization for those whose behavior offends the native-born Anglo mainstream. Embedded within the larger dynamics of international migration and economic globalization, conflicts over the shape of human-animal relations in Los Angeles highlight how the fragmented, heteropolitan city recasts our understanding of nature-society relations and enlarges the set of urban processes conventionally linked to understandings of race and place.

Claiming Space for Animals in the City

Los Angeles has less public open space per capita than almost any other major metropolis in the developed world. Not surprisingly, real estate developers seeking to maximize their profits routinely resisted efforts by planners to exact subdivision lands for public parks or other improvements. Moreover, subdivision after subdivision was sold to newcomers with the promise that each residence would have its own citrus grove or flower garden. Parks and gardens were, essentially, privatized and commodified. Later, postwar developers responded to the region's rapid growth in housing demand by constructing apartments, maximizing units per project by minimizing communal space. Thus, urbanization in Southern California not only eliminated, degraded, and fragmented the region's wildlife habitat, driving some species to the brink of extinction and many out entirely, but also left little open space for the many birds, small mammals, reptiles and amphibians, and insects able to coexist with humans and their activities. Appreciating the needs of household animals even less, such an urban pattern ignored the recreational requirements and desires of the city's domestic animals (dogs in particular), although by the 1980s, every second or third household included at least one canine; by some estimates, households were more likely to include a domestic animal than a child.

Social movements for *reclaiming* urban space for domestic and wild animals (as opposed to protecting fringe habitat from urban encroachment on the basis of endangered species) became widespread in the 1980s and 1990s. For most major environmental struggles in the region, the issue of wildlife habitat has not been a primary objective, but for those focused on various restoration efforts, enabling wildlife to reoccupy the city is typically an important secondary objective. For example, Friends of the Los Angeles River and the new Los Angeles-San Gabriel Watershed Council focus on large-scale riparian restoration and emphasize the benefits of such restoration for both flood control and public recreation. But an ancillary goal is creation of wildlife habitat within the city. Fights over specific developments—such as in Playa Vista, the last major wetland tract in the county—have centered not only on traffic congestion and pollution but on the destruction of in-town wildlife habitats.

Among those movements more directly focused on reclaiming or protecting space for animals in the fast-urbanizing region are those on behalf of domestic dogs. Wolch and Rowe, for example, analyzed a bitter conflict in Laurel Canyon Park over the presence of free dogs.[63] This four-acre park, located in the Hollywood Hills, had fallen into disrepair, becoming a site for drug transactions and prostitution. A small group of dog owners decided to "take back the park" by investing in improvements and security features and using the presence of large off-leash canines to discourage less desirable uses. As the park became more attractive, local residents decided that they, too, wanted to use the park once again—but objected to off-leash dogs, whose owners were violating a law against off-leash dogs in Los Angeles City parks. Antidog forces framed the issue as one of "dogs versus kids" and condemned the city for allowing dogs to usurp what should rightfully be open space for children. But dog owners organized an effective campaign to gain city council approval for off-leash dogs—a long struggle that ultimately succeeded when they discovered that the antidog forces were backed by real estate developers interested in converting the park into a property-value-enhancing amenity! Other off-leash areas have been planned and opened in the city, and many other cities across the Southland have established similar off-leash play areas for dogs.

In her analysis of golden eagle rehabilitation in San Diego County, Michel argues that conventional planning around endangered species and habitat conservation relies on scientific discourse and legitimacy and excludes a variety of alternative arguments based on the connections people feel with wild animals themselves.[64] Michel's participant-observation in a raptor rehabilitation center revealed the complex feelings that rehabilitators felt toward the golden eagles they worked with, many of the birds being injured as a result of urbanization. She characterizes their approach to the eagles as profoundly ecofeminist, with the everyday repetitive routines of care analogous to those of parents (especially mothers) caring for loved ones living in their midst. Michel describes the choice of these rehabilitators—distanced and largely excluded from scientific-rational debates about raptors in the public realm—to develop an alternative "politics of care" played out in local schools, churches, and other public institutions, where they bring recovering birds for demonstrations and educational lectures. This political practice is aimed at allowing children, and by extension their parents, into the world of the golden eagle and the birds' fight for survival and helping them voice their views to the larger public through letter-writing campaigns and special events. In this way, she suggests, such efforts may be recasting the nature of grassroots environmental activism in Southern California.

CONCLUSION

Using the case of Los Angeles, we have sought to demonstrate that urbanization produces profound changes in the physical environment. In turn, nature is a powerful player and a ubiquitous force, shaping everyday lives, life chances, perceptions of urban residents, and urbanization itself. The history of a city is in part inscribed in its nature, while infrastructure decisions, housing types, recreation, insurance rates, industrial location, and public health all reflect aspects of the natural environment and human perceptions of nature. Thus, the relationship of the city to its nature has shaped the region's past and present and will be significant to its future.

Given renewed theoretical interest in place, locality, community, and neighborhood, it is surprising how little attention has been given to the nature in which they are embedded and on which they depend. Yet within urban theory, human relations with nature are typically reduced to questions of growth versus growth control, jobs and transportation access versus environmental pollution, developers versus environmentalists. In our concluding comments, we set out an agenda for urban theory to begin to remedy these simplified characterizations by challenging urban theorists to rethink the many unexamined aspects of nature-society relations and to consider questions of justice for nature as well as for humans.

Incorporating Nature Into Urban Theory

Most urban analysis incorporates no theory of nature or else relies on weak, often unidimensional characterizations of nature and nature-society relations. Nature may enter the picture, perhaps, as "land" or "property" but not as an agent in urbanization or a resource appropriated by urban lifestyles and consumption practices. But even when urbanists more explicitly consider nature, the portrayal of the natural environment is typically limited and based on faulty, outdated assumptions.

For example, more often than not, the relevant nature involved in or alluded to in urban analysis consists only of environments linked directly to urbanized space (urban air or watersheds, open space). But as cities appropriate vast quantities of nature's bounty, they make an "urban footprint" many times the size of the region itself. Moreover, urban theory tends to view nature as a static container, rather than as a dynamic and potentially active agent, subject to disturbance. For the same reason, normative recommendations are grounded in outdated notions of ecological balance and harmony, rather than more current ideas of nature arising from disturbance ecology and disequilibrium models. Nature itself is treated like a monolith, transforming what is a profusion of animals, plants, rocks, and flowing waters into a black box. As we have tried to show, downtown coyotes and suburban debris flows do not fit nicely into such a box and often require consideration at the level of individual agency.

Even more pervasively, nature is treated as synonymous with wilderness, a place beyond the city and the realm of human habitation. Fights about nature in urban theory are thus often characterized as disputes about changes in the city-country boundary. But the relevant nature is not "out there" but within every human and throughout every city, however thoroughly manipulated and reordered, as well as far beyond the city. Such characterizations of nature as wilderness within urban theory rest on deeply ingrained beliefs in a nature-culture divide that is objective and fixed rather than fluid and socially constructed. This perpetuates the tendency to ignore vital aspects of nature operating within the city itself, aspects that affect human as well as nonhuman health; it also downplays how urban commodity chains appropriate nature at great remove from city limits.

Last, like nature itself, environmentalism as social theory and practice is too often portrayed as homogeneous and static. Environmentalists are just one more group of stakeholders locked in fights with growth machine politicians. But there are many (and often conflicting) environmentalisms that shape the activities of local social movements and actors. The diversity of environmental attitudes and ideologies, as well as the different actor networks involved in urban environmental struggles, influences activism and outcomes in such areas as pollution, environmental health, habitat protection, and resource conservation.

New Themes for Urban Analysis

Once recognized, these weaknesses open up a variety of new themes that can usefully be incorporated into the purview of urban theory. For example, urban land held as private property tends to be viewed by its owners and the state as somehow "not nature" but an exchange or use value to be transformed with relative impunity. Given its pervasiveness in larger society and its state-sanctioned legitimacy, this view goes largely unquestioned by urban theorists, whether they hail from a political economic or more mainstream perspective. How does the denaturalization of private property, ideologically and *de jure,* reinforce a false nature-culture divide, encourage a disregard for the life requirements of plants and animals, and exacerbate urban environmental degradation? How might land, land use, and land use planning and urban policy be reconceptualized in light of nature's agency and implication in urbanization? How can we incorporate alternative ideas from environmentalism to provide a better understanding of how ideologies of nature and pervasive nature-culture dualisms are manifest in everyday urban practices and landscapes?

Urban theory could also explore the diversity of more intimate relationships between urban residents and nature. Because of deep-seated notions of a rigid human-animal divide, animals have rarely been considered in urban theory, including domestic or companion animals with whom people may have close relationships. If many animals are not just genetically programmed bodies but sentient individuals, how can we understand the liminal spaces they occupy and the relationships they create with human inhabitants (and vice versa)? How do interactions with animals shape broader environmental commitments? How might the realization that the human-animal divide is socially constructed and variable, rather than biological and fixed, shape ideas about who "belongs" in the city?

Could the admission that people are also part of nature usefully focus attention on the ways that human bodies are compromised by urban environmental racism and, more generally, by urban environmental degradation that can affect residents regardless of their demographic or socioeconomic characteristics? Finally, at both cultural and political economic levels, urban theory could also wrestle with the many contradictions in nature-society relations as played out in cities. In particular, we need to understand why desires for access and proximity to nature seem to be rising, along with consumption practices that appear to serve such desires yet destroy their object, namely, nature itself. How do tropes about nature and the tranquility of wilderness become so powerful that they sell vast numbers of sports utility vehicles, although such vehicles are disproportionately polluting and ripping up the natural environment?

Social Justice, Nature, and the City

In light of the failure of most urban theory to include concerns for urban ecology and nature, it is not surprising that the normative approaches stemming from urban analyses ignore nature, opting, instead, to stress the importance of social justice in

cities. Such an emphasis is, in our view, fully warranted. We argue, however, that justice for nonhumans and nature is also a legitimate social goal for planners,
policymakers, and activists. For example, cities should be designed on the basis of
the normative assumption that animals and the quality of their lives do matter from
an ethical perspective. Moreover, many progressive social justice activists (excepting
environmental justice advocates) ignore environmental questions, even when it
means addressing the degradation of ambient urban environmental quality. Thus,
the urban agenda—designed to solve a list of urban ills such as racism, poverty, traffic congestion, fiscal stress, and so on—includes arguments for more jobs, better
jobs, better distributed jobs, more equitable taxation, regional burden sharing, and
so forth. Yet because the emphasis is almost always on more and faster growth, environmental impacts and the rights of nature are left out. This skewed approach needs
to be engaged with the dilemmas and trade-offs required to maximize social justice
but at the same time minimize urban ecosystem appropriation and urban habitat
destruction. Not only must we defend the rights of animals and nature and protect
the global climate, but we need to minimize Western urban consumption practices
that appropriate resources from residents of developing countries.

By the same token, "sustainable" planning and development discourses—coming
largely from developing countries, and even there highly contested—need careful
examination prior to their importation into cities in the developed world. Many
practices now identified in the development literature as sustainable are based on a
resourcist ideology of nature that legitimates the profound exploitation of nature.
For example, the promotion of sustainable urban architecture and design is vital, but
practical programs for sustainable urbanization have yet to be articulated for those
places that need them most, for example, large metropolitan regions. It is one thing
to herald the virtues of sustainable design in affluent retirement communities
such as Seaside, Florida, but quite another to forge a program for sustainable urbanization in megacities deeply polarized by race, class, and national origin and plagued
by fragmented, undemocratic administration. What would sustainable urbanism
look like in such a challenging context? Urban theorists and practitioners should
make it a priority to find out—the future of all of us, human and nonhuman,
depends on it.

NOTES

1. As quoted, pp. 126-127, in Robert L. Rothwell, ed., 1991, *An American Landscape:
Henry David Thoreau*, New York: Paragon House.

2. Eugenius Warming, *The Oecology of Plants*, rev. ed., Oxford, 1909; F. E. Clements,
Plant Succession, Washington, 1916; Charles C. Adams, *Guide to the Study of Animal Ecology*,
New York, 1913, all of which are mentioned in *The City*, pp. 68, 72, 145.

3. The bibliographic chapter that concludes *The City* is replete with references to works
by geographers; perhaps more than any other single field, geographical perspectives and research shaped Chicago School thinking.

4. Indeed, this brand of urban sociology is often termed *urban ecology.* See, for example, Brian J. L. Berry and John D. Kasarda, 1977, *Contemporary Urban Ecology,* New York: Macmillan. The wholesale importation of concepts developed in the natural sciences was a key strategy for institutionalizing sociology as a "rigorous" scientific discipline, deployed in other social science fields as well. Human geographers on the Chicago faculty and elsewhere during this period, also influenced by recent work in plant and animal geography, called for a recasting of the entire discipline of geography as *human ecology.* See Harlan H. Barrows, 1923, "Geography as Human Ecology," *Annals of the Association of American Geographers* 18, no. 1 (March).

5. William Cronon, 1991, *Nature's Metropolis: Chicago and the Great West,* New York: Norton.

6. There are some notable exceptions: the debates about urban sprawl and recent multidisciplinary work on environmental racism and environmental justice movements. The sprawl debates, however, focus on energy consumption, traffic congestion, and open space issues; much of the environmental racism-justice literature remains more closely connected to social movement research than to urban theory. New Western historians such as Limerick, Worster, Pisani, Cronon, Deverell, and others have begun to explore urban ecological issues from new perspectives, but this work has yet to strongly influence urban theorists.

7. John Logan and Harvey Molotch, 1987, *Urban Fortunes: The Political Economy of Place,* Berkeley: University of California Press, 95.

8. David Harvey, 1996, *Justice, Nature and the Geography of Difference,* Cambridge: Blackwell Books.

9. Carl Folke, Asa Jansson, Jonas Larsson, and Robert Costanza, 1997, "Ecosystem Appropriation by Cities," *Royal Swedish Academy of Sciences* 26: 167-172.

10. See Ann Whiston Spirn, 1984, *The Granite Garden: Urban Nature and Human Design,* New York: Basic Books; Michael Hough, 1995, *City Form and Natural Process,* New York: Routledge.

11. Effects on soil include increased impermeability, sterility, topsoil loss/degradation, contamination, slowed weathering, subsidence, and erosion.

12. Hydrological changes involve faster runoff rates, slowed storm water filtration, falling water tables, reduced groundwater table and recharge capability, loss of wetlands, increased variation in natural stream flows, greater flood risk because of channelization, and polluted and sediment-loaded surface runoff.

13. Changes in climate involve warming, heat island/dome effects, reduced precipitation, wind system changes, and increased dust.

14. Ambient quality deteriorated because of pollution and contamination related to industry, cars, and loss of wetlands/riparian flushing capacity, dust, elevated nutrient, and dissolved oxygen and suspended silt levels.

15. Impacts on vegetation include loss of native plant communities; invasion by exotic, weedy, or opportunistic species; high rates of urban forest stress; and disease.

16. See, for example, Marco Cenzatti, 1993, *Los Angeles and the Los Angeles School: Postmodernism and Urban Studies,* Los Angeles: Los Angeles Forum for Architecture and Urban Design.

17. According to Soja, for example, "The urblets lining the Saddleback Valley" and other areas created an "exopolis," or city beyond the city. Although acknowledging the implications of this urban form for species endangerment, he stopped short of exploring the dialectic relationships between urbanization and environmental transformation. See Edward Soja, 1992, "Inside Exopolis: Scenes From Orange County," in Michael Sorkin, ed., *Variations on a Theme Park: The New American City and the End of Public Space,* New York: Hill and Wang, Noonday Press, 94-122.

18. See Mike Davis, 1994, "Cannibal City," in Elizabeth A. T. Smith, *Urban Revisions,* Cambridge: MIT Press; Robert Gottlieb and Margaret FitzSimmons, 1993, *Thirst for Growth: Water Agencies as Hidden Government in California,* Tucson: University of Arizona Press; Margaret FitzSimmons and Robert Gottlieb, 1996, "Bounding and Binding Metropolitan Space: The Ambiguous Politics of Nature in Los Angeles," pp. 186-224 in Allen J. Scott and Edward W. Soja, eds., *The City: Los Angeles and Urban Theory at the End of the Twentieth Century,* Berkeley and Los Angeles: University of California Press; Mike Davis, 1996, "How Eden Lost Its Garden: A Political History of the Los Angeles Landscape," pp. 161-185 in Scott and Soja, *The City;* Stephanie Pincetl, 1999, "The Politics of Influence: Democracy and the Growth Machine in Orange County," in Andrew Jonas and Brian Wilson, eds., *The Urban Growth Machine: Critical Perspectives Twenty Years Later,* New York: State University of New York Press.

19. Roger Keil and Gene Desfor, 1997, "Making Local Environmental Policy in Los Angeles," *Cities* 13: 303-314; Mike Davis, 1998, *Ecology of Fear: Los Angeles and the Imagination of Disaster,* Chapter 3, New York: Metropolitan Books; John McPhee, 1989, "Los Angeles Against the Mountains," pp. 183-272 in *The Control of Nature,* New York: Noonday.

20. Laura Pulido, 1996, "Multiracial Organizing Among Environmental Justice Activists in Los Angeles," pp. 171-189 in Michael J. Dear, H. Eric Schockman, and Greg Hise, eds., *Rethinking Los Angeles,* Thousand Oaks, Calif.: Sage; Laura Pulido, Steven Sidawi, and Robert Vos, 1996, "An Archeology of Environmental Racism in Los Angeles," *Urban Geography* 17: 419-439.

21. Jennifer Wolch, Andrea Gullo, and Unna Lassiter, 1997, "Changing Attitudes Toward California's Cougars," *Society & Animals* 5, no. 2: 95-116; Jennifer Wolch, 1996, "Zoöpolis," *Capitalism, Nature, Socialism* 7: 21-48; Suzanne Michel, 1998, "Golden Eagles and the Environmental Politics of Care," in J. Wolch and J. Emel, eds., *Animal Geographies: Place, Politics and Identity in the Nature-Culture Borderlands,* London: Verso; Glen Elder, Jennifer Wolch, and Jody Emel, 1998, "Le Pratique Sauvage: Race, Place, and the Human-Animal Divide," in Wolch and Emel, *Animal Geographies;* Mike Davis, 1998, *Ecology of Fear: Los Angeles and the Imagination of Disaster,* Chapter 3, New York: Metropolitan Books.

22. Unless otherwise noted, basic environmental data are derived from Allan A. Schoenherr, 1992, "Cismontaine Southern California," Chapter 8, pp. 313-405 in *A Natural History of California,* Berkeley: University of California Press.

23. Mike Davis, 1997, "The Radical Politics of Shade," *Capitalism, Nature, Socialism* 8: 35-39, p. 38.

24. Ronald U. Cooke, 1984, *Geomorphological Hazards in Los Angeles,* London: Allen and Unwin, 25.

25. Efforts to control or eradicate nature to facilitate development also permeated public policies toward dealing with the region's natural hazards. Once declared disaster areas, parts of the city affected by floods, fires, or other "acts of nature" routinely attract public funds to subsidize rebuilding in the same high-risk zones and to underwrite additional hazard control projects.

26. Mike Davis, 1995, "Water Pirates and the Infinite Suburb," *Capitalism, Nature, Socialism* 7: 81-84.

27. A. F. Turhollow, 1975, *A History of the Los Angeles District, US Army Corps of Engineers, 1898-1965.* U.S. Army Engineer's Office, Los Angeles, 171, 189, as cited in Roger Keil and Gene Desfor, 1996, "Making Local Environmental Policy in Los Angeles," *Cities* 13: 303-314.

28. Mike Davis, 1996, "How Eden Lost Its Garden," in Scott and Soja, eds., *The City,* 179, 180.

29. California Department of Fish and Game Web site (www.dfg.ca.gov/endangered/lax.html), October 1997.

30. California Department of Fish and Game Web site.

31. Data in the rest of this section are derived from Mary Nichols and Stanley Young, 1991, *The Amazing L.A. Environment,* Los Angeles: Living Planet Press.

32. Stephanie Pincetl, 1999, "The Politics of Influence: Democracy and the Growth Machine in Orange County, USA," pp. 195-212 in Andrew E. G. Jonas and David Wilson, eds., *The Urban Growth Machine: Critical Perspectives Two Decades Later.* Albany: State University of New York Press.

33. Richard Beene, 1988, "Support of Slow-Growth Plan Soars," *Los Angeles Times,* February 7, p. A28.

34. Terry Timmons, 1993, *Structural Speculation as a Dynamic of Urban Growth: A Case Study of the Irvine Ranch Company,* Ph.D. diss., University of Michigan: University Microfilms International.

35. This immunity exists regardless of a change in political will or public opinion regarding the development, a change in fiscal status for the local jurisdiction, or any other unforeseen new set of circumstances. The landowner, however, can initiate change. Once passed by the city council, a DA can be appealed only by referendum and only within 30 days of the city's adoption of the ordinance.

36. The nexus criterion protects property owners from unjust regulatory takings (as defined by the courts) based on protections provided by the Fourteenth Amendment of the Constitution, which specifies just compensation by government for any property takings.

37. John F. O'Leary, 1995, "Coastal Sage Scrub: Threats and Current Status," *Fremontia* 23, no. 4 (October): 27-31.

38. Monica Florian, vice president of the Irvine Ranch Company, 1991, letter to Douglas P. Wheeler, Secretary of the Resources Agency, April 2.

39. Pincetl, 1999, "The Politics of Influence."

40. Some of this material has appeared in "Nature and the Reproduction of Endangered Space: The Spotted Owl in the Pacific Northwest and Southern California," with J. Proctor, *Environment and Planning D: Society & Space* 14, no. 6 (1996): 683-708.

41. J. Stephenson, 1991, "Spotted Owl Surveys on the National Forests of Southern California: A Status Report and Recommendations for the Future," U.S. Department of Agriculture, Forest Service, San Bernardino District.

42. The discussion of the spotted owl's biology and habitat is based on Jared Verner, K. McKelvey, B. Noon, R. Gutierrez, G. Gould, and T. Beck, 1992, *The California Spotted Owl: A Technical Assessment of Its Current Status,* USDA Forest Service General Technical Report PSW-GTR-133, USDA Forest Service Pacific Southwest Research Station, Albany, California (July).

43. John McPhee, 1989, "Los Angeles Against the Mountains," in *The Control of Nature,* 183-272.

44. Mike Davis, 1998, *The Ecology of Fear: Los Angeles and the Imagination of Disaster,* Chapter 3.

45. Davis, 1998, *Ecology of Fear,* 107.

46. For a discussion on racial and income inequality, see P. Ong and E. Bluemenberg, 1996, "Income and Racial Inequality in Los Angeles," in Scott and Soja, *The City,* 311-335.

47. United Church of Christ Commission on Racial Justice, 1987, *Toxic Waste and Race in the United States,* New York: United Church of Christ.

48. L. Pulido, S. Sidawi, and B. Vos, 1996, "An Archeology of Environmental Racism in Los Angeles," *Urban Geographies* 17, no. 5: 419-439; L. Burke, 1993, "Environmental Inequity in Los Angeles" (unpublished master's thesis, University of California, Department of Geography, Santa Barbara).

49. J. Sadd, M. Pastor, J. T. Boer, and L. Snyder, 1999, "Every Breath You Take: The Demographics of Point Source Air Pollution in Southern California," *Economic Development Quarterly* 13, no. 2: 107-123.

50. J. T. Boer, M. Pastor, J. Sadd, and L. Snyder, 1997, "Is There Environmental Racism? The Demographics of Hazardous Waste in Los Angeles County," *Social Science Quarterly* 78, no. 4: 793-810.

51. B. Baden and D. Coursey, 1997, "The Locality of Waste Sites Within the City of Chicago: A Demographic, Social and Economic Analysis," Working paper series: 97-2, University of Chicago, Irving B. Harris Graduate School of Public Policy Studies; D. Anderton, A. Anderson, J. Oakes, and M. Fraser, 1994, "Environmental Equity: The Demographics of Dumping," *Demography* 31: 229-248.

52. R. Acuna, 1996, *Anything But Mexican,* New York: Verso; G. Horne, 1995, *Fire This Time,* Charlottesville: University of Virginia Press; T. Almaguer, 1994, *Racial Fault Lines: The Historical Origins of White Supremacy in California,* Berkeley: University of California Press.

53. R. Morales and P. Ong, 1996, "The Illusion of Progress: Latinos in Los Angeles," in *Latinos in a Changing Economy,* ed. R. Morales and F. Bonilla, Newbury Park, Calif.: Sage, 55-84; A. Scott, 1996, "The Manufacturing Economy: Ethnic and Gender Divisions of Labor," in *Ethnic Los Angeles,* ed. R. Waldinger and M. Bozorgmehr, New York: Sage, 215-244.

54. Burke, 1993, "Environmental Inequity in Los Angeles."

55. For more on the Strategy Center's environmental justice organizing, see L. Pulido, 1996, "Multiracial Organizing Among Environmental Justice Activists in Los Angeles," in *Rethinking Los Angeles,* ed. M. Dear, G. Hise, and E. Schockman, 171-189; E. Mann, 1992, *L.A.'s Lethal Air,* Los Angeles: Labor/Community Strategy Center.

56. E. Mann and C. Mathis, 1997, "Civil Rights Consent Decree? Legal Tactics for Left Strategy," *Ahora/Now* 4: 1-11 (available from the Labor/Community Strategy Center).

57. This term is borrowed from M. Oliver and T. Shapiro, 1995, *Black Wealth/White Wealth,* New York: Routledge.

58. Mike Davis, 1998, Chapter 5 in *The Ecology of Fear: Los Angeles and the Imagination of Disaster,* New York: Metropolitan Books.

59. Jennifer Wolch, Andrea Gullo, and Unna Lassiter, 1997, "Changing Attitudes Toward California's Cougars," *Society & Animals* 5, no. 2: 95-116.

60. Mike Davis, 1998, Chapter 5 in *The Ecology of Fear.*

61. Glen Elder, Jennifer Wolch, and Jody Emel, 1998, "Le Pratique Sauvage: Race, Place, and the Human-Animal Divide," in J. Wolch and J. Emel, eds., *Animal Geographies: Place, Politics and Identity in the Nature-Culture Borderlands,* London: Verso.

62. Andrew Lam, 1989, "Cuisine of a Pragmatic People," *San Francisco Chronicle,* August 8, p. A17.

63. Jennifer Wolch and Stacy Rowe, 1992, "Companions in the Park: Laurel Canyon Dog Park," *Landscape* 31: 16-23.

64. Suzanne Michel, 1998, "Golden Eagles and the Environmental Politics of Care," in J. Wolch and J. Emel, eds., *Animal Geographies.*

Saber y Conocer
The Metropolis of Urban Inquiry

Cities do vitally important work. They house people, provide jobs, educate our children, and assist the needy; they are engines of entrepreneurial innovation, key players in world geopolitics, and indispensable cogs in our social fabric. The past five thousand years of human history have produced a world of cities, large and small. More than half the world's population is now living in urban areas. In 1950, there were seventy-eight cities with more than 1 million inhabitants; by 1985, there were 258. The United Nations estimates that by 2010, there will be more than 500 cities with populations in excess of 1 million. By that time, more than 1.25 billion people will live in urban areas greater than 4 million inhabitants.

The extracts that open this final chapter are comments by Morris Janowitz, who wrote an introduction to the 1967 edition of *The City*. In the first extract, Janowitz underscores the significance of the city in human affairs. I rephrase this sentiment in the following ways: that cities are the vital core of human civilization and that understanding what is happening to cities is vital to human survival and prosperity on this planet. There can be few more urgent scholarly and political imperatives than these.

The second quote from Janowitz emphatically echoes the Chicago School's intention to discover a science of society. Some contributors to this volume would, I think, be sympathetic to this goal. Yet if nothing else, this book has shown the need for a multiplicity of ways of knowing the city. To put it another way, we need all the theories we can lay our hands on to properly comprehend the urban. Therefore, it seems appropriate that we conclude our voyage with a chapter by historians Philip J. Ethington and Martin Meeker, who end (in essence) that we need insights from both the Chicago School and the L.A. School to understand the city. The choice of either/or is replaced by both/and.

QUOTES FROM
THE CITY

The city is not an artifact or a residual arrangement. On the contrary, the city embodies the real nature of human nature. It is an expression of mankind in general and specifically of the social relations generated by territoriality. Modern technology has altered but not eliminated territoriality as the city has come to equal civilization. . . . (viii)

. . . [T]he Chicago school of urban sociology was strongly motivated by a drive to view the city as an object of detached sociological analysis. These men were fascinated with the complexities of the urban community and the prospect of discovering patterns of regularity in its apparent confusion. (viii)

CHAPTER 15

Saber y Conocer
The Metropolis
of Urban Inquiry

PHILIP J. ETHINGTON

MARTIN MEEKER

The field of urban studies has been interpreting the human condition for more than a century, yet it seems locked in a timeless present of discovering the "urban crisis" and concocting interpretive schemas to deal with that crisis. We are haunted by the echoes of cities in crisis (poverty, violence, fear) and, at the same time, by the echoes of *knowledge* in crisis (modernism, objectivity, postmodernism, etc.). A multitude of theorists have proclaimed these urban and epistemological crises, regularly telling us that we have entered new conditions of experience and that our existing knowledge is no longer adequate to understand the problems they present, let alone solve them. Yet something is wrong with this picture, and this chapter is dedicated to the goal of ending this senseless contradiction of perpetual novelty.

Rather than viewing alternative interpretive models—such as the well-known Chicago School of urban sociology or postmodern urbanism—as occupying positions along a single narrative and historiographic line, with "better" or "more critical" interpretations succeeding older ones, we suggest viewing preceding, succeeding, and contemporaneous alternative interpretive schemas as contiguous neighborhoods in a "metropolis of inquiry." This chapter is, then, a guide for digesting the considerable variety of methodological and theoretical perspectives presented in this volume. Instead of reading the chapters in this volume as a din of cacophonous voices, each heralding the importance of its own interpretive approach, each might more profitably be viewed as residing in neighborhoods, cities, and suburbs in the ever-expanding metropolis of urban inquiry—and we might approach this body of theory as we would ideally approach a city, with the goal of getting to know it in all its complexity, understanding that each element has its "place."

AUTHORS' NOTE: We wish to thank Matt Roth and Michael Dear for their careful and helpful critiques of earlier drafts.

The chief task we have undertaken in writing this chapter has been to map the metropolis of urban inquiry to avoid senseless destruction and ruthless urban renewal. All of us inhabit one or more neighborhoods bounded by huge intellectual structures of practice. These intellectual discourses are similar to contrasting and interdependent metropolitan neighborhoods. There can be no truly isolated neighborhoods; the politics of ghettos rests on the investments and profit extractions of outsiders. Neither can there be genuinely isolated urbanist discourses, nor can they be reduced to one another. There are many fragmented, yet interlocking, practices in these metropolises of urban inquiry, as is true of everyday urban experience. In other words, the theorists and practitioners of each successive urbanist school still exist in the same tradition—they can build on but cannot escape the developing, sprawling, metropolis of inquiry.

THE MEANING OF *SABER Y CONOCER*

This is a chapter about urban epistemology, or ways of knowing cities. We "know" the metropolis according to two contradictory strategies, which nevertheless cannot be separated. The best urban studies have always united what is implied in two distinct definitions of *knowing*. Unfortunately, the distinct meanings are not linguistically evident in English, although they are in Latin tongues, such as Spanish and French. In Spanish, the verbs *saber* and *conocer* are both used in translations of the English verb "to know," and yet these two verbs convey different meanings. *Saber* means to know how, to learn, to find out, to know a fact, to know an address, to inform—depending on the context. *Conocer* also means to know, but more specifically, to know a person, to become acquainted with, to meet, to recognize, to know by name, or to know carnally—depending on context. Although the differences are sometimes subtle, they are critically important. Like all important root terms, *saber* and *conocer* are complex—sometimes overlapping—signifiers, and yet, in balance, they lead away from one another, expressing this split in strategies of knowing, which English does not have the capacity to signify. Because we cannot translate these two types of knowing directly into English, we translate them conceptually to our immediate project, with reference to knowing the city. We use these verbs to clarify what is jumbled together in the English *to know*—a sense of the contradictory urban epistemologies, loosely equivalent to "surveying the city" and "walking the city."[1]

The epistemological concept of "surveying the city" is signified by *saber,* the knowing of facts or research-oriented discoveries, represented in classic form by the "social survey." Begun by Charles Booth in *Life and Labour of the People in London* (17 vols., 1889-1903) and pioneered in the United States by Jane Addams et al. in *Hull House Maps and Papers* (1894), the social survey was used to "map" the empirical facts about the city. W. E. B. Du Bois opens his masterpiece of this genre, *The Philadelphia Negro* (1899), by explaining:

> This study seeks to present the results of an inquiry undertaken by the University of Pennsylvania into the condition of the forty thousand or more people of Negro blood now living in the city of Philadelphia. This inquiry extended over a period of fifteen months and sought to ascertain something of the geographical distribution of this race, their occupations and daily life, their homes, their organizations, and, above all, their relation to their million white fellow-citizens. The final design of the work is to lay before the public such a body of information as may be a safe guide for all efforts toward the solution of the many Negro problems of a great American city.[2]

Du Bois the social surveyor gives a precise description of the type of knowledge he seeks. Interestingly, just a few years later, he abruptly switched epistemological modes in his better-known masterpiece, *The Souls of Black Folk* (1903), in which he, just as clearly, conveys the precise meaning of the other kind of knowing, *conocimiento:* "How does it feel to be a problem?"[3] Although *The Philadelphia Negro* relies on statistics, *The Souls of Black Folk* is full of personal experiences. In the former, Du Bois finds "Negro problems" to survey, whereas, in the latter, the author *is* a problem (in the eyes of others).

Surveying's twin epistemological concept, "walking the city," *conocer,* is the intimate knowing of relations within and between selves, others, and places. Alfred Kazin's *A Walker in the City* is the modal type: "The block; *my* block. It was on the Chester Street side of our house, between the grocery and the back wall of the old drugstore, that I was hammered into the shape of the streets."[4] Another strong source of *conocimiento de la ciudad* is the long tradition of street photography, from the images of Jacob Riis (1849-1914), Arnold Genthe (1869-1942), Lewis Hine (1874-1940), Edward Steichen (1879-1973), Weegee/Arthur Fellig (1899-1968), Berenice Abbott (1898-1991), and continuing through Robert Frank and Mary Ellen Mark—to list a few of the more famous North American urban photographers. Taken sometime in the 1930s, Berenice Abbott's "Blossom Restaurant, The Bowery" provides the visual counterpart to Kazin's "feel" for his Brooklyn neighborhood, crowded as it is with textures of the everyday. The focal point of this image is the man emerging from a dark stairway where he has just had a shave for 10¢. A young man (loafing? we can't be sure) leans against a barber pole to watch the photographer. The Blossom, at 103, is a textual phenomenon: Every available surface, controlled by the owner/renter, is covered with menu items and prices. The Lamb-Oxtail Stew for 15¢ includes coffee. Does the Vienna Roast with beans for 10¢ also include coffee? We'd have to ask.

Had we been passengers in the elevated railway that once blighted the Bowery and gave this place its honky-tonk feel, we would never have noticed such detail. Only a pedestrian could have read the signs for the Blossom and its neighbor, the First Class Barber Shop. The whole image is saturated with the minutia of everyday life, from the subjectivity of boredom to the physicality of refuse. Examining such evidence decades after it was taken still provides the urbanist with a sense of the meaning invested in it by the thousands who passed by or lived above, behind, and around the block from this little forgotten restaurant and barber shop. What it

Berenice Abbott's "Blossom Restaurant, The Bowery," 1930s
SOURCE: Courtesy of the Library of Congress.

meant to live in Manhattan's Bowery in the 1930s cannot be approached without knowledge of this type.

The metropolis itself is the synthesis of the contradiction between these two strategies of knowing. Taking into account the variety of urban thought, we believe that the tensions and questions inherent in the ways of knowing embodied by *saber* and *conocer* provide us with a translation tool for moving between discourses. We can now start a dialogue not only between different fields and disciplines but also between academic and nonacademic urbanists. That metacontradiction may enable us to navigate—if not entirely to integrate—all the heterogeneous neighborhoods of urbanist thought and practice.

COUNTERPOINT: *SABER* VERSUS *CONOCER* IN THE MODERNIST METROPOLIS OF INQUIRY

By surveying the epistemological strategies of several classic figures from the period bounded by the 1890s and the 1960s, we see that the best work actually embodied the *saber* versus *conocer* contradiction: the search for systematic, predictable, holistic patterns of objective, quantifiable facts, on the one hand, and the search for fleeting, fragmentary phenomena of personal knowledge and experience, on the other. In Chicago circa 1910, Jane Addams first proposed what we now call *multiculturalism.* Building on William James's argument that there can be no single "truth," Addams argued that the various ethnic groups in Chicago had separate but equally valid ethical systems and that democracy required the dominant Protestant Yankees to respect the nation's ever-growing diversity.[5] Driven by an impulse to reform and advocate, Addams, John Dewey, George Herbert Mead, and W. I. Thomas developed a political activist base at Hull House, theories of intergroup understanding, multiculturalism, and a nonfoundational, intersubjective ethics. They laid the empirical groundwork in surveys of urban neighborhood conditions, typified by *Hull House Maps and Papers* (1895). Characterized collectively as "Chicago Pragmatism," this intellectual project has recently enjoyed rediscovery among advocates of its social democratic promise. The scholars, working from a modernist epistemology, pioneered a remarkably rich urban studies agenda, being most interested in manifestations of fragmentation: in truth claims, religious experience, ethnicity and race, gender, social classes, and generations. Dewey, Mead, and Thomas, more so than James and Addams, sought to fuse these fragments together in a democratic public.[6]

Jane Addams and her colleagues at Hull House founded the explicit practice of surveying the city with their classic report, *Hull House Maps and Papers* (1895). This volume, rendered in maps and statistics, exemplifies the *sabiendo* form of knowledge necessary for answering questions about the levels of wealth and poverty in these neighborhoods, about the types of immigrants and ethnic groups that live there, and about the structure of their families.

Yet to create such surveys, the surveyors had to walk from door to door and block to block and, thus, to adopt the *conocimiento* strategy. That was the well-understood purpose of the members of the social-settlement movement (for which Hull House was the model): to place the surveyor in the very place being surveyed so that the texture of everyday life there would allow the surveyor to experience something of the structure of feeling held by a neighborhood's inhabitants. Addams, in her many writings, then, worked simultaneously at both ends of the *saber-conocer* continuum, demonstrating an early, clear model of seamless applied urban theory.

But Dewey, Mead, Addams, and Thomas did not belong to the Chicago School that would come to dominate academic urban studies after World War I. Robert Park, once the protégé of Thomas, came to create and dominate that school after the social democratic pragmatists faded from the scene in the 1920s. Prior to arriving in Chicago, this eclectic thinker had worked for years, first as a newspaper reporter and later as Booker T. Washington's personal secretary and speechwriter (a position that put him in direct opposition to W. E. B. Du Bois, Washington's most prominent critic). Park's last nonacademic post at Tuskegee, Alabama, provided an important key to his later academic career. Just as his political mentor Booker T. Washington sought to avoid the politics of racial injustice and emphasize the economic process of "progress" for African Americans, so Park sought to distance urban sociology from

the political advocacy on behalf of juvenile delinquents and striking textile workers
that Jane Addams and her colleagues undertook at Hull House. He believed that sociology should be much more scientific and thus pushed it toward the surveying/
sabiendo mode of urban epistemology.[7]

Park's methodology—his way of knowing—marked an important transition in
urban studies in the United States.[8] Opening the epistemological split that now
forms a deep chasm within the works of individual urbanists and theorists, Park was
the first scholar to deliberately segregate the two ways of urban knowing discussed
here. To his credit, although Park demanded that surveying and walking be prac-
ticed distinctly, he did retain both ways of *knowing* a city; he was both an urban surveyor and a pedestrian *flâneur,* although at separate times. "The city," he wrote in
the classic article of the same name first published in 1915,

> is something more than a congeries of individual men and of social conveniences—
> streets, buildings, electric lights, tramways, and telephones, etc.; something more,
> also, than a mere constellation of institutions and administrative devices—courts,
> hospitals, schools, police, and civil functionaries of various sorts. The city is, rather,
> a state of mind, a body of customs and traditions, and of the organized attitudes
> and sentiments that inhere in these customs and are transmitted with this tradition.[9]

Park oversaw a huge body of empirical research into all aspects of the city described
in this passage. His students conducted both quantitative and institutional studies of
the "congeries of individual men," "social conveniences," and "institutions." Thus,
Park's school was strongly rooted in the social survey tradition of mapping and
counting. But members also conducted qualitative research into the "attitudes,"
"state of mind," and "customs and traditions" that make up the soul of the urban
environment, an epistemological strategy dedicated to more intimately knowing individuals through their experiences.[10]

But Park's ecological model of urban studies had an unfortunate influence.[11]
Throughout his large corpus, including his and Ernest Burgess's canonical 1921 sociology textbook, *Introduction to the Study of Society,* Park applied a crudely
"scientistic" approach to phenomena of the mind, freely positing "instincts" and
making facile comparisons between ant colonies, plant biology, and human collec-
tivities.[12] His insistence on treating urban communities as "natural areas" pushed
much of urban studies down an exclusively objectivist, quantitative track. On the
other hand, his strong interest in customs and traditions also fostered a qualitative
tradition, which has survived in case study, interview, and participant-observer
methods, designed to gain a more intimate knowledge of (*conocimiento de*) persons
and their urban experiences.

That the quantitative extreme of the surveying/*sabiendo* strategy seems so different from the qualitative studies to which it was once joined has little to do with the
necessities of the method itself and more to do with the imperative of *perpetual novelty.* There is no reason why quantitative and qualitative methods cannot be used
simultaneously. The questions of knowing as fact and knowing as personal experi-

ence apply to both quantitative and qualitative data and to objective and subjective data. Although Park understood this, his school also opened the rifts visible in contemporary U.S. urban studies.

That rift was at its widest in the immediate post-World War II years, when massive government-funded redevelopment projects applied social-surveying knowledge simultaneously to remove "blighted areas" as well as impoverished communities in the name of rational planning for social welfare. Three influential urbanists, Lewis Mumford, Jane Jacobs, and Robert Moses, asserted (eventually to the point of excess) the *sabiendo-conocimiento* contradictions during the period of high modernism (1930s to 1960s), and their public battles created a new agenda for urban studies and helped change the face of the American city.

The first of these three was a rather ambiguous figure who oscillated, as did Park, between the poles of *saber* and *conocer*. Lewis Mumford (1895-1990) sustained the dual epistemological strategies from his early connections with the first Chicago pragmatists. Mumford relentlessly criticized the industrial city as a spatial environment at odds with the ideal union of "Art and the Machine" voiced first by Frank Lloyd Wright in his 1901 Hull House lecture of the same title. In Mumford's *Story of Utopias* (1922), *The Culture of Cities* (1938), *The City in History* (1961), and innumerable writings (especially his "Skyline" column for the *New Yorker,* which ran from 1931 to 1963), Mumford set himself apart from the Parkian Chicago School by attempting to reassert an urban form within which urbanites could understand the wholeness of their social being through shared symbolic meaning inscribed in the aesthetic design and planning of the unified built environment.[13] Mumford's critique identified the two poles we have been exploring with the larger, systemic roles of industrial capitalism and nation-state militarism exerting a negative pressure on the spontaneous networks of social interaction that fostered humanistic, integrated urban culture and personalities.

In Mumford's account, the city has been shaped, through time, by two competing forces: "technics" versus "civilization." In contrast to his contemporary and fellow New Yorker, the master urban builder Robert Moses, Mumford appeared to be an advocate of the civilization side of urban history and closer to the walker/*conocimiento* epistemic strategy on our map of the metropolis of inquiry. An advocate of "progress" who believed that each era had an aesthetic consistent with its *zeitgeist* (such as Art Deco in the 1920s), Mumford strove throughout his work as a critic, consistent with the Chicago pragmatists, to strike a balance between these forces of technics and civilization. Yet given his leading role in the Regional Planning Association in the 1930s, Mumford appeared to later, more polemic advocates of the walker/*conocimiento* strategy to be simply a planner on the extreme end of the survey/*sabiendo* side of the spectrum.[14]

The famous introduction to Jane Jacobs's *The Death and Life of Great American Cities* (1961) contains one of the most notable indictments of Mumford's *sabiendo* version of knowing and planning the city. Jacobs expressed her ire by labeling Mumford, along with Catherine Bauer and Frank Lloyd Wright, "Decentrists" (i.e., advocates of urban decentralization) who "hammered away at the bad old city . . . were incurious about successes in great cities . . . [and] were interested only in failures. All was failure."[15] Yet although Jacobs thought Mumford and several other decentrists' treatment of the city unfair, she held practicing planners in even lower regard. According to Jacobs, the theories of respected urban planners, such as Ebenezer Howard and Sir Patrick Geddes, combined with the agendas of powerful federal agencies to create a perspective on the city that mandated a program of suburbanization, modernization, and single-use cityscapes—what Jacobs summarized as the death of American cities. The early pages of her book critique the theories of everyone from Howard to Mumford to Le Corbusier for their misguided and at times malevolent planning ideas that favored the planned over the unplanned, the dispersed over the dense, and the garden over the machine. The bulk of Jacobs's polemic masterpiece, however, is an extensive critique of the results of U.S. urban and governmental planning from midcentury onward. The bureaucratic planners put the theories of Howard and others to partial and distorted practice, creating an urban world that favored the automobile over the pedestrian, the freeway over the street, and the housing project over the tenement.

In her case study, which focuses primarily on the area below Midtown Manhattan, Jacobs touches on the way that the Federal Housing Administration, the New York City Housing Authority, and the New York City Planning Commission worked together with private developers to wreak havoc on the city by tearing down old neighborhoods, building freeways, and redeveloping sections of the city in favor of larger-scale commerce, contrary to the interests of local shopkeepers. We can tell much more about Jacobs's own project and the motivations of those she criticizes by considering their epistemological perspectives, the differing ways in which each came to know the city. Jacobs became acquainted with the city, the dense city she liked and "care[d] about . . . most," by literally walking the streets, talking to shop owners, watching children play in the streets, and simply participating in the "daily ballet" of urban life.[16]

Through this methodology, she offers prescriptions—that urban safety depends on a continuous and beneficial reconnaissance of watching eyes, that pedestrian-friendly streets should remain unobstructed by freeway overpasses or by Mumford's superblocks, and that governance happens most effectively at the local level where neighborhood residents, and not distant bureaucrats and zealous developers, regulate change. Such ideas, Jacobs claims, produce defensible, enjoyable space, creating a foundation for the sustained life of great American cities. This methodology and critique produce a plan for action. In one particular instance, Jacobs details a fight to preserve the actual sidewalks she traveled while getting to know the city.[17] The Manhattan Borough engineers, definitively employing the *sabiendo* strategy, planned to ease vehicular traffic in Greenwich Village by removing ten feet of sidewalk to widen roadways. In this confrontation between walkers and surveyors of the city, the neighborhood residents prevented the sidewalk demolition through pressure exerted by neighborhood associations and district governing bodies. In this pitched battle between two ways of knowing, appreciating, experiencing, and solving the problems of the city, Jacobs's *conocimiento* strategy prevailed. Yet we must consider the *sabiendo* side of this debate not only because it was more frequently victorious in post-1945 urban United States but also because much can be gained from seeing the subtle interrelationship of epistemological strategies.

Although much maligned by Jacobs—and for valid reasons—the surveyors who sought to widen roadways, build massive public housing projects, and construct modern superhighways had thoughtful and sometimes quite humane justifications for their work. They desired to create efficient roadways, provide sanitary housing for the poor (or simply "eliminate slums"), increase the ease and speed of transport for people and goods, and reduce urban crime through surveillance and policing. Like Jacobs, these urban planners and surveyors developed a critique and program for action based on their epistemology, the way in which they came to know the city. For instance, imagine Robert Moses on the job in the 1930s, confronted with the very real problem of crosstown traffic in Manhattan. Numerous schemes were introduced to improve the flow of automobiles and trucks from the bridges of the East River to the tunnels beneath the Hudson. Moses's idea was one of the most audacious and, for a time, popular. That his plan called for an expressway to run through New York's historic Washington Square Park demonstrates the degree to which Moses favored one strategy of knowing over another.[18] Although the crosstown expressway made sense on a map from above, *sabiendo la ciudad,* it was clearly an outrageous and destructive solution in the eyes of neighborhood residents and others who regularly walked in and around Washington Square. A single epistemological strategy is clearly a myopic one when it comes to getting to know the city and solving its problems.

The epistemological perspectives of Moses, Jacobs, and other urbanists not only helped shape varieties of emerging urbanisms but also demonstrate how epistemologies, like the material and ideological debates they stir, can lead to perpetual debates. The conflict we have traced—between William James, Jane Addams, Robert Park, Lewis Mumford, and Jane Jacobs—is exactly such a perpetual debate: the conflict between the walker's and the surveyor's ways of knowing; the conflict between *saber y conocer.* This continuous debate further demonstrates that much of the conflict in urban theory, planning, and studies, overall, is less political but more profound than we might have previously thought. Instead of casting the Addams-versus-Park or the Jacobs-versus-Moses disagreements as battles visible on the left-right political spectrum, we argue that the apparently intractable differences are primarily functions of epistemologies. Perhaps this is why, in the increasingly politicized environment of urban theory (including planning theory and practice) in the 1970s, it was virtually impossible to see that both strategies of knowing were necessary and compatible. The solution to the problem of perpetual novelty in urban theory, then, demands that urbanists augment their theories rather than trash the old and fetishize the new.[19] To make this point, we shall turn now to several thinkers, identified with postmodernism, who have been influential in U.S. urban studies of the 1980s and 1990s.

SABER VERSUS CONOCER AMONG
THE POSTMODERNISTS

> *So I come finally to my principal point here, that this latest mutation*
> *in space—postmodern hyperspace— has finally succeeded in*
> *transcending the capacities of the individual human body to locate*
> *itself, to organize its immediate surroundings perceptually, and*
> *cognitively to map its position in a mappable external world.*
>   —Fredric Jameson, 1984[20]

Postmodern urbanists have been the latest and perhaps most vocal in announcing
the emergence of a new chapter in human social, cultural, economic, political, and
urban arrangements. They also decry what they see as the ineptitude of earlier
epistemologies, especially modernist urban theory. Although there is no way to
make generalizations about postmodern urbanists as a unified group, there are at
least two camps: neo-Marxian urbanists, such as Fredric Jameson and David Harvey,
who have proclaimed the arrival of a "condition of postmodernity," and more self-
conscious postmodernists, such as Jean Baudrillard, Michael Dear, and Edward Soja
(in his recent work), who claim that the radical critique of modernism carried out by
such theorists as Jacques Derrida and Jean-François Lyotard should guide a post-
Marxian epistemology for interpreting the postmodern condition.

The postmodernists, like generations of urbanists before them, claim that the
urban condition manifestly disorients the urbanite and scholar alike, in a manner
genuinely new to all human history. We propose, however, that the wide range of
postmodern urbanist discourse that has arisen since Jameson's 1984 article cannot—and should not—escape the contradictions between the *saber* and *conocer*
epistemologies. Jameson's work itself beautifully embodies both strategies. There
can be little doubt that his interpretations of popular culture, fine art, and everything in between as manifestations of "late capitalism" are provocative and often
perceptive. He provides us with a clear map of postmodernity, reducing it, with min-
imal prevarication, to the "logic" of capitalist enterprise itself. Yet how ironic and
telling, then, is his claim in the same text, of "the incapacity of our minds, at least at
present, to map the great global multinational and decentered communicational
network in which we find ourselves caught as individual subjects."[21] This statement
fights with itself: It maps *and* denies the capacity to map at the same time. The
reader can easily imagine a great global network that disorients the subject, just as
Jameson must have mentally mapped such a thing as he wrote that phrase. Jameson
evidently cannot escape Hegel's dialectic: Every assertion of particularity immediately passes over into an assertion of universals.[22]

Using Jameson's thesis openly and examining more thoroughly the theme of
urban space and time, Harvey, in *The Condition of Postmodernity: An Inquiry Into the
Origins of Social Change* (1989),[23] announces the arrival of a postmodern condition
at a precise date.[24] Agreeing that a global capitalist system of fragmentation and cul-

tural commodification has disoriented workers and consumers alike, Harvey also attacks postmodernists—Derrida and Lyotard in particular—for failing to see what Marx taught: that the materialist logic is the foundation of all social interaction. Harvey goes further to accuse them not only of "political silence" but of complicity in the engine of capitalist exploitation that the contemporary city embodies. Harvey describes postmodernism as a "mask for the deeper transformations in the culture of capitalism," thus arguing that change, in the final instance, occurs in the economic sphere.[25]

To some who embrace postmodernism as a valid discourse, however, Jameson and Harvey are simply not "post" enough. Following Lyotard in defining post-modernism as "an incredulity toward all metanarratives," thoroughgoing post-modern urbanists deny the possibility that the metanarrative of Marxism can explain everything so neatly. Michael Dear was among the first and most eloquent to call their bluff, in a 1991 review of Harvey's *Condition of Postmodernity* and Edward Soja's *Postmodern Geographies.* Arguing that "by insisting on their totalizing and reductionist visions, Soja and Harvey squander the insights from different voices and alternative subjectivities,"[26] Dear calls for a postmodern urbanism other than the neo-Marxian one of Jameson, Harvey, and Soja.

Yet Dear shares with these other prophets of postmodernity the same contradiction between surveying and walking. In a chapter that seeks to show how "Los Angeles is the archetype of an emergent postmodern urbanism," Dear narrates "a progressive erosion of the rationalities of unity, control, and expert skills that characterized the newborn planning profession at the turn of this century." That "modernist" profession features "a totalizing discourse that facilitated the production of a modernist landscape." According to Dear, these "obsolescent institutional frameworks" have become "powerless to influence the city's burgeoning social heterodoxy." Dear claims to break with modernism's way of seeing the city, but his brief account is a survey (in the *sabiendo* tradition) *par excellence,* subduing history to a panoptic view whereby a postmodern fate is slowly unveiled.[27] In Dear and Steven Flusty's recent statement of what postmodernism really can be (Chapter 3, this volume), they identify eleven postmodern urbanisms and then proceed to map the global urban system.[28]

In similarly contradictory fashion, Edward Soja has described Los Angeles as paradigmatically postmodern (fragmented, postindustrial). In his influential *Postmodern Geographies,* Soja works as a researcher and surveyor, examining the factual statistics of employment and the Euclidean geography of residential and occupational segregation to prove that Los Angeles is a paragon of postmodernity.[29] Yet Soja, in his more recent *Thirdspace: Journeys to Los Angeles and Other Real-and-Imagined Places,* veers toward the *conocimiento,* or walking strategy of knowledge, in his call to embrace the metacontradiction between *saber* and *conocer,* something he calls "thirding"—a kind of spatial escape from the dialectics of modernism as well as an obvious return to the trap of perpetual novelty. Taking up his own challenge in a comparative study of Amsterdam and Los Angeles, Soja asks,

> Do we learn more about Amsterdam or Los Angeles or any other real-and-imagined
> cityspace by engaging in microgeographies of everyday life and perusing the local view
> from the city streets; or by seeing the city as a whole, conceptualizing the urban condi-
> tion on a more comprehensive regional or macrospatial scale?[30]

Soja's answer is, we believe, the most sensible one for an urbanist discourse always
defined by the two sides of its own contradiction: "Understanding the city must involve both views, the micro and the macro, with neither inherently privileged, but
only with the accompanying recognition that no city—indeed, no lived space—is
ever completely knowable no matter what perspective we take."[31]

Soja's *Thirdspace* is also an homage to Henri Lefebvre, the French geographer and
social theorist who has done so much to reassert the spatial dimension into urbanist
thought and to make decisive breaks with Marxist social science. Lefebvre, in turn, is
part of a long tradition that we have tried to detail in this chapter, one of the thinkers
who have given us an urbanist vision that is most engaging because it embraces the
epistemological contradiction between *saber* and *conocer,* rather than running away
from it. In concluding, then, we turn to a punctuated appreciation of that contradictory vision.

FORWARD TO THE METROPOLIS
OF INQUIRY: SURVEYS AND WALKS

Integrating the two strategies of knowing is possible because the metropolis is possible. The metropolis integrates without abolishing diversity; it promotes and generates interdependencies while promoting divisions of labor. It joins and splits, but it
is a place, an intersection. Perhaps no other urbanist in the Euro-American tradition
has better explained this than Henri Lefebvre. The city, Lefebvre writes, "is situated
at an interface, half-way between what is called the near order . . . direct relations between persons and groups which make up society (families, organized bodies, crafts
and guilds, etc.) . . . and the far order, that of society, regulated by large and powerful
institutions."[32] Lefebvre's detailed writings on the specificity of the city and of urban
phenomena demonstrate the profitability of keeping two dimensions of urbanism in
mind: (1) The far order yields a general and global view of urbanization, or what has
been called "modernization," and (2) the near order yields the uniqueness of each
urban node, which, for Lefebvre, is represented by the cities themselves. A unique
configuration of human labor in historical depth, each city presents itself as a text or,
in Lefebvre's terms, "an *oeuvre,* closer to a work of art than to a simple material product."[33] Lefebvre thus conceptualizes the city as a "mediation" of just those two
strands we have traced throughout urban studies: *saber* (abstract knowing) and
conocer (experiential knowing). In a memorable passage, Lefebvre encapsulates what
we believe is the metropolis of inquiry:

> The city is a mediation among mediations. Containing the *near order,* it supports it; it
> maintains relations of production and property; it is the place of their reproduction.

> Contained in the *far order,* it supports it; it incarnates it; it projects it over a terrain (the site) and on a plan, that of immediate life; it inscribes it, prescribes it, writes it. A text in a context so vast and ungraspable as such except by reflection.[34]

Lefebvre shows here how an urban place is both a systematic abstraction and a fragmentary, immediate life world of individualized experiences or group dynamics.[35] From this, we conclude that the various urbanisms are *neighborhoods* in a metropolis of inquiry. This metropolis of inquiry is nothing less or more than the metropolis that urbanism seeks to study. The vast accumulation of texts has given each successive generation of researchers-interpreters a growing set of *plazas,* places, *platzen,* each encased in the structures laid down thousands of years ago.

Our survey and walk through certain urbanisms have been intended to show how a common set of landmarks has accumulated. "Unlike Rome," Michel de Certeau observes, "New York has never learned the art of growing old by playing on all its pasts."[36] The same can be said of Los Angeles, which, by contrast, has made New York City look like de Certeau's Rome. But this comparison is not fair either to Los Angeles, which has gained a structure that will shape future development for many centuries, or to Rome, which has been demolished and rebuilt many more times during its thirty centuries of life. The point is that just as the Via Appia has served Rome well, so have Broadway and Sunset Boulevard served the evolving needs of New York and Los Angeles.

Gender studies, ethnic studies, cultural studies, rational choice theory, political economy, planning theory, econometrics, history, sociology, network analysis, time geography, media studies, immigration studies, political science, critical theory, American studies, queer theory, anthropology, post-Marxism, subaltern studies, postcolonialism, international relations, structure-functionalism, environmental studies, human or natural ecology, and many other distinct approaches to urbanism are, we believe, so many neighborhoods and communities. They operate in much the same way as urban communities—some with distinct territories, others not so spatially rooted. Many overlap, many have succumbed to the bulldozer of renewal, but many have resisted. Still, we can survey and walk through them all.

We do not suggest that all perspectives on a city are equally valid or that no one has gotten it wrong. Rather, we have argued that the battles between modernists and postmodernists, between humanists and social scientists, between totalizers and fragmenters, cease to be interesting or relevant because no dominant school of urban studies exists. The talk of an L.A. School coming to replace a Chicago School makes about as much sense as saying that the Upper East Side of Manhattan replaced the Lower East Side, or that Nezahualcóyotl is replacing the Distrito Federal in the metropolis of México, or that any city could ever be "the Paris of the West." The most perceptive urbanisms will draw as fully as possible on the methods and theories cultivated in so many neighborhoods in the metropolis of inquiry. The urban surveyor need no longer fear the approach of the city walker, or vice versa. We have fought many battles since urbanism first became codified in the 1890s. Perhaps the second century of intellectual urbanism will evolve more amicably, toward something like the Latin languages, the verbs *saber* and *conocer* dwelling productively together.

NOTES

1. The *American Heritage Larousse Spanish Dictionary* defines *saber* in the following terms: "to know, to know how, to learn, to find out, to inform (hacer saber), to know a thing or two (saber cuántas son cinco), to know by heart (saber de memoria)"; *conocer* is defined as "to know, to be acquainted with, to meet, become acquainted with, to recognize, to presume, to know carnally, to know by name (conocer de nombre), to know oneself (conocerse), and to know one another (conocerse)."

The Larousse *Dictionnaire Moderno Français/Español* confirms these equivalences. For example, *Connaitre comme sa poche* is rendered in Spanish as *conocer como la palma de la mano* (translated literally as "to know it like his/her pocket" and "to know like the palm of his hand," respectively).

In the Spanish language, it is telling that the definitions of each verb depend in part on forms of the other verb. The *Diccionario del Español Usual en México* (México, D.F.: El Colegio de México, 1991) gives as its first definition the following for *conocer:* "Llegar a saber lo que es algo, cuáles son sus características, sus relaciones con otros objetos, sus usos, etc aplicando la intelegencia; haber reunido los elementos necesarios para saber o entender algo: *conocer dos idiomas, conocer de albañilería, conocer del arte.*" For *saber,* the same dictionary gives the following as the first definition: "Tener in la mente ideas, juicios y conocimientos bien formados a propósito de alguna cosa: *saber mucho, saber matemáticas, saber historia.*"

2. W. E. Burghhardt Du Bois, *The Philadelphia Negro: A Social Study,* together with a *Special Report on Domestic Service* by Isabel Eaton (Philadelphia: Ginn and Co., 1899), 1.

3. Du Bois, *The Souls of Black Folk: Authoritative Text, Contexts, Criticism,* ed. Henry Louis Gates Jr. and Terri Hume Oliver (1903; New York: Norton, 1999). This line appears in the first paragraph of Chapter 1, "Our Spiritual Strivings."

4. Alfred Kazin, *A Walker in the City* (New York: Grove Press, 1951), 83.

5. William James, *A Pluralistic Universe* (Hibbert Lectures at Manchester College on the Present Situation in Philosophy, New York: Longmans, Green, 1912); *The Meaning of Truth,* ed. Fredson Bowers, textual editor; Ignas K. Skrupskelis, associate editor; introduction by H. S. Thayer (1909; Cambridge, Mass.: Harvard University Press, 1975); *Essays in Radical Empiricism,* ed. Fredson Bowers, textual editor; Ignas K. Skrupskelis, associate editor; introduction by John J. McDermott (1909; Cambridge, Mass.: Harvard University Press, 1976). See especially "Absolutism and Empiricism," in which he writes, "The through-and-through philosophy . . . seems too buttoned-up and white-chokered and clean-shaven a thing to speak in the name of the vast slow-breathing unconscious Kosmos with its dread abysses and its unknown tides," in *Essays in Radical Empiricism,* 142; Jane Addams, "Ethical Survivals in Municipal Corruption," *International Journal of Ethics* 8, no. 3 (April 1898): 879-889.

6. See, for example, Hans Joas, *Pragmatism and Social Theory* (Chicago: University of Chicago Press, 1993); Axel Honneth, *The Fragmented World of the Social: Essays in Social and Political Philosophy,* ed. Charles W. Wright (Albany: State University of New York Press, 1995); and Seyla Benhabib, *Democracy and Difference: Contesting the Boundaries of the Political* (Princeton, N.J.: Princeton University Press, 1996).

7. For important critical studies of the Parkian school, see Manuel Castells, "Theory and Ideology in Urban Sociology," in *Urban Sociology: Critical Essays,* ed. C. G. Pickvance (New York: St. Martin's Press, 1976), 60-84; Mary Jo Deegan, *Jane Addams and the Men of the Chicago School* (New Brunswick, N.J.: Transaction Books, 1988).

8. Several scholars have noted the importance of Park in the evolution of urban theory; most often, his thought is characterized as representing a synthesis of earlier perspectives, such as in William Sharpe and Leonard Wallock's introduction to the important collection titled *Visions of the Modern City* (New York: Columbia University, Heyman Center for the Humanities, 1983), which asserts that Park was born of both Booth's social surveys and Simmel's inquiries into the urban mind-set. Nevertheless, although not contesting the description of Park's intellectual lineage, in this chapter we take the opposite stance, seeing Park less as a figure of synthesis and instead as a scholar who precipitated breaks in the conversations between the surveyors and walkers.

9. Robert E. Park, "The City: Suggestions for the Investigation of Human Behavior in the Urban Environment," in *The City: Suggestions for Investigation of Human Behavior in the Urban Environment,* by Robert E. Park, Ernest W. Burgess, and Roderick D. McKenzie (Chicago: University of Chicago Press, 1925, 1967; Midway reprint, 1984), 1. Originally published in *American Journal of Sociology* 20, no. 5 (March 1915): 577-612.

10. For a positive appraisal of Park's influence, see Martin Bulmer, *Chicago School of Sociology: Institutionalization, Diversity, and the Rise of Sociological Research* (Chicago: University of Chicago Press, 1984).

11. Eugene Cittadino, "The failed promise of human ecology," in *Science and Nature: Essays in the History of the Environmental Sciences,* ed. Michael Shortland (Oxford: Alden Press, 1993), 251-283.

12. Park seriously compares human and ant society in a lengthy passage of "The City" chapter, in discussing the problem of corporate behavior (29-31). For his reliance on instincts to explain race prejudice, see Park and Burgess, *Introduction to the Science of Society* (Chicago: University of Chicago Press, 1921), Chapters 8-11.

13. Lewis Mumford, *Story of Utopias* (1922; New York: Viking, 1962); *The Culture of Cities* (1938; London: Routledge/Thoemmes, 1997); *The City in History: Its Origins, Its Transformations, and Its Prospects* (New York: Harcourt, Brace & World, 1961).

14. Casey Nelson Blake, *Beloved Community: The Cultural Criticism of Randolph Bourne, Van Wyck Brooks, Waldo Frank, and Lewis Mumford* (Chapel Hill: University of North Carolina Press, 1990).

15. Jane Jacobs, *The Death and Life of Great American Cities* (1961; reprint, New York: Vintage Books, 1992), 20. Jacobs was one of the earliest voices critical of postwar urban planning and redevelopment; also see Martin Anderson, *The Federal Bulldozer: A Critical Analysis of Urban Renewal, 1949-1962* (Cambridge: MIT Press, 1963); Bernard Frieden's slightly critical picture of redevelopment, *The Future of Old Neighborhoods: Rebuilding for a Changing Population* (Cambridge: MIT Press, 1964); Chester Hartman, *Yerba Buena: Land Grab and Community Resistance in San Francisco* (Berkeley: University of California Press, 1974); and Kevin Lynch's memorable *The Image of the City* (1960; reprint, Cambridge: MIT Press, 1994); also see Kevin Lynch, "Reconsidering the Image of the City," in *Cities of the Mind: Images and Themes of the City in the Social Sciences,* ed. Lloyd Rodwin and Robert Hollister (New York: Plenum Press, 1984).

16. Jacobs, *Death and Life,* 16, 54.

17. Jacobs, *Death and Life,* 124-125.

18. On Moses's expressway proposal and Jacobs's critique, see Jacobs, *Death and Life,* 69-71.

19. Thanks to Matt Roth, who helped us clarify this point.

20. This passage is quoted from Fredric Jameson, *Postmodernism, or, The Cultural Logic of Late Capitalism* (London: Verso, 1991), 44. It originally appeared in the article by that same title, in *New Left Review* 146 (July-August 1984): 59-92.

21. Jameson, *Postmodernism,* 44.

22. It is telling that in the earlier, article version of "Postmodernism, or, The Cultural Logic of Late Capitalism," the creation of cognitive or mental maps (inspired by the work of Kevin Lynch, who literally surveyed urban walkers) is posited as a potentially liberating—indeed necessary—way for gaining a sense of place and consequently reducing susceptibility to the premier modernist and postmodernist urban problems: alienation and the decentering of the subject, respectively.

23. David Harvey, *The Condition of Postmodernity: An Inquiry Into the Origins of Social Change* (Cambridge, Mass.: Basil Blackwell, 1989).

24. Harvey's fixation on this date is an obvious reference to Virginia Woolf's famous declaration of modernism, "in or about December, 1910, human character changed." The phrase appears in Woolf's *Mr. Bennett and Mrs. Brown* (London: L. and Virginia Woolf, 1924), 4.

25. Harvey, *The Condition of Postmodernity,* 354.

26. Michael J. Dear, "The Premature Demise of Postmodern Urbanism," in *Cultural Anthropology* 6 (November 1991): 549.

27. Michael J. Dear, "In the City, Time Becomes Visible: Intentionality and Urbanism in Los Angeles, 1781-1991," in *The City: Los Angeles and Urban Theory at the End of the Twentieth Century,* ed. Allen J. Scott and Edward W. Soja (Berkeley; University of California Press, 1996), 76-105; quotations at 85 and 97.

28. Ironically, perhaps, within this attempt to map the irreducible complexity of postmodern urbanisms, there are frequent references back to the modernist theories of Marxist urbanists; for example, one of the eleven postmodernisms that Dear and Flusty invoke is the idea of "Keno Capitalism," which closely resembles Harvey's thoroughgoing Marxian economic critique that he called "Casino Capitalism."

29. Edward Soja, *Postmodern Geographies: The Reassertion of Space in Critical Social Theory* (London: Verso, 1989), 223.

30. Soja, *Thirdspace: Journeys to Los Angeles and Other Real-and-Imagined Places* (Cambridge, Mass.: Blackwell, 1996), 310.

31. Soja, *Thirdspace,* 310.

32. Henri Lefebvre, "The Right to the City," in *Writings on Cities,* ed. and trans. Eleonore Kofman and Elizabeth Lebas (1968; reprint, Cambridge, Mass.: Blackwell, 1996), 101.

33. Lefebvre, "The Right to the City," 101.

34. Lefebvre, "The Right to the City," 101.

35. Along with theorizing the *saber-conocer* split in urban epistemology, Lefebvre's work itself embodies the split in its own *oeuvre;* although beyond the scope of this chapter, a comparison of Lefebvre's more structuralist and Marxist work (including "The Right to the City") with his influential works investigating the quotidian (such as *Critique of Everyday Life*) reveals a deep tension and perhaps inspiring contradiction within the writings of the urbanist himself. *Critique of Everyday Life,* trans. John Moore, preface by Michel Trebitsch (London and New York: Verso, 1991).

36. Michel de Certeau, *The Practice of Everyday Life,* trans. Steven Randall (Berkeley: University of California Press, 1984), 91.

The L.A. School
A Personal Introduction

QUOTES FROM
THE CITY

We are living in such a period of individualization and social disorganization. Everything is in a state of agitation—everything seems to be undergoing a change. Society is, apparently, not much more than a congeries and constellation of social atoms. Habits can be formed only in a relatively stable environment, even if that stability consists merely—as, in fact, it invariably does, since there is nothing in the universe that is absolutely static—in a relatively constant form of change. Any form of change that brings any measurable alteration in the routine of social life tends to break up habits; and in breaking up the habits upon which the existing social organization rests, destroys that organization itself. Every new device that affects social life and the social routine is to that extent a disorganizing influence. Every new discovery, every new invention, every new idea, is disturbing. Even news has become at times so dangerous that governments have felt it wise to suppress its publication. (107)

CHAPTER **16**

The L.A. School
A Personal Introduction

MICHAEL J. DEAR

Is there an L.A. School of urbanism? My personal answer to this question is a most emphatic *yes!* Even as certain contributors have expressed dissent from both the material and mental constructs of L.A.'s emergent urbanism, this volume has demonstrated beyond reasonable doubt that we urgently need to revision urban theory and that Los Angeles/Southern California is a prototypical example on which to base this effort. For some, this might be disturbing news, but I have not felt it wise to suppress its publication.

Two pervasive themes have dominated the discourses of this book: first, the notion that there has been a radical break in the *material conditions* that lead to the production of cities; and second, that there has been a radical break in the *ways of knowing* the city. It should come as no surprise that contributors to this volume evince a variety of (sometimes contradictory) opinions on each of these themes. There is, for instance, a world of difference separating Chapter 1's enthusiastic declaration of an L.A. School (Dear and Flusty) and Ethington and Meeker's rejection of the validity of *any* school of urbanism (Chapter 15). From these contradictions, however, has sprung a remarkable collection of insights regarding the city and urban theory. In this personal reflection, I conclude by highlighting those principal insights that I regard as points of departure for a revised theoretical and empirical inquiry into the nature and significance of the city.

Many of the themes taken up in the putative L.A. School were undoubtedly foreshadowed by the Chicago School. In particular, Louis Wirth's farsighted emphases on the suburbs, communications technologies, and globalization find expression in the presentation in Chapter 3 (Dear and Flusty). Nevertheless, we develop our theory of "postmodern urbanism" in exact contradiction to the precepts of the Chicago School. We assert that the tenets of modernist thought have been undermined and that in their place, a multiplicity of ways of knowing have been substituted; and analogously, in postmodern cities the logics of previous urbanisms have evaporated, and, absent a single new imperative, multiple forms of (ir)rationality have clamored to fill the vacuum.[1] The traditions of the Chicago School imagine a city organized

around a central core; in postmodern urbanism (of which Los Angeles is the prototype), the urban peripheries organize what remains of the center.

The *material conditions* of urbanism in contemporary Southern California offer
much support for the notion of a radical shift in the way in which cities are being
created.

- ▶ In demographic terms, most especially, rates of population growth, immigration, mobility, and multiethnicity, Los Angeles is prototypical—with cities
  such as New York, Chicago, and Washington, D.C., more and more coming
  to resemble Los Angeles (Myers, Chapter 2).

- ▶ The empirical manifestations of a postmodern urbanism (privatopia,
  heteropolis, etc.) proliferate in very high profile in Southern California landscapes (Dear and Flusty, Chapter 3).

- ▶ The patterns of industrial growth in twentieth-century American cities belied
  the theories of the Chicago School even as its adherents were propounding
  them, creating from such inbuilt obsolescence the imperative for a new theory
  (Hise, Chapter 4).

- ▶ Central to understanding the production of the urban economy (in both
  early-twentieth-century Los Angeles and contemporary Southern California)
  is the role of the local developmental state in the provision of urban infrastructure. This is in stark contrast to the Chicago School's emphasis on market-
  based processes of urban development (Erie, Chapter 5).

- ▶ In contemporary economic restructuring, the shift from a Fordist to a post-
  Fordist mode of flexible production and the rise of an information society can
  be regarded as radical breaks in industrial organization and its concomitant
  economic geography (Scott, Chapter 6).

- ▶ New waves of increasingly diverse immigration into Southern California are
  altering the ways in which community and citizenship are constituted
  (Straughan and Hondagneu-Sotelo, Chapter 7).

- ▶ Homelessness is an important indicator of social polarization associated with
  globalization, as well as a manifestation of significant revisions in the American social contract, that is, the terms and conditions under which peoples
  agree to live peaceably alongside one another (Stoner, Chapter 8).

- ▶ Los Angeles is prototypical of the enormous proliferation of street gang cultures in American cities, notable most especially for the sheer scale of the phenomenon in Los Angeles and the propensity for the diffusion of L.A.'s gang
  culture to other national and even international cities (Maxson and Klein,
  Chapter 9).

- ▶ Los Angeles has the most diverse, multiple-identity religious populations in
  the world. Religious institutions are transnational in character. They are recasting ideas of citizenship as religion becomes a matter of choice, not obliga-

tion, and governed by individuals, rather than religious institutions (Miller, Chapter 10).

▶ In a world of virtual reality—arriving faster in a fragmented cybermetropolis where almost everyone is getting connected—the terms of community and citizenship are being radically transformed (Dishman, Chapter 11).

This summary in no way does justice to the detailed analyses contained in Chapters 1 through 11 of this volume, but they are suggestive of across-the-board shifts in the practices of place production—demographic, economic, political, social, cultural, and virtual.

Yet it would be easy, even convenient, to subsume these adjustments under the rubric of existing categories, including (but not limited to) those of the Chicago School. To recognize the new, we also need adjustments in the way we see, know, and represent the urban. Thus, *altered ways of knowing* the city are vital to understanding the accumulating evidence of the changing material conditions of city making:

▶ In asking "Who speaks for Los Angeles?" Hunt insists on the need for a new "road map" of the city, one that recognizes Los Angeles as a mediated/contested place requiring multiple ways of seeing (Chapter 12).

▶ Vasishth and Sloane resurrect the human ecology metaphor so central to the Chicago School but present a revision based in a scale-hierarchic ecosystems approach, understanding that all models and theories are provisional and contingent (Chapter 13).

▶ Wolch, Pincetl, and Pulido take to task both the Chicago and L.A. Schools for ignoring environment, the animal question, and the rights of nature in urban theory. They recast urban ecology, not à la Chicago School but in the form of "zoöpolis," a transspecies urban theory that asks what a sustainable urbanism would look like and what social institutions it would generate (Chapter 14).

▶ Taking a longer view, Ethington and Meeker make the strongest case for merging the insights of both the Chicago School and the L.A. School, and indeed, for abolishing the emphases and distinctions that separate *all* schools of thought in urban studies. Their proposed map of the "metropolis of urban inquiry" insists that just as we should not exclude any neighborhood from our purview, so should we not allow any epistemology to supersede another. In short, they argue that the Chicago School and the L.A. School should coexist peacefully to better refine our understanding of the urban (Chapter 15).

In the final analysis, it must be left to others to judge the utility of these evidences and arguments. Personally, what strikes me most forcefully about the experiences of this book are the following:

- ▶ The intellectual harvest uncovered when one deliberately confronts the departures and continuities between the Chicago and the L.A. Schools
- ▶ The enduring legacies of the Chicago School, alongside the manifest potential of an L.A. School
- ▶ The inherent value and productivity of an interdisciplinary approach (these chapters are by scholars from geography, history, political science, religious studies, social work, sociology, and urban planning)
- ▶ The inherent value and productivity of adopting a variety of methodological approaches in examining the same object, in this case, the city (for instance, used in this book are quantitative and qualitative surveys, statistical analysis, archival searches, cross-disciplinary metaphors, critical interpretive exercises, nonhuman standpoints, intellectual histories, and so on)
- ▶ How a deliberate, open-minded juxtaposition of old and new (Chicago vs. L.A.) can lead to the (re)discovery of important and/or forgotten pieces of an intellectual puzzle (e.g., in our case, bringing back into urban theory questions of the state, economy, environment, and technological change)

The continuing validity of the Chicago School and the viability of an upstart L.A. School are issues that I hope will now engage the energies of urbanists around the world, all of whom bring different, valuable perspectives based on their experiences of other cities. This is as it should be, because comparative analysis is at the heart of a revitalized urban theory.

NOTE

1. This thesis is explored more fully in my book *The Postmodern Urban Condition* (Malden, Mass.: Blackwell, 2000).

Index

About the Contributors

Michael J. Dear is Professor of Geography and Director of the Southern California Studies Center at the University of Southern California. In 1996, he was a Fellow at the Center for Advanced Study in the Behavioral Sciences at Stanford, and he held a Guggenheim Fellowship in 1989. He received honors from the Association of American Geographers in 1995 and has also received the University of Southern California's highest honors for creativity in research, teaching, and service. His most recent book is *The Postmodern Urban Condition* (2000).

J. Dallas Dishman is a Ph.D. candidate in the Department of Geography at the University of Southern California. His master's thesis, "Digital Dissidents: The Formation of Gay Communities on the Internet," focused on the myriad ways that gay men engage with virtual communities on the Internet. He has received numerous awards from USC for his political and social activism as a graduate student. His doctoral dissertation work examines the role of place in antigay violence in the city of West Hollywood, California.

Steven P. Erie is Associate Professor of Political Science at the University of California, San Diego, and is a leading authority on urban political and public policy. His book, *Rainbow's End: Irish-Americans and the Dilemmas of Urban Machine Politics,* won the best urban book award from the American Political Science Association and the Robert Park award from the American Sociological Association. He has completed studies for the California Policy Studies Seminar on Latino and Asian American political empowerment and on international trade and job creation in Southern California. Currently, he is completing *Globalizing LA: The Politics of Trade Infrastructure and Regional Development,* a study of L.A.'s harbor and airport agencies and their roles in the region's emergence as a global trade center.

Philip J. Ethington is Associate Professor of History at the University of Southern California. He is the author of *The Public City: The Political Construction of Urban Life in San Francisco, 1850-1900* (1994) and *The Metropolitan Moment: Creating the Twentieth-Century United States in Boston, Chicago, New York, and San Francisco* (forthcoming).

Steven Flusty is a doctoral candidate in the Department of Geography, University of Southern California, where he is currently engaged in the study of quotidian globalization. He has previously been in the employ of architects, landscape restorationists, and the Community Redevelopment Agency of the city of Los Angeles, and he is author of numerous essays and the book *Building Paranoia: The Proliferation of Interdictory Space and the Erosion of Spatial Justice.*

Greg Hise is Associate Professor of Urban History in the School of Policy, Planning, and Development at the University of Southern California. He is coauthor (with William Deverell) of *Eden by Design: The 1930 Olmsted-Bartholomew Plan for the Los Angeles Region* (2000), author of *Magnetic Los Angeles: Planning the Twentieth-Century Metropolis* (1997), recipient of the 1998 Society of Architectural Historian's Spiro Kostof Book Prize, and coeditor of *Rethinking Los Angeles* (Sage, 1996). His current research focuses on nineteenth-century landscapes in Los Angeles and the environmental history of Southern California.

Pierrette Hondagneu-Sotelo is Associate Professor of Sociology at the University of Southern California and author of *Gendered Transitions: Mexican Experiences of Immigration* (1994), coeditor (with Mary Romero and Vilma Ortiz) of *Challenging Fronteras: Structuring Latina and Latino Lives in the U.S.* (1997), and coeditor (with Maxine Baca Zinn and Michael Messner) of *Through the Prism of Difference: Readings on Sex and Gender* (1997).

Darnell M. Hunt is Professor of Sociology at the University of California, Los Angeles. Previously, he was Chair of Sociology at the University of Southern California and worked within the media and as a media researcher, including as a staff social scientist for the United States Commission on Civil Rights. He has published in the areas of race, mass media, and popular culture.

Malcolm W. Klein is Emeritus Professor of Sociology at the University of Southern California. With specializations in juvenile delinquency, crime measurement, and comparative justice systems, he is internationally acknowledged as a leader in street gang research. His latest books are *Responding to Troubled Youth* (1997) and *The American Street Gang* (1996).

Cheryl L. Maxson is Assistant Professor of Criminology, Law, and Society at the University of California, Irvine. Her research interests include juvenile violence, street gangs, and community attitudes toward crime and policing. Recent books include *The Modern Gang Reader* (second edition, 2001), with Jody Miller and Malcolm W. Klein, and *The Eurogang Paradox* (2001) with Klein and Hans-Jurgen Kerner, and Elmar Weitekamp.

Martin Meeker received his Ph.D. in the Department of History at the University of Southern California for his dissertation *Come Out West: Communication and the Gay and Lesbian Migration to San Francisco, 1940's-1960's.* He has published in the *Journal of the History of Sexuality* and is the coeditor (with Joseph A. Boone, Martin Dupuis, and Karin Quimby) of the anthology *Queer Frontiers: Millennial Geographies, Genders, and Generations* (2000).

Donald E. Miller is the Leonard K. Firestone Professor of Religion at the University of Southern California. He is the author or editor of six books, including the recent published volumes *Gen X Religion* (2000) and *Reinventing American Protestantism: Christianity in the New Millennium* (1997). He is the Executive Director of the Center for Religion and Civic Culture at USC, which is compiling a large archive of research on faith-based community organizing and development in Southern California.

Dowell Myers is Professor and Director of the Master of Planning program at the University of Southern California. He is a specialist in urban growth and development with expertise as a planner and urban demographer. An adviser to the Bureau of the Census, he has authored the most widely referenced work on census analysis, *Analysis With Local Census Data: Portraits of Change* (1992). His program of research has pursued two contributions to the planning field: (1) bringing people back in as the focus of planning success, and (2) understanding planning as a temporal process of developing the future. He has published recent articles in the *Journal of the American Planning Association, Demography, American Sociological Review,* and *Journal of Housing Research.*

Stephanie Pincetl is Research Associate Professor of Geography and Coordinator for the Sustainable Cities Program at the University of Southern California. She earned her doctorate in urban planning at UCLA. She is an expert on the history and politics of land use and environmental planning in California. Her book *Transforming California: A Political History of Land Use and Development* was published in 1999. She has written on issues of natural resource management, environment, and urban growth in the United States and France, examining questions of governance, democratic participation, and immigration. She has received a V. S. Ciriacy Wantrup fellowship and two William Fulbright awards and has been a visiting scholar at the French Centre National de la Recherche Scientifique.

Laura Pulido is Associate Professor of Geography at the University of Southern California. She is the author of *Environmentalism and Economic Justice: Two Chicano Struggles in the Southwest* (1996) and is currently working on a comparative history of radical politics among various communities of color in Los Angeles in the 1960s and 1970s.

Allen J. Scott is Professor jointly appointed to the Departments of Policy Studies and Geography at the University of California, Los Angeles. He was a recipient of a Guggenheim Fellowship in 1986-1987 and was awarded honors by the Association of American Geographers in 1987. Born in England and educated at Oxford University, he was elected as Corresponding Fellow of the British Academy in 1999. In the winter of 1998-1999, he occupied the André Siegfried Chair in the Institut d'Études Politiques, Paris. His most recent books are *Regions and the World Economy* (1998) and *The Cultural Economy of Cities* (Sage, 2000).

David C. Sloane is Associate Professor in the School of Policy, Planning, and Development at the University of Southern California. His recent research includes projects on urban landscapes and environments, health care facilities, community health disparities, and community surveys on community policing and civil gang injunctions. He is author of *The Last Great Necessity: Cemeteries in American History* (1991) and coauthor (with Beverlie Conant Sloane) of *Medicine Moves Into the Mall: The Architecture of Health Care* (forthcoming).

Madeleine R. Stoner is Professor in the School of Social Work at the University of Southern California. She is the author of two books on homelessness, *The Civil Rights of Homeless People: Law,*

Social Policy, and Social Work Practice and *Inventing a Non-Homeless Future: A Public Policy Agenda for Preventing Homelessness,* and numerous journal articles dealing with the problem.

Jerome Straughan is a Ph.D. student in the Department of Sociology at the University of Southern California. He is currently researching Belizeans in Los Angeles.

Ashwani Vasishth is a doctoral candidate in the School of Urban Planning and Development at the University of Southern California, studying the historical relationships between theories of nature and of society. He has a research background in ecologically constrained vernacular architecture and settlement patterns in indigenous societies. His dissertation research focuses on the implications of contemporary knowledge in evolutionary ecosystem ecology for planning theory and nature management.

Jennifer Wolch is Professor of Geography at the University of Southern California, where she is also Co-Director of the Sustainable Cities Program. Her research on nature-society relations in cities and attitudes toward wildlife has been published in *Society & Animals; Capitalism, Nature, Socialism;* and *Environment and Planning D: Society & Space.* She is coeditor (with Jody Emel) of *Animal Geographies: Place, Politics, and Identity in the Nature-Culture Borderlands* (1998).